Southern Legal Studies

SERIES EDITORS

Paul Finkelman, Albany Law School
Timothy S. Huebner, Rhodes College

ADVISORY BOARD

Alfred L. Brophy, University of North Carolina School of Law
Lonnie T. Brown Jr., University of Georgia School of Law
Laura F. Edwards, Duke University
James W. Ely Jr., Vanderbilt University Law School
Sally E. Hadden, Western Michigan University
Charles F. Hobson, College of William & Mary
Steven F. Lawson, Rutgers, The State University of New Jersey
Sanford V. Levinson, University of Texas at Austin, School of Law
Peter Wallenstein, Virginia Polytechnic Institute and State University

Homicide Justified

Homicide Justified

THE LEGALITY OF KILLING SLAVES
IN THE UNITED STATES AND THE
ATLANTIC WORLD

Andrew T. Fede

The University of Georgia Press
ATHENS

Paperback edition, 2019
© 2017 by the University of Georgia Press
Athens, Georgia 30602
www.ugapress.org
All rights reserved
Set in 10.25/13.5 Minion Pro by Graphic Composition, Inc., Bogart, Georgia

Most University of Georgia Press titles are
available from popular e-book vendors.

Printed digitally

The Library of Congress has cataloged the hardcover edition of this book as follows:
Names: Fede, Andrew, author.
Title: Homicide justified : the legality of killing slaves in the United States and the Atlantic world / Andrew T. Fede.
Description: Athens, Georgia : University of Georgia Press, [2017] | Series: Southern legal studies | Includes bibliographical references and index.
Identifiers: LCCN 2016055418 | ISBN 9780820351124 (hardback : alk. paper) | ISBN 9780820351117 (ebook)
Subjects: LCSH: Slavery—Law and legislation—United States—History. | Slavery—Law and legislation—Atlantic Ocean Region—History. | Homicide—United States—History. | Homicide—Atlantic Ocean Region—History. | Slaves—Violence against—United States—History. | Slaves—Violence against—Atlantic Ocean Region—History. | Slaves—Legal status, laws, etc.
Classification: LCC KF4545.S5 F43 2017 | DDC 342.08/7—dc23
LC record available at https://lccn.loc.gov/2016055418

Paperback ISBN 978-0-8203-5618-5

For Daniele

CONTENTS

Preface   xi

Acknowledgments   xv

INTRODUCTION A Murder Trial and the Comparative Law of Slave Killing   1

CHAPTER 1 Ancient Approaches to the Law of Homicide and Slave Killing   11

CHAPTER 2 The Visigoth, Spanish, Portuguese, and French Laws on Slave Killing   22

CHAPTER 3 Creating a British Colonial Law of Slave Killing   33

CHAPTER 4 Decriminalization to Amelioration on Britain's Atlantic Island Colonies   43

CHAPTER 5 Slave Killing Law in Britain's Northern American Colonies and the Border States   68

CHAPTER 6 Slave Killing in Britain's Southern Mainland Colonies   91

CHAPTER 7 Slave Homicide Reform in Virginia   110

CHAPTER 8 Slave Homicide Reform in North Carolina and the Common Law of Slavery   130

CHAPTER 9 Slave Homicide Reform in Georgia and Tennessee   152

CHAPTER 10 South Carolina Joins the Homicide Law Reform Trend   173

CHAPTER 11 The Antebellum States' Law on Slave Homicide   192

CONCLUSION Breaking Out of the Box of Slavery Law   223

Notes   225

Index   333

PREFACE

When John Hoover was arrested on March 28, 1839, for killing his slave Mira, he declared that "the negro was his own property, and he had a right to do as he pleased with his property." Hoover overstated his case. By the next May he became the first of two North Carolina slave owners who were executed for killing one of their slaves.[1]

Hoover might have been correct if he had been a slave owner in a traditional society that lacked a centralized ruler or state. Family or clan members in many of these societies responded to homicides with customs such as the blood feud, although they often negotiated compensation to resolve disputes about homicides without resorting to more violence. But slave masters were free to kill their own slaves without retribution from the slaves' clan or kin.

In contrast, in many slave societies the law regulated the slave owners' rights to kill their own slaves. This book uses a comparative approach to examine and evaluate how this law evolved and how it was enforced in the Ancient Roman, Visigothic, Spanish, Portuguese, French, British, and U.S. jurisdictions. Although slave homicide law in the U.S. South was reformed after independence to make some slave murders capital offenses, this law continued to afford slaves' lives second-class status, much like the law in Ancient Rome and Visigothic Spain.

Any comparative study of slavery law must acknowledge sociologist Frank Tannenbaum's *Slave and Citizen: The Negro in the Americas*. Tannenbaum argued that Spanish and Portuguese laws better protected enslaved people than did the analogous Anglo-American laws and that this history caused South America to have better race relations than the United States.[2]

Tannenbaum wrote in 1946 when the separate but equal doctrine permitted de jure racial segregation in the United States and the dominant history narratives still included Ulrich B. Phillips's description of antebellum slavery as a beneficial institution. Tannenbaum replied to Phillips's slavery law interpretation by citing Thomas R. R. Cobb's incomplete antebellum treatise—on which Phillips relied—as well as the books of the abolitionists George Stroud and William Goodell, which Phillips eschewed because he thought their value was "somewhat vitiated by the animus of their authors."[3]

Tannenbaum was not the first to apply the comparative approach to study slavery in the Americas. Sir Harry Johnston and Mary Wilhelmine Williams used it previously.[4] But Tannenbaum's thesis triggered enlightening debates, especially after Stanley M. Elkins applied it in his controversial 1959 book, *Slavery: A Problem in American Institutional and Intellectual Life*.[5]

One does not have to agree with all of Tannenbaum's conclusions while using the comparative approach to explain how slave law evolved in different times and places.[6] Indeed, "a wide variety of scholars have recognized that Southern society is best understood in the context of slavery and other forms of unfree labour elsewhere in the modern world."[7] Historians have considered slavery's establishment and evolution among the British Atlantic island and American mainland colonies as part of "the Big Picture" depicting "the interrelationship that constituted an Atlantic Slave system as well as the place of [this] racial slavery in the evolution of the Western and modern worlds."[8]

These comparisons are based in part on more "narrowly focused studies—of slavery in one country or small region or even on one plantation over time, and of particular aspects of slavery (whether family life, flight, internal economy, or master-slave relations) in such specific localities."[9] These micro studies can be combined to identify and evaluate the law in action and the patterns of social, political, economic, and legal change over time in different jurisdictions to uncover "the reasons for legal development."[10] Thus, for example, we can explain how and why slavery law differed over time in jurisdictions that at times were controlled by different empires and nations.[11]

I use the comparative approach to advance the interpretation that I outlined in a 1984 review essay and in several articles, book reviews, and *People without Rights: An Interpretation of the Fundamentals of the Law of Slavery in the U.S. South*. I began work on this book after completing *Roadblocks to Freedom: Slavery and Manumission in the United States South* and while writing an article on Mississippi judge Joshua G. Clarke. I included some comparative passages in *Roadblocks*, and believe that new insights will continue to emerge from the use of the comparative approach to slavery's legal history.[12]

The introduction begins with a slave murder prosecution illustrating the law in action and introducing important slavery law principles. Chapters 1 and 2 discuss slave homicide law in traditional societies, in Ancient Rome, in Visigothic Spain, in more modern Spain and Portugal and their colonies, and in the French American colonies. Chapter 3 explains the history of British slavery, homicide law, and colonial policy. Chapters 4 and 5 review slave homicide law's evolution in Britain's Atlantic island and northern American mainland colonies and in the northern United States. Chapters 6 to 11 trace this law's evolution in Virginia, North and South Carolina, Georgia, and Tennessee and this law's movement west and south in the antebellum years. These chapters cite primary source materials, including prosecutions that have not been discussed in the scholarly literature and evidence shedding new light on the officially reported cases.

The conclusion suggests that, in the years before the Civil War, southern judges and legislators began to extend the slaves' inferior criminal law status to free African Americans. It proposes the need for further study of how slavery law may have influenced the attitudes that underlie the Jim Crow era criminal law in action.

"The word 'slave,'" according to Margaret Abruzzo, "has recently become controversial in historical scholarship." Writers use phrases including "enslaved persons" and "enslavers" to describe enslavement as "a process, not a natural state, and to emphasize the human dignity of the enslaved human being." But slave owners also "disliked the term *slave*, preferring *Negroes* or *servants*." Enslavers used these euphemisms to soften the public perceptions of slavery's everyday reality.[13] Although for stylistic reasons I use the terms "slave" or "enslaved" and "slave masters," "slave owners," or "enslavers," I do not suggest that—during slavery's long career in human history—enslaved people were better suited for their enslavement. Nor were the enslavers rightfully in their more advantageous position in life.

I also have retained the original archaic spelling used in the primary and secondary sources quoted, to give the reader a sense of the passage of time and to preserve the authenticity of the quoted texts. But consistent with the press's style, I do not indicate all punctuation alterations made within quotations, which I otherwise would have included according to the currently accepted legal writing style.[14]

ACKNOWLEDGMENTS

My career writing about slavery law began in the fall of 1980, with a paper for a Rutgers Law School–Newark course on law and social change in U.S. history. Professor and former Dean James C. N. Paul, who died on September 13, 2011, taught that class. He encouraged me to continue my project during my last three law school semesters—for independent study credit and an internship—and he gave me the confidence to publish my work. Before his long Rutgers tenure, Dean Paul was a founder and dean of the first law school in Ethiopia. He remained an advocate for human rights in Africa.[15]

I also acknowledge John Anthony (Tony) Scott, who died in June 2010. Professor Scott taught me much in a Rutgers course on the origins and development of Anglo-American law. Although he wrote a critical review of Eugene Genovese's *Roll, Jordan, Roll: The World the Slaves Made*, Scott and Genovese also provided a lesson in scholarly acceptance of diverse interpretations, confirmed by a letter Genovese sent to me requesting copies of my articles about which he learned from "[o]ur mutual friend Tony Scott."[16]

I thank the series editors, Paul Finkelman and Timothy S. Huebner, and Walter Biggins from the University of Georgia Press for their recommendations and support, and the two anonymous readers for their comments. I also thank the Harry A. Sprague Library staff at Montclair State University, where I have been an adjunct professor since 1986. As a practicing lawyer and independent scholar, I have benefitted from Internet sites and search engines, including Google Books, Ancestry.com, and GenealogyBank.com. Most important, I thank my wife Daniele Fede for enduring my books and boxes of documents.

Homicide Justified

INTRODUCTION

A Murder Trial and the Comparative Law of Slave Killing

Eliza Rowand's South Carolina trial for murdering a slave under her command illustrates the law in action and the legal principles discussed in the following chapters. It also reveals slavery's violent foundation, discussed by critics of slavery including Thomas Jefferson and Harriet Beecher Stowe.[1]

A "Lady of Respectable Family" and "Ordinary Domestic Discipline"

"Our community was deeply interested and excited yesterday, by a case of great importance and also of entire novelty in our jurisprudence," reported the May 6, 1847, *Charleston Courier*. Eliza Rowand, a thirty-seven-year-old "lady of respectable family and the mother of a large family," was tried for murdering Maria, a fifty-two-year-old enslaved woman. "The court-house was thronged with spectators of the exciting drama, who remained, with unabated interest and undiminished numbers," until the jury's verdict was announced. Although the *Courier*'s story included summaries of the trial testimony, Maria's killer's identity remains a mystery.[2]

Charleston, the courtroom drama's setting, was transformed between the 1670s and the 1730s "from a tiny provincial village to a rich and vital commercial center." By the years between 1840 and 1860, the city's population was almost forty thousand people. Charleston was unique among southern cities because between 1800 and 1850 slaves and free blacks outnumbered whites, and in 1820 and 1840 three-quarters of the heads of households owned slaves. Slaves were employed in various occupations, but most were household or domestic workers. The majority of slaves were women. Slave control was always a concern. Charleston in 1783 established the first urban police force in the United States. Fear of slave insurrection later increased, especially after the 1822 trials about the alleged Denmark Vesey rebellion.[3]

Eliza or her husband, Robert, owned Maria, who was described as Eliza's nurse. Eliza and Robert were married in 1833 and were the parents of five young children. Robert was a factor or broker in Charleston, where the family lived. A factor was the planters' merchant and banker who bought and sold the planters' crops and purchased goods for the planters.[4]

On the day Maria was killed, January 6, 1847, Eliza called on E. W. North, her medical doctor, to come to the Charleston home of Eliza's mother, Frances C. Bee. Dr. North stated at Eliza's trial that he arrived at one in the afternoon and found Eliza downstairs in the sitting room "in a nervous and excited state," which he said she had exhibited "for a month before." North attended to Eliza. Although he contended that Eliza said nothing to him about Maria, North nevertheless went upstairs and found Maria's body on the floor. He also noticed "a piece of pine-wood on a trunk or table in the room." Maria was lying on one side, where he presumed she died. He noted some slight marks on Maria's body and scratches about her face, but he did not examine her body before leaving the house.[5]

The next day, Charleston's district coroner, J. Porteous Deveaux, and a coroner's jury held an inquest into Maria's death. Before local police and prosecutors, homicide investigations and prosecutions began when a person notified the local coroner of a suspicious death. South Carolina law, like that in the other North American colonies and states, required coroners to assemble a coroner's jury to examine the body and ascertain the facts. If the jury found evidence of a crime, the sheriff would arrest the suspect for a grand jury appearance.[6]

The inquest began at Mrs. Bee's home, where Maria's body was found "in an out-building—a kitchen." Deveaux said the body was "of an old and emaciated person, between fifty and sixty years of age." The coroner's jury then went to Charleston City Hall, where Eliza was examined. She gave a written statement asserting that early in the morning of January 6, 1847, she and Maria were at Mrs. Bee's home. Her husband, Robert, was out of town. Eliza thought that Maria "misbehaved." At about seven that morning, Eliza sent Maria to the Rowand's home to be "corrected" by another slave named Simon. Maria returned to Mrs. Bee's house about two hours later and went to Eliza's chamber on the second floor, "where Maria fell down." Eliza tried to revive Maria but was unsuccessful. Eliza then left the chamber. Another slave named Richard later came down to the first floor and said that Maria was dead. According to

Eliza, no one struck Maria while she was in the second floor chamber. Maria died at about twelve o'clock.[7]

Deveaux and the coroner's jury next inspected the chamber in which Maria died. They observed wood pieces in the room and measured one piece, which was eighteen inches long, three inches wide, and one-half inch thick.[8]

Two physicians examined Maria's body at the coroner's request. According to Dr. Peter Porcher, Maria was "lacerated with stripes; abrasions about the face and knuckles; skin knocked of[f]." He found evidence of blood under Maria's scalp. He thought it likely she was hit one or more times on the top of her head and once just over the right ear and concluded that a heavy stick could have caused the damage. He found no other evidence of the cause of her death "except those blows." Dr. A. P. Hayne gave a similar description of Maria's body's condition. He attributed her death to blows to the head by "a large and broad and blunt instrument."[9]

The coroner's jury, after a more than ten-hour examination, found that "in the chamber of Mrs. Eliza Rowand, at the residence of Mrs. F. C. Bee, Maria came to her death in the forenoon of the 6th inst., by blows to her head, inflicted by Richard, the slave of Robert Rowand, by order of Mrs. Eliza Rowand." The jury concluded that Richard and Eliza "feloniously did kill [Maria], against the peace and dignity of the ... state aforesaid."[10] Eliza posted bail of ten thousand dollars on this charge.[11]

Richard was first tried for Maria's murder by a Magistrates and Freeholders Court, as South Carolina law required when slaves, some free Native Americans, and free blacks were accused of capital crimes. These defendants were denied the right to a grand jury review of the charges against them before their trials. They were instead tried quickly, not more than six days after their arrests, in an inferior court headed by one or two magistrates with a jury of between three and five freeholders.[12]

Moreover, a slave's testimony was inadmissible in trials against whites but not in the trials of other slaves. Therefore, Richard's trial may have included the testimony of slaves who may have been present when Maria was killed.[13]

Two magistrates presided over Richard's January 1847 trial, and five freeholders composed his jury. Unfortunately, the newspapers followed the magistrates' recommendation and did not publish even a summary of the testimony. Because Eliza's murder charge was pending in the Court of General Sessions, the press thought "it incorrect to prejudice the public mind." The magistrates charged the jury to acquit Richard if they thought that Eliza struck the fatal blows or if they found that Richard struck Maria at Eliza's direction. The jurors "merely retired a sufficient time to write the verdict 'Not Guilty,' which was concurred by the presiding magistrates, and Richard was discharged."[14]

Three months passed before a Charleston district grand jury, on May 3, 1847, considered Eliza's case. B. F. Hunt, representing Eliza, requested that the presiding judge, John B. O'Neall, charge the grand jury on the law of murder because "the case was a peculiar one." Judge O'Neall, who was one of South Carolina's most respected antebellum jurists, agreed. He charged the grand jury "that on an indictment for murder they should not find a Bill unless they were satisfied by the evidence that the deceased came under her death by the act of the accused—that the fact of the killing should be established by *legal* and not *hearsay* testimony." The grand jury indicted Eliza on the murder charge, and a bench warrant was issued for Eliza's arrest.[15]

Eliza, on May 5, 1847, was arraigned in the Court of General Sessions. With her husband and mother by her side, she pleaded not guilty. The trial was held on the same day before Judge O'Neall and a twelve-man jury. Eliza was represented by a team of Charleston lawyers: James Lewis Petigru, one of Charleston's most celebrated and respected lawyers; James S. Rhett; and B. F. Hunt. Attorney General Henry Bailey prosecuted the state's case.[16]

Judge O'Neall first granted Petigru's motion to permit Eliza to sit by her lawyers rather than at the bar. O'Neall stated that "he granted the motion only because [Eliza] was a woman, but that no such privilege would have been extended by him to any man."[17]

Bailey opened his case by noting that an 1821 South Carolina law imposed the death penalty even on slave owners who were convicted of slave murder. Deveaux then testified about his coroner's inquest, and Eliza's exculpatory statement was read to the jury. South Carolina law had stated since 1740 that a slave owner, or one in control of a slave, was presumed guilty of murder if the slave died while under his or her command. But if no white person was present, the defendant could give an exculpatory statement under oath, and the state had to prove the offense by the testimony of two witnesses. Eliza's written exculpatory statement thus came into evidence on the state's own case in chief, and she could not be cross-examined about her story.[18]

Hunt then made an opening statement on Eliza's behalf. In the end he relied upon Eliza's exculpatory statement and asked the jury to acquit Eliza because the state would offer only circumstantial evidence. Hunt also warned the jurors to consider only the testimony of "free white persons" presented under oath at trial. He expressed his trust that the jurors would not consider "unfounded accusations" or "legends of aggravated cruelty, founded on the evidence of negroes, and arising from weak and wicked falsehoods." "Truth has been distorted in this case," he stated, "and murder manufactured out of what is nothing more than ordinary domestic discipline." Masters were entitled to chastise slaves to the extent necessary to ensure slave subordination, he argued, and masters—not their neighbors—should judge the limits of their own permissible slave punishment.[19]

The defense team did not cross-examine Deveaux. The state offered no eyewitnesses to the crime. Dr. North testified of his visit to the scene of the crime and Drs. Porcher and Hayne testified about the condition of Maria's body. They were cross-examined by the defense team, which offered no witnesses.[20]

After the lawyers' closing statements, Judge O'Neall instructed the jury that the state offered no proof that Eliza struck Maria or that she directed Richard to do so. He also referred to Eliza's written exculpatory statement, noting "there was no sufficient evidence legally to contradict it." O'Neall criticized the exculpatory oath statute but conceded that he was bound to apply this law. He recommended that the jury "acquit the prisoner, to whom the painful actions of the day might be a rebuke and warning of great value." After twenty or thirty minutes the jury returned a not guilty verdict.[21]

Life went on for Richard and Eliza after the trial. They had another child, and according to the 1850 census, they owned nine slaves. Robert died in 1857, and in 1860 Eliza still was living in Charleston with five of her children.[22]

People in the South and North drew different conclusions from the case. According to the *Charleston Courier*, the trial demonstrated how South Carolina's law extended to slaves' lives "the aegis of protection, in the same manner as it does to that of the white man, save only in the character of the evidence necessary for conviction or defense." In contrast, Harriet Beecher Stowe called the trial an indictment of southern justice, noting that "the case is reported with the utmost apparent innocence that there was anything about the trial that could reflect in the least on the character of the State for the utmost legal impartiality."[23] One of Stowe's antebellum critics replied that Eliza "may have been guilty, but according to Mrs. Stowe's own showing, there was no evidence against [Eliza], and a good deal for [her]."[24]

Indeed, there was little admissible evidence against Eliza, in part because possible black or enslaved witnesses could not testify at Eliza's trial. The rules of evidence and procedure made it relatively easy for Eliza's dream team of lawyers to win her acquittal.

Thus, Maria's killer's identity remains unknown. It also is unclear how many other prosecutions were ditched as futile because enslaved people were not permitted to testify. Did the prevailing notions of "ordinary domestic discipline" permit slave masters to punish slaves by whacking them on their heads with planks? When did slave master homicide cross the line?[25]

Antebellum Southern Slave Homicide Law Reform

South Carolina was the only British North American colony that adopted colonial era laws based on a 1661 Barbados act declaring that malicious slave killers should be punished only with fines. The colonial lawmakers in Virginia, Georgia, and North Carolina in different ways decriminalized masters' slave killings, reduced the penalties for the killings that remained criminal offenses, or enacted both provisions. The legislatures in Virginia, North Carolina, Georgia, and Britain's Atlantic island colonies by 1805 reformed these laws, however, and defined slave murder as a capital crime on the defendant's first conviction. South Carolina followed sixteen years later.[26]

Historians have offered different interpretations of the masters' potential liability for slave homicide under these reform laws. Ulrich B. Phillips asserted, "In the nineteenth century the laws generally held the maiming and murder of slaves to be felonies in the same degree with the same penalties as in cases where the victims were whites: and when the statutes were silent the courts felt themselves free to remedy the defect."[27] Kenneth Stampp and Stanley Elkins responded that these laws continued to legitimize homicides when masters killed slaves who rebelled or who resisted their masters' authority and decriminalized killings caused by the masters' moderate slave correction.[28]

Moreover, I later argued that antebellum southern courts went beyond the statutes to legitimize even more violence by creating a common law of slavery that redefined justifiable homicide and the standards that could mitigate capital murders to lesser offenses. Both the statutory law and common law proved to be equally malleable.[29]

I also contended that the white community's social and economic class structure influenced the evolution of southern slave homicide law in the books and in action. Frontier settlements gave way to cash-crop-producing plantation economies, which included slave owners and hirers, slave traders, overseers, patrollers, poor whites, and other third parties to the master and slave relationship. A person's liability for slave killing was influenced by his or her place in this class structure.[30]

Even the antebellum slave homicide reform laws gave masters superior rights to kill their slaves while prohibiting some slave master homicides. These laws to some degree "collided with the [master's] right of personal autonomy in slave management," but "the community, not an abstract system of justice, determined the outcome."³¹ And even within the slave-owning class, an alleged slave killer's social status was relevant in the antebellum South's "honor" culture. Men who were "without much local standing ... were more likely to get caught in the toils of criminal justice than better placed masters, hardly surprising in the rank-conscious South."³²

Stampp and other historians also noted that procedural hurdles hindered successful slave master prosecutions. White citizens had to be willing to approach local coroners to initiate homicide inquiries against slave owners. Slaves did not lack all "agency"; they could activate local "gossip networks" by complaining about their masters' crimes. But southern slavery law, unlike the law in some other slave societies, did not provide formal legal venues or officials who were required to receive and prosecute slave complaints.³³

Therefore, some slave owners avoided trials when no one came forward to complain about a slave's death, when coroner's inquests found no cause for a murder charge, or when grand juries failed to indict the accused masters. After grand jury indictments, some masters were tried and acquitted by juries that, of course, were all white. Still other masters were convicted at trial of slave murders or manslaughters, but they appealed their convictions and avoided any penalty if the appellate courts reversed their convictions. Others evaded penalties by obtaining a governor's pardon.³⁴

Two evidence rules also benefitted white southerners who were accused of killing slaves. The law excluded in court slave testimony against whites.³⁵ And South Carolina, Louisiana, and colonial Georgia laws permitted slave owners to exculpate themselves on their own oaths to rebut charges of slave murders. These laws were contrary to the pre–Civil War rule generally prohibiting testimony by the parties in both criminal and civil cases.³⁶

Historians, including Thomas Morris, nevertheless contended that the antebellum southern slave homicide reform laws evidenced a "growing 'human sensibility'" in the eighteenth century, which gave people a higher "regard for the individual, and they were increasingly sensitive to human suffering." Examples include "the drive to eliminate corporal punishment for sailors" and a "campaign against capital punishment." These concerns, Morris wrote, "spilled over into a greater regard for the lives of slaves. State after state, whether through constitutions, judicial decisions, or statutes, extended greater legal security to slaves. Whether the practice followed theory is another question."³⁷ Morris also conceded that these reform laws denied to slaves the law's equal protection.³⁸

Lea VanderVelde recently called this type of explanation for legal change the "humanitarian impulse" progress narrative.³⁹ But the Enlightenment indeed also had a "dark side." Some planters more efficiently organized their plantations to get more work out of their slaves.[40] According to Joyce Chaplin, pleas for greater humanity toward slaves included the amelioration of wanton violence by slave owners as a way to better control slaves. And Margaret Abruzzo described how slavery's opponents and its supporters contended that their views advanced the demands of humanity toward slaves.[41]

The law in the books and its effect in practice raise related issues in jurisdictions, like the antebellum South, with representative assemblies that were free to adopt laws advancing the values of the slave-owning class. That class did not lack influence in the legislative halls and courtrooms.[42]

In contrast, I had contended that the patterns of legal change in the antebellum South's slavery law, including this slave homicide law reform and other legal measures that appear to be intended to protect slave humanity, are best understood as a process in which the courts and legislatures balanced what they believed were the salient interests. These interests were (1) the need to foster slave control, obedience, and submissiveness; (2) the individual slave owner's economic interest in his or her slave; (3) the slave master class interest in perpetuating the plantation economy and preserving slave property values; (4) the slave master class need to control overseers and slave hirers, while preserving these individuals' right to discipline slaves; and (5) the master class need to control poor white violence and slave abuse, while co-opting poor whites into becoming supporters of the slave economy. "The engines of legal change were the social, economic, and political changes that caused the slave owners' perceptions of the balance of these interests to shift, and their new attitudes and concerns were shared by judges and legislators who created the new standards for white slave abusers."[43]

VanderVelde called this type of analysis "a more sophisticated" progress narrative that recognizes how the "humanitarian impulse only tells half the story." She included Richard Morris and Derrick Bell among writers who argued that legal reforms were "precariously dependent upon a fortuitous conjunction of the humanitarian impulses and economic interests of those in power."[44]

How Did Other Slave Societies Regulate Slave Killings by Masters?

A broader comparative analysis permits us to fairly evaluate the southern antebellum slave homicide laws in a context that includes the laws of some ancient and other more modern societies. These antebellum reform laws justifying homicides when masters killed slaves, like the second- and fourth-century edicts of the Roman Emperors Antoninus Pius and Constantine and the reforms promulgated by the Visigothic kings of the 650s, limited the masters' rights to use their human property badly to discourage slave resentment and revolt and to encourage the social order on which a slave society depends.[45]

The comparative approach also reveals how in the more modern slavery era slave homicide law evolved in different places over time. The European colonists generally relied on law "to project European social and physical circumstances onto novel American environments," but the "settlers' orientations to law were not singular but plural."[46]

Different institutional and governmental forms contributed to divergent slave homicide laws. The Spanish, French, and Portuguese central governments adopted colonial slave laws with different degrees of local participation and input. These laws explicitly legitimized slavery and ordered the relationships among slave owners, slaves, third parties, and the state. The British colonies' slave laws, on the other hand, were almost entirely local. The colonists believed that, as transplanted Englishmen, they brought to the New World all of their customary, common law, and statutory rights—including the right to adopt local legislation.[47]

The British central colonial authorities at times suggested reforms, but they never imposed a slave code or slave killing laws. Three local variations in the early colonial homicide law followed from this passive policy. The law better protected enslaved people's lives in the northern British American mainland colonies. The more southern mainland colonies other than South Carolina afforded enslaved people's lives a middle level of protection. South Carolina and the Atlantic islanders offered the enslaved people the least protection.

Historians include the northern colonies among the societies with slaves in which slavery was only one of the labor forms. Enslaved people were fewer in number and slaveholdings were smaller than in Britain's other New World colonies. The mainland British southern colonies and some of the Atlantic island colonies, on the other hand, were among the world's slave societies. Slavery was the dominant economic and social institution.[48] In some of Britain's Atlantic colonies the enslaved population was more than 80 percent of the total. Although some counties in Britain's mainland colonies approached these percentages, only in South Carolina were enslaved people the majority.[49]

The late eighteenth- and early nineteenth-century Anglo-American slavery homicide reform laws also differed. The British Atlantic island colonists, under pressure from abolitionists and the central government that could abolish slavery, equated slave killing with common law murder. The antebellum lawmakers in the U.S. South did not copy the British island colonies' laws, maybe because they knew that the federal government could not abolish slavery. Instead, they defined some malicious slave killings as murder while continuing to permit slave owners to kill rebellious or resisting slaves. They also legitimized killings resulting from the masters' moderate slave correction. Thus they better protected "slave property from non-masters who killed slaves without cause and thereby threatened the master's interest in order and property."[50]

Conclusion

Slave homicide law in Britain's North American colonies and in the southern United States is exceptional, however, because there is significant evidence of this law in action. Sources include the appellate court decisions published after defendants challenged their convictions; the surviving trial court records; press reports of homicides, prosecutions, and court proceedings; and documents such as diaries and journals.

Generations of researchers have found evidence of four North American slave owners who were executed only for murdering slaves under their command: William Pitman of Virginia in 1775, John Hoover of North Carolina in 1840, Lewis A. J. Stubbs of South Carolina in 1853, and Christopher Robbins of North Carolina in 1856. These were among the 2,476 executions between 1608 and 1865 in the fifteen jurisdictions that took no steps to abolish slavery before the Civil War.[51] These slave master murder convictions suggest that antebellum southern legislators, judges, and juries justified slave owner killings except those that were among the most extreme examples of wanton or sadistic murders of slaves who were entirely submissive to their master's authority when they were killed.[52]

CHAPTER 1

Ancient Approaches to the Law of Homicide and Slave Killing

Homicide is the killing of one person by another person or persons. But not every homicide violates the legal norms of the society in which it occurs. Depending on the social and legal context, a homicide may be impermissible, permissible, or even required. Thus, many societies excused accidental killings, while others, including the Cherokees and the tribes of the northwestern United States and western Canada, established homicide liability by causation and not by the actor's intent. Some societies also permitted or required homicides through ritual human sacrifices.[1]

Homicide, Clans, Feuds, and the State

Nineteenth-century British scholar Henry Sumner Maine's comparative analysis can be used to analyze and fairly evaluate the diverse methods used to define, deter, prosecute, and punish impermissible homicides. Maine has been called "[t]he founding father of legal history and legal anthropology."[2] He divided societies into two types, Status and Contract. In Status societies, decentralized clans or families were the centers of social life and control. The clan members' legal rights and duties were determined by their kinship group position. Criminal responsibility for individual wrongdoing was viewed as a collective liability of the wrongdoer's group. A ruler or a more centralized state governed Contract societies and imposed criminal liability on individual wrongdoers.[3]

These social models are best viewed as types at the ends of a continuum. Even in societies toward the Contract end, such as the antebellum United States, some community members—including married women, people with mental disabilities, slaves, and children—may be denied equal legal rights because of their status.[4]

These models highlight the salient differences in the killers' potential liability for homicides—including slave killings by masters. In Status societies—which Max Weber called "traditional" and others have called primitive, clan, or tribal societies—people resolved disputes by customs and consensus. Examples include the Germanic tribes that the Roman writer and official Cornelius Tacitus described in 98 C.E. and the Native American tribes that Europeans encountered almost 1,400 years later.[5] No centralized state officials or institutions investigated, prosecuted, and punished suspected killers. No lawmaking rulers or bodies established the substantive rules distinguishing permissible from impermissible homicides. The law instead was "found . . . in the culture of the people."[6]

In many of these societies, if someone harmed another clan member "the loss was treated as a misfortune." The chief or leader most likely punished the offender, "although physical retaliation was rarely implemented to avoid duplicating the loss to the group."[7]

If someone caused harm to the member of another clan, "retaliatory rules specified the measures of acceptable retaliation to re-establish the equilibrium between the clans."[8] People on both sides applied customs to distinguish permissible from impermissible killings. If a homicide victim's clan members deemed the killing to be impermissible, they may even have been required—through the blood feud—to punish either the killer or another member of the killer's clan. But the blood feud was not anarchy. Those who violated their customs while enacting revenge risked starting another round of retribution. Thus, the "feud is a highly structured cultural practice that ingeniously maintains social harmony."[9]

Offended tribe members in some societies applied a multiplier; they took more than one life for a life. In others, the principle of *lex talionis* required that "retaliatory harms should be equal in magnitude to the harms suffered, popularly captured by the phrase, 'an eye for an eye.'" This norm was beneficial because it prevented "devastating spirals of reciprocal violence."[10]

Clan members also avoided violent revenge by agreeing on compensation for the offended clan's members. The Germanic and Anglo-Saxon tribes called this compensation the *wergeld* or *wergild*. This was blood money paid by the offending clan as an alternative to violent revenge.[11]

This decentralized model evolved in many societies into the Contract or centralized state model. The ruler or state enforced individual liability for an individual's wrongdoing and prohibited the blood feud, which "came to be regarded as an undesirable perpetuation of social and familial disorder."[12] The oldest written laws illustrate how this process occurred; they fixed schedules of the compensation to be paid by wrongdoers, including killers.[13]

In a centralized state, governmental officials define the elements of impermissible homicide and state-authorized officials or individuals prosecute, try, and punish unlawful killings. The state's official actors thus pursue what Max Weber called a monopoly, or near monopoly, of the legitimate use of physical force. The lawmakers may permit limited exceptions for state-sanctioned nonofficial killings that are justified or excused to advance public interests. Of course, some members of society, such as criminals, gangs, or lynch mobs, also continued to use extralegal self-help and violence.[14]

Slave Homicide, Clans, Feuds, and the State

It follows that societies exhibiting these two models would treat slave master homicides differently. We begin with the definition of slavery. Orlando Patterson's cross-cultural study of slavery's fundamentals through the ages discusses slavery's three constituent elements, which in their extremes distinguish slavery from other human relationships evidencing inequality or domination: (1) the master's legal power to use violence against the slave; (2) the slave's "natal alienation," which is defined as the absence of "all 'rights' or claims of birth"; and (3) the slave's dishonored condition. Patterson also contended that other forms of oppression, including European serfdom, are distinguishable from enslavement because at least one of these elements was lacking.[15]

Patterson cited Max Weber's view that "[a]ll human relationships are structured and defined by the relative power of the interacting persons." Power forces people to act, or refrain from acting, in conformance with the will of other people and contrary to their own wills. The masters' "power" or "domination" over their slaves began on the social level of interaction with their use of force, or the threat that they would use force, to coerce their slaves to behave in accordance with the masters' will. On the cultural level, natal alienation captures the slaves' isolation from the dominant community and their perpetual state of "otherness." The lack of honor relates to psychological coercion. It reinforces the notion that the master is all-powerful and honorable and that the slave is powerless and dishonorable.[16]

Patterson also noted that "slavery is always a relationship that rests ultimately on force," and masters enforced their will because every slave society authorized masters to inflict corporal punishment on their slaves. But "[s]ocieties varied considerably in the degree to which their legal codes or customs permitted the murder of slaves by their masters." He listed four models for the regulation and punishment of slave killings by masters that he found in his sample of forty-five societies: "(1) the same as that for the murder of a free person; (2) not the same, but very severe; (3) mild, amounting to no more than a small fine; or (4) negligible—the master was able to kill his slave with impunity."[17]

Patterson also found that "most societies considered the killing of a slave by a third party not only as an assault on another man's property but sinful. Even with murder, it was usually the case that the punishment beyond the payment of damages was rarely severe."[18]

With Maine's social models we can evaluate these four approaches to slave killing. In the decentralized traditional societies, masters generally were free to kill their slaves with impunity. No state existed to prosecute masters and no clan members pursued the blood feud to avenge a slave's death.[19]

There is, for example, evidence from Julius Caesar's time that a slave held among the German tribes "could be whipped and bound and he could be sold and killed with impunity at his owner's whim."[20] Tacitus noted that masters often killed their slaves "in a fit of passion as they might kill an enemy—except that they do not have to pay for it."[21]

As the Western Roman Empire declined, Germanic slave masters retained the privilege to kill their slaves. Only third-party slave killers were required to pay for their crimes. For example, the *Lex Salica*, which was written between 507 and 511 under Clovis I, codified customary law of the Salian Franks, a Germanic tribe that lived in the area that now includes Belgium and the Netherlands.[22] That code's section titled "Concerning Stolen Slaves or Other Chattels" provided that anyone stealing, killing, selling, or freeing another person's slave was required to pay to the owner fines of 1,400 denarii (35 solidi) for a male slave and 1,200 denarii (30 solidi) for a female slave, return the value of the slave, and reimburse the owner for the lost labor. No provision addressed slave killings by slave owners.[23] In contrast, the code required the killer of a free person to pay compensation of between 200 and 1,800 solidi based on the victim's status.[24]

Moreover, in premodern societies slave murder "for ritual purposes was, of course, widespread. It existed, at some time, on every continent and in the early periods of every major civilization."[25] People committed homicides when those captured in battle were either accepted as slaves or were tortured and then killed during rituals.[26] Even into the nineteenth century, the indigenous people of the North American Northwest coast practiced ritual slave killings, often during an important person's funeral.[27]

Centralized state lawmakers employed all four of Patterson's approaches to slave killings by masters. As state actors established and enforced the near monopoly of legitimate force, societies permitted slave masters to physically punish their slaves. Some continued to legitimize slave killings, by what Max Weber characterized as a "survival" of the master's traditional rights.[28]

Slave Homicide from Clan to State in Ancient Rome

Ancient Roman slave law illustrates how slave homicide law evolved as Rome's slave society matured. "From their earliest beginnings, the Romans practiced slavery on a small scale, using a few slaves as farmhands and household servants."[29] According to historians including Keith Hopkins, Moses I. Finley, and Keith Bradley, Ancient Rome evolved from a society with slaves to one of the few slave societies.[30] Hopkins defined a slave society as one "in which slaves play an important part in production and form a high proportion (say over 20%) of the population."[31] Finley cautioned about playing a "numbers game" with enslaved population percentages, but he nevertheless suggested a slightly higher enslaved population range of 30 to 35 percent. These scholars agree, however, that there have been only five true slave societies: Ancient Greece, Ancient Rome, "the West Indian Islands, Brazil and the southern states in the USA. These five societies in which slaves played a considerable role in production (and in ostentatious consumption) form a distinct category of 'slave society.'"[32]

"Rome became a true 'slave-owning society' only when slaves, both in the mines and, especially, on the latifundia (large landed estates), became a vital aspect of Roman production. Rome can be said to have become reliant on slave labor from this time on." This transition occurred during the third through first centuries B.C.E., following the influx of a large supply of people the Romans enslaved through conquest and the displacement of peasant farmers by the centralization of control over farmland. Enslaved people in Rome were agricultural, manufacturing, and mining workers. They also were household servants, secretaries, actors, mimes, and gladiators.[33]

The enslaved population in Roman Italy and the Roman Empire cannot be measured with precision, but it eventually reached the thresholds for slave societies.[34] Roman Italy's enslaved population is estimated to have been only about 10 percent between 225 and 200 B.C.E. Between 100 B.C.E. and 300 C.E., however, this enslaved population may have increased to as much as 30 to 35 percent. The enslaved population in the whole Roman Empire between 1 and 150 C.E. was between 16 and 20 percent, and it is estimated to have been between 10 and 15 percent in the late empire years between 275 and 425. But the concentrations of enslaved people varied in different locations. Sicily's enslaved population between 150 B.C.E. and 150 C.E. is estimated to have been as much as 66 percent. These estimates, although debated, confirm that the Roman Empire became one of the world's slave societies because of the numbers of slaves and the status associated with slave ownership.[35]

Roman slave homicide law also changed over time as Roman slavery evolved. The earliest sources confirm that homicide was a matter of "private vengeance" to be exacted by the victim's family.[36] According to Judy Gaughan, murder may have been a crime during the Roman monarchy, which ran from 753 to 509 B.C.E., but the law of the Roman Republic (509–27 B.C.E.) did not clearly define ordinary homicide as a crime to be prosecuted and punished by the state. The victims' relatives instead addressed and punished homicides privately. There were exceptions that Gaughan argues proved the general rule.[37]

This law changed "during the last days of the Roman republic," which was supplanted by the empire in 27 B.C.E. During the period "when the government was on the brink of a transition to empire and the creation of a centralized political institution that would last for centuries, murder became a crime."[38]

It should come as no surprise, then, that slave killing also was not initially clearly defined as murder to be punished by the state. Slave killing was addressed under *lex Aquilia*, a plebiscite from 287 B.C.E. regarding property owners' claims for damage to their property. Chapter 1 stated that a person who unlawfully killed a slave or a four-footed herd animal belonging to another was required to pay damages to the property owner. The damages were to be established at the property's highest value in the prior year.[39] This damages rule may have been intended to account for the seasonal fluctuation of agricultural slave values.[40]

This law has been called an "important turning point" in the history of Roman tort law because it "created for the first time the opportunity to get damages, laying the foundations for modern tort liability." A distinction thus arose between serious crimes (such as murder), which were publically punished, and lesser wrongs that were privately prosecuted by the victim's family, who could obtain damages from the wrongdoer.[41]

It follows that owners were free to kill their own slaves. But under the Roman Empire, law reforms incrementally limited the masters' rights to kill their slaves.[42] A statute known as *lex petronia* is the first example. The law's actual text and its date of adoption are unknown. It apparently predated the eruption of Vesuvius in 79, however, because evidence of this law was found in Pompeii. Historians have suggested promulgation dates including 19 and 61 C.E.[43] "For a host of crimes Rome punished criminals of low status with aggravated or ultimate punishments (*summa supplicia*), which included exposure to wild beasts, crucifixion, and burning alive."[44] The *lex petronia* denied to masters the right to sell their slaves to fight wild beasts in the arena. Both the buyer and the seller were liable to the penalty if they violated this law. Masters were instead required to bring their slaves before judges who could approve the slaves' punishment.[45]

This law in effect deprived masters of access to lucrative contracts of sale for their slaves and afforded slaves' lives some due process of law before facing death in the arena. At least to that extent it limited the masters' powers over their slaves' lives.[46]

But it is not clear whether the law at the time of *lex petronia* otherwise generally prohibited slave killings by masters. According to the Roman writer Suetonius, Emperor Claudius (41–54) issued an edict based on the emperor's "[f]inding that a number of sick or worn-out slaves had been abandoned by their owners on the Island of Aesculapius [in the Tiber river], to avoid the trouble of giving them proper medical attention." Claudius freed these slaves "and ruled that none who got well again should return to the control of his former owner; furthermore, that any owner who made away with a sick slave for the same mean reason should be charged with murder."[47]

This edict also suggests that the law may have protected slaves' lives from other arbitrary killings by masters, but it is not conclusive. Some historians have argued that Emperor Hadrian (117–38) decreed reforms protecting slaves, including a law that prohibited killings by masters without a court order. But others disagree.[48]

Hadrian also exiled for five years Umbricia, "a lady of family," because she "for the most trifling reasons subjected her serving women to appalling treatment."[49] Fixed-term exile was the "mildest form" of banishment in Roman law; it did not result in the forfeiture of citizenship or property. "It was overwhelmingly a sentence for crimes against the public order—political crimes—committed by persons of high status." Hadrian ordered this because unreasonable slave abuse disrupted the public order.[50]

According to Justinian's *Institutes*, which was compiled in 533, slave owners generally held "the power of life and death over slaves, and owners get whatever slaves acquire."[51] Emperor Antoninus Pius (138–61) declared, however, that "a man who kills his own slave without good grounds [was] liable to the same punishment as one who kills someone else's slave." He also restrained "excessive severity" by directing provincial governors to sell to new owners any mistreated slaves who fled to a temple or to an emperor's statue.[52] Antoninus Pius and the non-Christian emperors who followed did not more clearly define the conduct that afforded masters sufficient cause to kill their slaves. Nor did they define permissible or excessive severity in punishment.[53]

The first Christian emperor, Constantine, further explained his predecessors' reforms with two decrees that both legitimized and limited masters' power over their slaves.[54] According to Kyle Harper, these laws "are an interesting case study in the Roman state's desire to maintain order and decency without practically undermining the master's power."[55]

Constantine in 319 defined the permitted level of slave master punishment when he declared that a master could beat his or her slave "with a rod or whip or put him in chains to guard him, and if the slave dies, the master need have no fear of prosecution. Distinctions of time and questions of interpretation are abolished."[56]

Constantine also confirmed, however, that the master may not use this right "immoderately." Thus the master "will be charged with murder only if he killed the slave intentionally, by a blow from the fist or a stone, or, by using a weapon, he inflicted a lethal wound." A master also could be charged with murder if he "ordered [his slave] to be hanged by a noose, or by a wicked order instructed that he be thrown from a high place, or administered the virus of poison, or tore his body by public punishment, that is by tearing through his sides with the claws of wild beasts, or by burning him with fire applied to his limbs, or if, with the savagery of monstrous barbarians, he forced the slave to leave his life in the tortures themselves, with the destroyed limbs flowing with black blood." The claws of wild beasts "appear to have been instruments of torture which were made out of metal."[57]

This edict defined three classes of killings. Masters faced no liability for accidental or unintended killings that were caused by the usual forms of punishment. They could be liable in the second if they intentionally killed their slaves while employing these usual means of punishment. And third, masters were liable if they killed their slaves using one of the prohibited punishments listed in the law's "gruesome catalogue" of abuse.[58]

Harper called the law "morbid and voyeuristic. It combined the love of high-flown rhetoric in Constantine's legislation with the presentation of imperial benevolence." He concluded that Constantine attempted to distinguish "between death in the course of normal master-slave violence, which was perfectly acceptable, and deliberate death sentences or especially spectacular forms of death. Sadistic punishments were, notably, reserved for the state."[59]

Ten years later Constantine issued another edict affirming that masters should not be prosecuted for slave killings if their slaves died as a result of punishment for the slaves' misdeeds. He stated that slave owners have an interest in their own slave property, and thus should not be prosecuted "whether the punishment was simply inflicted or apparently with the intention of killing the slave." He added, "It is our pleasure that masters are not held guilty of murder by reason of death of a slave as often as they exercise domestic power by simple punishment." He concluded by declaring that when slaves died "after correction by beating . . . , the masters should fear no criminal investigation."[60] This was "the last time on record that a Roman emperor meddled with the works of private discipline."[61]

These provisions were in the next century included by Theodosius II in the Theodosian Code. But only the 319 edict was included in Justinian's Code of the sixth century.[62] William Harris called these laws of Constantine "a considerable step backwards from the legislation of Antoninus Pius."[63] And according to Harper, these edicts were "a regression from the standards of the high empire."[64]

This was not necessarily so, however. Constantine may have codified the specific types of moderate and immoderate correction and punishment that his predecessors may have recognized over time. He also clearly declared, however, that at least some killings by slave masters were murders, thus asserting some state control over slave masters.[65]

Why Did the Ancient Roman State Prohibit Slave Master Homicides?

Some scholars have argued that this effort to bring enslaved people under public control and regulation "reflects the growth of a humanitarian concern for slaves in the imperial age, a notion which, although perhaps containing some truth, is beyond proof and inconsistent with what can be determined of actual practice."[66] Miriam Griffin thus suggested that "even in an autocratic system, if the autocrat aims at conciliating opinion, the law usually follows average sentiment."[67]

On the other hand these reforms, and others imposing harsher penalties for slave criminals, may be seen as "utilitarian" responses to concerns about slave disquiet. Some apparently believed that "slavery was too important a social problem for control to be left any longer with individuals." Social changes may have influenced these legal changes, including the increased use of overseers by absentee land owners, the concentration of slaves in the cities, and the proliferation of governmental officials in the imperial system, which was "increasingly able and likely to intervene in social problems."[68] Or, as Niall McKeown suggested, these laws, like others promulgated in the first to third centuries

C.E., could, at least in part, "represent a new tendency to legislate, a change in the discourse between state and individual, rather than a change in attitudes towards slaves."[69]

Moses Finley thus concluded that laws regulating the masters' powers over their slave property were similar to any other legal regime regulating and legitimating owners' rights in their property. He called "[l]egal restrictions on the rights of a slaveowner ... a side issue" because "in modern sociological and juridical theories of any school, all property is understood to be a matrix of rights, rarely if ever unlimited. The precise rights that constitute the matrix vary with kinds of property and kinds of society."[70]

Justinian's *Institutes* further explained this legal change by admitting that "it is to the advantage of the state that no one use his property badly."[71] Justinian's summary was taken from Gaius's *Institutes*. In this Roman law textbook dating to 161, Gaius explained that the law limited the masters' power over their slaves "for the same reason prodigals are interdicted from the administration of their property." Prodigals or spendthrifts had demonstrated an inability to manage an inheritance. Roman law regulated their rights "in the interest of the relatives who will inherit their estate and who will suffer if it is squandered."[72]

The laws limiting an individual owner's right to wantonly kill his or her slaves similarly protected the interests of the slave owner's heirs, who would be deprived of a potential asset if a slave were to be killed without any cause. But they also distinguished between the individual master's interest in killing a slave without limitation and the competing interests of the master class, of the public in general, and of the state. Laws restricting an individual master's behavior balanced the "eternal tension in slave-owning communities—between protection of slaves from cruel masters" and the perceived need to confirm the individual master's right to exercise all necessary authority over his or her slaves.[73]

Accordingly, the Romans came to understand that, to advance the public order, homicide law could not be applied with equal force when masters were accused of killing their slaves. Slavery law had to legitimize the masters' powers to correct their slaves. The laws curbing the masters' unnecessary violence were designed to mitigate the slaves' "frustration," which, in turn, could "lead to slave revolt."[74] Killers could "be brought to justice only if fellow citizens laid complaint or if there was a spontaneous investigation by the authorities. Neither practice seems to have been common."[75]

This law in action cannot be compared with the practices in more recent slave societies. There is not sufficient evidence of cases in which Roman slave owners were prosecuted for violating these laws.[76]

Conclusion

The evolution of laws regulating the masters' right to mistreat and kill their slaves may best be understood along with the evolving limitations on the masters' right to bestow privileges on their slaves, including the ultimate benefit of manumission. When masters freed their slaves they severed the entire bundle of property rights embodied in the slaves, thus transforming slaves from property to people with the rights the law vested in them upon their release from bondage.[77]

Masters who killed and freed their slaves released their property rights in their slaves and compromised the interests of their creditors and heirs, and the public in general, because both the dead and the freed slaves no longer were human property. The better analogy for both the masters' right to kill and free their slaves, then, is with the owners' right to destroy their property. Both Roman and Anglo-American law afforded this right—*jus utendi et abutendi*—to property owners.[78]

An owner's decision to destroy his or her property may be perceived as having a wider effect on the prevailing notions of the public interest if the property has perceived public value, such as a historic building or a work of art. This is especially so if a property owner's will calls for the property to be destroyed after his or her death, because the destruction would have an impact on the present and future rights of others in the property and of the society at large.[79]

The following chapters illustrate how lawmakers advanced community interests while regulating unnecessary slave abuse and killings, which "endured as a real moral problem throughout the history of slavery." "Everyone agreed that in order to have slaves the owners needed the right to impose discipline as they saw fit, with as few questions as possible. But, the law also struggled with the fact that correction could and did go too far, and that premeditated homicide was a social problem that could not be ignored or treated as simply a foolish destruction of one's own property. Violence and discipline were a central legal issue, as was the slave's humanity." But slave humanity was an ambiguous concept. The law in different ways protected slaves' lives from homicide at the hand of their masters and generally did not limit the masters' right to beat or rape their slaves.[80]

CHAPTER 2

The Visigoth, Spanish, Portuguese, and French Laws on Slave Killing

When the Spanish and the Portuguese began their colonial empires, they "had well-developed slave cultures" and "a well-developed legal culture, based on Roman law, which allowed them to quickly create not just slaveholding, but a system of slavery."[1] The French did not have this contemporary slave culture. But they also adopted colonial slave codes explicitly legitimizing slavery and ordering the relationships among slave owners, slaves, third parties, and the state.[2] The laws in these regions illustrate two approaches to slave homicides, one affording to slave masters special privileges and immunities and another equating enslaved victims with free people.

The Visigothic Homicide Reform Statutes

Slavery was evident in Iberia, which the Romans called Hispania, "as far back as there are records." The Romans brought their slavery practices to Hispania, using slaves as household servants, artisans, and workers in gangs in agriculture, mining, and public works projects. The enslaved population is estimated to have been not more than 30 percent.[3]

Slavery later declined in third- and fourth-century Hispania. This society "was not a slave society by the end of the imperial period, if it ever had been one, but was a society with slaves."[4]

The Visigoths were Germanic people whose kings ruled Spain from about 415 until 711. Their society was stratified with slaves at the bottom. Even enslaved people were stratified; the minority at the top were slaves with skills, body guards, chamber maids, concubines, and the slaves of royalty, while the majority were menial household or agricultural workers.[5]

"The Visigothic economy, such as it was, was built on slavery. Impressed by the ubiquitous slave labor in the Late Roman Empire, the Goths adopted and spread plantation slavery across Northern Europe, where it had never flourished before." The Visigoths also "greatly reinforced" slavery "in those parts of the collapsed [Roman] empire where previously, as in Hispania, it had served the Roman landholders." Their slaves included Slavic people brought in to work the "vast cereal and cattle estates," which were the "Visigoth versions of the Roman *latifundia*." Visigothic Spain's slavery achieved its height in the sixth and seventh centuries, and its enslaved population is estimated to have reached 25 percent.[6]

The Visigoths were traditional tribal people who followed customs, including the blood feud. Slave masters had the unlimited right to kill their slaves. An enslaved person's injury or death was treated as damage to the owner's property interest.[7]

The Visigothic kings later compiled codes, which were "an amalgamation of Roman law with Germanic custom for the common use of all subjects in the realm."[8] The earliest known code, compiled under Euric (466–84), exists only in fragments, and the text of Leovigild's code, from about 586, is lost. The earliest surviving text, compiled under Recessvind (649–72), is called the Visigothic Code, *Liber Iudiciorum*, or *Leges Visigothorum*. Ervig in 681–82 and Egica (687–702) later promulgated revised versions.[9]

These kings sought to monopolize violence, with limited exceptions legitimizing private violence.[10] The code defined degrees of homicide and established punishment, including the death penalty for some intentional killings.[11]

The code also limited the masters' rights to kill their slaves according to the reform enacted by King Chindasvind (642–53), who was Reccesvind's father. This law asked, "If anyone who is guilty of crime, or of giving wicked counsel to another, cannot escape punishment, how much more liable is he who deliberately and maliciously commits homicide?" The law noted that slaves were "very frequently" killed "through the excesses of cruel masters, without having committed any crime," and it declared that "it is entirely proper that this license should be entirely abolished."

Masters thus could not kill their own slaves or slaves of another person "without an order of court." If a slave acknowledged that he committed a capital crime, the master was to "straightaway communicate" this to a local judge or to the governor. If "after an investigation, it is evident that the crime was committed," the official or the slave's master was to execute the slave. If the judge was not willing to order the slave's execution, he was to "commit his sentence of death to writing," and the master was authorized to kill or spare his or her slave's life.[12]

This law also included two exceptions legitimizing slave homicides. First, a master could "immediately" kill a resisting slave in self-defense if the slave "should strike him with a sword, stone, or with any weapon," or even if the slave attempted to strike the master. Masters had to prove this defense by their own oaths and the testimony of other slaves who were present. Second, slave master homicides were excused if the masters established by their oaths, or by the testimony of witnesses, that the killing occurred as a result of excessive punishment "influenced by a sense of injury, or by anger." But masters killing their slaves with "malice" were to be (1) deprived of the right to again testify in court "as a mark of infamy"; (2) exiled for the rest of their lives; (3) forced to do penance; and (4) deprived of their property, which was to be awarded to their "nearest heirs."[13]

The Visigoths viewed exile and public penance as serious penalties and "public penitence certainly involved excommunication." This "[p]enitential discipline was sometimes so severe that men preferred to commit suicide."[14] Ervig's code required accused masters to prove their justification but reduced the penalty to a seventy-two-solidi fine and the permanent loss of the master's right to testify. Egica later reintroduced penance for slave master killers.[15]

These codes continued to treat third-party slave homicides as property crimes. Slave owners had the "ultimate right and responsibility to seek a remedy. Regularly, this took the form of payment by the offender to the master. The deliberate and cold-blooded killing by a freeman of another's slave . . . was satisfied by the simple delivery of two substitutes" under Ervig's code.[16] Chindasvind's law also imposed "permanent exile" on offenders.[17]

The Visigothic Code included a schedule of compensation to be paid to free people who were the victims of nonfatal violence. But these values were cut in half when slaves were attacked, and the compensation was paid to the victims' owners. Free people who mutilated slaves also were to provide the owners with substitutes until the injured slaves recovered.[18]

This code also limited the masters' right to mutilate their own slaves, stating that "[b]y a former law we have restrained masters, actuated by unbridled rage, from putting their slaves to death." Therefore, masters "may not deform man, who was made in God's own image, while in the act of practising cruelty upon those who are subject to them, we must forbid corporeal mutilation." A master who "without a preliminary investigation in court, should openly and wickedly, deprive their slave of his nose, lip, tongue, ear, or foot; or should tear out his eye; or should mutilate any other part of his body; or should order anyone else to perpetrate any of these acts" was to be sentenced by the local bishop "to three years of exile, with penance."[19]

It is unclear why the Gothic kings enacted these laws after 240 years of their almost 300-year rule in Spain. Originally these kings were Arian Christians, and after 589 they were Catholics. Their religion may have motivated these reforms, or maybe they adapted Roman models after independently arriving at the same conclusions about the need to regulate the master and slave relationship.

The Spanish and Portuguese Slave Homicide Laws

The Visigothic Code influenced Spanish law after the Gothic era, but its effect on Spain's slave homicide law is unclear.[20] Almost six hundred years after King Reccesvind's slave homicide reform law, Alfonso X (Alfonso the Wise) compiled the Castilian legal code *Las Siete Partidas de Rey don Alfonso el Sabio*, which referred to slavery.[21]

Slavery "flourished" during Alfonso's reign. But Spain's enslaved population constituted a smaller percentage than in Ancient Rome, Gothic Spain, Medieval Europe, or Renaissance Italy. Slavery "was mostly an urban phenomenon, less frequently agricultural, mostly domestic and artisan. It was also largely female, to supply the maids, nannies, teachers, cooks, servants, cleaners, and the like for the affluent households." Enslaved males "rarely held menial jobs but rather [worked in] artisan occupations." Most of Spain's slaves after the reconquest were Muslims who typically lived with their owners as household members.[22]

Elsa Goveia asserted that "[i]n the *Partidas*, slavery is undoubtedly accepted as legal. It is not accepted as good. Liberty is the good which the law strives to serve: 'it is a rule of law that all judges should aid liberty, for the reason that it is a friend of nature, because not only men, but all animals love it.'" Indeed, under the *Partidas* slavery was "a misfortune, from the consequences of which slaves should be protected as far as possible, because they are men, and because man is a noble animal not meant for servitude."[23]

Las Siete Partidas defined three kinds of homicide: wrongful, justified, and accidental. Wrongful killings could be punished with death. Justified killings included those in which a person killed a man attempting to molest his wife or daughter, killed a thief at night breaking into the killer's house, or killed an arsonist setting the killer's property on fire. Soldiers also could kill deserters. Accidental killers were not punished if witnesses swore that there was no animosity between the killer and the victim. Careless killers faced five years of exile.[24]

The code also stated that one who intentionally killed another person "must suffer the penalty for homicide, whether the party killed is free or a slave; except where the homicide is committed in self-defense."[25] This code recognized that "[a] master has complete authority over his slave to dispose of him as he pleases. Nevertheless, he should not kill or wound him, although he may give cause for it, except by order of the judge of the district; nor should he strike him in a way contrary to natural reason, or put him to death by starvation; except where he finds him with his wife or his daughter, or where he commits some other offence of this kind, for then he has certainly a right to kill him."

This code also stated that if "a man is so cruel to his slaves as to kill them by starvation, or wound or injure them so seriously that they cannot endure it," the slaves "can complain to the judge; and the latter in the discharge of his official duty should investigate and ascertain whether the charge is true." Judges who verified the charges were to sell the slaves, pay the sales price to the offending master, and prevent the slaves from again being "placed in the power, or under the authority of the party through whose fault they were sold."[26]

Las Siete Partidas thus legalized the masters' right to impose moderate punishment in a provision that applied to free people, children, pupils, and slaves. Moderate punishment excluded the infliction of "severe wounds with stones, sticks, or other hard substances." Slave masters could be prosecuted and executed if they killed their slaves as a result of punishment that was intended to kill. Masters faced five years of banishment if their slaves died as a result of immoderate correction not intended to kill.[27]

This code also protected slave owner property interests. It required a "physician, a surgeon, or a farrier" caring for "a slave or an animal" of another person who "cuts, burns, or doses it" so that it "dies or is crippled" to compensate the owner. In contrast, physicians or surgeons who negligently caused the death of free people were punished "according to the discretion of the Judge."[28]

Slavery remained a part of Spanish law and culture when Spain began to establish American colonies. Colonists felt free to enslave Native Americans until the Crown abolished this form of slavery in 1542. Between 1492 and 1886, the Spaniards also imported almost a million and a half enslaved Africans to the Americas.[29]

The slavery provisions of *Las Siete Partidas* were applied in these colonies, including Florida and Louisiana when they were governed by Spain. Slavery's "nature" as an institution "was the same, in principle, in all of colonial Spanish America," even though "the circumstances that obtained in different colonies gave the institution a variety of distinctive features."[30] Elsa Goveia concluded that "this 'medieval' slave code was probably the most humane in its principles ever to be introduced in the West Indies."[31]

The colonists nevertheless enacted local laws regulating slaves.[32] Spain's monarchs also imposed slavery laws, including the 1680 compilation *Recopila-*

ción de las reyes de los reynos de las Indias. An eighteenth-century reform trend led to the 1785 *Código Negro Carolino* decreed for San Domingo, the 1789 *Real Cédula de su Majestad sobre la educación, trato y ocupaciones de los esclavos*, the 1826 *Reglamento para la educación, trato y ocupaciones de los esclavos* for Puerto Rico, and the 1842 Cuban slave code, which was replaced by another version in 1844. These laws in part sought to better enforce the slave homicide provisions of *Las Siete Partidas*, which remained in effect until 1886, when slavery was abolished in Spain's American colonies and the Philippines.[33]

Moreover, after the 1760s, a public official, called the *sindico procurador* or *defensor*, was authorized, among other things, to enforce the slaves' right to complain about abusive masters and request that they be sold to new owners. This process, which was called *papel de venta*, "gave a slave a set term, usually a month, to find a more congenial owner willing to pay the assessed price."[34]

Of course, murdered slaves could not invoke this right. But the law explicitly legitimizing the slaves' agency to complain was inconsistent with slavery law's general principles denying to the enslaved all legal rights, except the right to claim that they were not justly enslaved under law.[35]

The Portuguese also were enslaving people at home when they began their African slave trading and foreign empire. These slaves worked in various occupations, including in the domestic service and in the mines. The Portuguese, between 1441 and 1505, imported between 136,000 and 151,000 African slaves. These slaves were concentrated in the more urban areas and were at most 10 percent of Portugal's total population.[36]

The Portuguese also imported enslaved Africans to their colonies. These slaves worked in plantation agriculture, mining, and diverse jobs in urban settlements. Areas in these colonies, including Madeira, the Azores, the Cape Verde Islands, São Tomé, and Brazil, were suited for large-scale sugar plantations. But in Brazil "the characteristic elements of New World tropical slave plantations were first put together." Although Portuguese law permitted the enslavement of Native Americans until 1570, Brazil was the destination for more than four million enslaved Africans, the largest number in the Americas. Slaves were put to work in Brazil's mines and plantations that became models for the French, the English, and the Spanish sugar colonies.[37]

The Portuguese applied and supplemented their existing slavery laws in their colonies. These laws in 1603 were compiled during King Philip II's reign in the *Ordenações Filipinas*, and they formed the basis for Brazilian slavery law until the 1820s, when Brazil gained its independence.[38]

Portuguese slave homicide law generally was consistent with *Las Siete Partidas*. It "prescribed death for anyone, masters included, who murdered a slave."[39] Unlike the law that applied to free servants, however, the Portuguese did not at first regulate nonfatal slave owner punishments, and slaves who resisted or killed their masters faced severe penalties.[40] The *Ordenacoes Filipinas* later permitted owners to impose only moderate physical punishment upon their slaves. This law equated slaves with servants, pupils, wives, or children; its relationship to *Las Siete Partidas* "is readily apparent."[41] And a 1688 law permitted slaves to complain to officials about abusive masters, who could be ordered to sell their slaves to new owners if the masters' "continued ownership might result in unjust treatment."[42]

Brazil's 1824 constitution guaranteed citizenship and equal rights to all native-born free people without regard to race. It also declared that "whips, torture, branding, and all other cruel punishments" could not be imposed on free people. But slaves were excluded from these protections. Brazil did not abolish slavery until 1888.[43]

The French Colonial Statutes

Slaveholding customs and laws had all but died out in France by the end of the sixteenth century. The French New World colonists nevertheless became slaveholders and the law followed these customs.[44] "France was the last European power to enter the Atlantic game of conquest and colonization. In the first half of the seventeenth century, the French began a deliberate, sustained policy of exploration and colonization in American lands, resulting in the establishment of permanent settlements in what is now Canada, French Guiana (in South America), and the Caribbean islands." This effort began with the Atlantic island colonies in Martinique, Saint Christopher (St. Kitts), and Guadeloupe in 1635, and, in 1665, in Saint-Domingue (Haiti) and later expanded to other Atlantic islands and to the lands now in Canada and the United States—including Louisiana, Mississippi, Alabama, and Missouri.[45]

The king and the secretary of state in Versailles headed the French colonial bureaucracy. The king appointed for each colony a governor, "invariably a military officer from an old aristocratic family, and the intendant, who had financial and administrative oversight." Superior Councils of six of the colonies' most prominent males "were the highest judicial courts of appeal and generally represented the wealthiest slaveholders' interests."[46]

French Atlantic island colonists, from the 1630s to 1685, developed local slavery customs and rules. Scholars debate whether this early enslavement law was based on the local evolving customs and practices, Roman law, or both.[47]

Two Martinique prosecutions illustrate these evolving legal norms. On October 20, 1670, a militia lieutenant was impeached for mutilating his slaves by a court made up of his fellow officers.[48] And on May 10, 1671, the Council convicted Charles Brocard of inflicting excessive cruelty on his slave Anne. Governor Jean-Charles de Baas directed the attorney general to review the matter. A doctor examined Anne and reported that she was whipped, she suffered grievous injuries to different parts of her body, and her "shameful parts" were subjected to a "burning firebrand." The island's Council imposed a fine of five hundred pounds of sugar, with potential corporal punishment if Brocard repeated the offense.[49] Brocard had a previous brush with the authorities on October 6, 1664, when he was fined three hundred livres after trading a pocket pistol with the Caribe Indians.[50]

Louis XIV, in March 1685, enacted the law that later became known as the *Code Noir*, "the first integrated slave code written specifically for the Americas." It was "[d]erived from customary practices already developed in the colonies since the 1630s," and "was a collaborative effort by colonial officials and Catholic missionaries, modified by input from royal officials in Versailles."[51]

Malick Ghachem called the *Code Noir* "the last of the landmark royal ordinances of the late seventeenth century" promulgated by Louis XIV and his chief minister Jean-Baptiste Colbert de Seignelay.[52] It was "the product of a kind of preemptive strategy. Seen from the perspective of its own time, before the massive rise of African slavery on a systematic basis . . . , the Code Noir was an effort to grapple with a world of slave unrest and planter brutality that had not yet crystalized but was still coming into view."[53]

Article 42 permitted masters to chain or beat with canes or ropes slaves whom the masters believed "deserved" punishment, but it prohibited "masters from applying torture to their slaves or from inflicting any kind of mutilation, on pain of confiscation of the slaves and special prosecution of the masters."[54] Article 43 authorized the king's colonial officers to prosecute masters or overseers who killed slaves "under their power or under their direction," and these officers were to "punish the murder according to the atrocity of the circumstances." The code nevertheless "permitted the royal officers to 'absolve' such masters where appropriate, without the need to obtain a royal pardon."[55]

Article 26 permitted slaves to complain to prosecutors if they had "not been fed, clothed and maintained by their masters." If this evidence was "corroborated with testimonies from elsewhere," the prosecutors were to pursue masters who were guilty of "barbaric and inhumane treatment" of their slaves. But article 31 barred the admission in court of slave testimony except "to refresh the memory of the judges."[56]

Although the *Code Noir* did not by its own terms extend to New France, it appears that it was applied as if it were binding until 1763, when the British gained control of the colony. The New France colonists enslaved Native Americans and Africans beginning in 1629, before Louis XIV in 1689 declared black slavery to be a proper institution for that colony. Slaves were relatively few in number because plantation agriculture was not suited for the northern soil and climate. The majority of enslaved Canadians worked as domestic servants and lived in the towns. Of those whose ancestry is known, 65.1 percent were Native Americans and 34.9 percent were of African origin.[57]

A revised *Code Noir* for Louisiana, discussed in chapter 11, was adopted in 1724. Its slave homicide provisions are similar to those in the *Code Noir*.

The Visigothic, Spanish, Portuguese, and French Laws in Action

Although there is no evidence of slave homicide law enforcement under the Visigothic codes, historians have found prosecutions of Spanish, Portuguese, Brazilian, and French slave owners. These laws' true effect is hard to assess, however, because the evidence of prosecutions is limited.

Spain's criminal process in the fifteenth and sixteenth centuries had changed from the accusative model of the *Partidas* to an inquisitive model, under which magistrates investigated and prosecuted alleged illegal activity to maintain public order.[58] Spain's vast colonial empire was characterized by sparsely populated peripheral areas with few trained lawyers. The law's effect thus depended on the local administrators' willingness to enforce it.[59]

There is evidence of investigations of unlawful slave abuse and homicides, but the results are inconclusive or the masters only were fined.[60] For example, Jane Landers discussed two bilingual 1811 investigations conducted by Amelia Island justice of the peace Don James Santiago Cahsen. A slave named Yra accused Don Domingo Fernandez of using a stick to beat to death Fernandez's slave Yare. Cahsen heard the testimony of Yra, two other slaves, and Fernandez. A doctor examined Yare's body and concluded that the blows allegedly inflicted by Fernandez did not cause Yare's death. Fernandez was fined three hundred pesos and an embargo on his property was released.[61]

Don Guillermo Braddock that year was accused by his slave Rayna of "horribly" beating to death Braddock's slave Duncan. Rayna reported this killing to those on the plantation of Don Enrique Younge, who advised the authorities. Braddock, a small farmer who owned six slaves, and Younge were recent migrants from Georgia. Cahsen heard testimony of slaves and a neighboring planter, Don Eben O'Neill. After an examining doctor opined that the beating did not cause Duncan's death, Braddock was exonerated on the murder charge, was found guilty of cruel treatment, and was charged with the court costs.[62]

Portuguese colonial slave owners also were prosecuted for slave killings, but there is no evidence of any executions. The authorities used the death penalty "chiefly as a threat to force murderers to accept exile in the dangerous and unhealthy fortresses in Morocco, which were chronically in need of new men for their garrisons, or to encourage them to pay a considerable sum for the commutation or remission of their sentences."[63]

The law in action appears to have been the same after Brazilian independence.[64] For example, Antonio Concalves Carneiro was prosecuted in 1852 for killing his slave Andre, a shoe repairman and an *escravo de ganho*, a slave permitted to find his own work and pay his wages to his owner. Andre lost his job and, fearing punishment, went on the run. A slave named Aniceto alleged that Andre returned to his owner after three days and suffered the fatal beatings. The Council of State, an appointed body that advised the emperor, determined that the owner's "right of property outweighed the government's duty to prevent excessive cruelty and even murder in master-slave relations."[65]

Joao Argolo, an influential planter, in 1887 was accused of killing his slave Damian twelve years earlier. An escaped slave, Silvestre, saw Argolo kill Damian "with a blow to the head." Several other witnesses testified, including Argolo. On June 8, 1887, a judge dismissed the case because the evidence was "insufficient."[66]

The French colonial authorities also investigated slaves' allegations of unlawful abuse and homicides, but the results were inconclusive or the masters were only fined. For example, Saint Martin, a wealthy Saint-Domingue planter who owned three or four hundred slaves, allegedly killed more than two hundred of them. He was prosecuted, in September 1740, for the killing and complete mutilation of five slaves. Governor Marquis de Larnage and Intendant Jean-Pierre Maillart ended an investigation on March 1741 and accepted Saint Martin's 150,000 livres donation.[67] In a July 15, 1741, letter to the authorities in Paris, these officials acknowledged the need "to reprimand the abuses that inhumane masters can engage in because of their authority," but they concluded they could "not do anything that may give the slaves the wrong impression and allow them to move away from the confines of dependence and submission in which they must be kept." The colonial ministers disagreed but accepted the fine.[68]

The unsuccessful 1788 prosecution of Nicholas Lejeune on Saint-Domingue also illustrates the difficulties impeding slave master convictions. Lejeune's slaves complained to the authorities that he mistreated two female slaves, Zabeth and Marie-Rose. Both died soon after they were discovered in confinement on Lejeune's plantation. The local prosecutors pursued the case, but Lejeune was acquitted.[69]

Conclusion

Unlike the Visigothic code, the French, Spanish, and Portuguese laws protected enslaved people's lives from their masters' homicides without discrimination. Less clear was these laws' effect in practice. But they nevertheless expressed the ideal of the monarchs "not as oppressor-in-chief, but as the protector of all persons residing within the royal dominion, including slaves."[70]

CHAPTER 3

Creating a British Colonial Law of Slave Killing

British colonial slavery law evolved in a more revealing manner than did the law in the Spanish, Portuguese, and French colonies because the central government in London let the colonists enact in the positive law their evolving customs and practices, including those that put slaves' lives in jeopardy. The colonists believed that they could write this law on a blank slate because slavery had "vanished" from English society, culture, and law, "except in ancient texts."[1]

Indeed, by the 1600s, no law or court ruling expressly permitted or abolished slavery in Britain. The British also "had no Roman law tradition with its well-developed rules for slavery."[2]

The seventeenth-century British colonists were well aware of slavery as it was practiced elsewhere. But they did not copy the Spanish, Portuguese, or French homicide provisions. Like the early French colonists, they just assumed that they had the right to enslave Native Americans and Africans and accepted "[s]lavery as a social institution . . . without legal authorization. Thus, in the early days in the colonies overall, there were slaves but no law of slavery. The law came into being bit-by-bit, either by statute or by judicial precedent, sometimes based on what the people did." This local law was "more geared to local conditions than was the law in the Spanish or Portuguese colonies."[3]

Accordingly, as slavery became a social reality in the British colonies, the lawmakers and judges accommodated slavery's fundamental elements into the body of the English common law. They did not base this law on a code of Roman, medieval, or nonlocal origin. Instead, they made up the law as they went along to advance the salient public and private interests.[4]

From hereditary lifetime slavery's "very inception" in the British colonies "practical questions requiring legal answers arose every day" for which there were no precedents. These included "which heir should take how many slaves; what were the limits to a master's punishment of his slave; did a lessee have to pay when the slave died within the term of the lease. Whatever the substance of the answers, it was clear that English colonial slave law had to be homegrown."[5]

These "homegrown" laws included provisions trivializing or legitimizing homicides of enslaved people committed by slave owners and other free people. The laws followed three major trends in British history: (1) slavery's disappearance from Britain's society and law, (2) the British state's near monopolization of the roles of homicide prosecution and punishment, and (3) the British central government's failure to establish a slave code for the colonies.

Slave Master Homicide Law in British History

Slavery had for centuries been a part of Anglo-Saxon law and society before it "abruptly ended shortly after the Norman conquest of 1066."[6] Slaves made up almost 10 percent of the English population in 1086, and in some areas the enslaved population may have been as much as 20 percent to 25 percent. Enslaved people worked in the fields and in their masters' households.[7]

Medieval society in England included three major classes: the nobility, the *ceorlas*, and the slaves. The *ceorlas* made up the majority of the population. They worked in agriculture but were not enslaved; rather, they were members of the society who "could appeal to the protection of the customary law of the chiefdom in order to gain redress if wronged." Slaves, in contrast, had no legal recourse and "were regarded as chattels rather than persons." These "unfree" people "were not recognized as members of the chiefdom."[8]

As in the Germanic tribes, in Celtic and Anglo-Saxon Britain the blood feud was used to deter and punish homicide. The payment of compensation to a victim's family, the wergild, was an alternative to the blood feud and eventually replaced the feud as the preferred form of punishment. The victims' social status and their perceived value to their kin determined the payment.[9]

Because the Anglo-Saxon laws treated slaves as chattels, masters could recover compensation when other people committed wrongs against their slaves. But "[t]he slave had no wergild. He was a chattel, and if anyone killed him, he had merely to pay [the killed slave's] value to the owner. The usual price for a slave was a pound, the equivalent of eight oxen."[10]

The slave's kin thus did not recover the wergild when a slave was killed. "From a psychological point of view, this must have been a severe disability, since kinship was the strongest bond in Anglo-Saxon society."[11]

The first written English laws, which date to approximately 600, confirm that enslaved people's lives were devalued. These laws are attributed to Ethelbert I of Kent. They included provisions, also called dooms, establishing a standard schedule of the amounts of monetary compensation to be paid to homicide victims' families, "not as a radical substitute for feud but as a piece of it."[12]

This schedule of the relative perceived value of human lives reflected the social class structure. Ethelbert's laws "were plainly concerned with" providing, "in the form of fixed monetary payments, an alternative to retaliation and the feud." They also confirmed the slave's nonperson status, however, because they did not provide for any wergild if a slave was killed.[13]

The laws of Anglo-Saxon king Alfred the Great, codified around 892–93, were a synthesis of the laws of the Anglo-Saxon kingdoms that was influenced by Christian doctrine and Mosaic law. Alfred's code recognized slaves both as property and persons. According to David Pelteret, clauses 17 and 20 of the introduction included translations of Exodus 21:20–21 and 26 regulating slavery. Among these was a provision declaring a master guilty if a slave dies at his master's hands within the day of the abuse.[14]

Like Ethelbert's laws, however, Alfred's laws included a schedule of standardized wergild compensation values based on victims' social status. This schedule did not include slaves.[15]

Villeinage (also spelled *villainage* and *villenage*) also had a long career in English law and society. But it too had vanished when the English American colonization process began. Villeinage was "a form of serfdom superior to slavery."[16] The common law protected villeins from the violence of third parties and of their lords. Although lords could beat their villeins with impunity, they could not kill, maim, or rape them. Villeins "were never submitted to extremes of seigniorial constraint of the kind we label 'slavery.'"[17]

Jonathan Bush therefore concluded that "English colonial slave law had to be home-grown. Although English law had never abolished the category of 'villeinage'—common law serfdom—it was in complete desuetude, and the common law did not have another category for slaves."[18]

The British Common Law of Homicide

Before the Norman Conquest of 1066, "public authority had already taken over at least part of the responsibilities of the kin" for homicide prosecution, and "within two centuries after it the bloodfeud itself had been replaced by a concept of crime enshrined in a uniquely comprehensive system of royal justice."[19] Frederick Pollock and Frederic William Maitland thus concluded that the courts replaced the "elaborate system" of the wergild with a common law of homicide "with marvelous suddenness." Under this common law, the courts and juries punished killers as they enforced the king's peace. The state obtained and enforced a near monopoly on fatal violence and punishment for killers.[20]

This common law of homicide evolved over time. By the late sixteenth century, it established three classes of homicide: murder, manslaughter, and excusable homicide. Murder was the killing of another person with malice aforethought. It was punishable by death. Manslaughter was a sudden killing without premeditation based upon a legally adequate provocation, which did not extend to mere words or gestures. Manslaughter too was punishable by death. The definition of malice aforethought and the distinction between murder and manslaughter emerged more clearly in the early sixteenth century. Malice aforethought eventually came to include cold-blooded killings or killings committed while the defendant was perpetrating a felony.[21]

The common law afforded the benefit of clergy to murder and manslaughter defendants on their first offenses. The lives of defendants given this benefit were spared, but these killers were branded on the hand as evidence of their prior convictions. Those convicted of murder were denied this benefit by statutes adopted between 1496 and 1547.[22]

Defendants also could avoid criminal liability for homicides that were justified or excused. The common law, by the 1600s, narrowly defined justified and excusable homicides to advance the state's near monopoly on fatal violence. Justified homicides, in essence, could be committed with the king's express or implied permission. Examples included executions of felons after trials and convictions, killings of outlaws and thieves resisting capture, and killings to prevent felonies, for example, when the homicide defendant was an innocent victim of a violent crime such as robbery or rape and he or she killed the aggressor.[23]

Excusable killings, on the other hand, included homicides *per infortunium*, by misadventure, and homicides *excusable se defendendo*, in self-defense. Homicide by misadventure occurred when a defendant killed his victim while doing a lawful act without the intention to kill. But an accidental killing could have been manslaughter or murder if it occurred while the defendant was committing an unlawful act.[24]

The common law presumed that defendants charged with intentional killings acted with malice aforethought. These defendants had to establish legally adequate reasons to justify or excuse their homicides or provocations that would mitigate their homicides to manslaughter.[25]

The common law in the 1600s still permitted "superiors," such as parents and masters, to physically punish or correct misbehaving "inferiors," including children or servants, by striking them with their hands or with small sticks as long as the punishment was moderate and reasonable. This was an exception to the general rule providing that even a slight nonconsensual touching was wrongful. These "superiors" thus committed excusable homicides if unintended killings resulted from their lawful moderate punishment. But those who imposed immoderate and unlawful punishment could be convicted of murder or manslaughter.[26]

Accordingly, Michael Dalton's 1618 treatise included among killings by misadventure any deaths occurring while schoolmasters, parents, or masters in a "reasonable manner" corrected their students, children, or servants.[27] Sir William Hawkins in 1716 declared further that killings could be mitigated to manslaughter even if one of these "superiors" killed an "inferior" person by correction that was "barbarous as to exceed all Bounds of Moderation." The defendant would be guilty of murder, however, if he used an "instrument improper for correction, and apparently indangering the Party's Life, as an Iron Bar, or Sword, etc., or kick him to the Ground, and then stamp on his Belly and kill him."[28]

For example, John Grey, a blacksmith, in 1666 was convicted of murdering a servant, William Golden. Grey was not satisfied with Golden's work. During a discussion, "Grey, without any other provocation, struck ... Golden with a bar of iron, which ... Grey then had in his hand, and upon which he and Golden were working at the anvil." The blow hit Golden in the head, broke his skull, and killed him. Grey was convicted of murder because an iron bar was not considered to be among the usual or proper instruments of correction.[29]

Self-defense initially was not a common law legal defense to a homicide charge. Instead, those who killed in self-defense were considered for royal pardons based on the merits of their own cases.[30]

Self-defense eventually became a defense at law. An accused killer had to establish that an aggressor presented an imminent or immediate danger of unlawful bodily harm to the defendant, who used force to the extent that it was necessary to avoid the danger the aggressor posed. To establish this necessity element, defendants had to retreat to the wall if they could do so safely before killing their victims.[31]

Sir Matthew Hale's 1678 treatise thus declared that a homicide defendant claiming self-defense "is not excused, unless he give back to the Wall. But if the assault be so fierce, and in such a place that giving back would endanger his life, then he need not give back." The courts did not require a person to retreat if the homicide was justifiable, or if a killer responded to an attack in his or her home.[32]

Creating a Modern British Law of Slave Homicide

Accordingly, medieval and early modern English lawmakers shifted "personal disputes from field and street to the court of law. The state—that is, the Crown, insisted on monopolizing for itself the act of homicide."[33] But no pre-1600 British statutes or cases determined whether slave killings would or would not be murders or manslaughters. It also was not decided whether the mitigation standards for servants, apprentices, students, impressed sailors, or villeins applied to slaves. Nor were there any precedents defining the limits of slave master punishments or stating whether masters were required to retreat to the wall before killing aggressive slaves who were resisting the masters' punishment or authority.

These legal voids existed because slavery's oppressive human relations were unknown to the law that the British colonists brought to the New World. This absence of legal rules is consistent with the essential point that "the master and slave relationship is qualitatively different" from other forms of human relationships that are based on "inequality and domination."[34] As Christopher Brown concluded, "enslaved Africans suffered a degree of powerlessness in the colonies wholly without equal elsewhere in the British dominions." This powerlessness included the slaves' length of service, the treatment of slave parents and children, the slaves' lack of access to legal protections, and the degrees of dishonor and physical abuse that were characteristics of slavery.[35]

Indeed, Sir Moses Finley captured slavery's essential elements when he wrote, "The slaveowner's rights over his slave-property, were total in more senses than one. The slave ... suffered not only total loss of control over his labour but total loss of control over his person and his personality." Slavery was unique because "the labourer himself was a commodity, not merely his labour-power. His loss of control, furthermore, extended to the infinity of time, to his children and his children's children—unless ... the owner by a unilateral act broke the chain through unconditional manumission."[36]

Jedediah Purdy called this interpretation "the *anomaly* model," which understands "slavery as essentially different from other relationships and as resisting both conceptual and practical assimilation to the law of labor relations." He contrasts this with "the *conciliatory* model," in which the master-slave relationship is "part of a spectrum, analogous to the other legal bonds arising from agreement or status."[37]

Scholars advancing the conciliatory model include Justin Roberts, who argued that those who depict slavery as freedom's "polar opposite" or "as being uniquely different from other forms of coerced labor" have "fetishized" slavery as an "aberrant" institution. He conceded that slavery was "a brutal and violent institution," and that "the chattel principle, in some ways, made it distinct from other forms of coerced labor (such as naval impressment or indentured servitude)." But he asserted that slavery was only one example of "dependency in the hierarchical world of the eighteenth-century Atlantic. Thus, the violence within slavery must be understood as a point on a spectrum of violence in the early modern world."[38] Roberts concluded that in the British colonies he studied "the key difference between slaves and free laborers was that slaves lived under the constant threat of being sold or having their families separated from them or being beaten and tortured."[39]

These differences between slavery and other forms of domination suggest why the anomaly model permits twenty-first-century readers to best understand slavery as a point on a spectrum not of oppressive human relationships but of property ownership relationships. That spectrum defines the rights and duties of people and the state in property. The law applied different legal principles to living and nonliving property, taking into account the different natures of property, which in the past included human property. But by defining slaves as property, the law recognized that slavery was fundamentally different from other forms of human relationships that were characterized by varying levels of domination. Judges and legislators legitimized the slave's status by adapting common law property concepts "to fit the mold" of slavery's "social reality."[40]

British law did, of course, create for some people quasi-property rights in other people. Examples include relationships between or among husbands, wives, and children; masters and apprentices, servants, and day laborers; and the navy and impressed sailors. But enslaved people differed "not in being property, but rather in being nothing but property."[41]

Scholars have suggested that English customs and statutes approaching slavery's essence provided analogies for the British colonists who established slavery practices and laws. The Tudor-era Vagrancy Act of 1547 is cited as one example because it authorized procedures to enslave vagrants. But this law lasted only for about two years.[42]

Even in the seventeenth and eighteenth centuries, Andrew Fletcher (1689), George Berkeley (1735–37), and Francis Hutcheson (1755) authored proposals advocating the enslavement of England's poor. But they were not adopted and did not include true lifetime hereditary slavery and instead sought "to clothe and feed the destitute," who were to remain in society's "lower order."[43]

Slaveholding nevertheless was so appealing to the British colonists that they were not deterred by slavery's questionable legality. Thus, at a May 1652 joint meeting, the commissions of the towns of Providence and Warwick in Rhode Island adopted a law noting that by then it was "a common course practised amongst English men to buy negers, to the end they may have them for their service or slaves forever." The law declared that both whites and blacks "forced by covenant bond, or otherwise" were not to serve any longer than ten years, except for children who were younger than fourteen when they were imported; they could serve until they were twenty-four years old. These servants were to be freed when their terms ended "as the manner is with the English servants." Masters who violated the law were to pay fines of forty pounds.[44]

But this law may have been a "dead letter" as soon as 1654, when the Rhode Island towns were reunited. Rhode Islanders also began slaveholding practices and later legalized what they were already doing. These and other British colonial lawmakers at first generally resolved the legal issues that the early settlers found were the most pressing. As frontier settlement patterns gave way to plantation agriculture or other mature development patterns, the local legislatures adopted more comprehensive slave laws and judges developed a common law of slavery.[45]

This local colonial legislation controlled under what Mary Sarah Bilder called Britain's "transatlantic constitution." This was "an overarching arrangement of authority" both unwritten and written in colonial charters. Governors and councils of colonists appointed in London ran the colonies' day-to-day affairs, and locally elected assemblies or legislatures adopted local laws that they deemed necessary. These laws were not to be repugnant to and divergent from the laws of England.[46]

Thus as Jonathan Bush noted, under "the seventeenth-century version of the conquest doctrine, English law allowed *all the colonies* a private space in which planters and merchants could deploy slave labor with little oversight from England. The leash was never so long that colonists could take major or costly policy initiatives at will against the wishes of the Crown." Bush argued that "Westminster demanded the right to review local legislation and to reject unsuitable legislation. Often Westminster was able to make its claims and policies stick. But the momentum was with the colonists. By using the decentralized private space allowed them by prerogative constitutionalism, the colonists were able to erect a regime of slave law."[47]

This locally enacted legal regime included slave homicide law. The British Atlantic world colonists were aware of the Spanish and Portuguese slavery practices and copied these practices. But they did not copy the Spanish and

Portuguese slave homicide laws. This colonial slave law instead reflected local conditions in three "culture hearths," which were Barbados, New England, and Virginia in the Chesapeake.[48]

A culture hearth is an area where "new basic cultural systems and configurations are developed and nurtured before spreading vigorously outward to alter the character of much larger areas."[49] Colonists in these culture hearths developed "local cultures, including social institutions and ways of manipulating a particular kind of environment." With "appropriate modifications" these cultures were transferred "to other areas in the Anglo-American world."[50]

The plantation slavery system, in which most of the local population was enslaved, was "first articulated in Barbados." It "slowly spread to the nearby Leeward Islands in the eastern Caribbean and, after its capture from the Spaniards in 1655, to the large island of Jamaica in the central Caribbean." This culture, after 1750, was exported to Britain's other Atlantic island colonies. "[A] variant strain of that culture developed . . . in the Leeward Island colonies of St. Kitts, Antigua, Nevis, and Montserrat," as well as "in the new British West Indian island colonies of the Virgin Islands, St. Vincent, Dominica, and Tobago."

Slavery's development patterns in British North America were more diverse. The Barbados plantation culture reached the mainland in parts of South Carolina, the Cape Fear region of North Carolina, Georgia, and Florida. Virginia's colonists, in contrast, developed a "tobacco and mixed farming culture" that spread into Maryland, Delaware, North Carolina, and parts of Pennsylvania. And the "mixed-farming and fishing culture of Puritan Massachusetts Bay extended itself into offshoot societies in Connecticut, Rhode Island, New Haven, New Hampshire, Long Island, New Jersey, and Maine."[51]

Conclusion

It is not surprising, then, that the first wave of slave homicide laws adopted in Barbados, Virginia, and Massachusetts exhibited three different approaches, which were adapted in the British colonies with similar demographic and cultural conditions. Colonists in all areas based their laws on the notion that—without legislative action legitimizing violence against slaves—slave killings might be common law murder, manslaughter, or justifiable homicide.

What was surprising, however, was how the colonists in all of these regions openly defied the central British colonial authorities and monarchs who disapproved of many of the local colonial slave homicide laws. Chapters 4 to 6 illustrate how Britain's central government tried to influence these slave homicide laws but for many years failed to facilitate slave homicide reform.

The colonial legislators "at the top" accommodated slavery into the law, often in response to the actions of those "at the bottom"—slaves, masters, and third parties. They "claimed rights every bit as extreme as those enjoyed by their fellow subjects in England. Indeed, in many respects, the rights they claimed were broader. Nowhere was this more evident than with slavery."[52]

CHAPTER 4

Decriminalization to Amelioration on Britain's Atlantic Island Colonies

Seventeenth- and eighteenth-century British Atlantic island colonial lawmakers adopted statutes decriminalizing some slave homicides and abolishing capital punishment for others that would have been common law murders. These laws explicitly were based on the notion that Africans did not deserve the common law of crime's equal protection from fatal and nonfatal violence. These laws bucked the trend in England by which the number of capital crimes increased in the 130 years after 1688 from fifty to two hundred, although capital punishment was not imposed with regularity.[1]

These British colonists for almost a century disregarded the colonial authorities' directives urging them to adopt laws imposing the ultimate penalty on malicious slave killers. The central government did not adopt a colonial slave code or compel local criminal law reforms.[2]

These colonial legislators adopted ameliorative laws in the late eighteenth century, restoring the death penalty for slave murders and giving slave owners no superior right over their slaves' lives. But these laws' effects are hard to evaluate because there were few slave owner homicide prosecutions in slavery's final decades in the British colonies.

Early Colonial Barbados and Jamaican Laws

The Barbados slave homicide laws were models used by Britain's other Atlantic island colonies. The first British settlers landed on the island in 1627. Although British settlements had by then been established on Bermuda and Saint Kitts (Saint Christopher), Barbados soon became Britain's most important colony. The island's economy at first was based on small-scale farming and some tobacco and cotton exports. Sugar was the cash crop that by the 1660s enabled Barbados to become a slave society and Britain's most populous and lucrative Atlantic island colony, until it later was overcome by Jamaica.[3]

The Barbadian colonists established plantations on which the majority of the laborers at first were white indentured servants—many of whom were Irish and Scottish. Contracts limited this servitude to fixed lengths, and servants could assert their rights in local courts. Africans and Indians also were imported in small numbers at the start. The colony's population, by 1637, was about six thousand, but only about two hundred were African. Africans in 1643 were 25 percent of the total, and by 1650 they were about 26 percent.[4] The island's enslaved population increased by the 1650s to 50 percent and by 1680 to almost 70 percent. After 1750 the black population plateaued at about 80 percent.[5]

Some early Barbadian colonists may have been unsure about the Africans' status. Governor Henry Hawley and the Council, on July 21, 1636, apparently adopted a resolution declaring that, unless a contract provided otherwise, "Negroes that come here to be sold [would] serve for life."[6] Although Jerome Handler has questioned this resolution's existence, the colonists nonetheless enslaved Africans for life during the early years of settlement. And the island's assembly after 1641 began to adopt laws controlling servants and slaves, including a 1652 law requiring those leaving their plantations to have tickets or passes from their owners.[7]

It is not clear how Barbadians initially treated slave homicides. In one 1650s case, the island's Council ordered a justice of the peace to investigate whether a slave master, his wife, and their children killed a female slave "by cruel beating and other horrid misusage." Although there are no other records of this case, it suggests that some may have assumed—or feared—that common law homicide principles protected the island's enslaved people.[8] On the other hand, John Berkenhead in 1654 wrote "that Barbadians killed their slaves with impunity and ranked them with 'doggs.'"[9]

The island's legislators resolved this uncertainty with a 1661 statute titled An Act for the Better Ordering and Governing of Negroes, which followed "years of piecemeal legislation and discussion regarding slaves," many of which are lost to history.[10] The first Barbadian assembly to meet after the Restoration in September 1661 adopted this act, and the new acting governor, Humphrey Walrond, signed it the same month that the assembly approved An Act for the Good Governing of the Rights between Masters and Servants. This suggests "that the assembly worked out this legislation as one comprehensive project for the governance of laborers."[11]

The slavery act's preamble declared that the island had "many good laws and ordinances" that did not adequately regulate slavery. It called Africans "an heathenish, brutish and uncertaine, dangerous kinde of people" who must be governed by laws that were not "contradictory to the Laws of England." But the legislators confronted uncertainty, "there being in all the body of that Lawe noe track to guide us where to walke nor any rule sett us how to govern such slaves."

The preamble also asserted that slaves were property whom the legislators sought to protect "as wee doe men's other goods and Chattles." The legislators recognized, however, that "the right rule of reason and order" required that slaves not be left "to the Arbitrary, cruell and outragious wills of every evill disposed person." Slaves deserved greater legal protection than other property "as being created men, though without the knowledge of God in the world."[12]

This confirms that these lawmakers did not rely on the repealed 1547 British vagrancy law; nor did they rely on "the ancient villeinage laws, then scarcely extinct on British ground." Instead, they declared themselves free to write slavery laws reflecting their admitted racism and xenophobia.[13]

Clause 20 reconciled these biases and concerns by legitimizing the masters' right to punish and kill their slaves who misbehaved or ran away without having to comply with the common law requirement that the masters apply punishment in a reasonable manner. This clause stated, "if any Negro under punishment of his Master or his Order for Running away or any other Crimes or misdemeanor towards his said master shall suffer in his life or in member, no person whatsoever shall be accomptable to any law therefore." The clause then reduced to mere fines the penalties for slave killings that it did not decriminalize. It stated that anyone who "of wantonness or only mindedness and cruel intention willfully kill[s] any Negro of his owne," must pay a fine of "three thousand of [muscovado] sugar." One killing another person's slave was to pay to the slave's owner double the slave's value and pay a fine of "five thousand pounds of [muscovado] sugar." The killer also was "by the next Justice of the peace [to] be bound to the good behavior during the pleasure of the Governor and Council and not be liable to any other punishment or forfeiture for the same."[14]

Those killing "another man's Negro by accident [would not be] liable to any other penalty but the owner's action at law." But "if any poor small freeholder or other person kill a Negro by night out of the common path and stealing the provision, swine, or other goods He shall not be acceptable for it, any Law, Statutes or Ordinances to the contrary notwithstanding."[15]

Clause 2 of the act denied to enslaved people the common law privilege of self-defense in response to "Christian" violence, stating that "if any Negroe man or woman shall offer any Violence to any Christian as by striking or the like the Negroe shall for his and their first offence by information given to the next Justice of the peace bee severely whipped by the Constable by order of said Justice." The justices of the peace were to "severely" whip second offenders, slit their noses, and burn their faces. The governor and Council could impose on third-time offenders "such greater corporall punishment" that they thought necessary, provided "always that such striking or conflict bee not in the lawful defence of their Master[,] Mistress[,] or owner of their families[,] or of their goods."[16] This clause is best understood with a 1652 act providing that indentured servants who struck their masters could be punished with two years' additional service. The penalty in 1661 was reduced to one additional year of service.[17]

This 1661 slavery act thus illustrates three essential points. First, the colonists apparently believed that common law principles might apply absent a statute legitimizing some slave killings and reducing the penalties for others. Second, they denied to enslaved people the common law of homicide's equal protection because of their alleged racial characteristics. Third, they reduced the common law penalties for wanton and willful slave murder. Unlike a common law felony, this offense would not result in the killer's execution or the forfeiture of the offender's property.[18]

These lawmakers in the same month enacted a law better protecting servants from the "great violence and great oppression" of their masters, finding that some servants "have been murdered and destroyed." Servants who died during their term of service were not to be buried "before the body was examined by a justice of the peace or a constable" and two neighbors. Masters violating this act faced a fine of twenty thousand pounds of muscovado sugar, almost seven times the fine for maliciously killing an enslaved person.[19]

Governor Jonathan Atkins sent the Barbados slave laws to England for approval by the Lords of Trade and Plantations responding to the Lord's requests. Charles II created this body in 1675 to replace the Council on Trade and Plantations as a committee of the Privy Council. This committee and its 1696 successor known as the Board of Trade and Plantations, among other things, issued instructions to royal governors upon their appointments and reviewed the colonies' local legislation. But statutes involving race and slavery for the most part "were regarded as matters for the colonists themselves to sort out."[20]

The Lords of Trade, in July 1679, asked Sir Samuel Baldwin, one of the king's Sergeants at Law, to review the Barbados slave laws adopted between 1660 and 1672. Baldwin advised the Board, in June 1680, that these laws were "good, though not always consonant with the laws of England." He cited provisions calling for trials of slaves accused of capital offenses "summarily before two justices of the peace" instead of a jury, and provisions punishing "negroes... more severely than others for like offences." He did not mention the slave killing provisions. But he tacitly approved of them when he concluded that the laws he reviewed were "reasonable for by reason of their numbers [the enslaved] become dangerous, and being a brutish sort of people and reckoned as goods and chattels in the Island, it is of necessity or at least convenient to have Laws for Government of them different from the Laws of England, to prevent the great mischief that otherwise may happen to the Planters and Inhabitants in that Island."[21]

The colonial legislators on Britain's other Atlantic island colonies generally borrowed or built upon the Barbadian act's provisions, including the clause limiting the penalties for slave killers to fines. Slavery's development on these islands—other than Bermuda and the Bahamas—duplicated the Barbadian pattern. The colonists practiced plantation agriculture, and the islands' enslaved populations eventually by far exceeded the whites. These demographic patterns may have influenced the planters' and legislators' views about how the criminal law should protect their slaves' lives.[22] This transmission of experiences and approaches to colonial administration in the first half of the seventeenth century also was aided by what Alison Games called the "sequential migration of governors" from colony to colony, which assisted the colonies' survival and facilitated slavery's growth.[23]

Jamaica provides an example of this migration of both people and law. England acquired Jamaica from Spain in 1655. The island's population grew slowly at first. In 1660 it was about 2,200, and by 1662 it was about 3,500 whites and 550 blacks.[24]

Things began to change in June 1664 when Jamaica's new governor Sir Thomas Molyford and almost 1,000 other Barbadians brought the 1661 Barbados slave and servant acts to Jamaica. The local assembly, in the fall of 1664, adopted a copy of the Barbadian slavery act with only minor modifications.[25]

This code "was an instrument for instituting a slave labor system rather than a response to its emergence." Molyford sought to re-create the Barbados sugar economy on Jamaica and "provided the legal structure for its advance."[26] Jamaica's enslaved population in 1664 was only about 15 percent of the total, but the act adopted that year "reflected economic aspirations that quickly materialized." Cocoa production first fueled the island's enslaved population boom, and sugar production, which began in the late 1670s, carried this population to new heights. The island's black population in 1673 made up almost 50 percent of the total. By 1681 blacks outnumbered whites three to one. Blacks reached 85 percent of the total in 1693 and exceeded 90 percent from 1730 to 1788.[27]

Jamaica "came to dominate British sugar production at some point before the middle of the eighteenth century."[28]

The Colonists Resist Calls for Homicide Law Reform

Beginning in the 1680s, England's colonial authorities, including the Lords of Trade and Plantations and the Board of Trade and Plantations, asked Britain's colonists to adopt slave homicide reform laws. Instructions calling for these reforms were given to the governors of Jamaica and Virginia, and later to the governors of the islands including Barbados, the Leeward Islands, and the Bahamas, as well as the governors of Maryland, New England, Massachusetts, New Hampshire, New Jersey, New York, North and South Carolina, and Georgia.[29]

The British Atlantic island colonists resisted these instructions for more than a hundred years. For example, Jamaica's legislators revised the island's slave laws in the 1670s and the 1680s. A July 2, 1681, statute titled An Act for the Better Ordering of Slaves contained a new slave homicide provision stating that if a slave should die or lose a limb because of punishment from the owner for running away, "no person shall be liable for same, but if any through wantonness or cruelty shall kill a slave he or she shall forfeit twenty pounds to the King and forty pounds to the owner."[30]

The Lords of Trade, in a February 17, 1683, letter to Jamaica's Governor Thomas Lynch, stated that King Charles II had "confirmed the laws of Jamaica for seven years, except for some few remitted for amendment." These laws included the Act for Regulating Slaves. But the letter also declared, "A fine is imposed on all such as wilfully and wantonly kill a negro. The King will not confirm this clause, which seems to encourage the willful shedding of blood. Some better provision must be found than a fine to deter men from such acts of cruelty."[31]

Jamaica's Assembly responded on April 5, 1683, with a slavery act that included a provision stating, "If any slave by punishment from his owner for running away, or other offence, suffer life or limb, none shall be liable to the law for same; but whoever shall kill a slave out of wilfulness, wantonness, or bloody-mindedness, shall suffer three months' imprisonment" and pay a fine to the slave's owner of fifty pounds. Servants were punished with thirty-nine lashes and four years' additional service to be given to the owner of the murdered slave.[32]

Charles II, in May 1684, apparently approved at least some of the act's provisions. But before his sudden death in February 1685, he disapproved of the act's punishment for slave murder. The instructions given to Jamaican governors Sir

Phillip Howard, in 1685, and Christopher Monck, the Second Duke of Albemarle, in 1686 or 1687, thus stated, "You shall endeavor to get a law passed, for restraining of any unhuman severity, by reason of ill masters and overseers, that may be used towards their Christian servants or other Slaves." The instructions also declared that Charles II "did not think fit to confirm" the latest Jamaican slave homicide law stating that those who "wantonly and wilfully kill a Negro, are only liable to a fine, and three months imprisonment; which penalties not being equal to the guilt, might encourage the wilful shedding of blood; for which it is necessary some better provision be made, to deter all persons from such acts of cruelty." The governors were "to signify the same unto the next Assembly, and farther propose to them the enacting of a stricter clause in that behalf, which may be fit for our royal confirmation."[33]

Jamaica's assembly did not respond to this request until 1696, when it adopted An Act for the Better Order and Government of Slaves. This act continued to deny to slaves' lives the law's equal protection. It stated that any person "willingly, wantonly, or bloody-mindedly kill[ing] a Negro or Slave" would receive the benefit of clergy on his or her first offense. Only after a second willful slave killing was a defendant to be found guilty of murder without the benefit of clergy. These repeat offenders were to be punished "according to the Laws of *England*," except that the offender would not forfeit "Lands and Tenements, Goods and chattels."[34]

This act also imposed greater penalties on slaves who defended themselves from white violence. The 1664 act had stated that slaves who "offer any blow to any Christian" were to be whipped for the first offense, and, for a second offense, were to be whipped and have their noses split and faces burned. This section was amended in 1674 to apply to violence directed at any white Christian, and a 1677 revision deleted the reference to Christians. The 1696 act authorized the death penalty, or any other punishment imposed in the judges' discretion, if any slave "shall offer any violence, by striking or otherwise, . . . any white Person," unless the slave committed the violent act while defending his or her master's person or property or while complying with the master's lawful order.[35]

Meanwhile, the Barbadian assembly, between 1661 and 1688, adopted several acts addressing issues including Indian slavery and slave control. But the legislators continued to provide that slave killers should be punished with the payment of fines and damages to the slaves' owners.[36]

The Board of Trade's May 3, 1684, instructions to the island's governor, Sir Richard Dutton, found that the Barbadian laws "concerning Negroes" did not provide "sufficient punishment . . . for those that shall wilfully and wantonly kill a Negro." Dutton therefore was to "propose to the next assembly the enacting [of] some further penalty that may prevent same."[37]

This instruction shows how royal colonial policy had evolved. The December 19, 1673, instructions to Barbadian governor Sir John Atkins, in contrast, directed that he endeavor to convince the colonial legislators to adopt laws "for restraining inhuman severity by masters and overseers toward their Christian servants."[38]

The Barbados assembly ignored this request, as confirmed by the August 8, 1688, law titled An Act for the Governing of Negroes. This act "repealed all the earlier acts governing slaves and replaced them with a comprehensive law for slavery that remained in effect throughout the eighteenth century." It "simplified" the earlier acts' provisions "and streamlined their application."[39]

This act modified the fines and penalties imposed on slave killers. Masters who maliciously killed their slaves were to be fined fifteen pounds. Other malicious slave killers were to pay fines of twenty-five pounds, post bonds for their later good behavior, and pay the dead slaves' owners double the slaves' value. Those killing slaves by accident were liable only for damages in a suit by the slaves' owners.[40]

The Colonists Continue to Resist Calls for Reform

The British Leeward Island legislators emulated the Barbadian and Jamaican laws and imposed fines for slave murder. The original four Leeward Islands—Antigua, Montserrat, Nevis, and Saint Kitts—were settled "in the shadow" of Barbados and Jamaica. The Leeward Islands were under Barbadian jurisdiction until 1670, when the Board of Trade "reconstituted them as a separate federated colony." Although they shared a governor, each island had its own lieutenant governor, council, and assembly. Only the laws approved by a General Assembly of the Leeward Islands were binding on all of these islands.[41]

These islands' enslaved populations grew steadily at first. By 1678, "only Nevis had more black inhabitants that it did white, but by 1707 the whites on all four islands were outnumbered by the blacks by a factor of 2, a tendency that grew still more pronounced over the course of the eighteenth century. By 1756, the percentage ranged from 86.1 in Nevis to 90.2 in Antigua."[42]

Sugar plantations dominated the local economies and fueled this surge in the islands' slave populations. Slaves eventually outnumbered whites at rates even higher than on Barbados or Jamaica: 7.5 to 1 on Montserrat, 11 to 1 on Nevis, 12 to 1 on Saint Kitts, and 15 to 1 on Antigua.[43] "By the second quarter of the eighteenth century, the Leeward Islands, led by Antigua, took over from Barbados as the primary sugar producing region in the British Caribbean."[44]

The British Leeward Island slave homicide provisions included Antigua's 1697 act, which fined willful slave killers ten thousand pounds of sugar payable "to the King, for the public use, besides paying the owner." Those who could not pay the fine were to receive thirty-nine lashes on their bare backs, a six-month prison term without bail, and a four-year term of service to the dead slave's owner. The act also stated, "if any Slave lose Life or Limb by Punishment for a Crime, by his master, or the Justice's Order, No Person shall be liable to the law for the same."[45]

Upon his appointment as the Leeward Islands governor in 1705, Daniel Parke's instructions included the by then usual directive to get a law passed "(if not already done)," restraining "Inhumane Severity" by masters and overseers on their servants and slaves and making the "willful killing of Indians and Negroes" a crime punishable by death. Antigua's governors continued to receive this instruction, but the colonists refused to equate slave killing with murder.[46]

A December 9, 1723, slavery law thus again included provisions imposing only a fine for slave killings. The law's findings asserted that "several Cruel Persons, to gratify their own Humours, against the Laws of God and Humanity, frequently kill, destroy, or dismember" their own slaves or the slaves belonging to others, and that these killings "have hitherto gone unpunished, because it is inconsistent with the Constitution and Government of this Island." The legislators also found, however, that slave killers should not face the death penalty because this would encourage slaves to resist, and because the laws in the other British colonial islands did not require this equality. Although the Antiguans did not have the opportunity to review all of these laws, the act stated they "are found very effectual" crime deterrents.

Therefore, the act declared that anyone convicted of willfully killing a slave by "excessive punishment or otherwise" without an excuse provided by the laws of Great Britain or Antigua was liable for a fine of not less than one hundred pounds and not more than three hundred pounds. A convicted defendant would be imprisoned until the fine was paid and would have to post surety for good behavior for one year.[47]

Governor John Hart explained in a letter to the Board of Trade that, although he used his "utmost endeavours to make the murdering of a slave punishable with death," he could not get such a law passed. He nevertheless called this act "a great point" gained because there was "no law before this that laid any penalty on offenders for the crimes mentioned."[48]

According to David Barry Gaspar, this 1723 act was not intended "so much to prevent the brutal punishment of slaves for their own good but to control situations that could generate slave unrest or hostility." He quoted Elsa Goveia, stating that the reform "regulations were often intended to control behaviour which was held as impolitic as well as inhumane, and, for this reason, the context of particular clauses is always of the greatest importance for their proper interpretation."[49] Natalie Zacek added that "these rules can been seen as stemming not from Leeward slave owners' sense of power and confidence, but from their striking vulnerability."[50]

The law in Nevis followed the same pattern according to William Smith, who in 1745 wrote of his years between 1716 and 1721 as a Nevis clergyman. According to Smith, "If a White Man kills a Black one, he is not tried for his Life; however, the Law obliges him to pay Thirty Pounds, Nevis Money, to his Master for the loss of the Slave." Smith noted defensively, "You will say these Proceedings are very despotick; But if you consider, that we have near Ten Blacks to one White Person, you must own them to be absolutely necessary."[51]

Smith also wrote of one of his parishioners "who in a barbarous manner murthered one of his own Negroes." Smith reported that "the Law would not hang him for it; yet he underwent a grievous Punishment; for (excepting his own Relations) not a single Gentleman would ever vouchsafe to converse with him; or pay him Visit after he had committed the horrid Fact."[52]

These same gentlemen did not feel strongly enough to effectuate further homicide law reform in their local legislature. Thus Zacek asserted, "Under such circumstances, planters' overriding sense of themselves was that of people who were embattled rather than privileged."[53]

Slavery on Bermuda differed from the institution on Britain's other Atlantic island colonies, but its slave homicide law was consistent. Bermuda's enslaved population increased more slowly than on the other islands; in the 1670s the Barbadian population included 44,000 blacks and 21,000 whites, while on Bermuda the population was 1,500 blacks and 4,500 whites.[54] In the seventeenth and eighteenth centuries, the Bermudan black population remained less than 50 percent of the island's total population. Slaves did not exceed 50 percent of the island's population until the nineteenth century. The island was not suitable for large plantations growing cash crops. Instead, the colonists developed a diversified economy. Owners employed their slaves as field hands, shipbuilders, domestic workers, sailors, fishermen, whalers, and laborers.[55]

Bermuda's Assembly nevertheless adopted 1711, 1723, and 1730 laws enacting modified versions of the Barbados slave homicide laws. The 1730 statute, titled An Act for the Security of the Subject, to Prevent the Forfeiture of Life and Estate upon Killing a Negro or Other Slave, included findings confirming that the act preempted the common law of crimes when slaves were homicide victims. It first noted that "Negroes, Indians, Mulattoes, and other Slaves are very numerous within these islands, and that the wilful killing of such

Slave as aforesaid (by the strict laws of England) comes within the penalty of murder, the judgment whereof is forfeiture of life and estate." The legislators found that "the privileges of England are so universally extensive as not to admit of the least thing called Slavery, occasioned the making such laws for the preservation of each individual subject, in his or their lives, estates, and indisputable rights and properties." In contrast, "here, in His Majesty's colonies and plantations in America, the cases and circumstances of things are wonderfully altered."

The act then declared that "for the very kindred, nay sometimes the parents of these unfortunate creatures (upon the coast of Africa) expose their own issue to perpetual bondage and Slavery, by selling them unto Your Majesty's subjects trading there, and from thence are brought to these and other Your Majesty's settlements in America, and consequently purchased by the inhabitants thereof, they being (for brutishness of their nature) no otherwise valued or esteemed amongst us than as our goods and chattels, or other personal estates." The legislators admitted that they were influenced by "our prudent Neighbors in America as Barbadoes, etc.," who "have thought it fit (in the Case of killing any such Negro or Slave) to make Laws to prevent the penalty and forfeitures aforesaid . . . that then the aforesaid Owner or Possessor shall not be liable to any Imprisonment, Arraignment, or Prosecution . . . whatsoever."

The act therefore decriminalized accidental slave killings that resulted from correction imposed by slave owners and those controlling slaves. It imposed a fine of ten pounds current money payable to the king if slave owners maliciously and willfully killed their slaves. Other malicious and willful slave killers had to pay the ten-pound fine to the king and pay to the owners the dead slaves' value, as if still alive, established by a judgment of "five able and sufficient freeholders."[56]

The Reform Trend Begins

Jamaica's assembly began a reform trend with a December 14, 1751, slave homicide reform act, which once again fell short of the central government's instructions. According to Edward Long, this law was adopted after "[o]ne Lockwood (who was afterwards proved to be a lunatic) inhumanely butchered his slave."[57]

The legislators found that the 1696 act's slave homicide provisions were not "sufficient to deter Persons from committing such wicked and inhumane Practices," because the punishment of whites for slave killings was "of doubtful construction." The new act increased the penalty after a willful slave killer's first conviction to a prison term of not more than twelve months and a fine of sixty pounds to be paid to the slave's owner. Only second offenders would suffer the death penalty, but they would not forfeit any property.[58]

Not all agreed with even this halfway homicide reform. The Board of Trade, in 1751, asked the royal colonial governors to comment on their instructions. Barbadian governor Henry Grenville criticized the usual instruction directing the governors to "endeavor to get a Law passed" making all malicious slave killing a crime punished with death. "There seems to be sufficient provisions made by the Laws now in force, for restraining any inhuman Severities, which may be used by ill Masters and Overseers towards their Christian Servants, or their Slaves: of the First of these, the Number is now very small; but no provision has been made in any Law that the Willful Killing of Indians, or Negroes, shall be punished with death." Grenville cited two reasons: "there have been very few Instances of such Killing: and the Legislature here have probably been deterr'd from time to time from making such a provision, from an Apprehension of the Dangerous Effects it might have on the Spirits of the Negroes, by lessening that Awe which they ever ought to stand of their Masters."[59]

The Dominican assembly, in 1773, adopted a slave law that included a homicide provision that was consistent with these views. The French originally settled this island, which was among the islands that in 1763 were ceded to England. The British encouraged sugar production and the island's population increased from 1,718 whites, 500 free blacks, and 5,872 slaves in 1763 to 1,574 whites, 574 free blacks, and 14,309 slaves in 1778.[60]

A British-style assembly was created in 1770. That assembly's 1773 slavery act required those who willfully killed slaves to pay fines of between one hundred and three hundred pounds for every slave murdered and to serve a twelve-month jail term "without bail or mainprize." Killers who did not own their victims also were required to pay to the owners or renters the dead slaves' values. If the killers could not pay these damages, the owners or renters were to be compensated out of the public treasury.[61]

The Bahamas and Tobago assemblies, in contrast, adopted slave laws that complied with the Crown's instructions. British colonists from Bermuda settled in the Bahamas in the 1640s, but slaveholding was on a smaller scale when compared to Britain's other Atlantic island colonies.[62] Agriculture never prospered in the Bahamas. The cash crops grown on the other British islands' plantations did "not flourish in the arid climate and thin soil of the Bahamas."[63]

In the early decades of settlement, the white population outnumbered the black. The 1671 population on the Bahamas islands of New Providence and Eluthera included 1,077 whites and 443 slaves. Governor George Phenney reported in 1726 that the New Providence, Eluthera, and Harbour Island population included 670 whites and 310 blacks. By 1730 Governor Woodes Rogers recorded the islands' population as 925 whites and 453 slaves.[64] As late as 1750, the islands' 1,268 whites outnumbered its 1,145 enslaved people. With the influx of Loyalists from the United States after 1783, the enslaved population grew by 1830 to 9,503—almost double the 5,007 whites—but still a much lower percentage of enslaved people than on the other British Caribbean islands.[65]

Governor Phenney and the Council, on May 2, 1723, promulgated an order that included a provision authorizing a forty-shilling fine if slave owners abused their slaves in a "barbarous like manner by burning, cutting or maiming."[66] Phenney also called on the central government to authorize an assembly. After some delay, the first Bahamas assembly met in 1729. It adopted An Act for the Better Regulating and Governing Negroes and Other Slaves. Unfortunately, the act's terms are not known.[67] The Bahamas assembly in 1767 adopted a new slavery law stating that willful slave killers would be tried "according to the laws of England."[68]

Tobago's assembly adopted a 1775 statute explicitly defining slave murder as a capital crime on the first offense. The Spanish, Dutch, French, and British colonial empires fought over Tobago because of its strategic importance and timber resources, although the island was sparsely populated by Europeans until the 1750s. France agreed to Britain's claim in 1763 and a British-style local assembly was elected. After 1764, British settlers imported large numbers of enslaved people and began to establish sugar, cotton, and cocoa plantations. After 1785, sugar replaced cotton as the leading crop. The island's population in 1782 was 405 white, 118 free black, and 10,530 enslaved. By 1790, it grew to 541 white, 303 free black, and 14,471 enslaved. The French took the island in 1781, and the British regained control in 1793. In 1802 the French again obtained the island, which was returned to the British in 1814.[69]

Tobago's assembly adopted a homicide provision in a 1775 slavery act, when the British controlled the island. King George III approved this act in 1776. The assembly readopted it in 1794 after the British regained control of the island from the French.[70]

The 1794 version of the act stated that anyone who "willingly or wickedly" kills "a negro or slave," after a guilty verdict or confession, "shall be judged guilty of murder, and the offender [will] suffer death for said crime, according to the laws of England, forfeiture of lands and tenements, goods and chattels only excepted." Slave owners and hirers could put their slaves in chains and impose "a moderate whipping or some other moderate correction suitable to the fault," but punishment "with cruelty" was punishable with a fine or imprisonment.[71]

According to Thomas Southey, in 1776 on Tobago "a white man was hanged ... for the murder of a slave." It is not known if the killer owned his enslaved victim or if the crime occurred before or after the 1775 act went into effect. "The circumstance of slavery was urged in arrest of judgment, but [this motion was] overruled. The particulars of this most extraordinary fact are not given."[72] A motion in arrest of judgment asks the court to stay a judgment because the verdict differs materially from the pleadings or because the defendant cannot be convicted on the facts and the law.[73]

The British Virgin Islands colonists, in contrast, did not include a slave homicide provision in their 1783 slave code. The Spanish, French, and Dutch ruled the islands, which included Tortola, Virgin Gorda, Jost Van Dyke, Anegada, and forty smaller islands, until the British gained control in the mid-seventeenth century.[74]

The first British Virgin Islands settlers generally were yeoman farmers who raised tobacco, cotton, and provisions with a relatively small number of slaves. A shift to sugar plantations in the 1750s caused the islands' enslaved and free population to increase by 1805 to 9,220 blacks and 1,300 whites.[75]

The central government in 1701 and 1735 rejected these islanders' requests for their own assembly. But the sugar plantation boom persuaded the British central government, in 1773, to authorize a local assembly for Tortola, Spanish Town (Virgin Gorda), and Jost Van Dyke.[76]

That legislature in 1783 adopted the islands' first slave law. According to Elsa Goveia, this comprehensive law exemplified "the kind of provisions which were still considered acceptable elements of the slave law ... just before the slave trade agitation brought the whole question of amelioration to the forefront of the public mind."[77] Goveia stated that this very comprehensive act "passed over in silence" issues including the "powers of masters over their slaves." She noted that these issues "were left virtually unlimited, except in the cases of manumission and holidays, which were regulated in the interests of the public order. The master's power of correction was left to the governance of custom." She concluded, "The slave was left without protection against his master. For protection against others he had to rely upon the master's willingness to prosecute for damages to his property, rather than upon any privilege of appeal against maltreatment granted to him under the law."[78]

The statute may be interpreted to instead permit the common law prosecution of those who killed slaves. This was the prevailing law in the northern mainland colonies, which will be discussed in chapter 5. Indeed, the legal landscape regarding slavery law had changed by 1783. North Carolina's royal-appointed Loyalist chief justice Martin Howard had published a 1771 opinion declaring that slave killing was common law murder.[79] Chief Justice Lord Mansfield also had asserted, in his 1772 opinion in *Somerset v. Stewart*,[80] that slavery "is incapable of being introduced on any reasons, moral or political; but only [by] positive law."[81] And Jamaica's Grand Court, in 1777 and 1778, had upheld common law indictments of white third-party strangers for assaults and batteries on slaves.[82]

Moreover, in 1775 on Grenada, a white man named Bacchus Preston had been executed for murdering a slave belonging to another person. Preston was reputed to be a man "of a very bad character" who "had been obliged to leave Barbadoes upon that account." While living on Grenada, he was a bailiff's follower. "[F]rom his rigour in executing his office and bad character, he was particularly obnoxious to the inhabitants of the town of St. George."[83]

This prosecution also may have resulted from Grenada's colonial history. Grenada, Saint Vincent, Dominica, and Tobago were originally French colonies. Britain gained control over these Windward Islands in 1763 under the Treaty of Paris. Britain returned Saint Lucia to France, but regained control in 1778 and again in 1794. These islands' enslaved African populations increased after 1763 as British settlers cleared the forests and built sugar plantations and mills. Sugar plantations were especially successful on Saint Vincent and Grenada until 1795, when rebellions shook both islands. This unrest motivated some planters to move with their slaves to the more tranquil islands of Saint Lucia and Trinidad.[84]

These islands' history as French colonies also may have contributed to their relatively protective slave laws and to the slave homicide laws later adopted in Britain's Atlantic colonies. Indeed, Tortola in 1811 was the site of the murder trial of Arthur Hodge, the only British Atlantic island slave master convicted and executed on the allegation that he murdered one of his slaves.[85]

Slave Homicide Reform and Amelioration

The British colonial island assemblies, between 1780 and 1818, adopted slave homicide reform laws ending their hundred years of resistance to the metropole's instructions to make slave murder a capital offense according to the common law. The colonists acted during the decades in which parliament enacted ameliorative laws regulating the master and slave relationship and banning the African slave trade.[86]

Scholars have debated the causes and effects of these reforms, as well as the later ameliorative laws and the 1833 act abolishing slavery. Some have argued that material conditions and economics caused and determined the scope of these legal reforms. Others have cited the salutary effect of Enlightenment or religious principles, while others have interpreted these laws as responses to slave revolts.[87]

Whether motivated by one or all of these factors, it is undisputed that during this period many colonial legislators and their supporters in parliament changed their dominant attitudes toward slavery law—including slave homicide law. The largest plantations for many years had absentee owners living in Britain, some of whom never saw their plantations. Managers or attorneys in fact ran these plantations and employed overseers to manage the enslaved population. Plantation owners began to favor plantation management practices and laws that ameliorated the harsh treatment of slaves, at least in part to deter slavery's opponents, to better maintain order, and to increase the enslaved population's life span, fertility, and production.[88]

Claudius Fergus credited Grenada and Jamaica as the two principal sources of these reforms. He called Grenada's 1784 Guardian Act "a legacy of French rule," which was "modeled on the *Code Noir*." The act did not refer to slave homicides. But it stated that masters could not mutilate their slaves and required decent treatment of slaves by their masters. It also created guardians of slaves in each parish to enforce the law. New versions were reenacted in 1788 and 1797. "[T]he imperial government considered the New Grenada Slave Act the most advanced reform legislation and recommended its protector of slaves to all colonial assemblies."[89]

Fergus argued that Jamaica's post-1770 reform laws were "the offspring" of Edward Long's three-volume history of Jamaica and his "activism" favoring amelioration. Indeed, Long called for laws making slave murder a capital crime. He cited two examples for Jamaica to follow. One was "the law of Pennsylvania," which he said provided that "a white owner" who maliciously "kills his Negroe slave . . . is liable to suffer *death* for it." The other was the 1685 French *Code Noir*. Long included an English translation of the entire statute in his Jamaica history.[90]

Orlando Patterson also wrote of the trend beginning in the 1770s to further ameliorate Jamaica's slave laws. He divided the relevant period into "two fairly distinct phases: that beginning with the 1770s and ending with the abolition of the slave trade in 1808; and that between 1808 and total emancipation in 1838." During the first phase, abolition of the slave trade was "the main bone of contention and only a small number regarded the complete emancipation of the slaves as anything but the most remote of objectives."[91]

The Jamaican assembly, beginning in 1781, adopted a series of slave acts known as the Consolidated Acts, while the Privy Council conducted inquiries into the slave trade and the conditions slaves endured in the British colonies, especially Jamaica. The 1781 and 1787 versions included section 11, stating "[t]hat if any person shall murder any slave, whether his own property or not, he shall suffer death for such offence."[92]

Critics blasted these acts because they did not deny the benefit of clergy to slave murderers. "[B]y the common law, benefit of clergy is allowed, in all cases where it is not expressly barred by a statute; and here we see that the statute does not bar it, therefore the murder of negroes stood after these acts . . . just as it did before, that is to say, it was manslaughter, and the punishment, touching hand with a warm iron."[93]

In 1788 the assembly corrected "material errors," including the omission of the phrase "without benefit of clergy" from clause 11.[94] Accordingly, beginning with this act, the slave homicide clause stated "[t]hat if any person hereafter shall wantonly, willingly, or bloody-mindedly kill any negro or other slave, such person so offending shall, on conviction, be adjudged guilty of a felony without benefit of clergy, and shall suffer death accordingly for said offence." The conviction did not, however, "extend to the corrupting the blood, or forfeiture of lands or tenements, goods or chattels; any law, custom, or usage, to the contrary notwithstanding."[95]

An 1801 law also expanded the potential liability for slave homicides that were not murder. The act permitted juries to convict slave killers for manslaughter if they believed that the defendant tried for murder was not guilty of murder.[96]

The Bahamian assembly adopted a 1784 act that continued the 1767 act's provision requiring that willful slave killers be tried and punished "according to the laws of England, forfeiture of goods and chattels, lands and tenements, only accepted."[97] A Consolidated Slave Act followed in 1796, stating that any person who willfully and with malice aforethought kills or causes to be killed "any negro or other slave . . . shall be adjudged guilty of felony and murder, and shall suffer death without benefit of clergy." The act continued to exclude property forfeitures.[98]

The reform trend also extended to Bermuda. The island's assembly adopted a July 1789 act repealing the 1730 act limiting slave killers' punishments to fines. The 1789 act stated that "although no instance can be adduced of any person having claimed the benefit of the [1730] Act" and the old act was deemed "obsolete, yet it is right to place a question of such a nature beyond the possibility of a doubt."[99]

The Bahamian assembly, in April 1797, adopted a consolidated act repealing several earlier slavery laws. Section 9 of the new act stated that any person who "shall wilfully and with malice aforethought, kill, or cause to be killed any Negro or any other Slave . . . shall be adjudged guilty of felony and murder, and shall suffer death without benefit of Clergy." The conviction did not, however, "extend to the corruption of blood, or the forfeiture of lands or tenements, goods or chattels." The next section provided for fines, imprisonment, or both, for those convicted of "wantonly or cruelly" whipping, mistreating, imprisoning, or keeping in confinement "without sufficient support" any slave. If the defendant was not the slave's owner, the criminal prosecution was "without prejudice to any action that may be brought for recovery of damages" to the slave's owner.[100]

Leeward Island slave owners, and those sympathetic to their interests, also began to believe that they could best combat the threats to the slave trade and to slavery itself by offering their own local legal reforms ameliorating slavery's worst features.[101] The House of Commons, on April 6, 1797, debated a resolution offered by Charles Rose Ellis stating that, instead of adopting an act prohibiting the slave trade, parliament should request that the king recommend that the islands' legislators

> adopt such measures as shall appear to them best calculated to obviate the causes which have hitherto impeded the natural increase of the Negroes already in the islands; gradually to diminish the necessity of the Slave Trade, and ultimately to lead to its complete termination; and particularly, with a view to the same effect, to employ such means as may conduce to the moral and religious improvement of the Negroes, and secure to them, throughout all the British West-India Islands, the certain, immediate, and active protection of the law.[102]

Ellis said that he opposed the slave trade, but thought it best to encourage the local assemblies to adopt ameliorative measures to make the trade unnecessary.[103]

Bryan Edwards also argued in support of the resolution, relying, in part, on the ameliorative laws adopted in Jamaica, Dominica, Antigua, and Grenada. William Smith, arguing against the motion, cited, among other reasons, the Barbadian act that still permitted only fines for slave killers.[104]

Ellis's resolution was adopted by a vote of ninety-nine to sixty-three. The king approved the resolution, and it was sent to the islands.[105]

This request elicited several responses from the island assemblies. Antigua's assembly, on August 27, 1797, called a meeting of the General Council and Assembly of the Leeward Islands.[106]

Before the General Council met, the legislature on Saint Christopher appointed a committee to examine the island's slavery laws. The committee's October 1797 report found that "the necessity of the case made it essential at the first settlement of the Colony to pass several severe laws in order to preserve subordination and good order, yet few, if any instances, have happened, where the rigour of those Acts should be as soon as possible revised, corrected, and consolidated, as may appear expedient." The committee declared that the legislature adopted reform laws preventing "white or free persons from beating or ill-treating" slaves, by attacking them and taking from them goods that they were carrying to town for sale, as "was the practice of some of the lower class of white persons." The committee concluded that new laws were not needed because the courts had "always taken cognizance of barbarous treatment of slaves, in the same manner as crimes of a similar nature committed against white and free persons."[107]

The Antiguan legislators, in contrast, on December 28, 1797, adopted a law repealing the two slave murder sections of the 1723 law. This new law made slave murder a capital offense and provided that convicted slave killers would not forfeit any property or suffer the corruption of blood. The legislators found that this law was necessary because of "the alteration of times and circumstances."[108]

The General Council and Assembly of the Leeward Islands met on Saint Christopher, beginning on March 1, 1798. It adopted a statute on April 21, 1798, commonly known as the Leeward Islands Slave Amelioration Act of 1798.[109]

That statute, in section 21, stated that every white or "free Coloured-person" who is charged with murder or maiming his or her slave or a slave belonging to another person was to be "tried and punished ... without any sort of Distinction or Privilege" as if he or she had been charged with murdering or maiming any free person. Nevertheless, no conviction was to cause "any Corruption of Blood, or Forfeiture of Laws or Tenements, Goods or Chattels."[110]

Elsa Goveia suggested that more important than this provision punishing slave killers "as if the victims were white" was an enforcement provision.[111] That clause required coroners and justices of the peace to conduct inquiries when slaves not under six years of age died suddenly without being visited by a medical person within forty-eight hours of dying. Owners who did not comply with this requirement, or who buried the body in fewer than eighteen hours after giving this notice, were liable for fines of one hundred pounds.[112] A similar 1816 Jamaican act imposed a fine not to exceed five hundred pounds upon offending masters or overseers.[113]

This reform trend did not reach Barbados until the nineteenth century. The 1688 slave code's provision fining slave killers remained in effect in 1800 when Francis Humberston Mackenzie, Lord Seaforth, was appointed governor. He arrived on the island in early 1801 and created a controversy when he attempted to convince the island's assembly to adopt a law making slave killing a felony. The assembly rejected this proposal on March 17, 1802.[114]

Lord Seaforth admitted in a letter of the next day to Lord Hobart that the majority of the assembly members "had taken considerable offence at a message of mine, recommending an act to be passed to make the murder of a slave felony."[115] Indeed, one assembly member moved that a committee be appointed to prepare a response to the governor's message that would be "an answer, moderate and respectful, but calculated to repel insult, and evince that the House understood its interests and asserted its rights."[116]

In contrast, the assembly quickly enacted another 1801 Seaforth proposal, which increased the cost to masters who freed their slaves. Some legislators may have supported this limitation on masters' right to manumit their slaves because it would limit the island's free black population. Seaforth explained this as a humanitarian measure providing sufficient funds to support freed slaves who could not support themselves, but he added that this was necessary because of "their naturally idle and dissipated habits, [which] made by far the major part of them public nuisances."[117]

Lord Seaforth did not give up the fight for slave homicide law reform. He wrote November 13, 1804, and January 7, 1805, letters to Lord Camden documenting slave homicides.[118] In the earlier letter, Seaforth stated that "[b]ills are already proposed to make murders felony, but I fear they will be thrown out for the present in the Assembly. The Council are unanimous on the side of humanity."[119]

The Barbadian assembly, on April 9, 1805, finally adopted An Act for the Better Protection of Slaves of This Island. According to its preamble, "the penalties directed by the several Acts of this Island against the murdering of negro slaves have been found inadequate," and "the wilful and malicious murder of any fellow creature, whether it be a free person or a slave, ought to be punished with the death of the murderer." The act then stated that any person who "wilfully, maliciously, and wantonly, and without provocation" kills and murders a slave, "whether such slave be the property of the person so killing and murdering, or any other person," if convicted on the testimony "of one or more white person or persons, at a Court of Grand Session, shall suffer death without benefit of clergy." But the defendant would not "forfeit his lands, negroes, goods or chattels."[120]

Hilary Beckles contended that Seaforth succeeded "only . . . after the Secretary of the Colonies threatened to take measures against those Assemblymen who opposed the Governor's bill."[121] Jerome Handler also placed this vote in the context of the legislators' interest in controlling the island's free blacks. He quoted the assembly speaker, who argued in favor of the bill that "the [present] exemption from death . . . is not confined to white men, but extends equally to all free persons . . . and is there a man who will say, that the black or mulatto murderer ought not to suffer death."[122]

The 1805 act was criticized, however, as a "nugatory" law that was "passed merely for the purpose of delusion. Any provocation, however slight, though only in words, or in silent disobedience of the most frivolous order, would be a provocation, and consequently an excuse for the most cruel murder." It also hindered prosecutions by requiring the testimony of white witnesses.[123]

An 1818 act deleted the 1805 act's provocation clause and the white witness requirement. It stated that any person who "willfully and maliciously" kills and murders a slave, whether or not the slave's owner, and is convicted on the testimony "of one or more competent witness or witnesses at a Court of Grand Sessions, shall suffer death without benefit of clergy." But the defendant would not "forfeit his lands, negroes, goods or chattels."[124] Free blacks thus could testify in murder trials, but enslaved witnesses were not permitted to testify on Barbados until 1826, when a Consolidated Slave Law was adopted permitting slave testimony with strict conditions.[125]

This 1826 law confirmed the Barbadian legislators' concerns about the interests of slave owners and the public order. Accidental slave killers were to pay the slaves' owners for the value of the dead slaves, but not for slaves killed while attempting to commit crimes.[126]

The Atlantic island colonists' failure to reform their slave homicide laws until the eighteenth century prompted J. R. Ward to ask why it took so long for the planters to ameliorate their "extraordinarily harsh regime." Ward suggested that economic and political realities prompted this legal change, at least in part, to preempt the central government's potential imposition of more restrictive rules at the instigation of those advocating the abolition of slavery and the slave trade. The British island colonists began to believe that these legal reforms ameliorating their slaves' material living conditions made economic sense in the long run.[127]

Nevertheless, according to Goveia, these ameliorative laws did not all turn the masters' duties "into rights that slaves could enforce through an official guardian of slaves. The whites of the islands were prepared to ameliorate their slave laws, but they were more cautious about intervening between master and slave to ensure that the slave was adequately protected in practice."[128]

Prosecutions after the Amelioration Acts

There are seven recorded post-amelioration homicide prosecutions of slave owners or plantation managers on the British island colonies. Four of these defendants escaped punishment—one literally. Only one was executed.

Edward Huggins of Nevis, on January 23, 1810, ordered his son Peter to take two slave drivers and whip twenty of his worst behaved slaves (ten male and ten female) in the Charleston public marketplace. Three magistrates were in a crowd that stood by and watched as these slaves endured beatings of between 47 and 291 strokes. A female slave named Fanny died allegedly as the result of her beating. In response to the allegation of the coroner's failure to investigate, the Nevis Assembly adopted a resolution declaring that Huggins was "guilty of barbarity altogether unprecedented in this island."

Huggins was indicted by a grand jury for violating the Amelioration Act. But in May 1817, a jury packed with "men beholden to the defendant in one way or the other" acquitted Huggins. In response to Governor-General Hugh Elliot's protest, the three magistrates who stood by for the beatings were dismissed.[129]

Huggins in May 1817 once again was acquitted on a charge of excessive whipping, this time of slaves owned by his son-in-law Thomas Cottle. But Huggins's son, also named Edward, was not so lucky. He shot and killed a slave in October 1812 while in the street, allegedly thinking the slave was going to steal something. He was found guilty of manslaughter and was fined 250 pounds.[130]

In contrast, Arthur Hodge, "a leading inhabitant of Tortola," in 1811 was tried, convicted, and executed for murder. Hodge, in 1807 or 1808, whipped to death his slave Prosper. Hodge was indicted under the common law and the Amelioration Act.[131]

The key prosecution witness, Perreen Georges, was described as a "free woman of colour." She testified that, on Hodge's orders, Prosper "died by licks, confinement and starvation." She saw Hodge confront Prosper about a mango that fell from a tree. When Prosper could not pay the six shillings that Hodge demanded for the mango, Hodge had Prosper held down by four "negroes," and Prosper was whipped that day for "better than an hour." A second beating followed the next day while Prosper was tied to a tree. Prosper then was carried in irons to the sick house where he was confined and died within two weeks.[132]

Although the jury found Hodge guilty of murder, "they recommended the prisoner to mercy." The court nevertheless sentenced Hodge to die by hanging.[133]

Hodge may have been convicted and executed because his behavior was "beyond the pale of legitimate actions" and "offended the slave-holding white population of the community."¹³⁴ Hodge's fate also may have been sealed by the efforts of his powerful political enemies, who "maneuvered to send Hodge to the gallows" because they "had their own interests, and not those of the slaves, at heart."¹³⁵ The Hodge case was reported in Scotland and England, where it "became a lightning rod in debates about the regulation of slavery."¹³⁶

Two clergymen from Saint Kitts also were charged with killing slaves under their control, with mixed results. William Davis, an Anglican minister, was the attorney for Lord Romney's large estate and plantation. In late 1812, a female slave named Eliza died on the estate allegedly a result of a flogging that Davis ordered or administered. Davis, three of his sons, and his son-in-law, in March 1813, were accused of murdering Eliza. Their primary accuser was John Julius, the island's Council's president. He may have had a grudge against Davis because Davis replaced Julius as the estate's manager. At trial held a few months later, all of the defendants were exonerated.¹³⁷

The case caused a sensation in London, in part because Davis was a clergyman. The Bishop of London noted the jury's verdict but ordered that Davis cease plantation management.¹³⁸

Reverend Henry Rawlins, the manager of the Hutchinson plantation on Saint Kitts, was the other accused clergyman. In 1817, a slave called Congo Jack ran away from the plantation. He was captured and beaten. He died the next morning while chained to another slave, Tom Titley. Congo Jack's body, which was buried without a coroner's inquest, was examined, but the coroner's jury initially found that he died "by the visitation of God."¹³⁹

This verdict apparently was not satisfactory. A slave driver named Creole Jack, on September 27, 1817, was tried and found not guilty for Congo Jack's murder.¹⁴⁰

Rawlins then was charged with Congo Jack's murder. A jury at an October 16, 1817, trial found him not guilty of murder but guilty of manslaughter. He was sentenced to a three-month jail term and a two-hundred-pound fine.¹⁴¹ The Rawlins and Huggins prosecutions were discussed in Parliament in June 1818 as examples of cruelty to the enslaved.¹⁴²

Thomas Ludford was a Jamaican slave owner who in 1817 was accused of shooting his slave Cuffee after subjecting Cuffee to months of beatings for stealing sugar and rum from Ludford's store. After some delay, on June 16, 1817, a warrant issued for Ludford's arrest for murder, based on the statements of two free blacks, Mary Howel and Robert Williams, and two of Ludford's slaves, Alfred and Edward LaCruize Froth.¹⁴³ But Ludford escaped before his trial, prompting the governor to replace the local magistrate for not immediately issuing an arrest warrant.¹⁴⁴

Two Barbadian slave owners were prosecuted under that island's slave homicide reform laws. John Welch was indicted under the 1805 act for murdering his slave. A grand jury in 1806 found no true bill. John G. Archer, "a man of property," in December 1826, was indicted under the 1818 act for the murder of one of his slaves. After a trial in the Court of Grand Sessions, a jury found Archer guilty of manslaughter. He was sentenced to twelve months' imprisonment.[145]

A history of "archival depredations" limits the primary sources evidencing how these acts were enforced in practice. Moreover, the local authorities had to be motivated to initiate and pursue prosecutions, and local juries had to be persuaded to convict local slaveholder defendants. Slave and free black testimony was not permitted against white defendants until late in the slavery period. The Hodge case was a rare exception showing the importance of this evidence reform.[146]

The British central government addressed these concerns on Trinidad, which Spain ceded to Britain in 1802. The colony had been governed by Spanish law, and its white population was predominantly French. The British, in 1823 and 1824, established reforms for Trinidad and the other Crown colonies of Saint Lucia, British Guiana, Mauritius, and Cape of Good Hope. These laws created the position of protector of slaves to advance claims on behalf of abused slaves. These measures' effectiveness is subject to debate, but they were influential.[147]

A new parliamentary majority, under Thomas Fowell Buxton, in 1823 adopted three resolutions supporting further amelioration measures in all colonies. Colonial Secretary Earl Bathurst, on July 9, 1823, sent a circular calling on the local legislatures to adopt these reforms, which were to authorize the appointment of a protector of slaves for each colony and permit slaves to testify in the courts.[148] The colonial legislatures in the 1820s and 1830s adopted laws that, to different degrees, complied.[149] These law reforms permitted the local slave owners to retain "effective control of the legislative and legal machinery," and thus "protect themselves from prosecution for brutality and ensure the punishment of slaves who resisted."[150]

Conclusion

Slave homicide law in Britain's Atlantic island colonies evolved from the most extreme decriminalization and trivialization of slave master homicides to the formal equal protection of homicide law for slaves. These reforms may have contributed to the delay until August 1833 of the adoption of a law abolishing slavery in these colonies. But the incomplete evidence of enforcement limits the evaluation of the slave homicide reform laws' true effect.[151]

Orlando Patterson also asserted that Jamaican planters in the years before emancipation treated their slaves with "a new spirit of severity." By the 1820s "it was becoming increasingly clear" that the planters were losing the abolition debate. "All incentive for treating the slaves humanely was now gone and the general attitude among the masters was to exact mercilessly as much labour from the slaves as possible before emancipation."[152] Although the Enlightenment was an "era of amelioration" when many slaves' living conditions improved, "most planters were also focused on employing new technologies and agricultural innovations to extract increasingly higher levels of labor from their bondsmen."[153]

CHAPTER 5

Slave Killing Law in Britain's Northern American Colonies and the Border States

People were enslaved in all of Britain's North American colonies. The New England and Mid-Atlantic colonies and Canada were societies with slaves, while Virginia, the Carolinas, and Georgia evolved into slave societies. Between these ends of the continuum were the border colonies and states of Maryland, Delaware, and Kentucky.[1]

According to Edgar McManus, "Every Northern colony treated the deliberate killing of a slave as a capital crime, and none permitted maiming in the exercise of private discipline."[2] Nathan Dane, in his 1824 *General Abridgment and Digest of American Law*, agreed that a master had no right to kill his slave and "he was punishable as for killing a freeman." Dane added that the master who immoderately punished his slave would be liable, as would a "superior" correcting an apprentice or a child. The only authority Dane cited, however, was Tapping Reeve's 1816 Connecticut family law treatise, which did not cite any supporting authority.[3]

The positive law enacted or enforced in the northern American British colonies, including Canada after 1763, Maryland, Delaware, and later the state of Kentucky, did equate slave killings with common law homicide. This was established by legislative action in Massachusetts, New Hampshire, and New York, and by legislative silence in the other colonies and later states. Masters in most of these jurisdictions were prosecuted for slave killings, but only two, Peter Ball in Maryland and William Bullock of Philadelphia, were convicted of capital slave murder. They both avoided execution.[4]

The Development of Slavery in the North

The local social and demographic conditions in Britain's northern mainland colonies may have influenced the legislators who did not adopt slave homicide laws based on the Barbadian model. Slave holdings in these colonies were smaller, and slaves made up a smaller percentage of the total population than in the other British colonies. At the time of the American Revolution, Rhode Island was the New England colony with the largest percentage of enslaved population, but it was only about 5 or 6 percent. The enslaved population in the other New England colonies was less than 3 percent. Colonial New York's enslaved population was about 12 percent, and in New Jersey slaves made up about 8 to 10 percent of the population during the colonial years. Pennsylvania's statistics are less reliable, but that colony's total enslaved population may have been less than 3 percent.[5]

Enslaved people were not evenly distributed within these colonies, and over time the enslaved population percentages rose and fell. "During the half-century before the American Revolution, Kings [Brooklyn], Richmond, Queens, and Ulster counties in New York and Bergen County in New Jersey were all more than 20 percent slave, and Kings registered in excess of 30 percent after 1749." In Pennsylvania and some western New Jersey counties, however, the enslaved populations ranged between 2 and 9 percent.[6]

The northern slaves' labor was diverse. It included agricultural work, maritime work, various trades, and household service. Although some plantations or larger farms were established in Rhode Island's Narragansett region and in parts of Pennsylvania, New York, New Jersey, and Massachusetts, large plantations were few.[7]

Constitutions, statutes, or judicial decisions in these colonies and later states abolished slavery or started the first emancipation. This legal change was combined with social change, as those states' enslaved populations declined without war or bloodshed. But this trend ended in 1804, when New Jersey became the last state to adopt a gradual emancipation law. New Jersey's emancipation was so gradual, however, that slavery continued in modified form until the Thirteenth Amendment went into effect. But New Jersey's apprentices for life, as the "freed" slaves were defined by its last gradual emancipation law, totaled only 236 (0.048 percent) in 1850 and 18 (0.0026 percent) in 1860.[8]

The Statutes and Cases in Massachusetts, New York, and New Hampshire

Before any laws explicitly authorized slavery, the Massachusetts Bay and Plymouth colonists in the 1630s imposed slavery as a punishment for offenses. Native American captives also were enslaved. Some were enslaved in the Pequot War of 1636–38 and the King Philip's War in the 1670s. Indians also were sold into the seventeenth-century West Indies slave trade. Enslaved Africans were brought to the area in the 1630s.[9]

The 1636 Capitall Lawes of New-England and the 1641 Massachusetts Body of Liberties, in the "Capitall Lawes" section, confirmed that both murder and manslaughter were capital crimes. These laws did not afford slave masters any special immunity for slave killing.[10]

Massachusetts was the first British colony to adopt a law explicitly authorizing slavery. The Body of Liberties, in section 91, declared, "There shall never be any bond slaverie, villinage, or Captivitie amongst us; unles[s] it be lawfull Captives taken in just warres, and such strangers as willingly selle themselves or are solde to us," who were to "have all the liberties and Christian usages which the law of god established in Israell concerning such persons doeth morally require." But the law did not exempt from servitude those "who shall be Judged thereto by Authoritie."[11]

This provision legitimizing slavery was "[b]ased on the Mosaic code, [and] it is an absolute recognition of slavery as a legitimate status."[12] The Puritan settlers guaranteed "their own liberty without closing off the opportunity of taking it from others whom they identified with the biblical term, 'strangers.'"[13] And in 1670 they deleted the word "strangers," thus authorizing the enslavement of the children of their slaves.[14]

The Body of Liberties also prohibited slave master killings by reference to Exodus 21:12, which states that one who strikes another so that the victim dies "shall surely be put to death." According to verse 20, if a master strikes his slave with a rod and the slave dies "under his hand; he shall surely be punished." But verse 21 justifies a master's slave killing if the victim lives for "a day or two" after the beating, because the slaves are their masters' own "money."[15]

Although these verses do not state how offenders would be punished, scholars have suggested that the death penalty applied. According to Exodus 21:22–25, if while two people were fighting a pregnant woman, who was not one of the combatants, was injured and loses her child, the offender was to pay a fine determined by the woman's husband and the judges. "But if any harm follow, then thou shall give life for life, eye for eye, tooth for tooth, hand for hand, foot for foot, burning for burning, wound for wound, stripe for stripe."[16]

The Body of Liberties does not include a provision mirroring verses 20 and 21 excusing some killings by masters whose slaves died after fatal beatings. But section 87, following Exodus 21:26–27, stated, "If any man smite out the eye or tooth of his manservant, or maid servant, or otherwise mayme or much disfigure him, unlesse it be by meere casualtie, he shall let them goe free from his service. And shall have such further recompense as the Court shall allow him."[17]

Therefore, masters were prosecuted for killing slaves. Nathaniel Cane, on May 16, 1695, was tried and convicted in the Superior Court of Judicature for the Province of Maine for the murder "by cruel beating and hard usage" of his slave Rachel. He was fined five pounds, but the court stayed the fine until further court order.[18]

And Samuel Smith, a cooper from Sandwich, was charged with the June 16, 1719, murder of his slave Fortin. The indictment or presentment alleged that Smith assaulted Fortin's naked body and struck blows with a leather horsewhip. "Fortin then and there instantly or within the Space of an hour after dyed."[19]

Smith sent a letter from jail to the governor and Council declaring that he was "imprisoned for the Murther of his Negro Servant, which he is not guilty of." He requested "a Special Court of Oyer and Terminer" because it would not be a year until the next Court of Assize was to be held in his county.[20]

Smith got his speedy trial. The case was heard on July 22, 1719, in Plymouth before a "Special Court of assize and General Goal Delivery." The Justices were Addington Davenport, Paul Dudley, and Edmund Quincey. Smith entered a not guilty plea. No record survives of the witnesses' testimony. The case record states only that, after hearing the evidence, the jury deliberated and found that Smith was not guilty. He was to be discharged after paying the court costs.[21]

No Massachusetts slave master homicide convictions could be found. But Governor Thomas Hutchinson, in 1771, correctly asserted that the colony's laws gave masters "no right to the life of the servant, and a slave here is considered as a servant" bound for his or her life.[22]

New York and New Hampshire statutes, in contrast, confirmed that slave killings by masters could be murders. The British central government's instructions to these colonies' governors may have prompted these laws. King James II and the Lords of Trade, on May 29, 1686, directed New York's governor, Thomas Dongan, to convince the colonists to adopt a law restraining "any inhuman severity, which by ill masters or overseers may be used towards their Christian servants and their slaves, and provision be made therein that the wilfull killing of Indians and negroes may be punished with death, and that a fit penalty be imposed for the maiming of them."[23] Sir Edmund Andros, governor of New England, whose authority extended over New Hampshire, on April 16, 1688, also received instructions with this provision.[24]

Samuel Allen, in March 1692, was issued a commission to serve as New Hampshire's governor, and his son-in-law, John Usher, was appointed as the colony's lieutenant governor. Allen's instructions also included the provision quoted above on homicide and the mistreatment of servants. Usher arrived in New Hampshire first on August 11, 1692. His October 4, 1692, speech to the colony's assembly included the unheeded request for a law restraining "inhumanity to white servants or slaves."[25]

After Usher repeated this request on May 8, 1694, the assembly, on May 24, 1694, adopted an act restraining "inhuman Severitie which by evil masters or Overseers, may be used towards their christian servants." It declared that "if any man smites out the eye or tooth of his servant or maid Servant, or otherwise maime or disfigure them much, unless it be by meer casualitie," the servants were to be freed from their service and were permitted to recover damages in court. The statute also stated "[t]hat if any person or persons whatsoever within this Province shall willfully kill his Indian or Negroe Servant or servants, he shall be punished with death."[26]

This act was among the New Hampshire laws that Queen Anne and her Council disapproved on November 19, 1706, because they thought the act was too broad in scope. The Lords of Trade had asked Edward Northey, the attorney general, to review the colony's laws. His August 17, 1704, letter stated, as to the 1694 act, "I think it too Large, that willfully killing a man[']s own Negroe serv't shall Be punish'd with death, for that is not the description of Murder, w'ch is killing of Malice he that doth it in his own defence, doth it willfully, therefore it should be said without provocation, or of Malice."[27] The Lords of Trade adopted this recommendation and communicated it to the queen.[28]

The New Hampshire legislature, on May 14, 1718, nevertheless readopted the same law without the suggested revisions. This law later was among the acts repealed on June 20, 1792.[29]

Although this 1694 statute refers only to "servants" and not to "slaves," it has been interpreted to apply to slaves. The first Africans were brought to New Hampshire in 1645. Scholars have disagreed on the number of enslaved people in New Hampshire. Some have asserted that the enslaved population historically was less than 5 percent of the total, while others have argued that these estimates are understated because they were based on tax census data that accounted only for slaves between the ages of sixteen and forty.[30] Historians also do not agree when slavery was legally abolished in New Hampshire, with some concluding that "the abolition of slavery was not official in New Hampshire until 1857."[31]

Slave trader James DeWolf was indicted in Rhode Island for murdering a slave. DeWolf committed his alleged crime while his ship *Polly* was at sea. According to the depositions of two of DeWolf's crew members, DeWolf, in 1790, allegedly caused a middle-aged female slave to be thrown overboard because she became ill with smallpox.[32]

A grand jury in federal court, on June 15, 1791, indicted DeWolf for murder in violation of a 1790 U.S. law making murder and other crimes committed on the high seas crimes over which the U.S. courts had jurisdiction. DeWolf evaded trial by obtaining refuge on the Dutch West Indies island of Sint Eustatius. In April 1795, a judge on Saint Thomas dismissed the murder charges, even though the killing was not disputed. DeWolf brought two other alleged crewmen witnesses to the island to testify that DeWolf's actions were intended to protect the lives of his crew members and the remaining enslaved cargo. The New Hampshire arrest warrant later was dismissed and DeWolf was never tried. He continued his slave trading career and later became a wealthy planter, state legislator, and one of Rhode Island's U.S. senators.[33]

New York also attempted to comply with the British colonial slave homicide instructions after the British gained control of the colony from the Dutch. About three years after the Dutch established the New Netherlands colony in 1624, they imported the first black slaves. As slavery practices evolved in the New Netherlands, the colonial authorities did not enact a slave code or laws defining the punishments for slave killers. The Dutch, unlike the English, applied Roman law slavery concepts to their colonies.[34]

The English conquered the colony in 1664, when its population was about fifteen hundred, almost three hundred of whom were enslaved. The Duke of York, in 1664–65, promulgated the Duke of York's Laws, which included a provision on "bond slavery" that appears to be modeled on section 91 of the Massachusetts Body of Liberties. The Duke's version stated, "No Christian shall be kept in Bondslavery, villenage or Captivity," unless pursuant to a judgment "by Authority," a willing sale on record, or an indenture for a term of years or life. Although these laws omit the Body of Liberties' reference to the biblical slave code, they do not exempt slave master killers from the capital crimes provisions for murder and manslaughter.[35]

Seventeenth-century New York City "became an important trading center in [Britain's] slave-based New World empire." The colony's enslaved population grew to more than 20 percent of the total by midcentury. Enslaved New Yorkers "worked as domestic laborers, on the docks, in artisan shops, or on small farms in the city's rural hinterland," which included Brooklyn, "then a collection of farms and small villages" with a population that in 1771 that was one-third enslaved.[36]

The local legislators adopted slavery laws. These included 1702, 1712, and 1730 acts that legitimized the masters' right "to punish their slaves for their

Crimes and offenses [at the masters'] discretion." But these acts denied to masters the right to take their slaves' lives or limbs.[37]

New York's colonial era slave owner prosecutions, for the most part, were unsuccessful. Edgar McManus attributed this to the reluctance of juries "to convict if death resulted from disciplinary action."[38]

An early slave master prosecution is recorded among the complaints to the Court of Mayor and Aldermen in New York City. Sheriff Thomas Ashton on January 17, 1677, charged that John Cooley "unjustly and immoderately" beat an unnamed male slave to death. The slave died on January 19, 1677. The court's judgment is not reported, but Cooley later petitioned the court for a rehearing, claiming that a coroner's jury and four "Chirurgeons" cleared him. There is no report of the court's disposition of Cooley's rehearing request.[39]

William Pettit (also spelled Petit) was charged by a Newton, Queens County inquest jury with the December 19, 1734, fatal beating of a slave named Joe, who belonged to Pettit and Jonathan Hunt. Pettit was a "cordwainer." The jury found that "Pettit, with his fist and feet, beat, wounded, kicked and bruised the negro on his head, breast and other parts of his body to the degree that he instantly died thereof, for which Pettit is now in Jamaica jail." The final judgment is not reported.[40]

John Van Zandt allegedly beat his slave to death after finding the slave outside after the curfew. A New York City coroner's jury in 1735 found, "Correction given by the Master was not the Cause of his Death, but that it was by the Visitation of God."[41]

Charles Johnson, also of Newton, in 1788 was brought before a grand jury by the attorney general, who alleged that Johnson killed "Mary, a negro child" who was "the property of Charles and Catherine Johnson." The attorney general contended that Mary "died of wounds it [sic] had received in the head." The grand jury's verdict was "ignoramus, and Johnson was discharged."[42] When used in this context, "ignoramus" means: "We do not know. This notation, when written on a bill of indictment, indicated the grand jury's rejection of the bill." The terms "no bill" or "no true bill" later were used for the same decision by a grand jury.[43]

Also in 1788, John Allen of Flushing was indicted for killing his slave Michael by a chance medley and misadventure arising from correction. It appears that Allen had lost some money and flogged the slave until the slave died. According to press reports, Allen was not punished.[44]

Two successful prosecutions followed after New York adopted its 1799 gradual emancipation law. Samuel Cooper of Suffolk County, in 1807, was indicted for the murder of a slave whose identity is not disclosed. Jane, a slave belonging to John Howard, was permitted to testify as the state's only witness. A jury convicted Cooper of manslaughter. He was sentenced to twelve years of hard labor at a state prison.[45]

Carl A. Hoffman of New York City was convicted in 1804 for the mistreatment of his twelve- or thirteen-year-old slave James Wright. Hoffman tied James's hands together, drew them over his head with a rope attached to a wall, and fastened the child's feet to a staple on the floor. After whipping James with more than one hundred lashes, Hoffman rubbed salt and brandy in James's wounds. Hoffman also forced James to swallow salt. He then confined his victim to a room for two days without food or water. Hoffman was fined $250 and was required to post a $2,000 bond to guarantee his good behavior. But Hoffman again mistreated James and was again indicted. Hoffman responded by freeing James and the charges were dismissed.[46]

James Quimby of Marlborough in Ulster County also avoided prosecution for the February 1809 shooting of his slave. The details of the crime and the slave's name are not reported. Quimby was taken into custody but escaped "and has not been heard of since."[47]

The Pennsylvania and New Jersey Cases

The other northern colonies did not adopt laws explicitly criminalizing or legitimizing slave killings by masters or reducing the penalties for those offenses. This legislative silence presumptively subjected slave killers to prosecution under the common law of crimes. Slave owners were prosecuted for slave killings in these colonies and states. But they all avoided capital punishment.[48]

"Before William Penn and the Quakers ever arrived in what was to become Pennsylvania, racial slavery—or at least lifetime servitude for blacks—already existed in the area around the Delaware River."[49] Both Swedish and Dutch colonists held slaves when the British gained control of the region in 1664. The Duke of York's Laws, which recognized slavery, governed the colony until William Penn's 1681 grant from King Charles II. Pennsylvania statutes did not explicitly legitimize lifetime heredity slavery until the legislature adopted acts of 1700 and 1725. But the practice and customs of slaveholding evolved in the years before 1700.[50]

Pennsylvania's colonial criminal statutes confirmed that murder was a capital offense, and they did not legitimize "physical attacks on slaves by masters or third parties." The legislators also "never created a special list of justifications or excuses for the murder or beatings of slaves. The laws governing the physical abuse of slaves and blacks were the same as those that applied to whites."[51]

William Bullock was Pennsylvania's only colonial era slave master who was prosecuted for slave homicide. Bullock was a hatter who, in February 1742, was committed to Philadelphia's City Jail "on Suspicion of having been the Occasion of the Death of his Negro Boy, about 8 Years old, by beating and whipping him at sundry Times."[52] Bullock had "bought the Boy but a few Days before." Bullock's slave allegedly died after he was "most barbarously" beaten.[53]

A coroner's inquest followed. After viewing the boy's body, the inquest concluded that the boy's injuries received "from his Master were the Cause of Death."[54]

Bullock was indicted, tried, and convicted of murder in the court of Oyer and Terminer, but he was not immediately sentenced.[55] In April 1742, the Supreme Court held another hearing and sentenced Bullock to death. The Colonial Council then voted not to issue a warrant for Bullock's execution and he left Philadelphia.[56]

William Bullock's crime was not the first murder in the family. His brother John was convicted of murdering his wife, and in November 1741, John was executed.[57]

The Swedish professor Peter Kalm, while traveling in Pennsylvania in 1748, wrote that although Pennsylvania law made slave homicide a crime punishable by death, no "white man ever has been executed for his crime." He retold the story of a master, probably William Bullock, who "a few years ago" killed his slave. The master's friends, and even the magistrates, "secretly advised him to make his escape" to avoid prosecution and execution, which they thought was inevitable. Kalm was told that these actions were justified so that "the negroes might not have the satisfaction of seeing a master executed for killing his slave. This would lead them to all sorts of dangerous designs against their masters, and to value themselves too much."[58]

Pennsylvania adopted a 1780 gradual emancipation law, which freed the children who later were born to enslaved women. But these freeborn people were required to serve their mothers' masters until adulthood as indentured servants. Those who were enslaved when the law was adopted continued to be slaves.[59]

Pennsylvania, in 1794, also adopted an influential homicide reform law creating two degrees of murder. It limited capital punishment to first degree murder, which was defined as "all murder, which shall be perpetrated by means of poison, or by lying in wait, or by any other kind of wilful, deliberate and premeditated killing, or which shall be committed in the perpetration or attempt to perpetrate any arson, rape, robbery, or burglary." Second degree murderers faced prison terms. The act did not mention slaves or slavery.[60]

Slave owner John M'Alister and his brother William were tried under these laws in the Court of Oyer and Terminer in Carlisle, Cumberland County, on September 6, 1800, for the murder of John's slave Caesar. The defendants were "men far advanced in life, the youngest being above sixty years of age." William Yan, a farm worker John hired for the month, described in detail the fatal beating that the M'Alister brothers inflicted on Caesar for two hours during the morning of April 14, 1800, because John suspected that Caesar had stolen money. Caesar died after the defendants beat a confession out of him. The jury found the defendants guilty of second degree murder. They were sentenced to five-year prison terms, with six months in solitary confinement and the remainder at hard labor. The court's new president John Joseph Henry "admonished them in the most solemn manner to repentance for so great a crime. He mentioned that it was most probable the Jury would be justified in finding their offense murder in the first degree."[61]

In contrast, no New Jersey slave owner was convicted of murder for killing his or her slaves. Dutch and Swedish settlers first colonized New Jersey in the 1660s. The Dutch apparently brought the first slaves to the colony. Both Africans and Native Americans were enslaved in New Jersey.[62]

After the British gained control of the colony in 1664, the Duke of York's Laws applied. New Jersey was established as a proprietary colony that, in 1676, was divided into East Jersey and West Jersey. East Jersey became the home of more enslaved people than the West, which was settled by many Quakers. Only East Jersey legislators adopted slavery laws, but they did not adopt a slave homicide statute.[63]

James Wills of Burlington, a southwestern New Jersey Quaker settlement, was indicted on a charge that he murdered his "Negro woman," whose name is not mentioned in the case record. Wills plead not guilty and denied "giving the Negro woman any blowes that occasioned her death." He admitted to causing her to be buried "not knowing that the Law required there should have been an Inquest touching the cause of her death." Wills was tried in 1686 before the court made up of Governor John Skene, President George Hutcheson, five justices, and a jury of twelve men. Attorney General Christopher Snowden prosecuted the case for the king. The report does not state if Wills was represented by a lawyer. Eight witnesses testified at the trial.[64]

Katherine Greene testified that the enslaved victim was sent to Katherine's home because she "had some distemper upon her, that shee might have conference with a Negro that belongs to ... Katherine." The slave complained about a sore back, which she said was a result of the "Fum, fum, which is (beating)," and "Katherine found a small Scarr upon her Belly which was sore, which the

Negro told her came on the account aforesaid." Katherine "did not perceive any blowes that in her judgment might be the cause of her death." Thomas Greene confirmed this testimony.[65]

Four other witnesses testified about whippings that they heard or saw. William Myers heard from a considerable distance what he believed were the sounds of Wills beating his slave with a hundred lashes, along with the slave's cries in response. Myers responded by going home, closing his door, and complaining to his wife about this cruelty, "but he did not see James Wills beat his Negro." William Peachee and Thomas Gladwyn both heard Wills beat his slave with several stripes and heard her cries in response, while they were working in Gladwin's "Smithy." They went to the scene and saw "Wills beat his Negro Servant and give her many stripes which greeved" them both, but they responded by returning to their work.

James Hill saw Wills beat his victim, tie her hands, "and hang her up." He said "her feet reached the ground and might sustaine the weight of her body, but hee believes it was painful to her." Hill "tooke her downe, but sayth the Negro was soe stubborne and willfull that might well provoke any Master to use her sharply." Hill did not see anything done to the slave that in his judgment would cause her death, although he thought "she was unsound."

The jury found Wills not guilty but also found that because his slave was "unsound, it was a fault, that hee did not therefore be more spareing." Because Wills buried his slave without an inquest, the jury sentenced him to "pay all Court charges, which is assented to by the Bench."[66]

New Jersey became a royal colony in 1702. The first royal governor, Lord Cornbury, received instructions dated November 16, 1702, from Queen Anne, which directed him to get a law adopted "restraining of inhuman severities which by ill masters or overseers may be used towards their Christian servants," and that it also be provided that the willful "killing of Indians and Negroes may be punished with death, and that a fit penalty be imposed for the maiming of them."[67]

New Jersey's colonial legislators did not adopt a slave homicide law, but masters were unsuccessfully prosecuted for killing their slaves. Arthur Barcalow, of Allentown in the Township of Upper Freehold, Monmouth County, was suspected in the death of an enslaved "Black Woman Named Betty," who also was referred to as Barcalow's "Negro Wench Betty." Coroner James Cox assembled a coroner's jury of twelve men, which obtained statements from five witnesses.

According to Arthur's son Derick, Betty and Arthur were at Derick's home on April 9, 1784, when Arthur directed Betty to return home. She refused. Arthur then beat her "with a small whip." Derick declared "he would not have any quarreling in his house," and Betty left. Derick, "after some time," went to Arthur's house. He saw Betty "sitting in the kitchen, after sitting some time he went into the kitchen and found her dead."

John D. Warrick stated that he was at Derick Barcalow's house when Arthur gave Betty "some stripes" for refusing to return home. Warrick and Joseph Brown later went to Arthur's house "to see whether he would beat her any more." When they arrived, they found Arthur "beating her with a raw hide whip, and ... saw ... Barcalow strike the said wench one blow (with a broom stick) on the head as she was sitting in a chair, after which they went into the house." Derick Barcalow later "came into the house saying the wench was dead." Warrick "in company with the other went where she was and found her where they left her actually dead."

The coroner's jury, on April 17, 1784, found that Arthur Barcalow "did kill and murder" Betty.[68] But a grand jury in the Monmouth County Court of Oyer and Terminer on July 27, 1784, found "no bill against the Prisoner." Arthur was "ordered that he be discharged upon giving security."[69]

Another coroner's inquest was held on June 6, 1792, in Maidenhead, Hunterdon County (now the Township of Lawrence in Mercer County) into the killing of "a young Negro woman" who was owned by Samuel Hunt. The inquest reported that the slave's "death was occasioned by a most barbarous and inhuman whipping, which she survived but a few hours, inflicted by her master," who was seventy years of age. Samuel's nephew, Elias Hunt, also allegedly participated in the killing, which was "under the direction and superintendence" of Sarah Hunt, Samuel's wife.[70]

The coroner's jurors found "that from the mangled remains of the poor wretch, ... a more painful death than she must have suffered can scarcely be possible; refused by her mistress even a drink of water, which she supplicated with her last words; and yet these monsters are not even committed to prison." Elias was in the coroner's custody, but Samuel "has been suffered to slip away, and his connections are taking measures to have him bailed, while Mrs. Hunt, who is generally believed to be the most criminal of the three, it is believed will entirely elude punishment."[71]

The three alleged killers reportedly were, on July 11, 1792, confined in the Hunterdon County jail. This article suggested the Hunts' defense, stating, "It appears that the wench was a refractory obdurate jade—had been several times detected in attempts to poison the family;—and, that her last chastisement was for the same offence."[72]

"Philadelphiensis" published a response in the July 19, 1792, *Federal Gazette*. This writer probably was Benjamin Workman, who wrote several essays under that pen name critiquing the U.S. Constitution, in part because it condoned slavery.[73]

In the piece on the Hunt case, Philadelphiensis conceded that masters may moderately correct servants whom the masters believe "committed offences." He denied, however, that masters may kill their slaves, "self defence excepted." He also explained further the alleged facts of the Hunts' crime: "the poor creature was suspended by the arms to an apple tree in the orchard, and beat by the two men with hickory sticks. Fatigued with their exercise, they for a time" rested to drink. They resumed the beating, "nor did they desist, till they had given the poor wretch the deadly blow: while in the mean time the woman contrary to the natural tenderness of her sex not only remains a patient spectator, but even instigates them on to this scene of savage barbarity." Philadelphiensis also questioned the logic of the Hunts' defense, suggesting that no masters would keep slaves in their houses after suspecting that the slaves wanted to poison members of the masters' family. He asserted that "the unanimous opinion of the neighborhood" was that the Hunts killed this slave because, while Sarah was at church, the slave "instead of getting ready the dinner, according to orders, had been employed in gathering fruit."[74]

No reports of any trial could be found. Samuel died in Maidenhead in 1794. But there is no evidence that his death was as a result of a conviction for killing his slave. His will, dated December 16, 1783, was proved on October 27, 1794.[75] Sarah did not die until 1808.[76]

The Pattern of the Development of Slavery in the Border Jurisdictions

Slavery's development pattern in the border states of Maryland, Delaware, and Kentucky was a blend of the patterns in the northern societies with slaves and the southern slave colonies and states. These border slave states did not secede from the Union, although they included counties in which the portion of the enslaved population approached the large numbers found in the southern slave societies. But, on the whole, the enslaved people made up a lesser percentage of the population than in the states that seceded, and slaveholdings also were not as large as those in Britain's colonial slave societies. The enslaved people's work varied, and large-scale cash crop agriculture was not the dominant economic and social force.[77]

Maryland and Delaware at first became slave societies based on tobacco agriculture and enslaved labor. They exhibited four stages of the development of plantation agriculture: the frontier period, the slave population boom, the mature plantation period, and the decline of plantation cash cropping.[78]

Maryland evolved in its early years from a colony settled in 1634 for free whites and white indentured servants to a tobacco colony in which planters increasingly turned to enslaved black labor. The colony's black population grew from 9.0 percent of the total population in 1680 to 10.9 percent in 1700, 18.9 percent in 1720, and 30.8 percent in 1750.[79]

But the colony's black population fell short of its Chesapeake neighbor Virginia, and after an initial tobacco boom, Maryland's economy became more diversified, as many farmers, responding to soil exhaustion and other factors, abandoned tobacco to grow wheat and other crops. The colony's northern portion, including Baltimore, began to resemble the middle Atlantic colonies with slaves. Maryland's enslaved population fell from 32.2 percent of the total population in 1790 to 12.7 percent of the 1860 total, when Maryland was home to about 87,000 slaves and 84,000 free blacks.[80]

Maryland's colonists adopted statutes that more closely followed the English common law, when compared to the colonists in Virginia and New England. The Maryland legislators enacted modifications, however, including the provisions that they deemed necessary to accommodate slavery into the common law.[81]

Nevertheless, Maryland's assembly never adopted a statute decriminalizing slave killings by masters and imposing a reduced penalty for masters who killed their slaves, but it also failed to adopt a statute expressly equating slave killing with capital murder.[82] The British colonial Board of Trade on at least five occasions between 1691 and 1713/14 included in its instructions to Maryland's governors requests that they persuade the colonial legislators to pass a law expressly confirming that the death penalty would be imposed on those who willfully killed slaves and establishing appropriate punishments for those who dismembered them.[83]

This legislative silence nevertheless may have been understood to leave open the possibility that Maryland slave masters could face common law murder prosecutions and convictions. This view is supported by a 1751 Maryland law that decriminalized killings of slaves who refused to surrender themselves contrary to law or who were unlawfully resisting any officer or other person who was seeking to apprehend the slaves.[84]

According to Thomas Morris, the Maryland experience "although thin, suggests that in the absence of a statute modifying the common law, people were reluctant to deal with the killers of slaves."[85] In 1658, Symon (or Simon) Overzee, a thirty-one-year-old Dutch-born merchant, was the first Maryland slave owner prosecuted for killing his or her slave. Overzee was "one of the most prominent men in the colony."[86] Nevertheless, another colonist apparently

82 CHAPTER FIVE

informed on Overzee. The Provincial Court prosecuted Overzee on a charge of manslaughter for killing his slave Antonio or Tony, who, in 1656, allegedly died under Overzee's correction.[87]

The prosecution apparently was based on the depositions of Hannah Littleworth and William Hewes, which were taken on November 27, 1658, before Judge Philip Calvert, the half-brother of the colony's proprietor, Cecil Calvert, the second Lord Baltimore. Littleworth alleged that, in September 1656, she was present with Hewes and Matthew Stone when Overzee unchained Tony, who had been restrained at Overzee's wife's command that was given while Overzee was abroad. Overzee ordered Tony to get to work. But Tony stayed down on the ground and did not stir.[88]

Overzee then beat Tony's bare back with pear tree "wands or twiggs," which were the size of a man's finger. Tony pretended to have a fit, which Littleworth said Tony was inclined to do. Overzee responded by ordering Littleworth to heat a shovel and to bring him some lard. Overzee had an Indian slave tie Tony to a ladder by his wrists. Overzee again beat Tony and he poured the heated lard on Tony, who was still tied up. Tony remained "mute or stubborne" and made no signs of conforming to Overzee's will for about a quarter of an hour or less, when Mr. and Mrs. Overzee left the scene to go home. Littleworth did not hear Overzee give any orders about Tony. She and Hewes asked Stone to cut Tony down because they thought that Tony was dying. Stone refused. Tony then was exposed to the wind from between three and four o'clock in the afternoon until six or seven o'clock the next morning, when he was found dead and was buried. Hewes also gave similar testimony, and added that Tony had in the past run away from the Overzees. Calvert apparently asked if Tony's feet were on the ground when he was tied up. According to Littleworth they were, but Hewes was not as sure.[89]

Governor Josias Fendall and his Council heard the case on December 20, 1658. Fendall asked the Council whether they thought they had the power to judge the case. Overzee "humbly requested" that the court "end it" and that he be acquitted. Instead, the Court, noting that Stone's statement had not been taken, required Overzee to post bond of a hundred thousand pounds of tobacco and appear at the next Provincial Court.[90]

The Provincial Court heard the case again in February 1659, and a grand jury of twelve men was impaneled. There is no record that Stone testified, but Overzee's brother-in-law, Job Chandler, who also was a prominent colonist, did. He was a court councilor and receiver general of the colony. According to Chandler, Overzee bought Antonio in March 1656. He called Antonio a runaway slave who would not work and who did not speak English, adding,

"I never knew such a Brute; for I could not perceive any speech or language hee had, only an ugly yelling Brute beast like."[91]

The grand jury then deliberated, and "[a]fter some time spent," returned a verdict of ignoramus. "The Evidence being fownd not pregnant [against] the Prisoner," the sheriff proclaimed that Overzee "stood uppon his Justification," and with no one coming to give evidence "for the Lord Proprietary," Overzee was acquitted.[92]

Overzee's case reveals how Maryland's masters could be prosecuted for killing their slaves, although no statute supplemented the common law of crimes. Overzee's trial may have been orchestrated by his rivals in the ruling colonial elite as "a piece of political theater meant to rankle Overzee."[93]

Three other slave owners avoided convictions after they were indicted by grand juries. Richard Sweatnam, of Talbot County, was indicted on January 29, 1692/93, for the murder of his slave Sambo. The grand jury found that Sweatnam allegedly knocked out Sambo's right eye with a cudgel. Sambo instantly died. A trial jury found Sweatnam not guilty. Samuel Pottenger was indicted on August 1, 1761, for the murder of his slave Natt. According to the grand jury, Pottenger hit Natt's left eye with a club, inflicting a wound two inches long and one inch deep. Natt immediately died. A Provincial Court jury, in September 1763, found Pottenger not guilty. And James Lee Jr. twice was indicted for slave manslaughter. A Baltimore County grand jury, in September 1763, charged Lee with the killing of his slave Nace, but Governor Horatio Sharpe later pardoned Lee. In April 1773, Lee again was indicted for the manslaughter of his slave Joe. There is no record of a trial. It appears that Lee's lawyers obtained a *nolle prosequi* ending the prosecution.[94]

Grand juries in two other cases refused to indict slave masters, or their family members, who were suspected slave killers. A coroner's jury charged Richard and Susanna Harris, of Somerset County, with the October 1688 death of a thirteen-year-old slave girl named Anne. Susanna had a life estate interest in Anne, who later was to be the property of Elizabeth Richardson, Susanna's daughter from a prior marriage.

The coroner's jury began its investigation into the cause of Anne's death on October 25, 1688, "as it is Credibly reported amongst the Neighbors" that she "hath been used after a very Violent & barbarous manner." Three witnesses provided depositions to the coroner and testified in court before the grand jury. They alleged that, on October 2 or 3, 1688, Richard and Susanna stripped off Anne's clothes, tied her to a well post, beat her with switches, and then set a pile of straw at her feet on fire. Anne died apparently as a result of the beating and the burns. Richard and Susanna then buried Anne in a shallow grave. They later lied to their neighbors who inquired about Anne, stating that she "was in being" and "was gon[e] abroad."

The coroner's jury found and dug up Anne's body "in an Obscure place by the side of a greate poplar in the Corne field & three Chuncks of wood laid length waies over the grave." Anne's body was described as being "extremely burnt in soe much that most of the skin was peeld from all her lower parts & Arm & her flesh appeared in some places blackish & Crispey as it is usuall for flesh to looke when scoarched with fire & in many other places where skin was off it appeared as red as fire & the Skin laying loose in flacks in severall places where it was burnt." The jurors concluded "that the death of the said Negro girle was hastened by meanes of the said burning or Roasting."

A grand jury, on November 13, 1688, found Richard and Susanna not guilty, but they were ordered to post security that they would convey to Richard Richardson's heirs all of their inheritance when demanded, apparently to reimburse the Richardson heirs for the destruction of their remainder interest in Anne. The Court also required Richard and Susanna to post security to guarantee their future good behavior.[95]

In the second prosecution, Parker and Matthew Selby, of Worcester County, in 1744, were charged with the killing of Tom, an enslaved man who was owned by their father Philip. Parker allegedly killed Tom, at Matthew's direction or incitement, by hitting Tom on the right side of his head with an oak staff. The blow inflicted a wound that was two inches long and two inches deep. Tom immediately died, but the grand jury's verdict was ignoramus.[96]

In contrast, Maryland slave owner Peter Ball was indicted, tried, and convicted on the charge that he murdered one of his slaves. There is no court record of this Kent County case. We know of the conviction because acting Governor Benjamin Tasker, on December 19, 1752, signed a death warrant calling for Ball's December 29, 1752, execution. But, on December 28, 1752, Tasker pardoned Ball, in response to a petition of many of Kent County's "principal Inhabitants."[97]

At least two other Maryland defendants avoided punishment when slaves under their command were killed. John McAtee, a minor planter and slave owner in Charles County, Maryland, was charged with the murder of Peter, a slave of Ann Berry. McAtee was accused of beating and stabbing Peter to death after hoisting him in the air for a period of six hours from the beams of McAtee's house. At a trial that was held in 1779, witnesses testified that McAtee beat Peter with a birch rod that was four feet long and one inch thick. Peter's wounds were six inches long and a half inch deep. Although the evidence confirmed that Peter had been lashed on his back, shoulders, sides, and stomach, the jury found McAtee not guilty.[98]

Luke Tiernan Williamson also was cleared of any suspicion of wrongdoing that apparently arose in the minds of some neighbors when Tom Kell, a fifteen-year-old slave owned by Luke's mother, died after enduring a beating administered by Luke. Luke was a descendent of Luke Tiernen and David Williamson, two of Baltimore's leading business, social, religious, and political leaders in the early 1800s.

The incident occurred in August or September 1843 at Lexington, a country home of the Williamson family, which was about seven miles outside of Baltimore. Luke whipped Tom with a leather strap for about ten minutes in a barn, according to Thomas Dorsey, an overseer employed by Luke. Luke returned from the barn, put down the whip, and asked Dorsey if he had seen Tom. Luke then left for a meeting of magistrates when another slave reported that Tom was found dead in a granary, which was about five hundred yards from the barn. Tom had a bridle rein around his neck and was hanging from a beam, with his feet three or four feet from the floor. Dorsey saw four wounds on Tom's body.

Dorsey then sent for Luke, who soon returned with two magistrates, William and James Owings. They then conducted an inquest, in which the jurors, including Dorsey, concluded that Tom committed suicide. Luke later sued the *Baltimore Sun* for libel after it reported, on September 8, 1843, Tom's death and the alleged belief of some neighbors that Tom "was indebted to his master not only for the chastisement, but also the hanging—a story which, we hope, farther developments will entirely refute." The next day the *Sun* printed a retraction, but Luke nevertheless pursued his libel suit, and in February 1845 won a hundred-dollar verdict. His reputation apparently was not tainted—the next year he was appointed as a District Court judge.[99]

Delaware's recorded slave homicide prosecutions all were unsuccessful. That colony's tobacco bust following its boom was swifter and steeper than Maryland's decline. The Swedish and the Dutch originally settled Delaware in the first half of the seventeenth century, and they attempted to develop tobacco farming in the colony. The British first gained control in 1664. They increased Delaware's enslaved population as colonists from the southern Chesapeake moved north to southern Delaware in search of new land for tobacco cultivation. Nevertheless, Delaware's tobacco farms generally were smaller than those in Maryland and Virginia. Delaware's colonists soon exhausted the soil and in the 1740s began to abandon tobacco farming. By the 1770s, grain farming generally replaced tobacco agriculture, and colonists began freeing their excess slaves. Slavery, moreover, was a less important institution in northern Delaware, which was influenced by Quakers from Pennsylvania.[100]

Delaware's enslaved population thus declined in the nineteenth century. The colonial enslaved population is hard to estimate, but in 1790 it was 15.9 percent of the total population. By 1800 Delaware's enslaved population fell to 9.6 percent, by 1820 it was 6.2 percent, and by 1840 it was 3.3 percent.[101] By 1860, only 1.4 percent of Delaware's population was enslaved.[102]

Delaware did not adopt a "statutory discrimination of the crime of killing a slave."[103] William Williams found four Delaware cases between 1781 and 1827 in which masters or other whites were prosecuted for killing slaves, but he found no convictions on record.[104]

The case about which the record is most complete is that of Benjamin Walmsley. He was indicted on the charge that, in 1811, he murdered his slave Michael. Until the day before his death, Michael had been a slave of William Corbit, a tanner who lived in New Castle County, Delaware.

Walmsley suspected that Michael gave poison to Michael's niece Judith, who was Walmsley's slave, so that she could put the poison in Walmsley's tea. Judith did this, but apparently had second thoughts and removed the poison from the tea. Walmsley learned of the plot. He confronted Corbit, demanding that Corbit either sell Michael out of state or sell him to Walmsley. Delaware law prohibited the sale of slaves out of state unless the seller obtained a license. Corbit agreed to sell Michael to Walmsley. On the sale day, Walmsley began to beat and torture Michael to find out the source of the poison. Michael refused to tell. By the next day Michael was dead. Walmsley was found not guilty after a trial during the Court of Oyer and Terminer's April 1814 session.[105]

Kentucky law in the books and in action followed the same pattern as that of Delaware and Maryland, although one master was convicted of manslaughter. The land that became the state of Kentucky, while a part of Virginia, evolved in the 1770s from a western frontier outpost with few slaves to a colony with an increasing number of slaves, as Virginians moved west with their slaves. Kentucky's slaveholdings nevertheless were smaller than those in the more southern states, because large-scale plantation agriculture was not typical of the state's economy.[106]

Kentucky was admitted to the union in 1792. Efforts to prohibit slavery failed, and the state's 1792, 1799, and 1850 constitutions included substantially similar articles confirming slavery's legality. These articles authorized laws requiring slave owners to treat their slaves "with humanity, to provide for their necessary clothing and provision, to abstain from all injuries to them, extending to life or limb; and in case of their neglect or refusal to comply" with these laws to have the offending owners' slaves sold for the owners' benefit.[107]

Slavery "flourished" under these constitutions. Kentucky's enslaved population in 1777 was 9.6 percent of the total, and by 1830 it reached a peak of 24 percent. By 1860 the state's enslaved population fell to 19.5 percent, although between 1840 and 1850 the number of the state's enslaved population increased by 16 percent.[108]

Kentucky's statutes did not include slave homicide provisions. Thus, the state's general homicide laws governed slave killings.[109] Moreover, for almost forty years, Kentucky's legislature failed to adopt a law enforcing the constitution's anticruelty provisions. The legislators in December 1811 defeated a bill that would have made cruelty to slaves an offense with a hundred-dollar fine and a jail term of up to three months on a first offense. A second offender's slave would be sold to a new owner. Instead, the legislators adopted an 1816 act permitting a slave owner to file a trespass action against any person who should "whip, strike, or otherwise abuse the slave of another, without the slave owner's consent," although the act was not to be "construed to prevent any person from inflicting such punishments on slaves as the laws now in force permit."[110] And a 1798 slavery law included a provision, based on Virginia law, stating, "If any negro, mulatto, or Indian, bond or free, shall at any time lift his or her hand in opposition to any person not being a negro, mulatto or Indian, he or she so offending, shall for every such offence, proved by the oath of the party before a justice of the peace of the county where such offence shall be committed, receive thirty lashes on his or her bare back, well laid on, by order of such justice."[111]

It was not until January 28, 1830, that the legislature adopted a statute authorizing any person to file a petition alleging cruel treatment of a slave. The offending owners' slaves would be sold for the masters' benefit.[112]

The recorded slave homicide cases include two 1804 prosecutions of masters in Livingston County, which is on the northwestern Kentucky border neighboring Illinois. It appears that both masters escaped punishment.

A coroner's jury accused John Strong, on September 12, 1804, of beating his runaway slave to death. On September 24 and October 1, 1804, in the Circuit Court, the charges were dismissed.[113] Another coroner's jury, on December 9, 1804, held an inquest into the death of "a negro woman named Rachel," who was a slave of Thomas Hawkins. The inquest reported that Rachel sustained "an exceeding bad wound behind the right ear, supposed to be struck with a club or some other unlawful weapon. The appearance of the wound had affected the side of the head unto the left nostril and Blood appeared to issue therefrom, together with sundry smaller wounds appeared to be from severe whipping and the appearance of being seeded in a number of places by large blisters." The jurors found that Hawkins and his wife murdered Rachel with malice aforethought. On December 19, 1804, the charges were dismissed.[114]

Kentucky's successful slave master prosecution was pursued against Zaba Campfield. He was indicted in 1807 for murdering "his own mulatto slave boy" in Boone County, another northern Kentucky border county adjacent to both Ohio and Indiana. After a trial held in 1808 in the Circuit Court, a jury found Campfield guilty only of manslaughter. He was ordered to serve a four-year prison term. But in January 1811 Governor Charles Scott pardoned Campfield after the prosecuting attorney admitted "the proof was only presumptive and light."[115]

Thomas Jefferson's nephews, Lilburne and Isham Lewis, in March 1812 were indicted by a Livingston County grand jury for the murder of Lilburne's seventeen-year-old slave George. The Lewis brothers avoided a trial after Lilburne allegedly committed suicide and Isham escaped from the county jail and fled the state.[116] This case nevertheless became an example of "the gruesome tribulations of the body [that] became a staple of antislavery literature."[117]

In contrast, a man identified in press reports only as Brasfield (or Brashfield) voluntarily appeared in the Franklin County Circuit Court in 1830 to refute an indictment charging him with killing a slave. Brasfield hired his victim, who had run away and was being held in a jail. Brasfield took possession of the slave, tied the slave's arms, and "compelled him to walk before him, he being on horseback and having hold of a rope fastened around the slave." After traveling about twelve miles in four hours, Brasfield beat the slave because the slave was "inclined to apoplexy, and occasionally rendered his motion more uneasy by being sulky." Brasfield then put the slave "into a sitting posture, and he fell backwards. He was found to be very ill, and dragged across the road out of the sun. Means were ineffectually used to restore him; and it was found that a blood vessel had burst in the head." After airing this testimony Brasfield was acquitted.[118]

Abyer (or Abyger) McGuire, on the other hand, absconded after he and a white hired man named Murphy tied up, beat, punched, and stomped to death Jem, a slave McGuire had recently purchased. The beating occurred during the afternoon of Wednesday, July 31, 1839, in a stable at the corner of Main and Clay Streets in Louisville. Jem died early that evening. McGuire had a grave prepared, and before daylight the next morning he "conveyed the body to the grave and interred it; immediately after which he rode off."

The coroner, Mr. Spurrier, was not informed until Friday, August 2, 1839. The coroner's jury's verdict was murder, and a warrant was issued for McGuire's arrest. The Clay Street neighbors spread rumors that McGuire suspected that Jem, who "was scarcely 30 years of age," was having an affair with "a black woman whom McGuire had lately bought, and with whom [McGuire] had formed an intimacy." There are no reports that McGuire was caught and prosecuted.[119]

Third parties to the master and slave relationship also were prosecuted in Kentucky for fatal and nonfatal violence directed against slaves. Theodore H. Davis was charged with murder by a Mercer County grand inquest jury in October 1850 after Davis, on September 25, shot a slave named Jack, who was owned by James Telford. Davis contended that Jack was known as a "violent fellow." Davis and Jack were working in a garden when Jack, "with a rake in his hands, threatened to beat Davis's brains out." Davis claimed that he "was obliged to do what I did to save my life." The prosecutor entered a *nolle prosequi* and the charge was dropped in April 1852.[120]

But the Court of Appeals in 1860 reversed the dismissal of an indictment charging the defendants Lee and Bledsoe with assault and battery on George, Betsy, and Tabitha, who were slaves owned by A. B. Watkins. The opinion of Judge Belvard J. Peters cited general common law principles. But he also relied on North and South Carolina decisions that were part of the common law of slavery that will be discussed in the following chapters. Peters noted that third-party attacks on slaves generally were "a great provocation to the master," who might feel "resentment," tending to cause "breaches of the peace" that "may end in fatal conflict." He also cited the rule of unequal protection providing "many circumstances which would not constitute legal provocation for one white man to commit a battery upon another, would justify it when committed upon a slave."[121]

Conclusion

Lawmakers in Maryland, Delaware, Kentucky, and the more northern mainland societies with slaves rejected the Barbadian slave homicide law model and adopted no laws justifying slave homicides or trivializing slave killer penalties. Edward Long's 1774 critique of Jamaica's slave laws thus cited with approval Pennsylvania law because "a white owner, who kills his Negroe slave with malice prepense, is liable to suffer *death* for it." But Long recognized that the authorities needed the will to enforce these laws.[122]

Local coroners' juries, grand juries, and trial juries also had to be convinced that accused slave owners committed unjustified homicides. The cases in this chapter confirm that often these jurors were not convinced. And community members intervened to prevent the executions of the two convicted slave master murderers.

Frederick Douglass wrote that while he was enslaved on Maryland's eastern shore he heard of owners who killed their slaves but "never knew a solitary instance in which a slaveholder was either hung or imprisoned for having murdered a slave." He explained that "[t]he usual pretext for killing a slave is, that the slave has offered resistance. Should a slave, when assaulted, but raise his hand in self-defense, the white assaulting party is fully justified by southern, or Maryland, public opinion, in shooting the slave down."[123]

Douglass's experiences support Graham Russell Hodges's view that when masters in the northern mainland jurisdictions killed their slaves the "[l]ocal authorities invoked the law only in the most horrific cases."[124] And the lack of slave master prosecutions prompted Dinah Mayo-Bobee to conclude that laws protecting slaves' lives "although espousing humanitarianism and justice cloaked an often vicious and coercive labour system in lofty but useless rhetoric. For the most part, such laws were seldom if ever enforced. When their lives or persons were threatened, slaves had little recourse other than fleeing from violent masters."[125] It is possible, however, that the masters' "knowledge that [they] could not escape the odium of a trial with its attendant inconveniences and costs, as well as a public censure" deterred wanton killings, as did the possibility that a trial might result in a capital sentence.[126]

In contrast, the following chapters will show how the legislators and judges in the more southern mainland jurisdictions rejected the notion that enslaved people's lives deserved the criminal laws' equal protection. They adopted laws explicitly legitimizing slave master killings that were deemed necessary.

CHAPTER 6

Slave Killing in Britain's Southern Mainland Colonies

Lawmakers in colonial Virginia, the Carolinas, and Georgia adopted statutes that in different ways explicitly legitimized slave killings by masters, which would have been common law murders. Moreover, legislators in the Carolinas and Georgia abolished or modified the common law's imposition of capital punishment when slaves were murdered. Before American independence, these colonists ignored the British authorities' requests for slave homicide reform laws. As a result, some masters may have known that they could murder slaves with impunity and avoid even the possibility of the odium of a trial.

Scholars have suggested that the mainland lawmakers followed the Barbadian or Jamaican laws. This was not so, however, with the colonial era slave homicide laws adopted in Britain's North American colonies other than South Carolina.[1]

Virginia's Partial Decriminalization

After almost twelve years of what some have called martial law under the Virginia Company, Virginia's first legislative assembly met in 1619, the year that the first Africans arrived. Scholars have drawn from the sketchy data differing conclusions about these first Africans' legal status. Virginians eventually imposed lifetime and hereditary enslavement on some Africans and Indians and adopted laws ratifying these practices.[2]

Virginia's development pattern differed from that in Britain's sugar island colonies and South Carolina. Tobacco, Virginia's first successful cash crop, did not require the large slaveholdings found in the sugar and rice colonies.[3]

Virginia's tobacco planters at first used indentured servants and later turned to more enslaved labor. Virginia's enslaved population grew less dramatically than those in the Atlantic islands and South Carolina. It increased from 0.09 percent in 1620 to 5.6 percent in 1670 and 6.9 percent in 1680. It then jumped to 17.6 percent in 1690 and grew more steadily to 30 percent by 1720. Between 1790 and 1840 Virginia's enslaved population hovered around 40 percent.[4]

Virginia's slaves were concentrated in the Chesapeake region. But the enslaved population's percentage in no county reached the 80 to 90 percent concentrations in South Carolina's low country counties.[5]

Historians have debated the extent to which the Barbadian slavery culture influenced Virginia's colonists. According to April Hatfield, in the 1600s, many planters moved from Barbados to Virginia, and there were "many parallels" between these colonies' slave laws. Virginia Bernhard also wrote of the connections between the early Virginia and Jamaica colonists, while Richard S. Dunn noted differences between them.[6]

Virginia's legislators did not copy the Barbadian laws substituting fines for the common law homicide penalties. They instead accommodated slave killing into the common law of crimes with statutes maintaining at least the potential for some common law capital murder convictions when whites killed slaves.[7]

The legislators thus adopted a 1669 act concerning the "casuall killing of slaves." This act confirmed that some people were already enslaved in Virginia for life, with the finding that the usual punishment for "refractory" servants, which was the extension of the servants' term of service, could not be applied to these lifetime slaves, and that the "obstinancy of many of them" required "violent meanes" of discipline. The act declared that if any slave resisted his or her master, or any other person correcting a slave by the master's order, "and by the extremity of the correction should chance to die," the killing would not be a felony, and "the master (or that other person appointed by the master to punish him) be acquit from molestation, since it cannot be presumed that propensed malice (which alone makes murther a ffelony) should induce a man to destroy his owne estate."[8]

This act exempted slave owners, and other people acting on their orders, from the common law rule that would have required these disciplinarians to retreat to the wall before killing slaves who resisted discipline. It also exempted these slave killers from the moderate correction standard that limited the privilege of "superiors" to discipline their "inferiors," including servants, apprentices, and children.

According to Paul Finkelman, Virginia's colonial legislators based this act on the "faulty" notion that masters would not unnecessarily kill their own slaves, when "we know that some slave masters killed slaves for pleasure, out of anger, or when drunk." He also noted that the statute "ignored the possibility that a master's callous and reckless disregard for the life of a slave could be punished by a charge other than premeditated murder. This statute treated the slave as property—a commodity—and not a person." Slaves thus were "not protected from the whims or anger of their masters."[9] And Finkelman asserted that this act gave slave masters greater freedom to kill their slaves than the slave code in Exodus 20. That provision legitimized the killings of slaves by their masters' correction only if the slaves survived a fatal beating for a day or two.[10]

This statute illustrates "how the Virginia colonists viewed themselves as governed by English common law, not Biblical or civil law." The colonists instead passed this statute in derogation of the common law permitting strangers to their enslaved homicide victims and some slave masters to be charged with murder if the killings "did not fit within the four corners of the statute."[11]

Virginia's legislators apparently believed that they "were bound by the common and statute law of England in so far as that was applicable to their situation. English law was supplemented or amended by those laws of the General Assembly that were approved by the King and Council but the basic law, including all the more serious criminal offenses, was the law of England." This colonial legislation modified the English law of crimes "to fit colonial conditions," which included enslavement.[12]

Moreover, laws adopted in 1680 and 1691 legitimized killings when enslaved people ran away from their owners. The 1680 law also declared that slaves could not carry weapons without their masters' written permission and authorized whippings of thirty lashes "if any negroe or other slave shall presume to lift up his hand in opposition against any [C]hristian."[13]

Virginia's legislators included these provisions in a more comprehensive 1705 slavery law.[14] Although some slave murders remained capital offenses, these laws ignored at least the spirit of the colonial authorities' instructions that, as early as January 27, 1681/82, directed Governor Sir Thomas Lord Culpeper to "endeavor to get a law passed for the restraining of any inhuman severity which by ill masters or overseers may be used towards their Christian Servants or Slaves."[15] Later versions more explicitly directed the governors to call for laws punishing with death the willful killers of slaves and Indians.[16]

Another 1705 act "diverged from English procedure by introducing a new court to hear evidence of serious crimes."[17] It authorized justices of the peace who were holding in the county jails those accused of serious crimes to summon a court of the county's justices to meet within five to ten days to examine the prisoner, the witnesses, and the "circumstances relating to the matter." The examining court could send the case to the General Court in Williamsburg, retain the case because the offense was not so serious and could be heard in the county, or acquit the defendant. This act thus afforded slave owners with a procedure to obtain the dismissal of serious charges including murder.[18]

Slave owners were prosecuted after their slaves died under correction. One such owner was the Reverend Samuel Gray who, between 1693 and 1698, was a pastor in Middlesex County, Virginia. His slave Jack ran away and was recovered. Gray, along with Thomas Williamson and Gray's "Negroe Peter," proceeded to beat Jack to death. Gray had Jack tied to a mulberry tree. Jack first was beaten "about the head, chest, and abdomen until the lash itself had broken." Gray complained that the lash was no good, and he asked for another one. Gray then obtained a branding iron and approached Jack, who cried out, "Pray Master lett me down." Gray responded by hitting Jack in the head with two or three blows from the branding iron. Gray then "sat him selfe down and bidd the Negroe Whipp him some more." Gray admitted his excesses and was not convicted of any crime.[19]

Frances Wilson was suspected of whipping to death Rose, one of her husband's slaves. Andrew Woodley, an Isle of Wight County justice of the peace and coroner, had Rose's body exhumed. The inquest jury on November 26, 1713, found that Rose was killed "by hard useage," there being "no mortal wounds but only stripes." Attorney General John Clayton nevertheless persuaded Governor Alexander Spotswood to instruct the County Court, on February 18, 1713/14, to examine the case and prosecute Wilson based on Mary Lupo's evidence. The County Court did not comply. But Clayton in April 1714 proceeded before the General Court made up of the governor and Council in Williamsburg.[20]

Clayton obtained a grand jury indictment against Wilson for murdering Rose with "forty mortal strokes each of the length of three inches & the breath of half an inch." Spotswood later reported to the Board of Trade that he charged the grand jury that "no Master has such a Sovereign Power over his Slave as not to be liable to be called to Account whenever he kills him; that at the same time, the Slave is the Master's Property, he is likewise the King's Subject, and the King may lawfully bring to Tryal all Persons here, without exception, who shall be suspected to have destroyed the Life of his Subject."[21]

William Byrd II presided over Wilson's General Court trial during the October Term 1714. Samuel Seldon appeared for Wilson, but the only record of Wilson's defense is Seldon's contention that Wilson should not be "molested for killing the s[ai]d Slave." The jury acquitted Wilson.[22]

Possibly in response to the concerns raised by cases such as these, Virginia's 1723 and 1748 slave laws declared that "no person indicted for murder of a slave, and upon a trial found guilty of manslaughter only, shall incur any forfeiture or punishment, for such offence, or misfortune." The acts stated that they did not bar the slave owners' rights to sue and potentially recover damages from those who wrongfully killed their slaves.

These acts also declared that if a slave "shall happen to die, by reason of any stroke, or blow given, during his, or her correction, by his, or her owner, or by reason of any accidental blow whatsoever, given by such owner, no person concerned in such correction, or accidental homicide, shall be liable to any prosecution, or punishment for the same, unless upon examination before a county court, it shall be proved, by the oath of at least one lawful and credible witness, that such slave was killed wilfully, or maliciously, or designedly."[23] This act thus vested Virginia's examining courts with additional powers to dismiss criminal prosecutions instituted against masters.

Virginia's homicide law remained unchanged until after independence. But a 1753 act authorized death without benefit of clergy for anyone stealing a slave "out of, or from the possession of the owner or overseer of such slave."[24]

Anthony Parent argued that these laws evidenced the "dangerous fissures within Virginia's white society." Virginia's white colonists were divided between slave owners and those who did not own slaves.[25] And Philip Morgan's comparative study of South Carolina and Virginia noted that Virginia's slave-owning elites had greater concerns about slave and poor white fraternization and violence because Virginia's non-slave-owning and poor white populations were larger than those in South Carolina. These poorer white classes allegedly disrupted the social order both by cooperating with slaves in committing crimes and by getting into violent confrontations with slaves.[26]

Overseers also were prosecuted under Virginia's colonial slave homicide laws. Andrew Bourne (or Byrn) was charged with subjecting a frequent runaway slave to "such immoderate Correction that the Fellow dyed under it for which the Jury found him guilty of Murder." Lieutenant Governor William Gooch in June 1729 requested that the Privy Council pardon Bourne. Gooch stated the trial judge favored mercy because it did not appear that Bourne intended to kill his victim and because Bourne's execution would "make the slaves very insolent, and give them occasion to condemn their Masters and Overseers, which may be of dangerous Consequences in a Country where the Negroes are so numerous and make the most valuable part of the People's Estates."[27]

In contrast, overseer Charles Quinn and an accomplice, David White, were tried and convicted in Essex County for murdering an enslaved man owned by Charles Braxton. The November 23, 1739, *Virginia Gazette* reported that these defendants were hung for whipping to death their victim "in a most cruel and barbarous manner."[28]

Four years later, William Lee was jailed in Lunenburg Parish, Richmond County, and was charged with the felonious killing of John Barber's slave Will. Lee was the overseer for Barber, who was described as a "Gentleman." The County Court examined a coroner's inquest report and the evidence of four witnesses, including Barber.

Will was a runaway who was captured on May 2, 1743. The next morning, Barber tied and whipped Will. He then sent for Lee and directed him to take Will to Barber's smith to have Will "Ironed" to prevent him from running away again. Barber said that late that night he heard Lee tell Barber's wife that "he was obliged to Beat Will in Carrying him to the Smiths five Times as Much as he had done Before." It also appeared that Barber whipped Will "a Considerable time" before calling for Lee. Lee whipped Will at Barber's direction with a "catt of Nine tails and Cowskin whip." Will was subjected to about two hundred lashes.

The next day, Lee hit Will with a switch after Will refused to obey Lee's demand that Will take off his jacket. Will tried to escape but was caught. Lee kicked Will in the mouth, stripped him, whipped him, and washed him with brine. Will complained of pain in his stomach and shoulders on May 6 and died on May 10.

The examining court sent the case to Williamsburg for prosecution and released Lee on bail. There is no record of Lee's indictment or trial. It appears that Barber was not prosecuted for his actions.[29]

Virginia also retained the threat of capital punishment for some slave owners. Morgan referred to differences in "tone" as slavery evolved in Virginia and South Carolina. He wrote that in the Chesapeake, seventeenth-century "patriarchalism" evolved during the eighteenth century into an "enlightened patriarchalism."[30]

Thomas Morris cited four colonial prosecutions of slave owners or their wives. These cases illustrate the limits of this enlightened patriarchalism. Hannah Crump (1747), William Cox (1752), and Sarah Scott (1762) all were discharged from prosecution.[31]

William Pitman was the only Virginia master who was tried, convicted, and executed for murdering his slave. His son and daughter testified at his April 1775 General Court trial. Pitman, "in the heat of passion, and when in liquor, had, for some trifling offence, tied his poor negro boy by the neck and heels, beat him most cruelly with a large grape vine, and then stamped him to death." The *Virginia Gazette* opined that "this man has justly incurred the penalties of the law, ... which ought to be a warning to others to treat their slaves with moderation, and not give way to unruly passions, that may bring them to an ignominious death, and involve their families in their unhappy fate."[32] Pitman was executed on May 12, 1775, "and attributed his unhappy fate to the effect of intemperate drinking."[33]

Pitman's conviction may have been influenced by his involvement in seven civil King George County lawsuits between 1759 and 1765. Pitman may have made enemies.[34]

The prosecution also may have been in part "due to the talk of liberty in the air of 1775."[35] Indeed, 1775 was a year of turmoil. The Virginians' fears of slave insurrection intensified in the spring and summer with heightened tensions between the increasingly rebellious colonists and the Royal Governor Lord Dunmore. These tensions led to Dunmore's November proclamation offering freedom to slaves and indentured servants who helped Dunmore suppress the rebellious Virginians.[36]

Class-based "fissures" among Virginia's elite slave owners and "smallholders" may also have influenced Pitman's prosecution.[37] By 1775, Virginia's white class structure included convicts and indentured servants, apprentices, free wage laborers, overseers, tenant farmers and non-slaveholding small landholders, poorer slaveholders and substantial landholders, and the elites with hundreds of slaves and thousands of acres. The slave-owning elites may have viewed masters like Pitman—who lost control of their drinking and their slaves—as members of the "middling" to lower subclasses that threatened their slave society on the eve of the revolution.[38]

South Carolina Adopts the Barbados Approach to Slave Killing

South Carolina, in contrast, followed the 1661 Barbadian law abolishing capital punishment for slave killers. These colonies' different development and slaveholding patterns may have contributed to different perceptions among the elites, and thus the differences in the slavery laws.

Although a small number of Africans arrived in South Carolina with Spanish, French, and English explorers as early as 1526, the colony's enslaved population did not expand significantly until after 1663, when Charles II established the colony as a proprietorship. "[T]he leading men in this endeavor ... all had extensive experience."[39]

The proprietors issued the colony's Fundamental Constitutions of 1669, edited by their secretary John Locke. It declared, "Every freeman of Carolina shall have absolute power and authority over negro slaves, of what opinion or religion soever."[40] Although this provision offers "crucial insight into how the project of settling Carolina was imagined," these constitutions never legally went into effect and "were quickly replaced by the settlers' own visions for the new polity."[41]

South Carolina had the most significant connection with Barbados among Britain's North American colonies. Indeed, Peter Wood called it the colony of the Barbados colony, and Barbadians contributed to the colony's first successful settlement.[42] South Carolina was "a successful extension of the Barbados culture hearth," and its development pattern paralleled Jamaica's.[43]

The first settlers began to develop an economy focusing on cattle, pork, corn, and lumber exports, along with trade in "pelts and deerskins procured from Indians and shipped to England." Rice cultivation experiments did not begin until 1689–90. It was not until 1699 that "a considerable harvest was exported."[44]

"What sugar was for the West Indian colonies, rice became for South Carolina."[45] As rice cultivation spread, South Carolina's estimated black population increased from 16.7 percent in 1680 to about 40 percent in 1690. This population grew to 42.8 percent in 1700 and to 70.4 percent in 1720. It leveled off at more than 60 percent in 1750 and 1770.[46] Not all blacks were enslaved, and Indians were enslaved in growing numbers until the end of the Yamasee War in 1717. South Carolina became the only British mainland colony in which enslaved blacks consistently outnumbered whites.[47]

South Carolina was divided into three regions: the low country, the up country, and the mountains in the extreme northwest corner. The low country developed into a mature plantation society, which peaked in the eighteenth century. It had the largest enslaved population, which was 80 percent of the total at the time of the revolution. This region's plantation development pattern over time moved into the up country. The mountains, on the other hand, were settled from the north and remained in many ways distinct.[48]

In some low country areas the ratio of blacks to whites reached nine to one, "a figure well beyond that found in Barbados and only slightly below that found on Jamaica."[49] Accordingly, "[i]t is understandable that 'on a rice plantation in South Carolina where within a five-mile radius there were ten slaves for every white person . . . one of the major daily concerns of responsible men was the effective control of the masses of slaves.'"[50]

As slavery emerged as South Carolina's primary labor form, the colony's legislature, then dominated by Barbadians known as the Goose Creek men, enacted the colony's first slave code in 1690. This law, and those that followed, adapted the 1661 Barbadian act's premise that most slave killers should only pay fines, although the South Carolinians more closely copied the text of Jamaica's 1683/84 code.[51]

The 1690 act, titled An Act for the Better Ordering of Slaves, stated in section 12 "[t]hat if any slave, by punishment of the owner for running away or other offense, shall suffer in life and limb, no person shall be liable to the law for the same, but if any one out of willfulness, wantonness, or bloody mindedness, shall kill a slave, he or she, upon due conviction thereof, shall suffer three months imprisonment, without bail or mainprize, and also shall pay the sum of fifty pounds" to the slave's owner. Servants were to receive thirty-nine lashes on their bare back and serve their victims' owners for four years after the end of their current terms of service. The act also decriminalized a killing by a person catching "a slave stealing in his house or plantation by night" if the slave refused "to submit himself, . . . any law, custom or usage to the contrary notwithstanding." The act, in contrast, made the theft of a slave out of the colony a felony without benefit of clergy and imposed for attempted slave theft a fine of sixty pounds, ten pounds more than the fine for slave killing.[52]

The proprietors rejected all of the colony's 1691 acts, as part of their disputes with the Goose Creek men. But the colonists reenacted the slave law in 1693 and 1695. Governor John Archdale is credited with working with the political factions to create new laws, called Archdale's laws, which included a March 16, 1695/96, slavery act.[53]

A 1712 act, titled An Act for the Better Ordering and Governing of Negroes and Slaves, included in section 30 a slave homicide provision that decriminalized any killing or maiming occurring during the punishment of a slave who ran away or committed "any other crimes or misdemeanors," while declaring that this type of slave killing "seldom happens." Masters who "violently" killed their own slaves out of "wantonness, or only bloody-mindedness, or cruel intention" were liable for fifty-pound fines. Other slave killers were to pay their victims' full value and twenty-five-pound fines, but not "any other punishment or forfeiture for the same." Servants were punished with thirty-nine lashes, a three-month jail term, and four years' service to the dead slave's owner. Accidental killers were liable only to "the owner's action at law." The act also permitted people to kill slaves caught stealing and resisting demands for submission.[54]

South Carolina became a royal colony in 1720. The August 30, 1720, instructions to the first royal governor, Francis Nicholson, contained the by then usual request that he "endeavor to get a law passed, if not already done, for restraining of any inhuman severity which by ill masters or overseers may be used towards their christian servants or their slaves, and that provisions be made therein that the unlawful killing of Indians and Negroes may be punished with death." Nicholson also was to seek a "fit penalty" for the maiming of servants and slaves.[55]

The legislators instead adopted acts continuing to impose fines for slave killers. A 1722 act restated the fine for malicious killing as "fifty pounds, proclamation money." Servants killing slaves continued to be subject to thirty-nine lashes. But they were no longer imprisoned; instead they were to serve the dead slaves' masters for five years.[56] A 1735 act increased these fines to "five hundred pounds current money," and authorized informers to sue to recover one half of the fine. Killers were liable to the owner for the slaves' value, and if they did not pay these fines, they were subject to thirty-nine lashes and were to serve the dead slaves' owners for three years.[57]

A 1740 slavery act, titled An Act for the Better Ordering and Governing Negroes and Other Slaves in This Province, was "the tenth return to the basic law of slavery since 1690/1." It was a response to the 1739 Stono slave rebellion and remained in effect for the next 125 years.[58] Although it included "new polite language of legality and humanity," it "reenacted all of the familiar features" of the colony's earlier laws.[59] Lieutenant Governor William Bull sealed it during a May 10, 1740, ceremony in the Charleston council chambers.[60]

Section 37, addressing slave killings, found that "cruelty is not only highly unbecoming those who profess themselves [C]hristians, but is odious in the eyes of all men who have any sense of virtue or humanity." This provision thus was adopted "to restrain and prevent barbarity being exercised towards slaves." It stated that "any person or persons whosoever, shall wilfully murder his own slave, or the slave of any other person, . . . shall, upon conviction thereof, forfeit and pay the sum of seven hundred pounds, current money, and shall be rendered and is hereby declared altogether and forever incapable of holding . . . any office, place or employment, civil or military, within this Province." Killers who could not pay their fines were to serve seven years of hard labor.

This section, for the first time in South Carolina, imposed a fine of 350 pounds for slave killings "on a sudden heat or passion, or by undue correction." But it continued to decriminalize killings resulting from necessary and ordinary punishment when it imposed a 100-pound current-money fine upon any person who "shall wilfully cut out the tongue, put out the eye, castrate, or cruelly scald, burn, or deprive any slave of any limb or member, or shall inflict any other cruel punishment, other than by whipping or beating with a horsewhip, cow-skin, switch or small stick, or by putting irons on, or confining or imprisoning such slave."[61]

Section 39 provided slave masters with a procedural advantage. It began with the findings that plantations were far from each other and that offenses against slaves may be committed when "no white person may be present to give evidence of same." Owners or others having charge over slaves were presumed to be guilty of offenses under the act if their slaves were found to have been killed, maimed, or abused contrary to the act while in the defendants' possession. But these defendants could exculpate themselves by offering "good and sufficient evidence," or simply by making their own oaths sworn in court, "if clear proof of the offence be not made by two witnesses at least; any law, usage, or custom to the contrary notwithstanding."[62]

Slave owners could use this provision to avoid prosecution if they killed their slaves when no other whites were present. The 1740 law thus protected slave property from unwarranted violent destruction by overseers and third parties, including poor whites, while permitting masters and overseers to impose ordinary discipline.[63]

This act also denied to slaves who were accused of murdering white people the common law right to mitigate their murder charges to manslaughter. These homicides were capital crimes unless they were "by misadventure" or were in the defense of the slaves' masters or others controlling of the slaves.[64] In contrast, a 1754 law continued to impose death without the benefit of clergy on those convicted of stealing slaves.[65]

According to Robert Olwell, between 1769 and 1776, five white men in South Carolina were convicted of "inveigling or stealing negroes" and three were executed, while only one of four convicted murderers was executed. For example, on October 30, 1772, in the Charleston Court of General Sessions, Dempsey Griffin was sentenced to death for slave stealing while John Milner pled guilty to slave killing, was fined fifty pounds, and was released.[66]

As late as June 1770, the royal instructions to South Carolina governor William Campbell contained the usual direction that he get a law adopted restraining any "inhuman severity" on the part of masters or overseers toward their "Christian servants and slaves, and that provision be made therein that the willful killing of Indians and Negroes may be punished with death."[67] South Carolina's lieutenant governor William Bull II, also in 1770, suggested why the colony's slave-owning elite continued to defy these requests for slave homicide law reform. He declared that the 1740 slave code was "calculated to punish offending and to protect abused slaves." He acknowledged that "[t]he royal humanity has often recommended to governors that a white man who murders a Negro should be punished with death. It is so in all of the English *colonies north of Maryland*, where the number of Negroes is small."

But Bull opposed these reforms for Maryland, Virginia, South Carolina, and the British island colonies because "it has been thought dangerous to the public safety, to put [slaves] on a footing of equality in that respect with their masters." This equality at law "might tempt slaves to make resistance, and deter masters and managers from inflicting punishment with exemplary severity tho' ever so necessary." Slavery in these southern colonies was made as "comfortable" as possible, according to Bull. Although at times masters acted like "monsters of cruelty," Bull said these offenders were "punished and abhorred." He concluded that "the general humanity of masters" made the Crown's proposed legal reforms unnecessary.[68]

North Carolina's Moderate Correction Exception

North Carolina's and Georgia's legislators adopted slave homicide laws that were variations on the Virginia and South Carolina acts. North Carolina was legally separated from South Carolina when it became a royal colony in 1729, but these colonies' economies, legal cultures, and slaveholding patterns had long before diverged.[69]

Unlike Virginia and South Carolina, "colonial North Carolina did not become a slave society but rather a culture where slavery became significant but not institutionally dominant."[70] North Carolina had fewer slaves and lacked an extensive plantation economy and planter elite.[71]

Africans, as early as 1585, were brought to the outer banks of what would become North Carolina as a part of the failed Ralph Lane Colony, which soon was abandoned.[72] Permanent settlers began to move from Virginia into the Albemarle Sound area in the 1650s and 1660s, before Charles II established the charter for the Carolina Colony in 1663. Few Africans lived in North Carolina during the next fifty years. In the 1720s, South Carolina whites and their slaves began to settle the Cape Fear region. This is when slavery became more significant in North Carolina.[73]

The colony's patterns of settlement and slaveholding were diverse. Before the American Revolution, North Carolina's slaves worked in three main agricultural areas. Slaves in the northeastern and central counties worked on tobacco farms that were similar to those in the Chesapeake regions of Virginia and Maryland. Along the Cape Fear and Tar Rivers and the Albemarle Sound's inlets, enslaved workers made tar and pitch. And in the low tidewater areas and the Sea Islands near Wilmington, planters from South Carolina established rice and indigo plantations. Rice soon became the region's major cash crop. Settlers from the North also moved into western and central regions and brought fewer enslaved people to these regions.[74]

The dominant patterns of economic development and slaveholding concentration varied in these regions, as the colony's slave population increased from about 3.9 percent in 1680 and 1700 to 6 percent in 1710, 14 percent in

1720, 20 percent in 1730, 22 percent in 1755, 25 percent in 1767, and 30 percent in 1775. The lower Cape Fear area slaves, in 1767 and 1775, made up as much as 62 percent of the population. In contrast, slaves in the far west constituted only between 4 and 8 percent of the population in those years. North Carolina's slave population in the years between 1780 and 1860 floated between 25 and 33 percent, still a significant portion but less than in Virginia and South Carolina.[75]

The colony's first slave code of 1715 did not address slave murders.[76] The king's December 14, 1730, letter instructed Governor George Burrington to endeavor to get a law adopted restraining "inhuman severity" by "ill masters or their overseers," making willful slave killing a crime punished with death, and imposing a "fit penalty" on those who maim slaves.[77] The legislators did not follow this instruction, although their 1741 slavery law declared that convicted slave thieves who sold slaves out of the colony were to be "adjudged and condemned as guilty of Felony, and shall suffer accordingly."[78]

This legislative silence on slave homicide left open the possibility that North Carolina would follow the example of the northern colonies. The 1741 act explicitly legitimized slave homicides occurring "in the dispersing of any unlawful Assemblies of rebel Slaves or Conspirators" or in the apprehensions of runaway or outlawed slaves. A slave would be declared an outlaw if he ran away from his master, concealed himself, and killed a hog or cattle for substance.[79]

The prosecution of Matthew Hardy, a medical doctor, suggests there was uncertainty about the masters' potential liability for slave killings. A Northampton County coroner's inquest jury on September 1, 1743, found that Hardy murdered "his Negro girl Lucy." On August 27, 1743, Hardy ordered that Lucy be brutally whipped. He then caused her to be tied to a ladder and burned. Lucy died two days later. A grand jury indictment was prepared during the October 1743 General Court term accusing Hardy of murdering Lucy, "formerly belonging to William Little deceased." But it appears that Hardy was discharged.[80]

Governor Arthur Dobbs, pursuant to his June 1754 instructions from the colonial authorities, on September 30, 1756, urged the legislators to adopt a law "to prevent maiming and killing Negro Slaves." The legislators did not comply.[81]

Fifteen years later a defendant whose name is unknown was prosecuted for murdering a slave. The facts are not reported; nor is it known if the defendant was the slave's master. North Carolina's chief justice Martin Howard's grand jury charge, echoing Virginia governor Alexander Spotswood's views expressed almost sixty years earlier in the Frances Wilson case, asserted that an accused slave killer could be indicted at common law for murder. But the grand jury failed to indict the defendant, returning the bill ignoramus.[82]

Howard was a slave owner who was moved to publically affirm his opinion that malicious slave killing could be common law murder. Portions of his charge were reported in North Carolina and Rhode Island newspapers.[83]

Howard began by noting that although the grand jury's reasoning was unknown, they may have thought "THAT IT IS NOT MURDER FOR A WHITE MAN TO KILL A NEGRO SLAVE." Howard criticized slavery as a matter of humanity and morality. But his main legal argument was that, under the common law, "'[m]urder is, when a man of sound mind and memory, and of the age of discretion, unlawfully killeth any REASONABLE CREATURE, being under the king's peace.' So that if we persuade ourselves, that a negro slave is a reasonable creature, it must be murder in any one that shall feloniously slay him."

Howard also asserted that cruelty toward slaves "is ever bad policy." The best way to "preserve us from the horrors of a BELLUM SERVILE, or a rebellion of slaves," was "a mild, humane and gentle treatment" of slaves. This policy, he offered, was less likely to cause the slaves to "seize the first occasion to revenge all past injuries, and oppressions."[84]

Howard was not a southern native. He was born in either England or New England. While serving as a Rhode Island legislator, in February 1765, he published a pamphlet in favor of the Stamp Act. He became so unpopular that, by August 1765, he and his family sailed to England. Howard was rewarded, in July 1766, with an appointment as North Carolina's chief justice. Howard remained a Loyalist whose slave homicide charge was consistent with the Crown's instructions to royal governors. In 1778 he returned to England.[85]

There also is a record of a 1771 case in which Peter Lord was indicted for murdering his "Negroe man slave." After a trial in the Wilmington District Superior Court term beginning on November 27, 1771, the jury found that Lord was pursuing and located his slave, who had hidden "for a few hours." Lord had a knife and cut his slave's ear in a struggle that followed. The slave died a few hours later. The jurors stated, however, that because they did not know whether the killing was "murder, manslaughter, or homicide by misadventure, we pray the advice of the Court." The court allowed Lord to post bond of a thousand pounds as security for his appearance at the Court's November 1772 term. There is no further record of the case.[86]

North Carolina's legislators responded in 1773 when Whig lawyer William Hooper introduced a bill providing fines as the punishment for slave killings. The General Assembly passed the bill, but Governor Josiah Martin rejected it. He explained in a letter to William Legge, the Earl of Dartmouth, that the bill's "general scope and design" was in his "opinion good, but it was inconsistent with his Majesty's instructions to pass it, as it did not reserve the fines imposed by it pursuant to their direction."[87] Martin also may have acted "as part of an ongoing war with the radical Whig members of the Assembly."[88]

The legislators, in 1774, replied with An Act to Prevent the Willful Killing of Slaves, which included a finding that "[d]oubts have arisen with Respect to the Punishment proper to be inflicted upon such as have been guilty of willfully and maliciously killing Slaves." It declared that malicious slave killing was murder, but in two ways it provided slaves with inferior legal protection.

First, it imposed a twelve-month prison term on a killer's first conviction and authorized the death penalty without benefit of clergy only on a second conviction, consistent with the 1696 Jamaican slave law. The act also required first-time killers who were not the slave's owner to pay the owner the slave's value. Second, the act excused the killing of an outlawed slave, a slave "in the Act of Resistance to his lawful Owner or Master, or to any Slave dying under moderate Correction."[89] William M. Wiecek called this the "notorious 'moderate correction proviso.'" John Spencer Bassett asserted, "It is impossible to fail to see that the last proviso . . . went far toward annulling the whole law."[90]

This clause may have legitimized killings such as Peter Lord's offense. Even if jurors believed masters were guilty of immoderate correction, they could find that the slaves' resistance justified or excused the killing. The clause also referred to the 1741 act that legitimized slave homicides occurring "in the dispersing of any unlawful Assemblies of rebel Slaves or Conspirators" or in the apprehensions of runaway or outlawed slaves.[91]

Governor Martin did not reject this law but expressed reservations in a letter to the Earl of Dartmouth. Although "the laws of humanity require more rigorous punishment than is allotted by this Act to the first offense," Martin wrote that the act had a "salutary and humane tendency, and will operate, I hope, to the restraint of the inhuman Masters of Slaves." He called this new law "a manifest improvement" because "the Courts of Justice having heretofore doubted of the propriety of punishing this offense capitally."[92]

Georgia's Changing Law of Slave Homicide

Colonial Georgia's slave homicide laws evolved significantly over time. Georgia's trustees were granted a 1732 charter to establish "a common man's utopia" of "small-scale agriculture and limited landholdings." The colony was to supply desirable commodities such as silk and wine and be South Carolina's defensive buffer.[93]

The trustees also initially prohibited slavery in Georgia, but opposition to this prohibition grew within the colony. On August 8, 1750, the trustees permitted slavery and adopted Georgia's first slave law.[94]

This law's homicide provision was similar to the law in the northern colonies. It legitimized the masters' right to chastise their slaves and provided fines only if the chastisement endangered a slave's limb. "But in the Case of Murder of a Negroe or Black the Criminal [was] to be tried according to the Laws of Great Britain."[95]

The trustees gave up control of Georgia to the Crown in 1752. Georgia was later transformed into "a full-blown slave society ... based on rice. A planter elite class rose to political power and created a slave society modeled on South Carolina and the West Indies."[96] Georgia's enslaved population grew from 19 percent in 1750 to 45 percent in 1770. In the years after 1780, it was between 35 and 44 percent.[97]

Georgia's enslaved population was unevenly disbursed. The black and white population ratios in the low country's eastern region, focused on coastal rice production, approached those in South Carolina and the Caribbean colonies. Thus, in 1790, blacks were 69.6 percent of the population in the lower country counties but only 25.8 percent in the higher elevation, more western region.[98]

Georgia's slave laws later included provisions that were approved by the colony's local leaders, also the growing plantation elite. The Assembly, on March 7, 1755, adopted An Act for the Better Ordering and Governing Negroes and Other Slaves in This Province, which generally was based on South Carolina's 1740 slave law.[99]

Georgia's legislators copied the slave homicide provisions of South Carolina's slave law and Jamaica's 1696 slave law. Georgia's version authorized all white persons to examine, apprehend, and moderately correct slaves who were away from their plantations without a white person present and if the slaves refused to "undergo examination." If any slave who was apprehended assaulted or struck the white person, "such slave may be lawfully killed."[100]

Willful slave killers were felons if they were convicted on the proof of two witnesses under oath. But this law granted the benefit of clergy to first-time slave killers, who were to pay restitution to the dead slaves' owners. Killers who could not pay this restitution were to serve seven years of hard labor. Only a slave killer's second conviction "shall be deemed Murther and the Offender Suffer to the said Crime according to the Laws of England," except that the defendant was to forfeit property only to the extent necessary to reimburse the slave's owner for the dead slave's value. The law imposed a fifty-pound fine on those who killed slaves "on a Sudden heat or Passion or by undue Correction."[101]

The act also included a section modeled on the South Carolina 1740 code's provision stating that owners or others having charge over slaves were presumed to be guilty if their slaves were found to have been killed, maimed, or abused contrary to the act while in the defendants' possession. But these defendants could exculpate themselves by offering "good and Sufficient Evidence," or simply by making their own exculpatory oaths sworn in court, "if clear proof of the Offence be not made by Two Witnesses at least any Law[,] Usage[,] or Custom to the Contrary notwithstanding."[102]

The 1755 law's anticruelty provision was based on South Carolina's 1740 law, but instead of a hundred-pound fine, Georgia imposed a fine of ten pounds for each offense. The act applied to a person who "shall wilfully cut out the Tongue[,] put out the Eye[,] Castrate[,] or Cruelly Scald[,] burn[,] or deprive any Slave of any Limb or Member, or shall inflict any other Cruel punishment." But the statute expressly legitimized "whipping or beating with a Horse Whip[,] Cow Skin[,] Switch[,] or Small Stick or by putting Irons on or Confining or Imprisoning" any slave.[103] The act also imposed a six-shilling fine if a slave was "beaten Bruised Maimed or Disabled" by a person "not having sufficient Cause or Lawfull authority for doing so."[104]

Georgia's legislators adopted slave laws in 1765 and 1770.[105] The Board of Trade disapproved the 1765 law because it changed the slaves' legal status from real to personal property. The board apparently intended to limit the slave owners' right to break up their plantations, which would be of no value without slaves. Governor James Wright convinced the board that if slaves were defined as personal property creditors could more easily recover slave owners' debts. The board approved the Georgia Assembly's May 10, 1770, code.[106]

The 1765 and 1770 codes included homicide provisions that were similar to those in the 1755 act. First-time malicious slave killers remained felons with the benefit of clergy if they compensated the slaves' owners for the loss of the slaves, but they faced seven years of hard labor if they could not pay. First offenders also were to be incapable of "holding any place of Trust, or exercising, enjoying or receiving the profits of any Office, place or employment, civil or Military within this Province." Only second-time offenders were to be guilty of murder and punished according to the laws of England, except that they forfeited property only to the extent necessary to compensate the owners' losses.

The 1765 act increased the fine for killings on a sudden heat or passion or undue correction to 150 pounds. But the 1770 act effectively legitimized slave owners' manslaughters committed upon their slaves when it required those convicted of manslaughter to pay to the slaves' owners the slaves' value "as appraised by any three or more freeholders."[107]

The 1765 act also permitted masters to refute by their own oath a presumption of guilt that arose when a slave died with no other white person present. Proof by two witnesses was required to refute the master's denial, or the master was to be acquitted. The legislators omitted this provision from the 1770 code.[108]

These codes also included anticruelty provisions that were similar to those in the 1755 act. The 1770 law imposed a fine not exceeding fifty pounds sterling for each offense.[109] It also imposed a five-shilling sterling fine plus damages if a slave was "beaten, bruised, maimed, or disabled" by a person "not having sufficient cause for authority for so doing."[110]

According to Watson Jennison, the 1765 code expressed the views of Georgia's elite planters, who "sought a new model" that "better reflected their vision of a well-ordered society." He quoted Governor Wright's letter to the Board of Trade asserting that the 1765 code was drafted "with great care & attention" to the "Negro Laws of Jamaica, So. Carolina & Virginia."[111] Jennison stated that Georgia's elites believed that "[b]y blending" these codes' provisions, the legislators "improved" slavery. Jennison also quoted a May 19, 1768, letter from a committee including James Habersham to Benjamin Franklin, then Georgia's agent in England. The letter objected to the Board of Trade's rejection of the 1765 law, which "was framed on more extensive and humane principles than our former Law or that now in Force in So[uth] Carolina."[112]

Betty Wood, in contrast, stated that the 1765 code was adopted in response to Georgia's growing enslaved population and was "noticeably harsher" than the 1755 law.[113] Jennison acknowledged that these codes allowed masters to discipline their slaves and that "[m]any planters . . . did not embrace the humanitarian reform of slavery."[114]

Jennison also cited evidence of growing white social class tensions as Georgia's elite planters dominated the society and government. Governor Wright in the 1770s owned eleven Georgia plantations and more than five hundred slaves. James Habersham owned several plantations and about two hundred slaves. Although Habersham called for more humane slave treatment, he favored the abolition of Georgia's slavery prohibition. He thought slavery was essential for Georgia's development and was "a positive good for slaves."[115]

But these elites "tended to regard nonelite whites with veiled contempt," and "valued and respected the skills of their slaves. Planters created a slave society that benefitted the elite class at the expense of the nonelite class."[116]

Conclusion

According to Ralph Flanders, Georgia's colonial statutes reflected "the altruistic dispositions and ideas of the provincial leaders."[117] We can debate this assumption about the leaders' altruism. But the colonial legislators in Virginia, the Carolinas, and Georgia adopted statutes that clearly limited the common law's application to slave killings by masters, while protecting slaves from wanton killings by third parties, including overseers and other whites who did not own slaves. These laws, which in different ways defied the British colonial authorities' instructions to apply the common law to willful slave murders, remained in force for more than a decade after American independence.

CHAPTER 7

Slave Homicide Reform in Virginia

Virginia's legislature adopted a 1788 act reforming the state's slave homicide laws. Virginia was the logical state to lead the way for this reform trend. Its colonial legislature had not reduced the common law penalties when slaves were murder victims, therefore requiring less extensive legal change than in the Carolinas and Georgia.

Virginia, in 1790, was the state with the largest number of slaves. They constituted about 39 percent of the state's total population. This percentage remained steady until 1840, when it fell to 36 percent. It later declined to 33 percent in 1850 and to 30 percent in 1860. In each decade from the 1790s to the 1860s, Virginia's total of net slave exits exceeded entries. Some enslaved Virginians were freed by their owners and moved out of the state, while others were taken west and south with their owners or were sold into the interstate slave trade.[1]

Antebellum Virginia continued to evolve into a complex slave society made up of masters, slaves, merchants, skilled tradesmen and professionals, slave traders, and poor whites who did not own slaves. Social stratification within the white community intensified, as elite planters could be contrasted with the owners of few slaves and non-slave-owning whites. In 1790, 44.9 percent of Virginia's slave-owning families owned between one and five slaves. By 1850 the percentage was 48.9 percent, but only about 10 percent of these families owned more than twenty slaves. Most white households owned no slaves throughout the antebellum South. Virginia in 1790 had the highest percentage of slave-owning households, only 44.9 percent, and by 1850 this percentage had declined to 32.9 percent.[2]

Virginia's 1788 Slave Homicide Reform Law

Virginia's leaders debated criminal law reforms based on revolutionary and Enlightenment ideas, including proposals limiting the crimes for which free persons could be executed. The legislature in 1776 authorized a committee, which included Thomas Jefferson, George Wythe, and Edmund Pendleton, to draft a criminal reform law. The committee's 1779 proposal did not include slave homicide law reform. The assembly did not consider the bill until 1785, when it was not approved.[3]

The legislators nevertheless adopted a November 21, 1788, slave homicide reform law. It repealed the provisions of the 1723 and 1748 acts that legitimized slave killings resulting from the masters' correction and accidents; that allowed masters a pretrial review and dismissal of a murder charge, unless "at least one lawful and credible" witness testified that the killing was willful, malicious, or by design; and that decriminalized slave homicides that would have been common law manslaughter.[4]

No legislative history explains why Virginia's lawmakers adopted this statute. "One proffered explanation for the change in the law is that some of the revolutionary notions of liberty and humanity engendered by the American Revolution carried over into the treatment of slaves." But as Philip Schwarz noted, "the problem was that all these apparent reforms effectively perpetrated bondage. They were intended to prevent another revolution."[5]

St. George Tucker contended that with the adoption of the 1788 law, in Virginia "homicide of a slave stands now upon the same footing, as in the case of any other person," thus falling in line with the northern slave states, Maryland, and Delaware.[6] Tucker also asserted that John Huston's indictment for slave murder prompted the legislature to act. During the General Court's December 1788 term, a jury found Huston guilty of manslaughter. But the court granted Huston's motion in arrest of judgment, apparently under the 1723 and 1748 laws. According to Tucker, the general assembly was in session, and "some members of the court mentioned the case to some leading characters in the legislature." The 1788 act followed, permitting a jury to convict a slave killer of the lesser offense of manslaughter if it believed that the defendant's crime was not murder.[7]

Tucker does not report if Huston was the slave's owner, but other cases suggest that tensions within the white class structure may have highlighted the need for slave homicide law reform. Thomas Sorrell, for example, was accused of murdering a slave he hired from Ebenezer Moore. The Westmoreland County Court on December 22, 1785, found Sorrell potentially guilty of manslaughter and ordered a trial. Sorrell argued that the court should dismiss this charge after affording him the initial review allowed to slave owners under the 1723 and 1748 statutes. The Virginia Supreme Court of Appeals disagreed, and a grand jury indicted Sorrell for murder. The General Court on April 6, 1786, denied Sorrell's motion to reconsider its decision denying Sorrell the masters' statutory privilege. Sorrell then was tried before a jury that found him not guilty, a verdict that St. George Tucker asserted was "directly contrary to evidence."[8]

The *Sorrell* case illustrates how the slave owners' long-term economic interests in their slaves conflicted with the hirers' short-term interests. Hirers rented slaves for a period of time—usually a year in the southern states. Masters may have favored criminal prosecution to punish hirers like Sorrell to deter future hired slave homicides.

Similar conflicts are exhibited in cases in which overseers, patrollers, and other third parties to the master and slave relationship injured or killed slaves, and thus damaged the individual owners' interests in their slaves. Wanton white violence directed at slaves also threatened the broader slave master class's social and political interests in slave property and the public order.[9]

The 1788 law would have permitted the jury to convict Sorrell for manslaughter, thus supplementing the slave owners' right to sue for monetary damages when others killed or injured their slaves. The courts evaded two common law rules that could have been applied to limit these suits. First, when slaves were killed, the courts did not follow the common law rule that prohibited wrongful death actions. Second, the courts, other than those in Alabama, did not require that slave killers be prosecuted before slave owners could sue to recover their economic damages. Slave owners thus "had a choice of remedy based upon the social and economic class of the white slave killer, and his concurrent ability to pay the master damages. Civil damages for dead slaves often exceeded $1,000, if a 'gentleman' could pay an owner for his loss the master probably thought that the punishment was adequate." But the statutes reserved capital punishment "to deter slave killings by poor whites who were unable to pay the dead slave's owner his just due."[10]

Concerns about conflicts among the white community's members leading to breaches of the peace also may have prompted the slave homicide reform laws, as illustrated by the 1790s case *Hoomes v. Kuhn*.[11] Jacob Kuhn suspected that a slave belonging to John Hoomes had robbed Kuhn's store. "[A]t the Bowling Green, Kuhn whipt [the slave] very severely." Hoomes, who lived about half a mile away, "upon hearing of the whipping, went to the Bowling Green; and, after a short altercation with Kuhn, struck him: the latter returned the blow, and a fight ensued, in which Kuhn was much worsted."

Kuhn filed an assault and battery suit against Hoomes in the district court of Fredericksburg. He also unsuccessfully pursued a theft prosecution against the slave, whose name is not mentioned in the reports. Hoomes responded by suing Kuhn for damages caused by the slave whipping, and Hoomes recovered a seventeen-pound judgment against Kuhn. At the first trial of Kuhn's suit against Hoomes, the jury did not reach a verdict. At the second trial, two of Hoomes's witnesses did not appear, and the jury awarded Kuhn one hundred pounds in damages. Hoomes's new trial motions were denied, and the Supreme Court of Virginia in 1792 affirmed the judgment.[12]

The legislators also may have responded to the similar threats to public order raised by overseers' violence, as evidenced by the January 1791 murder trial of a slave named Moses. He was acquitted by a divided Fairfax County Court in Alexandria on the charge that he murdered Hezekiah Williams, the overseer of his owner, a Mr. Alexander. According to the local press report, Williams had previously been cleared on the charge that he beat to death Bob, who was a brother of Moses. Moses admitted taking Williams's gun and shooting him with it after Williams beat and chained Moses and threatened "to treat him the next morning in the manner he had done his brother Bob."

Moses's lawyer, who is not identified, argued that by statute a master "had no right to deprive his slave of life or member," and that a slave "notwithstanding his degraded station, still retained some natural rights, particularly that of self-preservation." He thus argued if "a master inflicts on his slave cruel and severe punishment, which endangers the limits of his authority, and trespasses on the retained natural rights of the slave . . . , the slave has the same right to defend those rights that a freeman has." In view of Williams's "character . . . , his threats, and the cruel treatment [Moses] had received from him, [Moses] had sufficient reason to believe that his life was in imminent danger—and to prevent that danger he discharged his gun at [Williams] in doing so he was prompted by self-preservation; a principle which actuates the meanest reptile in the animal creation." The divided court agreed and acquitted Moses. The *Virginia Gazette and Alexandria Advertiser* reported that those in the large courthouse crowd "generally were satisfied with the verdict."[13]

That newspaper, in February 1791, printed two long letters to the editor, one criticizing the verdict and one in support. The first also noted a legal anomaly; Moses would have suffered thirty lashes for raising a hand to Williams even in self-defense, but he successfully invoked the privilege of self-defense in response to a charge of murder.[14]

A December 17, 1792, act followed, which revised the then-current provision mandating the whipping of any "negro or mulatto who lifted a hand" in opposition to anyone who was not a "negro or mulatto." The new act excluded from these mandatory whippings slaves like Hoomes's slave and Moses who were "wantonly assaulted" and then lifted their hands in self-defense.[15]

The 1788 and 1792 reform laws also expanded the state's regulation of the slave masters' potential liability for slave homicide. They followed a 1782 general manumission reform law permitting masters, in their wills or in their lifetimes, to free some or all of their slaves, as long as the masters satisfied certain conditions.[16] But this amelioration was in part reversed by an 1806 act requiring all manumitted slaves to leave the state within a year after they were freed, although, in the following years, the legislature permitted exceptions to this rule of exclusion.[17]

Evolving social customs and attitudes toward all homicides also may have encouraged Virginia's slave homicide law reform. According to Randolph Roth, the colonial era homicide rates for black victims in New England and in Virginia's Chesapeake regions exceeded the homicide rsates for whites, but these rates all began to fall in the late seventeenth and early eighteenth centuries. The late seventeenth-century Virginia data reveal a homicide rate of 15 per 100,000 persons per year for black victims, and about 10 per 100,000 for whites. In New England the rates after the Pequot War were 10 black and fewer than 5 white victims per 100,000 persons per year. These rates for blacks fell by the American Revolution to about 5 per 100,000 persons in Virginia and to fewer than 4 per 100,000 in New England, although the black homicide rates continued to exceed those of whites.[18]

Roth suggested that the early black homicide rates were higher than those for whites because "[s]lavery and violence were inextricably linked in the years when racial slavery was being established in the colonies. Slaveowners had to use force to persuade newly enslaved people that they had no choice but to accept their position at the bottom of a new social hierarchy." He noted that masters and overseers did not always use force in a "rational way," and that enslaved people did not always submit to violence. In these "early days of colonial slavery whites who killed slaves often revealed the profound ignorance that lay at the root of racial prejudice."[19]

Roth concluded that "[m]urders of blacks by whites began to decline everywhere in the mid-eighteenth century as slavery became more firmly established and whites became more confident of their ability to keep blacks in their place." He cited several potential causes for this change, as frontier regions evolved into plantation societies, although antebellum homicide rates in the South continued to exceed those in the North.[20]

Indeed, Roth noted that by the end of the eighteenth century, southerners began to assert "that abusive owners undermined the institution. Every time they flew into 'fits of passion,' [slave owners or overseers] sowed the seeds of rebellion in all slaves. Humane treatment and moderate correction were the best ways to ensure loyal service and social place." Roth quoted the *Virginia Gazette*'s editorial comment supporting William Pitman's 1775 execution.[21]

But Pitman was the only Virginia slave master who was executed for slave murder. Moreover, Virginia's legislators later amended the state's slave homicide law to put the enslaved person's life on a lesser footing than any free person. These statutes regulating the masters' rights to wantonly kill their slaves, along with the laws restricting manumission, are examples of the antebellum laws that William Novak stated regulated perceived hazards to the "population, social order, and civil government."[22]

Virginia's Homicide Reform Laws of 1796 and 1803

The homicide reform drive continued until December 15, 1796, when Virginia's legislature adopted a comprehensive statute that included a provision based on Pennsylvania's 1794 law limiting capital punishment. Virginia became the first of twelve states to adopt this homicide law. George Keith Taylor sponsored the bill, which also authorized and funded a state penitentiary.[23]

Virginia's law declared that "no crime whatsoever committed by any free person against this commonwealth, (except murder in the first degree) shall be punished with death." The legislators found that "the several offences which are included under the general denomination of murder, differ so greatly from each other in the degree of their atrociousness, that it is unjust to involve them in the same punishment." The act thus stated that "all murder which shall be perpetrated by means of poison, or by lying in wait, or by any other kind of wilful, deliberate, and premeditated killing, or which shall be committed in the perpetration or attempt to perpetrate any arson, rape, robbery, or burglary shall be deemed murder in the first degree." Any other murder was "murder of the second degree" with a jail term of five to eighteen years. Those convicted of voluntary manslaughter were to serve sentences of between two and fourteen years for the first offense, with security given for future good behavior, and on a second offense the prison term was from six to fourteen years. In cases of involuntary manslaughter resulting from an unlawful act, the prosecutor was permitted to waive the felony and prosecute the defendant for a misdemeanor.[24]

General Court judge Robert White, citing the statute's preamble, stated that the legislature had not intended "to make any change in the *crime of murder*, but that it thought that this *crime*, as it might be committed under an almost infinite variety of circumstances, ought to be punished in each case according to the degree of atrocity or extenuation under which each offence was committed." The legislature "intended to graduate the punishment of each murder by a scale to be established by itself, according to the circumstances under which it should be committed."[25]

This law also created two types of first degree murders. Killings in the first class were characterized by evidence of the killer's willful, deliberate, and premeditated intention to kill. Killings in the second class were felony murders, according to which juries could find that a homicide committed in one of the four listed felonies was first degree murder, even if the jury did not find that the defendant acted with a willful, deliberate, and premeditated intention to kill.[26] Virginia's legislature, in January 1799, also abolished capital punishment as the penalty for stealing slaves and imposed a prison term for this offense.[27]

These acts did not mention slave homicides, but a January 28, 1803, amendment did. This law, which remained in effect for forty-four years, addresses questions that arose under the 1796 act. The new law's section 1 accommodated slave murder into the 1796 law's scheme. It redefined first degree murder as "all murder ... perpetrated by means of poison, or by lying in wait, or by duress of imprisonment or confinement, or by starving, or by wilful, malicious and excessive whipping, beating or other cruel treatment or torture, or by any other kind of wilful, deliberate, and premeditated killing, or which shall be committed in the perpetration, or attempt to perpetrate any arson, rape, robbery or burglary." Any other murder was "of the second degree."

Sections 2 and 3 prohibited malicious maiming and malicious stabbing and shooting intended to maim and kill any person and established jail terms of two to ten years and fines not to exceed one thousand dollars. These provisions did not "extend to any case of a slave accused or convicted" of violating the act. But the courts applied them to cases in which slaves were the victims of this nonfatal violence.[28]

This act implicitly recognized the masters' right to use ordinary means to correct their slaves, as long as the slaves were not killed, maimed, stabbed, or shot, thus in part rolling back the 1788 homicide reform law. Killings following punishments that juries found to be ordinary and not excessive would be no more than second degree murders, unless the juries found that the killings were willful, deliberate, and premeditated. Killings by masters or others that were the result of excessive punishments nevertheless could be first degree murders.

But the statute was ambiguous when applied to killings that juries found were caused "by duress of imprisonment or confinement, or by starving, or by wilful, malicious and excessive whipping, beating or other cruel treatment or torture." Would the crime be first degree murder based on the evidence of this conduct alone, or were juries required to find that the death was the result of the defendant's willful, deliberate, and premeditated killing?

General Court judge William Nelson sent a November 30, 1810, letter to Governor John Tyler on behalf of the General Court judges suggesting that several statutes be revised, including the 1803 law. Nelson asked, "Was it or was it not the intention of the Legislature that if a murder [is] perpetrated by duress of imprisonment or confinement, or by starving, or by wilful, malicious and excessive whipping, beating or other cruel treatment or torture these acts in themselves should supply malice, and a sufficient wilful deliberation and premeditation in the killing, or is any other wilfiulness, deliberation and premeditation in the killing to be required?" All did not agree; according to Nelson. "The lenity of our countrymen to individuals, perhaps sometimes, induces them to adopt the latter construction." He suggested that the legislature enact the less lenient interpretation, but it did not adopt this revision.[29]

Lawyers for homicide defendants used this ambiguity to avoid first degree murder convictions. The law went into effect on April 1, 1803. It was soon tested in a May 16, 1803, inquest, cited by Melvin Patrick Ely, into the death of a Prince Edward County slave named Bob. A coroner's jury found that Bob's owner John Andrews, on May 13, 1803, killed Bob with a blow to the head from "the helve of a hoe" that Andrews had in his hands. Ely did not find any further evidence of the prosecution of this case.[30]

A defendant named Sledd (or Slead), according to an article in the December 20, 1810, *Lynchburg Star*, "[w]ithin the last 16 to 18 months," had been charged with the murder of "a negro wench, belonging to the estate of the late Henry L. Davies, Esq. of Bedford county." Sledd hired his victim, who ran away "and sought refuge and protection from one of her old master's sons." Unfortunately, the son returned the slave to Sledd and, "with mild language, endeavored to appease [Sledd] and to soften down gusts of passion, which appeared to be excessive." Sledd was not appeased. He instead stripped, tied down, and repeatedly "scored and cut, and bruised, and battered" his victim. He also bathed her in a concoction of red pepper and tobacco.

Sledd's lawyer argued that a master's right to correct a slave was unlimited. If the correction should result in a slave's death, "unless the determination in the master to kill, was plainly proved, the crime did not amount to or constitute murder." The jury agreed that Sledd was not guilty of first degree murder, and he was sentenced to two years in the penitentiary.[31]

A slave owner named William Myers, "a substantial freeholder," in 1810 also was convicted "for murdering a female negro slave." The press report does not reveal the facts, except that Myers was sentenced to eight years' imprisonment, thus confirming that Myers was convicted of second degree murder. But Myers did not serve any jail time because "he shot himself on the way to Richmond."[32]

In contrast, Tom Johnson of Bedford County, also in 1810, was acquitted on the charge of murdering "a negro wench of Turpin's estate," for which Johnson was the manager. The case is similar to Sledd's. "The ill fated victim had withdrawn from Mr. Johnson's superintendence, and sought relief and protection from her master, at his residence in Cumberland county," but the slave was returned to Johnson. "[I]n conducting her home by a rope fastened around her neck, in broad day, on the public highway in Buckingham county, the wench was murdered. Johnson was charged with the crime—taken up—committed to the jail of Buckingham—there tried and acquitted!"[33]

Nine years later, Joseph Cohen was indicted for the February 14, 1819, murder of Samuel Hardin's slave. Cohen, in Lynchburg, allegedly shot his victim, who "instantly expired." Cohen was first examined by the Lynchburg Corporation Court. Cohen was convicted of second degree murder at a trial held in the Superior Court of Law for Campbell County. Virginia's Supreme Court of Appeals rejected Cohen's appeal challenging the examining court's jurisdiction and affirmed the conviction.[34]

Ely's study of antebellum Prince Edward County cited three unsuccessful prosecutions or inquests between 1803 and 1814 when slaves were killed, including the case of John Andrews. Ely concluded that "[t]he prohibition of slave testimony against white defendants helped ensure that none of the prosecutions yielded a conviction. Those meager results hardly encouraged people to bring charges in the future. At the same time, the tenacious efforts of some whites to pursue people who killed slaves may have discouraged such crimes in the years that followed."[35]

But the substantive law written by the legislature and applied by the judges and juries permitted lawyers to argue that their clients who were accused of slave homicides should avoid convictions—or at least the death penalty. This state of legal affairs continued until the Civil War.

Virginia's 1819 Code, the Revision, and the *Souther* Case

Virginia's legislature, on March 12, 1819, adopted a code that, for the most part, compiled the state's existing laws, according to Benjamin Watkins Leigh, one of five judges and lawyers whom the legislature authorized to prepare the code.[36] The 1819 Code defined murder in the first and second degrees consistent with the 1803 act.[37] It continued to provide the death penalty for first degree murderers. Second degree murderers faced jail terms of between five and eighteen years. Those found guilty of voluntary manslaughter could be sentenced to jail terms of between two and ten years. Defendants who were guilty of involuntary manslaughter "happening in consequence of an unlawful act" could have their offenses reduced to misdemeanors at the prosecutor's discretion.[38]

This code thus repeated the ambiguity in the 1803 act. It remained unclear if juries could find that killings of slaves by masters were capital murders if the jurors believed the homicides were the result of willful, malicious, and excessive abuse that somehow was not intended to kill. Moreover, killings would not be first degree murder if they resulted from what juries believed were cases of ordinary correction or whipping that was not excessive. Instead, these offenses would be second degree murder, manslaughter, or justifiable homicide as juries might find on the facts of each case. And manslaughter resulting from a master's lawful correction of his or her slave would not be involuntary manslaughter.

Slave owners therefore were not convicted of first degree murder, although some were convicted of second degree murder or manslaughter. Thomas Alsop, who in December 1823 was tried in Fredericksburg "on a charge of causing, by ill treatment, the death of his slave, a boy about 12 years of age," was found guilty of the lowest grade of manslaughter, which called for a two-year jail term. But "from some extenuating circumstances the verdict was accompanied with a recommendation of mercy to the governor, for 18 months of the time to be remitted."[39]

More details are available about the case of William (aka Hill) Wilson. He was a Rockbridge County "yeoman" charged with murder in 1826 after he allegedly beat to death his slave Adam. Four witnesses testified at Wilson's trial— William White, James White, James Trimble, and Dr. William A. Caruthers. But Wilson escaped the death penalty when a jury found him guilty of second degree murder.

William White testified that early in the morning of October 16, 1826, "he heard a great noise up the river he got up and went to see and about two hundred yards above his house near the river he found [Wilson] sitting astride of & beating some person and asked him who it was he said it was Adam." White told Wilson "that he had given him enough and to let him go." Wilson "then let Adam get up keeping hold of his clothes and ordering him to go home. Adam said if he would let him go that he would go home but that he would not be led." Wilson "commenced beating & choaking Adam and they fell together, Adam rather on or across [Wilson], who said never mind I will soon fix you & immediately turned Adam under & commneced beating him."

William White then went home and returned with James Trimble, James White, and Shelton Camden. They found Wilson beating Adam with stones he held in his hand, striking Adam "on the head & face and sometimes throwing them at him. At one time [Wilson] took a hoop pole & struck Adam several times with it over the shoulders near the head." White several times asked Wilson to stop the beating. Wilson declared, apparently to Adam, "I am bound to kill you." White and the others "frequently told [Wilson] that he would kill Adam if he did not let him alone."

White and his group then "left the prisoner beating Adam and went down to near [White's] house where they heard blows." Wilson later "came to them and said boys come up and see where the old deceitful rascal has crawled into the river pretending to drown himself. All the company refused to go at first," but Wilson insisted. The group eventually agreed and they "found Adam with his feet in the river & head on the bank, his clothes wet." White and the others "removed Adam made a fire & put a blanket about him during which time [Wilson] bid them good morning and went away." White and "those with him thought it would be dangerous to interfere with [Wilson]." James White and James Trimble confirmed William White's account, although Trimble said that "he did not see the prisoner beat Adam . . . with a hoop pole."

Dr. Caruthers testified that on Monday morning, October 16, he and Dr. Robert McCluer "on crossing the river at the boat yard" found Adam lying on "the further side bloody and wet." Adam's head was bruised, "his left eye mashed out, his nose split open, his teeth knocked out, the inner part of his lips cut into many wounds or gashes, the exterior skin being entire on his head. They counted upwards of twenty wounds on one side as he lay and many on the other." Caruthers stated that he thought "that Adam could not live" because the wounds were sufficient to cause his death. The doctor saw Adam again "about sundown" the next day "and again dressed his wounds." Adam died during the night or morning of October 17/18.

The jury convicted Wilson of second degree murder, and he was sentenced to thirteen years in the penitentiary. Although Wilson brutally beat Adam and then left him by a river bank apparently to die, the jury found that Wilson's acts were not sufficiently excessive or cruel or deliberate to warrant a first degree murder conviction.[40]

Virginia's legislature, during its 1847–48 term, adopted an amended homicide law deleting killings by "beating or other cruel treatment or torture" from the list of homicides that were first degree murders. First degree murder was redefined as "[m]urder committed by poison, lying in wait, duress of imprisonment, starving, wilful and excessive whipping, cruel treatment, or any kind of wilful, deliberate and premeditated killing," or in an attempt to commit or in the commission of arson, rape, robbery, or burglary.[41]

The legislature also deleted from the section on involuntary manslaughter the phrase "happening in consequence of an unlawful act."[42] This deletion suggests that the legislators intended to criminalize unintentional killings resulting from a slave owner's lawful whipping or other correction of his or her slave. Virginia's General Court, in 1827, had held that slave masters could not be prosecuted for assault or battery upon their slaves. Thus a master's slave correction was not an unlawful act as long as the enslaved victim did not lose life or limb.[43]

The extreme abuse that crossed the line between ordinary and excessive whipping and cruel treatment is illustrated by the gruesome murder detailed in *Souther v. Commonwealth*,[44] the official report in the appeal of Virginia slave owner Simeon Souther. A Hanover County Circuit Court grand jury indicted Souther, on April 2, 1850, for the September 1, 1849, murder of his slave Sam. The court granted Souther's motion to quash the indictment. A second indictment followed during the court's October 1850 term.[45]

Souther most likely was in his fifties at the time of his trial. According to the 1840 census, he was single and owned eleven slaves. Eight of the people in the household were listed as employed in agriculture.[46]

The fifteen-count indictment "sets forth a case of the most cruel and excessive whipping and torture." It alleged that Sam "was tied to a tree and whipped with switches. When Souther became fatigued with the labour of whipping, he called upon a negro man of his, and made him cob Sam with a shingle. He also made a negro woman of his help to cob him." Souther then "applied fire to [Sam's] body," and "his back, belly and private parts." Souther next caused Sam "to be washed down with hot water, in which pods of red pepper had been steeped." Sam "was also tied to a log and to the bed post with ropes, which choked him, and he was kicked and stamped by Souther. This sort of punishment was continued and repeated until the negro died under its infliction." Souther apparently contended that he decided to punish Sam "for the offense of getting drunk, and dealing as the slave confessed and alleged, with Henry and Stone, two of the witnesses for the Commonwealth."[47]

A jury found Souther guilty of second degree murder, and he was sentenced to the minimum five-year jail term. Souther filed an appeal alleging, among other things, that he should have been convicted only of manslaughter.[48]

Souther's lawyer argued "that a man cannot be indicted and prosecuted for the cruel and excessive whipping of his own slave. That it is lawful for the master to chastise his slave; and that if death ensues from such chastisement, unless he was intended to produce death, it is like the case of homicide, which is committed by a man in the performance of a lawful act, which is manslaughter only." He relied on the court's 1827 decision in *Commonwealth v. Turner*,[49] which held that a slave owner cannot be indicted for assault and battery for the malicious, cruel, and excessive beating of his own slave.[50]

Judge Richard H. Field's opinion for Virginia's Supreme Court rejected Souther's claim that he should have been convicted of manslaughter and affirmed Souther's conviction. Field powerfully condemned Souther's crime: "It is believed that the records of criminal jurisprudence do not contain a case of more atrocious and wicked cruelty than was presented upon the trial of Souther; and yet it has been gravely and earnestly contended here by his counsel, that his offence amounts to manslaughter only."[51]

Field distinguished *Souther* from *Turner*, which involved nonfatal violence, stating:

> it by no means follows when . . . malicious, cruel and excessive beating results in death, though not intended and premeditated, that the beating is to be regarded as lawful, for the purpose of reducing the crime to manslaughter, when the whipping is inflicted for the sole purpose of chastisement. It is the policy of the law in respect to the relation of master and slave, and for the sake of securing proper subordination and obedience on the part of the slave, to protect the master from prosecution in all such cases, even if the whipping and punishment be malicious, cruel and excessive. But in so inflicting punishment for the sake of punishment, the owner of the slave acts at his peril; and if death ensues in consequence of such punishment, the relation of master and slave affords no ground of excuse or palliation.

Field concluded on this point: "The principles of the common law in relation to homicide, apply to his case, without qualification or exception; and according to those principles, the act of the prisoner, in the case under consideration, amounted to murder. Upon this point we are unanimous."[52]

The court, in dictum, also debated the ambiguity in Virginia's homicide law, which Judge Nelson noted forty years earlier. Field asserted that the jury should have found that Souther's crime was first degree murder, as defined by the 1847–48 revision of the 1819 Code that was still in effect, because Sam died as a result of Souther's willful and excessive whipping and other cruel treatment. Judge William Leigh dissented from this conclusion. He believed that the statute required that Souther must be proven to have had a willful, deliberate, and premeditated intention to kill by excessive punishment to be guilty of first degree murder.[53]

Souther's crime is hard to square with a verdict of less than first degree murder. While this case was pending, Virginia's legislature was adopting a revised code that again amended the state's slave homicide laws.[54]

The 1849 Code and the Cases

Virginia's General Assembly in 1846 authorized the preparation of a revised civil and criminal code. The codifiers, John Mercer Patton and Conway Robinson, on July 3, 1849, submitted a report that included a revised criminal code with amendments to the section on homicide. The legislature in August 1849 adopted this section, with a minor revision, as a part of Virginia's 1849 Code, which went into effect on July 1, 1850.[55]

The new code redefined first degree murder to include any killing committed "by poison, lying in wait, imprisonment, starving, or any wilful, deliberate and premeditated killing, or in the commission of, or attempt to commit, arson, rape, robbery or burglary." All other murders were second degree murders. The punishments for first and second degree murderers remained the same as in the 1819 Code. The penalty for voluntary manslaughter was between one and five years.[56]

The codifiers explained that they deleted references to "wilful and excessive whippings and cruel treatment" from the section on first degree murder after the legislature, in the 1847–48 revision, deleted references to "beating and torture." They added, "We think the words 'imprisonment and starving' may also be omitted."[57]

The General Assembly did not accept this latter suggestion. But it did eliminate the phrases that some had read to suggest that a jury could infer a slave master's intention to kill his or her slave, which was necessary for a first degree murder conviction, from evidence of the master's excessive whipping or other cruel treatment and torture of his or her slave. The legislature abolished first degree murder convictions in cases of extreme abuse of slaves by masters allegedly not perpetrated with a willful, deliberate, and premeditated intention to kill, contrary to the majority opinion in *Souther*.

The codifiers' report also noted that the section on involuntary manslaughter in the 1847–48 revision deleted the phrase "happening in consequence of an unlawful act." They recommended, "It may be best to insert some such words in this section." The legislature did not follow this recommendation.[58]

In another section, however, this code addressed the legislators' continued concern about the insolence of both enslaved blacks and free blacks. It listed various offenses for which a "negro shall be punished with stripes." One example occurred "if he use[d] provoking language or menacing gestures to a white person."[59]

Three murder trials after 1849 illustrate how Virginia's courts and juries continued to validate killings resulting from what they perceived to be the masters' infliction of usual punishment and correction, or even excessive punishment by masters whom the jurors found did not intend to kill. The first is the 1851 trial and acquittal of Colonel James Castleman and his son Stephen D. Castleman. In August 1851, they were indicted on the charge that they murdered Stephen's slave Lewis, after a coroner's jury found sufficient evidence that Lewis's death was caused by foul play. The Castlemans were released on five thousand dollars bail each.[60]

The Castlemans were tried on two days beginning on October 13, 1851, in the Clarke County Circuit Court in Berryville before Judge Green B. Samuels and a jury. Clarke County is in northeastern Virginia on the Shenandoah River across from what now is West Virginia. It is about 120 miles north of Hanover County, where Souther was tried. James Castleman apparently had social and economic status and political connections that Souther may have lacked.[61]

James Castleman was about fifty-five years old when he was tried for murder and was a prominent member of the community. According to the 1850 census he owned twenty-four slaves.[62] He also owned "a splendid estate on the Shenandoah [R]iver, in the midst of the richest and most populous portion of the Valley," and he was an "enthusiastic and experienced breeder of cattle."[63] Governor John B. Floyd in 1849 entrusted James with the care of two Khaisi cattle from Syria because James was "a great stock raiser."[64] These cattle were so noteworthy that they were taken to Washington for a presidential visit.[65]

James Castleman also was reported, in December 1850, to be the president of a steamboat company that launched the towboat *Shenandoah*, the first steamboat on the river, from Castleman's Ferry, Virginia.[66] He was an active member of the Democratic Party who even was mentioned as a potential congressional candidate.[67]

Stephen was about thirty-three years old at the time of the trial. According to the 1850 census he had nine slaves in his household.[68] Stephen operated a tavern. For many months before Lewis was killed, money was missing from the tavern's cash drawer. Liquor stored in bulk also was missing. "Suspicion had from various causes been directed to Lewis, and another negro named Reuben, (a blacksmith,) the property of James Castleman, but by the aid of two of the house servants they had eluded the most vigilant watch."

Stephen "accidentally discovered a clue," on August 20, 1851, that caused the Castlemans to be suspicious of Lewis and Reuben. The Castlemans immediately launched their own investigation, acting as detectives, torturers, prosecutors, judges, and jurors. In an upper-room warehouse in Stephen's store, the Castlemans first beat a confession out of Lewis. They whipped him "by stripes with a broad leathern strap." Lewis admitted that the theft "had been effected by false keys, furnished by the blacksmith, Reuben." The Castlemans then confined Lewis "by a chain around his neck." The chain "was attached to a joist above his head." Lewis's hands were tied in front. The Castlemans left "a white man, who had been at work with Lewis during the day," to watch Lewis while they searched for Reuben.

This white man, whose name is not mentioned in the press reports, testified for the prosecution "that Lewis asked for a box to stand on, or for something that he could jump off from." Lewis "expressed a fear that when they came back, he would be whipped again; and said if he had a knife and could get one hand loose he would cut his throat." The witness said Lewis "'stood firm on his feet'; that he could turn freely in whatever direction he wished, and that he made no confinement." He "remained with Lewis about half an hour," and then he went home.

The Castlemans meanwhile found Reuben and also beat a confession out of him. Reuben "produced the false key; one fashioned by himself, by which the theft had been effected." The Castlemans then returned with Reuben to the storeroom. They found Lewis "hanging by the neck, his feet thrown behind him, his knees a few inches from the floor, and his head thrown forward—the body warm and supple (or relaxed;) but life was extinct." The surgeons who examined the body for the coroner's jury opined that "the death was caused by strangulation by hanging." Other "eminent surgeons" testified that Lewis could not have fainted before his strangulation.

After both sides presented their evidence, "the jury from their box, and of their own motion . . . informed the court that they agreed upon their verdict." The lawyers agreed to this unusual trial procedure. The jury's verdict was not guilty. The attorney general promptly decided not to try Stephen and entered a *nolle prosequi*. Judge Samuels dismissed all charges, stating that he agreed with the verdict and would have set aside a guilty verdict.[69]

Newspaper articles describing the trial were based upon the notes of counsel for the defendants, which the friends of James Castleman provided to the press. Harriet Beecher Stowe printed one of these articles in her book *The Key to Uncle Tom's Cabin*. But she also included a letter to the editor of the *National Era*, an antislavery newspaper that published Stowe's *Uncle Tom's Cabin*. The letter's author was "an old and highly-respected citizen of this place" who "is very far from being an Abolitionist." This correspondent asserted that he or she was acquainted with three members of the community who were staying with the Castlemans when Lewis was killed. They were not present in the warehouse, but "[t]hey heard the dreadful lashing and the heart-rending screams and entreaties of the sufferer." They "implored" the trial witness "to interpose;

but for a long time he refused, on the ground that he was a dependent, and was afraid to give offense." The witness also stated that the Castlemans "had been drinking." The witness eventually went to the scene and returned, describing Lewis's lashing and chaining.

The next morning, when Lewis was reported to be dead, the Castlemans' guests "reproached Castleman with his cruelty. He expressed his regret that the slave died, and especially as he had ascertained that he was innocent of the accusation for which he had suffered. The idea was that he had fainted from exhaustion; and, the chain being round his neck, he was strangled." The correspondent stated that his or her sources were "themselves slaveholders" who would have testified if they had been called as witnesses at the trial.[70]

The Castlemans' torture and restraint of Lewis by his neck nevertheless apparently did not rise to the level of a willful, deliberate, or premeditated killing, or even a death caused by excessive cruelty according to the jury's verdict. Maybe James's local standing, political connections, and renown as a cattleman contributed to that verdict. James apparently was not shunned by the influential community members. Just six months after the trial, in March 1852, he was one of two Clarke County residents chosen to serve on a committee that was to pursue a railroad extension.[71] He died at his residence on March 16, 1854, "after a lingering illness, caused by an attack of paralysis."[72]

Henry Birdsong, of Sussex County in southeastern Virginia, in 1854 also successfully defended a slave murder prosecution for the 1853 fatal beating of one of his young slaves. Birdsong was a farmer who, according to the 1850 census, was about forty-eight years old. His wife Rebecca was forty-one, and their household included six children, ages two to nineteen, and twelve slaves. Birdsong's reported slaveholding in the 1840 census was twenty-one.[73]

Birdsong had the misfortune to make headlines twice in 1853—once as a crime victim and again as the alleged criminal. Birdsong and his twelve-year-old son, in July 1853, were shot while they were in bed. Birdsong survived, but his child died. Three of Birdsong's slaves were tried, convicted, and hanged for this crime.[74]

Birdsong again made news when, in November 1853, he killed one of his slaves, whose name is not mentioned in the press reports. Birdsong, after recovering from the shooting, ordered his slaves "to report themselves to him at his dwelling every night at an early hour." On the night of the killing, the slaves failed to report. One of Birdsong's young slaves came to the house to clean Birdsong's shoes. Birdsong began asking the child about the slaves' failure to report, and the child, expecting a whipping, "ran out of the house to escape it."

Birdsong "followed him closely, and calling a very ferocious dog, (of the bull species) started the animal in pursuit of the fugitive also. The dog soon overtook [the child], and bit him very seriously; before he was taken off." Birdsong "then tied the boy, and whipped and beat him so that he died in a few hours." This beating was so severe that Birdsong knocked out one of his victim's eyes with a stick. A coroner's inquest jury found that the child "came to his death by sundry blows, ect, inflicted by his master, Henry Birdsong." Birdsong was then arrested and jailed.[75]

Birdsong's spring of 1854 trial "resulted in an acquittal."[76] Even a manslaughter verdict would be hard to justify if the facts as initially reported in the press were proven at trial. Maybe the jury felt that Birdsong's status as a crime victim excused his excesses, even though the slaves who allegedly shot Birdsong and his son had been executed. Birdsong survived this ordeal. According to the 1860 census his household included his wife Rebecca and four of their children. Their slaveholding had increased to fourteen.[77]

In contrast, Charles Hudson's September 1860 trial ended with a second degree murder verdict. Hudson was indicted in the Mecklenburg County Circuit Court for the murder of his slave Jane. According to the 1850 census, Hudson was single. He owned five slaves.[78]

On July 4, 1860, Hudson, who was about sixty-eight years old, "stripped" his victim "naked as when she came into the world, tied her to a persimmon tree, and whipped her for three consecutive hours, with occasional intermissions of a few minutes, until he had worn out to stumps fifty-two switches, and until the bark of the body of the tree was rubbed to smooth and greasy by the attrition of" Jane's body. "One witness testified that he heard distinctly, at the distance of 600 yards, both the noise of the switches and screams and entireties of the woman." Hudson then buried Jane's body in a shallow grave "in a rough box, without any shroud." He rejected his overseer's suggestion that the neighbors be permitted to see the body before the burial.

Jane's body was exhumed two days later, "but [it] was in such a state of decomposition that the external marks of violence were well nigh obliterated." Nevertheless, the testimony of the doctors who examined the body and several others who testified as expert witnesses "was distinct and positive that the violence used was sufficient to produce death."

Hudson was tried before Judge Thomas Saunders Gholson and a jury. He was represented by a team of lawyers—Wood Bouldin, Wood Bouldin Jr., and Edward R. Chambers. The jury apparently rejected Hudson's attempt to prove that the beating did not cause Jane's death. The jurors "hesitated much between a conviction for murder in the first and murder in the second degree." But they finally agreed to convict Hudson for second degree murder and imposed an eighteen-year term in the penitentiary—"the longest term known to the law."

Gholson confirmed this sentence and condemned Hudson's "crime against human and divine law." He expressed two other concerns, however: "You have outraged the feelings of the community among whom you lived. You have enabled their enemies to fan the flame of fanaticism, by charging against them the enormity and cruelty of your hard and unfeeling heart, although that community cordially loathe and condemn cruelty towards black and white."[79]

Gholson's condemnation of Hudson's crime illustrates how judges and lawmakers could restrain what they perceived to be slave owner excesses while remaining dedicated to slavery. Gholson served on Virginia's Fifth Judicial Circuit from 1859 until 1863, when he was elected to the Confederate Congress. He was viewed as an ally of Jefferson Davis and had been "an early proponent of secession while sitting as a state judge before the war."[80]

Gholson nevertheless opposed the proposals of Davis and General Robert E. Lee to enlist slaves in the Confederate forces. Gholson stated in a February 1, 1865, speech delivered in the Confederate House of Representatives, "Nature seems to have fitted our slaves, as a race above others, for servants. They are loyal, obedient, submissive and grateful, but timid and unstable as children. Kept at home, and subjected to proper discipline they are useful and happy." But when slaves were "[f]reed from restraint, and exposed to evil influences, they become licentious and fanatical."[81]

Virginia's juries also may have been willing to extend the benefit of the doubt to hirers and overseers who were accused of slave murder, as illustrated by the prosecution of George Monroe. Monroe was charged with the November 1857 murder of an enslaved man who was identified only as "an old and much respected family servant, the property and sole support of an aged lady." The slave was hired to a person not named in the news reports. Monroe was this hirer's overseer. The enslaved victim was "unwell" and was "not capable of performing much labor. Monroe became irritated at his moving about slowly; whipped him severely, and stabbed him with a knife in several places." Physicians testified that the slave died from pneumonia caused by Monroe's attack; "but, there was some doubt in the minds of the jury as to the cause of the fatal termination."

After a trial during the Nelson County Circuit Court's spring 1858 term, the jury found Monroe guilty of second degree murder. He was sentenced to a five-year jail term. The trial judge, Lucas P. Thompson, denied Monroe's motion for a new trial, stating "that in his opinion the verdict of the jury was right, as he regarded it as a most atrocious murder."[82]

Conclusion

It is unclear why Virginia's slave homicide law reforms fell short of St. George Tucker's ideals, the homicide laws in the northern states, and the reforms in Britain's Atlantic island colonies. Between 1608 and 1865 Virginia's 877 executions (plus 43 in what would become West Virginia) led the nation. But only one Virginia slave owner was executed for killing his slave.[83]

Both the law on the books and that in practice denied Virginia's slaves the criminal law's equal protection. Wilson, Souther, the Castlemans, Birdsong, and Hudson all avoided first degree murder convictions in cases of extreme whipping, cruel treatment, or torture.

Moreover, before masters were tried for slave murders, their neighbors had to be convinced that the masters' acts reached extreme levels of unnecessary brutality imposed on submissive slaves. For example, after a July 1859 Prince Edward County inquest into the death of Robin, a slave of Overton, "[t]he jurors all agreed that 'the slave [had] been flogged' on more than one occasion '& paddled severely' on the buttocks, yet they doubted that those beatings had caused the man's death. 'I have seen negroes as badly whipped before, who are still living,' one juror [Samuel W. Bondman] explained." Another examiner named Giles Cockran agreed, "saying, 'I have seen a great many negroes worse whipped than I thought Robin had been.'"[84]

It is unknown how many other slave masters may have evaded prosecution if their jurors would not condemn other accused slave owners because they too knew of slaves who had been "worse whipped."

CHAPTER 8

Slave Homicide Reform in North Carolina and the Common Law of Slavery

The North Carolina, Tennessee, and Georgia legislatures also made slave murder a capital offense, while explicitly protecting the masters' prerogatives to kill their own slaves when it was deemed to be necessary. North Carolina's 1791 slave homicide law led the way. But the state's courts limited this law's effect by modifying the common law standards for mitigation and extenuation when whites were accused of killing slaves.

North Carolina's total enslaved population in 1790 was the fourth largest among the states after Virginia, South Carolina, and Maryland. About 25 percent of North Carolina's population then was enslaved, the fifth highest percentage among the states, trailing Virginia, South Carolina, Maryland, and Georgia. This percentage of enslaved North Carolinians grew steadily to 33 percent in 1830, and it remained constant until 1860, although North Carolina's net slave exports exceeded imports in each decade after 1800.[1]

Antebellum North Carolina, like Virginia, had a relatively large white non-slave-owning population. In 1790, 31 percent of white families owned slaves, but by 1850 the percentage had fallen to 26.8 percent. During this period slaveholding became more concentrated. In 1790, 82.6 percent of slave owners held fewer than ten slaves, and that percentage fell in 1850 to 67.2 percent. In 1790 the average number of slaves per slaveholding family was 6.7, and by 1850 the figure had risen to 10.2. Slaveholdings were more highly concentrated in the state's eastern portion.[2]

The North Carolina 1791 Reform Law and the Court's Responses

North Carolina's 1791 slave homicide reform statute declared that the 1774 act's double standard for "the murder of a white person and of one who is equally an human creature, but merely of a different complexion, is disgraceful to humanity and degrading in the highest degree to the laws and principles of a free, [C]hristian and enlightened country." Accordingly, the new act provided "[t]hat if any person shall hereafter be guilty of wilfully and maliciously killing a slave, such offender shall upon the first conviction thereof be adjudged guilty of murder, and shall suffer the same punishment as if he killed a free man; any law, usage or customs to the contrary notwithstanding." The act did not extend "to any person killing a slave outlawed by virtue of any act of Assembly of this state, or any slave in the act of resistance to his lawful owner or master, or to any slave dying under moderate correction."[3]

Heightened humanitarian motives may have finally persuaded some legislators to comply with the principles they asserted in the 1791 act's preamble, after years of resisting the British colonial authorities' repeated requests that the colony clearly define slave murder as a capital offense. But because the law explicitly legitimized killings by slave masters, the shifting and conflicting interests of slave owners and non-slave-owning whites also may have been relevant.

Indeed, the new state's legislators, in 1778, made slave stealing a capital offense. They condemned both "the promiscuous practice of stealing or other ways carrying away slaves the property of others" and the sale of free blacks into slavery. The act punished slave theft by "death without benefit of Clergy."[4]

These slave theft and slave homicide reform laws can be read as expressions of master class concerns about the crimes of third parties to the master and slave relationship, including hirers, overseers, patrollers, and strangers, whose violence directed against slaves threatened the interests of slave owners in their property and in the public welfare and peace. The slave stealing law was more direct, however, when it declared the punishment for slave thieves. The legislators' concern for the public welfare also motivated an act adopted in the 1791 term outlawing public gambling tables.[5]

North Carolina's antebellum legislatures nonetheless resisted calls for the criminal law reforms pioneered in other states such as Pennsylvania and Virginia. Instead, North Carolina retained a modified version of the older British model imposing capital punishment for many crimes, requiring the state's governors often to decide whether to pardon convicts in individual cases. It was not until 1854 that the legislature adopted a Revised Code reducing the number of capital crimes to twelve. But the legislature continued to refuse to build a state penitentiary.[6]

Moreover, the courts gave little weight to the 1791 slave homicide act's preamble expressing concern for slaves' lives, and instead read the statute strictly in favor of white defendants. Judge John Haywood, during the Halifax Superior Court's April 1797 term, broadly interpreted the exception for homicides of resisting slaves in *State v. Weaver*.[7] Weaver was indicted for murdering Lewis, a slave he hired from Smith. Haywood instructed the jury to find the killing justifiable if Weaver killed Lewis while he was resisting Weaver or if Lewis "offered to resist by force when he was killed." Haywood thus extended to a hirer the statutory exemption in favor of a slave's "lawful owner or master." He also extended this privilege for those who killed slaves "in the act of resistance" to those who killed slaves threatening to resist. The jury acquitted Weaver, thus relegating Smith to his civil damage remedies.[8]

The Superior Court, during the Newbern March 1799 term, in *State v. Piver*,[9] interpreted the act to legitimize all slave killings that would have been common law manslaughter, even if the killer was a stranger to the master and slave relationship. In a *per curiam* decision, the court, probably made up of Judges Haywood and Alfred Moore, held that in the act "against the malicious killing of slaves there is no punishment affixed to manslaughter." The court thus acquitted the defendant, who would have been guilty of manslaughter if his victim had not been enslaved.[10]

Nevertheless, some North Carolinians recognized that an orderly slave society should limit free people's conduct to prevent wanton killings of slaves owned by others. Simon Bright and John Boon were prosecuted under the 1791 act for violating these norms.

Bright was a Revolutionary War veteran who had served in various public offices, including justice in Lenoir County from 1795 until the summer of 1799, when he briefly was clerk of the county court. But on September 11, 1799, Bright declared to his friends and neighbors John and Slade Gatlin that two of his turkeys were missing. Bright suspected these turkeys "were stolen by some Negro and that he would charge his gunn and shoote the first Negro he met until he killed the right one." Bright then shot Mary, "a highly respected slave woman belonging to Captain Jesse Cobb, another justice and the town's leading merchant." Bright was charged with Mary's killing. But "his mental condition and general health deteriorated rapidly." He died in 1802 before he was tried for his alleged offense. Cobb nevertheless sued Bright for damages and continued the suit against Bright's heirs after Bright's death.[11]

Meanwhile, in the 1801 case *State v. Boon*,[12] John Boon was indicted for murdering a slave belonging to Daniel Dodson in violation of the 1791 act. A jury found Boon guilty of murder after a trial in the Superior Court, Hillsborough

District, during the court's October 1801 term. Boon made a motion in arrest of judgment, which the trial judge sent to the North Carolina Court of Conference. Boon's lawyers included John Haywood, who in 1800 had resigned from the Superior Court.[13]

The Court of Conference was not an appellate court. It instead made recommendations to the judges in cases pending in the trial court.[14] The court granted Boon's motion, holding that the 1791 statute was too vague to be enforced because, unlike the slave stealing law, it did not identify death without benefit of clergy as the penalty for malicious slave killers. Four judges wrote opinions. They all agreed that the legislature clearly expressed an intent to define slave homicide as "murder," but the law created an ambiguity when it stated that upon a murder conviction a slave killer was to "suffer the same punishment as if he had killed a free man." The common law punished killers of free people in different ways, depending on whether the crime was murder or manslaughter. Or the killers might not be punished at all if the killings were excusable or justified.

Judge Spruce Mccay's opinion addressed only the statute's defects.[15] Judges John Louis Taylor and Samuel Johnston found that the statute was ambiguous. But they also contended, in dictum, that slave killing could be common law murder. Taylor wrote that "the killing of a slave, if accompanied with those circumstances which constitute murder, amounts to that crime, in my judgment, as much as the killing of a free man." He argued that a "slave is a reasonable creature; may be within the peace, and is under the protection of the State, and may become the victim of preconceived malice." He asserted that the law should not permit masters to kill slaves without any limits, noting "[i]t is not the necessary consequence of the state of slavery, for that may exist without it, and its natural inconveniences ought not to be aggravated by an evil, at which reason, religion, humanity and policy equally revolt." He admitted, however, that "[p]olicy may occasionally dictate the propriety of enhancing or mitigating the punishment; may at one time subject the offender to a year's imprisonment, and at another to death; yet amidst all these mutations the crime is unchanged in its essence, undiminished in its enormity. The scale of its guilt exists in those relations of things which are prior to human institutions, and whose sanctions must forever remain unimpaired."[16]

Judge Johnston agreed, calling slave murder "a crime of the most atrocious and barbarous nature; much more so than killing a person who is free, and on an equal footing. It is an evidence of a most depraved and cruel disposition to murder one so much in your power that he is incapable of making resistance, even in his own defense." He added that if a slave's "conduct becomes so obnoxious that it can not be longer borne by his master, he has it in his power to dispose of him and remove him to any distance he thinks proper." It was "unnecessary to consider what punishment was annexed to the murder of slaves in other countries, either in ancient or modern times; the definition of murder, as laid down in our books, applies as forcibly to the murder of a slave as to the murder of a freeman." Had the Assembly not adopted the ambiguous 1791 law, he would "not hesitate on this occasion to have pronounced sentence of death on the prisoner."[17]

Judge John Hall also found the statute defective, but he asserted that slave killing was not common law murder because in pure slavery masters had the right to kill their slaves. He acknowledged that the laws in some countries denied masters the right to wantonly kill or cruelly punish their slaves. But because slavery did not exist in the common law, he contended that North Carolina masters retained the right to kill their slaves until the legislature altered this state of slavery. He admitted that lords did not have the unlimited right to kill villeins, but concluded, "Villeinage, however, as it existed in England, reflects but little on our subject; it had, attached to it, certain rights, that were unknown to a pure state of slavery."[18]

The legislature responded with an 1801 statute asserting that "doubts have arisen" about the 1791 slave homicide act. The new act stated "[t]hat if any person shall hereafter be guilty of feloniously, wilfully and maliciously killing any slave, such offender, upon conviction thereof, on being arraigned stands mute, or challenge peremptorily more than thirty-five jurors, shall suffer death without benefit of clergy."[19]

Augustus Benton was indicted for murder under this statute, but he apparently escaped a trial. An Orange County, Saint Thomas District inquest jury, on September 8, 1806, found that Benton murdered "a mulattoe girl named Lucinda, a Slave late in the possession of Augustus Benton, late a Merchant at the University," based primarily on three affidavits.[20]

Dr. Elias Hawes asserted that Benton summoned him on the evening of August 31, 1806, to come to Benton's house. Benton asked Hawes to agree to confidentially and "to prescribe something to a little girl who was in a deplorable situation, for [Benton] had whipped her smartly" because she broke some china. Benton "apprehended that serious consequences might ensue ... because he already had the name of a cruel master. [T]his circumstance if known might be magnified by the several enemies which he had, into a crime for which he might be prosecuted."

Hawes then examined Lucinda, who had scars on her entire body. Her pulse was "remarkably low, and her flesh cold." After overcoming Benton's resistance, Hawes took off a cap on Lucinda's head, which was "much bruised and swollen in several places." Her eyes were "mostly closed," and she was in a "languid stupor." Hawes also recorded the "intolerable smell" of her wounds. Hawes returned early the next morning. Benton reported that Lucinda was much better.[21]

But at about noon that same day Benton contacted Benjamin Yeargin, claiming that an accident occurred and "one of the little Negroes was dead." Benton asked Yeargin's help in digging a grave because Benton "appeared to dread the handle his father in law Wm. Taylor and family might make of it." Yeargin assisted Benton, although he previously told Benton that his whipping "was too hard for a child and [Yeargin] reproached [Benton] for it and he promised [Yeargin] he would not beat her again."[22]

Hugh Nunn stated that he saw Lucinda about three weeks before and "she walked stooping." His wife asked what was wrong. Lucinda exhibited injuries to her shoulder, including "a hole about an half inch deep."[23]

A grand jury indicted Benton for murder in the Superior Court, Hillsborough District, October term 1806. But Benton somehow avoided a trial.[24] As late as 1820 he was "seen at large," and he also escaped punishment when he was pardoned in 1795 by a private act of the legislature.[25]

Newspaper reports of other slave murder prosecutions confirm that some North Carolinians favored further reforms. The *Raleigh Star* published an unsigned April 19, 1810, letter, "A Caution to Slave Drivers," stating, "Altho' there is no danger of a mans being hurt by the law for killing a negro, it might be well for some people to know how to punish without killing them." The author reported that a man, not identified by name, was recently tried in Tarboro, in Edgecombe County, "for whipping a negro to death." An inquest doctor testified that the victim's body exhibited seventy stripes "on the belly, which cut through the skin—he made an incision with a knife through the cavity of the belly, and he found that there was one continued bruise from the breast to the waistband." The injuries "appeared more than commensurate to the [two or three hundred] stripes that were counted" and "were sufficient to produce such deep bruise; and consequent death."[26]

This small item must have caused some disquiet in the community. The author, four months later, wrote that he feared his "hasty remarks" might be "misunderstood, and lead to the idea that the practice of killing Negroes is a common amusement with us." He further described the crime, calling the killer "a man of a respectable family" who was "addicted to drinking" and who thought his slave had stolen seventy dollars. While intoxicated, he attempted to beat a confession out of his slave. The defendant "was arraigned at the bar, but he was acquitted; though not without murmurs from many of the byestanders, who thought that retributive justice was improperly dispensed with on the occasion." In view of the defendant's intoxication and his belief that his slave was a thief, the letter suggested that a term of imprisonment should have been an available alternative to the death penalty.[27]

The *Star* also reported on the October 1815 indictments of John R. Cooke, John Davis, Wes Heflin, and Samuel Bailey for murdering Bailey's slave Stephen. Cooke, Davis, and Bailey were arraigned in the Wake County Superior Court before Judge Henry Seawell. Heflin apparently had absconded. Cooke was tried first. His two young lawyers, Frederick Nash and Thomas Ruffin, later served as North Carolina's chief justice.[28]

Attorney General Hutchins G. Burton called five witnesses for the state in Cooke's trial, including the defendant's brother, Joseph Cooke. They described a twenty-plus-mile trail of whippings and other abuse that the defendants inflicted on Stephen, on July 4, 1815, apparently to get information from him about a runaway slave. They forced Stephen to trot with their horses as they left Raleigh about two o'clock in the afternoon and headed to Bailey's house. They denied Stephen water and splashed "spirits" in his face, among other violent and psychological abuses.

According to Joseph Cooke, the other defendants were met by Bailey after dark. John Cooke and Heflin then inflicted another fifteen to thirty stripes each, and Davis offered to whip Stephen further the next day. Bailey declared he would whip Stephen "on the belly." Stephen "asked to rest," and the witness said that he "turned aside a few steps, (but for what, he did not in any manner pretend to account,) *when he heard an exclamation* from the prisoner and Davis." He returned to see Stephen "lying on his back." Stephen died ten or fifteen minutes later.

The Wake and Granville County coroners did not examine the body until July 10. Stephen's neck was broken and his body "bore the marks of much whipping." But the Granville coroner "said he thought that he had seen slaves worse whipped."

The jury returned a guilty verdict in less than five minutes. Davis and Bailey "were then arranged at the bar; and after a few moment's consultation, the Jury returned a verdict of *Not Guilty*."[29]

Governor William Miller pardoned Cooke after receiving "[n]umerous petitions" in Cooke's favor. The *Star* reported,

> Many thought it hard to hang Cooke, when it was believed that Davis and Hefflin were equally guilty, and his brother Joe Cooke, almost equally so. Some thought, as this was the first instance in which a white man had ever been convicted for killing

a negro, it would be impolitick to hang him so unexpectedly. And others believed that it would be wrong in all respects, to hang a white man for killing a negro. But whatever might have been the motives of his excellency, we hear no dissatisfaction expressed by any at this act of clemency.

The editor also cautioned "the unwary against a repetition of the too common practice of whipping negroes to death, as the courts have shown a disposition to bring offenders to account and executive interposition may not be expected in all cases."[30]

The November 10, 1815, *Star* published a letter from "A Constant Reader" warning that "[g]ood men, lovers of justice and order, will hereafter look upon the attempt to bring criminals to justice as useless trouble, if the governor is to step in and screen them from justice." According to the letter, "Cooke's former *good* character certainly did him no service, and his getting drunk and exercising more than brutal rage upon a poor dumb beast as soon as he left the *Gallows*, speak little in commendation of that act of *clemency* of which you seem to boast." The writer called for limits on the governor's pardon power or "if death cannot be inflicted let us have a Penitentiary."[31]

A week later, the paper printed a letter from "Americanus" defending the pardon because Cooke "was very much intoxicated" and had "not the smallest idea" that the "whipping he gave" would cause his victim's death. According to the letter, a petition supporting Cooke's pardon was signed by "no less than a thousand or fifteen hundred" of the area's "respectable citizens." The writer agreed the law should provide jail terms for slave killers like Cooke, whose "crime of whipping the negro, was not enough . . . to take his life."[32]

The 1817 Reform Act and the *Tackett* Doctrine

During the legislative term beginning on November 17, 1817, North Carolina's legislators adopted An Act to Punish the Offense of Killing a Slave. It stated that slave killing would be "homicide, and shall partake the same degree of guilt when accompanied with the like circumstances that homicide now does at common law."[33]

The legislators during that term also debated a petition for the pardon of John Walker of Rockingham, whose slave murder conviction the Supreme Court had affirmed in *State v. Walker*.[34] Walker was charged with murdering a twenty-one-year-old male slave who was a runaway belonging to John Guy. Walker tortured and beat his victim to death while he was transporting the slave on a nine-mile journey back to his owner. The trial judge instructed the jury that, under these facts, they were to either convict Walker of murder or acquit him. The jury convicted Walker and he was sentenced to death.

After the Supreme Court affirmed Walker's conviction, Governor Miller stayed the November 14, 1817, execution. He later pardoned Walker in response to legislative support for Walker's petition.[35]

The *Walker* decision did not state how trial judges might instruct juries when there was evidence of provocation. The 1817 act appears to express the legislators' intent to equate slave homicides with other homicides.

North Carolina's Supreme Court, which was reformed in 1818, soon interpreted the statute to the contrary after two 1819 slave killings by white non-slave owners. This court at the start was made up of three justices—Chief Justice John Louis Taylor and Justices John Hall and Leonard Henderson.[36]

Mason Scott on July 16, 1819, killed Caleb, a slave belonging to Frederick S. Marshall, in Raleigh late at night and without any provocation while Scott was "drunk with liquor."[37] Scott, who was about eighteen years old, was indicted and tried for murder on April 1, 1819, in Wake County Superior Court before Judge John Paxton and a jury. Charles Manly, Anthony G. Glynn, and former Superior Court judge Henry Seawell represented Scott. Judge Paxton charged the jury after ten in the evening. At about two o'clock the next morning they found Scott guilty of murder. Judge Paxton denied Scott's motion for a new trial, denied him the benefit of clergy, and sentenced him to death.[38]

Scott filed an appeal with the new Supreme Court, which, during its June 1820 term, affirmed the conviction and death sentence, despite the arguments of Seawell, who was described as "one of the strongest criminal lawyers who ever appeared at the Bar in North Carolina."[39] Seawell by then already had an extensive legislative and judicial career. He had been elected to North Carolina's House of Commons and Assembly, and in 1821 he was elected to the State Senate. He also served on the Superior Court until the beginning of 1819, when he was not appointed to the new Supreme Court. Seawell was the trial judge for John Cooke's trial and wrote an opinion that affirmed John Walker's slave murder conviction. Seawell again served as a judge from 1832 to his death in 1835. In that year, he also was a delegate to the state's constitutional convention.[40]

Seawell argued that the 1817 statute "is very lamely drawn, and being darkly expressed, points out no one object in the body of it plainly." He thus contended that Scott should enjoy the benefit of clergy because the statute did not clearly exclude this benefit. In essence, Seawell asked the court to restore the provisions of the 1774 act that permitted the death penalty only on a slave killer's second offense.[41] The Supreme Court's opinion by Judge Henderson rejected this argument, as well as the other arguments offered by Seawell and his co-counsel.[42]

Judge Joseph J. Daniel, on October 7, 1820, sentenced Scott to be executed on October 22, 1820. The execution was delayed while Governor John Branch considered and denied Scott's pardon request. Scott was hanged on November 10, 1820. He was the first North Carolina slave killer who was executed.[43]

Branch denied this pardon although he received "[a] perfect avalanche of petitions and protests from practically the entire population of Raleigh," including "several State officers, one hundred and twenty-three ladies, and young Frederick Sterling Marshall, owner of the slave who had been killed." The petitioners' concerns included the fear that "insolence and insubordination ... would be encouraged among the negroes by putting the life of a freeman and a slave upon the same footing."[44]

William Tackett, in contrast, avoided execution after Seawell convinced the Supreme Court, in *State v. Tackett*,[45] to ignore the 1817 statute's plain language and keep slave killings on a different footing. Tackett (also spelled Tacket) was a journeyman carpenter employed by Millington Richardson in Raleigh. Tackett was indicted for the December 18, 1819, murder of Daniel, William Ruffin's slave. His trial was held in Raleigh during the fall 1820 Superior Court term, when Joseph J. Daniel was the presiding judge.

Tackett shot Daniel after they argued and fought because Daniel believed that Tackett "kept" Daniel's "wife" Lotty, although under southern law slave contracts, including marriage contracts, were unenforceable.[46] Tackett offered to prove that Daniel was a "turbulent man" who was "insolent and impudent to white people." The trial judge "refused to hear such testimony, unless it would prove that the deceased was insolent and impudent to the prisoner in particular."

The trial judge also instructed the jury "that under the act of 1817, this case was to be determined by the same rules and principles of law as if the deceased had been a white man; that murder was the felonious killing of a human being, with malice aforethought, which might either be expressed, as by declarations or lying in wait, or implied, as from the instrument used: that no words would justify or extenuate homicide, and make it less than murder."[47] The jury found Tackett guilty of murder. Tackett sought a new trial "because proper evidence had been rejected; and because the Court erred in the charge to the Jury: but it was refused, and sentence of death was pronounced upon the prisoner."[48]

On Tackett's appeal to North Carolina's Supreme Court, Seawell first contended that the 1817 act "had no other effect than ... to create the offence of manslaughter, as applied to the homicide of slaves."[49] He also asked the court to modify the common law of crimes to account for "the wide distinction [that] exists in the grades of our society between freemen and slaves—whites and blacks." He contended that "the policy of the Law as well as the inveterate habits of our population, and the best feelings of our nature enjoin it upon us to keep these classes as distinct in every respect as possible, and, to that end, to enforce the superiority of the one, and the subordination due from the other, a new rule must be laid down fitted to this state of things, and adapted to this particular relation and the exigency of our situation." He suggested "that a word from a slave was a provocation equal to a blow from a free man; and the most trifling assault, to a deadly stroke."[50]

The court, in its December 1820 term, reversed Tackett's murder conviction. Chief Justice Taylor wrote the court's opinion that first held that the trial judge should have permitted Tackett to offer evidence that Daniel "was a turbulent man, and that he was insolent and impudent to white people" in general. This evidence, Taylor stated, "might have an important bearing on" the mitigation issue.[51]

Second, Taylor held that the trial judge should not have instructed the jury to apply "the same rules and principles of law as if the deceased had been a white man." Taylor held that the legislators "had no design beyond that of authorising a conviction for manslaughter, in cases where a slave was killed under a legal provocation." He contended that before the 1817 act was approved "a white person [who] had killed a slave under such circumstances as constituted murder, ... might have been convicted and punished for that offence; but if the homicide was extenuated to manslaughter, no punishment was annexed to that offence, and the accused persons were uniformly acquitted." Therefore, "[i]t seemed just to the Legislature, that the manslaughter of a slave should be punished in the same manner with that of a white person. This they have provided for, and it is all they intended to provide for."[52]

Taylor then asserted that the legislators did not intend to require that slave killings "could be only extenuated by such a provocation as would have the same effect where a white person was killed. The different degrees of homicide, they left to be ascertained by the Common Law of the country—a system which adapts itself to the habits, institutions and actual conditions of the citizens, and which is not the result of the wisdom of any one man, or society of men, in any one age, but of the wisdom and experience of many ages of wise and discreet men." Taylor explained that white supremacy was at the root of this interpretation: "It exists in the nature of things, that where slavery prevails, the relation between a white man and a slave differs from that, which subsists between free persons; and every individual in the community feels and understands, that the homicide of a slave may be extenuated by acts, which would not produce a legal provocation if done by a white person." Taylor did not "define and limit these acts." He left these issues for "the sense and feelings of Jurors, and the grave discretion of Courts," to balance "the rights respectively belonging to the slave and white man—to the just claims of humanity, and to the supreme law, the safety of the citizens."[53]

And third, Taylor rejected the "rule of law, that neither words of reproach, insulting gestures, nor a trespass against goods or land, are provocations sufficient to free the party killing from the guilt of murder, where he made use of a deadly weapon." He stated that "it can not be laid down as a rule, that some of these provocations, if offered by a slave, well known to be turbulent and disorderly, would not extenuate the killing, if it were instantly done under the heat of passion, and without circumstances of cruelty."[54]

This decision is relevant for all slave homicides because it set a trend in the southern common law of slavery declaring that the prevailing standards of mitigation and extenuation did not apply to slave homicides, thus echoing the principles dating back to the 1661 Barbados act denying the common law's equal protection to slaves because of their race. The legislature did not adopt a statute in response, confirming that its command that slave homicides be determined on "like circumstances" meant that the courts and juries were to mitigate slave homicides from murder to manslaughter under "unlike circumstances."[55]

The *Tackett* case arose out of a pattern of poor white and slave fraternization and violence about which Taylor expressed further concerns in his 1823 opinion in *State v. Hale*.[56] The *Hale* court held that a free person could be indicted for "inhuman assault and battery" on a slave that he or she did not own.[57]

North Carolina's Supreme Court, in *State v. Jarrott*,[58] later extended both the *Tackett* "mere words" exception and the rule denying to enslaved defendants the equal protection of the common law's mitigation standards to an enslaved man named Jarrott who allegedly killed a white stranger named Thomas Chatham. Justice William Gaston wrote the court's opinion reversing Jarrott's murder conviction. But the court affirmed trial judge John M. Dick's rejection of the defendant's requested jury charge language, which stated, "in trials affecting life, a negro slave should not be convicted of murder, unless a white man would be convicted on the same evidence." Gaston instead applied the *Tackett* rule legitimizing white violence against insolent slaves.[59] Gaston thus limited his holding in *State v. Will*,[60] which reversed Will's conviction for murdering his overseer, because Will should have been permitted to attempt to mitigate his murder charge to manslaughter.[61]

North Carolina's Supreme Court in 1823 affirmed another slave murder conviction in *State v. Reed*,[62] which suggests that the courts also may have been concerned about free black violence directed at slaves. The March 1823 indictment identified the defendant Thomas Reed as a free black man who, on December 10, 1822, in Hertford County, allegedly struck an enslaved man called Tom. Tom lingered until January 7, 1823, when he died. Reed pled not guilty and was tried before Judge Frederick Nash and a jury.[63]

Reed went to Tom's house armed with a large stick. He asked Tom if he had said that Reed "had stole [sic] his bacon." Tom answered that he had. Reed then hit Tom with the stick. Judge Nash instructed the jury that "words of reproach however insulting would not extenuate a homicide from murder to manslaughter more particularly in a case like this when the prisoner had gone to the house of the deceased and brought upon himself the insulting language." The jury convicted Reed of murder. The Supreme Court affirmed the conviction. Because Reed was a "free man of colour," his lawyers apparently did not contend that the *Tackett* rule applied in favor of their client.[64] At least two other North Carolina free blacks, Trueman Goode in 1826 and Louis Hart in 1851, were prosecuted and acquitted for slave homicides.[65]

Hoover, Robbins, and the 1817 Law's Limits

Several slave masters were prosecuted for murdering their own slaves under the 1817 law. The results of these cases were mixed.

Warner Taylor of Granville County was in 1819 found by an initial coroner's inquest to have beaten his slave Betty to death. But a grand jury found no evidence of "wicked intent," which was necessary for a murder indictment. Accordingly, Taylor was indicted for manslaughter and a trial jury found him not guilty. Only six years later, Taylor and his overseer Thomas Huff were indicted for murdering another slave owned by Taylor. Huff was acquitted. Taylor was found guilty only of manslaughter. His hand was burned to mark his conviction. Archibald D. Murphey, who with George E. Badger successfully defended Huff, asserted in a September 10, 1825, letter to Thomas Ruffin that Taylor "was guilty of a most foul Murder."[66]

Jacob Pope, in April 1822, was tried in the Halifax Superior Court for murdering his female slave "by inflicting on her naked body and limbs, between two and three hundred lashes with a cow-skin." Pope's overseer testified about this brutal beating, which occurred after Pope tied the slave's body and arms to an apple tree. Pope was exhausted after inflicting at least 260 lashes. He directed his overseer to continue the beating, but the overseer "declined with entreaties that she had received enough." The slave, whose name and alleged offense are not reported, died a day or two later. The jury found Pope guilty of manslaughter, and the court imposed a two-hundred-dollar fine plus costs.[67]

David Yates (sometimes spelled Yeates), in September 1825, was indicted for murder by a Wilkes County grand jury, which found that, on September 1, 1825, he beat his slave Jim to death. Yates was tried before Judge Frederick Nash and a jury, which found Yates not guilty of murder but guilty of manslaughter. Yates's lawyer asked Judge Nash to grant his client the benefit of clergy to avoid the death sentence. Judge Nash agreed. He sentenced Yates to eleven months in jail and two separate whippings of thirty-nine lashes on his bare back. Yates filed an appeal with the North Carolina Supreme Court challenging only the whippings. The Court, by a two to one vote, invalidated the whippings based on its interpretation of an 1816 statute that abolished the burning of the hands of those convicted of clergiable felonies.[68]

In contrast, Henry Sides in 1827 escaped prosecution for killing his male runaway slave who was being held at the Wilkesboro jail for a few days before June 4, 1827, when Sides and his brother-in-law Jonas Bradshaw recovered the enslaved man from the jail. They tied a rope around his neck; kicked, beat, and choked him to death; and left his body along the side of a road seven miles outside of Wilkesboro, where it was found on the following morning.

Samuel Finley Patterson's June 10, 1827, letter to Governor Hutchins G. Burton called this a crime "of a most brutal and savage character." Patterson also sent Burton a coroner's jury's inquest report concluding that Sides and Bradshaw were guilty of murder. He stated that the sheriff pursued Sides and Bradshaw without success for "some days." He called on Burton to bring the suspects to justice because of the crime's "atrocious character" and "extreme barbarity," and because Sides was of "general bad character." Patterson feared that the suspects may have absconded to some "Western State."[69] Sides and Bradshaw were from Lincoln County, which is in southwestern North Carolina. Wilkesboro is in Wilkes County, which is farther to the north. The North Carolina newspapers published versions of Patterson's letter in June 1827. Some opined, "We never heard of an instance of such thoughtless, savage barbarity."[70]

Governor Burton was going to issue a proclamation for the "capture of the culprits" when the state assembly "blocked its dissemination." The alleged killers never were returned for a trial.[71]

Twenty years after deciding *Tackett*, North Carolina's Supreme Court extended that decision's mitigation and extenuation standards while affirming

John Hoover's conviction for the March 1839 murder of his slave Mira. Chief Justice Thomas Ruffin's opinion in *State v. Hoover* legitimized slave homicides by masters,[72] which were less arbitrary and brutal than Hoover's crime.[73]

The official case report and Ruffin's opinion describe Hoover's brutality and sadism, which also are preserved in the record of the trial testimony in the North Carolina Supreme Court's file.[74] Hoover was a farmer in a rural area near Statesville in Iredell County, in western North Carolina. Statesville then "was a small town with a population of no more than two hundred people. On the surface Statesville was probably typical of other developing southern communities, except that there were fewer slaves than elsewhere in this part of the state."[75]

Hoover was about fifty-seven years old when he killed Mira. He married Regina Lipe (or Leib) on August 27, 1806. The first of their ten children, Leah, was born nine months before their marriage.[76]

According to Carolyn Powell, it is not clear how many slaves Hoover owned, but "in comparison to his neighbors, [he] was land rich; at the time of his death he had amassed a total of 1,914 acres of land, and a considerable amount of property." Hoover "was not only a master of brutality" but also "a cheat" who "at various times . . . owned more land than he actually paid taxes on, and he also owned an undetermined number of slaves who never appeared in the census records or county tax lists."[77]

The Iredell County coroner William B. Jones, on March 28, 1839, led an inquiry into Mira's death. Hoover at first cooperated. He admitted that Mira died the previous morning. But he claimed that venereal disease caused her death and offered to prove this by some of his family members and neighbors, apparently to deter the exhumation of Mira's body. When this failed, Hoover used threats to obstruct the exhumation. These efforts also proved fruitless. Mira's body was examined, and John McLaughlin, one of the examiners, testified that he saw head wounds from one-half inch to two inches, including a fresh wound one and one-half inches long. He asserted that Mira's body "from the back of her head to her heels was literally a continued wound."[78]

Hoover was immediately arrested and charged with Mira's murder. While he was being transported to Statesville, Hoover offered to bribe the inquest members. McLaughlin testified that this was "repelled with indignation." According to McLaughlin, Hoover also asserted that "the negro was his own property, and he had a right to do as he pleased with his property." Hoover alleged that Mira "had attempted to burn his barn or still house and he was afraid she would burn him up. He also stated that she had put something in the food to poison the family."[79]

A grand jury, during the fall term 1839, indicted Hoover for Mira's murder. Hoover entered a not guilty plea.[80]

Hoover was tried on September 12, 1839, in the Iredell Superior Court in Statesville before Judge John M. Dick and a jury. Twelve witnesses testified for the prosecution, including three men who had worked for Hoover—James Wordy, Henry Philer, and John Bales—and five neighbors—Andrew Steele, Jacob Hill, James G. Flemming, Jacob Wooliver, and Christian Barringer. Their testimony supported the charge that Mira's death followed "a series of the most brutal and barbarous whippings, scourgings and privations" that Hoover inflicted from December 1838 until Mira died on March 27, 1839, while she was in the latter stages of pregnancy and continuing after she gave birth to her child. Carolyn Powell argued that Hoover's actions suggest an intent to induce Mira "to abort her child."[81]

According to these witnesses, Hoover declared that he killed Mira because "she stole his turnips and sold them to the worthless people in the neighborhood, and that she had attempted to burn his barn, and was disobedient and impudent to her mistress; at another, that she had attempted to burn his still house, and had put something in a pot to poison his family. There was no evidence except her own confessions, extorted by severe whippings, that the deceased was guilty of any of the crimes imputed to her."[82]

Coroner Jones and John H. McLaughlin testified about the inquest, including Hoover's statements and conduct.[83] Dr. Moore, the physician who participated in the inquest, stated that he observed "five wounds" on Mira's head, "four of which appeared to have been inflicted a week or more before her death: that the fifth was a fresh wound, about one and a half inches long, and to the bone." These injuries "were sufficient to have produced her death: that there were many other wounds on different parts of her body, which were sufficient, independent of those on the head, to have caused death." He concluded that he "did not discover the slightest symptom of [venereal] disease."[84]

The prosecution also called a Mr. Allison, whose father "raised" Mira. He and his brother sold Mira to Hoover. He described her as "an obedient and humble negro when his Father owned her."[85] The report of the case thus concluded that it did not "appear that [Mira] was disobedient or impertinent to her master or mistress; on the contrary, she seemed, as some of the witnesses testified, to do her best to obey the commands of her master, and that when she failed to do so, it was from absolute inability to comply with orders to which her condition and strength were unequal."

Hoover offered no trial testimony supporting his allegations of Mira's misconduct or refuting the evidence of his extreme abuse. Judge Dick nevertheless charged the jury "that they must be satisfied, beyond a reasonable doubt" that Hoover killed Mira, that he intended to kill her, and that he had no legal provocation at the time of killing her, before they could find him guilty of murder. He also instructed "that if [Mira] attempted to burn the barn, still house, or kitchen of the defendant, or if she put poison in a pot to poison the family, or stole turnips, or disobeyed the orders of her master, these were all acts of legal provocation." If Hoover killed Mira "upon the discovery of any of the aforesaid offences, or in so short a time thereafter that the passion of the defendant had not a reasonable time to subside, the slaying would be manslaughter, and not murder."[86]

The jury convicted Hoover of murder. Hoover's lawyer "moved for a new trial on the ground that the jury was misdirected by the court." Judge Dick denied Hoover's motion.[87] He sentenced Hoover to be held until October 25, 1839, when he was to "be taken the place of public Execution and hung by the neck until he be dead."[88]

The North Carolina's Supreme Court, in February 1840, heard oral argument on Hoover's appeal, but no lawyer appeared for Hoover. The court's opinion by Chief Justice Ruffin affirmed the conviction.[89]

Ruffin contended that Judge Dick's jury charge was more favorable to Hoover than it should have been because there was no evidence of immediate provocation. He also stated that the jury could have inferred Hoover's intent to commit murder: "The intent, by severe and protracted cruelties and torments, to inflict grievous and dangerous suffering, or, in other words, to do great bodily harm, imports, from the means and manner thereof, a disregard of consequences; and consequently, the party is justly answerable for all the harm he did, although he did not specially design the whole."[90]

Although Ruffin thought Hoover's appeal lacked any merit, he explained at length why some slave master killings should be murder. He cited the rule he established in *State v. Mann*:[91] "A master may lawfully punish his slave, and the degree must, in general, be left to his own judgment and humanity, and cannot be judicially questioned." Ruffin then distinguished Mann's case because "the master's authority is not altogether unlimited. He must not kill. There is, at least, this restriction upon his power: he must stop short of taking life." Ruffin noted that the courts had held, "independent of the act of 1791," that slave killing may be murder, whether committed by a master or a stranger to the slave.[92]

Ruffin did not mention the 1817 act's requirement that slave homicide should "partake the same degree of guilt when accompanied with the like circumstances that homicide now does at common law."[93] Instead, he extended Taylor's *Tackett* doctrine, asserting, "It must indeed be true, in the nature of things, that a killing by the owner may be extenuated by many circumstances, from which no palliation could be derived in favor of a stranger."[94]

Ruffin explained further, "If death unhappily ensue from the master's chastisement of his slave, inflicted apparently with a good intent, for reformation or example, and with no purpose to take life, or to put it in jeopardy, the law would doubtless tenderly regard every circumstance which, judging from the conduct generally of masters towards slaves, might reasonably be supposed to have hurried the party into excess." But, in contrast, "the acts imputed to this unhappy man do not belong to a state of civilization. They are barbarities which could only be prompted by a heart in which every humane feeling had long been stifled; and indeed there can scarcely be a savage of the wilderness so ferocious as not to shudder at the recital of them." Thus he concluded Hoover's "acts cannot be fairly attributed to an intention to correct or to chastise. They cannot, therefore, have allowance, as being the exercise of an authority conferred by the law for the purposes of the correction of the slave, or of keeping the slave in due subjection."

Ruffin found that Hoover's crime "must have flowed from a settled and malignant pleasure in inflicting pain, or a settled and malignant insensibility to human suffering. There was none of that *brief fury* to which the law has regard, as an infirmity of our nature." Ruffin then reasoned,

> On the contrary, without any consideration for the sex, health or strength of the deceased, through a period of four months, including the latter stages of pregnancy, delivery, and recent recovery therefrom, by a series of cruelties and privations in their nature unusual, and in degree excessive beyond the capacity of a stout frame to sustain, the prisoner employed himself from day to day in practising grievous tortures upon an enfeebled female, which finally wore out the energies of nature and destroyed life. He beat her with clubs, iron chains, and other deadly weapons, time after time; burnt her; inflicted stripes over and often, with scourges, which literally excoriated her whole body; forced her out to work in inclement seasons, without being duly clad; provided for her insufficient food; exacted labour beyond her strength, and wantonly beat her because she could not comply with his requisitions. These enormities, besides others too disgusting to be particularly designated, the prisoner, without his heart once relenting or softening, practised from the first of December until the latter end of the ensuing March; and he did not relax even up to the last hours of his victim's existence. In such a case, surely, we do not speak of provocation; for nothing could palliate such a course of conduct.

Ruffin concluded, "Punishment thus immoderate and unreasonable in the measure, the continuance, and the instruments, accompanied by other hard usage and painful privations of food, clothing and rest, loses all character of correction *in foro domestico*." Instead Hoover's violence "denotes plainly" that he "must have contemplated the fatal termination, which was the natural consequence of such barbarous cruelties."[95]

Superior Court judge Thomas Settle later sentenced Hoover to death. Official records of Hoover's execution have not been found. But it appears that, on May 15, 1840, in Statesville, Hoover was executed.[96]

Hoover's anticipated execution may have caused Ruffin to write his dictum for trial judges, lawyers, and the public. Ruffin further cut down the scope of illegal slave homicide when masters were accused of killing their slaves. Like his dictum in *Mann*, Ruffin explained the necessary limits to the violence that was inherent in the master-slave relationship.[97]

Hoover's hanging may have deterred slave owners who were inclined to kill their slaves, but some slave killers evaded prosecution. Local community members decided to "overrule" Mary Hinkel's murder conviction and exercise their "right" to impose vigilante "justice." Hinkel, in 1842, was accused of beating to death with a ladle a slave girl whom she owned. After Hinkel's conviction and death sentence, 190 citizens urged Governor John Moorehead to pardon Hinkel. They called her an "uneducated and weak-willed woman of violent passions" who must have been insane to kill her own property. Governor Moorehead denied the pardon. But Hinkel evaded the death penalty when "the community resorted to the simpler procedure of letting her break jail and flee."[98]

John A. and Mary Ann Holloway successfully escaped prosecution after Mary Ann was charged with the February 5, 1845, murder of Sarah, a slave owned by her husband John. John was a member of a leading Person County family. In 1842 and 1843, he served in the state legislature. Haywood Williams, the Person County coroner, held an inquest, which found that Mary Ann murdered Sarah "in a most cruel manner." John was charged "with being present, [and] feloniously abetting and encouraging the murder." After the Holloways absconded, Governor William A. Graham, on March 6, 1845, offered a four-hundred-dollar reward (two hundred each) for the capture and return of the Holloways.[99]

Press reports published in April 1845 asserted—"from indubitable authority"—that the Holloways escaped "to parts unknown to their neighbors, doubtless Texas," after Mary Ann "beat and tortured... to death" her enslaved victim. She "prevailed upon" John to tie Sarah's hands before the killing. Sarah "was privately buried eight feet deep, in an obscure place."[100]

The Holloways turned up in Texas in March 1845 with their four children and nine slaves. John died the next year. Mary Ann in 1848 married Phillip J.

Shaver, who was a North Carolina native. They had five children.[101] Mary Ann died on January 2, 1912, at the age of ninety-two. An obituary did not mention her escape from a murder prosecution. It instead remembered her as "a lovely type of the old time Southern womanhood. Kind and courteous to all, the soul of hospitality."[102]

Ira Westbrook, a slave hirer, also avoided a murder conviction when Judge Richmond Pearson, who later served on the North Carolina Supreme Court, extended the rule permitting masters to kill rebellious slaves. Westbrook allegedly killed a slave named Lot during the term of hiring and was indicted and tried in the Jones County Superior Court in 1847. "Westbrook was an illiterate whom the 1850 census lists as owning no real estate. He was a poor man in a rich neighborhood."[103]

Lot was "insolent and impudent in his language toward" Westbrook, who "took down a cowhide to whip him." Lot told Westbrook "that he would not be whipped by any such man, and began to move off. Westbrook then took down his gun, upon which the negro in an impudent manner told him to shoot—repeating it three times." Westbrook shot Lot, "and lodged the contents of gun" in one of Lot's calves. Lot fell, but soon crawled back to the door of Westbrook's house "and told him in an impudent manner, to shoot the other barrel of the gun into his head, which the prisoner did not do." Lot died of his wounds three days later.

James W. Bryan argued for Westbrook that Lot "was in a state of rebellion and resistance" to Westbrook

> who for the *time being* was [Lot's] *owner*, and had all the rights of [Lot's] *actual* master. That but for this resistance and rebellion, it would be at most a case of manslaughter. Judge Pearson charged the jury that if they believed Westbrook killed Lot upon the *provocation* of *impudence* and *insolence*, it was in the eye of the law but a case of manslaughter. But if the deceased was in an actual state of *rebellion*, and resistance to the prisoner, then he would have a right to kill him, and would not be liable criminally for the act, but would be justified in law for so doing.

Judge Pearson then defined "what he deemed rebellion and resistance, on the part of a slave toward his master. The Jury found the prisoner not guilty."[104]

Christopher (Kit) Robbins in contrast was convicted in the Wilkes County Superior Court for the 1855 murder of his slave Jim. North Carolina's Supreme Court applied the *Hoover* decision's limitations on a master's criminal liability for slave killing while affirming the conviction in *State v. Robbins*.[105]

Robbins was a slave trader and slave driver in a six-county area that included Surry County, in northwestern North Carolina. Wilkes County is adjacent to Iredell County, where John Hoover had been convicted sixteen years earlier.[106]

Robbins came home from tax paying on the evening of July 20, 1855. He believed that Jim, who was about sixty years old, failed to feed a horse. Robbins beat Jim with an axe handle, stomped on him, whipped him with a wagon whip, poured hot water on him, and whipped him again. Robbins then poured salt in Jim's wounds and repeatedly whipped him four or five times. Jim of course died. At about four o'clock the next morning, Robbins forced his youngest stepdaughter Martha to help him drag Jim's body to Jim's cabin and shut and nail the door from the inside. Martha came out "by raising a plank of the floor." Robbins also made Martha "wash up the blood from the kitchen floor, and put sand on the floor," because "there was much blood on the floor before it was washed off."[107]

A coroner's inquiry was held the next day. Robbins absconded, but he was caught, indicted, and tried before a jury in the Wilkes County Superior Court. Robbins's three stepchildren—Mary Jane (seventeen), Pinkney (fifteen), and Martha (thirteen)—were among the witnesses for the prosecution. Robbins offered no testimony, and the jury found him guilty of murder.[108]

On appeal Robbins argued that the trial judge's jury charge was erroneous, and that he should have been found guilty of no crime greater than manslaughter.[109] North Carolina's Supreme Court disagreed and affirmed the conviction. Justice William H. Battle's opinion relied on Ruffin's opinion in *State v. Hoover*.[110] Evidence strongly suggests that Robbins was hanged on April 4, 1856.[111]

Jurors provided a final check on the 1817 law's effect. Jason Franklin was acquitted after he, Robert Binkly, and Albert Vann were indicted for murdering an enslaved man named Lamb, who was about sixty years old. Franklin had hired Lamb for the year 1857. All three defendants were tried in October 1858 in the Superior Court in Gates County before Judge Jesse G. Shepherd and a jury. Franklin's eleven-year-old daughter Cornelia, the state's principal witness, described the fatal beating, the defendants' efforts to destroy the evidence of their crime, and how she was directed to assist in this effort to cover up the homicide. The defense contended that Jason Franklin "heard that the negro told his children that no white man had ever whipped him, and that none ever should." The defense argued that Lamb "was insolent, and disposed to resist rightful authority." The defendants thus contended they "were engaged in a lawful act, and, in order to expel the negro from the premises, they had the perfect right to use any measures and exert any force that was necessary in order to subdue him in case he resisted."

Judge Shepherd instead charged the jury "that there was no evidence that the negro was insolent," or that he resisted Franklin's "lawful authority." If the jurors believed Cornelia's testimony they were to find the defendants guilty of murder. But they found the defendants not guilty, allegedly because Cornelia's testimony "was unreliable, on account of her youth."¹¹²

Conclusion

North Carolina's legislators adopted laws making slave murder a capital crime, but they unambiguously legitimized slave master killings of resisting slaves and killings from moderate correction. And the courts went further, modifying the common law to grant masters special privileges to kill slaves. Only the wanton extremes of violence exhibited by Hoover and Robbins sank to the level of depravity warranting the ultimate punishment.¹¹³

It is not apparent why North Carolina's statutes differed from Virginia's. But the cases suggest that these statutory distinctions may have made little difference in practice. And the Virginia and North Carolina courts agreed that slave masters and hirers could not be indicted for assault and battery on slaves under their command.¹¹⁴

The Granville County, North Carolina, criminal prosecutions between 1791 and 1839 studied by Laura Edwards put this all in context. She found three slave homicide prosecutions, one of William Ball, a third party, and the two prosecutions involving slave owner Warner Taylor. The other twenty-two arose out of third-party nonfatal assaults against slaves involving twenty-nine defendants.¹¹⁵

These slave homicide reform laws and cases thus echoed the slave-owning class concerns about third-party violence directed against slaves. They also reflected the white social class structure when imposing standards for criminal liability for fatal and nonfatal slave abuse.

CHAPTER 9

Slave Homicide Reform in Georgia and Tennessee

Georgia's 1798 state constitution and Georgia and Tennessee statutes enacted in the 1790s made slave murders capital crimes. But they also included the North Carolina 1791 act's exemptions for slave killings by masters as a result of moderate correction and the assertion of the masters' authority over resisting slaves. These states, also like North Carolina, provided slave owners with criminal and civil remedies against others who killed their slaves. This similarity in the law on the books is mirrored by the law in action—no Georgia or Tennessee slave master was executed for murdering his or her own slave.[1]

Georgia's Constitution, Statutes, and Cases

Most of Georgia's antebellum slaves were held in the central and coastal areas where the soil and climate made cotton or rice plantation agriculture most suitable. In the late antebellum years, almost half of Georgia's wealth was embodied in its enslaved people. Although some areas in Georgia were in decline because of overcultivation and soil exhaustion, new acreage was cultivated. In 1859, Georgia produced its first 700,000-bale cotton crop, trailing only Alabama, Mississippi, and Louisiana. With this increased cotton cultivation, Georgia's enslaved population grew from 33.5 percent in 1790 to 43.7 percent in 1860.[2]

Some Georgians in the late 1790s began to favor slave law reform, as confirmed by a September 16, 1797, editorial in the *Augusta Chronicle and Gazette of the State*, which Watson Jennison attributed to the paper's editor John E. Smith.[3] Smith reported, "A late enquiry into the treatment of slaves, brought to light instances of barbarity, abhorrent to human nature, and even a reproach to it. Words cannot describe them. But if they could, the humane could hardly be persuaded to believe." Smith urged Georgia's legislators to end slave importation into the state and to better protect Georgia's slaves "not merely as acts of mercy," but also as "acts of *justice* not only to the unhappy bond-men, but to themselves." These reforms, he argued, would deter slave disquiet and rebellion.[4]

This editorial must have caused some controversy. Smith wrote a follow-up on October 7, 1797, confirming that he was not opposed to slavery. He also argued in favor of discipline within families and in the relationship between masters and slaves, noting, "*Some must command; and some must obey*." He nevertheless cited five Jamaican legal reforms for Georgia's legislators to follow, including the law providing that "any person wantonly, or bloody mindedly killing a slave, shall suffer death."[5]

Georgia's May 30, 1798, constitution, which remained in effect until 1861, followed calling for slave homicide law reform, but it did not endorse Jamaica's 1788 law or the 1750 Georgia colonial law equating slave killing with common law homicide. Instead, it declared that those who "maliciously dismember" or kill a slave would suffer the same punishment as if they committed the offense against "a free white person, and on the like proof, except in the case of insurrection by such slave, and unless such death should happen by accident in giving such slave moderate correction."[6]

Georgia's December 2, 1799, act was consistent with this constitutional provision. It applied to slave killers the same substantive and procedural standards for murder and manslaughter that applied to those who killed free white people. The act nevertheless excused killings "in case of insurrection by such slave, and unless such death should happen by accident in giving such slave moderate correction."[7]

Georgia's 1816, 1817, and 1833 penal codes also legitimized slave homicides, stating, "Killing a slave in the act of revolt, or when the said slave forcibly resists a legal arrest, shall be Justifiable Homicide." But they added, "In all cases, the killing or maiming of a slave, or person of color, or Indian, in amity with the United States, shall be put upon the same footing of criminality as the killing or maiming of a white person."[8]

Although these codes appear to eliminate the moderate correction defense, it remained in Georgia's state constitution. Georgia's Supreme Court, in 1857, held that the 1833 code did not repeal the 1799 act. Howell Cobb's 1859 compilation of Georgia laws thus included the 1799 law.[9]

These Georgia criminal codes also defined as a misdemeanor, punished by a fine, imprisonment, or both, cruelty "by unnecessary and excessive whipping, by withholding proper food and sustenance, by requiring greater labor from such slave than he ... [is] able to perform, or by not affording proper clothing, whereby the health of such slave ... may be injured and impaired." An 1851 amendment applied this provision to overseers and also prohibited "beating, cutting or wounding, and unnecessarily biting or tearing with dogs." In 1860, the legislature deleted the requirement that the cruelty by masters and overseers injure or impair the slaves' health. These provisions thus legalized the usual punishments imposed by slave masters and employers. In contrast, they prohibited all beating, whipping, or wounding by others "without sufficient cause or provocation" by the enslaved victim.[10] Thomas Morris found evidence of only one Georgia master who was prosecuted for cruel punishment in a perjury case that was filed against the accuser.[11]

The Georgia legislators did not clearly state why they enacted these laws redefining the differing levels of fatal and nonfatal violence that slave owners, hirers, overseers, and others could inflict on slaves. Georgia did not have a state Supreme Court until 1846.[12]

Several Georgia slave masters were prosecuted for killing their own slaves, but there was no murder conviction until 1858. A December 1822 trial court decision, *State v. Abbot*,[13] was issued by Judge James M. Wayne after John Abbot Jr. was charged by a coroner's jury with the "felonious homicide" of Abbot's slave Ezekiel. The May 2, 1822, coroner's inquest found that, while in Effingham County, Abbot shot Ezekiel's left side. Abbot admitted this shooting to the physician who attended to Ezekiel, "narrating at length the causes which impelled him to the deed."[14]

Judge Wayne denied Abbot's application to be released on bail. He also denied Abbot's request for a presumption of innocence caused by the solicitor general's delay in prosecuting the case before the grand jury.[15]

The outcome of Abbot's case is not known, but he appears to have been a controversial person. He was born in 1799, and his father was the naturalist and artist John Abbot. Savannah records identified the junior Abbot as a merchant, slave trader, and attorney. He operated the John Abbot Jr. Company, which in 1808 defaulted on its taxes and was dissolved. He formed a business partnership with Burrel Lathrop in 1810, but that partnership was dissolved. He married Eliza Rawls in Savannah in April 1812 and the next year purchased forty-five acres of real estate, which he called "Three Mile." The property was mortgaged in 1816 to secure a thousand-dollar debt owed to James Jones of Screven County. John Junior defaulted on the mortgage, and his father apparently paid the debt in the penal sum of two thousand dollars. In 1817 the property was sold. John Senior, in 1819, was a witness in a suit in which his son was sued for debt. John Junior died on August 18, 1826, because of "liver complaint." The Savannah death records identify his occupation as "watchman."[16]

Ralph Betts Flanders cited three cases in which Georgia masters were tried for slave homicide and were found not guilty. Elijah Cotton, of Bibb County, in 1827 was indicted for manslaughter after using a large stick to beat to death his slave Ned. The jury found Cotton not guilty. John E. Bartlett, in 1849, was indicted for the murder of his slave Ellen by beating her "with a sharp, blunt weapon." According to the testimony at the October 1849 term trial held in Houston County, Bartlett fractured Ellen's skull and killed her. But a jury failed to convict Bartlett. And Solomon Haddock, also of Houston County, in 1853 was indicted for killing his slave Chaney. Haddock allegedly beat Chaney with a stick, tied a rope around her neck, and choked her to death. At a trial held during the April 1853 court term, the jury found that Haddock was not guilty, but Haddock's criminal career continued. Three years later he shot and killed William Knight, a white man.[17]

Michael Boylan also was accused of killing his slave Stepeny, but the outcome of his case is unknown. Boylan, who was described as "a German," lived near Savannah. He and Philip Martin were charged with murder after an examination before three magistrates.[18]

Three doctors testified that they examined Stepeny's body and found that "the beating inflicted was sufficient to cause death." According to several witnesses, Stepeny was a runaway who, on February 8, 1857, was arrested by Constable Jones. He took Stepeny to Boylan "who employed the officer to whip [Stepeny]." Jones then inflicted "some thirty lashes with a riding whip or a small cowhide." This whipping apparently did not satisfy Boylan. The witnesses "saw the negro tied up by the hands to a tree, and the prisoner Martin, [was] beating him with a heavy trace strap."

Robert Curry testified that he arrived at Boylan's place, witnessed the beating, and "remonstrated with Boylan against the inhumanity of the punishment, when the negro was released and fell to the ground, speechless and prostrate. Martin ordered him to rise, and dealt him several blows with a wagon whip," while Stepeny was "on the ground insensible." Martin then dragged Stepeny into the house where he died the next day.

Sergeant Wilson also testified that he was notified of the crime on the day Stepeny died. Upon arriving at Boylan's place, he found Stepeny's body lying on the floor. The body was "still warm, and a coffin [was] in readiness for his burial." Boylan and Martin then were arrested and charged with murder. After hearing this testimony, the magistrates "committed the prisoners to answer the charge of murder in the Superior Court."[19]

The *Savannah Republican* declared, "We are shocked to record such a crime in our midst, and trust the law will be rigidly enforced against the offender." Although the arrest and the preliminary hearing were widely reported in the press, no reports of the final resolution of Boylan's or Martin's prosecution could be found.[20]

Georgia's Supreme Court in the 1850s decided five reported slave homicide cases. In two of these cases the court reversed slave master convictions, and in the others the court affirmed two non-masters' manslaughter convictions and reversed another.

Two Georgia slave owners, Pierce Bailey and Green Martin, were indicted and tried for murdering one of their slaves. Bailey, a wealthy plantation owner in Warren County, filed two appeals with Georgia's Supreme Court after he was convicted of manslaughter. These appeals arose out of the charge that, in July 1852 in Taliaferro County, Bailey shot and killed one of his slaves. The facts of the crime are not recited in either of the two reported decisions.[21]

According to the 1850 census, Bailey was a fifty-year-old single planter whose real estate was worth thirty thousand dollars. His household included a twenty-two-year-old male, James Battle, who was listed as the manager. Bailey owned eighty slaves in Warren County and another three slaves in Taliaferro County.[22]

A Taliaferro County grand jury, during its August 1852 term, indicted Bailey for murder.[23] Bailey allegedly "fled from justice," prompting Governor Howell Cobb, on August 31, 1852, to authorize a two-hundred-dollar reward for Bailey's capture.[24]

Bailey was tried before Judge Thomas W. Thomas and a jury during the August 1856 Taliaferro County Superior Court term. The jury found Bailey guilty of voluntary manslaughter.[25]

Bailey filed an appeal to the Georgia Supreme Court, which during its November 1856 term affirmed the judgment, rejecting Bailey's argument that Judge Thomas should have applied an 1856 statute to the jury selection.[26] But during that same term the court also reversed the conviction, holding that Judge Thomas should have required "the questions mentioned in the bill of exceptions to be put to the jurors as requested by the accused."[27]

The case came on for trial again during the February 1858 term. Bailey withdrew his not guilty plea and argued that he could not be tried again on the murder charge because the first jury found him guilty only of manslaughter. The Supreme Court affirmed the trial judge's decision rejecting Bailey's argument.[28]

It does not appear that Bailey was tried again before he died in September 1863. According to the 1860 census, Bailey was living alone in Warren County and was sixty-three years old. His real estate was again valued at $30,000 and his personal estate was valued at $70,000.[29]

Bailey's September 7, 1861, will was challenged in *Cobb v. Battle*,[30] which Georgia's Supreme Court decided in 1866. The evidence in that case confirmed that Bailey was survived by one sister, he owned more than one plantation, and he was a moneylender. His estate's estimated value was between $150,000 and $200,000 before emancipation.[31]

Although not legally married, Bailey admitted to having a special relationship with his slave Adeline and that her child Tolbert (or Talbert) was his child. He asked his lawyer if he could free Adeline and Tolbert in his will. When his lawyer advised him that Georgia law prohibited this postmortem manumission, Bailey decided to leave his estate to his trusted nephew, Lawrence Battle. Bailey's last will directed Battle to confer special treatment in favor of Adeline and Tolbert.[32]

The Georgia Supreme Court sustained Bailey's will, in an opinion by Justice Iverson L. Harris. But it also invalidated the will's provision in favor of Adeline and Tolbert under Georgia's pre-emancipation laws.[33]

Georgia's Supreme Court also reversed Green Martin's murder conviction in *Martin v. State*.[34] Martin was indicted for murder at the March 1858 term of the Superior Court of Washington County, in Sandersville. Martin's victim was his slave Alfred, about twelve years old when he died after enduring a fatal afternoon of torture and abuse inflicted by Green Martin and his son Godfrey (sometimes spelled Godfry).

According to the 1850 census, Green Martin owned eleven slaves, was forty-eight years old, and was married to Lucy Martin who was fifty-three. Five of their children lived with them. Martin's real estate's value was reported at $1,300. Sometime after 1850 Mrs. Martin died.[35]

Godfrey apparently absconded before the trial. Green was tried alone before a jury and Judge William W. Holt. The trial witnesses included Alexander Orr, the coroner; Lucein Q. Taylor, a physician; three of Green's daughters, Catherine (twenty-one), Mary (nineteen), and Sarah (sixteen); and John A. Bedgood (fifteen), who was working for Green Martin on May 9, 1857, the day Alfred was killed.[36]

Dr. Taylor testified that, on May 11, 1857, he was called by Green Martin. Alfred's body was disinterred from a shallow grave on an "old field" on Thomas Wright's property, which was about a mile and a half from Green's property. Dr. Taylor "found the boy disfigured by bruises" that "were on his breast, sides, wrists, and ankles, and his face." He "borrowed a pocket-knife and cut into the boy's neck, and found a dislocation of the neck," which he opined caused Alfred's death. He called the bruises "severe, and on the side the skin was broken, produced by violence; they were caused by something hard; the appearance of the bruises around the wrists and ankles were caused by a rope." He also stated that a violent fall could have caused the dislocation: "a fall backwards from a chair has produced it; a jerk may produce it; choking without a jerk will not."[37]

Orr testified at the trial that, also on May 11, 1857, he held an inquest into Alfred's death after receiving information from four "gentlemen living in that neighborhood." These "gentlemen" included Thomas Wright.[38]

Martin's daughters and Bedgood testified that Green Martin and his son Godfrey began punishing Alfred at about noon on May 9, 1857. According to Catherine, Godfrey that year was controlling Green's field slaves. Alfred had been whipped the week before. On the day of his death, Green and Godfrey apparently thought Alfred had told Godfrey to kiss his backside. The abuse continued until Alfred was killed late in the afternoon. Green and Godfrey took turns beating Alfred, put a saddle on him and rode him like an animal, tied him with a rope, and poured water on him. Bedgood testified that he saw Green Martin riding on Alfred's back and choking Alfred while sitting on him. Sarah testified that while Alfred was on the ground, she saw Godfrey kick Alfred. She said that Alfred never got up after that kick.[39]

The jury, on March 14, 1858, convicted Green Martin of murder. His lawyer made a motion for a new trial, which Judge Holt denied.[40]

Green Martin then filed an appeal with Georgia's Supreme Court, and Joseph P. Lumpkin, one of the court's leaders, wrote the court's opinion.[41] The court reversed the conviction and ordered a new trial because one of the jurors, Rueben Osborn, allegedly admitted after the trial that the jurors considered in their deliberations their knowledge of an incident the year before in which Green Martin allegedly beat another slave, Peace, almost to death.[42]

Nevertheless, Lumpkin, like Thomas Ruffin, wrote at length about a case that he asserted was "rather peculiar in several respects." After describing the three fatal hours of punishment inflicted on Alfred, Lumpkin wrote that it was "not disputed" that the slave owner

> has the right to correct him for his misconduct. And the mode and measure of punishment must in the main, be left to the master. It must not be cruel and excessive. The manner of punishing slaves, is different with different persons. The *unusual* modes of punishing slaves resorted to by some owners, are not necessarily, nor always the most cruel or severe. It is frequently so in the *seeming* only. From the nature of the case there can not be any uniform rule prescribed upon the subject. It can hardly be supposed that the Martin's [sic] intended to kill the boy. Still if the circumstances show, that their treatment was such, as was likely to produce death, the law will infer malice and the offence may be adjudged murder.[43]

No new trial is reported, but the death of Green Martin, a widower, was recorded in Ware County Georgia in February 1860. The cause of death was inflammation.⁴⁴

Lumpkin's call for limits on the masters' right to kill their slaves is significant. He was a legislator, lawyer, legal educator, and longtime judge who advocated temperance and legal reforms. He even delivered an 1833 speech in Boston publicly criticizing slavery.⁴⁵

But Lumpkin later viewed slavery a positive good and a biblical imperative: "To inculcate care and industry upon the descendants of Ham, is to preach to the idle winds. To be the 'servants of servants' is the judicial curse pronounced upon their race." This principle was a "Divine decree" that was "unreversible." He declared that "[i]t will run on parallel with time itself. And heaven and earth shall sooner pass away, than one jot or tittle of it shall abate." According to Lumpkin, only "[u]nder the superior race and no where else, do [blacks] attain to the highest degree of civilization." God's "ways are higher than ours; and humble submission is our best wisdom, as well as our first duty!"⁴⁶

Lumpkin also advocated reforms that closed what he perceived to be unwarranted loopholes in Georgia's manumission laws.⁴⁷ Lumpkin argued, however, that masters should treat their slaves "with paternalistic kindness to provide moral uplift."⁴⁸ Lumpkin thus was devoted to slavery while supporting limits on the masters' rights to commit homicides of enslaved people, provided that the law legalized the masters' right to punish their slaves using methods that were not "cruel and excessive."⁴⁹

In contrast, the court affirmed the manslaughter convictions of non-slave owners Randal S. Jordan, in *Jordan v. State*,⁵⁰ and Newton Camp, in *Camp v. State*.⁵¹ A grand jury indicted Jordan for the July 23, 1853, murder of Mariah, a young enslaved girl owned by John H. Dawson. Jordan, the overseer on a plantation owned by Dawson and a Mr. Collier, was tried during the June 1857 term in Dougherty County before Judge A. A. Allen and a jury.⁵²

Allen T. Mallard, the state's main witness, was an overseer on another plantation. Mariah was a runaway who was brought to Mallard by another slave. He returned Mariah to Jordan at the Dawson and Collier plantation at about eleven in the morning of the killing. Jordan proceeded to beat Mariah to death with a heavy whip, which Mallard testified was "much heavier" than "the straps commonly used." The whipping continued for about an hour until Mariah died. Mallard estimated that Jordan hit Mariah with "between four hundred and a thousand" strokes and stated that "[t]he girl seemed to be suffering great pain."⁵³ A member of the inquest jury and a doctor also testified and described Mariah's wounds.⁵⁴

The jury found Jordan guilty of voluntary manslaughter and recommended the defendant "to the mercy of the Court." Judge Allen denied Jordan's motions in arrest of judgment and for a new trial. Jordan then filed an appeal with Georgia's Supreme Court, asserting several legal objections and challenging the jury's finding of guilt. The court, in an opinion by Justice Charles J. McDonald, rejected Allen's arguments. McDonald also questioned but affirmed the jury's decision to reduce the crime from murder to manslaughter, stating "we confess that it is difficult for us, under our construction of the law, to come to the same conclusion." Nevertheless, the court could not order a new trial.[55]

A Marion County grand jury indicted Newton Camp for manslaughter, alleging that, on June 12, 1857, he used a leather strap known as a carriage trace to beat to death Willis, a slave belonging to James M. Harvey. The case report does not include a summary of the evidence presented at trial, nor does it state whether Camp was an overseer. The jury found Camp "guilty of involuntary manslaughter, in the commission of a lawful act, which probably might produce such a consequence in an unlawful manner."[56]

Camp moved for arrest of judgment, and after the trial judge denied the motion, Camp filed an appeal. He argued that slave manslaughter was not a crime in Georgia and that slave killing was either murder or justifiable homicide.[57]

Justice McDonald wrote the court's opinion affirming Camp's conviction. He rejected Camp's manslaughter argument, relying on the Georgia Penal Code's provision stating "that the killing or maiming of a slave shall be put on the same footing of criminality as a killing or maiming of a white person."[58]

The court also sustained the jury's finding that the killing was involuntary manslaughter of the lowest degree, apparently because the jury found that Camp acted lawfully when he began correcting Willis. The Penal Code, for this grade of homicide, permitted the courts to impose any fine, term of imprisonment in the county jail, or both. The code imposed a penalty of between one and three years for the more serious crime of involuntary manslaughter in the commission of an unlawful act.[59]

Justice McDonald did not state in these decisions whether Georgia's code preempted the *Tackett* mitigation rule when slaves were homicide victims. But in 1854 the court, in *Jim v. State*,[60] applied the *Tackett* rule of unequal protection in an appeal of Jim, an enslaved man who was convicted of murdering his overseer. The court also went beyond the holding in *Tackett* and held that enslaved people could not be permitted to mitigate homicides from murder to manslaughter when reacting to the excessive violence of their masters and overseers. Slaves could not make judgments "as to the reasonableness or unreasonableness of the extent and degree" of the "patriarchal discipline which the master is permitted to exercise." This rule was required to discourage "insubordination, ... servile insurrection and bloodshed." Accordingly, "the homicide of his master, overseer, or employee ... by a slave, in resistance to an assault made upon him by that master, overseer, or employer, must, in all cases, be either justifiable homicide or murder."[61]

Three years after deciding Camp's appeal, the court reversed Thomas W. Cox's voluntary manslaughter conviction in *Cox v. State*.[62] This case illustrates the inherent tensions between slave owners and other whites, including overseers, who killed or abused slaves, as well as the difficult task prosecutors faced because of the rule prohibiting slave testimony.

A Polk County grand jury indicted Cox for murder, finding that, on January 11, 1858, Cox shot Humphrey, a slave owned by Abraham Jones. Jones, in late November or early December 1857, hired Cox as an overseer. Cox was tried in October 1860 before Judge Dennis F. Hammond and a jury.

At least one enslaved man named Claiborne was an eyewitness to the shooting, but, of course, he was not permitted to testify at the trial. Both the prosecuting and the defense lawyers therefore based their proofs on the testimony of eight white witnesses who arrived at the scene of the crime after the shooting or who heard admissions or other statements made by Cox and Humphrey.

Jones was one of the state's witnesses. Before the shooting, he and Cox disputed whether Humphrey should be whipped for allegedly putting a rock in a cotton basket. Jones, on the day of the shooting, "heard a pistol fire, and then heard some one hallooing; that on being told that Humphrey was killed, he went to him, and found him in a dying condition; that he was shot in the back of the head, and his brains were running out at the bullet hole." Jones also heard "some one hallooing in the swamp." Jones "went to the place and found Cox wringing his hands and crying." Cox asked Jones "if he was going to shoot him, to which witness replied, 'no, if you will do right'; Cox said he had done wrong, and begged witness not to shoot him." Jones asked Cox for his pistol, which Cox returned to Jones. Jones took Cox to the scene of the crime. Cox did not tell Jones that Humphrey resisted him, and if he had, Jones said he would not have believed it because "the negro had never resisted anybody." Humphrey died that day.[63]

Lucius Thompson testified that he lived about a mile from Jones and heard a shot while heading to Jones's land. Upon arriving at the crime scene, about two or three minutes later, Thompson saw that Humphrey was wounded. Cox told Thompson that "he went up to the negro, and the negro took hold of him and he shot him."

In contrast, Chapley Echols testified for the state about the more detailed and somewhat contradictory confession that Cox made to him an hour or an hour and a half after the shooting. Echols asked Cox why he shot Humphrey, to which Cox answered

> that he went up behind the negro, where he was chopping on the log, and took hold of him, and witness thinks that Cox said the negro dropped the axe and turned upon him, and took him by the throat, and threw him down over a log or brush, and that he then called Claiborne, another negro, to take hold of him, which Claiborne did, and that deceased then let go his hold on Cox and broke to run, and as he, Cox, rose from his position, he drew his pistol and fired at him; witness saw a singed place in Claiborne's hat that looked like the touch of a ball; Humphrey was shot in the back part of the head, rather on the left side, the ball ranging upward, as if it would have come out near the upper part of the forehead.[64]

Cox's lawyers asked Judge Hammond to instruct the jury based upon Cox's alleged statement to Thompson

> that if a master or overseer undertake to whip a slave belonging to such master, or under the control of such overseer, and the slave refuses to submit to the whipping, or resists the whipping, such refusal or resistance is an act of revolt, and if the master or overseer kill the slave in such act of revolt, the killing is justifiable homicide; and if you believe such to be the facts of this case, from the evidence, you must find the defendant not guilty, and if you have a reasonable doubt as to whether such are the facts of this case, still you must give the defendant the benefit of the doubt, and find him not guilty.

But Judge Hammond instead charged the jury based on the testimony of Echols:

> That if defendant went and laid hold on the negro man, Humphrey, for the purpose of chastising him, and said negro resisted, and shoved defendant down, and took defendant by the throat, and if said negro was taken off and ran, that said negro was not in revolt at the time when he ran, and if said defendant shot said negro at that time, he would be guilty of murder if he shot with a deliberate intention to take the negro's life. If he shot said negro at that time, under sudden heat of passion, he would be guilty of manslaughter.

After the jury returned a verdict of voluntary manslaughter, Cox's counsel moved for a new trial. The judge denied the motion and Cox filed an appeal, challenging the charge.[65]

Justice Richard F. Lyon and Chief Justice Lumpkin voted to reverse Cox's conviction. Lyon wrote the court's opinion. Justice Charles J. Jenkins dissented without an opinion. Lyon held that Judge Hammond's jury charge erred because it was based on one version of the testimony and thus was misleading to the jury. Lyon reasoned,

> The circumstances of the killing are ascertained entirely from the declarations of the defendant. The first reason given by the accused was made, in two or three minutes after the shooting, to the witness, Thompson. Cox then said, that "he went up to the negro, and the negro took hold of him, and he shot him." This declaration was a part of the *res gestæ*; was evidence for the prisoner, and was made at or near the time of the shooting, when the true inducement or necessity for shooting was impressed most strongly on his mind. From that impression of the mind he is supposed to have spoken and acted. It was the version on which the defence was put, and was the evidence of the defendant.
>
> Now, if the prisoner shot while the negro had hold of him, or upon the idea that it was necessary to do so in his defence, he is not guilty of a crime, and ought not to be convicted of one. The Court, by the charge made in effect, excluded this view; he rejects this evidence as furnishing a basis on which the jury should act in their deliberations, and instead, takes the version or declaration of the prisoner as testified to by the witness, Chapley Echols, which was put in evidence by the prosecution. Although the Court does not, in so many words, direct the jury that this first declaration was not evidence, and should not be considered by them, yet by not including it in his hypothesis, he not only left them at liberty to disregard it altogether as he had done, but his failure to do so was well calculated to impress the jury with the idea that it was worthless as evidence. For this reason we think the charge had a tendency to mislead the jury, and was therefore erroneous. In so holding, however, we do not hold that it is the duty of the Court, in his charge to the jury, to sum up or state the facts in proof by hypothesis or otherwise, but if he undertakes to do so, he must include all that might be important to the defense.[66]

The conflicting social and economic interests of slave masters and other whites are further illustrated by the cases in which owners sued those who killed or injured their slaves to recover monetary damages to compensate the owners for their property losses. The Georgia Supreme Court facilitated these suits with its 1851 decision in *Neal v. Farmer*.[67] William Neal admitted that he killed Nancy Farmer's slave. After a jury awarded Farmer $825 in damages, Neal filed an appeal, alleging that he could not be held liable for damages because he had not been prosecuted for homicide. The Supreme Court's opinion by Justice Eugenius A. Nisbet affirmed the judgment. Following the rule in the majority of southern states, Nisbet held that slave killing was not a common law crime in Georgia, and thus did not have to be prosecuted before a slave owner could recover his or her damages in a suit against a slave killer.[68]

The Tennessee Statutes and Cases

Similarly in Tennessee, no slave master was executed for slave murder, and none was convicted for the murder or manslaughter of one of his or her slaves. The territory that became the state of Tennessee was a part of North Carolina until 1790, when this land was ceded to the United States. North Carolina's law was applied in Tennessee until it was replaced by local law. The April 2, 1790, act of cession, among other things, stated "that no regulation made or to be made by Congress shall tend to emancipate slaves."[69]

Tennessee entered the union in 1796. Its first state constitution did not mention slavery, except regarding taxation.[70]

Tennessee's enslaved population grew steadily from about 9 percent of the total population in 1790 to 25 percent in 1860. Enslaved people's net entries exceeded exits in each decade until the 1850s. By 1860, Tennessee's enslaved population ranked eighth among the fifteen slaveholding states and eleventh in the enslaved population's percentage of the state's total population.[71]

The state's economy and agriculture were diverse. Crops included cotton, tobacco, and corn. Cotton production increased from 2,500 bales in 1801 to 50,000 in 1820, 194,532 in 1850, and 296,464 in 1860. Tobacco and corn production also increased between 1840 and 1860.[72]

"In some ways, Tennessee is three states rather than one. Throughout most of its history, the state has been divided into three distinct 'grand divisions,' East, Middle, and West Tennessee."[73] Tennessee's enslaved population also was not uniformly distributed. Middle Tennessee had the largest number of slaves, but enslaved people were more highly concentrated in the state's western region as a percentage of the total population. The sizes of individual slaveholdings also were the largest in West Tennessee. Accordingly, "slavery was most important in West Tennessee and least important in East Tennessee."[74]

In the early years of statehood, many eastern Tennesseans openly supported either immediate or gradual emancipation or colonization of the state's slaves to Africa. As late as 1834, these slavery opponents tried to force a debate at a constitutional convention on the merits of thirty petitions calling for gradual emancipation of the state's slaves. A motion by Mathew Stephenson to create a committee to study the issue was tabled. Instead, the convention formed a committee of three delegates, which included as chair John A. McKinney, "a distinguished lawyer" and native of Ireland, to explain why the convention rejected emancipation. The antislavery delegates criticized the committee's June 19, 1834, report, calling it a "kind of apology for slavery."[75]

The convention, in response, authorized the committee to prepare a second report further justifying its conclusions. The convention ultimately approved a provision confirming the emancipation proposals' defeat and stating that "the General Assembly shall have no power to pass laws for the emancipation of slaves without the consent of their owner or owners."[76]

Support for even gradual emancipation or colonization later eroded in East Tennessee. In the decade before the Civil War, East Tennessee was becoming better integrated into the South's slave economy, and the region's enslaved population increased by 21 percent.[77]

North Carolina's 1774 slave homicide law applied in Tennessee until 1799, when the legislature adopted an act that was similar to North Carolina's 1791 act. Tennessee's version provided that any person who willfully or maliciously killed "any negro or mulatto slave, on due conviction thereof ... shall be deemed guilty of murder, as if such person so killed had been a free man, and shall suffer death without benefit of clergy." This act also decriminalized the killing of any slave who was outlawed by an act of the legislature, "any slave in the act of resistance to his lawful owner or master, or any slave dying under moderate correction."[78] The Tennessee legislature in 1799 also adopted laws including among the state's capital crimes the theft of slaves and of horses.[79]

Tennessee's 1799 slave homicide law remained in effect until 1858, when the legislators adopted a code that continued to legitimize homicides of slaves who were killed in the act of resisting their masters or slaves who died as a result of "moderate correction." The code also permitted the killing of a runaway slave who was the "ringleader or chief instigator of any plot to rebel, or to murder any white person ... if it be not practicable otherwise to arrest and secure him."[80]

Moreover, an 1813 act, by implication, legitimized nonfatal violence by masters against their slaves. It provided that any person who "wantonly, and without sufficient cause" beats or abuses a slave "of another person" was subject to indictment "under the same rules, and subject to the same pains and penalties as for the commission of similar offenses on the body of any white person."[81] The Tennessee Supreme Court also applied to enslaved victims the 1829 criminal code's provision prohibiting malicious dismemberment, including castration.[82]

Although there are no officially reported cases in which Tennessee masters were successfully prosecuted for murdering their slaves, evidence suggests that some Tennessee slave masters may have gotten away with slave murders. Ezekiel Birdseye, a Connecticut native who lived in several southern states including Tennessee and who opposed slavery, wrote of two slave murders in

166 CHAPTER NINE

Greene County, in East Tennessee, which Birdseye believed were committed by Daniel Allen.[83]

Allen owned a thirteen-hundred-acre farm, a roller grain mill, and an ore bank in Greene County and was a moneylender who held promissory notes. He also owned many slaves. Birdseye reported on Allen's crimes in one of his many letters to Gerrit Smith, a wealthy New York financier who opposed slavery. Birdseye wrote to Smith describing his observations of slavery in the South.[84]

According to Birdseye's September 24, 1842, letter, one of Allen's slaves "visited his wife some miles distant," and "came in the morning later than usual." Allen took this offender "into his cellar" and "made his slaves hold him or assist in tying him." Allen then "emasculated" his victim, who "died soon after" and was "thrown into the river Nolichucky." This slave's body floated down the river and was found lodged in a fish trap in the Nolichucky River. The slave's "wounds were apparent, and the report which went out from [Allen's] slaves [is] not doubted." But Birdseye relied on evidence an enslaved witness to the alleged crime told to his enslaved son Jeremiah, who then told his owner J. Huff, who later told Birdseye of the crime. The enslaved witnesses, of course, could not testify about the alleged killing.

Huff also told Birdseye that, the summer before, Allen killed another one of his slaves. This time Allen allegedly committed the homicide with a pitchfork. Birdseye stated that these facts were "well known" in East Tennessee, but no action was taken against Allen. According to Birdseye, "no man doubts" the reports of Allen's acts, "but there is no legal proof as a slave cannot testify against a white man and none but slaves saw him commit the murders." Birdseye thus concluded that, even in East Tennessee, "[t]he law does not restrain a despot in the treatment of his slaves unless he kills them [and] then slaves are not admitted to testify against him, so that the protection that the law affords is very little."[85]

Arthur Howington's study of the antebellum criminal court records in nineteen Tennessee counties tends to support Birdseye's views. Howington found fifty-four felony prosecutions against forty-seven whites for killing or physically abusing slaves. Thirty-three of these cases were slave homicides. "Only three of the cases involved owners of the slave victims. All three were murder cases in which the owner was indicted for whipping or beating his slave to death. None of the owners accused of murdering their slaves ever came to trial. In each case, the cause eventually was 'stricken' because the defendant 'was not to be found.'"[86]

For example, Ellen Bolton was accused of the September 18, 1855, murder of Silvie, a slave owned by Ellen's husband James. Williamson County coroner Joel Nichol held an inquest that found Silvie's body "was terribly mutilated, besides having her neck dislocated." Ellen reportedly confessed to the killing, "but says it was in self defense." Two justices of the peace conducted a preliminary examination. Ellen was indicted for second degree murder and she was released on bail of a thousand dollars. According to press reports, Ellen killed Silvie because Ellen was "exasperated by jealousy." Representative William Ewing later stated, on the Tennessee General Assembly floor, that Ellen beat her victim with a shovel, hung her, and scalded her body with boiling water. He also asserted that after the justices of the peace released Bolton on a "nominal bail" she never appeared for trial.[87]

Three years later, Hugh C. Hurst was indicted in Bedford County after a coroner's inquest exhumed the body of his slave Almira. Hurst also apparently avoided a trial.[88]

Nevertheless, whites who killed slaves belonging to others were successfully prosecuted in Tennessee. Howington cited several cases of non-master homicide defendants who, in the 1820s, were convicted of manslaughter. Another slave killer, Benjamin Rowe, in 1849, allegedly "shot a negro through the back of the head and instantly killed him . . . without the least provocation." These killings may have implicated greater concerns about slave property values and social order in the minds of the slave-owning community, as evidenced by the newspaper report that Rowe's neighbors were "so exasperated . . . at the unprovoked murder, that they erected a gallows and hung a rope to it for the purpose of hanging the murderer." The lynching was prevented, however, and Rowe was tried before the Shelby County Circuit Court. He was convicted of second degree murder and was sentenced to a ten-year prison term. Tennessee's Supreme Court affirmed Rowe's conviction.[89]

Rowe's case illustrates how interclass tensions may have favored the prosecution of whites such as Rowe who wantonly killed slaves belonging to others. These concerns also are illustrated by the May 16, 1858, conviction of William Hagar for the killing of Isaac, a slave owned by John J. Allen. Isaac was at a corn husking held in the fall of 1857 on the property of W. E. Jones. Hagar stabbed Isaac to death without any provocation. Hagar was sentenced to a three-year prison term. Allen later sued Jones for damages, and the Tennessee Supreme Court reversed a $1,050 judgment that a jury awarded to Allen.[90]

Tennessee's Supreme Court decided only one reported slave homicide case—*Fields v. State*.[91] William Fields was one of the defendants identified by

Howington among those convicted of the manslaughter of a slave belonging to another person. Fields was indicted in Maury County, which is in Middle Tennessee, for the murder of Peter, a slave owned by David Jefferies. The jury found Fields not guilty of murder but guilty of manslaughter. The official report of the case does not describe the details of the crime. In addition to being burned on the hand, Fields was sentenced to a thirty-day prison term, and he was ordered to pay the costs of the prosecution.[92]

Fields filed an appeal with the Tennessee Supreme Court contending that the 1799 act did not make slave manslaughter a crime. The court in 1829 rejected this argument and affirmed the conviction. Judges Robert Whyte and Jacob Peck each wrote opinions. Judge John Catron concurred.[93]

According to Peck's opinion, Fields's lawyer cited "2 Haywood Rep.; 1 Taylor Rep.; act of 1799" to support the argument that the manslaughter of a slave was not a crime. The first citation was to Judge Haywood's North Carolina decision in *State v. Piver*, holding that the similarly worded 1791 North Carolina statute legitimized slave manslaughter. The second reference was to *State v. Boon*, in which the North Carolina Conference Court found that the North Carolina statute was too vague to be enforced.[94]

Judges Whyte and Peck rejected these North Carolina decisions and adopted the reasoning of the North Carolina judges who believed that enslaved people were entitled to the protection of the common law of crimes. Judge Whyte discussed in detail the legislation on slave murder in North Carolina and Tennessee. He ruled by analogy to the evidence that, in the past, the common law in England protected the lives of villains even against killings by their lords.[95]

Judge Peck also rejected the notion that masters were free to kill their slaves under the common law, a view that he attributed to "a jurist," probably referring to North Carolina Judge Hall's opinions first expressed in *State v. Boon*. Instead, Peck relied on the common law "suited to Christian communities." Guided by "[t]he four gospels upon the clerk's table," Peck found that "[l]aw, reason, Christianity and common humanity, all point out one way."[96]

Judges Whyte, Peck, and Catron were slave owners who may have expressed their sincere concerns about the need to protect the lives of enslaved people from homicide, at least from people like Fields who would kill slaves belonging to others. I have not found a Tennessee case deciding whether the *Tackett* mitigation doctrine applied to whites who were accused of slave homicide. But Tennessee's Supreme Court, in opinions by Justices William Turley and Nathan Green, applied the *Tackett/Jarrott* mitigation doctrine in cases in which slaves were convicted of manslaughter of masters or strangers who wantonly attacked slaves or who went too far while correcting insolent slaves.[97]

Peck, moreover, was unique among southern antebellum judges because he publically expressed his opposition to slavery and became a friend of the abolitionist Ezekiel Birdseye. Peck served on Tennessee's Supreme Court until 1834, when a new court was convened under the state's 1835 constitution. Peck and Birdseye later worked together in unsuccessful efforts to acquire land and establish a free labor mineral extraction colony in East Tennessee. Their goal was to demonstrate free labor's superiority over slavery, while making a profit for themselves and potential investors, like Gerrit Smith.[98]

These slave homicide prosecutions also illustrate how the statutes and case law decisions that made some slave killings crimes protected the interests of both individual slave owners and the slave-owning class as a whole in preventing wanton white violence directed at slaves by hirers, overseers, and strangers. The conflict between masters and overseers is illustrated by the press reports of a June 1834 trial in the Davison County Circuit Court, which was "of more than usual interest to the public." A slave owner named Meeks sued his overseer named Philips for damages after Philips beat one of Meeks's slaves to death after the slave "had disobeyed Philips's orders in going away one night without permission." The jury found for Meeks, and there is no evidence of a criminal prosecution.[99]

Tennessee's Supreme Court also expressed concerns about white third-party violence directed against slaves while ruling in favor of slave owners who filed damage suits when their slaves were the victims of third-party violence. The Court, in *James v. Carper*,[100] in 1857 ruled in favor of Jane G. James, who filed a tort action of trespass *vi et armis* in the Hardeman County Circuit Court against Sampson Carper. The case was tried during the February 1857 term before Judge Humphreys.

James alleged that she hired her slave Bill to a man identified only as Champ. He was "the keeper of a public-house in the town of Bolivar." Champ hired Bill "for a few days during the June term of the circuit court, to assist as a servant in the house, at 75 cents per day." Carper was a guest at the public house. When Carper went to bed he "placed his pocket book, containing about $120, under the head of his bed, and in the morning forgot to remove it. On missing the pocket book-from his pocket, [Carper] mentioned the matter to Champ."

Champ "immediately enquired of the slave Bill—who made up the bed that morning—for the pocket-book." Bill "replied that he put it back where he found it, under the head of the bed." Champ went up to the room, where he found the pocket book with no money. "Without further enquiry, Champ immediately ordered" Bill to go to the stable. Champ then "stripped the slave, 'and,' in the language of the bill of exceptions, 'bucked him over a wheelbarrow';

took out his knife, and threatened to castrate the slave if he did not give up the money, the slave earnestly declaring his innocence of the charge. Champ then took a martingale and inflicted some twelve or fifteen blows on the slave, when he was called to the house." Champ then left the stable. He told Carper to "whip the God damned negro's guts out, unless he gave up the money." Carper tied Bill "up to a stall, and continued to beat him with the martingale, the slave all the time protesting his innocence. Champ then took the slave and returned him to the plaintiff."

Bill did not confess, apparently because he "was entirely innocent." Immediately after the beating, "it was ascertained that a vagrant white man about the house had committed the theft." This white man was arrested and surrendered almost all of the stolen the money, was convicted of the theft, and was sent to the penitentiary.

A physician was called and testified that Bill's "shoulders and back were bruised and wounded, that the skin was broken in several places, and that some of the injuries had the appearance of having been done with the ring of a martingale, and his shirt was stained with blood." Bill also "complained of his kidneys being affected, and also of an injury in his head."

Judge Humphreys instructed the jury that a slave's owner "had the right to inflict chastisement on him, and that the law had made no provision to determine whether it was right or wrong, nor held the owner amenable for inflicting chastisement on his slave, except that the master had not the right to take away life or limb, or inflict great or unnecessary torture." Slave hirers during the hiring term were "substituted to the rights of the owner, and [they had] the same right to punish or chastise the slave that the master would." Therefore, "if the chastisement inflicted on the slave was by the special direction of Champ, and no other or greater chastisement was inflicted by [Carper] than Champ directed, then the jury should find for [Carper]." The jury's verdict was for Carper and James appealed.[101]

Tennessee's Supreme Court reversed the judgment. Justice Robert J. McKinney's opinion did not address the trial judge's discussion of "the extent of the owner's right to inflict punishment on his slave," because this issue did not "properly" arise in the case. Instead, McKinney held that a slave hirer may not "take the law into his own hands, and avenge the crime committed by the slave without appeal to the law." He also noted that "[o]ne of the great dangers" to slave owners was "the recklessness and wanton disregard, on the part of hirers, of the safety of the slave and the interests of the owners." Thus "[t]he interests of the owner, sound policy, and humanity alike forbid that the hirer of a slave should be clothed with any such power; and if the hirer is possessed of no such authority, of course he can communicate none to a third person."[102]

Indeed, McKinney held it was a master's duty to "protect the person of his slave, and, in a lawful mode, seek redress for injuries done to him." A rule denying James her right to recover her damages would "ignore the plainest principles of reason and of right," and "would be justly esteemed a reproach to humanity in any condition of civil society above the level of barbarism."[103]

Daniel Flanigan argued that the *James* decision "demonstrated how slavery could warp the values of the slaveholders. Civil suits to recompense masters for the value of the labor or lives of their slaves did not reduce but instead encouraged 'barbarism.'" Indeed, McKinney applied the common law rule holding a hirer or bailee of a chattel, such as a horse, liable for the owner's damages caused by the intentional misuse of the chattel.[104]

The court expressed similar concerns about social order and slave humanity in *Kirkwood v. Miller*,[105] while affirming George Miller's eight-hundred-dollar judgment against Kirkwood, Denning, and Osborn, who captured, confined, and killed one of Miller's slaves.[106] Justice Robert Caruthers, writing for the court, found "no justifiable cause" for the defendants' actions because the slave "had not misbehaved himself in any way, had done no wrong, threatened none, and was entirely submissive and docile." Caruthers rejected the defendants' contention that their alleged belief that the slave was engaged in a suspected insurrection justified the killing:

> The wild panic, and vague, undefined apprehensions about a "rising or insurrection of the slaves," at that time, cannot be allowed to save parties from liability for the destruction of their neighbor's property. To justify this, they must stand upon facts, and not rumors and groundless alarms. This species of property, above all others, must be protected by the law from *wanton* abuse. All proper principle, as well as the general interest of slaveholders, unite in establishing the necessity for the most stringent laws on this subject. Humanity, as well as the general interest, demand the enforcement of these laws.
>
> Obedience and strict subordination, are indispensable on the part of slaves; and so far as it has been thought necessary, for these ends, power has been given to magistrates, and, in particular cases, to individuals, other than the owner. But all this is, as it should be, well defined and limited.
>
> The Legislature has been very careful in guarding slaves against the cruelty and violence of those having no interest in or authority over them. They are property: but have souls and feelings, and claims upon humanity. Those who take it upon

themselves, in these periods of groundless panic, to slay and destroy, without the sanction of law, must do so at their peril. Every description of mob-law, and reckless invasion of the rights of others, should be visited with the highest penalties. If this lawless spirit is tolerated, or allowed to display itself with impunity, no man would be safe, in his person or property, in any community. Almost any other evil would be preferable to this. The law is, in general, sufficient for the redress of all wrongs, public and private. But, if it should fall short, in particular instances, the evil had far better be endured than to throw off its restraints, and permit men to take vengeance into their own hands.[107]

Tennessee's Supreme Court, in 1858, also held that owners could recover punitive damages from those who intentionally killed the owners' slaves. But Justice Caruthers based this ruling on an 1817 New York decision affirming a jury's punitive damage award against a defendant who beat to death the plaintiff's horse.[108]

In these cases, then, the courts permitted owners to obtain monetary judgments against slave killers. Although McKinney and Caruthers both referred to slave humanity, they were enforcing the owners' rights to collect their damages for injuries to the owners' economic interests, thus obscuring the identity of the true victims of these killings.[109]

Conclusion

The Georgia and Tennessee legislatures adopted slave homicide reform statutes that were consistent with North Carolina's law. But no slave masters were executed for slave murder in these states. The courts did, however, permit masters to sue and recover damages from others who killed their slaves without good reasons. Non-masters also were successfully prosecuted for homicides in both states. As in Virginia and North Carolina, the reasons for these reforms are not clear, but South Carolina's long reluctance to join the reform trend provides some clues.

CHAPTER 10

South Carolina Joins the Homicide Law Reform Trend

South Carolina reformed its slave homicide laws almost thirty years after its North Carolina neighbor. This legal inertia was rooted in the state's unique social, political, and economic history, which caused its legislators to have heightened concerns about slave control. South Carolina had the highest enslaved population percentage in the United States. In 1790 and in 1800 this population was 43 percent and 42 percent, respectively, of the total. It grew to 47 percent in 1810, to 51 percent in 1820, and to 57 percent in both 1850 and 1860. In comparison, Virginia's total enslaved population fell to 30 percent by 1860.[1]

Furthermore, by the American Revolution, enslaved blacks were 80 percent of the state's low country population, a percentage that was similar to Britain's Atlantic island sugar colonies.[2] South Carolina and Georgia in 1790 also had the largest average of number of slaves, at 12.1 per slaveholding household. By 1850, this average increased to 15 in South Carolina, while it fell to 9.9 in Georgia. South Carolina's percentage of slaveholding families also grew during this period, from 34.2 percent in 1790 to 48.4 percent in 1850.[3] Although the state's net slave exits outnumbered entries in each decade after 1820, the state's planters remained committed to slave labor while their cash crops shifted in the early nineteenth century from tobacco and rice to cotton.[4]

South Carolina's low country legislators dominated both the state's politics and its legislature until the early nineteenth century. By the 1750s, settlers migrated into the colony's middle region and in effect moved the low country plantation model west. In 1820, 54 percent of the middle districts' population was black. The planter interests in the low country and the midcountry dominated South Carolina's legislature after the state's 1808 constitutional convention; "the Low Country with its unparalleled concentration of wealth retained a disproportionate grip on the levers of state."[5]

The Calls for Reform and the Failed Reform Efforts

After repeated revivals, the legislature in 1783 made the 1740 slave law permanent. This was later confirmed by the state's 1790 constitution, which stated that all laws would remain in effect until they were amended or repealed by the legislature.[6]

Many South Carolinians continued to believe that the 1740 slave code struck the right balance of the relevant interests when it provided that even willful slave murderers should be punished with fines. Some nevertheless favored slave homicide law reform, as illustrated by the 1791 report of the case *State v. Gee*.[7]

Gee, who is identified only by his last name, was convicted at trial, "after the clearest evidence for the prosecution," of the willful murder of "a negro boy named Sawney, the property of Abraham Cohen, by shooting with a gun loaded with shot." Gee failed to pay his seven-hundred-pound fine. The court therefore ordered that Gee serve a seven-year term of hard labor.[8]

Gee's lawyers asked the Court of Common Pleas and General Sessions to mitigate the sentence under the state's insolvent debtor's act. Judge Elihu Hall Bay's opinion rejected that claim based in part on the argument of the prosecutors Pinckney and Ford, who noted that the court sentenced Gee to prison to punish him "for the atrocity of the offence, which had deserved death." They added "[t]hat the frequency of the offence was owing, in a great measure, to the nature of the punishment, which was only a pecuniary fine, where the party was able to pay."[9]

Indeed, the court decided another slave homicide case during its May 1791 term. A defendant identified only as Welch, the prior September, had been indicted for murdering a slave owned by a Mr. Radcliffe. Welch "had taken the negro on some pretext or other, and afterwards carried him on board of a schooner he then commanded; where, either in attempting to tie him, or secure him from going off, he threw a lead-line round the negro's neck, and strangled him." Welch's lawyer Pinckney attempted to invoke the 1740 slave code provision permitting slave owners and others in control of slaves to exculpate themselves on their own oaths, if no other white person witnessed the killing. The court denied this privilege to killers like Welch, "who have not immediately the direction of [their victims]." Welch was found guilty of manslaughter, was sentenced to pay a fifty-pound fine, and was to "stand committed 'till paid."[10]

The slave homicide law reform debate continued, as illustrated by John Slater's 1806 prosecution. Slater, like Welch, was a boat captain. He became angry at a slave known as Abe, who was working on a Charleston dock. While "a few yards" from the Charleston Harbor shore, Slater had Abe's hands and feet bound and ordered another slave to chop off Abe's head with an ax and throw Abe's body parts into the harbor "unblushingly in the face of open day."[11]

A jury found Slater guilty of willfully killing Abe. Judge Samuel Wilds in February 1806 sentenced Slater under the 1740 law. His eloquent sentencing memorandum, which was published throughout the nation, stated, "From the peculiar situation of this country, our fathers felt themselves justified in subjecting to a very slight punishment, him who murders a slave." He noted that a local grand jury "deeply impressed with [Slater's] daring outrage, against the laws both of God and man, have made a very strong expression of their feelings on the subject to the legislature; and from the wisdom and justice of that body, the friends of humanity may confidently hope to see this blackest in the catalogue of human crimes, pursued by appropriate punishment." Wilds also declared, "I never felt more forcibly the want of power to make respected the laws of my country, whose minister I am."[12] Although there is no record of Slater's fine, Wilds likely imposed the maximum.[13] The local press reported on Slater's death the next year in Nassau.[14]

The *Charleston Currier* published a letter in January 1806 calling the maximum fine for slave killing an insufficient penalty for Slater's crime.[15] A June 1806 letter in the *Charleston Times* also asserted that blacks were frequent homicide victims while the penalty for killing slaves was less than for stealing slaves.[16]

And on February 3, 1806, a Kershaw District justice of the peace ordered the arrest of Samuel Nettles for "burning a Negro man" with straw that was set on fire. That November, it was alleged before a grand jury in the Kershaw District Court of General Sessions that Nettles, on February 2, 1806, applied this burning straw to "several parts of the head, body, and limbs" of his male slave, whose name is not mentioned. The indictment charging Nettles with a common law assault and a violation of the anticruelty statute is marked "No Bill" and is signed by the foreman Thomas Gardner.[17] When a grand jury returns an indictment signed "no bill" by the foreman "the party is discharged without further answer. But a fresh bill may afterwards be preferred by a subsequent Grand Jury." There is no evidence of a further prosecution.[18]

Also in November 1806, Theodore Gaillard proposed a bill in the General Assembly increasing the penalty for slave killing. The General Assembly appointed a committee to recommend changes to the criminal code. The committee called for increased punishment for "the crime of manslaughter and murdering a slave." A bill accompanying this report was introduced in November 1807, but it was not adopted.[19]

Three Kershaw District slave homicide prosecutions followed in 1808 and 1809—two alleging killings by third parties and one by a master and another person. These cases illustrate the conflicting interests between slave owners and other whites such as hirers, overseers, patrollers, and strangers, which may have convinced some South Carolinians to favor slave homicide reform.[20]

In one of these cases John Kershaw, a lawyer who over his long career served as a judge, mayor, state legislator, and congressman, signed an April 1, 1808, statement alleging that his overseer, Davis Cooper, contrary to Kershaw's "express and repeated orders," on February 7, 1808, cruelly beat a slave named Will, "who was not under [Cooper's] management." Will was owned by John's sister Mary Kershaw. John alleged that Will died of his wounds on March 24, 1808, after being given "every medical aid." He accused Cooper of seeking "occasion to create a difference" with Will "in order that he might have a plea for inflicting so severe and fatal a punishment." The grand jurors' April 1808 indictment is signed as a "True Bill" by foreman John Chestnut, but it also is signed "Not Guilty," apparently by the trial jury foreman.[21]

Possibly in response to this case, the Kershaw grand jury issued a November 14, 1808, presentment. It complained that the state's laws were "entirely inadequate to prevent the too prevailing crime of murdering negroes whereby our land is becoming stained with Blood and the pages of our Records crowded with instances of unexpiated murder."[22]

Years again passed with no homicide law reform. Governor John Drayton issued a June 4, 1810, proclamation offering a two-hundred-dollar reward for the capture of an unknown person who in late April or early May of that year "wantonly and cruelly murdered" Abel, a slave of Dennis Carpenter of the Edgefield District.[23] Later that year, Charleston City Coroner James Browne held a November 8, 1810, inquest into the death of a "Negro Man, belonging to John Ashe, esq." The victim "was inhumanly dragged on shore from a wood boat lying at Prioleau's warf, by a rope tied round his neck, which produced a dislocation of the part, and caused instant death." The coroner's jury found that David Mathews, the "patroon of said boat," committed "brutal and inhuman murder."[24]

Dr. Philip Moser was a South Carolina legislator who in 1810 took up the slave homicide reform cause. Called "a great humanitarian" who successfully advocated laws establishing public schools, Moser also sponsored an antiduel-ing law, which was adopted in 1812. He introduced bills in 1810 and 1812 that would have established the death penalty for the willful murderer of any free or enslaved blacks. These homicide reform bills failed.[25]

Grand jury presentments calling for slave homicide reform continued after Moser's unsuccessful reform effort. An 1816 Charleston grand jury denounced as a "serious evil the many instances of Negro Homicide" committed in the city "for many years." Masters exercised "unlimited control" over their slaves and "in the indulgence of malignant and cruel passions in the barbarous treatment of slaves," used "them worse than beasts of burden, . . . thereby bringing on the community, the state and the city the contumely and opprobrium of the civilized world."[26] A Darlington District 1816 trial jury even recommended mercy for a convicted slave thief because he faced the death penalty and slave killers did not. The court imposed the death sentence on the defendant.[27] A Kershaw grand jury, on April 14, 1818, complained about the "inadequacy of the punishment attached to the crime, in preventing persons of malignant disposition from murdering slaves." A Fairfield District grand jury, on November 19, 1818, also referred to "the great evil" of "many instances of murder and cruel treatment of slaves in this District and other parts of the State." And a November 1819 Kershaw grand jury found that slave owners suffered from the "fast increasing" evil of "slaves wantonly ambushed and crippled by loose and licentious men who very often do not profess sufficient property from which compensation can be obtained."[28]

Laura Edwards discussed two more slave homicide prosecutions in the Kershaw District during this period. John Havis, a farmer, was charged with killing his slave Elsey "based on the complaint of two free white men and evidence that Havis's 'small negro boy' gave at the inquest." A grand jury indicted Havis in November 1819 for this killing, which allegedly occurred on October 14, 1819, in Camden. Havis was found guilty of willful murder, according to the jury foreman's note on the indictment, but Havis's fine was not recorded. The 1810 Kershaw census data reported that Havis's household included fourteen slaves, and in 1815 Havis was a Kershaw District justice of the peace. But in 1817 he was indicted for a November 23, 1816, assault of Johannes Arrents. And the 1820 census reported that Havis, after killing one of his slaves, owned nine slaves, while eight people in his household were engaged in agriculture.[29]

Also in 1820, Ephraim Strafford, Joiner Middleton, and Douglas Minton were indicted for killing Sam Sinclair, who was John Chestnut's slave. The defendants allegedly were in a slave patrol that found Sinclair out at night, and they beat him to death. Two were convicted at a trial in the General Sessions Court, but Edwards states that the records do not reflect the degree of the homicide convictions.[30]

There is evidence that slave homicide reform was gaining support among the state's newspapers and its elected officials. The *Southern Patriot* on December 1, 1819, published a letter to the editor advocating the death penalty for white persons who murdered slaves.[31] Governor John Geddes's November 27, 1820, final annual message to the legislature included a recommendation for slave homicide reform. Geddes, a lawyer who was governor from 1818 to 1820, asserted "again" that the state's slave homicide law was "so very inadequate to the demands of justice, that the State has suffered in its reputation for humanity." He argued that "[t]he rules of reason, justice and religion, require that the punishment for wilful and deliberate murder, should be the same in all cases"; and that "a slave being deprived of his natural right of self-defense against a white man, the killing of him by the latter receives from the circumstances additional aggravation, and demands at least equal punishment." If because of "the situation of our country" there was insufficient support for this proposal, Geddes asked the legislature to consider the "annexing of other severe penalties to the commission of this barbarous deed." Geddes also asked the legislators to abolish the magistrates and freeholder courts and grant slaves the rights to jury trials and appeal, "to ensure the protection of the innocent and the conviction of the guilty."[32]

The legislature did not in 1820 adopt these reform laws. It instead enacted two of Geddes's other proposals that sought to limit the state's free black population by prohibiting free black immigration into the state and requiring that masters freeing their slaves obtain acts of the legislature permitting the manumissions.[33]

South Carolina's newspapers continued to report on slave homicides. The *Charleston Times* published a February 20, 1821, letter signed by "A Preacher," which discussed the alleged slave murder by Samuel Lewis. A coroner's jury in Prince William's Parish, Beaufort District, found that the slave died "in consequence of sundry blows of an axe, inflicted on his neck and head, by hands of his master, Samuel Lewis." After killing his slave, Lewis "mounted his horse, rode to some of his neighbors, who were indebted to him, and after making some collections, went off and has not returned. His wife, an amiable woman, lately the mother of a smiling infant, lies sick, and even unto death!"[34]

And the *Charleston Courier* in November 1821 published an appeal signed by "Beccaria." The letter's author invoked the name of Cesare Beccaria, whose 1764 book *On Crimes and Punishment* was widely read and cited. Cesare Beccaria favored the abolition of capital punishment, except in limited cases of treason and rebellion, and opposed lifetime slavery, except as punishment for those convicted of crimes. The letter instead suggested that the death penalty be extended to slave killers because the author did not believe "that the wise ordinance of Heaven had special regard to color or complexion" when punishing an "abandoned villain, who wantonly sports with the life of his fellow creature."[35]

The Legislature Finally Acts

Dr. Moser, in November 1821, again introduced a slave homicide reform bill. The legislature on December 20, 1821, finally approved this law, and Moser is credited with "push[ing] it through the Assembly."[36]

The law's first section imposed "death without benefit of clergy" for any person who "wilfully, maliciously, and deliberately murdered any slave within this State." According to the second, those killing any slaves "on sudden heat and passion" will "be fined in a sum not exceeding five hundred dollars, and shall be imprisoned not exceeding six months."[37]

Howell M. Henry and Edward McCrady suggested that a master's well-known killing of a runaway slave may have caused the legislature to finally act.[38] That prosecution resulted in a reported Court of Appeals decision, *State v. Taylor*.[39]

William H. Taylor was convicted in the Charleston Circuit Court for the murder of his slave Jacob. Jacob and another slave had run away. They were "absent for some considerable length of time" when Taylor received information as to the slaves' location. He then pursued and caught them "some where about Wappoo Creek." Taylor caused the slaves' hands to be tied behind their backs and put them in the bottom of a boat bound for Charleston "while he sat in the stern with a loaded double barreled gun beside him."

The boat on June 7, 1821, approached the landing near the end of Beaufrain Street in Charleston. Taylor "took up his gun and deliberately took aim at Jacob, saying, 'damn you, you shall never kill any more hogs,' and then fired off one of the barrels at him." The shot hit Jacob in the knee. A witness named Robert Hume was standing on the shore looking at the boat. He saw the flash and heard the report of the gun. After the boat landed, Hume saw Jacob tied up in the boat bleeding from his wounds. Hume then questioned Taylor, who denied firing the gun. Hume demanded to see the gun. When Taylor refused, Hume "forcibly" retrieved the gun and saw that one of the two barrels had been fired. Hume had Jacob taken to a doctor, but Jacob later died of his wounds.

The trial testimony of Hume and another witness was essential for Taylor's conviction. The appellate court sustained the conviction and fine.[40]

Public aversion to this one homicide does not explain why the legislators broke the grip of the legal inertia that, until then, stifled other calls for reform in response to the earlier infamous slave killings. Ryan A. Quintana recently read the 1821 statute in the context of other South Carolina antebellum legal reforms, including laws authorizing state funding and the construction of roads, bridges, and other internal improvements. He asserted that the state's legislators exhibited a preoccupation with "creating and maintaining what historian William J. Novak has called the 'well-regulated society,' whereby the practice of governance provided for the general welfare—economic, but also moral—of its inhabitants." Thus the slave homicide act should be read "in part, as the state privileging the property claims of slaves' white owners, shielding the enslaved—as property—from unjustified violence."[41]

Indeed, South Carolina's legislature adopted this homicide reform act sixty-seven years after it made slave stealing a capital offense. The theft of slaves and wanton slave killing both threatened individual slave owners' interests in their own slaves and the master class's interest in the social order.[42]

The law imposing capital punishment for the property crime of slave theft thus was consistent with the new capital crimes created in eighteenth-century England, such as forgery. These crimes "struck at the heart of the emerging commercial economy and were perceived by the elite as a threat to salient class interests." As the plantation economy matured in South Carolina and the rest of the antebellum South, the lawmakers also came to believe that wanton slave killings by third parties posed a similar "serious threat to both the individual economic interests of slave owners as well as the master class interest in maintaining the power and authority of the slave-owning regime."[43]

The threat of capital punishment supplemented the slave masters' civil damage remedies when whites wantonly killed slaves. Indeed, these civil suits illustrate the slave owners' concerns about this violence. For example, a 1796 Constitutional Court of Appeals decision affirmed a damage award for Sims White against James Chambers who beat White's slave, whose name is not mentioned in the case report. The slave "had the care of his master's fishing canoe in Sullivan's island, when the defendant went down to the landing place where it was, and said he would take it, and go fishing in it." The slave refused, stating that "his master had given him orders to let no one take it away." A dispute then arose "upon which some high words passed between them on both sides, whereupon the defendant struck [the slave] with a blow with his fist, and then took up a paddle, which was in the canoe, and knocked him down, and afterwards beat him very severely, which laid him up for several days before he was able to go about his master's business again."[44] The appellate court affirmed a five-pound judgment for White, noting that "very often an injury offered to a slave, in the execution of his master's commands, is a direct injury offered to the master who gave the orders, or an affront to his authority, which would too often lead on to quarrels and bloodshed, if some adequate remedy was not provided for this kind of injury offered to a slave."[45]

Two 1818 South Carolina Constitutional Court of Appeals decisions further illustrate these concerns. The court, in *Arthur v. Wells*,[46] affirmed a jury verdict in favor of Hargrove Arthur. He sued David Wells, who admitted that he shot and killed one of Arthur's slaves after Wells saw the slave running away from Arthur's overseer.[47] Justice Charles J. Colcock's opinion for the court declared, "It may be the policy of a country, holding slaves, to subject them to the partial control of the freemen of the country, when not under the immediate control of their masters. But it can never be considered politic to subject a valuable species of property to the disposal of any unprincipled, unfeeling man in society; nor is it less impolitic with regard to the slaves themselves—for where there is no protection to life, there is no incitement to action."[48]

And in *Witsell v. Earnest*,[49] the court reversed a jury verdict denying Laurence Witsell monetary damages in his suit against John Earnest and Joshua Parker, who allegedly killed Witsell's slave. Colcock again expressed the court's disdain for the "violent and unthinking" people who threatened slave property values and public order: "The peace of society, and the safety of individuals required that slaves should be subjected to the authority and control of all freemen, when not under the immediate authority of their masters. And while it is conceded, that this is necessary, it is equally obvious, that both principle and policy require, that their lives should be protected from the attacks of the violent and unthinking part of the community."[50]

Colcock's views appear fairly to represent those of the states' opinion leaders. He was born in Charleston, the son of John Colcock, a lawyer who served in the American Revolution. John died when Charles was twelve years old. Charles graduated from Princeton and studied law under the well-respected Chancellor William DeSaussure. Charles was elected to the state legislature before beginning his judicial career, which extended from 1811 to 1830. He resigned from the courts in that year and served as the president of the Bank of South Carolina until he died in 1839.[51]

The majority of the state's legislators may have shared Colcock's concerns and biases toward poor whites when they reformed the state's slave killing statutes. The courts in several other cases—both civil and criminal—condemned white third parties, even slave patrollers, who directed wanton violence at slaves. And Thomas Motley and William Blackledge were executed in 1854 after their convictions were affirmed for brutally killing of Joe, a slave whose owner was unknown.[52]

The South Carolina Court of Appeals of Law and Equity also approved of the *Tackett* unequal mitigation doctrine, however, when whites were accused of slave homicides. For example, in *State v. Cheatwood*,[53] the appellate court's 1834 opinion by Justice William Harper affirmed the murder conviction of Bob Cheatwood (or Chatwood), "a desperate, gambling, dissolute fellow," who would persuade slaves to steal from their owners so they could gamble with him. Cheatwood's murder victim was a slave who beat Cheatwood one night at his own game. The slave "instantly snatched up the money and ran off. Bob soon overtook him and in the scuffle which ensued, finding the black man too strong, he ran a knife into his throat and mortally wounded the poor fellow, who had just strength to get home, tell his story, and expire." Cheatwood thus "committed the unpardonable sin of playing at cards with a *slave* for stolen property."[54]

Trial judge Baylis J. Earle instructed the jury to decide the case under the 1821 act "according to the principles and rules of the common law, and that he could admit no other distinction between the killing of white men and that of negroes, than this—that in the latter class of cases, a smaller degree of provocation would have the effect of extenuating or excusing, as the case might be." Justice Harper did not disapprove of this charge, which was consistent with decisions of Judge Earle and Justice O'Neall two years earlier in a case involving a free black criminal defendant.[55]

The 1821 slave homicide reform law also authorized the death penalty when slave owners murdered their own slaves. This required a more delicate balance of the slave masters' social and economic interests in the control of and investment in their slaves against the broader concerns arising when slave owners wantonly killed their slaves. The timing of the 1820 and 1821 laws limiting the masters' right to free and kill their slaves is telling. These laws both regulated the slave masters' conduct that the legislators deemed to be too lenient or too severe.[56]

Accordingly, South Carolina's legislators, like those on the Barbadian culture hearth, voted to limit slave homicides soon after they imposed stricter limits on the masters' rights to free their slaves. This similar pattern of legal change may have been a coincidence, or it may be evidence of similar thinking by the slaveholding elites.

The 1821 act continued to be controversial. Twenty-three Christ District Parish planters signed an 1829 petition calling for the law's repeal. The petitioners termed the act both useless, because no jury would inflict capital punishment on a white slave killer, and dangerous, because it encouraged slaves to run away and be insubordinate. The legislators referred the petition to the judiciary committee, and the act was not repealed.[57]

The South Carolina Courts and the 1821 Act

Public concern about the 1821 law's effect on slave owners may have ebbed over time because the courts held that the act did not repeal the 1740 law's provisions permitting masters to exculpate themselves on their own oaths and limiting the slaves' ability to mitigate killings to manslaughter.[58] Thus, in *State v. Raines*,[59] Guy Raines killed Isaac, William Gray's slave, in an altercation that occurred while Raines was transporting Isaac from a Columbia jail. Raines was convicted of manslaughter after the trial judge denied Raines the right to exculpate himself by his own oath. The Court of Appeals reversed the conviction. It extended to masters and others acting in their place the privilege to exculpate themselves on their oaths if they killed slaves without two white witnesses present.[60]

Justice Colcock's opinion sustained the masters' privilege because the 1740 act's "necessity or propriety originated in a state of things not materially changed since 1740. The slave and his owner or possessor is perhaps as much secluded from the views of other white persons now as formerly; he is still even now for days and weeks, in many parts of the country, left entirely with the master or overseer, and if in this situation an accidental killing should happen, why not permit the person killing to prove how it happened?" The 1821 law provided "no reason why [a master] should not be permitted to shew that he was free from all guilt; and this is what the law intends."[61]

Colcock also suggested that the 1821 act legitimized slave killings by masters resulting from both immoderate and moderate punishments because the act referred only to killings on a "sudden heat and passion."[62] The Court of Appeals, twenty-two years later, in *State v. Fleming*,[63] overruled this interpretation. Josiah Fleming was indicted in that case for murdering his slave Marcus. Fleming was convicted of manslaughter during the Sumter Circuit Court's fall 1847 term before Judge Josiah J. Evans and a jury. The reported decision does not state the facts of the case. Fleming's lawyer made a motion in arrest of judgment, which Judge Evans directed be filed with the Court of Appeals.

Judge Evans wrote for the Court of Appeals majority that a master who inflicts punishment on a slave either with malice or with the willful and deliberate purpose to kill will be guilty of murder. He also stated that the statute replaced the broader lesser offense of common law manslaughter with a killing in a "sudden heat and passion," which included killings resulting from undue correction, but not killings resulting from ordinary domestic discipline.[64]

Other South Carolina slave masters were prosecuted for slave homicides after 1821, including Charleston watchmaker Andrew Montgomery and his wife Priscilla. They were indicted for killing a slave by undue correction in violation of section 37 of the 1740 act. Andrew was acquitted, but Priscilla was convicted and fined 350 pounds, $212.28 at the time. Judge Baylis J. Earle denied the state's attempt to collect this debt from Andrew during the May 1839 trial court term. The Court of Appeals affirmed this ruling.[65]

Russel Harden of Edgefield District apparently absconded in 1845 after he killed a slave he owned. Governor William Aiken, on October 14, 1845, offered a two-hundred-dollar reward for Harden's capture, alleging that Harden committed "an atrocious murder" of his unnamed slave at Harden's residence on Beach Island near the Savanah River. Harden was described as being forty to forty-five years old, "of sallow complexion," and being in the habit of talking "loud and gross in common conversation." The notice also expressed fear that Harden had escaped to Georgia.[66] Edgefield is in the state's southwestern portion along the Savannah River and the Georgia border. It had a reputation for violence and a comparatively high murder rate during the antebellum years, in part because it retained its frontier character.[67]

Harden eventually was indicted for this murder and was tried in the Edgefield District Court of Sessions during its March 1846 trial term. A jury convicted Harden of murder, but recommended mercy. South Carolina's Court of Appeals reversed Harden's conviction because the trial court session was not properly extended.[68]

Harden was tried again in the Edgefield Court of Sessions before Judge Andrew Butler and a jury on October 6, 1846, two months before Butler was appointed to serve in the U.S. Senate. The jury found Harden guilty of manslaughter. Neither the officially reported decision nor the newspaper articles describe Harden's crime, although the *Edgefield Advertiser* reported that this was a case of "peculiar aggravation." Judge Butler sentenced Harden to a five-hundred-dollar fine and a six-month prison term. The local sheriff later advertised the sale of 150 acres of Harden's land, plus two slaves, six horses, and one mule.[69]

Seven months after Harden's second trial, Eliza Rowand was acquitted after her trial in Charleston, discussed in the introduction. Rowand escaped punishment for killing her alleged victim Maria, or ordering an enslaved man named Richard to strike the fatal blows, on the strength of Rowand's written sworn denial, which the state could not refute with two white witnesses.[70]

In contrast, Martin Posey of Edgefield District was the first South Carolina slave owner on record to be executed after killing one of his slaves; but Posey was more than a slave killer. He was about thirty-four years old, was drinking heavily, and was obsessed with his wife Matilda's younger sister Eliza when he and his slave Appling in February 1849 agreed that Martin would free Appling if Appling killed Matilda. Appling upheld his end of this deadly bargain by beating and drowning Matilda, and then burying her body. But rather than freeing Appling as promised, Martin shot and killed him and buried his body. Martin also married Eliza, thus evading South Carolina's strict divorce prohibition.[71]

This double murder was soon exposed, however, and Martin was tried for both killings in the Edgefield District Court of Sessions during the fall 1849 term before Judge Thomas Jefferson Withers and two juries. Although Martin was not at the scene when his slave killed his wife, the first jury found Martin guilty as an accessory before the fact to Appling's murder of Matilda.[72] An accessory before the fact is a person "who by hire, command, counsel or conspiracy, or by assenting to another's committing a felony, abets and encourages him to commit it, and is so far absent when he actually commits it that he could not be encouraged by the hope of any immediate assistance from [the accessory]."[73] The state's principal witness was Martin's overseer, Wilson Kirkland, who in court recounted Martin's and Appling's admissions.[74] The second jury convicted Martin for Appling's murder, again based in part on Martin's admissions repeated at trial by Wilson and Caleb Kirkland.[75]

Martin appealed his convictions to South Carolina's Court of Appeals, which, during its December 1849 term, issued two opinions by Judge Withers affirming the verdicts.[76] A footnote in the opinion on Matilda's murder quoted the court's unreported 1836 opinion affirming Elizabeth Green's conviction as an accessory before the fact who facilitated her husband Henry's murder by an unknown person. A free man named Head and Tommy Ray's "negro man, Edom" had been acquitted of this murder.[77] These and other cases in which slave owners were prosecuted as accessories to slave crimes suggest that the state had a strong interest in getting at the truth to deter slave owners from ordering or inducing their slaves to murder free or enslaved people and then making their slaves scapegoats or, even worse, murder victims like Appling.[78]

Lewis Andrew Jackson (aka L. A. J.) Stubbs was the only South Carolina slave owner executed only for murdering a slave under his control. But he was not the legal owner of the young child he so brutally abused and killed, and his status in his community and family may have contributed to his demise.

On August 6, 1852, Stubbs was arrested by Marlboro District Sheriff B. F. McGilvary for killing Maria, an eight-year-old enslaved girl who was under Lewis's control when she died. Coroner James H. Bolton held an inquest, and a coroner's jury that same day found that Stubbs, two days before, "feloniously killed" Maria "by blows or exposure long continued of which she died."[79]

This prosecution may not have been a surprise to all. Stubbs, "with others of the same family name, had been more than once indicted for cruelty to slaves and general disturbance of the peace of the community."[80]

The Marlboro District, now Marlboro County, is in northeastern South Carolina. "This low-country but not tidewater district is tucked between the Great Pee Dee River and the westward bend that the South Carolina/North Carolina border makes about 120 miles from the Atlantic Ocean."[81] It was in 1785 separated from the Cheraw District. After an initial period of growth, its population declined between 1805 and 1819, when many Quakers who came to oppose slavery moved out as slavery spread into the region. The district's population later doubled from 6,425 in 1820 to 12,434 in 1860, while its enslaved population increased from 47.2 to 55.4 percent of the total population. By 1830, Marlboro was among the thirteen of twenty-eight South Carolina districts in which more than 50 percent of the people were enslaved.[82]

The Stubbs family had resided in the area since the 1740s, when Lewis's great-grandfather, John Stubbs, settled there. Various Stubbs family members were planters and slave owners in the Brightsville area, near the North Carolina border.[83]

Lewis A. J. Stubbs was born in or about 1815, most likely soon after General Andrew Jackson's January 8, 1815, victory in the Battle of New Orleans. His parents, Benjamin and Clarissa Hubbard Stubbs, were first cousins. He had three siblings, Mary Ann, Clarissa, and Thomas J. Stubbs. Benjamin died in 1825, and Clarissa married another first cousin, Benjamin's brother Thomas Stubbs Jr. First cousin marriages were more common in southern slaveholding families than in the rest of the nation.[84]

It once seemed that Lewis would be a successful planter like his paternal great uncle and maternal grandfather, Lewis Stubbs Sr. In or about 1835, Lewis A. J. Stubbs married Mary Ann Hubbard. They had one child, Mary Ann. Their household in 1840 included ten slaves. Six household members were employed in agriculture.[85]

Lewis's fortunes began to change for the worse after 1840, however, after his first wife died. Lewis soon married Mary Jane Crosland. Between 1841 and 1853, they had six children.[86]

Lewis Stubbs Sr.'s 1845 will suggests that the elder Lewis had concerns about his grandson and great nephew. The fifth paragraph of that will devised seven slaves and some land to be divided equally among Lewis A. J. and his two surviving siblings, Mary Ann Hayes and Clarissa Newton. The slaves included "Agnes and her child Maria." Unlike his sisters, who were direct beneficiaries under the will, Lewis's share of these assets was devised to Clarissa's husband, Cornelius S. (Stubbs) Newton, in trust for Lewis's children. The will authorized Cornelius to permit Lewis A. J. to use his one-third share during Lewis A. J.'s life.[87]

Lewis A. J.'s household by 1850 included two enslaved females, one aged sixteen and the other six, who may have been Maria. The sixteen-year-old probably was a "negro girl" Lizett (or Lisette) in whom Mary Jane Crosland Stubbs was given a life interest by her mother's 1841 will. Upon Mary Jane's death, Lizett and "her increase" would pass to Mary Jane's daughters.[88]

A grand jury issued an eight-page handwritten murder indictment on the second Monday of October 1852, finding that on May 1, 1852, Cornelius S. Newton gave Lewis A. J. Stubbs possession and control of Maria. Between that date and August 4, 1852, when Maria died, Lewis allegedly maliciously chained, confined, beat, whipped, starved, and killed her. No witness testimony is preserved in the court file, but three local medical doctors testified, William J. David, James H. Lane, and William D. Wallace. The only grand juror identified was the foreman Benjamin D. Townsend, who with his brother Meekin ran a Bennettsville mercantile business. Benjamin in 1866 was elected as the Cheraw and Coalfields Railroad Company's president, and his wife was a schoolteacher. Reverend J. A. W. Thomas, writing in 1897, called Benjamin a "patron of temperance."[89]

Twenty-three witnesses were ordered to testify on the first Monday in October 1852 at the murder trial in the Court of General Sessions, at the district's Bennettsville courthouse. These witnesses included three of Lewis's blood relatives—Thomas E., Lewis E., and John J. Stubbs.[90]

The only trial court record is the notation "guilty" written on the indictment that was signed by John L. McLucas, who is designated foreman. Reverend Thomas later wrote that John, a farmer, and his brother Hugh McLucas "are both remembered as good citizens."[91]

Newspapers throughout the nation reported both the jury's October 1852 guilty verdict and Lewis's January 7, 1853, execution in Bennettesville's courthouse square, which is only about 135 miles from Statesville, North Carolina, where John Hoover was executed.[92] Mary Jane Stubbs, her six children, and her slave Lizett later moved to Tennessee, where Mary Jane remained until she died in 1882.[93]

The local *Cheraw Gazette*'s reporting included an editorial comment declaring that Maria's murder "consisted as much of the neglect of [Lewis's] duty as a master as of any other ingredient." This assertion clashed with the jury's finding that Lewis A. J. Stubbs murdered Maria. The newspaper also declared that the case "speaks volumes in behalf of our laws enacted for the protection of our slave population; and puts to blush thousands of the lies invented and propagated by Northern fanaticism to disparage this institution of slavery."[94]

Nevertheless, when Lewis A. J. Stubbs killed Maria he had the right only to possess her, like a slave hirer. We do not know if the coroner's jury, the grand jury, and the trial court jury members who condemned Lewis's heinous murder all were slave owners. But, according to the 1860 census, the coroner Bolton owned six slaves, Townsend thirteen, and McLucas four.[95]

This case also highlights the ripple effect that a master's decision to kill a slave had on the interests of others. Lewis's misdeeds reduced the value of both his own children's inheritance and the property interests he held jointly with his sisters and their heirs. They may have been motivated by intrafamily rivalries to support action against Lewis.[96]

Three years later, Jackson Bradley was to be hanged for murdering one of his slaves, but he literally escaped punishment. Bradley was indicted along with William Adkins for murdering George, who was between six and eight years of age when he was killed. Adkins was not arrested. Bradley was tried alone and was convicted in the Kershaw General Sessions Court's 1855 fall term before Judge Robert Munro and a jury. Kershaw is about sixty-seven miles west of Bennettesville, where Lewis A. J. Stubbs was executed.[97]

Wilkes Thurlow Caston on December 11, 1855, argued Bradley's appeal to the Law Court of Appeals. Caston, a temperance advocate, was described as "an excellent man and promising lawyer" who died suddenly in 1858 at the age of thirty-seven.[98]

The court affirmed Bradley's conviction in *State v. Bradley*,[99] but the official report does not state the facts. The trial witnesses included two physicians, as well as Wiley Bradley, Jane and John Williams, and the wife of William Adkins. Wiley's relationship to Jackson Bradley is not stated. It appears that Jackson may have been guilty of concealing or destroying the "*corpus delicti*," a reference most likely to George's body or its condition. Judge Munro referred to the testimony "on this point" of the two doctors and Wiley Bradley.[100] Circumstantial evidence of guilt was insufficient under nineteenth-century evidence law "unless the *corpus delicti*, the fact that the crime has been actually perpetrated, be first established." Accordingly, a defendant in homicide cases was not to "be convicted unless the death be first distinctly proved, either by direct evidence of the fact, or by inspection of the body."[101]

The appellate court focused on Judge Munro's ruling that Mrs. Adkins could not "testify that her husband was alone guilty of murder."[102] Judge Munro's opinion affirmed this ruling on appeal, permitting Mrs. Adkins to testify on behalf of Jackson Bradley while excluding her testimony incriminating her husband.[103]

Bradley was sentenced to be hanged on March 14, 1856. But on February 18, 1856, Bradley broke the lock on his Kershaw District jail cell and escaped. The local sheriff initially offered a three-hundred-dollar reward for Bradley's capture, which Governor James H. Adams later increased to a thousand. There is no evidence that Bradley was caught and executed.[104]

Two more defendants were later convicted for slave killings. Mary McKewn, in May 1858, was arraigned in the Charleston Court of General Sessions for the murder on Sullivan's Island of her slave Louisa. McKewn was tried on June 1, 1858, before Judge David L. Wardlaw and a twelve-man jury. James Simons, a lawyer and state legislator who served as speaker of the South Carolina house from 1850 to 1861, defended McKewn.[105] The attorney general called "[a] large number of witnesses," and Simons, "on the part of the defence, also produced a mass of testimony in favor of the prisoner and her uniform kind treatment of the girl *Louisa*." The testimony and argument concluded at eight o'clock in the evening. Judge Wardlaw charged the jury, which deliberated until eleven, when they reported they "had not agreed upon a verdict."[106] The next day the jury returned. They received additional instructions and "in a few minutes" returned with a manslaughter verdict.[107] Judge Wardlaw imposed a $250 fine and a three-month prison term.[108]

And Caroline Hertzer, on February 5, 1861, was indicted for murdering a slave whose name is not mentioned in the reports of the case. A trial was held before Judge Munro and a twelve-man jury. The jury deliberated for four hours and found Hertzer guilty of manslaughter.[109]

Judge Munro later that month sentenced Hertzer to an eighteen-month prison term, but she was to be released after nine months "upon the payment of $500." Munro rejected Hertzer's argument, which was supported by two physicians' certifications, that her "health was such as to render confinement in jail very likely to prove fatal to the life of the prisoner." Munro said this might provide a strong case for a governor's pardon, but he "must take the case as he found it," which evidenced "an act of great atrocity." The jury "took a very merciful view of the case, and [Munro] thought they might very well have convicted the prisoner of murder. It was a brutal act; an idiot slave cruelly beaten to death to compel him to work." The judge found that Hertzer's husband bought the slave knowing of his condition and that "his former owner never attempted to make him work." As soon as she obtained the slave, Mrs. Hertzer attempted to beat "into him what his Creator had denied him—intelligence. She might as well have beaten a stick or a stone."[110]

Other slave masters avoided homicide prosecutions when coroner's juries or grand juries found that slave deaths were not caused by foul play. For example, a coroner's jury on Saint Helena in South Carolina's Sea Islands in 1849 found insufficient evidence of James H. Sandiford's culpability for the death of his disabled slave Roger. Thomas B. Chaplin was a juror who wrote in his diary that his "*individual* verdict would be" that Roger was "*deliberately* but *unpremeditatedly* murdered by his master James H. Sandiford."[111]

W. J. Megginson cited three unsuccessful slave master homicide prosecutions from Anderson District, in northwestern South Carolina. Coroner's juries found that John W. Beson in 1834 and Reverend Albert A. Moore in 1863 caused the deaths of their slaves Sam and Jane, but Megginson found no convictions. Alfred Hester also allegedly beat to death his slave Amy. But a grand jury discharged Hester, who, in 1836, unsuccessfully sued Benjamin Hagood for malicious prosecution. Hagood had alleged that Amy had periodically run away and that Hester turned his dogs on her, perhaps killed her, and then tried to prevent her body from being examined.[112]

These prosecutions may have been unsuccessful for good reasons. Or maybe jurors agreed with the jury foreman who, in Francis R. M'Kee's case, said he would not convict M'Kee "or any other white person, of murdering a slave."[113]

South Carolina's governors also pardoned some masters, like James Kelly, who was pardoned after being fined fifty pounds in Orangeburgh District "for killing a negro by undue correction."[114] Executive pardons were not automatic. Governor Pierce M. Butler, in October 1838, denied Nazareth Allen a pardon after a Richland District jury found Allen guilty of slave murder. Allen's relationship to his victim is not reported. The jurors and a number of respectable petitioners sought mercy for the young defendant. Butler wrote that "[t]he case is undeniably clear, of deliberate, or rather wanton homicide." He rejected Allen's "extreme youth" and chance for reform as reasons for a pardon.[115]

Local residents in at least one case even took the law into their own hands so a suspected slave killer could evade justice. A February 5, 1858, *Laurensville Herald* editorial referred to a slave owner who allegedly caused the "death of his slaves by ill treatment." A committee of community members "waited upon this particular slaveowner and demanded that he leave the community at once, which he did."[116]

Conclusion

When South Carolina finally imposed the death penalty on at least some slave murderers, it continued to permit masters and others standing in the masters' place to kill slaves when "necessary." Procedural exceptions also favored masters, including the exculpatory oath privilege, which Justice O'Neall in 1848 labeled "the greatest temptation ever presented to perjury." He asked the legislature "to speedily remove it."[117] O'Neall restated his critique five years later, while commenting on Eliza Rowand's case in a letter to the editor reviewing Stowe's *Key to Uncle Tom's Cabin*.[118] Also in 1853, a Fairfield District grand jury presentment, among other things, cited "informal complaints ... of ill treatment of slaves which cannot be corrected by the present law. If such be the case we respectfully recommend that the Legislature provide a law that will correct this evil."[119]

South Carolina's pre–Civil War legislature did not repeal the masters' exculpatory oath privilege. But it did adopt an 1858 act imposing fines and prison terms on slave owners or other persons "having the care, management, or control of any slave" who imposed "cruel or unusual punishment." This act stated, however, that it did not "prevent the owner or person having charge of any slave from inflicting on such slave such punishment as may be necessary for the good governance of the same."[120]

CHAPTER 11

The Antebellum States' Law on Slave Homicide

The slave homicide law that evolved in the Old South migrated with the antebellum settlers who moved to the Mississippi and Florida Territories, the Louisiana Purchase, and the Texas annexation, which became parts of the vast Cotton Kingdom.[1] "In the span of a single lifetime after the 1780s, the South grew from a narrow coastal strip of worn-out plantations to a sub-continental empire." More than one million enslaved people were moved west and south as the U.S. enslaved population "increased five times over, and all this expansion produced a powerful nation."[2]

These states and territories imposed capital punishment on slave murderers. But no slave owners were executed for killing their own slaves in these jurisdictions, which enforced capital punishment 565 times between the years 1800 and 1865.[3]

Louisiana Law

Slavery law in Louisiana evolved as a mixture of French and Spanish codes and Roman law. But this civil law had a similar effect on slave homicide prosecutions when compared with the law in the common law slave states.

The land that became the state of Louisiana was included in territory that was controlled by France from 1712 to 1763 and by Spain from 1763 until 1803, when France regained and sold it to the United States.[4] Slavery grew slowly when France first ruled the colony. "Between 1803 and 1860 Louisiana changed from a frontier territory to a state wherein all the accessible good land and much marginal land was under cultivation." Slavery flourished as enslaved workers turned the swamps into rice and sugar fields.[5]

The enslaved population in Louisiana and New Orleans grew slowly in the early years of French rule because the economy was similar to that in New France. "By the late 1710s, however, slavery emerged as a competing form of economic and social organization." Thousands of Africans were imported to the region. They soon became a majority of the population as the economy "moved away from that of New France, with its dependence on Indian trade and family farms, toward the Caribbean model of plantation agriculture and enslaved labor."[6]

Scholars have debated whether Louisiana "was from its origin a slave society with a black majority."[7] The colony's enslaved population nonetheless in 1763 and 1785 was about 51 percent of the total, and between 1810 and 1860 this population ranged between 45 percent and 47 percent. Louisiana also was the state with the largest median slaveholdings of 38.9 and 49.3 slaves per household in 1850 and 1860.[8]

A revised *Code Noir* for Louisiana was adopted in 1724 under Louis XV as "the Crown looked to the islands to determine how to govern Louisiana."[9] This code's homicide and slave abuse provisions were similar to those in the original *Code Noir*.[10] And a law adopted while Louisiana was under Spanish rule provided that "the slave is entirely subject to the will of his master, who may correct and chastise him, though not with unusual rigor, not so as to maim, or mutilate him, or to expose him to the danger of the loss of life, or to cause his death."[11]

After Louisiana became a U.S. territory, the local legislators adopted modified versions of these slave codes. The territory's 1806 Black Code, in section 16, stated that any person willfully killing a slave "shall be tried and condemned agreeably to the laws of the territory." Those inflicting upon slaves "any cruel punishment, except flogging, or striking with a whip, leather thong, switch or small stick, or putting in irons, or confining such slave" were to pay fines of between two and five hundred dollars.[12] This section has to be read along with an 1821 act mandating fines not exceeding two hundred dollars or no more than six months' imprisonment for those found guilty of "wantonly or maliciously" killing "any horse, mare, gelding, mule, or jack-ass, or any milk cow, cow, or beast of the cow kind, or a dog . . . without some lawful excuse for so doing." Offenders also were liable to compensate the owners for their losses. Persons convicted of cruelly beating, maiming, or disabling these animals were subject to one-hundred-dollar fines and liability for the owners' damages.[13]

The Black Code's drafters also borrowed the South Carolina exculpatory oath provision. According to section 17, if a slave was "mutilated, beaten, or ill treated" when no other person was present, the owner or person in charge of the slave was to be presumed guilty of the offense and could be "prosecuted without further evidence," unless the accused "can prove the contrary by means of good and sufficient evidence, or can clear himself by his own oath."[14]

The 1808 Louisiana Digest and the 1825 Louisiana Code, which the legislature adopted after Louisiana became a state in 1812, reaffirmed these principles. Article 173 of the 1825 code stated, "The slave is entirely subject to the will of his master, who may correct and chastise him, though not with unusual rigor, nor so as to maim or mutilate him, or to expose him to the danger of loss of life, or to cause his death." And article 192 declared that after an abusive master was "convicted of cruel treatment of his slave," the judge, "besides the penalty established for such cases," could order that the slave "be sold at public auction, in order to place him out of the reach of the power which his master has abused."[15]

Louisiana's courts imposed the death penalty at least 195 times between 1722 and 1861. Yet during these years no white person was executed in Louisiana for killing a slave or a free black person. Only Pierre Antoine Douchenet, a French soldier, in 1752 was executed after stabbing but not killing two female slaves. One of his victims was owned by the Ursuline nuns and the other by the king.[16]

Louisiana's Supreme Court decided only two appeals following slave master convictions, in part because that court did not have criminal appeal jurisdiction until 1846.[17] The court applied the exculpatory oath provision in *State v. Morris*.[18] Morris allegedly beat to death his slave "'in a cruel and barbarous manner ... causing sundry dangerous and severe bruises and wounds upon the thigh, loins, and other parts of the body.' A hole in the abdomen, the size of a dollar and appearing to have been 'gouged out,' was the immediate cause of death." No eyewitnesses testified at the trial in the District Court of Saint Helena. Morris presented his affidavit denying liability, which the district judge instructed the jury was not conclusive proof of Morris's innocence. The jury found Morris guilty.[19]

Louisiana's Supreme Court, in an opinion by Justice George King, affirmed the verdict, holding that the jury need not accept Morris's exculpatory oath as conclusive proof of his innocence. Instead, the jury could consider the affidavit along with all other evidence. "No greater weight is to be given to the oath of the accused in such cases than to other testimony." The case report does not refer to Morris's sentence.[20]

In the other officially reported slave master homicide case, George White and Clarence Ward were indicted in 1857 for mistreating a slave belonging to one of them contrary to Black Code sections 16 and 17. The case report does not state the slave's name or the facts. White was found guilty and was fined four hundred dollars. Chief Justice Edwin Merrick's opinion affirmed this conviction, rejecting White's argument that a later statute repealed the Black Code's anticruelty provisions.[21]

The other Louisiana slave owner prosecutions resulted in one conviction for slave killing, but the defendant avoided the death penalty. Bennett H. Barrow, a planter in Louisiana's Florida Parishes, on May 21, 1839, recorded in his diary the case of a slave killer whom he thought got away with murder. Barrow "Went to Town" and learned of a "man tried for Whipping a negro to Death." He noted, "trial will continue till tomorrow—deserves death—Cleared!"[22]

About six years later, Joseph Louapre, of the New Orleans baking firm Marks & Louapre, was charged with beating to death a slave of the firm, who was referred to as Chat Botte, William, or Moustache. Botte's body was buried after a Dr. Barbe, on December 1, 1845, certified that Botte died the evening before "from tetanus produced by cold." Alfred Beaufeau, a neighbor of the bakery, then filed an affidavit with Recorder Joseph Genois describing repeated beatings that Beaufeau heard in the days before Botte's death. The recorder issued a warrant for Louapre's arrest and ordered a coroner's inquest. Botte's body was exhumed. It exhibited the results of the beatings that Beaufeau described. A coroner's jury found that Botte died as a result of the beatings.[23]

The recorder then heard testimony from Beaufeau and his mother. They said they heard Botte being "whipped unmercifully for months past; that he had run away, was put to the police jail; and on his return to Louapre's bakery, was again severely punished, when he died." Dr. Barbe testified in reply that slaves "had occasionally died of tetanus after the infliction of thirty lashes, but not immediately." Several of Louapre's journeymen bakers "testified that Moustache was idle and refractory, and on one occasion struck his master."

The Beaufeaus said that before Botte died he "had received some hundreds of lashes, while the bakers admitted only six or seven, on the night of Sunday, and on Monday, when the slave died." Louapre's lawyer Robert Preaux, a prominent attorney, free mason, and leading member of the City's French-speaking community, argued that "the most that could be made of it was manslaughter." District Attorney Cyprian Dufour concurred. Recorder Genois "admitted Louapre to bail in $5,000, to appear before the Criminal Court." Although these preliminary hearings received extensive press coverage, I have not found further reports of a prosecution.[24]

Nine years later Aimes Dietz and her daughter Eliza Dimitry were charged with the November 1854 murder of Leda, a thirteen-year-old enslaved girl who was owned by Mr. Lachaumette. Leda was found dead in a house on Rampart Street. After an inquest, a coroner's jury found that Leda "came to death by cruel inhumane punishment inflicted upon her person with a cowhide, while sick, by the hands of Mrs. John Dimitry and Mrs. Deitz, her mother." According to the testimony at the inquest, Leda "had been in the employ of Mrs. Dimitry about three months, during which time she and her mother had been in the constant habit of beating and ill-treating her." Leda's body "was cut and scarred from head to foot in a most horrible manner—four days ago she got her last whipping, and was put to bed—being very sick with worms, Dr. [Charles] Turpin was sent for, who treated her for worms, but she died on Sunday morning." Doctors Turpin, Fagot, and Mercier certified that Leda died of a combination of worms and ill treatment. A warrant for the defendants' arrest was issued, "but, on the request of counsel, [the defendants] were committed for trial before the First District Court."[25]

A grand jury then indicted the defendants, who were arrested and jailed to await their trial. Their lawyer, John Larue, requested that they be released on bail. Judge John Blount Robertson set bail at ten thousand dollars each because of the defendants' "ill health and infirmities; also on account of some doubts as to the guilt of the parties of the charges on which they had been indicted." Larue had been Judge Robertson's predecessor as a First District Court judge.[26]

The case was tried on January 23, 1855, in the First District Court before Judge Robertson and a jury. Larue and Joaquim (Joachim) Bermudez, also a former judge whose son later served as the state's chief justice, represented the defendants. They asked Judge Robertson to sever the trials so that Dimitry might appear as a witness for Deitz. Judge Robertson denied this request.

Several witnesses then testified about the whippings the defendants inflicted on Leda. Mary Clark, "a servant of the family from the week prior to the death of the decedent to the present time," stated that the defendants whipped Leda "for stealing, but not in a cruel manner; and that when the slave was taken sick, they were very kind and attentive to her up to the hour of her death." Doctors Fauet and Valette attributed her death to the whippings, but Mercier and Turpin, who was called by the defense, opined that illness was the cause of death. At about seven in the evening, one of the jurors became so ill that Judge Robertson released the jury and declared a mistrial. Although this trial was widely covered in the press, I have not found any reports of a retrial of the defendants.[27]

Three years later, Francis (or Francois) Roueche, who operated a New Orleans shoe shop, was convicted on the charge that, during a period of eight months ending in March 1858, he beat to death an eleven- to twelve-year-old slave named Jourdan. Roueche was about twenty-eight years old and was a native of France or Germany. The initial case reports stated that Roueche was married to Catherine, who was pregnant and had two children. Roueche obtained a certificate from Dr. H. Allain declaring that Jourdan died of "diagnostic phthistic." Roueche was in the process of getting ready to bury the body when his neighbors reported Jourdan's death to the coroner. Deputy Coroner Osborne arrested Roueche, impaneled a jury, and conducted an inquiry. Jourdan's body was found to be covered with marks of wounds and bruises that Dr. Alfred Mercier concluded could have been the cause of death. The coroner's jury also heard the testimony of several of the Roueches' neighbors and charged the Roueches with murder. They also charged Dr. Allain as an accessory after the fact, but these charges were dismissed.[28]

The Roueches later that month appeared before Recorder J. L. Fabre. He committed Francois Roueche for trial for the murder and found insufficient evidence to charge Catherine.[29] Later that year, Judge T. G. Hunt sentenced Roueche to fifteen years' hard labor in the penitentiary. The press reports asserted that Roueche "was morally depraved and unprincipled, living openly with and having a family by a mistress," but Roueche's life was spared.[30]

The Louisiana Supreme Court also decided several appeals filed by defendants convicted of killing or cruelly abusing slaves belonging to others, and slave owners filed civil suits to collect damages from those who killed or injured their slaves. As in the common law slave states, Louisiana afforded slave masters a choice of criminal and civil remedies that protected their interests in their slaves.[31]

Mississippi Law

The lawmakers in the other new slave states followed the slave laws of the older common law southern jurisdictions. But Mississippi and Alabama followed different paths to confirm the masters' right to kill their resisting slaves.

The land that was included in the states of Mississippi and Alabama was in the empires of France, England, and Spain. But when Spain's rule began in 1781 the area "was thoroughly anglicized."[32] Spain ceded this territory to the United States in 1795. Congress, in April 1798, created the Mississippi Territory, which included the states of Mississippi and Alabama. Mississippi entered the Union in 1817. Mississippi's enslaved population in 1800 made up 39 percent of the total population, and this percentage increased steadily in the following years. After 1840, Mississippi's enslaved population exceeded 50 percent and by 1860 reached 55 percent.[33]

Mississippi received the English common law and not the civil law of its French and Spanish colonial past. The governor and a three-judge Supreme

Court made up the territory's first legislative body. The early territorial laws, known as Sargent's Code, were forty-six acts promulgated between 1799 and 1800 under the first territorial governor, William Sargent.[34]

These laws included A Law Respecting Crimes and Punishments, promulgated on February 28, 1799, which codified common law murder: "If any person or persons, shall with malice aforethought, kill or slay another person, he, she or they so offending, shall be deemed guilty of murder, and upon conviction thereof, shall suffer the pains of death." The code also included the common law definition and penalties for manslaughter. It listed justified or excused killings in self-defense, in the defense of the life of others, or in the prevention of felonies.[35]

Sargent's Code included A Law for the Regulation of Slaves, promulgated on March 30, 1799. One section imposed thirty lashes on the bare back of "any negro or bond mulatto" who was convicted of "lift[ing] his or her hand in opposition to any person not being a negro, or mulatto." The code also included a section that was adopted because "it has been the humane policy of all civilized nations, where slavery has been permitted, to protect this useful but degraded class of men, from extreme cruelty, and oppression." It imposed a fine not to exceed one hundred dollars on any owner convicted of authorizing or permitting "cruel or unusual punishment . . . on any slave within this Territory."[36]

Sargent and this code became so unpopular among the territory's residents that, on May 10, 1800, Congress authorized the territory's first general assembly. The territorial legislators adopted criminal codes in 1802 and 1807, which, like Sargent's Code, codified the common law definitions of murder and manslaughter without any slave homicide provisions.[37]

Mississippi's state legislature, in 1820, adopted a comprehensive criminal statute that included murder and manslaughter provisions that were for the most part consistent with the common law of crimes, Sargent's Code, and the territorial laws.[38] An 1805 territorial law increased the maximum fine for "cruel or unusual" slave punishment to two hundred dollars.[39]

Mississippi's Supreme Court, in *State v. Jones*,[40] held that slave killing could be common law murder in an opinion written by Judge Joshua G. Clarke.[41] The defendant, Isaac Jones, was found guilty at trial of murdering a slave. Judge Clarke did not state the deceased slave's name or when or how the homicide occurred. Jones probably was a white stranger to the slave he killed.[42]

The case came to the Supreme Court in its June 1821 term on a "motion in arrest of judgment, transferred on doubts from Adams [County] superior court."[43] These courts applied the statutory procedure by which the territorial trial courts referred to the higher court cases in which there was "doubt as to the law, rule or decision."⁴⁴ Adams County, the site of the trial, included the Natchez District, which was Mississippi's largest population center in 1817.⁴⁵ Its 1818 population of 10,600 included 6,709 enslaved people and 125 free blacks, some of whom owned slaves.⁴⁶

Jones's lawyer asked the court to decide "whether in this state, murder can be committed on a slave."⁴⁷ Clarke concluded that it could: "Because individuals may have been deprived of many of their rights by society, it does not follow, that they have been deprived of all their rights." He acknowledged that "[i]n some respects, slaves may be considered as chattels, but in others, they are regarded as men."⁴⁸

Clarke relied on statutes holding slaves liable for their crimes "as reasonable and accountable beings." He asserted that "it would be a stigma upon the character of the state, and a reproach to the administration of justice, if the life of a slave could be taken with impunity, or if he could be murdered in cold blood, without subjecting the offender to the highest penalty known to the criminal jurisprudence of the country." Then he asked, "Has the slave no rights, because he is deprived of his freedom? He is still a human being, and possesses all those rights, of which he is not deprived by the positive provisions of the law, but in vain shall we look for any law passed by the enlightened and philanthropic legislature of this state, giving even to the master, *much less to a stranger*, power over the life of a slave." The emphasized language suggests that Jones was a stranger to the slave he killed. Clarke defined "positive" law to include statutes, as did other antebellum judges.⁴⁹

Clarke repeated, without citation, Chief Justice Lord Mansfield's 1772 opinion in *Somerset v. Stewart*.⁵⁰ Mansfield asserted that slavery "is incapable of being introduced on any reasons, moral or political; but only [by] positive law."⁵¹ According to Clarke, the master's right over the slave "exists not by force of the law of nature or of nations, but by virtue only of the positive law of the state," and Mississippi's positive law gave "the master no right to take the life of the slave."⁵²

The Supreme Court thus overruled Jones's motion. On July 27, 1821, Jones was sentenced to hang, but no records confirm that the sentence was carried out.⁵³

Clarke's opinion echoed the views of North Carolina's Chief Justices Martin Howard and John Louis Taylor, who like Clarke were not southern natives. Clarke moved from Pennsylvania to the Mississippi Territory before 1804, prompting William Wiethoff to suggest that Clarke's rhetoric in *Jones* "reflects more his rearing in Pennsylvania than his planting in the Mississippi territory."⁵⁴

Clarke's holding in *Jones* is consistent with the slave homicide law that had evolved in the other states. South Carolina's legislators later that year made malicious slave killing a capital offense. Moreover, a 1788 Pennsylvania decision had upheld a common law indictment for malicious horse killing.[55] Of course, horse killing was not murder. But, like horses, slaves were valuable property. Mississippi's legislators included among capital felonies the theft of a "negro or mulatto slave" from his or her master's possession and the knowing sale of free persons as slaves.[56]

It is not clear whether Judge Clarke would have applied his *Jones* dicta to guarantee to the enslaved the common law of crime's equal mitigation standards, contrary to Justice Taylor in *Tackett*. Soon after he wrote the *Jones* opinion, Clarke became Mississippi's first chancellor. He died in 1828 without writing any other slavery law opinions.[57]

Mississippi's legislature, on June 14, 1822, adopted a revised criminal act again codifying the common law crimes of capital murder and manslaughter. Convicted murderers were to "suffer death." Those convicted of manslaughter were to be punished by fines and jail terms to be determined by the court and were to be branded on the hand with the letter "M" while in open court. Repeat offenders were to be executed. The act excused killings in self-defense, in the defense of others, "by misfortune," and by a defendant "in lawfully chastising his, her, or their child or servant."[58] Four days later, the legislature adopted an act regulating slaves, which increased the maximum fine for "cruel or unusual punishment" to five hundred dollars.[59]

The legislature adopted another comprehensive criminal code on February 15, 1839, redefining murder and manslaughter. This act listed among excusable killings those committed "[b]y accident and misfortune, in lawfully correcting a child or servant, or by doing any other lawful act by lawful means, with usual and ordinary caution, and without any unlawful intent."[60]

Several Mississippi slave owners were unsuccessfully prosecuted for slave homicides. Stephen Lewis in March 1831 was charged in Warren County with burning and beating to death his slave Daniel. People in the community had noticed that Daniel, who had a medical condition, apparently disappeared. Lewis told Wylin Bohannon that this condition motivated Lewis to kill Daniel. Several other neighbors urged the local officials to investigate. Daniel's body was found in a shallow grave. He had been burned and skin had been beaten off his back. A coroner's jury found that Lewis caused Daniel's death, and a grand jury indicted Lewis. Lewis's lawyers obtained a change of venue for the trial, which was held in Madison County. The trial records are lost, but Lewis apparently was not convicted. According to Warren County records, he returned home in 1832 and owned ten slaves, but by 1840 he was living alone with no property.⁶¹

Another slave owner, James Paul, also apparently evaded a murder trial on a charge that, in 1843, he killed and buried his slave Aaron. In 1819 or 1820 Paul moved from Tennessee to Tuscaloosa, Alabama, where he established a successful metalworking shop. He later moved to Mississippi.⁶²

The Lowndes County, Mississippi, coroner's inquest records state that Aaron had run away from Paul but was caught. Aaron then was "ironed, including an iron gag in his mouth, and whipped. Paul then left. When he returned he and his brother discovered that Aaron was dead. The body was taken to a log heap and buried. A neighbor suspected that the bones were Aaron's and Paul was responsible." The inquest concluded that Aaron "came to his death by maltreatment."⁶³

Paul apparently was not "very popular" and was "known to have punished this slave repeatedly" before the homicide. Paul fled in response to the charge. Mississippi's governor authorized a reward for Paul's capture and return.⁶⁴ Paul was captured in Texas in 1847 by two men from Tuscaloosa and David Walker of Grimes County, Texas. They took Paul to Walker's house, but Paul's Texas neighbors pursued him and freed him. The local press initially reported that Paul was a wealthy man who was kidnapped in an extortion attempt.⁶⁵ But later reports admitted that "Paul was arrested under a requisition of Governor of Mississippi, charging him with murder."⁶⁶

Walker again found Paul and captured him on April 6, 1848, in Mobile, Alabama. Paul was denied bail and was committed to jail.⁶⁷ "It is said that the evidence against Paul, though possibly not conclusive, was such as to put him in supreme dread of a trial, and that he spent the whole of his large fortune and the remainder of his life fighting *off a trial*."⁶⁸

William Johnson, a free black Natchez barber, property owner, and slave owner, noted another unsuccessful prosecution. His diary entry for August 18, 1844, states that "[r]eports were in circulation" that "Simon Murcherson [also spelled Murcheson] had beat his man Arther [sic] very Severely on Friday night with a Picket that he pull[e]d off of a fence and that the Picket had a nail in it which Struck in the Poor fellow[']s head, and that the man Arther Died Last night." Johnson noted that "[t]here was Considerable talk about it. So much that Several Persons had went to Esqr Woods," who wrote a note to Murcheson. Murcheson replied that he had already buried the body. "Reports Seys that he beat the Poor man" between nine and ten in the evening, "when he was herd to hallow no more." An inquest jury of fourteen the next day examined the victim's head and "found it very much Bruised. Did cut it Open." But they did not strip the victim's body or examine his back, apparently because of a dispute about the charges due to a doctor. "So they closed the man up again and Said he Died with Congestion of the Brain."[69]

Later Mississippi High Court of Errors and Appeals decisions applied the *Tackett* rule to mitigate slave homicides. That three-judge court in 1833 succeeded the Supreme Court as Mississippi's highest court.[70]

Archibald Kelly and Archibald Little, in April 1844, were indicted in the Circuit Court of Smith County for murdering "one Jack, a negro man" who was Kelly's slave. The case report does not state any of the facts, noting only that the defendants claimed that they were intoxicated when the crime occurred. They were tried before a jury on April 26, 1844, and were found guilty of first degree manslaughter. The next day they were sentenced to seven-year prison terms. On their appeal, the High Court of Errors and Appeals, in an opinion by Justice Joseph S. B. Thacher, affirmed the convictions but reversed the sentences.[71]

Thacher affirmed the trial judge's decision denying the defendants' lawyer's request to charge the jury contrary to *Jones*: "There being no system of domestic slavery known to the Common Law of England, the relation of master and slave known in this State, as well as that between slave and overseer not having existed in England, there is nothing in the Common Law on the subject of murder, that has strict and complete application to a case of killing, as arising from the chastisement of a slave by his master, or overseer, or both."[72] Thacher nonetheless affirmed the assumption that the courts should modify the common law to permit slave masters to inflict what the judges and juries believed was necessary punishment:

> Now, by the Common Law of England, masters were allowed to punish their servants with moderation. 1 Hale's P. C. 454. What was moderation at Common Law was a question of fact for a jury, who might be masters, and here, what is a cruel and unusual punishment, is likewise in all cases a question of fact for a jury, who most generally are slave owners. It is not contended that a greater degree of punishment may not be inflicted here by the master upon his slave, than by the master upon the servant at Common Law, because such here may be usual from necessity; but the same general principle of law holds in both cases, so that the Court did not err in refusing the instruction.[73]

The court also rejected Kelly's and Little's intoxication defense but reversed the sentences because the defendants were not present in court for the sentencing and because the trial judge did not state the date on which the sentences were to begin. The case was remanded so the trial court could again impose its sentence.[74]

Almost ten years later, Justus Hurd was indicted for murdering one of his slaves. Hurd "was a wealthy citizen of Amite County, originally from New England, but a resident of Mississippi for twenty years." Hurd was convicted of some grade of homicide after a January 1855 trial in Wilkinson County and was sentenced to a seven-year prison term.[75]

Meanwhile, the Mississippi legislature in 1854 authorized the Errors and Appeals Court justices to appoint three commissioners to revise, digest, and codify the state's laws. William L. Sharkey, Samuel S. Boyd, and Henry T. Ellett initially served. William L. Harris replaced Boyd after he resigned. In 1857 the legislature enacted the Commission's revised code, which again redefined the crimes of murder and manslaughter without explicitly referring to slave killings. It listed among excused killings those committed:

> By accident and misfortune, in lawfully correcting a child or servant, or by doing any other lawful act by lawful means, with usual and ordinary caution, and without any unlawful intent; or,
>
> By accident and misfortune, in heat and passion, upon any sudden and sufficient provocation, or upon sudden combat, without any undue advantage being taken, and without any dangerous weapon being used, and not done in a cruel or unusual manner.[76]

Three years later, the Mississippi Errors and Appeals Court did not even cite *Jones* when, in *Oliver v. State*,[77] it adopted the reasonable resistance or rebellion exception after George W. Oliver's manslaughter conviction for killing his slave John. Oliver, "a wealthy planter with 48 slaves," was indicted for murder and tried in the Lafayette County Circuit Court.[78]

Oliver's overseer Bramel testified at the trial that, on March 14, 1859, John, "a violent, turbulent, and rebellious slave," and "several other slaves" were "put to shelling corn on a corn-sheller" in Oliver's corncrib. They used "a stick, about five feet long, about two and a-half inches in diameter at the large end, and gradually tapering to the other." A slave named Dick used this stick to push ears of corn into the sheller. John was not allowed to use the stick "on account of his awkwardness."[79]

Bramel left the corncrib while Dick was using the stick and John was "engaged in another department of the shelling." Upon returning about fifteen minutes later, Bramel found Oliver in the corncrib. He heard Oliver "say, in a quiet and unexcited tone, 'Give up the stick'; and then in a short time he said, violently, 'Give up the stick.'" When Bramel "could see what was going on" he saw John and Oliver "struggling together for the possession of the stick . . . , both having hold of it." John's "countenance . . . at the time had a very vicious and savage look. Very soon [Oliver] succeeded in wresting the stick from the hands of [John], and he immediately struck [John] with the same on the head, and [John] fell and almost immediately expired." Right after John fell Oliver "struck in rapid succession two other blows at [John], but neither of them struck him." Bramel also testified that John "had been guilty, on the day before, of an act of disobedience, which was usually punished on the plantation by whipping."[80]

Trial judge John W. Thompson instructed the jury "[t]hat when death ensues from the correction of parent, master, and others having lawful authority, and such correction be considered nothing more than reasonable, the death will be considered accidental." But he added that when "the correction exceeds the bounds of due moderation, either in the measure of it, or in the weapon made use of for the purpose, it will be murder or manslaughter, according to circumstances. If done with a cudgel or other thing not likely to kill, though improper for the purpose of correction, it will be manslaughter. But if it is done with a dangerous weapon, likely to kill or maim, as a pestle or great staff, it will be murder." Thus he stated that a master may enforce his authority by "lawful means and lawful instruments of correction and not with a staff or such means as are likely to maim, and also with due and proper caution."[81]

After the jury convicted Oliver of manslaughter, Judge Thompson denied Oliver's new trial motion and Oliver filed an appeal.[82] His appellate lawyer, Hugh A. Barr, was a prominent Mississippi lawyer and political leader who argued that Thompson's instruction "that a master must overcome resistance with lawful instruments of correction, and has no right to use a staff, or such means as are likely to kill or maim in enforcing his authority," should be "limited to a mere case of correction, where the slave made no resistance," otherwise the rule would "result will be the supremacy of the slave. The slave population will be incited to insubordination and rebellion, the land will be filled with violence and bloodshed, and the institution of slavery will become a curse."[83]

William L. Harris wrote the Court of Errors and Appeals opinion. In 1858 he had been appointed to the court. He reversed the conviction and ordered a new trial, asserting that when a slave is in a state of "resistance and rebellion" the master's "authority and power"

> is only to be limited by the necessity occasioned by unlawful resistance to lawful authority. If, without necessity, or apparent necessity, in reducing his rebellious slave to subjection, the master wantonly take his life, he would certainly be guilty of murder or manslaughter, according to the circumstances. Or if the master, by inhuman or brutal treatment, endangering the life or limb of the slave, induce resistance necessary on the part of his slave to save his life or limb, and the master, in the further

prosecution of his unlawful conduct, take the life of the slave in such conflict, it is equally certain that the master would be guilty of murder. But if the master, in the exercise of lawful authority, in a lawful manner, be resisted by his slave, then the master may use just such force as may be requisite to reduce his slave to obedience, even to the death of the slave, if that become necessary to preserve the master's life, or to maintain his lawful authority.

This rule followed from the slave's "imperative duty" to afford "[u]nconditional submission and obedience" to the master's "lawful commands and authority." Harris traced this rule's "wisdom and origin ... to the humane reason that upon its proper observance the happiness and welfare of both races, in that relation, necessarily depend."[84]

Harris was a Georgia native and a "staunch secessionist" who, like Justice Joseph Lumpkin of Georgia, wrote of slavery as a positive good. He carved out a limited potential for murder convictions when slave masters imposed excessive violence on entirely submissive slaves.[85]

Mississippi's legislators and courts also afforded slave owners criminal remedies if their slaves were killed by others without cause, while protecting what they perceived to be the masters' necessary prerogatives. The Errors and Appeals Court decided two appeals in which defendants were prosecuted for killing slaves whom they did not own.[86]

The courts also enforced the masters' right to sue and collect damages from those who wantonly killed the masters' slaves. Thus, the Court of Errors and Appeals, in 1855 in *Thompson v. Young*,[87] affirmed a judgment entered in a trespass action that William Young filed against John J. Thompson for shooting and killing one of Young's slaves. Thompson alleged that the slave, whose name is not mentioned, "was a runaway, prowling about the premises of the defendant in the night-time and that defendant attempted to arrest him and restore him to his master; the said slave being armed with deadly weapons, to wit, a large knife and club, refused to submit to an arrest, but resisted, and by such resistance made it necessary for the defendant to shoot and wound the said slave." Thompson relied on a statute that "makes it the duty of every citizen to arrest a runaway slave. It follows therefore, necessarily, that if any person, in essaying to capture a runaway, shall meet with resistance, he may lawfully oppose force to force. He may even justifiably, in such cases, slay the resistant, if the resistance offered be of such a character as to threaten imminent danger to the life or great injury to the person of the captor."[88]

Chief Justice Cotesworth P. Smith's opinion for the court rejected this argument, stating some "rules" that are essential to the good government of the slave population, and necessary to the safety of the community. The laws for the government of slaves should be enforced firmly and wisely; and of course without unnecessary severity. The law is careful of the safety of the slave within his prescribed sphere. Regarded in the twofold aspect of persons and of property, the same law which protects the master, guards their rights as persons.

It would, hence, be no justification of the homicide of a runaway, that he was slain by the captor, in an effort to avoid an arrest, by flight. For the same reason, a person in an attempt to arrest a runaway, who offered resistance, would not be justified in taking the life of a slave, unless by such resistance his own person or life were put in imminent danger. [*Witsell v. Earnest*] 1 Nott & McCord [S.C.] 182; [*Copeland v. Parker*] 3 Iredell [N.C.] 513; [*Smith v. Hancock*] 7 Ky. 222, 4 Bibb 222; [*Richardson v. Dukes*] 15 S.C.L. 156, 4 McCord 156; [*Jennings v. Funderburg*] 15 S.C.L. 161, 4 McCord 161.[89]

The court held that because Thompson did not allege "that his person or life was ... placed in the slightest danger," the homicide "cannot be justified by any principle of morality, of law, or of policy growing out of the institution of slavery."[90]

Alabama Law

Congress created the Alabama territory after Mississippi's statehood, and Alabama entered the Union in 1819. By 1820, slaves were 33 percent of the state's population. This percentage increased steadily to 45 percent by 1860.[91]

Alabama's 1819 constitution stated, "Any person who shall maliciously dismember or deprive a slave of life, shall suffer such punishment as would be inflicted in case the like offense had been committed on a free white person, and on the like proof, except in case of insurrection of such slave."[92] It directed the legislature to enact a penal code "founded on principles of reformation, and not of vindictive justice."[93] It was not until 1839 that the legislature authorized this code, which was drafted by Supreme Court Justices Henry W. Collier, Henry R. Goldthwaite, and John J. Ormond.[94]

The code, which was adopted in 1841, in chapter 3 defined the accused slave killers' potential criminal liability in reference to their relationships to their enslaved victims. By implication, it legitimized killings that resulted from usual punishment and slave resistance.

Section 5 stated that any person who "with malice aforethought" caused a slave's death "by cruel, barbarous or inhuman whipping or beating, or by any cruel or inhuman treatment, or by the use of any instrument in its nature calculated to produce death" was guilty of first degree murder. Thus it excluded nonmalicious killings that were caused by humane whippings and beatings.

Section 6 added that overseers or managers of slaves committed second degree murder if they caused a slave's death "by such cruel, barbarous or inhuman whipping or beating, or by any cruel or inhuman treatment, although without intention to kill," or if they killed a slave "by the use of any instrument in its nature calculated to produce death, though without intention to kill, unless in self defence."

And section 7 expanded the slave owners' right to use all force necessary to secure the obedience of resisting slaves. It stated that owners committed second degree murder if they killed slaves "by cruel, barbarous or inhuman whipping or beating, or by any cruel or inhuman treatment without intent to kill," or "by the use of any instrument in its nature calculated to produce death, though without intention to kill, unless in self defence, or in the use of so much force as is necessary to precure obedience on the part of the slave."[95]

Alabama's legislature adopted a comprehensive 1852 code that included a slave homicide section stating, "Any person who with malice aforethought causes the death of a slave by cruel whipping or beating, or by any inhuman treatment, or by the use of any weapon in its nature calculated to produce death, is guilty of murder in the first degree." The next section continued, "Any owner, overseer, or other person having the right to correct any slave, who causes the death of such slave by cruel whipping or beating, or by any other cruel or inhuman treatment, or by the use of any instrument in its nature calculated to produce death, though without intention to kill, is guilty of murder of the second degree, and may be guilty of murder in the first degree." First degree murderers faced death or life imprisonment, while second degree murder carried a prison term of not less than ten years.[96]

Alabama's legislature in 1819 created the state's first Supreme Court, consisting of the five trial level circuit court judges. In 1832, the legislature created a separate three-justice Supreme Court, which decided two cases in which masters were prosecuted for killing their slaves.[97]

William H. Jones, of Perry County, was indicted for murdering his slave Isabel. The indictment's first count followed the common law charge that Isabel was Jones's property and that her death was "caused by beating with clubs, sticks and whips." The second count alleged that Jones, contrary to code section 7, "feloniously, wilfully and of his malice aforethought" committed "an assault" on Isabel, and that he did "feloniously, wilfully, and of his malice aforethought, cruelly, barbarously and inhumanly beat and whip, of which said beating and whipping the said Isabel ... died." The third count alleged assault and battery and cruel punishment.[98]

Jones's lawyer moved to quash the indictment, contending that it contained a misjoinder of offences. The trial judge agreed but allowed William M. Brooks, who prosecuted the state's case, to elect on which counts he would proceed. Brooks proceeded on the first and second counts, and Jones entered a not guilty plea. A trial jury found Jones guilty of second degree murder, and the judge sentenced him to be confined in the penitentiary for ten years.[99] Alabama's Supreme Court, in its June 1843 term, affirmed the conviction, but the officially published case report does not describe the facts presented at trial.[100]

Fourteen years later, the court released Benjamin Howard on bail after he posted a five-thousand-dollar bond to secure his appearance at a Macon County murder trial. Howard had been indicted for second degree murder of his slave Jake "by cruel whipping, or beating, or by any other cruel or inhuman treatment, or by the use of any instrument in its nature calculated to produce death, though without any intention to kill," in violation of Alabama Code. There is no report of the trial.[101]

The unsuccessful prosecutions of Henry M. Hall and Malachi Warren shed more light on the cruelty prohibited by the Alabama Code. Hall was charged in Autauga County with whipping one of his slaves to death. Hardy Vickers Wooten, then a young medical doctor from neighboring Lowndes County, recorded in his journal, on February 10, 1837, that he "attended a coroner's inquest on the body of a Negro boy, which the jury thought was murdered by his master, Henry M. Hall." According to witness M. B. Smith's statement,

> I first saw the negro on Friday. He was tied with his hands over his head in a very peculiar manner and seemed to be in great pain. He begged to be untied, upon which his master struck him over the head three or four times with a large hickory stick. The boy fell ... and while lying on the floor, Hall kicked him on the forehead once or twice. The boy's head bled quite profusely, but deponent does not know whether it was from the blows with the stick or the kicks he received while laying on the floor. The boy was taken out and tied to a tree. Deponent did not go out immediately, but hearing the sound of the lash, he finally did so, and after begging for the boy for some time without effect, he went back into the house with Hall still whipping the boy. Hall must have whipped the boy without cessation, with the exception of the few minutes when the deponent, as before said, interceded.

Two months later, Wooten wrote in his diary, "I attended court at Autauga as a witness in the case of the killed negro aforesaid. Hall was convicted of manslaughter and imprisoned two months and fined five hundred dollars."[102]

This verdict is inexplicable if the jury heard Smith's evidence. Even if Hall initially responded to provocation, after Smith intervened the killing was not a sudden act in response to immediate provocation.

Malachi Warren, a Lowndes County planter, was tried in the Circuit Court in Haynesville on charges of murder and the infliction of cruel and unusual punishment causing the death of his slave Dick. Warren allegedly killed Dick, between November 1 and 10, 1842, by "putting 'divers iron rods and bands' around Dick's belly, chest, and neck—all held together by an iron rod up and down [Dick's] back," leaving Dick's body "bruised wounded and cut." The jury found Warren not guilty of both charges.[103]

Alabama's Supreme Court applied the statutory definition of slave resistance in an 1853 decision reversing a slave named Dave's conviction for assaulting with the intent to kill the son of a man who had hired Dave. Justice Lyman Gibbons approved of the trial judge's jury charge asserting, "if the slave, is in open hostile rebellion against the master, and is resisting his legal authority by physical force, the master has the right to employ so much force as shall be sufficient to overcome such resistance. But if the slave is not resisting the master by physical force, or by hostile acts, but is simply in a state of disobedience, without personal violence towards the master, then the latter can only administer such punishment as is appropriate to the case, without endangering life or limb." The court thus extended the masters' prerogative to kill resisting slaves to the family members of those who hired slaves.[104]

Alabama's Supreme Court decided only two reported cases in which the defendants appealed convictions for killing slaves they did not own.[105] And, contrary to the other southern state courts, it held that slave masters could not sue others who killed their slaves before the killers were acquitted of the felony. The court nevertheless decided several cases in which masters sued those who caused their slaves' deaths.[106]

Missouri Law

Missouri's slave homicide law confirmed the masters' prerogative to kill resisting slaves consistent with the common law of slavery. French rule over Missouri extended from 1720 until 1763, when the land was transferred to Spain. Governor-General Alejandro O'Reilly implemented Spanish law in 1769 for the Louisiana Territory, which then included Missouri.[107]

Harriet Frazier found no evidence of slave master prosecutions for killing their slaves under this French and Spanish rule. An overseer, Jean-Baptiste Lacroix, was charged with the November 15, 1783, killing of Tacoua, a slave of Jean

Datchurut, a wealthy slave owner. At an inquest held the day after the killing, another slave named Jacob testified that Lacroix hit Tacoua with one fatal blow to the head after Tacoua failed to comply with Lacroix's demand that Tacoua stop explaining why a salt furnace was not lit. A physician confirmed the cause of death, but there is no record that Lacroix was punished. Four years later, he was recorded as a member of the same household.[108]

Missouri in 1804 became the District of Louisiana, in 1805 the territory of Louisiana, and in 1812 the territory of Missouri. Migrants from the southern states moved to the territory, which in 1821 entered the Union as a slave state. These settlers, mostly from Virginia, the Carolinas, Tennessee, and Kentucky, re-created "their small slave holding paradigm" instead of the Deep South's plantations.[109] Missouri's enslaved population was about 15 percent in 1810 and 1820, and although it increased to 18 percent in 1830, by 1860 it fell to 9.8 percent.[110]

The state evolved into "not one Missouri, but several." It included the cities of St. Louis, Westport, Kansas City, and St. Joseph. "There was the northern fringe, so close to Iowa, so like Iowa, with nearly all-white towns and family farms. There was the white and very poor southern fringe, the Ozark fringe, where scattered farmers scratched a bare subsistence out of the unforgiving hills. And then there was the heart and central artery of the state, the counties arrayed along the Missouri River, the region that would be known as Little Dixie."[111]

Little Dixie, in north-central Missouri, was a seven-county region in which, in 1850, enslaved people made up at least 24 percent of the population.[112] This region's enslaved population by 1860 grew to more than 28 percent as the settlement patterns increasingly resembled the more southern states. Although slaveholdings were smaller than the Deep South average, the percentage of enslaved people living on farms with more than twenty slaves increased from 8 percent in 1830 to 19 percent by 1860. This region's cash crops included tobacco and hemp.[113]

Missouri's first territorial slavery law, adopted in 1804, was based on modified versions of Virginia's and Kentucky's laws. Although this law did not include a slave homicide provision, it stated that a "negroe or mulattoe, bond or free," who lifted "his or her hand in opposition to any person not being a negroe or mulattoe" was liable for a whipping by a justice of the peace, "not exceeding thirty lashes on his or her bare back well laid on," unless the accused "was wantonly assaulted," and acted in self-defense.[114]

Missouri's 1820 constitution required the legislature to pass laws "[t]o oblige the owners of slaves to treat them with humanity, and to abstain from all injuries to them extending to life or limb." It also stated that any person "who shall maliciously deprive of life or dismember a slave, shall suffer such punishment as would be inflicted for the like offense if it were committed on a free white person."[115]

Missouri's Revised Statutes of 1835 made first degree murder a capital crime, which included killings "committed by means of poisons, or by laying in wait, or by any other kind of wilful, deliberate and premeditated killing, or which shall be committed in the perpetration or attempt to perpetrate any arson, rape, robbery, burglary, or other felony." All other murders were of the second degree and were punished by jail terms of not less than ten years. The statute also included lesser penalties for manslaughter.[116]

Two types of homicides were "excusable when committed by action or misfortune," including slave homicides. First were homicides "[i]n lawfully correcting a child, apprentice, servant or slave, or doing any other lawful act by lawful means, with usual and ordinary caution, and without unlawful intent." Second were homicides "[i]n the heat of passion, upon any sudden and sufficient provocation, or upon sudden combat without any undue advantage being taken, and without any dangerous weapon being used, and not done in a cruel and unusual manner."[117]

The statute also reduced the penalties for some killings of slaves caused by cruel and unusual violence. It defined second degree manslaughter as "[t]he killing of a human being, without a design to effect death, in a heat of passion, but in a cruel and unusual manner, unless it be committed under such circumstances as to constitute excusable or justifiable homicide." That crime was punished by a jail term of between three and five years. Fourth degree manslaughter included "[t]he involuntary killing of another by a weapon, or by means neither cruel or unusual, in the heat of passion, in any cases other than justifiable homicide." It was punished by a jail term in the penitentiary of two years, by imprisonment in the county jail of a term not exceeding one year, by a fine not exceeding one thousand dollars, or both imprisonment and a fine.[118]

The legislature suggested the limits of the uncruel and usual when it imposed a prison term of between five and ten years for any person who should "on purpose, and of malice aforethought, cut or bite off the ear, or cut out or disable the tongue, put out an eye, or slit, cut or bite off the nose or lip, or shall cut off or disable any limb or member of any person, with intent to kill, maim or disfigure such person."[119] The legislators also adopted statutes "against public morals and decency, or the public police." These included provisions prohibiting malicious cruelty to any "horse, ox or other cattle" and cruel or inhuman torture, beating, wounding, or abuse of a slave under the defendant's control.

The fine for animal abusers was not to exceed fifty dollars. Slave abusers faced jail terms not to exceed one year, fines not exceeding one thousand dollars, or both.[120]

Harriet Frazier found "no known instance" in which a white person was convicted for murdering a slave "in Missouri's history."[121] A defendant named Prinne was found not guilty in 1820 in the St. Louis General Court on the charge that he murdered his slave Walter by confining him "in a dungeon or cell dangerous to his health."[122]

Two years later, Marshall Mann was found not guilty on a charge that he killed Fanny, a slave owned by Charles C. Traube. According to a January 1, 1824, written agreement, Mann paid thirty-five dollars to hire Fanny for one year. He also had a right to purchase Fanny if he paid to Traube two installments of two hundred dollars, one on June 1, 1824, and the second on December 25, 1824.

Fanny died on March 22, 1824. Mann was indicted for manslaughter and assault and battery in connection with Fanny's death, but a jury acquitted him. Traube then sued Mann for damages caused by Mann's failure to return Fanny, in breach of their agreement. Traube won a judgment at trial, which the Missouri Supreme Court affirmed.[123]

Frazier told a "chilling account" of Obadiah Malone's escape from the charge that, in Cape Girardeau County, he killed his slave Louese. This homicide was triggered by the July 1824 death of Obadiah's twenty-four-year-old wife Eliza. Obadiah was a farmer, and he and Eliza, the daughter of John and Polly Johnson, had five daughters. After Eliza died, Obadiah delegated his child care duties to Louese. Obadiah became "enraged" when he discovered that, on April 22, 1826, Louese had whipped his four-year-old daughter Polly "on her legs and buttocks with sufficient severity to leave bruise marks."

Obadiah's abuse of Louese began on Saturday, April 22. The next day, Louese appeared at the residence of the Johnsons. Polly Johnson testified at the coroner's inquest that she heard Louese screaming before opening the door to see Louese appearing "very bloody" with a rope tied around her upper leg. Louese asked John Johnson to "save her life" because Obadiah "was coming with a gun to kill her." John said that he could not "hinder" Obadiah "from killing her, but he thought he would not."

Obadiah later came after Louese "with a loaded gun, called her a 'damm bitch,' and ordered her out of his former in-laws' home. She asked him to spare her life and assured him that she would not disobey him by running away. Malone drank whiskey at the Johnsons' house and afterward continued to beat [Louese] with a hickory stick, a stool, and a club." Obadiah's neighbor, Malinda Jenkins, testified that while returning from church on Sunday, "she heard Louese cry out that if her master whipped her any more that she would put an end to her existence. Someone did."

A coroner's inquest was held the next day at the Malone house. The coroner's jury of twelve Apple Creek Township householders found Louese's body hanging from a tree by her neck. She had "at least 40 bruises . . . from her neck to her ankles, 9 visible bruises on her head, and her skull [was] dented." After John, Polly, and John M. Johnson, the Johnsons' son, testified, the jury found that Obadiah beat Louese to death. Obadiah was arrested and indicted for Louese's murder.

The trial in the Cape Girardeau County Circuit Court began on Friday, May 6, 1826, and by ten o'clock the next evening the jurors began their deliberations. On the following Tuesday, the jurors declared that they could not reach a verdict and were discharged. Obadiah's lawyer obtained a change of venue to Scott County. After a trial held in June, the jury found Obadiah not guilty.[124]

U.S. Army Major William S. Harney also may have gotten away with murder. While he was stationed at Jefferson Barracks in Missouri, in October 1833 Harney married Mary Mullanphy, a daughter of wealthy St. Louis entrepreneur John Mullanphy. In April 1834, William and Mary moved into the St. Louis house of Mary's sister Ann Biddle, while Ann traveled in France. William later believed that an enslaved woman named Hannah had hidden misplaced keys. He tried to beat a confession out of her with a piece of rawhide. She died the next day.[125]

A June 28, 1834, coroner's inquest found that Hannah "came to her death by wounds inflicted by William S. Harney."[126] Harney was confronted by an angry mob and fled to Washington, D.C., where he sought a transfer. A grand jury on July 28, 1834, indicted Harney for Hannah's murder, finding that he beat her repeatedly with a cowhide on her "head, stomach, sides, back, arms, and legs."[127]

Harney returned to St. Louis in November 1834, submitted to arrest, and sought a change of venue. Judge Luke E. Lawless, on November 5, 1834, transferred the case to Franklin County. The trial began on March 23, 1835, before Judge Charles H. "Horse" Allen. The prosecution and defense attorneys presented their cases on the two following days. The testimony of the fifteen witnesses was not recorded. On March 25, 1835, the jury found that Harney was not guilty. Major Harney later rose to the rank of major general.[128]

Harney may have been prosecuted because he made enemies in St. Louis. Two years before the homicide, he was involved in a public altercation regarding the merits of his hero Andrew Jackson.[129] St. Louis resident Nathan Cole, in a July 2, 1834, letter to abolitionist Arthur Tappan, asserted more details about the alleged homicide. While Harney was beating Hannah, Cole alleged that her husband "had become suspected of telling some neighbor of what was going on, for which Major Harney commenced torturing him, until the man broke from him and ran into the Mississippi and drowned himself." Cole described Hannah's husband as "a pious and very industrious slave, perhaps not surpassed by any in this place." Hannah had "been in the family of John Shackford, Esq., the present doorkeeper of the Senate of the United States, for many years; was considered an excellent servant—was the mother of a number of children—and I believe was sold into the family where she met her fate, as a matter of conscience to keep her from being sent below."[130] Cole also asserted that he was "not an advocate of immediate emancipation of the slaves of our country, yet no man has ever yet depicted the wretchedness of the situation of the slaves in colors too dark for the truth."[131]

About eight years later, Thomas B. Finley was accused of whipping to death his slave Rachel in Black Water Township on April 13, 1842, because he objected to her table manners. He buried Rachel in a coffin that he built, but he did not keep her death a secret. A coroner's jury on April 19, 1842, found that Rachel's death was caused by a blood clot on the brain. After a preliminary hearing, Finley was charged with second degree murder or manslaughter. On May 13, 1842, Finley and two other men posted a two-thousand-dollar recognizance bond to secure Finley's appearance at a trial before the Saline County Circuit Court in Marshall on July 18, 1842. Harriet Frazier found no evidence of Finley's trial.[132]

Conrad Carpenter also apparently escaped a murder prosecution when he failed to appear for his trial. He had been indicted in July 1842 for murdering his slave Minerva. Carpenter and three other men posted a two-thousand-dollar recognizance bond to secure Carpenter's appearance at a trial before the Montgomery County Circuit Court in October 1842, but there is no record of any trial.[133]

In another unsolved case, a St. Louis newspaper described a coroner's inquest and report after the death of an enslaved girl named Sarah, who was only eight years and two months old when she died. Leona Campbell, Sarah's owner, had hired her out to Edwin Tanner.[134]

The coroner's jury found that Sarah "came to her death by violence inflicted on her person." The August 13, 1847, report of the coroner Esrom Owens explained that Sarah "came to her death by blows by some person unknown while in the employ of Mr. Tanner." Owens added that—of the 317 inquests he had conducted—this "crime far surpasses anything I have ever seen of human depravity and cruelty." The *Missouri Republican* on August 16, 1847, recounted the details of the alleged crime:

Death by Cruelty.... The body exhibited evidence of the most cruel whipping and beating we have ever heard of. The flesh on the back and limbs were beaten to a jelly—one shoulder bone was laid bare—there were several cuts from a club, on the head and around the neck was the indentation of a cord, by which it was supposed she had been confined to a tree. She had been hired by a man name of Tanner, residing in the neighborhood, and was sent home in this condition. After coming home, her constant request until her death was for bread, by which it would seem that she had been starved as well as unmercifully whipped.

"As in other cases wherein white men murdered slaves in Missouri," Frazier wrote, "the perpetrator was neither hanged nor sent to the penitentiary."[135] The Missouri courts did, however, permit slave owners to sue and recover damages from those who killed or injured their slaves, even after the defendants were found not guilty in criminal prosecutions.[136]

Arkansas Law

There are no recorded slave owner homicide prosecutions in Arkansas or Florida, but the courts applied the common law of slavery although these states had been in the French and Spanish empires. By 1803, Arkansas's total population was only 874, and 12.2 percent were enslaved. Slaves, by 1810, made up 13 percent of the total, and by 1820 this population fell to 11 percent. Arkansas became a U.S. territory in 1819, along with most of what became the state of Oklahoma. It entered the union in 1836, and with growth in the state's cotton production the enslaved population grew steadily, from 15 percent in 1830 to 26 percent in 1860.[137]

Most of Arkansas's enslaved population came to be concentrated in the Mississippi Delta low country region in the state's southern and eastern portions, where cotton production was concentrated. The enslaved population in some of these counties exceeded 50 percent of the total and in one county was 81 percent in 1860.[138]

The 1836 Arkansas constitution did not address slave homicides. It authorized laws "[t]o oblige the owner of any slave or slaves to treat them with humanity," but no such statute was adopted.[139] The legislators also did not enact laws explicitly permitting masters to kill rebellious or resisting slaves. There are no reported appeals following convictions of white defendants accused of slave killings.[140]

The Arkansas Supreme Court nonetheless applied the common law of slavery in *Austin v. State*,[141] an appeal by an enslaved man named Austin who was convicted of murder. Austin, who was owned by Benjamin Watson, allegedly murdered Hiram Payne, "a white man," after Austin had run away from Watson. Payne, Watson, and several others formed a pursuit team that found and approached Austin, who retreated while holding an ax. The pursuers overtook Austin and ordered him to drop the weapon. Austin refused, declaring that "he would not be whipped by Watson, or anybody else, and that he would kill the first man that attempted to take him."

Austin then began to walk away and his pursuers followed. "In a short time [Austin] stopped again and was conversing with Watson, but what was said does not appear." Payne, with "a piece of pine plank" in his hand, "walked directly up to Watson and Austin . . . and drew his stick upon Austin." Austin "stood with his axe drawn" and then "warded off the blow of Payne with his left arm, and with his right struck Payne with the axe." This blow fatally injured Payne.[142]

The Arkansas Supreme Court's opinion by Justice Christopher C. Scott reversed Austin's conviction. But it approved the trial judge's self-defense instructions, stating that if Austin "was in rebellion to the authority of his master, Payne had a right to take [Austin] and to use such force as was necessary to take him." If Austin "then attacked Payne and slew him," Austin "was guilty of murder, and his offense could not be reduced to manslaughter," although Payne's acts "would have been evidence to show an extenuation of the killing of Payne by [Austin] from murder to manslaughter, if the slave had not been at fault in acting in rebellion to the authority of his master." Scott felt "free to say, that the tranquility of the public at large, the security of the master, the value of the slave as property, and the just protection and comfort of the slave himself, all depend so essentially upon his entire subordination to the lawful authority of his master." He thus "would hesitate long before we would declare otherwise than that the principle, laid down in this charge, was any other than a sound general principle of the common law of slavery, as it exists in our slave States."[143]

Accordingly, Scott preserved the slave's "lawful subordination upon which the best interests of the community, of the master, and of the slave, so radically depend, every citizen in common with the master, has an abiding interest." He added that "when a slave is in rebellion to the lawful authority of his master, whatever force may be necessary to bring him within the pale of subordination, graduated upon principles of law and humanity, let it come from what quarter it may, invades no right of the slave, and consequently does him no such wrong as the law can recognize as a mitigation or excuse for crime."[144]

The court extended these principles when James Martin sued Robert A. Brunson, who hired Martin as his overseer for a year beginning on March 1, 1853. Martin alleged that Brunson breached their contract when he failed to pay Martin $250 for his work during the period March 1 to October 15, 1853.

That was the date on which Martin shot and killed Nath, one of Brunson's slaves. Brunson responded that Martin owed him Nath's value of fifteen hundred dollars.[145]

The evidence offered at the trial in the Hempstead Circuit Court revealed that Martin contended that Brunson's slaves "'were a hard set to manage,' and often found idle, in the absence of the overseer. The overseer of the previous year had found it necessary to flog some of them for idleness and other faults common to negroes, and he also had found them 'harder to manage than some negroes he had managed.'" At about eleven o'clock on the morning of October 15, 1853, Martin while at a neighborhood store complained that he "had a rough and saucy set of hands to manage" and said "if he ever overseed again, he would make the negroes obey him, or he would kill them." One witness said Martin "remained at the store until two or three o'clock, and 'was drinking,' but 'seemed to be in a good humor, and laughed and talked a good deal,' and among other things, said, he was going to prove a mule for his employer, which had been taken up as an estray." Another witness recalled that by three that afternoon Martin "showed no signs of being intoxicated."

Martin returned to Brunson's plantation, and "having his whip in his hand," he "went into the field where the hands were picking cotton." He approached Nath and said "that he had 'come for his shirt; to which, *Nath* replied that he had pulled off his shirt to the last overseer.'" Martin then drew a revolver and repeated that he "had come for his shirt, and intended to have it or hurt him." Nath replied, "shoot and be damned." Martin "simultaneously exploding a cap in his first effort to shoot, and at the same moment Nath commenced advancing upon [Martin], with some cotton in one hand, and nothing in the other." Martin shot Nath "three or four times; until, at the last fire, Nath was near enough to knock the pistol up — Nath at the same moment himself falling down."

A physician testified that Nath's body exhibited "the wounds of three balls," and that "the third struck him on the left side of the abdomen, and . . . produced his death." The doctor asserted that "all the shots were made by some one, on the left side of the negro. The wounds could not have been made upon one who advanced directly to the shooter; if at all, while advancing, it must have been done while advancing with his left side to the shooter."[146]

The trial judge told the jury that they could find for Brunson if they believed that Nath's death "was the result of [Martin's] mismanagement," and that Martin "negligently and without necessity" killed Nath. The jury found for Martin. The trial judge denied Brunson's new trial motion.[147]

Justice Scott wrote the Arkansas Supreme Court's opinion affirming the judgment on Brunson's appeal. Citing his opinion in *Austin v. State*, he held the jury instructions were appropriate "in view of the just protection of the slave, which the common law of slavery, as it has grown up in the slave States of this Union, humanely affords to him." He could not "safely displace the word '*necessity*,' as it appears in the charge of the court," adding that "the stern mandates of that same common law of slavery" mitigate "some of its absoluteness of signification, in the absolute right it recognizes, not only of the master or his representative, but also of a stranger, as against the slave, to overcome by proper means, graduated upon principles of humanity and law, the slave's rebellion against the lawful authority of his master."[148]

The jury, Scott wrote, could "determine from the evidence" whether the means Martin "used for overcoming the rebellion in this case, were graduated upon the principles of humanity ... as matter of fact and law, of which latter, *necessity*, in the slayer, as thus understood, was given them by the court as a standard." Although Scott was "loth to subscribe to the verdict, it is still more difficult to say, that it is totally unsupported by the evidence."[149]

Scott's biography suggests how the southern common law of slavery migrated west. Born in 1807 in Virginia, he was orphaned at a young age and moved to Alabama to live with his siblings. Scott returned Virginia to attend Washington College, graduated at the age of twenty, and returned to Alabama. After an unsuccessful business career, he returned to Virginia to study law at the Staunton Law School. He married Elizabeth Smith, whose father Judge Daniel Smith later served on Virginia's Court of Appeals. The Scotts moved to Alabama, where Christopher began to practice law. There he killed a man named Smith in 1838, was fined, and was pardoned by the governor. Scott moved to Arkansas in 1844 and two years later began his judicial career that ended with his death in 1859.[150]

Florida Law

Enslaved Africans were brought to Florida during Spain's reign between 1565 and 1763. More enslaved people were imported by rice and indigo planters when the British controlled Florida between 1763 and 1784. Spain regained control in 1784, and slave imports continued after the United States outlawed the slave trade. Spain ceded Florida to the United States in a February 2, 1819, treaty. It was organized as a territory in 1821 and entered the Union in 1845.[151]

Florida's enslaved population growth continued, and by 1830 slaves were 45 percent of the territory's total population, a percentage that remained about the same until the Civil War, while Florida's total population grew from 34,730 in 1830 to 140,424 in 1860. Most of Florida's enslaved population resided in middle Florida near the Georgia border.[152]

Florida's crimes act of 1828 did not exclude slaves from the general law of homicide. But an 1832 act asserted that "[t]he killing of a slave in the act of revolt shall be deemed justifiable homicide."[153]

James Denham and Randolph Roth argued that antebellum Florida's unstable frontier areas propelled the homicide rate to levels that were high even in the antebellum South. And the white homicide rate exceeded the rate at which blacks, almost all of whom were enslaved, were killed.[154]

Denham nonetheless cited several white Floridians who were prosecuted for killing slaves, but none owned their victims. Three overseers were convicted of slave manslaughter, including George Thompson, who in 1853, was indicted in the Orange County Circuit Court for the murder of a slave under his command at a St. Johns River plantation. He was fined three hundred dollars. The other two overseers, both named Williams, were sentenced respectively in 1856 and 1843 to jail terms of eight months and thirty days.[155]

Florida slave owners also recovered damages from slave killers. Florida's Supreme Court in 1849 reversed a judgment dismissing a suit that Daniel McRaeny filed as trustee for a married woman named Rebecca Williams against William Johnson and Wormley Moore for assaulting and beating to death Sam, a slave owned by a trust for Williams. Justice Thomas Baltzell's opinion stated,

> In cases of injury to this peculiar species of property, the American courts, by a spirit of enlightened humanity, have extended a more enlarged protection than prevails in cases of mere chattels; it is said, slaves are, by the operation of our law, deprived of all personal rights, yet they are moral agents, subject to the same feelings, and have a right to protection from abuse, as other human beings. Whilst different remedies have been used, they all, either impliedly or expressly, admit the right of the master to sustain trespass for any battery of his slave.[156]

Baltzell brought his views on American slavery to Florida in 1825 after earning his law license in Kentucky. He was "known for a fiery temper." Before his judicial career, he challenged Florida's Territorial Secretary James D. Westcott to a duel. Baltzell wounded Westcott, who survived and later became a U.S. senator.[157]

Texas Law

The Texas legislature adopted an 1856 penal code restating the common law of slave homicide. Anglo-Americans began to migrate to Texas with their slaves in the 1820s after Texas gained its independence from Mexico. Most of these immigrants came from southern states. They "brought with them a thorough familiarity with every aspect of the South's peculiar institution, including its legal framework."[158]

The Congress of the Republic of Texas adopted a February 5, 1840, act stating, "if any person or persons shall murder any slave, or so cruelly treat the same as to cause death, the same shall be felony, and punished as in other cases of murder." The act also imposed a fine of between two hundred fifty and two thousand dollars on "any person" convicted of "unreasonably or cruelly treat[ing] or otherwise abus[ing] any slave."[159]

Texas entered the Union as a slave state in 1845. Its enslaved population grew from 27 percent in 1850 to 30 percent in 1860.[160] Enslaved people, in 1850, were more than 50 percent of the total population in six eastern counties. By 1860, thirteen eastern counties had more than 50 percent enslaved populations, while in many western counties this population was less than 25 percent.[161]

The first Texas state constitution stated, "Any person who shall maliciously dismember, or deprive a slave of life, shall suffer such punishment as would be inflicted, in case the like offence had been committed upon a free white person, and on the like proof—except in case of insurrection of such slave."[162]

The Texas Supreme Court applied this law in 1847 in *Chandler v. State*.[163] David Chandler was indicted for murdering Claiborne, a slave owned by David Conner. A Travis County jury convicted Chandler of manslaughter. Chandler argued that the trial judge should have instructed the jury that manslaughter was not a crime in Texas. The trial judge did, however, instruct the jury, as Chandler requested, "that the relation between a white man and a slave is different from that between white men—that if a slave raises his hand against a white man, the white man has then a right to use force sufficient to put down the opposition." The judge also stated that the killing "might or might not be manslaughter according to the circumstances of the case."[164] Justice Royall T. Wheeler's Supreme Court opinion affirming the conviction did not comment on the trial judge's instruction recognizing the unequal relationship between white people and slaves.[165]

The Texas state legislature adopted a February 14, 1848, act imposing a fine of between twenty and five hundred dollars "if any person or persons shall cruelly or unreasonably treat or abuse any slave belonging to him, her, or them, or to another or others," thus reducing the fine imposed by the 1840 act. The Texas Supreme Court in 1855 held that these statutes would "govern or regulate" the conduct of masters and others having custody and control of slaves, while sustaining indictments against J. D. Nix for common law assault and battery with a knife on a slave named Lucy, who was the property of Mrs. McRea.[166]

The Texas legislature adopted a February 11, 1854, law with a section stating that "murder or manslaughter committed upon the body of a slave, shall be punished in the same manner as murder or manslaughter committed upon the body of a free white person."[167] The previous day, the legislature adopted an act requiring the governor to appoint a commission to codify the state's civil and criminal laws. The commissioners John W. Harris, Oliver Cromwell Hartley, and James Willie proposed four codes. But the legislature in August 1856 adopted only the Code of Criminal Procedure and, "with very material amendments," the Penal Code.[168]

The Penal Code defined homicide as "the destruction of the life of one human being by the act, agency, procurement, or culpable omission of another."[169] Article 564 included among justifiable homicides:

1. When a slave is in a state of insurrection.
2. When a slave forcibly resists any lawful order of his master, overseer, or other person, having legal charge of him, in such manner as to give reasonable fear of loss of life, or great bodily harm, in enforcing obedience to such order.
3. Where a runaway slave forcibly resists a person attempting to arrest him, in such manner as to cause reasonable fear of loss of life, or great bodily harm, in making such arrest.
4. Where a slave forcibly resists any patrol or officer of the law, in such manner as to cause reasonable fear of loss of life, or great bodily harm, in executing such order.
5. When a slave uses weapons, calculated to produce death, in any case other than those in which he may lawfully resist with arms, under the provisions of part III of this Code.[170]

Article 565 stated that a slave was in a "state of insurrection" when he or she was "acting in concert with at least four others, and they are armed with the intention of freeing one or more of their number from a state of slavery." The next article stated that "[f]light on the part of a slave, except when in a state of insurrection, does not justify homicide, by either the master or any other person," and that "the killing of a slave, under any other circumstances, except those [enumerated in article 564], is the same offense as the killing of a free person."[171]

Article 575 defined excusable homicide as a killing that "happens by accident or misfortune, though caused by the act of another, who is in the prosecution of a lawful object by lawful means." The next section applied this excuse to the lawful chastisement by parents, guardians, schoolmasters, or masters of their children, wards, scholars, or slaves or apprentices, "yet if done with an instrument likely to produce death, or if with a proper instrument the chastisement be cruelly inflicted, and death result, it is murder."[172]

Article 670 increased the fines for the unreasonable abuse or cruel treatment of slaves to between two hundred fifty and two thousand dollars. One would be guilty of unreasonable abuse, according to article 671, if one were "to inflict a chastisement by whipping, or otherwise greatly disproportioned to the nature of the offense which provoked such chastisement, or beat with unusual implements any such slave." The next section defined cruel treatment of a slave as "to inflict an unusual degree of punishment without just provocation, or to torture, or cause unusual pain and suffering to a slave by the use of means, or subject such slave to punishment so severe as to become injurious to his health, or calculated greatly to depreciate his value."[173]

Article 674 also stated, "If, by reason of abuse or cruel treatment to a slave, death shall result, the offence is murder." But all white people were empowered by article 678, which declared, "Insulting language or gestures from a slave to a free white person will justify reasonable chastisement, whether such person has lawful control over the slave or not."[174]

Several Texans were prosecuted for killing slaves. The courts also permitted masters to file civil suits to recover damages from third parties who killed the masters' slaves.[175]

William R. Wilson was the only Texas slave owner convicted of killing his slave. He was indicted in 1861 for murdering his slave Nat by inflicting "six hundred stripes with a gutta-percha strap." The case was tried in May 1865 before Judge James A. Baker and a jury, which found Wilson not guilty of murder but guilty of slave abuse in violation of the Texas Code. They imposed the maximum two-thousand-dollar fine.[176] The Texas Supreme Court reversed the conviction. Justice Stockton P. Donley's January 1867 opinion was based on the Texas Code, but he added, "Human life cannot be held so cheap that a party wrongfully depriving another of it may be discharged on paying a fine to the state, as is believed was done in the earlier history of our ancestors in certain cases of homicide."[177]

Conclusion

Although the law that the antebellum southern settlers brought west and south included slave murders among the capital crimes, this law also confirmed the underlying notion that enslaved people were not entitled to the common law's equal protection. This law supplemented the masters' civil remedies with potential criminal liability for third-party slave killers, thus protecting the masters' economic interests in their slaves as well as the master class interests in the social order. This law, to a lesser extent, applied to slave owners who wantonly and brutally killed their own submissive slaves, thus limiting the threat to the master class interest posed by excessive or unnecessary slave owner violence.

CONCLUSION

Breaking Out of the Box of Slavery Law

The sometimes shifting standards for the enslavers' homicide liability can be placed on a continuum based on Orlando Patterson's four homicide categories discussed in chapter 1. On one end are the customs of traditional societies, including those in Europe, Britain, and the Americas, which permitted masters to kill their slaves with impunity. On the other end are the written laws in the societies that applied the general homicide standards to masters who killed their slaves. Examples are found in the Spanish, Portuguese, and French codes, and the laws adopted by the elected legislatures in Britain's northern American colonies, in the northern United States, and in the late 1700s in Britain's Atlantic island colonies.

Between these ends of the spectrum were the laws of the Roman and Visigothic rulers, of the early British Atlantic island colonies, and of the British colonies of Virginia, the Carolinas, and Georgia. The slave homicide laws of these Old South states and Tennessee, as well as the slave states added in the antebellum years, exposed even slave owners to execution for murdering their slaves. But they continued to permit masters to kill their slaves as a result of moderate correction or if their slaves dared even to threaten to resist their masters' authority, thus denying to slaves the criminal law's equal protection.[1]

The recorded antebellum U.S. slave master capital convictions enforcing these laws were among the most brutal, sadistic, and wanton killings. They confirm that, in practice, this antebellum law enabled enslavers who legally enforced their power to "rest assured that no one would interfere with their dominion over their slaves." Slave owners could boast of their "benevolence" or "paternalism"—as a class and as individuals—while inflicting "ordinary domestic discipline," which subjected "their slaves to unthinkable cruelties."[2]

The comparative approach reveals how the antebellum U.S. slave homicide reform laws, like the reforms dictated by the Ancient Roman emperors and the Visigothic kings of Spain, were the products of the lawmakers' changing perceptions of the interests of the public, of the individual slave owners, and of the slave owners' families, heirs, and creditors. These laws advanced the slave-owning class's interest by protecting valuable enslaved property from wanton destruction by hirers, overseers, and poor whites who did not own slaves. The legislators and judges, who for the most part were slave owners, also intervened against the most brutal masters, not "because of moral outrage alone; [they] intervened to protect [their] interests. Or rather, [their] strong sense of interest informed [their] moral sensibilities."[3]

In the pre–Civil War years this unequal protection doctrine migrated from the slavery law box to mark free African Americans as second-class citizens when they were accused of crimes against whites, beginning with the decisions of Justices John B. O'Neall of South Carolina and Richmond Pearson of North Carolina.[4] And the 1856 Texas Code restated and applied this rule to "free colored" people, whom the code defined as people with "one-fourth African blood" or more.[5]

But that code did not apply this unequal protection rule when slaves or free persons of color were tried for killing or injuring a white person who "was in the habit of association with slaves or free negroes, and by his general conduct placed himself upon an equality with these classes of persons." The rights of those slaves or free persons of color were to be determined as if their white victims were slaves or free persons of color, unless the white victims were "under the age of eighteen years" or if "the injury was done to the master of the slave" or to any member of the master's family.[6]

Historians have long noted how racial caste laws subjected antebellum southern free African Americans "to special disabilities attaching to them as Negroes, regardless of their legal status as slaves or freemen," and that many of the northern state laws and social norms also imposed some of these disabilities.[7] But the antebellum southern judges and legislators also began explicitly to impose upon free African Americans de jure "racially invidious over-enforcement of the criminal law" and "under-enforcement" that denied them the criminal law's equal protection.[8] This case and statutory law, which had its roots in the laws legitimizing slave master homicides, suggest the need for further comparisons of this law's impact on the customs that Sidney Fant Davis called the "negro law" and I. Bennett Capers called the "white letter law," which persisted even after the postwar constitutional amendments required formal legal equality for all.[9]

NOTES

PREFACE

1. See Testimony of John H. McLaughlin, Trial Record, *State of North Carolina v. John Hoover*, Superior Court, Iredell County, Fall Term 1839, in State Archives of North Carolina, case 2637.

2. See Frank Tannenbaum, *Slave and Citizen: The Negro in the Americas* (New York: Vintage, 1946), 48–82, an expanded version of a March 1946 *Political Science Quarterly* article, reprinted in Frank Tannenbaum, "The Destiny of the Negro in the Western Hemisphere," in *The Balance of Power in Society and Other Essays* (New York: McMillan, 1969), 119–58.

3. See Ulrich B. Phillips, *American Negro Slavery: A Survey of the Supply, Employment and Control of Negro Labor as Determined by the Plantation Regime* (New York: Appleton, 1918), 75–77, 98–114, 327–38, 489–514, 489n1. On Phillips and the related Dunning School critique of Reconstruction, see the essays in *The Dunning School: Historians, Race, and the Meaning of Reconstruction*, ed. John David Smith and J. Vincent Lowery (Lexington: University Press of Kentucky, 2013).

4. Harry H. Johnston, *The Negro in the New World* (New York: MacMillan, 1910), 47n1 ("in the opinion of the negroes themselves the slave-holding nations stood in order of merit as regards the treatment of slaves: the Portuguese first; then the Spaniards, the Danes, the French, English, and Dutch"; emphasis omitted); Mary Wilhelmine Williams, "Slavery, Modern," in *Encyclopedia of the Social Sciences*, ed. Edwin A. Seligman (1930–35; New York: Macmillan, 1937), 14:80–84; Mary Wilhelmine Williams, "The Treatment of Negro Slaves in the Brazilian Empire: A Comparison with the United States of America," *Journal of Negro History* 15, no. 3 (July 1930).

5. See, e.g., Robert J. Cottrol, *The Long, Lingering Shadow: Slavery, Race, and Law in the American Hemisphere* (Athens: University of Georgia Press, 2013), 1–21; Stanley M. Elkins, *Slavery: A Problem in American Institutional and Intellectual Life*, 3rd ed. (Chicago: University of Chicago Press, 1976), 1–26; Philip S. Foner, *History of Black Americans: From Africa to the Emergence of the Cotton Kingdom* (Westport, Conn.: Greenwood, 1975–83) 1:131–34; Michelle McKinley, "Fractional Freedoms: Slavery, Legal Activism, and Ecclesiastical Courts in Colonial Lima, 1593–1689," *Law and History Review* 28, no. 3 (August 2010): 752–55; Alejandro de la Fuente, "Slave Law and Claims-Making in Cuba: The Tannenbaum Debate Revisited," *Law and History Review* 22, no. 2 (Summer 2004): 339–53, and the other articles in "Forum: What Can Frank Tannenbaum Still Teach Us about the Law of Slavery?," *Law and History Review* 22, no. 2 (Summer 2004): 339–87.

6. See McKinley, "Fractional Freedoms," 755.

7. Peter Kolchin, "The American South in Comparative Perspective," in *The American South and the Italian Mezzogiorno: Essays in Comparative History*, ed. Enrico

Dal Lago and Rick Halpern (New York: Palgrave, 2002), 39; see also, e.g., Cottrol, *Long, Lingering Shadow*, 25–109; Peter Kolchin, *A Sphinx on the American Land: The Nineteenth Century South in Comparative Perspective* (Baton Rouge: Louisiana State University Press, 2003), 74–115; Elkins, *Slavery*, 52–80, 223–42; Eugene D. Genovese, *Roll, Jordan, Roll: The World the Slaves Made* (New York: Vintage, 1976), 39–49; Carl N. Degler, *Neither Black nor White: Slavery and Race Relations in Brazil and the United States* (New York: Macmillan, 1971), 3–92; Eugene D. Genovese, *In Red and Black: Marxian Explorations in Southern and Afro American History* (New York: Pantheon Books, 1971), 79–92; Herbert S. Klein, *Slavery in the Americas: A Comparative Study of Virginia and Cuba* (Chicago: University of Chicago Press, 1967), 37–85; David Brion Davis, *The Problem of Slavery in Western Culture* (Ithaca, N.Y.: Cornell University Press, 1966), 100–106, 223–88; Marvin Harris, *Patterns of Race in the Americas* (New York: Walker, 1964), 65–94; Hilary McD. Beckles, "Social and Political Control in Slave Society," in *General History of the Caribbean: Volume III, The Slave Societies of the Caribbean*, ed. Franklin W. Knight (London: UNESCO Publishing, 1997), 194–221; Elsa V. Goveia, "The West Indian Slave Laws of the Eighteenth Century," in *Slavery in the New World: A Reader in Comparative History*, ed. Laura Foner and Eugene Genovese (Englewood Cliffs, N.J.: Prentice Hall, 1969), 113–37; Ariela J. Gross, "Race, Law, and Comparative History," *Law and History Review* 29, no. 2 (May 2011): 549–65; Keila Grinberg, "Freedom Suits and Civil Law in Brazil and the United States," *Slavery & Abolition* 22, no. 3 (December 2001); George M. Fredrickson, "From Exceptionalism to Variability: Recent Developments in Cross-National Comparative History," *Journal of American History* 82, no. 2 (September 1995): 593–94, 597–98; Judith Schafer, "The Long Arm of the Law: Slave Criminals and the Supreme Court in Antebellum Louisiana," *Tulane Law Review* 60, no. 6 (June 1986): 1247–68; David C. Rankin, "The Tannenbaum Thesis Reconsidered: Slavery and Race Relations in Antebellum Louisiana," *Southern Studies* 18, no. 1 (Spring 1979); Mark Tushnet, "The American Law of Slavery, 1810–1860: A Study in the Persistence of Legal Autonomy," *Law & Society Review* 10 (1975): 181–84; Eugene D. Genovese, "Materialism and Idealism in the History of Negro Slavery in the Americas," *Journal of Social History* 1, no. 4 (Summer 1968); Arnold A Sio, "Interpretations of Slavery: The Slave Status in the Americas," *Comparative Studies in Society and History* 7, no. 3 (April 1965). For comparative studies, see, e.g., Seymour Drescher, *Abolition: A History of Slavery and Antislavery* (New York: Cambridge University Press, 2009); Stanley L. Engerman, *Slavery, Emancipation, and Freedom: Comparative Perspectives* (Baton Rouge: Louisiana State University Press, 2007); Orlando Patterson, *Slavery and Social Death: A Comparative Study* (Cambridge, Mass.: Harvard University Press, 1982); George M. Fredrickson, *White Supremacy: A Comparative Study of American and South African History* (New York: Oxford University Press, 1981).

8. David Brion Davis, "Looking at Slavery from Broader Perspectives," *American Historical Review* 105, no. 2 (April 2000): 454; see Sue Peabody, "Slavery, Freedom, and the Law in the Atlantic World, 1420–1807," in *The Cambridge History of Slavery: Volume 3 AD 1420–AD 1804*, ed. David Eltis and Stanley L. Engerman (Cambridge: Cambridge University Press, 2011), 594–630; Peter Kolchin, "The Big Picture: A Comment on David Brion Davis's 'Looking at Slavery from Broader Perspectives,'" *American Historical*

Review 105, no. 2 (April 2000). For comparative studies in the British colonies, see, e.g., Richard S. Dunn, *A Tale of Two Plantations: Slave Life and Labor in Jamaica and Virginia* (Cambridge, Mass.: Harvard University Press, 2014), 1–22; Paul M. Pressly, *On the Rim of the Caribbean: Colonial Georgia and the British Atlantic World* (Athens: University of Georgia Press, 2013); Virginia Bernhard, *A Tale of Two Colonies: What Really Happened in Virginia and Bermuda* (Columbia: University of Missouri Press, 2011); Philip D. Morgan, *Slave Counterpoint: Black Culture in the Eighteenth-Century Chesapeake and Lowcountry* (Chapel Hill: University of North Carolina Press, 1998).

9. See Peter Kolchin, *American Slavery 1619–1877*, rev. ed. (New York: Hill & Wang, 2003), "Afterword," 248; but see, expressing concerns about the comparative method, Joseph C. Miller, *The Problem of Slavery as History: A Global Approach* (New Haven, Conn.: Yale University Press, 2012), 22–24, 121–30; Eric Hinderaker and Rebecca Horn, "Territorial Crossings: Histories and Historiographies of the Early Americas," *William and Mary Quarterly*, 3rd ser., 67, no. 3 (July 2010): 412–32.

10. Alan Watson, *Slave Law in the Americas* (Athens: University of Georgia Press, 1989), ix; see ibid., xi–xv; Jack P. Greene, "Early Modern Southeastern North America and the Border Atlantic and American Worlds," *Journal of Southern History* 23, no. 3 (August 2007): 529. On the law in action, see, e.g., Sidney W. Mintz, *Caribbean Transformations* (Chicago: Aldine, 1974), 72; David Lowenthal, *West Indian Societies* (New York: Oxford University Press, 1972), 39–40; Harris, *Patterns of Race in the Americas*, 76. On making judgments and evaluations, see Andrew Fede, *Roadblocks to Freedom: Slavery and Manumission in the United States South* (New Orleans: Quid Pro Books, 2011), 5–6; Eric L. Muller, "Judging Thomas Ruffin and the Hindsight Defense," *North Carolina Law Review* 87, no. 3 (March 2009): 760.

11. See, e.g., for Florida, Larry Eugene Rivers, *Slavery in Florida: Territorial Days to Emancipation* (Gainesville: University of Florida Press, 2000), 1–15, 66–67; for Louisiana, Thomas Ingersoll, *Mammon and Manon in Early New Orleans: The First Slave Society in the Deep South* (Knoxville: University of Tennessee Press, 1999), 134–43, 232–39, 322–29; and for Canada, Afua Cooper, *The Hanging of Angelique: The Untold Story of Canadian Slavery and the Burning of Old Montreal* (Toronto: HarperCollins, 2006), 74–84; Robin W. Winks, *The Blacks in Canada: A History* (New Haven, Conn.: Yale University Press, 1971), 1–60. For a history of one family providing a comparative analysis, see Rebecca J. Scott and Jean M. Hebrard, *Freedom Papers: An Atlantic Odyssey in the Age of Emancipation* (Cambridge, Mass.: Harvard University Press, 2012).

12. See Andrew Fede, *People without Rights: An Interpretation of the Fundamentals of the Law of Slavery in the U.S. South* (New York: Garland, 1992; repr., New York: Routledge, 2011); Andrew T. Fede, "Judging Against the Grain? Reading Mississippi Supreme Court Judge Joshua G. Clarke's Views on Slavery Law in Context," *FHC Annals: Journal of the Florida Conference of Historians* 20 (May 2013): 11–29; Andrew T. Fede, review of *The Bondsman's Burden: An Economic Analysis of the Common Law of Southern Slavery*, by Jenny Bourne Wahl, *American Journal of Legal History* 62, no. 4 (October 1998); Andrew T. Fede, review of *Southern Slavery and the Law, 1619–1860*, by Thomas D. Morris, *American Journal of Legal History* 61, no. 3 (July 1997); Andrew Fede, "Legitimized Violent Slave Abuse in the American South, 1619–1865: A Case Study of Law

and Social Change in Six Southern States," *American Journal of Legal History* 29, no. 2 (April 1985); Andrew Fede, "Toward a Solution of the Slave Law Dilemma: A Critique of Tushnet's 'The American Law of Slavery,'" *Law and History Review* 2, no. 2 (Fall 1984); see also Andrew Fede, "Legal Protection for Slave Buyers in the U.S. South: A Caveat Concerning *Caveat Emptor,*" *American Journal of Legal History* 31, no. 4 (October 1987); Andrew T. Fede, "Gender in the Law of Slavery in the Antebellum United States," *Cardozo Law Review* 18, no. 2 (November 1996).

13. See Margaret Abruzzo, *Polemical Pain: Slavery, Cruelty, and the Rise of Humanitarianism* (Baltimore: Johns Hopkins University Press, 2011), 14–15; see generally Miller, *Problem of Slavery as History*, 4.

14. See Bryan A. Garner, *The Elements of Legal Style*, 2nd ed. (New York: Oxford University Press, 2002), 86–89.

15. See Sally A. Downey, "James C.N. Paul, 85, Helped Found First Law School in Ethiopia," *philly.com*, accessed July 18, 2015, http://articles.philly.com/2011-09-22/news/30189839_1_eritrea-and-ethiopia-addis-ababa-university-meles-zenawi.

16. See William Weber, "In Memoriam: John Anthony ('Tony') Scott (1916–2010)," *Perspectives on History*, accessed July 18, 2015, https://www.historians.org/publications-and-directories/perspectives-on-history/december-2010/in-memoriam-john-anthony-(tony)-scott; John Anthony Scott, *Hard Trials on My Way: Slavery and the Struggle Against It 1800–1860* (New York: Mentor, 1974); John Anthony Scott, "Roll, Jordan, Roll: The World the Slaves Made," *Challenge*, May/June 1975, 65–71; Eugene Genovese to author, March 1, 1988.

INTRODUCTION. A Murder Trial and the Comparative Law of Slave Killing

1. See, e.g., Andrew Fede, *Roadblocks to Freedom: Slavery and Manumission in the United States South* (New Orleans: Quid Pro Books, 2011), 6–7. For the divergent views of southern whites and slaves on the relationship between slavery and violence, see Dickson D. Bruce, Jr., *Violence and Culture in the Antebellum South* (Austin: University of Texas Press, 1979), 114–60.

2. See Harriet Beecher Stowe, *The Key to Uncle Tom's Cabin* (Boston: John P. Jewett & Co., 1853; repr., New York: Arno Press, 1968), 177, 182. Stowe quotes and comments on the article "The Trial for Murder," *Charleston Courier*, May 6, 1847, 2. See ibid., 175–88; see also "An Extraordinary Trial," *National Era* (Washington, D.C.) 1, no. 22 (June 3, 1847): 1.

3. See Amrita Chakrabarti Myers, *Forging Freedom: Black Women and the Pursuit of Liberty in Antebellum Charleston* (Chapel Hill: University of South Carolina Press, 2011), 21–32, 26; see also Robert N. Rosen, *A Short History of Charleston*, 2nd ed. (Columbia: University of South Carolina Press, 1992), 67–70, 75–77; Frederic Cople Jaher, *The Urban Establishment: Upper Strata in Boston, New York, Charleston, Chicago, and Los Angeles* (Urbana: University of Illinois Press, 1982), 317–451; Stephanie E. Yuhl, "Hidden in Plain Sight: Centering the Domestic Slave Trade in American Public History," *Journal of Southern History* 73, no. 3 (August 2013): 593–624. On the Vesey matter, see, e.g., Lacy K. Ford, *Deliver Us from Evil: The Slavery Question in the Old South* (New York:

Oxford University Press, 2009), 205–96; Michael P. Johnson, "Denmark Vesey and His Co-conspirators," *William and Mary Quarterly*, 3rd ser., 58, no. 4 (October 2001): 915–76; and the articles in "*Forum*: The Making of a Slave Conspiracy, Part 2," *William and Mary Quarterly*, 3rd ser., 59, no. 1 (January 2002): 135–202.

4. See 1850 Census, St. Michael and St. Phillip, Charleston, S.C.; roll: M432; p. 99A; image 38, accessed July 23, 2013, http://search.ancestry.com; John H. Honour, "A Directory of the City of Charleston and Neck for 1849," in James W. Hagy, *Directories for the City of Charleston, South Carolina for the Years 1849, 1852, and 1855* (Baltimore: Clearfield, 1998), 38; Mabel L. Webber, "Records from the Elliot-Rowand Bible," *South Carolina Historical and Genealogical Magazine* 11, no. 1 (January 1910): 71. On factors, see Harold D. Woodman, *King Cotton and His Retainers: Financing and Marketing the Cotton Crop of the South 1800–1925* (Lexington: University Press of Kentucky, 1968), 8–14; Alfred Holt Stone, "The Cotton Factorage System in the Southern States," *American Historical Review* 20, no. 3 (April 1915): 557, 561.

5. See Stowe, *Key to Uncle Tom's Cabin*, 185. Stowe refers to Eliza's mother as "Mrs. T. C. Bee." Eliza's parents were Peter Smith Bee and Frances Caroline Ward Bee. See Barnwell Rhett Heyward, "The Descendants of Col. William Rhett of South Carolina," *South Carolina Historical and Genealogical Magazine* 4, no. 1 (January 1903): 71.

6. See Stowe, *Key to Uncle Tom's Cabin*, 181. On the coroner's role, see "An Act Concerning the Office, Duties and Liabilities of Coroner," in *The Statutes at Large of South Carolina, Volume XI, Containing the Acts from 1838* (Columbia, S.C.: Republican Printing, 1873), 55–62; "An Act Relating unto the Office and Duty of a Coroner, and for Settling and Ascertaining the Fees of the Same," in *The Statutes at Large of South Carolina, Volume Second, 1682–1716*, ed. Thomas Cooper (Columbia, S.C.: A. S. Johnston, 1837), 269–73; Benjamin James, *A Digest of the Laws of South-Carolina* (Columbia, S.C.: Telescope Press, 1822), 32–37; *The South-Carolina Justice of Peace*, 3rd ed. (New York: T. & J. Swords, 1810), 126–31; see generally Jeffrey M. Jentzen, *Death Investigation in America: Coroners, Medical Examiners, and the Pursuit of Medical Certainty* (Cambridge, Mass.: Harvard University Press, 2009), 1–30; Stephen Berry, "The Historian as Death Investigator," in *Weirding the War: Stories from the Civil War's Raged Edges*, ed. Stephen Berry (Athens: University of Georgia Press, 2011), 178–81; Elizabeth Dale, "Criminal Justice in the United States, 1790–1920: A Government of Laws or Men?," in *The Cambridge History of Law in America*, ed. Michael Grossberg and Christopher Tomlins (Cambridge: Cambridge University Press, 2008), 2:148–49.

7. See Stowe, *Key to Uncle Tom's Cabin*, 181–82.

8. See ibid., 182.

9. See ibid., 185–86.

10. See "From the Charleston News, Jan. 8," *New York Commercial Advertiser*, January 15, 1847, 1. The article refers to Maria as Mrs. Bee's slave. See ibid.

11. See "Odds and Ends," *Cape Ann Light and Gloucester (Mass.) Telegraph*, January 23, 1847, 1.

12. See David J. McCord, ed., *Statutes at Large of South Carolina* (Columbia: A. S. Johnston, 1840), 7:427, 400–402, 354–55, 346; *Ex parte Boylston*, 33 S.C.L. (2 Strob.) 41 (Court of Appeals of Law 1847); see also Bruce Eelman, *Entrepreneurs in the Southern*

Upcountry: Commercial Culture in Spartanburg, South Carolina, 1845–1880 (Athens: University of Georgia Press, 2008), 92–98; Robert Olwell, *Masters, Slaves, and Subjects: The Culture of Power in the South Carolina Low Country, 1740–1790* (Ithaca, N.Y.: Cornell University Press, 1998), 63, 71–101; Michael Stephen Hindus, *Prison and Plantation: Crime, Justice, and Authority in Massachusetts and South Carolina, 1767–1878* (Chapel Hill: University of North Carolina Press, 1980), 129–33; Howell Meadoes Henry, *The Police Control of the Slave in South Carolina* (Emory, 1914; repr., New York: Negro Universities Press, 1968), 58–65; John Belton O'Neall, *Negro Law of South Carolina Collected and Digested by John Belton O'Neall* (Columbia: John G. Bowman, 1848), 33–36 (noting that Charleston's procedures were "better" than elsewhere in the state but criticizing these procedures as "the worst system which could be devised").

13. See McCord, *Statutes at Large*, 7:401–2, see also, e.g., Thomas D. Morris, *Southern Slavery and the Law, 1619–1860* (Chapel Hill: University of North Carolina Press, 1996), 229–39; Thomas R. R. Cobb, *An Inquiry into the Law of Negro Slavery in the United States of America* (Philadelphia: T. & J. W. Johnson & Co., and Savannah: W. Thorne Williams, 1858; repr., Athens: University of Georgia Press, 1999), 226–34.

14. See "Trial for Murder," *Edgefield (S.C.) Advertiser*, February 10, 1847, 4; see also "The Charleston Case," *Pennsylvania Freeman* (Philadelphia), January 28, 1847, 3; "Trial of a Slave for Murder," *Albany (N.Y.) Evening Journal*, January 28, 1847, 2; "Trial of a Slave for Murder," *Brooklyn Daily Eagle*, January 27, 1847: 2; "Trial of a Slave for Murder," in *The Law Reporter*, ed. Peleg W. Chander, 9 (1847): 524. On the law regarding a slave's liability for crimes committed at the master's direction, see Cobb, *Inquiry into the Law of Negro Slavery*, 265–66; Craig Buettinger, "Did Slaves Have Free Will? *Luke, a Slave, v. Florida* and Crime at the Command of the Master," *Florida Historical Quarterly* 83, no. 3 (Winter 2005): 257.

15. See "In the Court of General Sessions and Common Pleas—Spring Term, 1847," *Charleston Courier*, May 5, 1847): 2. On O'Neall, see, e.g., Fede, *Roadblocks to Freedom*, 372–73; Bernie D. Jones, *Fathers of Conscience: Mixed-Race Inheritance in the Antebellum South* (Athens: University of Georgia Press, 2009), 140–46; Alexander M. Sanders, Jr., "O'Neall, John Belton," in *The Yale Biographical Dictionary of American Law*, ed. Roger K. Newman (New Haven, Conn.: Yale University Press, 2009), 410–11; A. E. Keir Nash, "Negro Rights, Unionism, and Greatness on the South Carolina Court of Appeals: The Extraordinary Chief Justice John Belton O'Neall," *South Carolina Law Review* 21 (1969): 141–90; see also Laura F. Edwards, *The People and Their Peace: Legal Culture and the Transformation of Inequality in the Post-revolutionary South* (Chapel Hill: University of North Carolina Press, 2009), 34–35 (discussing O'Neall among the antebellum legal reformers).

16. See Stowe, *Key to Uncle Tom's Cabin*, 178–79. On Petigru, see William H. Pease and Jane H. Pease, *James Louis Petigru: Southern Conservative, Southern Dissenter* (Athens: University of Georgia Press, 1995); Warren Moise, *Rebellion in the Temple of Justice: The Federal and State Courts in South Carolina during the War between the States* (Lincoln, Neb.: iUniverse, 2003), 40–41; Elizabeth Fox-Genovese and Eugene Genovese, *The Mind of the Master Class: History and Faith in the Southern Slaveholder's Worldview* (New York: Cambridge University Press, 2005), 98.

17. Stowe, *Key to Uncle Tom's Cabin*, 180.

18. See ibid., 180–82.

19. See ibid., 182–84. On the slaves' "gossip networks," see Edwards, *People and Their Peace*, 7–8, 102–3, 117–21, 124–25.

20. See Stowe, *Key to Uncle Tom's Cabin*, 185–86.

21. See "The State vs. Eliza C. Rowand," *Charleston Courier*, May 14, 1847, 2; see also Stowe, *Key to Uncle Tom's Cabin*, 186.

22. See *Census of Charleston South Carolina for 1861* (Charleston: Evans and Cogswell, 1861), 58; 1860 Census, Charleston Ward 2, Charleston, S.C., roll: M653, p. 224, image 82, accessed August 5, 2013, http://search.ancestry.com; 1850 Census, St. Michael and St. Phillip, Charleston, S.C., roll: M432, p. 99A, image 38, accessed July 23, 2013, http://search.ancestry.com; U.S. Bureau of the Census, Seventh Census of the United States, 1850, Washington, D.C.: National Archives and Records Administration, M432, accessed July 23, 2013, http://search.ancestry.com; Charleston City Death Records 1821–1914, accessed August 5, 2013, http://search.ancestry.com.

23. See Stowe, *Key to Uncle Tom's Cabin*, 177; see also "Southern Justice," *Maine Cultivator and Hallowell Gazette*, 1.

24. See E. J. Stearns Jr., *Notes on Uncle Tom's Cabin: A Logical Answer to the Allegations and Inferences against Slavery as an Institution* (Philadelphia: Lippincott, 1853), 201.

25. See Andrew Fede, *People without Rights: An Interpretation of the Fundamentals of the Law of Slavery in the U.S. South*, (New York: Garland, 1992; repr., New York: Routledge, 2011), 86–87; Hindus, *Prison and Plantation*, 91–93, 133–36; Henry, *Police Control of the Slave*, 70–76.

26. See, e.g., chapters 6 to 11; Christopher Tomlins, *Freedom Bound: Law, Labor, and Civic Identity in Colonizing English America, 1580–1865* (New York: Cambridge University Press, 2010), 427–52; Fede, *People without Rights*, 62–70; Eugene D. Genovese, *Roll, Jordan, Roll: The World the Slaves Made* (New York: Vintage, 1976), 37–38; Henry, *Police Control of the Slave*, 67–68; George M. Stroud, *A Sketch of the Laws Relating to Slavery in the Several States of the United States of America* (2nd ed., 1856; repr., New York: Negro Universities Press, 1968), 20–28; see also Anthony W. Neal, *Unburdened by Conscience: A Black People's Collective Account of America's Ante-Bellum South and the Aftermath* (Lanham, Md.: University Press of America, 2009), 36–37. On the criminal law and the death penalty in colonial America, see, e.g., Douglas Greenberg, "Crime, Law Enforcement, and Social Control in Colonial America," *American Journal of Legal History* 26, no. 4 (October 1982): 53–85. The geographic area included within the term "southern law" may have different meanings in different times. See Paul Finkelman, "Exploring Southern Legal History," *North Carolina Law Review* 64, no. 1 (November 1985): 85–87. In the colonial period it includes the six colonies south of Pennsylvania, and, in the antebellum period, the fifteen states that had not by the Civil War taken steps to abolish slavery. Ibid., 86. I will refer to the southern colonies and states to include the eleven states that seceded from the Union and the border states to include Delaware, Maryland, Kentucky, and Missouri. See Stanley Harold, *Border War: Fighting over Slavery before the Civil War* (Chapel Hill: University of North Carolina Press, 2010), 4–7.

27. Ulrich B. Phillips, *American Negro Slavery: A Survey of the Supply, Employment and Control of Negro Labor as Determined by the Plantation Regime* (New York: Appleton, 1918), 509; see also Alfred H. Stone, "The Early Slave Laws of Mississippi," in *Publications of the Mississippi Historical Society*, ed. Franklin Riley (Oxford, 1899), 2:141–45.

28. See Stanley M. Elkins, *Slavery: A Problem in American Institutional and Intellectual Life*, 3rd ed. (Chicago: University of Chicago Press, 1976), 57–59; Kenneth M. Stampp, *The Peculiar Institution: Slavery in the Ante-Bellum South* (New York: Vintage, 1956), 218–20.

29. See Fede, *People without Rights*, 70–97; Daniel Flanigan, *The Criminal Law of Slavery and Freedom 1800–1868* (New York: Garland, 1987), 145–69; Andrew Fede, "Legitimized Violent Slave Abuse in the American South, 1619–1865: A Case Study of Law and Social Change in Six Southern States," *American Journal of Legal History* 29, no. 2 (April 1985): 114–17; compare A. E. Keir Nash, "A More Equitable Past? Southern Supreme Courts and the Protection of the Antebellum Negro," *North Carolina Law Review* 48 (1969–70): 203–42; A. E. Keir Nash, "Fairness and Formalism in the Trials of Blacks in the State Supreme Courts of the Old South," *Virginia Law Review* 56, no. 1 (February 1970): 67–76; see also Morris, *Southern Slavery and the Law*, 171–81.

30. See Fede, *People without Rights*, 3–15, 61–97; Fede, "Legitimized Violent Slave Abuse," 101–26, 149; see also Fede, *Roadblocks to Freedom*, 9–12. For a discussion of the development pattern for plantation slavery in the U.S. South, which included the frontier period, the plantation boom, the mature plantation period, and the decline of plantation slavery, see Fede, "Legitimized Violent Slave Abuse," 101–10, citing Lewis C. Gray, *History of Agriculture in the Southern United States to 1860* (1932; repr., Gloucester, Mass.: Peter Smith, 1958), 1:14–22, 42–59, 213–34, 312–41, 437–62; Phillips, *American Negro Slavery*, 73–186; Ulrich B. Phillips, "Introduction," in *A Documentary History of American Industrial Society, Plantation and Frontier Documents: 1649–1863 Illustrative of Industrial History in the Colonial and Ante-Bellum South*, ed. Ulrich B. Phillips (Cleveland: Arthur H. Clark, 1909), 1:69–104; Ulrich B. Phillips, "The Origin and Growth of the Southern Black Belts," *American Historical Review* 11, no. 4 (July 1906): 798–816 (the latter two articles are reprinted in Ulrich B. Phillips, *The Slave Economy of the Old South: Selected Essays in Economic and Social History*, ed. Eugene Genovese [Baton Rouge: Louisiana State University Press, 1968], 3–22, 95–116). See also Ira Berlin, *Generations in Captivity: A History of African-American Slaves* (Cambridge, Mass.: Harvard University Press, 2003), 2–144; Philip D. Morgan, *Slave Counterpoint: Black Culture in the Eighteenth-Century Chesapeake and Lowcountry* (Chapel Hill: University of North Carolina Press, 1998), xviii, citing Willie Lee Rose, "The Domestication of Domestic Slavery," in *Slavery and Freedom*, ed. William W. Freehling (New York: Oxford University Press, 1982), 18–36; Ira Berlin, "Time, Space, and the Evolution of Afro-American Society in British Mainland America," *American Historical Review* 85, no. 1 (February 1980): 44–78. See also, listing seven phases of South Carolina low country slave society evolution, Robert Olwell, "The Long History of a Low Place: Slavery on the South Carolina Coast, 1670–1870," in *Slavery in the American South*, ed. Winthrop Jordan (Jackson: University Press of Mississippi, 2003), 123–26.

31. Bertram Wyatt-Brown, *Southern Honor: Ethics and Behavior in the Old South* (New York: Oxford University Press, 1982), 375.

32. Ibid., 376.

33. See Edwards, *People and Their Peace*, 7–8, 102–3, 117–21, 124–25, 193–94; Genovese, *Roll, Jordan, Roll*, 41–43; Stampp, *Peculiar Institution*, 222–24; Walter Johnson, "On Agency," *Journal of Social History* 37, no. 1 (Fall 2003): 115–16.

34. See, e.g., Genovese, *Roll, Jordan, Roll*, 37–38; Stampp, *Peculiar Institution*, 220–23.

35. See, e.g., Genovese, *Roll, Jordan, Roll*, 38–39; Stampp, *Peculiar Institution*, 222.

36. See, e.g., Dale, "Criminal Justice in the United States," 150; George Fisher, "The Jury's Rise as a Lie Detector," *Yale Law Journal* 107, no. 3 (December 1997): 575–713; see also Fede, *People without Rights*, 187–89 (discussing masters' right to testify in favor of their slaves).

37. See Morris, *Southern Slavery and the Law*, 171–72; see also, e.g., Peter Kolchin, *American Slavery 1619–1877*, rev. ed. (New York: Hill & Wang, 2003), 59–62; Winthrop D. Jordan, *White over Black: American Attitudes toward the Negro 1550–1812* (Chapel Hill: University of North Carolina Press, 1968), 366–67; Elizabeth B. Clark, "'The Sacred Rights of the Weak': Pain, Sympathy, and the Culture of Individual Rights in Antebellum America," *Journal of American History* 82, no. 2 (September 1995): 492–93.

38. See Morris, *Southern Slavery and the Law*, 181.

39. See Lea VanderVelde, "The Last *Legally* Beaten Servant in America: From Compulsion to Coercion in the American Workplace," *Seattle University Law Review* 39, no. 3 (Spring 2016): 749.

40. See Justin Roberts, *Slavery and the Enlightenment in the British Atlantic, 1750–1807* (New York: Cambridge University Press, 2013), 6, 55.

41. See Margaret Abruzzo, *Polemical Pain: Slavery, Cruelty, and the Rise of Humanitarianism* (Baltimore: Johns Hopkins University Press, 2011); Joyce E. Chaplin, *An Anxious Pursuit: Agricultural Innovation and Modernity in the Lower South, 1730–1815* (Chapel Hill: North Carolina University Press, 1993).

42. See Ely Aaronson, *From Slave Abuse to Hate Crime: The Criminalization of Racial Violence in American History* (New York: Cambridge University Press, 2014), 41; Fede, *People without Rights*, 51–53; James Oakes, *Slavery and Freedom: An Interpretation of the Old South* (New York: Norton, 1990), 158; Willie Lee Rose, "The Domestication of Domestic Slavery," in *Slavery and Freedom*, ed. William W. Freehling (New York: Oxford University Press, 1982), 24.

43. See Fede, "Legitimized Violent Slave Abuse," 96; see also Fede, *People without Rights*, 22, 84–85. See, using a similar "multi-factored" analysis, Morris, *Southern Slavery and the Law*, 2–9.

44. See VanderVelde, "Last *Legally* Beaten Servant in America," 749–50, quoting Richard B. Morris, *Government and Labor in Early America* (New York: Columbia University Press, 1946), 523. For Derrick Bell's analysis contending that "[t]he interest of blacks in achieving racial equality will be accommodated only when it converges with the interests of whites," see, e.g., Derrick A. Bell, Jr., "*Brown v. Board of Education* and the Interest-Convergence Dilemma," *Harvard Law Review* 93, no. 3 (January 1980): 523.

45. See chapters 1 and 2.

46. See Christopher Tomlins, "Introduction: The Many Legalities of Colonization: A Manifesto of Destiny of Early American Legal History," in *The Many Legalities of Early America*, ed. Christopher L. Tomlins and Bruce H. Mann (Chapel Hill: University

of North Carolina Press, 2001), 13; see also William E. Nelson, *The Common Law in Colonial America: Volume I, The Chesapeake and New England, 1607–1660* (New York: Oxford University Press, 2008), 6; David S. Clark, "Comparative Law in Colonial British America," *American Journal of Comparative Law* 59, no. 3 (Summer 2011): 647–53; see generally Lauren Benton, *A Search for Sovereignty: Law and Geography in European Empires 1400–1900* (New York: Cambridge University Press, 2010), 1–39, 270–99. Historians have recently critiqued the terms "settlers" and "settlement" for their implied assumptions. When I use these terms, I am referring to "colonists" or "European settlers," who in many cases replaced or displaced Native American settlements. See, e.g., Wendy Warren, *New England Bound: Slavery and Colonization in Early America* (New York: Liveright, 2016), 89–91; James H. Merrill, "Second Thoughts on colonial Historians and American Indians," *William and Mary Quarterly*, 3rd ser., 69, no. 3 (July 2012): 473–84. Scholars also have used the terms "colonies of settlers" and "colonies of exploiters" to describe colonization patterns. Settler colonies were extensions of the metropolitan culture and society for the settlers' own occupation, with or without imported enslaved labor. The settlers either excluded the indigenous population or ruled that population. Exploitation colonies were characterized by "a small, intrusive, managerial class; a numerically preponderant, ethnically differentiated laboring class; and an economic activity that supported the community." Labor was supplied by a dominated indigenous population, imported slaves, or both. See Franklin W. Knight, *The Caribbean: The Genesis of a Fragmented Nationalism*, 2nd ed. (New York: Oxford University Press, 1990), 68–83, 78; see also Philip D. Curtin, *The Rise and Fall of the Plantation Complex*, 2nd ed. (New York: Cambridge University Press, 1998), 10–16.

47. See chapters 3 and 4.

48. See Kolchin, *American Slavery*, 255–56; Ira Berlin, *Many Thousands Gone: The First Two Centuries of Slavery in North America* (Cambridge, Mass.: Belknap, 1998), 7–11; Moses I. Finley, *Ancient Slavery and Modern Ideology*, expanded, ed. Brent D. Shaw (Princeton, N.J.: Markus Wiener, 1998), 147–49; Keith Hopkins, *Conquerors and Slaves: Sociological Studies in Roman History*, vol. 1 (New York: Cambridge University Press, 1978), 99–100.

49. See, e.g., Kolchin, *American Slavery*, 252, 254; Orlando Patterson, *Slavery and Social Death: A Comparative Study* (Cambridge, Mass.: Harvard University Press, 1982), 354–64; Stanley L. Engerman and B. W. Higman, "The Demographic Structure of the Caribbean Slave Societies in the Eighteenth and Nineteenth Centuries," in *General History of the Caribbean: Volume III, The Slave Societies of the Caribbean*, ed. Franklin W. Knight (London: UNESCO Publishing, 1997), 49–51; Raymond T. Diamond, "Condemned by Substance and Process: A Comment on 'Doubly Condemned': Adjustments to the Crime and Punishment Regime in the Late Slavery Period in the British Caribbean Colonies and 'Under the Present Mode of Trial, Improper Verdicts are Very Often Given': Criminal Procedure in the Trials of Slaves in Antebellum Louisiana," *Cardozo Law Review* 18, no. 2 (November 1996): 757.

50. See Fede, *People without Rights*, 67; see also Eliga H. Gould, *Among the Powers of the Earth: The American Revolution and the Making of a New World Empire* (Cambridge, Mass.: Harvard University Press, 2012), 57–58; Paul Finkelman, *Slavery and the Founders: Race and Liberty in the Age of Jefferson*, 2nd ed. (New York: M.E. Sharpe, 2001),

3–36; Paul Finkelman, "How the Proslavery Constitution Led to the Civil War," *Rutgers Law Journal* 43, no. 3 (Fall/Winter 2013): 407–38.

51. Wyatt Espy and John Ortiz Smykla, "Executions in the U.S. 1608–2002: The Espy File Executions by State," 193, Death Penalty Information Center, accessed March 10, 2015, http://www.deathpenaltyinfo.org/documents/ESPYstate.pdf.

52. See Fede, *People without Rights*, 80; Fede, "Legitimized Violent Slave Abuse," 120.

CHAPTER 1. Ancient Approaches to the Law of Homicide and Slave Killing

1. See John Phillip Reid, *Patterns of Vengeance: Crosscultural Homicide in the North American Fur Trade* (Pasadena, Calif.: Ninth Judicial Circuit Historical Society, 1999), 20–24, 40–50; John Phillip Reid, *A Law of Blood: The Primitive Law of the Cherokee Nation* (New York: New York University Press, 1970), 73–84; "Homicide," in *Black's Law Dictionary*, deluxe 9th ed., ed. Bryan A. Garner (St. Paul: West, 2009), 802. On human sacrifice, see, e.g., Andres Resendez, *The Other Slavery: The Uncovered Story of Indian Enslavement in America* (New York: Houghton Mifflin Harcourt, 2016), 3, 64; Fernando Santos-Granero, *Vital Enemies: Slavery, Predation, and Amerindian Political Economy of Life* (Austin: University of Texas Press, 2009), 49, 63, 86, 91, 130, 139, 142, 152, 211, 220–21; Donald G. Kyle, *Spectacles of Death in Ancient Rome* (New York: Routledge, 1998), 36–37; Jan N. Bremmer, "Human Sacrifice: A Brief Introduction," in *The Strange World of Human Sacrifice*, ed. Jan N. Bremmer (Leuven: Peeters, 2007), 1–8.

2. See Mark S. Weiner, *The Rule of the Clan: What an Ancient Form of Social Organization Reveals about the Future of Individual Freedom* (New York: Farrar, Straus & Giroux, 2013), 10.

3. See Henry Sumner Maine, *Ancient Law: Its Connection with the Early History of Society and Its Relation to Modern Ideas*, 4th ed. (London: John Murray, 1870), 165–70; see also, e.g., Weiner, *Rule of the Clan*, 3–14.

4. See Holly Brewer, *By Birth or Consent: Children, Law, and the Anglo-American Revolution in Authority* (Chapel Hill: University of North Carolina Press, 2005), 5–8, 352–59; Martha Minow, *Making All the Difference: Inclusion, Exclusion, and American Law* (Ithaca, N.Y.: Cornell University Press, 1990), 121–28; Paul Diesing, *Patterns of Discovery in the Social Sciences* (Chicago: Aldine Atherton, 1971), 201–2.

5. See Christina Snyder, *Slavery in Indian Country: The Changing Face of Captivity in Early America* (Cambridge, Mass.: Harvard University Press, 2010), 19–20; Harold J. Berman, *Law and Revolution: The Formation of the Western Legal Tradition* (Cambridge, Mass.: Harvard University Press, 1983), 52–61; John Phillip Reid, *A Better Kind of Hatchet: Law, Trade, and Diplomacy in the Cherokee Nation during the Early Years of European Contact* (University Park: Pennsylvania State University Press, 1976), 1–12; Reid, *A Law of Blood*, 49–71; Tacitus, "Germania," in Tacitus, *The Agricola and The Germania*, trans. Harold Mattingly, trans. revised S. A. Handford (New York: Penguin, 1948, revised 1970), 111–12; Mark D. Walters, "The Extension of Colonial Criminal Jurisdiction over the Aboriginal Peoples of Upper Canada: Reconsideration of the *Shawanakiskie* Case (1822–26)," *University of Toronto Law Journal* 46, no. 2 (Spring 1996): 304. On the definitions of primitive and primitivism, see Kaius Tuori, *Lawyers and Savages: Ancient History and Legal Realism in the Making of Legal Anthropology* (New York: Routledge,

2015), 9–11. On Weber, see Max Weber, "Politics as a Vocation," in *From Max Weber: Essays in Sociology*, ed. and trans. H. H. Gerth and C. Wright Mills (New York: Oxford University Press, 1946), 78–79; David M. Trubek, "Max Weber on Law and the Rise of Capitalism," *Wisconsin Law Review* 1972, no. 3 (1972): 732–35.

6. See Tuori, *Lawyers and Savages*, 37; see also Reid, *Patterns of Vengeance*, 40–50.

7. See Francesco Parisi and Giuseppe Dari-Mattiacci, "The Rise and Fall of Communal Liability in Ancient Law," *International Review of Law and Economics* 21, no. 4 (December 2002): 492; see also Martin Daly and Margo Wilson, *Homicide* (New York: Aldine De Gruyter, 1988), 270–72; Reid, *Law of Blood*, 86–92; Richard A. Posner, "A Theory of Primitive Society, with Special Reference to Law," *Journal of Law and Economics* 23, no. 1 (April 1980): 50.

8. See Parisi and Dari-Mattiacci, "Rise and Fall of Communal Liability," 492.

9. Weiner, *Rule of the Clan*, 18; see ibid., 36–37, 117–26; see also Tuori, *Lawyers and Savages*, 18–34; William Ian Miller, *Eye for an Eye* (New York: Cambridge University Press, 2006), 17–30; Snyder, *Slavery in Indian Country*, 80–84; Paul R. Hyams, *Rancor and Reconciliation in Medieval England* (Ithaca, N.Y.: Cornell University Press, 2003), 6–13; Richard Fletcher, *Bloodfeud: Murder and Revenge in Anglo-Saxon England* (New York: Oxford University Press, 2003), 7–9; Daly and Wilson, *Homicide*, 221–36; Christopher Boehm, *Blood Revenge: The Enactment and Management of Conflict in Montenegro and other Tribal Societies*, 2nd ed. (Philadelphia: University of Pennsylvania Press, 1987), 54–142, 195–227; Reid, *Better Kind of Hatchet*, 7–12; Reid, *Law of Blood*, 73–112; Paul R. Hyams, "Was There Really Such a Thing as Feud in the Middle Ages," in *Vengeance in the Middle Ages: Emotion, Religion and Feud*, ed. Susanna A. Throop and Paul R. Hyams (Burlington, Vt.: Ashgate, 2010), 151–76; Tacitus, "Germania," chap. 21, 119; Christopher Boehm, "Retaliatory Violence in Human Prehistory," *British Journal of Criminology* 51, no. 3 (May 2011): 525–31; James Lindgren, "Why the Ancients May Not Have Needed a System of Criminal Law," *Boston University Law Review* 76 (February/April 1996): 51–55; Warren Winfred Lehman, "The First English Law," *Journal of Legal History* 6, no. 1 (1985): 8–9; see generally Elizabeth Colson, *Tradition and Contract: The Problem of Order* (Piscataway, N.J.: Transaction, 1974), 37–44; Max Gluckman, *Politics, Law and Ritual in Tribal Society* (New York: Basil Blackwell, 1965), 112–16.

10. See Francesco Parisi, Daniel Pi, Barbara Luppi, and Iole Fargnoli, "Deterrence of Wrongdoing in Ancient Law" (University of Minnesota Law School, Legal Studies Research Paper Series Research Paper No. 14–38, 2014), 6; see also Miller, *Eye for an Eye*, 20–22.

11. See Tuori, *Lawyers and Savages*, 35–36; Miller, *Eye for an Eye*, 9, 40–42, 104–16; Daly and Wilson, *Homicide*, 236–37; Reid, *Law of Blood*, 100–108; Frederick Pollock and Frederic William Maitland, *The History of English Law before the Time of Edward I*, 2nd ed. (Boston: Little, Brown, 1898), 1:47–48; Tacitus, "Germania," chap. 21, 119; Parisi et al., "Deterrence of Wrongdoing in Ancient Law," 15–21; James Q. Whitman, "At the Origins of Law and the State: Supervision of Violence, Mutilation of Bodies, or Setting Prices?," *Chicago-Kent Law Review* 71, no. 1 (January 1995): 41–84.

12. Stanley Rubin, "The *Bot*, or Composition in Anglo-Saxon Law: A Reassessment," *Journal of Legal History* 17, no. 2 (August 1996): 144.

13. See Daly and Wilson, *Homicide*, 237–51; Alexander Grant, "Murder Will Out: Kingship, Kinship and Killing in Medieval Scotland," in *Kings, Lords and Men in Scotland and Britain, 1300–1625: Essays in Honor of Jenny Wormald*, ed. Steve Boardman and Julian Goodare (Edinburgh: Edinburg University Press, 2014), 193–214; Parisi et al., "Deterrence of Wrongdoing in Ancient Law," 13–21; James Lindgren, "Measuring the Value of Slaves and Free Persons in Ancient Law," *Chicago-Kent Law Review* 71, no. 1 (January 1995): 149–215; Jenny Wormald, "Bloodfeud, Kindred and Government in Early Modern Scotland," *Past and Present* 87 (May 1980): 55–57; Volodymyr Machuslyy, "The Right of the Blood Feud in Kyvian Rus," *Ukrainian Blog*, accessed January 18, 2015, http://ukrainianlaw.blogspot.com/2015/01/the-right-of-blood-feud-in-kyivan-rus.html; but see Saul Levmore, "Rethinking Group Responsibility and Strategic Threats in Biblical Texts and Modern Law," *Chicago-Kent Law Review* 71, no. 1 (January 1995): 85–121.

14. See, e.g., Max Weber, *Basic Concepts in Sociology*, trans. H. P. Secher (New York: Philosophical Library, 1962; repr., Westport, Conn.: Greenwood, 1969), 122; Weber, "Politics as a Vocation," 78; Boehm, "Retaliatory Violence in Human Prehistory," 529–31; see also Weiner, *Rule of the Clan*, 135–46.

15. See Orlando Patterson, *Slavery and Social Death: A Comparative Study* (Cambridge, Mass.: Harvard University Press, 1982), 1–14, 17–101; see also Orlando Patterson, *Freedom: Freedom in the Making of Western Culture* (New York: Basic Books, 1991), 347–62; David Brion Davis, *Inhuman Bondage: The Rise and Fall of Slavery in the New World* (New York: Oxford University Press, 2006), 27–47; M. L. Bush, *Servitude in Modern Times* (Cambridge: Polity, 2000), 12–17; Moses I. Finley, *Ancient Slavery and Modern Ideology*, expanded. ed. Brent D. Shaw (Princeton, N.J.: Markus Wiener, 1998), 145; Robin Blackburn, "Slave Exploitation and the Elementary Structures of Enslavement," in *Serfdom and Slavery: Studies in Legal Bondage*, ed. M. L. Bush (New York: Longman, 1996), 158–80; Claude Meillassoux, *The Anthropology of Slavery: The Womb of Iron and Gold*, trans. Alide Dasnois (Chicago: University of Chicago Press, 1991), 9–12, 33–40, 99–175; M. I. Finley, "Slavery," in *International Encyclopedia of the Social Sciences*, ed. David L. Stills (New York: Macmillan, 1968), 14:307–9. For critiques of Patterson's approach, see Joseph C. Miller, *The Problem of Slavery as History: A Global Approach* (New Haven, Conn.: Yale University Press, 2012), 20–22, 31–33, 70–71; Vincent Brown, "Social Death and Political Life in the Study of Slavery," *American Historical Review* 114, no. 5 (December 2009): 1231–49; see also Daragh Grant, "'Civilizing' the Colonial Subject: The Co-evolution of State and Slavery in South Carolina, 1670–1739," *Comparative Studies in Society and History* 57, no. 3 (July 2015): 608n16 (suggesting the term "civic death" to distinguish the slaves' legal status from their social status in practice).

16. Patterson, *Slavery and Social Death*, 1, 10–14, 1, quoting Weber, *Basic Concepts in Sociology*, 117.

17. Patterson, *Slavery and Social Death*, 190–91.

18. Ibid., 193–94; see also, discussing slave killing in China, Pamela Kyle Crossley, "Slavery in Early Modern China," in *The Cambridge History of Slavery: Volume 3 AD 1420–AD 1804*, ed. David Eltis and Stanley L. Engerman (Cambridge: Cambridge University Press, 2011), 191.

19. See Snyder, *Slavery in Indian Country*, 128–29, 140–41; Reid, *Law of Blood*, 193; Denise I. Bossy, "Indian Slavery in Southeastern Indian and British Societies, 1670–1730," 212–13, and Brett Rushforth, "'A Little Flesh We Offer You': The Origins of Indian Slavery in New France," 355–59, both in *Indian Slavery in Colonial America*, ed. Alan Gallay (Lincoln: University of Nebraska Press, 2009).

20. See E. A. Thompson, "Slavery in Early Germany," in *Slavery in Classical Antiquity: Views and Controversies*, reprint, ed. M. I. Finley (New York: Barnes & Noble, 1968), 18.

21. See Tacitus, "Germania," chap. 25, 122; see also R. Samson, "Slavery, the Roman Legacy," in *Fifth-Century Gaul: A Crisis of Identity?*, ed. John Drinkwater and Hugh Elton (New York: Cambridge University Press, 1992), 221.

22. See Weiner, *Rule of the Clan*, 139–41; see also M. Stuart Madden, "Paths of Western Law after Justinian," *Widener Law Journal* 22, no. 3 (June 2013): 815–25.

23. See Katherine Fisher Drew, *The Laws of the Salian Franks* (Philadelphia: University of Pennsylvania Press, 1991), 74–75, quoting Title X, (3) and (4), "Concerning Stolen Slaves or Other Chattels"; see also ibid., 47–49, 163–64.

24. See ibid., 50; see also William D. Phillips, Jr., *Slavery from Roman Times to the Early Transatlantic Trade* (Manchester: Manchester University Press, 1985), 47.

25. See Patterson, *Slavery and Social Death*, 191.

26. See Brett Rushforth, *Bonds of Alliance: Indigenous and Atlantic Slaveries in New France* (Chapel Hill: University of North Carolina Press, 2012), 45–46; Snyder, *Slavery in Indian Country*, 35, 92–96; Patterson, *Slavery and Social Death*, 191.

27. See Leland Donald, *Aboriginal Slavery on the Northwest Coast of North America* (Berkeley: University of California Press, 1997), 34–35, 80–81, 165–81; Leland Donald, "Slavery in Indigenous North America," in Eltis and Engerman, *Cambridge History of Slavery*, 233–38; Leland Donald, "The Northwest Coast as a Study Area: Natural, Prehistoric, and Ethnographic Issues," in *Emerging from the Mist: Studies in Northwest Coast Culture History*, ed. R. G. Matson et al. (Vancouver: UBC Press, 2003), 300–302, 322.

28. See Weber, *Basic Concepts in Sociology*, 122.

29. Phillips, *Slavery from Roman Times*, 16.

30. See Finley, *Ancient Slavery and Modern Ideology*, 147–49; Keith Bradley, *Slavery and Society at Rome*, Key Themes in Ancient History (New York: Cambridge University Press, 1994), 29–30; K. R. Bradley, *Slaves and Masters in the Roman Empire: A Study in Social Control* (New York: Oxford University Press, 1987), 13–14; Keith Hopkins, *Conquerors and Slaves: Sociological Studies in Roman History*, vol. 1 (New York: Cambridge University Press, 1978), 99–100.

31. See Hopkins, *Conquerors and Slaves*, 99.

32. See Finley, *Ancient Slavery and Modern Ideology*, 147; see also Hopkins, *Conquerors and Slaves*, 10; Finley, "Slavery," 308; see also David Turley, *Slavery*, New Perspectives on the Past (Malden, Mass.: Blackwell, 2000), 4–5, 62–100.

33. See Matthew Dillon and Lynda Garland, *Ancient Rome: From the Early Republic to the Assassination of Julius Caesar* (New York: Routledge, 2005), 295–96; see also Thomas R. Martin, *Ancient Rome: From Romulus to Justinian* (New Haven, Conn.:

Yale University Press, 2012), 121–23; Kyle Harper, *Slavery in the Late Roman World AD 275–425* (New York: Cambridge University Press, 2011), 100–200; Phillips, *Slavery from Roman Times*, 11, 16–18; Hopkins, *Conquerors and Slaves*, 99–132; Walter Scheidel, "Slavery," in *The Cambridge Companion to the Roman Economy*, ed. Walter Scheidel (New York: Cambridge University Press, 2012), 90.

34. See Walter Scheidel, "Human Mobility in Roman Italy, II: The Slave Population," *Journal of Roman Studies* 95 (2005): 66.

35. See Harper, *Slavery in the Late Roman World*, 60; Sandra R. Joshel, *Slavery in the Roman World* (New York: Cambridge University Press, 2010), 7–9; Niall McKeown, *The Invention of Ancient Slavery?* (London: Duckworth, 2007), 124–40; Finley, *Ancient Slavery and Modern Ideology*, 147–48; Davis, *Inhuman Bondage*, 43–44; Phillips, *Slavery from Roman Times*, 18; Patterson, *Slavery and Social Death*, 354; Hopkins, *Conquerors and Slaves*, 99–102; William L. Westermann, *The Slave Systems of Greek and Roman Antiquity* (Philadelphia: American Philosophical Society, 1955), 69; Scheidel, "Slavery," 89–113; Walter Scheidel, "The Roman Slave Supply," in *The Cambridge World History of Slavery Volume I: The Ancient Mediterranean World*, ed. Keith Bradley and Paul Cartledge (New York: Cambridge University Press, 2011), 287–310; Walter Scheidel, "Demography," in *The Cambridge Economic History of the Greco-Roman World*, ed. Walter Scheidel, Ian Morris, and Richard Saller (New York: Cambridge University Press, 2017), 38–86; Scheidel, "Human Mobility in Roman Italy," 64–79.

36. See Wolfgang Kunkel, *An Introduction to Roman Legal and Constitutional History*, 2nd ed., trans. J. M. Kelly (New York: Oxford University Press, 1973), 26–27.

37. Judy E. Gaughan, *Murder Was Not a Crime: Homicide and Power in the Roman Republic* (Austin: University of Texas Press, 2010), 1–140.

38. Ibid., 141; see, e.g., Andrew M. Riggsby, *Roman Law and the Legal World of the Romans* (New York: Cambridge University Press, 2012), 200; Richard Saller, "The Hierarchical Household in Roman Society: A Study of Domestic Slavery," in Bush, *Serfdom and Slavery*, 117–21.

39. See George Mousourakis, *The Historical and Institutional Context of Roman Law* (Hampshire: Ashgate, 2003), 162–63; Milton Meltzer, *Slavery: A World History*, updated ed. (New York: DaCapo Press, 1993), 176–77; Alan Watson, *Roman Law and Comparative Law* (Athens: University of Georgia Press, 1991), 18, 71; Alan Watson, *Studies in Roman Private Law* (Rio Grande, Ohio: Hambledon Press, 1991), 261; Barry Nichols, *An Introduction to Roman Law* (Oxford: Oxford University Press, 1962), 218; Westermann, *Slave Systems of Greek and Roman Antiquity*, 82–83; W. W. Buckland, *The Roman Law of Slavery: The Condition of the Slave in Private Law from Augustus to Justinian* (Cambridge: Cambridge University Press, 1908), 36; Jane F. Gardner, "Slavery and Roman Law," 416, 432, and Keith Bradley, "Slavery in the Roman Republic," 245, both in Bradley and Cartledge, *Cambridge World History of Slavery*.

40. See Alan Watson, *The Spirit of Roman Law* (Athens: University of Georgia Press, 1995), 144.

41. See Parisi et al., "Deterrence of Wrongdoing in Ancient Law," 17; see also Ari Z. Bryen, *Violence in Roman Egypt: A Study in Legal Interpretation* (Philadelphia: University of Pennsylvania Press, 2013), 54–55, 75–76, 299n9, 310n77 (violence against slaves

referred to in Roman Egyptian petitions for relief not as *hybris*, violence to persons, but as *bia*, violence against property).

42. See, e.g., Paul du Plessis, *Borkowski's Textbook on Roman Law*, 4th ed. (New York: Oxford University Press, 2010), 93; Richard A. Bauman, *Human Rights in Ancient Rome* (New York: Routledge, 2000), 118–19; Meltzer, *Slavery*, 177–78; Alan Watson, *Roman Slave Law* (Baltimore: Johns Hopkins University Press, 1987), 120–25; Bradley, *Slaves and Masters*, 126–27; Alan Watson, *The Law of the Ancient Romans* (Dallas: Southern Methodist University Press, 1970), 46; Buckland, *Roman Law of Slavery*, 36–38; Niall McKeown, "Greek and Roman Slavery," in *The Routledge History of Slavery*, ed. Gad Heuman and Trevor Bernard (New York: Routledge, 2011), 28; Gardner, "Slavery and Roman Law," 433–34; Alan Watson, "Roman Slave Law: An Anglo-American Perspective," *Cardozo Law Review* 18, no. 2 (November 1996): 595–98; Alan Watson, "Roman Slave Law and Romanist Ideology," *Phoenix* 37, no. 1 (Spring 1983): 59–65.

43. See, e.g., William V. Harris, *Restraining Rage: The Ideology of Anger Control in Classical Antiquity* (Cambridge, Mass.: Harvard University Press, 2001), 330; Miriam T. Griffin, *Seneca: A Philosopher in Politics* (Oxford: Oxford University Press, 1976), 278.

44. Kyle, *Spectacles of Death in Ancient Rome*, 53.

45. See Watson, *Roman Slave Law*, 121–22; Buckland, *Roman Law of Slavery*, 36; Gardner, "Slavery and Roman Law," 433.

46. See Bauman, *Human Rights in Ancient Rome*, 119.

47. See Gaius Suetonius Tranquillus, *The Twelve Caesars*, trans. Robert Graves, James B. Rives, revised with introduction and notes (New York: Penguin, 2007), 194–95; see also Watson, *Roman Slave Law*, 122; Griffin, *Seneca*, 268; Buckland, *Roman Law of Slavery*, 36–37; Gardner, "Slavery and Roman Law," 433.

48. See, e.g., attributing the reform to Hadrian, du Plessis, *Borkowski's Textbook on Roman Law*, 93; Bauman, *Human Rights in Ancient Rome*, 119; Paul A. Zoch, *Ancient Rome: An Introductory History* (Norman: University of Oklahoma Press, 1998), 270; Watson, *Roman Law and Comparative Law*, 40; Westermann, *Slave Systems of Greek and Roman Antiquity*, 115; Buckland, *Roman Law of Slavery*, 37; Ferdinand Gregorovius, *The Emperor Hadrian: A Picture of the Graeco-Roman World in His Time*, trans. Mary E. Robinson (New York: Macmillan, 1898), 229; Gardner, "Slavery and Roman Law," 433. For the opposite view, see Harris, *Restraining Rage*, 330.

49. See *The Digest of Justinian*, 1.6.2., trans. Alan Watson (Philadelphia: University of Pennsylvania Press, 1985), 18; see also Harris, *Restraining Rage*, 330; Peter Garnsey, *Ideas of Slavery from Aristotle to Augustine* (New York: Cambridge University Press, 1996), 92; Griffin, *Seneca*, 268; Gardner, "Slavery and Roman Law," 433.

50. See Lauren Benton, *A Search for Sovereignty: Law and Geography in European Empires 1400–1900* (New York: Cambridge University Press, 2010), 166–67, 166; Mary V. Braginton, "Exile under the Roman Emperors," *Classical Journal* 39, no. 7 (April 1944): 396.

51. See *Justinian's Institutes*, 1.8.1, trans. Peter Birks and Grant McLeod (Ithaca, N.Y.: Cornell University Press, 1987), 41.

52. See ibid., 1.8.2, 41; see also Harper, *Slavery in the Late Roman World*, 232; du Plessis, *Borkowski's Textbook on Roman Law*, 93; *Justinian's Institutes*, 7–16; Harris,

Restraining Rage, 330–31; Bradley, *Slaves and Masters*, 129; Watson, *Roman Slave Law*, 120; Griffin, *Seneca*, 268, 273; Westermann, *Slave Systems of Greek and Roman Antiquity*, 115; Buckland, *Roman Law of Slavery*, 37–38; Gardner, "Slavery and Roman Law," 433; McKeown, "Greek and Roman Slavery," 26.

53. See Harris, *Restraining Rage*, 330–31; Griffin, *Seneca*, 268–69; McKeown, "Greek and Roman Slavery," 26.

54. See, e.g., Steven A. Epstein, *Speaking of Slavery: Color, Ethnicity, and Human Bondage in Italy* (Ithaca, N.Y.: Cornell University Press, 2001), 63; Harris, *Restraining Rage*, 335–36; Watson, *Roman Slave Law*, 124–25; Griffin, *Seneca*, 269; Buckland, *Roman Law of Slavery*, 38.

55. Harper, *Slavery in the Late Roman World*, 232.

56. Watson, *Roman Slave Law*, 124.

57. Ibid., 124–25; see Phillips, *Slavery from Roman Times*, 27.

58. See Harper, *Slavery in the Late Roman World*, 233n88.

59. See ibid., 233; see also Richard P. Saller, *Patriarchy, Property and Death in the Roman Family* (New York: Cambridge University Press, 1994), 133–53.

60. Watson, *Roman Slave Law*, 125.

61. See Harper, *Slavery in the Late Roman World*, 233.

62. See Watson, *Roman Slave Law*, 127.

63. See Harris, *Restraining Rage*, 335–36.

64. See Harper, *Slavery in the Late Roman World*, 233.

65. See Watson, *Roman Slave Law*, 125–27; Harold J. Berman, *Law and Revolution: The Formation of the Western Legal Tradition* (Cambridge, Mass.: Harvard University Press, 1983), 167–68; see also John Noel Dillon, *The Justice of Constantine: Law, Communication, and Control* (Ann Arbor: University of Michigan Press, 2012) (discussing Constantine's efforts to expand central control of governmental administration and bureaucracy).

66. See Bradley, *Slaves and Masters*, 127, citing Alison Burford, *Craftsmen in Greek and Roman Society* (Ithaca, N.Y.: Cornell University Press, 1972), 50–51; Westermann, *Slave Systems of Greek and Roman Antiquity*, 116–17, and contrasting Griffin, *Seneca*, 268–74.

67. Griffin, *Seneca*, 268.

68. See ibid., 273; see also Bradley, *Slaves and Masters*, 129.

69. See McKeown, *Invention of Ancient Slavery?*, 70.

70. See Finley, *Ancient Slavery and Modern Ideology*, 141.

71. See Watson, *Roman Slave Law*, 120, quoting Justinian, *Institutes*, 1.8.2. Birks and McLeod translated the quotation: "It is in the public interest that nobody should treat his property badly." See *Justinian's Institutes*, 41.

72. See Watson, *Roman Slave Law*, 120–21; see also Harris, *Restraining Rage*, 331–32; *The Institutes of Gaius*, trans. W. M. Gordon and O. F. Robinson (Ithaca, N.Y.: Cornell University Press, 1988), 45, quoting 1.53: "We ought not to abuse our rights; that is also the reason why spendthrifts are forbidden to administer their own property." See on Gaius and Justinian's *Institutes*, e.g., Mousourakis, *Historical and Institutional Context of Roman Law*, 299–301; Watson, *Roman Law and Comparative Law*, 15; Karen Wagner,

"Gaius," in *From Polis to Empire—The Ancient Word c. 800 B.C.–A.D. 500: A Biographical Dictionary*, ed. Andrew G. Traver (Westport, Conn.: Greenwood, 2002), 166; *Justinian's Institutes*, 16–18. On prodigals, see Watson, *Spirit of Roman Law*, 14; Watson, *Roman Law and Comparative Law*, 37–38.

73. Watson, *Roman Slave Law*, 120–21; see Joshel, *Slavery in the Roman World*, 72; David Johnston, *Roman Law in Context* (New York: Cambridge University Press, 1999), 43.

74. See Watson, *Roman Slave Law*, 127; see also Harper, *Slavery in the Late Roman World*, 232; Harris, *Restraining Rage*, 331–32; Bradley, *Slaves and Masters*, 129.

75. See Watson, *Roman Slave Law*, 125; see also Harris, *Restraining Rage*, 332–36; Bradley, *Slaves and Masters*, 126–27; McKeown, "Greek and Roman Slavery," 26; Watson, "Roman Slave Law: An Anglo-American Perspective," 597–98.

76. See Harper, *Slavery in the Late Roman World*, 233; Bradley, *Slaves and Masters*, 127; Hopkins, *Conquerors and Slaves*, 119n44; Griffin, *Seneca*, 269.

77. See Andrew Fede, *Roadblocks to Freedom: Slavery and Manumission in the United States South* (New Orleans: Quid Pro Books, 2011), 36.

78. See ibid., 36–37, citing Edward J. McCaffery, "Must We Have the Right to Waste?," in *New Essays in the Legal and Political Theory of Property*, ed. Stephen R. Munzer (New York: Cambridge University Press, 2001), 76–91; Lior Jacob Strahilevitz, "The Right to Destroy," *Yale Law Journal* 114, no. 4 (January 2005): 783–96; but see, questioning this concept's historical basis, Joseph L. Sax, *Playing Darts with a Rembrandt: Public and Private Rights in Cultural Treasures* (Ann Arbor: University of Michigan Press, 1999), 203n2.

79. See Strahilevitz, "Right to Destroy," 796–854.

80. Epstein, *Speaking of Slavery*, 63–64; see Bradley, *Slavery and Society at Rome*, 49–50. On rape, see, e.g., Diane Miller Sommerville, *Rape and Race in the Nineteenth-Century South* (Chapel Hill: University of North Carolina Press, 2004), 64–71; Peter W. Bardaglio, *Reconstructing the Household: Families, Sex, and the Law in the Nineteenth Century South* (Chapel Hill: University of North Carolina Press, 1998), 64–78; Jeffrey J. Pokorak, "Rape as a Badge of Slavery: The Legal History of, and Remedies for, Prosecutorial Race-of-Victim Charging Disparities," *Nevada Law Journal* 7, no. 1 (Fall 2006): 6–11; *George v. State*, 37 Miss. 316, 320 (1859).

CHAPTER 2. The Visigoth, Spanish, Portuguese, and French Laws on Slave Killing

1. Paul Finkelman, "Defining Slavery under a 'Government Instituted for Protection of the Rights of Mankind,'" *Hamline Law Review* 35 (2011–12): 553; see William D. Phillips, Jr., *Slavery in Medieval and Early Modern Iberia* (Philadelphia: University of Pennsylvania Press, 2014), 153–55; Robert J. Cottrol, *The Long, Lingering Shadow: Slavery, Race, and Law in the American Hemisphere* (Athens: University of Georgia Press, 2013), 28–29, 54–55; William D. Phillips, Jr., "Slavery in the Atlantic Islands and the Early Modern Spanish Atlantic World," in *The Cambridge History of Slavery: Volume 3 AD 1420–AD 1804*, ed. David Eltis and Stanley L. Engerman (Cambridge: Cambridge

University Press, 2011), 330–31; Philip D. Curtin, "Slavery and Empire," in *Comparative Perspectives on Slavery in the New World Plantation Societies*, Annals of the New York Academy of Sciences vol. 292, ed. Vra Rubin and Arthur Tuden (New York: New York Academy of Sciences, 1977), 3–11.

2. See Mary Wilhelmine Williams, "Slavery, Modern," in *Encyclopedia of the Social Sciences*, ed. Edwin A. Seligman (1930–35; New York: Macmillan, 1937), 14:82.

3. See Phillips, *Slavery in Medieval and Early Modern Iberia*, 15.

4. See ibid., 16.

5. See P. D. King, *Law and Society in the Visigothic Kingdom* (New York: Cambridge University Press, 1972), 1–22, 159–69; E. A. Thompson, *The Goths in Spain* (Oxford: Oxford University Press, 1969), 267–69; Pierre Bonnassie, "Society and Mentalities in Visigothic Spain," in *From Slavery to Feudalism in South-Western Europe*, trans. Jean Burrell (Cambridge: Cambridge University Press, 1991), 60–103.

6. See David Levering Lewis, *God's Crucible: Islam and the Making of Europe, 570–1215* (New York: Norton, 2008), 109–12, 112; see also Robin Blackburn, *The Making of New World Slavery: From the Baroque to the Modern, 1492–1800* (New York: Verso, 1997), 36–38; Orlando Patterson, *Slavery and Social Death: A Comparative Study* (Cambridge, Mass.: Harvard University Press, 1982), 354; King, *Law and Society in the Visigothic Kingdom*, 160; Bonnassie, "Society and Mentalities in Visigothic Spain," 71–75.

7. See Herwig Wolfram, *History of the Goths* (Berkeley: University of California Press, 1988), 103; E. A. Thompson, *Romans and Barbarians: The Decline of the Western Empire* (Madison: University of Wisconsin Press, 1982), 45; Thompson, *Goths in Spain*, 138, 269; Bonnassie, "Society and Mentalities in Visigothic Spain," 63.

8. See Floyd Seyward Lear, "The Public Law of the Visigothic Code," *Speculum* 26, no. 1 (January 1951): 2.

9. See, e.g., Roger Collins, *Visigothic Spain, 409–711* (Malden, Mass.: Blackwell, 2004), 223–39; King, *Law and Society in the Visigothic Kingdom*, 7–22; Thompson, *Goths in Spain*, 238–46; J. H. W. G. Liebeschuetz, "Goths and Romans in the *leges visigothorum*," in *Integration in Rome and in the Roman World: Proceedings of the Tenth Workshop of the International Impact of Empire (Lile, June 23–25, 2011)*, ed. Gerda de Klejin and Stephane Benoist (Leiden: Brill, 2014), 90–91.

10. King, *Law and Society in the Visigothic Kingdom*, 85–93, 259–63; Liebeschuetz, "Goths and Romans in the *leges visigothorum*," 91n10; Luis A. Garcia Moreno, "Legitimate and Illegitimate Violence in Visigothic Law," in *Violence and Society in the Early Medieval West*, ed. Guy Halsall (Woodbridge: Boydell Press, 1998), 55–57.

11. See *The Visigothic Code (Forum Judicum)*, trans. S[amuel] P. Scott (Boston: Boston Book Company, 1910), 209–31; see also Phillips, *Slavery in Medieval and Early Modern Iberia*, 98; King, *Law and Society in the Visigothic Kingdom*, 172; Thompson, *Goths in Spain*, 138–39, 261, 269; Pierre Bonnassie, "The Survival and Extinction of the Slave System in the Early Medieval West (Fourth to Eleventh Centuries)," in *From Slavery to Feudalism in South-Western Europe*, 20–21; Bonnassie, "Society and Mentalities in Visigothic Spain," 73. Scott's introduction and his translation received mixed reviews, but the negative comments do not apply to the passages cited in this chapter. See

Timothy G. Kearly, "The Enigma of Samuel Parsons Scott," *Roman Legal Tradition* 10 (2014): 20–23.

12. See *Visigothic Code (Forum Judicum)*, 222.

13. See ibid., 222–23; see also Thompson, *Goths in Spain*, 269–70.

14. See King, *Law and Society in the Visigothic Kingdom*, 127, 127n2.

15. See Phillips, *Slavery in Medieval and Early Modern Iberia*, 98; King, *Law and Society in the Visigothic Kingdom*, 127, 127n9, 177; Thompson, *Goths in Spain*, 270.

16. See King, *Law and Society in the Visigothic Kingdom*, 172.

17. See *Visigothic Code (Forum Judicum)*, 223; see also Phillips, *Slavery in Medieval and Early Modern Iberia*, 98; King, *Law and Society in the Visigothic Kingdom*, 172.

18. See *Visigothic Code (Forum Judicum)*, 209, 216–17; see also James Lindgren, "Measuring the Value of Slaves and Free Persons in Ancient Law," *Chicago-Kent Law Review* 71, no. 1 (January 1995): 149–215, 194–98.

19. See *Visigothic Code (Forum Judicum)*, 225–26; see also Thompson, *Goths in Spain*, 245–46, 270–71; Bonnassie, "Survival and Extinction of the Slave System," 21n74.

20. See Lewis, *God's Crucible*, 105–32; Alan Watson, *Slave Law in the Americas* (Athens: University of Georgia Press, 1989), 40–42; King, *Law and Society in the Visigothic Kingdom*, vii–viii; Thompson, *Goths in Spain*, 29–51; Bonnassie, "Society and Mentalities in Visigothic Spain," 86–90; Lear, "Public Law of the Visigothic Code," 2–3.

21. See Samuel Parsons Scott, trans., Robert I. Burns, ed., "Introduction to the Fourth *Partida*," in *Las Siete Partidas*, vol. 4, *Family, Commerce and the Sea: The Worlds of Women and Slaves* (Philadelphia: University of Pennsylvania Press, 2001), xxiii–xxv; see also Phillips, *Slavery in Medieval and Early Modern Iberia*, 19–21.

22. See Scott and Burns, "Introduction to the Fourth *Partida*," xxiii; see also Phillips, *Slavery in Medieval and Early Modern Iberia*, 19; Hugh Thomas, *Rivers of Gold: The Rise of the Spanish Empire from Columbus to Magellan* (New York: Random House, 2003), 32–33.

23. See Elsa V. Goveia, "The West Indian Slave Laws of the Eighteenth Century," in *Slavery in the New World: A Reader in Comparative History*, ed. Laura Foner and Eugene Genovese (Englewood Cliffs, N.J.: Prentice Hall, 1969), 115, quoting *Las Siete Partidas*, pt. 4, title 34, law i.

24. See Samuel Parsons Scott, trans., Robert I. Burns, ed., *Las Siete Partidas*, vol. 5, *Underworlds: The Dead, the Criminal, and the Marginalized* (Philadelphia: University of Pennsylvania Press, 2001), xxiii–xxiv; ibid., pt. 7, title 8, laws 10–16, 1342–50; see also Samuel Astley Dunham, *History of Spain and Portugal* (New York: Harper & Brothers, 1860), 4:121–22. See generally Lauren Benton, *A Search for Sovereignty: Law and Geography in European Empires 1400–1900* (New York: Cambridge University Press, 2010), 167–76 (noting that Spanish and Portuguese law imposed exile or banishment, following the Roman model).

25. *Las Siete Partidas*, vol. 5, pt. 7, title 8, law 2, 1342.

26. *Las Siete Partidas*, vol. 4, *Family, Commerce and the Sea: The Worlds of Women and Slaves*, pt. 4, title 21, law 6, 979; see Phillips, *Slavery in Medieval and Early Modern Iberia*, 98–100.

27. See *Las Siete Partidas*, vol. 5, *Underworlds: The Dead, the Criminal, and the Marginalized*, pt. 7, title 8, law 9, 1348; see also Watson, *Slave Law in the Americas*, 45–46.

28. *Las Siete Partidas*, vol. 5, pt. 7, title 15, law 9, 1397.

29. Sue Peabody and Keila Grinberg, "Introduction: Slavery, Freedom, and the Law," in *Slavery, Freedom, and the Law in the Atlantic World: A Brief History with Documents*, Bedford Series in History and Culture, ed. Sue Peabody and Keila Grinberg (Boston: Bedford/St. Martin's, 2007), 15; see Franklin W. Knight, *The Caribbean: The Genesis of a Fragmented Nationalism* 2nd ed. (New York: Oxford University Press, 1990), 68–75; Frederick P. Bowser, *The African Slave in Colonial Peru 1524–1650* (Stanford, Calif.: Stanford University Press, 1974), 1–12. On Native American slavery, the 1542 New Laws, and the challenges in enforcement, see Andres Resendez, *The Other Slavery: The Uncovered Story of Indian Enslavement in America* (New York: Houghton Mifflin Harcourt, 2016), 1–75.

30. See Norman A. Meiklejohn, "The Implementation of Slave Legislation in Eighteenth-Century New Granada," in *Slavery and Race Relations in Latin America*, ed. Robert Trent Toplin (Westport Conn.: Greenwood, 1974), 182–83, 197, 197; see also Thomas Ingersoll, *Mammon and Manon in Early New Orleans: The First Slave Society in the Deep South* (Knoxville: University of Tennessee Press, 1999), 134–38, 234, 322–23; Jane Landers, *Black Society in Spanish Florida* (Urbana: University of Illinois Press, 1999), 7–8, 192–95; Derek N. Kerr, *Petty Felony, Slave Defiance, and Frontier Villainy: Crime and Criminal Justice in Spanish Louisiana, 1770–1803* (New York: Garland, 1993), 3–39; Thomas Ingersoll, "Slave Codes and Judicial Practice in New Orleans, 1718–1897," *Law and History Review* 13, no. 1 (Spring 1995): 42–60.

31. See Goveia, "West Indian Slave Laws," 115.

32. See Bowser, *African Slave in Colonial Peru*, 150, 156–57, 166–67; see also, e.g., William F. Sater, "The Black Experience in Chile," in Toplin, *Slavery and Race Relations in Latin America*, 28–35.

33. See "Royal Instruction on the Education, Treatment and Occupation of Slaves," May 31, 1789, in *Slavery: Oxford Readers*, ed. Stanley L. Engerman, Seymour Drescher, and Robert Paquette (New York: Oxford University Press, 2001), 127–34; "The Slave Code of 1842" and "Slave Regulations of 1844," in Robert L. Paquette, *Sugar Is Made with Blood: The Conspiracy of La Escalera and the Conflict between Empires over Slavery in Cuba* (Middletown, Conn.: Wesleyan University Press, 1988), 80, 267–74; see also, e.g., Cottrol, *Long, Lingering Shadow*, 29–47; Watson, *Slave Law in the Americas*, 40–42, 59–60; Franklin W. Knight, *Slave Society in Cuba during the Nineteenth Century* (Madison: University of Wisconsin Press, 1970), 121–36; Ana Hontanilla, "Sentiment and the Law: Inventing the Category of Wretched Slave in the *Real Audiencia* of Santo Domingo, 1783–1812," *Eighteenth-Century Studies* 48, no. 2 (Winter 2015): 181–90; Michelle McKinley, "Fractional Freedoms: Slavery, Legal Activism, and Ecclesiastical Courts in Colonial Lima, 1593–1689," *Law and History Review* 28, no. 3 (August 2010): 752–53; Manuel Barcia, "Fighting with the Enemy's Weapons," *Atlantic Studies* 3, no. 2 (October 2006): 165; Alejandro de la Fuente, "Slave Law and Claims-Making in Cuba: The Tannenbaum Debate Revisited," *Law and History Review* 22, no. 2 (Summer 2004): 349, 367–68;

Meiklejohn, "Implementation of Slave Legislation," 182–83; Goveia, "West Indian Slave Laws," 114–18; Norman Arthur Meiklejohn, "The Observance of Negro Slave Legislation in Colonial Nueva Granada" (Ph.D. diss., Columbia University, 1968), 44–66.

34. See Lyman L. Johnson, "'A Lack of Legitimate Obedience and Respect': Slaves and Their Masters in the Courts of Late Colonial Buenos Aires," *Hispanic American Historical Review* 87, no. 4 (November 2007): 632; see also Kerr, *Petty Felony, Slave Defiance, and Frontier Villainy*, 18, 213; Bianca Premo, "An Equity Against the Law: Slave Rights and Creole Jurisprudence in Spanish America," *Slavery and Abolition* 32, no. 4 (December 2011): 499–501; Alejandro de la Fuente, "Slaves and the Creation of Legal Rights in Cuba: *Coartacion* and *Papel*," *Hispanic American Historical Review* 87, no. 4 (November 2007): 665, 669–72; Meiklejohn, "Implementation of Slave Legislation," 184–97; but see Ingersoll, *Mammon and Manon in Early New Orleans*, 323.

35. See Andrew Fede, *Roadblocks to Freedom: Slavery and Manumission in the United States South* (New Orleans: Quid Pro Books, 2011), 13, 150–51; see also, e.g., William Frederick Sharp, *Slavery on the Spanish Frontier: The Colombian Choco 1680–1810* (Norman: University of Oklahoma Press, 1976), 138, note *; Hontanilla, "Sentiment and the Law," 191–93; Premo, "Equity Against the Law," 501; de la Fuente, "Slaves and the Creation of Legal Rights in Cuba," 672–76; Johnson, "'A Lack of Legitimate Obedience and Respect,'" 632n2; Barcia, "Fighting with the Enemy's Weapons," 170–77; Sater, "Black Experience in Chile," 34–35.

36. See Cottrol, *Long, Lingering Shadow*, 29; Herbert S. Klein and Francisco Vidal Luna, *Slavery in Brazil* (New York: Cambridge University Press, 2010), 3–11; Blackburn, *Making of New World Slavery*, 113–14; Stuart B. Schwartz, *Sugar Plantations in the Formation of Brazilian Society: Bahia, 1550–1835* (New York: Cambridge University Press, 1985), 3–6; A. C. de C. M. Saunders, *A Social History of Black Slaves and Freedmen in Portugal 1441–1555* (New York: Cambridge University Press, 1982), 1–34, 47–88, 176–77.

37. Philip D. Curtin, *The Rise and Fall of the Plantation Complex*, 2nd ed. (New York: Cambridge University Press, 1998), 46–57, 190–95, 46; see Klein and Luna, *Slavery in Brazil*, 11–18; Peabody and Grinberg, "Introduction," 22–23; Blackburn, *Making of New World Slavery*, 108–12, 163–213; Schwartz, *Sugar Plantations in the Formation of Brazilian Society*, 6–27; Saunders, *Social History of Black Slaves and Freedmen*, 177–78; Joao Fragoso and Ana Rios, "Slavery and Politics in Colonial Portuguese America: The Sixteenth to the Eighteenth Centuries," in Eltis and Engerman, *Cambridge History of Slavery*, 350–77; Sidney M. Greenfield, "Madeira and the Beginning of New World Sugar Cane Cultivation and Plantation Slavery: A Study in Institution Building," in Rubin and Tuden, *Comparative Perspectives on Slavery*, 536–52. On slavery in Brazil's mining region, see A. J. R. Russell-Wood, *The Black Man in Slavery and Freedom in Colonial Brazil* (New York: St. Martin's, 1982), 104–27.

38. See Peabody and Grinberg, "Introduction," 21–22; Watson, *Slave Law in the Americas*, 91–101; Schwartz, *Sugar Plantations in the Formation of Brazilian Society*, 261; Saunders, *Social History of Black Slaves and Freedmen*, 113–33; A. J. R. Russell-Wood, "Centers and Peripheries in the Luso-Brazilian World, 1500–1808," in *Negotiated Empires: Centers and Peripheries in the Americas 1500–1820* (New World in the Atlantic World), ed. Christine Daniels and Michael V. Kennedy (New York: Routledge, 2002),

107; Robert Conrad, "Nineteenth-Century Brazilian Slavery," in Toplin, *Slavery and Race Relations in Latin America*, 158–61.

39. See Saunders, *Social History of Black Slaves and Freedmen*, 115.

40. See ibid., 108, 128, 130.

41. Watson, *Slave Law in the Americas*, 92.

42. See Schwartz, *Sugar Plantations in the Formation of Brazilian Society*, 134–35; see also ibid., 261, 527n17.

43. See Cottrol, *Long, Lingering Shadow*, 53, 63–79; Alexandra K. Brown, "'A Black Mark on Our Legislation': Slavery, Punishment, and the Politics of Death in Nineteenth-Century Brazil," *Luso-Brazilian Review* 32, no. 2 (Winter 2000); 100; Mary Wilhelmine Williams, "The Treatment of Negro Slaves in the Brazilian Empire: A Comparison with the United States of America," *Journal of Negro History* 15, no. 3 (July 1930): 325–26.

44. See Watson, *Slave Law in the Americas*, 83–85; see also Vernon Valentine Palmer, *Through the Codes Darkly: Slave Law and the Civil Law in Louisiana* (Clark, N.J.: Lawbook Exchange, 2012), 5; Peabody and Grinberg, "Introduction," 6.

45. Peabody and Grinberg, "Introduction," 5; see James Pritchard, *In Search of Empire: The French in the Americas, 1670–1730* (New York: Cambridge University Press, 2004), 3–122; Laurent Dubois, "Slavery in the French Caribbean, 1635–1804," in Eltis and Engerman, *Cambridge History of Slavery*, 431–49.

46. See Peabody and Grinberg, "Introduction," 5; see also Pritchard, *In Search of Empire*, 230–63.

47. See Palmer, *Through the Codes Darkly*, 6–9; Watson, *Slave Law in the Americas*, 83–90; see also Malick W. Ghachem, *The Old Regime and the Haitian Revolution* (New York: Cambridge University Press, 2012), 43–76; Philip P. Boucher, *France and the American Tropics to 1700: Tropics of Discontent?* (Baltimore: Johns Hopkins University Press, 2008), 212, 285; Brett Rushforth, *Bonds of Alliance: Indigenous and Atlantic Slaveries in New France* (Chapel Hill: University of North Carolina Press, 2012), 73–122; Bernard Moitt, *Women and Slavery in the French Antilles, 1635–1848* (Bloomington: Indiana University Press, 2001), 2–18; Robin W. Winks, *The Blacks in Canada: A History* (New Haven, Conn.: Yale University Press, 1971), 1–17; Finkelman, "Defining Slavery," 554.

48. See "Arret du Conseil de la Martinique, contre un Particulier mauvais Mari et Maitre cruel. Du 20 Octobre 1670," in Moreau de Saint-Mery, *Loix et Constitutions des Colonies Francoises de l'Amerique sous le vent*, 6 vols. (Paris: by author, 1784–90), 1:203; see also Ghachem, *Old Regime*, 59n94; Boucher, *France and the American Tropics to 1700*, 285.

49. See "Arret du Conseil de la Martinique, contre un Maitre cruel, Du 10 Mai 1671," in Moreau de Saint-Mery, *Loix et Constitutions des Colonies Francoises de l'Amerique*, 1:224–25; see also Ghachem, *Old Regime*, 59n94; Boucher, *France and the American Tropics to 1700*, 285; Rushforth, *Bonds of Alliance*, 130.

50. See Pierre Regis Dessalles, *Histoire Legislative des Antilles, ou Annales du Conseil Souverain de la Martinique* (Paris, 1847), 1:65.

51. See "French Crown, The *Code Noir* 1685," in Peabody and Grinberg, *Slavery, Freedom, and the Law in the Atlantic World*, 31; see also Palmer, *Through the Codes Darkly*, 3–42; Boucher, *France and the American Tropics to 1700*, 212–13; Rushforth, *Bonds of Al-*

liance, 122–32, 355; Watson, *Slave Law in the Americas*, 83–90; Vernon Valentine Palmer, "The Origins and Authors of the Code Noir," *Louisiana Law Review* 56 (1995): 363–407; Alan Watson, "The Origins of the Code Noir Revisited," *Tulane Law Review* 71 (March 1997): 1041–57; Goveia, "West Indian Slave Laws," 126–35; William Renwick Riddell, "Le Code Noir," *Journal of Negro History* 10, no. 3 (July 1925): 321–29.

52. Ghachem, *Old Regime*, 43.

53. Ibid., 55; see Boucher, *France and the American Tropics to 1700*, 160, 212, 285–87.

54. See Ghachem, *Old Regime*, 177n27; see also ibid., 63.

55. See ibid., 177; see also ibid., 63; Palmer, *Through the Codes Darkly*, 34; Rushforth, *Bonds of Alliance*, 128–30.

56. See Louis Sala-Molins, *Dark Side of the Light: Slavery and the French Enlightenment* (Minneapolis: University of Minnesota Press, 2006), 33–35; Moitt, *Women and Slavery in the French Antilles*, 104; see also Ghachem, *Old Regime*, 176; Joan Dayan, *Haiti, History, and the Gods* (Berkeley: University of California Press, 1995), 209–11.

57. See Marcel Trudel, *Canada's Forgotten Slaves: Two Hundred Years of Bondage*, trans. George Tombs (Montreal: Vehicule Press, 2013), 29–122, 254–63; Rushforth, *Bonds of Alliance*, 122–32; Afua Cooper, *The Hanging of Angelique: The Untold Story of Canadian Slavery and the Burning of Old Montreal* (Toronto: HarperCollins, 2006), 74–76; Harvey Amani Whitfield, *Blacks on the Border: The Black Refugees in British North America, 1815–1860* (Lebanon, N.H.: University Press of New England, 2006), 10–14; Maureen G. Elgersman, *Unyielding Spirits: Black Women and Slavery in Early Canada and Jamaica* (New York: Garland, 1999), 3–16; Daniel G. Hill, *The Freedom-Seekers: Blacks in Early Canada* (Agincourt, Ontario: Book Society of Canada, 1981), 3–4; Leo W. Bertley, *Canada and Its People of African Descent* (Pierrefonds, Québec: Bilongo, 1977), xi–xii, 25–36; Winks, *Blacks in Canada*, 5, 10–11.

58. See Charles R. Cutter, *The Legal Culture of Northern New Spain* (Albuquerque: University of New Mexico Press, 1995), 107–8. For a detailed description, see ibid., 113–46; Kerr, *Petty Felony, Slave Defiance, and Frontier Villainy*, 11–39, 89–95.

59. See Cutter, *Legal Culture of Northern New Spain*, 34–35; Knight, *Slave Society in Cuba*, 123; but see M. C. Mirow, "Law in East Florida, 1783–1821," *American Journal of Legal History* 55, no. 1 (January 2015): 113–17; Sharp, *Slavery on the Spanish Frontier*, 225n44; see also Alexander Von Humboldt and Aime Bonpland, *Personal Narrative of Travels to the Equinoctial Regions of America, Volume III: During the Years 1799–1804*, trans. and ed. Thomasina Ross (London: George Bell and Sons, 1889), 270–84.

60. See, for Peru, Bowser, *African Slave in Colonial Peru*, 231; for New Grenada, Kristen Block, *Ordinary Lives in the Early Caribbean: Religion, Colonial Competition, and the Politics of Profit* (Athens: University of Georgia Press, 2012), 19–64; Meiklejohn, "Observance of Negro Slave Legislation in Colonial Nueva Granada," 239; for Spanish Louisiana, Gilbert C. Din, *Spaniards, Planters, and Slaves: The Spanish Regulation of Slavery in Louisiana, 1763–1803* (College Station: Texas A&M Press, 1999), 133; Kerr, *Petty Felony, Slave Defiance, and Frontier Villainy*, 95, 237; for six Louisiana counties, Adams County in Mississippi, and New Orleans, Din, *Spaniards, Planters, and Slaves*, 91, 275n7; James Thomas McGowan, *Creation of a Slave Society: Louisiana Plantations in the Eighteenth*

Century (Ph.D. diss., University of Rochester, 1976), 246–47, 259n45, 260n47; Gwendolyn Midlo Hall, "African Women in French and Spanish Louisiana: Origins, Roles, Family, Work, Treatment," in *The Devil's Lane: Sex and Race in the Early South*, ed. Catherine Clinton and Michele Gillespie (New York: Oxford University Press, 1997), 257.

61. See Landers, *Black Society in Spanish Florida*, 192–93.

62. See ibid., 193–95; see also Andrew McMichael, *Atlantic Loyalties: Americans in Spanish West Florida, 1785–1810* (Athens: University of Georgia Press, 2008), 37.

63. See Saunders, *Social History of Black Slaves and Freedmen*, 115–16, 208n9, 268, 115; see also Schwartz, *Sugar Plantations in the Formation of Brazilian Society*, 134–35, 261, 527n17.

64. See Klein and Luna, *Slavery in Brazil*, 190n4, citing Luis Francisco Carvalho Filho, "Impunidade no Barisil—Colonia e Imperio," *Estudios Avancados* 18, no. 51 (2004): 187–88; Mary C. Karasch, *Slave Life in Rio de Janeiro 1808–1850* (Princeton, N.J.: Princeton University Press, 1987), 116–17.

65. See Roger A. Kittleson, *The Practice of Politics in Postcolonial Brazil, Porto Alegre, 1845–1895* (Pittsburgh: University of Pittsburgh Press, 2006), 78; see also A. J. R. Russell-Wood, *The Black Man in Slavery and Freedom in Colonial Brazil* (New York: St. Martin's, 1982), 35.

66. See Dale Torston Graden, *From Slavery to Freedom in Brazil Bahia, 1835–1900* (Albuquerque: University of New Mexico Press, 2006), 178–79.

67. See Bernard Moitt, "Transcending Linguistic and Cultural Frontiers in Caribbean Historiography: C.L.R. James, French Sources, and Slavery in San Domingo," in *C.L.R. James: His Intellectual Legacies*, ed. Selwyn R. Cudjoe and William E. Cain (Boston: University of Massachusetts Press, 1995), 154.

68. See ibid., 154–55, quoting "Lettre du Ministre a MM. de Lanage et Maillart, sur les mauvais traitemens des Maitres pour leurs Esclaves," Du 25 Juillet 1741, in Moreau de Saint-Mery, *Loix et Constitutions des Colonies Francoises de l'Amerique*, 3:674–75; see also Moitt, *Women and Slavery in the French Antilles*, 104–6.

69. See Ghachem, *Old Regime*, 167–210; see also Moitt, *Women and Slavery in the French Antilles*, 107; Dayan, *Haiti, History, and the Gods*, 215–17.

70. Ghachem, *Old Regime*, 210; see ibid., 121–210.

CHAPTER 3. Creating a British Colonial Law of Slave Killing

1. Sally E. Hadden, "The Fragmented Laws of Slavery in the Colonial and Revolutionary Eras," in *The Cambridge History of Law in America*, ed. Michael Grossberg and Christopher Tomlins (Cambridge: Cambridge University Press, 2008), 1:257; see David A. E. Pelteret, *Slavery in Early Medieval England: From the Reign of Alfred until the Twelfth Century* (Rochester, N.Y.: Boydell Press, 1995), 251–54; Doris Mary Stenton, *English Society in the Early Middle Ages 1066–1307*, The Pelican History of England, vol. 3, 4th ed. (New York: Penguin, 1965), 138–39; David A. E. Pelteret, "Slavery in Anglo-Saxon England," in *The Anglo-Saxons: Synthesis and Achievement* (Waterloo, Ontario: Wilfrid Laurier University Press, 1985), 126–33.

2. Paul Finkelman, "Defining Slavery under a 'Government Instituted for Protection of the Rights of Mankind,'" *Hamline Law Review* 35 (2011–12): 555; but see Lukasz Jankorporwicz, "Roman Law in Roman Britain: An Introductory Survey," *Journal of Legal History* 33, no. 2 (August 2012): 143; John Frederick Winkler, "Roman Law in Anglo-Saxon England," *Journal of Legal History* 13, no. 2 (August 1992): 109, 124n134; see generally Michael E. Jones, "The Legacy of Roman Law in Post-Roman Britain," in *Law, Society and Authority in Late Antiquity*, ed. Robert W. Mathisen (Oxford: Oxford University Press, 2001), 52–67.

3. See Alan Watson, *Slave Law in the Americas* (Athens: University of Georgia Press, 1989), 64; see also Michael Guasco, *Slaves and Englishmen: Human Bondage in the Early Modern Atlantic World* (Philadelphia: University of Pennsylvania Press, 2014), 4–5.

4. See Andrew Fede, *Roadblocks to Freedom: Slavery and Manumission in the United States South* (New Orleans: Quid Pro Books, 2011), iv–vi; Lorena S. Walsh, *Motives of Honor, Pleasure, and Profit: Plantation Management in the Colonial Chesapeake, 1607–1763* (Chapel Hill: University of North Carolina Press, 2010), 113–45, 203–5, 383–85; Robin Blackburn, *The Making of New World Slavery: From the Baroque to the Modern, 1492–1800* (New York: Verso, 1997), 31–63; Thomas D. Morris, *Southern Slavery and the Law, 1619–1860* (Chapel Hill: University of North Carolina Press, 1996), 37–57; Andrew Fede, *People without Rights: An Interpretation of the Fundamentals of the Law of Slavery in the U.S. South* (New York: Garland, 1992; repr., New York: Routledge, 2011), 17, 29–30, 51–53; Robert J. Steinfeld, *The Invention of Free Labor: The Employment Relation in English and American Law and Culture, 1350–1870* (Chapel Hill: University of North Carolina Press, 1991), 1–121; Winthrop D. Jordan, *White over Black: American Attitudes toward the Negro 1550–1812* (Chapel Hill: University of North Carolina Press, 1968), 103–10; Lorena S. Walsh, "Slavery in the North American Mainland Colonies," in *The Cambridge History of Slavery: Volume 3 AD 1420–AD 1804*, ed. David Eltis and Stanley L. Engerman (Cambridge: Cambridge University Press, 2011), 413–14.

5. See Jonathan A. Bush, "Free to Enslave: The Foundations of Colonial American Slave Law," *Yale Journal of Law and the Humanities* 5, no. 2 (Summer 1993): 423.

6. William D. Phillips, Jr., *Slavery from Roman Times to the Early Transatlantic Trade* (Manchester: Manchester University Press, 1985), 59.

7. See Guasco, *Slaves and Englishmen*, 25; Hugh M. Thomas, *The Norman Conquest: England after William the Conqueror*, Critical Issues in History (Lanham, Md.: Rowman & Littlefield, 2008), 5; David Eltis, *The Rise of African Slavery in the Americas* (New York: Cambridge University Press, 2000), 5.

8. Pelteret, *Slavery in Early Medieval England*, 29, 31, 32, 32.

9. See ibid., 29; see also Richard Fletcher, *Bloodfeud: Murder and Revenge in Anglo-Saxon England* (New York: Oxford University Press, 2003), 8–17; Dorothy Whitelock, *The Beginnings of English Society*, Pelican History of England, vol. 2 (Baltimore: Penguin, 1952), 38–46; Frederick Pollock and Frederic William Maitland, *The History of English Law before the Time of Edward I*, 2nd ed. (Boston: Little, Brown, 1898), 1:46–55; Pelteret, "Slavery in Anglo-Saxon England," 124; Jenny Wormald, "The Blood Feud in Early Modern Scotland," in *Disputes and Settlements in the West*, ed. John Bossy (New York:

Cambridge University Press, 1983), 101–44; Stanley Rubin, "The *Bot*, or Composition in Anglo-Saxon Law: A Reassessment," *Journal of Legal History* 17, no. 2 (August 1996): 144–47; William Ian Miller, "Choosing the Avenger: Some Aspects of the Bloodfeud in Medieval Iceland and England," *Law and History Review* 1, no. 1 (Fall 1983): 159–75; see generally Harold J. Berman, *Law and Revolution: The Formation of the Western Legal Tradition* (Cambridge, Mass.: Harvard University Press, 1983), 49–61; M. Stuart Madden, "Paths of Western Law after Justinian," *Widener Law Journal* 22, no. 3 (June 2013): 772–73, 782–83, 796–803, 816–17, 827–28.

10. Whitelock, *Beginnings of English Society*, 108; see Pelteret, *Slavery in Early Medieval England*, 32, 81, 84; Pelteret, "Slavery in Anglo-Saxon England," 124.

11. Pelteret, "Slavery in Anglo-Saxon England," 124; see William Ian Miller, *Eye for an Eye* (New York: Cambridge University Press, 2006), 111–13.

12. Warren Winfred Lehman, "The First English Law," *Journal of Legal History* 6, no. 1 (1985): 17; see Miller, *Eye for an Eye*, 113–16; Lisi Oliver, *The Beginnings of English Law* (Buffalo: University of Toronto Press, 2002), 3–20.

13. A. W. B. Simpson, "The Laws of Ethelbert," in *Legal Theory and Legal History: Essays on the Common Law* (London: Hambledon Press, 1987), 12; see Oliver, *Beginnings of English Law*, 16–17, 67–69, 90–93, 96–97; Martin Daly and Margo Wilson, *Homicide* (New York: Aldine De Gruyter, 1988), 241–41; F. L. Attenborough, *The Laws of the Earliest English Kings* (Cambridge: Cambridge University Press, 1922), 2–17; James F. Stephen, *A History of the Criminal Law of England* (London: Macmillan, 1883), 3:23; James Lindgren, "Measuring the Value of Slaves and Free Persons in Ancient Law," *Chicago-Kent Law Review* 71, no. 1 (January 1995): 149–215, 198–200; Patrick Wormald, "The Age of Bede and Aethelbald," in *The Anglo-Saxons*, ed. James Campbell (Ithaca, N.Y.: Cornell University Press/Phaidon Books, 1982), 98–99.

14. See Pelteret, *Slavery in Early Medieval England*, 84; see also Benjamin Merkle, *The White Horse King: The Life of Alfred the Great* (Nashville: Thomas Nelson, 2009), 197–207; Justin Pollard, *Alfred the Great: The Man Who Made England* (London: John Murray, 2005), 255–59; Alfred Smyth, *King Alfred the Great* (New York: Oxford University Press, 1995), 238, 515, 525.

15. See Richard Abels, *Alfred the Great: War, Kingship and Culture in Anglo-Saxon England* (Harlow: Longman, 1998), 29–37; Attenborough, *Laws of the Earliest English Kings*, 62–93.

16. See John V. Orth, "When Analogy Fails: The Common Law & *State v. Mann*," *North Carolina Law Review* 87, no. 3 (March 2009): 987n49.

17. See Paul R. Hyams, *Kings, Lords, and Peasants in Medieval England: The Common Law of Villeinage in the Twelfth and Thirteenth Centuries* (Oxford: Clarendon, 1980), ix, 125–31; see also Pollock and Maitland, *History of English Law*, 1:412–32; Paul Vinogradoff, *Villainage in England: Essays in English Mediaeval History* (Oxford: Clarendon, 1892), 67–88; William Blackstone, *Commentaries on the Laws of England*, ed. John L. Wendell (New York: Harper & Brothers, 1854), 2:*92–*93; Stanley L. Engerman, "Slavery, Serfdom and Other Forms of Coerced Labour: Similarities and Differences," in *Serfdom and Slavery: Studies in Legal Bondage*, ed. M. L. Bush (New York: Longman, 1996),

18–41; Morris, *Southern Slavery and the Law*, 52–55; Thomas D. Morris, "'Villeinage . . . as It Existed in England, Reflects but Little Light on Our Subject': The Problem of the 'Sources' of Southern Slave Law," *American Journal Legal History* 32, no. 2 (April 1988): 127–31; but see Guasco, *Slaves and Englishmen*, 25–33, 242n42.

18. See Bush, "Free to Enslave," 423; see also Jordan, *White over Black*, 49; Stenton, *English Society in the Early Middle Ages*, 139–59; Finkelman, "Defining Slavery," 555n26.

19. See Wormald, "Bloodfeud, Kindred and Government," 57; see also Alexander Grant, "Murder Will Out: Kingship, Kinship and Killing in Medieval Scotland," in *Kings, Lords and Men in Scotland and Britain, 1300–1625: Essays in Honor of Jenny Wormald*, ed. Steve Boardman and Julian Goodare (Edinburg: Edinburg University Press, 2014), 207–8.

20. See Pollock and Maitland, *History of English Law*, 2:458, 485–88, 458; see also Michael P. Roth, *Crime and Punishment: A History of the Criminal Justice System*, 2nd ed. (Belmont, Calif.: Wadsworth, 2011), 36–37; Daly and Wilson, *Homicide*, 244–45; Richard L. Keyser, "'Agreement Supersedes Law, and Love Judgment': Legal Flexibility and Amicable Settlement in Anglo-Norman England," *Law and History Review* 30, no. 1 (February 2012): 83–85; Thomas A. Green, "Societal Concepts of Criminal Liability for Homicide in Mediaeval England," *Speculum* 47, no. 4 (October 1972): 669, 687–89.

21. See Blackstone, *Commentaries*, 4:*176–*204; see *also* J. M. Beattie, *Crime and the Courts in England, 1660–1800* (Princeton, N.J.: Princeton University Press, 1986), 77–79; Stephen, *History of the Criminal Law of England*, 3:44; Michael H. Hoffheimer, "Murder and Manslaughter in Mississippi: Unintentional Killings," *Mississippi Law Journal* 71 (Fall 2001): 37–52; Thomas A. Green, "The Jury and the English Law of Homicide, 1200–1600," *Michigan Law Review* 74, no. 3 (January 1976): 412–22, 472–87; Francis Bowes Sayre, "Mens Rea," *Harvard Law Review* 45, no. 6 (April 1932): 996–98.

22. See Lawrence M. Friedman, *A History of American Law*, 3rd ed. (New York: Touchstone, 2005), 34; Jeffrey K. Sawyer, "'Benefit of Clergy' in Maryland and Virginia," *American Journal of Legal History* 33, no. 1 (January 1990): 49–68; Kathryn Preyer, "Crime, the Criminal Law and Reform in Post-revolutionary Virginia," *Law and History Review* 1, no. 1 (Spring 1983): 54n6; Kathryn Preyer, "Penal Measures in the American Colonies: An Overview," *American Journal of Legal History* 26, no. 4 (October 1982): 331–32n93; Green, "Jury and the English Law of Homicide," 487–97.

23. See, e.g., Cynthia Lee, *Murder and the Reasonable Man: Passion and Fear in the Criminal Courtroom* (New York: New York University Press, 2003), 127; Richard Maxwell Brown, *No Duty to Retreat: Violence and Values in American History and Society* (New York: Oxford University Press, 1991), 3–4; Beattie, *Crime and the Courts in England*, 79; Pollock and Maitland, *History of English Law*, 2:478–84; Garrett Epps, "Any Which Way but Loose: Interpretative Strategies and Attitudes toward Violence in the Evolution of the Anglo-American 'Retreat Rule,'" *Law and Contemporary Problems* 55, no. 1 (Winter 1992): 307–8; Green, "Jury and the English Law of Homicide," 436–44.

24. See, e.g., Guyora Binder, *Felony Murder* (Stanford, Calif.: Stanford University Press, 2012), 104–5; Beattie, *Crime and the Courts in England*, 79–80; Stephen, *History of the Criminal Law of England*, 3:45–49; P. Luevonda Ross, "The Transmogrification

of Self-Defense by National Rifle Association-Inspired Statutes," *Southern University Law Review* 35, no. 1 (Fall 2007): 4–8; Guyora Binder, "The Origins of American Felony Murder Rules," *Stanford Law Review* 57, no. 1 (October 2004): 80–81; Richard Singer, "The Resurgence of Mens Rea: II—Honest but Unreasonable Mistake of Fact in Self-Defense," *Boston College Law Review* 28, no. 3 (May 1987): 471–74; Green, "Jury and the English Law of Homicide," 444–52.

25. Blackstone, *Commentaries*, 4:*201; see *State v. Zellers*, 7 N.J.L. 220, 243–44 (Sup. Ct. 1824).

26. See Holly Brewer, *By Birth or Consent: Children, Law, and the Anglo-American Revolution in Authority* (Chapel Hill: University of North Carolina Press, 2005), 193; Steinfeld, *Invention of Free Labor*, 16, 59, 217n17; Beattie, *Crime and the Courts in England*, 86; Richard B. Morris, *Government and Labor in Early America* (New York: Columbia University Press, 1946), 461–500; Lea VanderVelde, "The Last *Legally* Beaten Servant in America: From Compulsion to Coercion in the American Workplace," *Seattle University Law Review* 39, no. 3 (Spring 2016): 729–30; Evelyn Atkinson, "Out of the Household: Master-Servant Relations and Employer Liability," *Yale Journal of Law and the Humanities* 35, no. 2 (Summer 2013): 219.

27. Michael Dalton, *The Countrey Justice, Conteyning the Practice if the Justices of the Peace of Their Sessions, Gathered for the Better Helpe of Such Justices of the Peace as Have Not Beene Much Conversant in the Studie of the Lawes of This Realme* (London: Societie Stationers, 1618), 216; see Morris, *Southern Slavery and the Law*, 162–63.

28. William Hawkins, *A Treatise of the Pleas of the Crown; or, A System of the Principal Matters relating to That Subject Digested under Their Proper Hands* (London: Eliz. Nutt, 1716), 73–74; see Morris, *Southern Slavery and the Law*, 163; Joel Prentiss Bishop, *Commentaries on the Criminal Law* (Boston: Little, Brown, 1882), 365, 371, 383–84; William Oldnall Russell, *A Treatise on Crimes and Indictable Misdemeanors* (London: Joseph Butterworth, 1826), 532–33.

29. See *Rex v. Grey* (Newgate Sessions 1666), in Courtney Stanhope Kenny, *A Selection of Cases Illustrative of English Criminal Law* (Cambridge: Cambridge University Press, 1901), 105–6; see also *State v. Shaw*, 64 S.C. 566, 43 S.E. 14 (1902) (affirming employer's conviction for murdering young boy servant), with annotation in Burdett A. Rich and Henry P. Farnham, *The Lawyers Report Annotated 1903 Extra Annotated Edition of 1913* (Rochester: Lawyers Co-Operative Publishing, 1915), 801–5.

30. See Helen Lacey, *The Royal Pardon: Access to Mercy in Fourteenth-Century England* (York: York Medieval Press, 2009), 19–81; Naomi D. Hurnard, *The King's Pardon for Homicide before AD 1307* (Oxford: Clarendon, 1969), 68–170; Thomas J. McSweeney, "The King's Courts and the King's Soul: Pardoning as Almsgiving in Medieval England," *Reading Medieval Studies* 40 (2014): 169–73; Green, "Jury and the English Law of Homicide," 419–21, 428–36, 457–72; Green, "Societal Concepts of Criminal Liability," 672–73.

31. See, e.g., Onder Bakircioglu, *Self-Defence in International Criminal Law: The Doctrine of Imminence* (New York: Routledge, 2011), 40–43; Roth, *Crime and Punishment*, 37; Lee, *Murder and the Reasonable Man*, 127, 312–13n24; Brown, *No Duty to Retreat*, 4–5; Epps, "Any Which Way but Loose," 308–10; Singer, "Resurgence of Mens Rea," 471–72;

Joseph H. Beale, Jr., "Retreat from a Murderous Assault," *Harvard Law Review* 16, no. 8 (June 1903): 567–76.

32. See Matthew Hale, *Pleas of the Crown; or, A Methodical Summary of the Principal Matters Relating to That Subject* (London: Assigns of Richard Atkins and Edward Atkins, 1678), 41; see also Wyatt Holliday, "Comment: 'The Answer to Criminal Aggression Is Retaliation': Stand-Your-Ground Laws and the Liberalization of Self-Defense," *University of Toledo Law Review* 43, no. 2 (Winter 2012): 410–11; Benjamin Levin, "Note: A Defensible Defense? Reexamining the Castle Doctrine Statutes," *Harvard Journal on Legislation* 47, no. 2 (Summer 2010): 527–32; Denise M. Drake, "The Castle Doctrine: An Expanding Right to Stand Your Ground," *St. Mary's Law Journal* 39 (January 2008): 573–613; Catherine L. Carpenter, "The Enemy Within, the Castle Doctrine, and Self-Defense," *Marquette Law Review* 86 (Spring 2003): 653–700; Singer, "Resurgence of Mens Rea," 474–75.

33. Brown, *No Duty to Retreat*, 4.

34. See Fede, *People without Rights*, 18.

35. See Christopher Leslie Brown, *Moral Capital: Foundations of British Abolitionism* (Chapel Hill: University of North Carolina Press, 2006), 44–46, 44; see also Christopher Tomlins, *Freedom Bound: Law, Labor, and Civic Identity in Colonizing English America, 1580–1865* (New York: Cambridge University Press, 2010), 411; Susan Dwyer Amussen, *Caribbean Exchanges: Slavery and the Transformation of English Society, 1640–1700* (Chapel Hill: University of North Carolina Press, 2007), 15–19, 142–44; Eltis, *The Rise of African Slavery in the Americas*, 71–84; Seymour Drescher, *Capitalism and Antislavery: British Mobilization in Comparative Perspective* (New York: Oxford University Press, 1986), 15–16; Jonathan A. Bush, "The First Slave (and Why He Matters)," *Cardozo Law Review* 18, no. 2 (November 1996): 599–629; Bush, "Free to Enslave," 420–56.

36. Moses I. Finley, *Ancient Slavery and Modern Ideology*, expanded, ed. Brent D. Shaw (Princeton, N.J.: Markus Wiener, 1998), 142–43 (citation and internal quotation omitted).

37. See Jedediah Purdy, *The Meaning of Property: Freedom, Community, and the Legal Imagination* (New Haven, Conn.: Yale University Press, 2010), 89.

38. See Justin Roberts, *Slavery and the Enlightenment in the British Atlantic, 1750–1807* (New York: Cambridge University Press, 2013), 2–5, 2–3.

39. See ibid., 291; see also, defining "the other slavery" to include slave-like relationships resulting after Spain's 1542 abolition of Native American slavery and other general emancipations, when the officials did not enact or enforce laws preventing the continuation of slavery's badges and incidents, Andres Resendez, *The Other Slavery: The Uncovered Story of Indian Enslavement in America* (New York: Houghton Mifflin Harcourt, 2016), 4, 295–314.

40. Fede, *People without Rights*, 3–44, 18; see Fede, *Roadblocks to Freedom*, 6–19; see also Guasco, *Slaves and Englishmen*, 288n15 (stating that the common law "did not address slavery in a systematic fashion," but that the colonists' selective reception of the common law legitimized slavery, and that "historians should pay less attention to what common law said and more to how it was constructed and legitimated over time").

41. Teresa Michals, "'That Sole and Despotic Dominion': Slaves, Wives, and Game in Blackstone's *Commentaries*," *Eighteenth-Century Studies* 27 (1993–94): 202.

42. See C. S. L. Davies, "Slavery and Protector Somerset: The Vagrancy Act of 1547," *Economic History Review*, New Series 19, no. 3 (1986): 533–49. See, e.g., discussing English customs and statutes that, it is suggested, may have provided analogies for colonial slave laws, Tomlins, *Freedom Bound*, 418–20; Eltis, *Rise of African Slavery in the Americas*, 5–7, 70–71; Sidney W. Mintz, *Caribbean Transformations* (Chicago: Aldine, 1974), 70–72; Jordan, *White over Black*, 48–56; Holly Brewer, "Power and Authority in the Colonial South: the English Legacy and Its Contradictions," in *Britain and the American South: From Colonialism to Rock and Roll*, ed. Joseph P. Ward (Jackson: University Press of Mississippi, 2003), 27–51; Bradley J. Nicholson, "Legal Borrowing and the Origins of Slave Law in the British Colonies," *American Journal of Legal History* 38, no. 1 (January 1994): 41–53; David Konig, "'Dale's Laws' and the Non-Common Law Origins of Criminal Justice in Virginia," *American Journal of Legal History* 26, no. 4 (October 1982): 354–75.

43. See Michal Jan Rozbick, *Culture and Liberty in the Age of the American Revolution* (Charlottesville: University of Virginia Press, 2011), 43–55.

44. See John Russell Bartlett, ed., *Records of the Colony of Rhode Island and Providence Plantations in New England, Volume 1: 1636–1663* (Providence: J. Crawford Greene and Brothers, 1856), 243; see also John Donoghue, *Fire under the Ashes: An Atlantic History of the English Revolution* (Chicago: University of Chicago Press, 2013), 265; Patrick T. Conley and Robert G. Flanders, Jr., *The Rhode Island State Constitution*, Oxford Commentaries on the State Constitutions of the United States (New York: Oxford University Press, 2011), 69–70; Robert J. Cottrol, *The Afro-Yankees: Providence's Black Community in the Antebellum Era* (Westport, Conn.: Greenwood, 1982), 14–18; Lorenzo Johnston Greene, *The Negro in Colonial New England*, Studies in American Negro Life (New York: Columbia University Press, 1942; repr., New York: Atheneum, 1971), 18, 125–26; Elizabeth Donnan, *Documents Illustrative of the History of the Slave Trade to America: New England and the Middle Colonies* (Washington, D.C.: Carnegie Institution, 1932), 3:108–9; Thomas Williams Bicknell, *The History of the State of Rhode Island and Providence Plantations* (New York: American Historical Society, 1920), 3:996–97. This law apparently was advocated by Samuel Gorton of Warwick. See Jordan, *White over Black*, 70n58; Adelob Gorton, *The Life and Times of Samuel Gorton* (Philadelphia: George S. Ferguson, 1907), 93–94.

45. See Conley and Flanders, *Rhode Island State Constitution*, 70; Helen T. Catterall, ed., *Judicial Cases Concerning American Slavery and the Negro* (1926–37; repr., New York: Negro Universities Press, 1968), 4:448; see also Fede, *People without Rights*, 44.

46. See Mary Sarah Bilder, *The Transatlantic Constitution: Colonial Legal Culture and the Empire* (Cambridge, Mass.: Harvard University Press, 2004), 1–50; see also Mary Sarah Bilder, "English Settlement and Local Governance," in Grossberg and Tomlins, *Cambridge History of Law in America*, 1:83–103.

47. See Bush, "Free to Enslave," 458–59; see also Ken MacMillan, *The Atlantic Imperial Constitution: Center and Periphery in the English Atlantic World* (New York: Palgrave Macmillan, 2011), 1–30; Amussen, *Caribbean Exchanges*, 108–44; Larry Gragg, *Englishmen Transplanted: The English Colonization of Barbados, 1627–1660* (New York: Oxford University Press, 2003), 5–10; Seymour Drescher, *Capitalism and Antislavery:*

British Mobilization in Comparative Perspective (New York: Oxford University Press, 1986), 12–24; Lauren Benton and Kathryn Walker, "Law for the Empire: The Common Law in Colonial America and the Problem of Legal Diversity," *Chicago-Kent Law Review* 89, no. 3 (May 2014): 950–53; Thomas Konig, "Regionalism in Early American Law," in Grossberg and Tomlins, *Cambridge History of Law in America*, 1:156–77; Eliga H. Gould, "Zones of Law, Zones of Violence: The Legal Geography of the British Atlantic, circa 1772," *William and Mary Quarterly*, 3rd ser., 60, no. 3 (July 2003): 474–75, 497–501; but see, noting a "resurgence of imperial history" stressing "the metropole's critical role in seventeenth-century colonial affairs," Justin Roberts, "Surrendering Surinam: The Barbadian Diaspora and the Expansion of the English Sugar Frontier, 1650–75," *William and Mary Quarterly*, 3rd ser., 73, no. 2 (April 2016): 227.

48. See Jack P. Greene, "Colonial South Carolina and the Caribbean Connection," *South Carolina Historical Magazine* 88, no. 4 (October 1987): 192; see also Jack P. Greene, *Pursuits of Happiness: The Social Development of Early Modern British Colonies and the Formation of American Culture* (Chapel Hill: University of North Carolina Press, 1988), 7–54.

49. See D. W. Meinig, *The Shaping of America: A Geographical Perspective on 500 Years of History: Volume I, Atlantic America, 1492–1800* (New Haven, Conn.: Yale University Press, 1986), 52.

50. See Greene, "Colonial South Carolina and the Caribbean Connection," 192; see also Meinig, *Shaping of America*, 252; Jack P. Greene, "Early Modern Southeastern North America and the Border Atlantic and American Worlds," *Journal of Southern History* 23, no. 3 (August 2007): 532–33.

51. See Greene, "Colonial South Carolina and the Caribbean Connection," 192–93; see also Matthew Mulcahy, *Hubs of Empire: The Southeastern Lowcountry and British Caribbean*, Regional Perspectives in Early America (Baltimore: Johns Hopkins University Press, 2014), 1–8.

52. See Eliga H. Gould, *Among the Powers of the Earth: The American Revolution and the Making of a New World Empire* (Cambridge, Mass.: Harvard University Press, 2012), 52–53.

CHAPTER 4. Decriminalization to Amelioration on Britain's Atlantic Island Colonies

1. See, e.g., Douglas Hay, "Property, Authority and the Criminal Law," in *Albion's Fatal Tree: Crime and Society in Eighteenth-Century England*, ed. Douglas Hay et al. (London: Allen Lane, 1975), 17–23; Hugo A. Bedau, "General Introduction," in *Capital Punishment*, ed. James A. McCafferty (Chicago: Aldine-Atherton, 1972), 7–12; Frederick C. Millett, "Will the United States Follow England (and the Rest of the World) in Abandoning Capital Punishment?," *Pierce Law Review* 6, no. 3 (Spring 2008): 552; see also A. E. Keir Nash, "Reason of Slavery: Understanding the Judicial Role in the Peculiar Institution," *Vanderbilt Law Review* 32, no. 1 (January 1979): 49.

2. See, e.g., Susan Dwyer Amussen, *Caribbean Exchanges: Slavery and the Transformation of English Society, 1640–1700* (Chapel Hill: University of North Carolina Press,

2007), 108–44; Jack P. Greene, *Peripheries and Center: Constitutional Development in the Extended Polities of the British Empire and the United States 1607–1788 (The Richard B. Russell Lecture Series)* (Athens: University of Georgia Press, 1986), 9–18; Jack P. Greene, "Transatlantic Colonization and Redefinition of Empire in the Early Modern Era: The British-American Inheritance," in *Negotiated Empires: Centers and Peripheries in the Americas 1550–1820*, ed. Christine Daniels and Michael V. Kennedy (New York: Routledge, 2002), 267–82; Jonathan A. Bush, "Free to Enslave: The Foundations of Colonial American Slave Law," *Yale Journal of Law and the Humanities* 5, no. 2 (Summer 1993): 432–34, 456–70; Elsa V. Goveia, "The West Indian Slave Laws of the Eighteenth Century," in *Slavery in the New World: A Reader in Comparative History*, ed. Laura Foner and Eugene Genovese (Englewood Cliffs, N.J.: Prentice Hall, 1969), 118–26.

3. See Matthew Mulcahy, *Hubs of Empire: The Southeastern Lowcountry and British Caribbean*, Regional Perspectives in Early America (Baltimore: Johns Hopkins University Press, 2014), 9–53; Matthew Parker, *The Sugar Barons: Family, Corruption, Empire, and War in the West Indies* (New York: Walker & Company, 2011), 32–66; David Eltis, *The Rise of African Slavery in the Americas* (New York: Cambridge University Press, 2000), 195–204; Jan Rogozinski, *A Brief History of the Caribbean: From the Arawak and Carib to the Present*, rev. ed. (New York: Plume, 1999), 69–70, 91–92; Jerome S. Handler, "Custom and Law: The Status of Enslaved Africans in Seventeenth-Century Barbados," *Slavery and Abolition* 37, no. 3 (June 2016): 233–34.

4. See Larry Gragg, *Englishmen Transplanted: The English Colonization of Barbados, 1627–1660* (New York: Oxford University Press, 2003), 117–30; Eltis, *Rise of African Slavery in the Americas*, 47–56. On Indian slavery, see Linford D. Fisher, "'Dangerous Designes': The 1676 Barbados Act to Prohibit New England Slave Importation," *William and Mary Quarterly*, 3rd ser., 71, no. 1 (January 2014): 101–3.

5. Christopher Tomlins, *Freedom Bound: Law, Labor, and Civic Identity in Colonizing English America, 1580–1865* (New York: Cambridge University Press, 2010), 428; see Carrie Gibson, *Empire's Crossroads: A History of the Caribbean from Columbus to the Present Day* (New York: Atlantic Monthly Press, 2014), 90–91; Mulcahy, *Hubs of Empire*, 53–58; Simon P. Newman, *A New World of Labor: The Development of Plantation of Slavery in the British Atlantic* (Philadelphia: University of Pennsylvania Press, 2013), 246–54; Rogozinski, *Brief History of the Caribbean*, 70–72; Hilary McD. Beckles, *A History of Barbados: From Amerindian Settlement to Nation State* (New York: Cambridge University Press, 1990), 20–40; Jerome S. Handler, *The Unappropriated People: Freemen in the Slave Society of Barbados* (Baltimore: Johns Hopkins University Press, 1974), 12–21; Richard S. Dunn, *Sugar and Slaves: The Rise of the Planter Class in the English West Indies, 1624–1713* (Chapel Hill: University of South Carolina University Press, 1972), 49–76, 87–89, 230, 312; Fisher, "'Dangerous Designes,'" 104–5; Hilary McD. Beckles and Andrew Downes, "The Economics of Transition to the Black Labor System in Barbados, 1630–1680," *Journal of Interdisciplinary History* 18, no. 2 (Autumn 1987): 225–47.

6. See Gragg, *Englishmen Transplanted*, 114; Robert H. Schomburgk, *The History of Barbados* (London: Longman, Brown, Green & Longmans, 1848), 199, 265–66; Betty Wood, "The Origins of Slavery in the Americas, 1500–1700," in *The Routledge History of Slavery*, ed. Gad Heuman and Trevor Bernard (New York: Routledge, 2011), 72; Ed-

ward B. Rugemer, "The Development of Mastery and Race in the Comprehensive Slave Codes of the Greater Caribbean during the Seventeenth Century," *William and Mary Quarterly*, 3rd ser., 70, no. 3 (July 2013): 433–34.

7. See Gragg, *Englishmen Transplanted*, 116, 157–59; Handler, "Custom and Law," 242–46.

8. See Gragg, *Englishmen Transplanted*, 130, citing "Minutes of the Council of Barbados, 1654–1658" (Typescript, 1934), Public Records Office, London.

9. See Rugemer, "Development of Mastery and Race," 434.

10. See David Barry Gaspar, "With a Rod of Iron: Barbados Slave Law as a Model for Jamaica, South Carolina, and Antigua, 1661–1697," in *Crossing Boundaries: Comparative History of Black People in Diaspora*, ed. Darlene Clark Hine and Jacqueline McLeod (Bloomington: Indiana University Press, 1999), 345; see also Mulcahy, *Hubs of Empire*, 56; Parker, *Sugar Barons*, 148; Amussen, *Caribbean Exchanges*, 110, 129–35; Dunn, *Sugar and Slaves*, 238–41; Rugemer, "Development of Mastery and Race," 436–38. I quote the version of the original manuscript cited by Christopher Tomlins in *Freedom Bound*, 428–29. I am grateful for his generosity in providing me with a copy of his typescript. Portions of the act are published as "An Act for the Better Ordering of Negroes" [Barbados 1661 (Public Records Office Kew, CO 30/2/16–26, 32–3)], in *Slavery: Oxford Readers*, ed. Stanley L. Engerman, Seymour Drescher, and Robert Paquette (New York: Oxford University Press, 2001), 105–13. I will include citations to this published version.

11. See Rugemer, "Development of Mastery and Race," 438; see also Jenny Shaw, *Everyday Life in the Early English Caribbean: Irish, Africans, and the Construction of Difference* (Athens: University of Georgia Press, 2013), 15–16; Handler, "Custom and Law," 246, 254–55n48.

12. See "An Act for the Better Ordering of Negroes," in Engerman, Drescher, and Paquette, *Slavery: Oxford Readers*, 105; Parker, *Sugar Barons*, 148; Gragg, *Englishmen Transplanted*, 118–19.

13. See, e.g., Sidney W. Mintz, *Caribbean Transformations* (Chicago: Aldine, 1974), 70–71, quoting the "racist proslavery" writer, George Wilson Bridges, *The Annals of Jamaica* (London: John Murray, 1827), 1:507; Edward Long, *The History of Jamaica* (London: T. Lowndes, 1774), 2:493–96.

14. See "An Act for the Better Ordering of Negroes," in Engerman, Drescher, and Paquette, *Slavery: Oxford Readers*, 111–12. Muscovado sugar is a sticky, brown-colored product of the sugar-making process. See J. H. Galloway, *The Sugar Cane Industry: An Historical Geography from Its Origins to 1914* (New York: Cambridge University Press, 1989), 108; Dunn, *Sugar and Slaves*, 195–96. It became the island's dominant commodity and "served as a sort of currency in Barbados, much like tobacco did in Virginia." See Fisher, "'Dangerous Designes,'" 111n39.

15. See "An Act for the Better Ordering of Negroes," in Engerman, Drescher, and Paquette, *Slavery: Oxford Readers*, 112.

16. Ibid., 106.

17. See Rugemer, "Development of Mastery and Race," 441.

18. See K. J. Kesselring, "Felony Forfeiture in England, c. 1170–1870," *Journal of Legal History* 30, no. 3 (December 2009): 201–26.

19. See Newman, *New World of Labor*, 94.

20. Robin Blackburn, *The Making of New World Slavery: From the Baroque to the Modern, 1492–1800* (New York: Verso, 1997), 265; see Ken MacMillan, *The Atlantic Imperial Constitution: Center and Periphery in the English Atlantic World* (New York: Palgrave Macmillan, 2011), 2–8; Greene, *Peripheries and Center*, 13–17; Elmer Beecher Russell, *The Review of American Colonial Legislation by the King in Council* (New York, 1915), 15–43; Winfred T. Root, "The Lords of Trade and Plantations," *American Historical Review* 23, no. 1 (October 1917): 20–41; Mary Patterson Clarke, "The Board of Trade at Work," *American Historical Review* 17, no. 1 (October 1911): 17–43.

21. See W. Noel Sainsbury and J. W. Fortescue, eds., *Calendar of State Papers, Colonial Series, America and West Indies, 1677–1680, Preserved in the Public Records Office* (London: Her Majesty's Stationary Office, 1896), 387–88, 401–2, 548–51, quoting no. 1391, Samuel Baldwin to Lords of Trade and Plantations, June 14, 1680; see also Amussen, *Caribbean Exchanges*, 111–12; April Lee Hatfield, *Atlantic Virginia: Intercolonial Relations in the Seventeenth Century* (Philadelphia: University of Pennsylvania Press, 2004), 155; Edmund S. Morgan, *American Slavery, American Freedom: The Ordeal of Colonial Virginia* (New York: Norton, 1975), 314; Dunn, *Sugar and Slaves*, 245; David Barry Gaspar, "'Rigid and Inclement' Origins of the Jamaica Slave Laws of the Seventeenth Century," in *The Many Legalities of Early America*, ed. Christopher L. Tomlins and Bruce H. Mann (Chapel Hill: University of North Carolina Press, 2001), 91.

22. See Dunn, *Sugar and Slaves*, 312.

23. See Alison Games, *The Web of Empire: English Cosmopolitans in an Age of Expansion, 1560–1660* (New York: Oxford University Press, 2008), 175–79; see, generally, Amussen, *Caribbean Exchanges*, 140–41; Dunn, *Sugar and Slaves*, 239–46; Gaspar, "With a Rod of Iron," 349, 354, 356, 359.

24. See Parker, *Sugar Barons*, 97–111; Rugemer, "Development of Mastery and Race," 443.

25. Dunn, *Sugar and Slaves*, 243; Orlando Patterson, *The Sociology of Slavery: An Analysis of the Origins, Development and Structure of Negro Slave Society in Jamaica* (Rutherford, N.J.: Fairleigh Dickinson University Press, 1965), 16–23; Rugemer, "Development of Mastery and Race," 430, 443.

26. See Amussen, *Caribbean Exchanges*, 140; see also Justin Roberts, "Surrendering Surinam: The Barbadian Diaspora and the Expansion of the English Sugar Frontier, 1650–75," *William and Mary Quarterly*, 3rd ser., 73, no. 2 (April 2016): 241–56.

27. See Rugemer, "Development of Mastery and Race," 443–45, 444; Patterson, *Sociology of Slavery*, 23–27; Trevor Burnard, "European Migration to Jamaica, 1655–1780," *William and Mary Quarterly*, 3rd ser., 53, no. 4 (October 1996): 772.

28. Justin Roberts, *Slavery and the Enlightenment in the British Atlantic, 1750–1807* (New York: Cambridge University Press, 2013), 11; Mulcahy, *Hubs of Empire*, 63–83.

29. See L. W. Labaree, *Royal Instructions to British Colonial Governors 1670–1776* (New York: Appleton, 1962), 2:506–8; see also John Marshall, "Whig Thought and the Revolution of 1688–91," in *The Final Crisis of the Stuart Monarchy: The Revolutions of 1688–91 in the British, Atlantic, and European Contexts*, ed. Tim Harris and Stephen Taylor (Rochester, N.Y.: Boydell Press, 2013), 85.

30. See J. W. Fortescue, *Calendar of State Papers, Colonial Series, America and West Indies, 1681–1685* (London, 1898), 82; see also Amussen, *Caribbean Exchanges*, 141; Patterson, *Sociology of Slavery*, 74–75.

31. See Lords of Trade and Plantations to Gov. Sir Thomas Lynch, February 17, 1683, in "America and West Indies: February 1683, 17–28," *Calendar of State Papers Colonial, American and West Indies, Volume 11: 1681–1685* (1898), 385–400, accessed March 16, 2014, http://www.british-history.ac.uk/report.aspx?compid=69873; see also Amussen, *Caribbean Exchanges*, 142; Patterson, *Sociology of Slavery*, 74; Gaspar, "'Rigid and Inclement,'" 93.

32. See "An Act for the Better Ordering of Slaves," in *The Laws of Jamaica Passed by the Assembly, and Confirmed by His Majesty in Council, April 17, 1684, to Which Is Added, the State of Jamaica, as It Is Now under Government of Sir Thomas Lynch. With a Large Mapp of the Island* (London, 1684), 147; see also Rugemer, "Development of Mastery and Race," 449n71.

33. See William Dickson, "Letter XI, Farther Considerations on the Confirmation of the Slave-laws, etc.," in *Mitigation of Slavery, in Two Parts* (London: R. and A. Taylor, 1814), 340; Long, *History of Jamaica*, 2:493–94; see also Dunn, *Sugar and Slaves*, 245; Labaree, *Royal Instructions*, 2:507–8.

34. See "An Act for the Better Order and Government of Slaves," in *Acts of Assembly Passed in the Island of Jamaica: From the Year 1681 to the Year 1768, Inclusive* (Saint Jago de la Vega, Jamaica: Lowry and Sherlock, 1769), 1:63; see also Dunn, *Sugar and Slaves*, 245; Patterson, *Sociology of Slavery*, 75, 82; Rugemer, "Development of Mastery and Race," 455–56; Gaspar, "With a Rod of Iron," 354; Gaspar "'Rigid and Inclement,'" 94–95.

35. See "Act for the Better Order and Government of Slaves," 61; see also Patterson, *Sociology of Slavery*, 85–86.

36. See Amussen, *Caribbean Exchanges*, 135–38; Fisher, "'Dangerous Designes,'" 99–100, 109–20, 122–24.

37. See Labaree, *Royal Instructions*, 2:507; see also Amussen, *Caribbean Exchanges*, 138; "Additional Instructions to Sir Richard Dutton," May 3, 1664, in "America and West Indies: May 1684, 1–15," *Calendar of State Papers Colonial America and West Indies, Volume 11: 1681–1685*, ed. J. W. Fortescue (1898), 623–36, accessed March 24, 2014, http://www.british-history.ac.uk/report.aspx?compid=69892.

38. See Labaree, *Royal Instructions*, 2:506–7; "Instructions to Sir John Atkins, Governor of Barbados," December 19, 1673, in "America and West Indies: December 1673," *Calendar of State Papers Colonial America and West Indies, Volume 7: 1669–1674*, ed. J. W. Fortescue (1898), 535–44, accessed March 24, 2014, http://www.british-history.ac.uk/report.aspx?compid=70243.

39. Amussen, *Caribbean Exchanges*, 138; see Fisher, "'Dangerous Designes,'" 120–21.

40. See Beckles, *History of Barbados*, 34–35; see also Amussen, *Caribbean Exchanges*, 135–40; Dunn, *Sugar and Slaves*, 241–42; Ulrich B. Phillips, *American Negro Slavery: A Survey of the Supply, Employment and Control of Negro Labor as Determined by the Plantation Regime* (New York: Appleton, 1918), 491–92, citing Richard Hall, ed., *Acts Passed in the Island of Barbados from 1643 to 1762 inclusive* (1764), 112–21. For the case of Peter Bascom, who on November 18, 1729, was required by the Barbados Court of Exchequer

to be bound over to his good behavior for six months after killing an unnamed female slave of Mrs. Ashby, see Marisa J. Fuentes, *Dispossessed Lives: Enslaved Women, Violence, and the Archive* (Philadelphia: University of Pennsylvania Press, 2016), 116, 196n78.

41. See Natalie A. Zacek, *Settler Society in the English Leeward Islands, 1670–1776* (New York: Cambridge University Press, 2010), 7, 45, 206–7, 7; see also Parker, *Sugar Barons*, 129–42, 167–68. The Leeward Islands, until 1816, included Antigua, Barbuda, Montserrat, Nevis, Anguilla, Saint Christopher or Saint Kitts, and the British Virgin Islands. See Zacek, *Settler Society in the English Leeward Islands*, 15–19; Elsa V. Goveia, *Slave Society in the British Leeward Islands at the End of the Eighteenth Century* (New Haven, Conn.: Yale University Press, 1965), vii; Mindie Lazarus-Black, "Slaves, Masters, and Magistrates: Law and the Politics of Resistance in the Caribbean, 1736–1834," in *Contested States: Law, Hegemony and Resistance*, ed. Mindie Lazarus-Black and Susan F. Hirsch (New York: Routledge, 1994), 269n2.

42. See Zacek, *Settler Society in the English Leeward Islands*, 29, 46–65, 29.

43. See Jack P. Greene, "Colonial South Carolina and the Caribbean Connection," *South Carolina Historical Magazine* 88, no. 4 (October 1987): 193–205; see also Zacek, *Settler Society in the English Leeward Islands*, 29, 46–64, 242.

44. Roberts, *Slavery and the Enlightenment*, 10; see Mulcahy, *Hubs of Empire*, 58–62; Eltis, *Rise of African Slavery in the Americas*, 204–22.

45. David Barry Gaspar, *Bondmen and Rebels: A Study of Master-Slave Relations in Antigua* (Baltimore: Johns Hopkins University Press, 1985), 158–59; Gaspar, "With a Rod of Iron," 359.

46. See Gaspar, *Bondmen and Rebels*, 302n22.

47. See "An Act for Attaining Several Slaves Now Run-Away from Their Masters' Services, and for Better Government of Slaves," in *The Laws of Antigua: Consisting of the Acts of the Leeward Islands, November 8, 1690 to April 21, 1798*, ed. Anthony Brown (London: Samuel Bagster, 1805), 1:229–30; see also Gaspar, *Bondmen and Rebels*, 159–60.

48. See Governor Hart to the Council of Trade and Plantations, "America and the West Indies: March 1724, 11–20," Calendar of State Papers Colonial, America and West indies, Volume 34: 1724–1725 (1936), 56–71, *British History Online*, accessed November 2, 2014, http://www.british-history.ac.uk/report.aspx?compid=72383&strquery=antigua %20act%201723%20murder.

49. Gaspar, *Bondmen and Rebels*, 160; see Goveia, *Slave Society*, 173.

50. See Zacek, *Settler Society in the English Leeward Islands*, 35.

51. William Smith, *A Natural History of Nevis, and the Rest of the English Charibee Islands in America* (Cambridge: J. Bentham, 1745), 233.

52. Ibid., 233–34; see Raymond Phineas Stearns, *Science in the British Colonies of America* (Champaign: University of Illinois, 1970), 337.

53. Zacek, *Settler Society in the English Leeward Islands*, 35; see, discussing Leeward politics, ibid., 206–66.

54. See Virginia Bernhard, *Slaves and Slaveholders in Bermuda 1616–1782* (Columbia: University of Missouri Press, 1999), 66.

55. See Cyril Outerbridge Packwood, *Chained to the Rock: Slavery in Bermuda* (New York: Eliseo Torres & Sons, 1975), 11–82.

56. See "Act for the Security of the Subject to Prevent the Forfeiture of Life and Estate upon Killing a Negro or Other Slave," in *Acts of Assembly Made and Enacted in the Bermuda or Summer Islands* (London, 1737), 98, quoted in Bernhard, *Slaves and Slaveholders in Bermuda*, 215–16; James E. Smith, *Slavery in Bermuda* (New York: Vantage Press, 1976), 99; *Second Report of the Committee of the Society for the Migration and Gradual Abolition of Slavery through the British Dominions* (London: Ellerton & Henderson, 1825), Appendix G, 144–45, note *; James Stephen, *The Slavery of the British West India Colonies Delineated* (London: Joseph Butterworth & Son, 1824), 1:278–79, note *; William Dickson, "Letter X, Have Any, and Which of the Slave-Laws Been Ever Confirmed?," in *Mitigation of Slavery*, 333–36.

57. See Long, *History of Jamaica*, 2:493; see also Patterson, *Sociology of Slavery*, 75, 82; Miles Ogborn, "The Power of Speech: Orality, Oaths and Evidence in the British Atlantic World, 1650–1800," *Transactions of the Institute of British Geographers* 36, no. 1 (January 2011): 115; Frank Wesley Pitman, "The Treatment of the British West Indian Slaves in Law and Custom," *Journal of Negro History* 11, no. 4 (October 1926): 623.

58. See "An Act to Explain Part of an Act Entutled An Act for the Better Order and Government of Slaves and for Inflicting Further and Other Punishment on Persons Killing Negroes or Slaves," in *Acts of Assembly Passed in the Island of Jamaica*, 1:337–38.

59. See Pitman, "Treatment of the British West Indian Slaves," 622, quoting Letter of Governor Henry Grenville to the Board of Trade, December 14, 1752; see also W. Stitt Robinson, *James Glen: From Scottish Provost to Royal Governor of South Carolina* (Westport, Conn.: Greenwood, 1996), 79.

60. See Lennox Honychurch, *The Dominica Story: A History of the Island* (Oxford: Macmillan Education, 1995), 53, 60–61, 100; Patrick L. Baker, *Centering the Periphery: Chaos, Order and the Ethnohistory of Dominica* (Montreal: McGill-Queens University Press, 1994), 67.

61. See "An Act for Suppressing Runaway Slaves, and for the Better Government of Slaves, etc.," quoted in Philip Francis, *Proceedings of the House of Commons on the Slave Trade, and State of the Negroes in the West India Islands* (London: Caroline Ridgeway, 1796), 98–99.

62. See Rogozinski, *Brief History of the Caribbean*, 91; W. Hubert Miller, "The Colonization of the Bahamas, 1647–1670," *William and Mary Quarterly*, 3rd ser., 2, no. 1 (January 1945): 33–46.

63. Rogozinski, *Brief History of the Caribbean*, 92.

64. See Michael Craton, *A History of the Bahamas*, rev. ed. (London: Collins, 1968), 70, 110, 116.

65. See Engerman and Higman, "The Demographic Structure of the Caribbean Slave Societies," in *General History of the Caribbean: Volume III, The Slave Societies of the Caribbean*, ed. Franklin W. Knight (London: UNESCO Publishing, 1997), 49, 51; Jack P. Greene, *Pursuits of Happiness: The Social Development of Early Modern British Colonies and the Formation of American Culture* (Chapel Hill: University of North Carolina Press, 1988), 153–54; Craton, *History of the Bahamas*, 166.

66. See Michael Craton and Gail Saunders, *Islanders in the Storm: A History of the Bahamian People Volume One: From Aboriginal Times to the End of Slavery* (Athens: University of Georgia Press, 1992), 128.

67. See ibid., 136.
68. See ibid., 154.
69. See K. O. Laurence, *Tobago in Wartime 1793–1815* (Kingston: The Press, University of the West Indies, 1995), 2–9, 94–100.
70. See ibid., 94–100.
71. See "An ACT for the Good Order and Government of Slaves, and for Repealing an Act of This Island, Intituled, 'An Act for the Good Order and Government of Slaves, and for Keeping Them under Proper Restraint; for Establishing the Method of Trial in Capital Cases and Other Regulations for the Greater Security of That Part of the Inhibitants Property,'" in *Miscellaneous Papers Private Bills: Agriculture; Finance; Vaccine etc. 1 February–2 July 1816 Vol. XIX* (1816), 185; Laurence, *Tobago in Wartime*, 98–100.
72. See Thomas Southey, *Chorological History of the West Indies* (London: Longman, Rees, Orme, Brown, and Green, 1827), 2:425; see also F. W. N. Bayley, *Four Years' Residence in the West Indies* (London: William Kidd, 1833), 687.
73. See "Arrest of Judgment," in *Black's Law Dictionary*, deluxe 9th ed., ed. Bryan A. Garner (St. Paul: West, 2009), 125.
74. See Katherine A. Smith, "Economy, Politics, and the Early Formation of Cultural Identity in British Virgin Islands' Slave Society," in *Slavery in Africa and the Caribbean: A History of Enslavement and Identity since the Eighteenth Century*, ed. Olatunji Ojo and Nadine Hunt (New York: J. B. Tauris, 2012), 144.
75. See Michael E. O'Neal, *Slavery, Smallholding and Tourism* (New Orleans: Quid Pro, 2012), 11–13; Susanna Henighan Potter, *Moon Virgin Islands*, 5th ed. (Berkeley: Avalon Travel, 2012), 304–13; Smith, "Economy, Politics, and the Early Formation of Cultural Identity," 144–48.
76. See Rogozinski, *Brief History of the Caribbean*, 77.
77. Goveia, *Slave Society*, 176; see Smith, "Economy, Politics, and the Early Formation of Cultural Identity," 154–56.
78. Goveia, *Slave Society*, 185. For a summary of the act, see ibid., 168, 171–85.
79. See chapter 6, notes 80–85.
80. *Somerset v. Stewart*, Lofft 1, 98 Eng. Rep. 499, 20 How. St. T. 1 (K.B. 1772).
81. See *Somerset v. Stewart*, Lofft, 19; see, e.g., Andrew Fede, *Roadblocks to Freedom: Slavery and Manumission in the United States South* (New Orleans: Quid Pro Books, 2011), 153, 289–92; Steven M. Wise, *Though the Heavens May Fall: The Landmark Trial That Led to the End of Human Slavery* (Cambridge: DaCapo Press, 2006).
82. See *Rex v. Jones* (June 1778) (jury found Jones not guilty of assault and battery of slave); *Rex v. Fell* (June 1777) (jury convicted Fell who was fined twenty pounds for beating a slave and taking from him meat purchased for the slave's owner), in John Grant, *Notes of Cases Adjudged in Jamaica from May 1774 to December 1787* (Edinburgh: Adam Neill Company, 1794), 29, 45.
83. See *An Abstract of the Evidence Delivered before a Select Committee of the House of Commons, in the Years 1790 and 1791* (Society in Newcastle for Promoting the Abolition of Slave Trade, 1791), 79–80; see also Laurence, *Tobago in Wartime*, 245n4.
84. See Beverly A. Steele, *Grenada: A History of Its People* (Oxford: Macmillan, 2003), 30–172; George Brizan, *Grenada: Island of Conflict* (London: Macmillan, 1998), 19–115; Rogozinski, *Brief History of the Caribbean*, 119–20, 170.

85. See notes 131–36.

86. See, e.g., Lauren Benton, "Just Despots: The Cultural Construction of Imperial Constitutionalism," *Law, Culture and the Humanities* 9, no. 2 (June 2013): 224–25; Lauren Benton, "Abolition and Imperial Law, 1790–1820," *Journal of Imperial and Commonwealth History* 39, no. 3 (September 2011): 355–74; Trevor Burnard, "Powerless Masters: The Curious Decline of Jamaican Sugar Planters in the Foundational Period of British Abolitionism," *Slavery & Abolition* 32, no. 2 (June 2011): 185–98.

87. See, e.g., Claudius K. Fergus, *Revolutionary Emancipation: Slavery and Abolitionism in the British West Indies* (Baton Rouge: Louisiana State University Press, 2013), ix–xii.

88. See, e.g., ibid., 36–97; Roberts, *Slavery and the Enlightenment*, 54–55; J. R. Ward, *British West Indian Slavery 1750–1834: The Process of Amelioration* (New York: Clarendon, 1988), 1–7, 61–118, 208; W. L. Burn, *Emancipation and Apprenticeship in the British West Indies* (London: Jonathan Cape, 1937; repr., New York: Johnson Reprint, 1970), 28–74; Keith Mason, "The Absentee Planter and the Key Slave: Privilege, Patriarchalism, and Exploitation in the Early Eighteenth-Century Caribbean," *William and Mary Quarterly*, 3rd ser., 70, no. 1 (January 2013): 79–85.

89. See Fergus, *Revolutionary Emancipation*, 44–45; see also "An ACT for the Better Protection and for Promoting the Natural Increase and Population of Slaves within the Island of Grenada, and Such of the Grenadines as Are Annexed to the Government Thereof, for Compelling an Adequate Provision for and Care of Them, as Well in Sickness and Old Age as in Health; and for Constituting and Appointing Guardians to Effectuate and Carry into Execution the Regulations and Purposes of This Act [9 Dec. 1797]," in *Miscellaneous Papers Private Bills: Agriculture; Finance; Vaccine etc. 1 February–2 July 1816 Vol. XIX* (1816), 67–75; Steele, *Grenada*, 100–101; Brizan, *Grenada*, 84–85.

90. See Fergus, *Revolutionary Emancipation*, 44; Long, *History of Jamaica*, 2:493, 498, 3:921–34.

91. See Patterson, *Sociology of Slavery*, 76.

92. See *Notes on the Two Reports from the Committee of the Honourable House of Assembly of Jamaica by a Jamaica Planter* (London: James Phillips, 1789), 27; see also Vincent Brown, *The Reaper's Garden: Death and Power in the World of Atlantic Slavery* (Cambridge, Mass.: Harvard University Press, 2008), 180–85; Maureen G. Elgersman, *Unyielding Spirits: Black Women and Slavery in Early Canada and Jamaica* (New York: Garland, 1999), 51–55; Goveia, *Slave Society*, 167–68; Patterson, *Sociology of Slavery*, 76–77; Pitman, "Treatment of the British West Indian Slaves," 624–26.

93. See *Notes on the Two Reports*, 28.

94. See ibid., 46.

95. "An Act to Repeal an Act Intitled 'An Act to Repeal Several Acts and Clauses of Acts Respecting Slaves, and for Better Order and Government of Slaves, and for Other Purposes'; and Also to Repeal the Several Acts and Clauses of Acts, Which Were Repealed by the Act Intituled as Aforesaid; and for Consolidating, and Bringing into One Act, the Several Laws Relating to Slaves, and for Giving Them Further Protection and Security; for Altering the Mode of Trial of Slaves Charged with Capital Offences; and for Other Purposes," in Stephen Fuller, *The New Act of Assembly of the Island of*

Jamaica (London: B. White and Son, 1789), 5; for the later versions of the Consolidated Act, see, e.g., Bryan Edwards, *The History, Civil and Commercial, of the British Colonies in the West Indies: In Two Volumes* (London, John Stockdale, 1793), 161 (1792 version); see also "An Act for the Subsistence, Clothing, and Better Regulation and Government of Slaves; for Enlarging the Power of the Council of Protection; for Preventing the Improper Transfer of Slaves; and for Other Purpose," in *An Abstract of the Laws of Jamaica Relating to Slaves*, ed. John Lunan (Jamaica: Saint Jago de la Vega Gazette, 1819), 113 (1816 version); Patterson, *Sociology of Slavery*, 77–78.

96. See "An Act for Explaining and Amending the Laws Relating to Manslaughter," in Lunan, *Abstract of the Laws of Jamaica*, 66.

97. See Francis, *Proceedings of the House of Commons*, 96.

98. See "An ACT to Consolidate and Bring into One Act, the Several Laws Relating to Slaves, and for Giving Them Further Protection and Security; for Altering the Mode of Trial of Slaves Charged with Capital Offences; for Suspending the Several Acts and Clauses of Acts Therein Mentioned, and for Other Purposes," in *Miscellaneous Papers, 1 February–2 July 1816 Vol. XIX*, 18.

99. See "An ACT to Repeal an Act, Intituled 'An Act for the Security of the Subject, to Prevent the Forfeiture of Life and Estate upon Killing a Negro or Other Slave,'" in *Miscellaneous Papers, 1 February–2 July 1816 Vol. XIX*, 38; see also Smith, *Slavery in Bermuda*, 99.

100. See "An Act to Consolidate and Bring into One Act, the Several Laws Relating to Slaves, and for Giving Them Further Protection and Security; for Altering the Mode of Trial of Slaves Charged with Capital Offences; for Suspending the Several Acts and Clauses of Acts Therein Mentioned; and for Other Purposes," in *Papers Presented to the House of Commons on the 7th May 1804, Respecting the Slave-Trade* (1804), 5B.

101. Goveia, *Slave Society*, 26–33; David Barry Gaspar, "Ameliorating Slavery: The Leeward Island Slave Act of 1798," in *The Lesser Antilles in the Age of European Expansion*, ed. Robert L. Paquette and Stanley R. Engerman (Gainesville: University Press of Florida, 1996), 241; see Goveia, *Slave Society*, 189–91, 198; David Brion Davis, *The Problem of Slavery in the Age of Revolution, 1770–1823* (Ithaca, N.Y.: Cornell University Press, 1975), 411–13; Mindie Lazarus-Black, *Legitimate Acts and Illegal Encounters: Law and Society in Antigua and Barbuda*, Smithsonian Series in Ethnographic Inquiry (Washington, D.C.: Smithsonian Institution Press, 1994), 68–69.

102. *The Parliamentary Register; or, History of the Proceedings and Debates of the House of Commons . . . , during the First Session of the Eighteenth Parliament of Great Britain* (London: J. Debrett, 1797), 2:247; see Fergus, *Revolutionary Emancipation*, 91–97; Goveia, *Slave Society*, 33–34.

103. See *Parliamentary Register*, 2:229–47.

104. See ibid., 264, 268.

105. See ibid., 273–74.

106. Davis, *Problem of Slavery*, 413; Goveia, *Slave Society*, 33–34; Gaspar, "Ameliorating Slavery," 242.

107. See "Report of the Committee Appointed to Examine All the Laws Respecting the Government of Slaves by Their Owners, and to Examine into the Proceeding of the

Courts of Justice Where Persons Have Been Tried, and Punished, for Offences Committed against Slaves," in *Papers Presented to the House of Commons on the 7th May 1804, Respecting the Slave-Trade* (1804), H 6–7; see also Gaspar, "Ameliorating Slavery," 242–43.

108. "An Act to Repeal the Fortieth and Forty-First Clauses of an Act of This Island, Intituled, 'An Act for Attaining Several Slaves Now Run Away from Their Masters Services, and for Better Government of Slaves, Dated the Ninth Day of December in the Year of Our Lord One Thousand Seven Hundred and Twenty Three'; and to Make Persons Charged with and Found Guilty of the Murder of Slaves, Liable and Subject to the Same Pains and Penalties as Are Inflicted for the Murder of Free Persons," in *Miscellaneous Papers, 1 February–2 July 1816 Vol. XIX*, 9–10 and Brown, *Laws of Antigua*, 2:287–88; see Goveia, *Slave Society*, 191; Gaspar, "Ameliorating Slavery," 243–44.

109. "An Act More Effectually to Provide for the Support, and to Extend Certain Regulations for the Protection of Slaves, to Promote and Encourage Their Increase, and Generally to Meliorate Their Condition," in *Papers Presented to the House of Commons on the 7th May 1804, Respecting the Slave-Trade*, 15 H–28 H; see Brown, *Laws of Antigua*, 1:21–43; see also Lazarus-Black, *Legitimate Acts and Illegal Encounters*, 68–71; Goveia, *Slave Society*, 191–98; Gaspar, "Ameliorating Slavery," 243–58; Lazarus-Black, "Slaves, Masters, and Magistrates," 258.

110. "An Act More Effectually to Provide for the Support, and to Extend Certain Regulations for the Protection of Slaves, to Promote and Encourage Their Increase, and Generally to Meliorate Their Condition," in *Papers Presented to the House of Commons on the 7th May 1804, Respecting the Slave-Trade*, 21 H; see Goveia, *Slave Society*, 191; Brown, *Laws of Antigua*, 1:30–31.

111. See Goveia, *Slave Society*, 191.

112. See "An Act More Effectually to Provide for the Support, and to Extend Certain Regulations for the Protection of Slaves, to Promote and Encourage Their Increase, and Generally to Meliorate Their Condition," in *Papers Presented to the House of Commons on the 7th May 1804, Respecting the Slave-Trade*, 20 H–21 H; Goveia, *Slave Society*, 191.

113. See Lunan, *Abstract of the Laws of Jamaica*, 145–47; see also Brown, *Reaper's Garden*, 80–81.

114. See Rose-Marie Belle Antoine, *Commonwealth Caribbean Law and Legal Systems*, 2nd ed. (New York: Routledge, 2008), 20; Karl Watson, "Capital Sentences Against Slaves in Barbados in the Eighteenth Century: An Analysis," in *In the Shadow of the Plantation—Caribbean History and Legacy*, ed. Alvin O. Thompson (Jamaica: Ian Randle, 2002), 212; see also H. M. Chichester, "Mackenzie, Francis Humberston, Baron Seaforth and Mackenzie of Kintail (1754–1815)," rev. Jonathan Spain in *Oxford Dictionary of National Biography* (Oxford: Oxford University Press, 2004; online ed., May 2006), accessed April 2, 2014, http://www.oxforddnb.com/view/article/14126.

115. See "Extract of Lord Seaforth's Letter to Lord Hobart, March 18, 1802," in *A Letter to Mr. Corbbett on His Opinions Respecting the Slave-Trade*, ed. Thomas Clarke (London: J. Hatchard, 1806), 96.

116. See Samuel Romilly, *Memoirs of the Life of Sir Samuel Romilly*, 2nd ed. (London: John Murray, 1840), 3:255.

117. Handler, *Unappropriated People*, 41, quoting Lord Seaforth to Duke of Portland, July 27, 1810.

118. See "Extract from Lord Seaforth, Dated Barbadoes, November 13, 1804," in *The Horrors of the Negro Slavery Existing in Our West Indian Islands* (London: J. Hatchard, 1805), 3–15; "Lord Seaforth to Lord Camden, Jan. 7. 1805," 97–102, and "Extract from Lord Seaforth's (Governor of Barbadoes) Letter to Lord Camden, November 13, 1804," 97, both in *Memoirs of the Life of Sir Samuel Romilly*.

119. See "Lord Seaforth to Lord Camden, Jan. 7, 1805," in *Memoirs of the Life of Sir Samuel Romilly*, 97.

120. See "An Act for the Better Protection of Slaves of This Island," in *Miscellaneous Papers, 1 February–2 July 1816 Vol. XIX*, 36; see also Beckles, *History of Barbados*, 85–88; Stephen, *Slavery of the British West India Colonies Delineated*, 1:38.

121. See Hilary Beckles, *Black Rebellion in Barbados: The Struggle against Slavery, 1622–1838* (Bridgetown, Barbados: Antilles Publications, 1984), 151n112.

122. See Handler, *Unappropriated People*, 70.

123. See Romilly, *Memoirs of the Life of Sir Samuel Romilly*, 3:256; Claude Levy, "Slavery and the Emancipation Movement in Barbados 1650–1833," *Journal of Negro History* 55, no. 1 (January 1970): 2–3.

124. See Schomburgk, *History of Barbados*, 421–22; Claude Levy, "Barbados: The Last Years of Slavery 1823–1833," *Journal of Negro History* 44, no. 4 (October 1959): 318.

125. See Levy, "Barbados," 317–18; see also Schomburgk, *History of Barbados*, 422n2, for the Barbados act of 1831 on slave testimony, which went into effect on May 30, 1832. Schomburgk stated that this act facilitated several convictions of whites on slave testimony. Ibid., 432.

126. See Levy, "Barbados," 318.

127. See Ward, *British West Indian Slavery*, 208; see also Dunn, *Sugar and Slaves*, 324–25; Goveia, *Slave Society*, 198.

128. Goveia, *Slave Society*, 200.

129. See Brian Dyde, *Out of Crowded Vagueness: A History of the Islands of St. Kitts, Nevis and Anguilla* (Oxford: Macmillan Education, 2005), 140–41; see also Goveia, *Slave Society*, 200–201; Lauren Benton and Lisa Ford, "Magistrates in Empire: Convicts, Slaves, and the Remaking of Plural Legal Order in the British Empire," in *Legal Pluralism and Empires, 1500–1850*, ed. Lauren Benton and Richard J. Ross (New York: New York University Press, 2013), 175–78; Lauren Benton, "The Melancholy Labyrinth: The Trial of Arthur Hodge and the Boundaries of Imperial Law," *Alabama Law Review* 64, no. 1 (2012): 91–110.

130. See Dyde, *Out of Crowded Vagueness*, 141, 143–44.

131. See Goveia, *Slave Society*, 201; A. M. Belisario, *A Report of the Trial of Arthur Hodge, Esquire* (Middletown: Tertius Dunning, 1812), 40–47; see also, e.g., John Andrew, *The Hanging of Arthur Hodge: A Caribbean Anti-slavery Milestone* (Bloomington, Ind.: Xlibris, 2000); Paul Finkelman, *Slavery in the Courtroom: An Annotated Bibliography of American Cases* (Washington, D.C.: Library of Congress, 1985), 290–92; Benton and Ford, "Magistrates in Empire," 178–79; Benton, "Melancholy Labyrinth," 91–110; Benton, "Abolition and Imperial Law, 1790–1820," 367–68; Natalie Zacek, "Voices and Silences:

The Problem of Slave Testimony in the English West Indian Law Court," *Slavery and Abolition* 24, no. 3 (December 2003): 32.

132. See Belisario, *Report of the Trial of Arthur Hodge*, 94–97.

133. Ibid., 183.

134. Finkelman, *Slavery in the Courtroom*, 291–92; see Zacek, "Voices and Silences," 32.

135. Benton, "Melancholy Labyrinth," 110; see Goveia, *Slave Society*, 201; Benton, "Abolition and Imperial Law, 1790–1820," 367–68.

136. Benton, "Melancholy Labyrinth," 92.

137. See Dyde, *Out of Crowded Vagueness*, 95–96, 141.

138. See ibid., 142.

139. See "A Copy of the Correspondence Which Passed between the Governor of the Island of Saint Christopher and the Secretary of State of the Colonial Department; Relative to the Trial of the Reverend Henry Rawlins, for Murder," in *Miscellaneous Papers: Ionian Islands; Slaves in the Colonies, Session 27 January–10 June, 1818, Volume XVII* (Ordered to Be Printed 28 May 1818), 3–10.

140. See "Evidence on the Trial of Creole Jack, a Slave Belonging to Hutchinson's Estate, the Property of Henry Rawlins, Esq. on the 27th day of September 1817," in *Miscellaneous Papers: Ionian Islands*, 5–7.

141. See "Evidence on the Trial of the Rev. W. H. Rawlins, for Murder of a Slave at St. Christopher's, 16th day of October 1817," in *Miscellaneous Papers: Ionian Islands*, 8–9.

142. See *The Annual Register, or a View of the History, Politics, and Literature, for the Year 1818* (London: Baldwin, Cradock, and Joy, 1819), 109–18; *The Parliamentary Debates from the Year 1803 to the Present Time Volume XXXVII Comprising the Period from the Thirteenth Day of April to the Tenth Day of June, 1818* (London: T.C. Hansard, 1818), 1201–7.

143. See "Copy of a Letter from His Grace the Duke of Manchester to Earl Bathurst; with Two Enclosures, 21st June 1817," in *Miscellaneous Papers: Ionian Islands*, 259–67.

144. See "Copy of a Letter from His Grace the Duke of Manchester to Earl Bathurst; with Two Enclosures, 22nd October 1817 and Copy of a Letter from His Grace the Duke of Manchester to Earl Bathurst, 29th August 1817," in *Miscellaneous Papers: Ionian Islands*, 267–69; see D. A. Dunkley, *Agency of the Enslaved: Jamaica and the Culture of Freedom in the Atlantic World* (Lanham, Md.: Lexington Books, 2013), 37, 46; D. A. Dunkley, "The Life of Rev. George Wilson Bridges: The Jamaica Experience," in *Readings in Caribbean History and Culture: Breaking Ground*, ed. D. A. Dunkley (Lanham, Md.: Lexington Books, 2011), 89.

145. See Schomburgk, *History of Barbados*, 421–22; see also Levy, "Slavery and the Emancipation Movement," 3.

146. See Zacek, "Voices and Silences," 24 (discussing the Hodge case and two others in which free black or slave testimony was permitted).

147. See Fergus, *Revolutionary Emancipation*, 123–75; Noel Titus, *The Amelioration and Abolition of Slavery in Trinidad, 1812–1834: Experiments and Protests in a New Slave Colony* (Bloomington, Ind.: AuthorHouse, 2009), 1, 9–15; Levy, "Barbados," 310–12.

148. See William A. Green, *British Slave Emancipation: The Sugar Colonies and the Great Experiment 1830–1865* (New York: Clarendon, 1976), 101–4; Olwyn M. Blouet,

"Earning and Learning in the British West Indies: An Image of Freedom in the Pre-emancipation Decade, 1823–1833," *Historical Journal* 34, no. 2 (June 1991): 393; Levy, "Slavery and the Emancipation Movement," 7–10; Levy, "Barbados," 309–12.

149. See *An Abstract of the British West Indian Statutes for the Protection of Slaves* (London: James Ridgeway, 1830), 6, 7, 10, 13, 17, 19, 23, 24, 29, 32, 34, 40, 42; see also Steele, *Grenada*, 156–59; Brizan, *Grenada*, 108–9; Green, *British Slave Emancipation*, 104–12; Schomburgk, *History of Barbados*, 422n2; Blouet, "Earning and Learning in the British West Indies," 393–94; Levy, "Slavery and the Emancipation Movement," 9–11; Levy, "Barbados," 315–21; see also Melanie J. Newton, *The Children of Africa in the Colonies: Free People of Color in Barbados in the Age of Emancipation* (Baton Rouge: Louisiana State University Press, 2008), 97–98.

150. See B. W. Higman, *Slave Populations of the British Caribbean 1807–1834* (Kingston, Jamaica: The Press, University of the West Indies, 1995), 200.

151. See "An Act for the Abolition of Slavery throughout the British Colonies; for Promoting the Industry of the Manumitted Slaves; and for Compensating the Persons Hitherto Entitled to the Services of Such Slaves," August 28, 1833, in *A Collection of Statutes Connected with the General Administration of the Law*, 3rd ed., ed. Anthony Hammond and Thomas C. Granger (London: Thomas Blenkarn, 1836), 10:837–56. The act emancipated slaves in Great Britain and Ireland, converted colonial slaves to apprentices in 1834 to be emancipated in 1838 or 1840 (depending on their status), and compensated slave owners. It did not apply "to any of the Territories in the Possession of the East India Company, or to the Island of Ceylon, or to the Island of Saint Helena." Ibid., sec. LXIV, 856; Burn, *Emancipation and Apprenticeship in the British West Indies*, 118–20; see, e.g., David Brion Davis, *The Problem of Slavery in the Age of Emancipation* (New York: Knopf, 2014), 261–71, 284, 397n71; Fergus, *Revolutionary Emancipation*, 176–98; Thomas C. Holt, *The Problem of Freedom: Race, Labor, and Politics in Jamaica and Britain, 1832–1938* (Baltimore: Johns Hopkins University Press, 1992), 13–53; Beckles, *History of Barbados*, 90–99; Green, *British Slave Emancipation*, 112–27; Michael Craton, "Emancipation from Below? The Role of the British West Indian Slaves in the Emancipation Movement, 1816–1834," in *Out of Slavery: Abolition and After* (Totowa, N.J.: Frank Cass, 1985), 110–31.

152. See Patterson, *Sociology of Slavery*, 78–79.

153. See Roberts, *Slavery and the Enlightenment*, 55.

CHAPTER 5. Slave Killing Law in Britain's Northern American Colonies and the Border States

1. See Russell R. Menard, "Making a 'Popular Slave Society' in Colonial British America," *Journal of Interdisciplinary History* 43, no. 3 (Winter 2013): 380–81.

2. Edgar J. McManus, *Black Bondage in the North* (Syracuse, N.Y.: Syracuse University Press, 1973), 90.

3. See Nathan Dane, *A General Abridgment and Digest of American Law, with Occasional Notes and Comments* (Boston: Cummings, Hilliard, 1824), 313; Tapping Reeve, *The Law of Baron and Femme; of Parent and Child; of Guardian and Ward; of Master and Servant; and of the Powers of the Courts of Chancery* (New Haven, Conn.: Oliver Steele,

1816), 340; see also Lorenzo Johnston Greene, *The Negro in Colonial New England*, Studies in American Negro Life (New York: Columbia University Press, 1942; repr., New York: Atheneum, 1971), 177.

4. See Joanne Pope Melish, *Disowning Slavery: Gradual Emancipation and "Race" in New England, 1780–1860* (Ithaca, N.Y.: Cornell University Press, 1998), 25; McManus, *Black Bondage in the North*, 90–91; Greene, *Negro in Colonial New England*, 234. On Maryland and Delaware law, see Thomas D. Morris, *Southern Slavery and the Law, 1619–1860* (Chapel Hill: University of North Carolina Press, 1996), 164. This chapter includes sections on colonies, excluding Canada, and states in which I have found slave homicide statutes or slave master prosecutions. See, on Canada, Afua Cooper, *The Hanging of Angelique: The Untold Story of Canadian Slavery and the Burning of Old Montreal* (Toronto: HarperCollins, 2006), 81–84; Robin W. Winks, *The Blacks in Canada: A History* (New Haven, Conn.: Yale University Press, 1971), 24–60.

5. See Allan Kulikoff, *From British Peasants to Colonial American Farmers* (Chapel Hill: University of North Carolina Press, 2000), 248–49; Ira Berlin, *Many Thousands Gone: The First Two Centuries of Slavery in North America* (Cambridge, Mass.: Belknap, 1998), 47–63, 177–94; Jack P. Greene, *Pursuits of Happiness: The Social Development of Early Modern British Colonies and the Formation of American Culture* (Chapel Hill: University of North Carolina Press, 1988), 71–72, 131–35; David Brion Davis, *Slavery and Human Progress* (New York: Oxford University Press, 1984), 75; A. Leon Higginbotham, Jr., *In the Matter of Color: Race and the American Legal Process: The Colonial Period* (New York: Oxford University Press, 1978), 302, 465n146; Arthur Zilversmit, *The First Emancipation: The Abolition of Slavery in the North* (Chicago: University of Chicago Press, 1967), 3–7; Greene, *Negro in Colonial New England*, 72–99; Stuart Gold, "The 'Gift' of Liberty: Testamentary Manumission in New Jersey—1791–1805," *Rutgers Race & Law Review* 15, no 1. (2014): 7–11; Gary B. Nash, "Slaves and Slaveowners in Colonial Philadelphia," *William and Mary Quarterly*, 3rd ser., 30, no. 2 (April 1973): 232–38; William D. Johnston, *Slavery in Rhode Island, 1755–1776*, Papers from the Historical Seminary of Brown University (Providence: Rhode Island Historical Society, 1894), 18–19. Colonial era black population estimates did not generally distinguish between enslaved and free people. Historians thus have equated these populations, realizing that not all blacks were enslaved and some slaves were Native Americans. See Menard, "Making a 'Popular Slave Society,'" 384–85.

6. See Greene, *Pursuits of Happiness*, 132; see also James J. Gigantino, II, *The Ragged Road to Abolition: Slavery and Freedom in New Jersey, 1775–1865* (Philadelphia: University of Pennsylvania Press, 2014), 2; Gold, "'Gift' of Liberty," 10–11.

7. See Richard Shannon Moss, *Slavery on Long Island: A Study in Local Institutional and Early African-American Communal Life* (New York: Garland, 1993), 69–91; Davis, *Slavery and Human Progress*, 75; McManus, *Black Bondage in the North*, 1–44; Zilversmit, *First Emancipation*, 7–53; Greene, *Negro in Colonial New England*, 100–123; see also, e.g., Mac Griswold, *The Manor: Three Centuries at a Slave Plantation on Long Island* (New York: Farrar, Straus and Giroux, 2013); Katherine Howlett Hayes, *Slavery before Race: Europeans, Africans, and Indians at Long Island's Sylvester Manor Plantation, 1651–1884* (New York: New York University Press, 2013); C. S. Manegold, *Ten Hills Farm: The*

Forgotten History of Slavery in the North (Princeton, N.J.: Princeton University Press, 2010); William Davis Miller, "The Narragansett Planters," *Proceedings of the American Antiquarian Society*, new series, 43, no. 1 (April–October 1933): 49–115; Edward Channing, "The Narragansett Planters: A Study of Causes," *Johns Hopkins University Studies in Political Science*, fourth series, no. 3 (March 1886): 23–127.

8. See Ira Berlin, *The Long Emancipation: The Demise of Slavery in the United States* (Cambridge, Mass.: Harvard University Press, 2015), 57–71; Patrick Rael, *Eighty-Eight Years: The Long Death of Slavery in the United States, 1777–1865* (Athens: University of Georgia Press, 2015), 62–69, 126–35; Gigantino, *Ragged Road to Abolition*, 4–5, 64–239; Melish, *Disowning Slavery*, 64–79; Ira Berlin, *Many Thousands Gone: The First Two Centuries of Slavery in North America* (Cambridge, Mass.: Belknap, 1998), 228–55; Robert B. Shaw, *A Legal History of Slavery in the United States* (Potsdam: Northern Press, 1991), 253–73; Zilversmit, *First Emancipation*, 55–229; Henry Scofield Cooley, *A Study of Slavery in New Jersey*, Johns Hopkins University Studies in Historical and Political Science (Baltimore: Johns Hopkins University Press, 1896), 20–31; Gary K. Wolinetz, "New Jersey Slavery and the Law," *Rutgers Law Review* 50, no. 4 (Summer 1998): 2228, 2246; Simeon F. Moss, "The Persistence of Slavery and Involuntary Servitude in a Free State (1685–1866)," *Journal of Negro History* 35, no. 3 (July 1950): Table III, 311.

9. See, e.g., Wendy Warren, *New England Bound: Slavery and Colonization in Early America* (New York: Liveright, 2016), 49–151; Margaret Ellen Newell, *Brethren by Nature: New England Indians, Colonists, and the Origins of American Slavery* (Ithaca, N.Y.: Cornell University Press, 2015), 4–44, 238; Christopher Tomlins, *Freedom Bound: Law, Labor, and Civic Identity in Colonizing English America, 1580–1865* (New York: Cambridge University Press, 2010), 479–81; Oscar Reiss, *Blacks in Colonial America* (Jefferson, N.C.: McFarland, 1997), 65; Shaw, *Legal History of Slavery*, 10–11; Higginbotham, *In the Matter of Color*, 61–82; George Lee Haskins, *Law and Authority in Early Massachusetts: A Study in Tradition and Design* (Lanham, Md.: University Press of America, 1960), 101; George H. Moore, *Notes on the History of Slavery in Massachusetts* (New York: Appleton, 1866), 1–11; Daragh Gray, "The Treaty of Hartford (1638): Reconsidering Jurisdiction in Southern New England," *William and Mary Quarterly*, 3rd ser., 72, no 3 (July 2105): 481–84.

10. See "Body of Liberties, 1641," in *The Colonial Laws of Massachusetts*, ed. William H. Whitmore (Boston: Rockwell and Churchill, 1890), 55; Frederick C. Millett, "Will the United States Follow England (and the Rest of the World) in Abandoning Capital Punishment?," *Pierce Law Review* 6, no. 3 (Spring 2008): 585.

11. "The Liberties of Massachusetts Collonie in New England, 1641," in *Slavery: Oxford Readers*, ed. Stanley L. Engerman, Seymour Drescher, and Robert Paquette (New York: Oxford University Press, 2001), 103; see Warren, *New England Bound*, 34–35; Newell, *Brethren by Nature*, 44–45; Tomlins, *Freedom Bound*, 479–80; Shaw, *Legal History of Slavery*, 10; Higginbotham, *In the Matter of Color*, 62; McManus, *Black Bondage in the North*, 68; Winthrop D. Jordan, *White over Black: American Attitudes toward the Negro 1550–1812* (Chapel Hill: University of North Carolina Press, 1968), 66–70; Haskins, *Law and Authority in Early Massachusetts*, 129; Greene, *Negro in Colonial New England*, 63; Helen T. Catterall, ed., *Judicial Cases Concerning American Slavery and the Negro* (1926–37; repr., New York: Negro Universities Press, 1968), 4:455–56, 469–70; Moore, *Notes on*

the *History of Slavery in Massachusetts*, 11–19. On this law and the process leading to its adoption, see Tomlins, *Freedom Bound*, 424–25; William E. Nelson, *The Common Law in Colonial America: Volume I, The Chesapeake and New England, 1607–1660* (New York: Oxford University Press, 2008), 67–72; Haskins, *Law and Authority in Early Massachusetts*, 119–40; John Codman Hurd, *The Law of Freedom and Bondage in the United States* (1858/1862; repr., Boston: Little, Brown, 1968), 1:258–61.

12. Moore, *Notes on the History of Slavery in Massachusetts*, 18; see Greene, *Negro in Colonial New England*, 64–68, 167–68; Lorenzo J. Greene, "Slave-Holding New England and Its Awakening," *Journal of Negro History* 13, no. 4 (October 1928): 501.

13. See Jordan, *White over Black*, 68.

14. See Tomlins, *Freedom Bound*, 424–25n82; Shaw, *Legal History of Slavery*, 11; Greene, *Negro in Colonial New England*, 65–66, 126; Moore, *Notes on the History of Slavery in Massachusetts*, 16–17.

15. See Exodus 21:12, 20–21 (American Standard Version); "Liberties of Massachusetts Collonie," 101–2; see also William Ian Miller, *Eye for an Eye* (New York: Cambridge University Press, 2006), 33.

16. See Exodus 21:22–25 (American Standard Version); see also Richard H. Hiers, *Justice and Compassion in Biblical Law* (New York: Continuum, 2009), 15–21; Konrad Schmid, "The Monetization and Demonetization of the Human Body: The Case of Compensatory Payments for Bodily Injuries and Homicide in Ancient Near Eastern and Ancient Israelite Law Books," in *Money as God? The Monetization of the Market and Its Impact in Religion, Politics, Law, and Ethics* (Cambridge: Cambridge University Press, 2014), 271–79; Andrew R. Simmonds, "Measure for Measure: Two Misunderstood Principles of Damages, Exodus 21:22–25, 'Life for Life, Eye for Eye,' and Matthew 5:38–39, 'Turn the Other Cheek,'" *Saint Thomas Law Review* 17, no. 1 (Fall 2004): 126–31.

17. "Liberties of Massachusetts Collonie," 103; see Exodus 21:26–27 (American Standard Version); Miller, *Eye for an Eye*, 21.

18. "Letter from George H. Moore, Esq., to the Editor," in *Slavery in Massachusetts, Two Letters from the Historical Magazine, September and October 1866* (New York, 1866), 7; see Greene, *Negro in Colonial New England*, 232, 234–36.

19. "Letter from George H. Moore, Esq., to the Editor," 8–9.

20. Ibid., 4.

21. Ibid., 9.

22. See Bernard Bailyn, *The Ordeal of Thomas Hutchinson* (Cambridge, Mass.: Harvard University Press, 1974), 378; Greene, *Negro in Colonial New England*, 177; Richard Frothingham, *Life and Times of Joseph Warren* (Boston: Little, Brown, 1865), 167; Moore, *Notes on the History of Slavery in Massachusetts*, 131–32. Hutchinson's letter to Lord Hillsborough explained why he opposed a bill that would have banned slave imports into Massachusetts. See ibid., 130–44.

23. John Romeyn Brodhead, ed., *Documents Relative to the Colonial History of the State of New York* (Albany: Weed, Parsons, 1853), 3:347; see Graham Russell Hodges, *Root and Branch: African Americans in New York and East Jersey 1613–1863* (Chapel Hill: University of North Carolina Press, 1999), 38; William Renwick Riddell, "The Slave in Early New York," *Journal of Negro History* 13, no. 1 (January 1928): 65.

24. Brodhead, *Documents Relative to the Colonial History of the State of New York*, 3:547; see Greene, *Pursuits of Happiness*, 233; Greene, "Slave-Holding New England and Its Awakening," 514; Riddell, "Slave in Early New York," 65.

25. See *Calendar of State Papers, Colonial Series, America and West Indies, 1689–1692* (London: Mackie, 1901), 606, 727–29; see also *Laws of New Hampshire Volume One Province Period* (Manchester: John B. Clarke Company, 1904), xvc. For Allen's instructions, see ibid., 499–501, 514.

26. See "An Act of Restraining of Inhuman Severeties," in *Provincial Papers: Documents and Records Relating to the Province of New-Hampshire from 1692–1722*, ed. Nathaniel Bouton (Manchester: John B. Clarke, State Printer, 1869), 3:16, 200; see also *Laws of New Hampshire Volume One Province Period*, 570; see generally McManus, *Black Bondage in the North*, 90; Greene, *Negro in Colonial New England*, 233–34; Dinah Mayo-Bobee, "Servile Discontents: Slavery and Resistance in Colonial New Hampshire, 1645–1785," *Slavery & Abolition* 30, no. 3 (September 2009): 341.

27. See *Laws of New Hampshire Volume One Province Period*, 646.

28. See ibid., 861.

29. See *Laws of New Hampshire Volume Two Province Period 1702–1745* (Concord: Rumford Printing Company, 1913), 292; Hurd, *Law of Freedom and Bondage*, 1:267; "An ACT to Repeal Sundry Acts and Laws Therein Mentioned," in *Constitution and Laws of the State of New-Hampshire* (Dover: Samuel Bragg, Jr., 1805), 404.

30. See Mayo-Bobee, "Servile Discontents," 340–42.

31. See ibid., 355.

32. See Cynthia Mestad Johnson, *James DeWolf and the Rhode Island Slave Trade* (Charleston: History Press, 2014), 23–25.

33. See ibid., 26–130; Leonardo Marques, "Slave Trading in a New World: The Strategies of North American Slave Traders in the Age of Abolition," *Journal of the Early Republic* 32, no. 2 (Summer 2012): 233–60.

34. See Eric Foner, *Gateway to Freedom: The Hidden History of the Underground Railroad* (New York: Norton, 2015), 28; Thelma Wills Foote, *Black and White Manhattan: The History of Racial Formation in Colonial New York City* (New York: Oxford University Press, 2004), 23–52; Leslie M. Harris, *In the Shadow of Freedom: African-Americans in New York City, 1626–1863* (Chicago: University of Chicago Press, 2003), 13–26; Shaw, *Legal History of Slavery*, 14–15; George M. Fredrickson, *White Supremacy: A Comparative Study of American and South African History* (New York: Oxford University Press, 1981), 80; Higginbotham, *In the Matter of Color*, 100–114; Edgar J. McManus, *A History of Negro Slavery in New York* (Syracuse, N.Y.: Syracuse University Press, 1966), 15–22; Christopher Moore, "A World of Possibilities: Slavery and Freedom in Dutch New Amsterdam," in *Slavery in New York*, ed. Ira Berlin and Leslie M. Harris (New York: New Press, 2005), 31–56.

35. See "The Duke of York's Laws, 1665–75," in Charles Z. Lincoln, *The Colonial Laws of New York from the Year 1664 to the Revolution* (Albany: James B. Lyon, State Printer, 1896), 1:18, 20; see also Foner, *Gateway to Freedom*, 28; Moss, *Slavery on Long Island*, 18–19; Shaw, *Legal History of Slavery*, 15–16; Higginbotham, *In the Matter of Color*, 115, 270–71; Jordan, *White over Black*, 84; Robert C. Cumming, "Historical Note," in Lincoln,

Colonial Laws of New York, 1:ii–xxi. The Duke of York in 1667 filed an initial draft that included a final sentence stating: "This Law shall not extend to sett at liberty any Negroe or Indian Servant who shall turne Christian after he shall have been brought by Any Person." See Tomlins, *Freedom Bound*, 425n83.

36. Foner, *Gateway to Freedom*, 28–29; see Foote, *Black and White Manhattan*, 53–88; Harris, *In the Shadow of Freedom*, 26–47; Jill Lepore, "The Tightening Vise: Slavery and Freedom in British New York," in Berlin and Harris, *Slavery in New York*, 63.

37. See "An Act for Regulateing of Slaves," in Lincoln, *Colonial Laws of New York*, 1:520, which was adopted on November 27, 1702, and was to remain in effect for one year. On August 5, 1705, the legislators revived and reenacted this act. See "An Act for Reviving and Continuing an Act, Entituled, an Act for Regulating Slaves," in Lincoln, *Colonial Laws of New York*, 1:588. A December 10, 1712, act with a similar provision was adopted in response to an April 1712 slave revolt. See "An Act for Preventing the Conspiracy and Insurrection of Negroes and Other Slaves," in Lincoln, *Colonial Laws of New York*, 1:762. An October 29, 1730, act also contained a similar provision. See "An Act for the More Effectual Preventing and Punishing the Conspiracy and Insurrection of Negro and Other Slaves, for the Better Regulating Them and for Repealing the Acts Herein Mentioned Relating Thereto," in Lincoln, *Colonial Laws of New York*, 2:680; see Foote, *Black and White Manhattan*, 132–39; Higginbotham, *In the Matter of Color*, 119, 123–24; Lepore, "Tightening Vise," 76–81; Edwin Olson, "The Slave Code in Colonial New York," *Journal of Negro History* 29, no. 2 (April 1944): 155.

38. See McManus, *Black Bondage in the North*, 91; see also McManus, *History of Negro Slavery in New York*, 93.

39. See Complaints to Court of Mayor and Aldermen in Liber 19B, in *Collections of the New-York Historical Society for the Year 1894: Abstracts of Wills on File in the Surrogate's Office, City of New York, Vol. III, 1730–1744* (New York, 1895), 433–35; see also Edwin Olson, "Social Aspects of Slave Life in New York," *Journal of Negro History* 26, no. 1 (January 1941): 74.

40. See Henry Onderdonk, Jr., *Queens County in Olden Times: Being a Supplement to the Several Histories Thereof* (Jamaica, N.Y.: Charles Welling, 1865), 20; see also Moss, *Slavery on Long Island*, 100.

41. See McManus, *Black Bondage in the North*, 91; Charles R. Foy, *Ports of Slavery: How Slaves Used Northern Seaports' Maritime Industry to Escape and Create Trans-Atlantic Identities, 1713–1783* (Ph.D. diss., Rutgers, State University of New Jersey, 2008), 156; Juninus P. Rodriguez, "Murder," in *Encyclopedia of Slave Resistance and Rebellion*, ed. Juninus P. Rodriguez (Westport, Conn.: Greenwood, 2007), 1:335; John C. Miller, *The First Frontier: Life in Colonial America* (Lanham, Md.: University Press of America, 1966), 156.

42. See Onderdonk, *Queens County in Olden Times*, 72; see also Moss, *Slavery on Long Island*, 100.

43. See "Ignoramus," in *Black's Law Dictionary*, deluxe 9th ed., ed. Bryan A. Garner (St. Paul: West, 2009), 814.

44. See Onderdonk, *Queens County in Olden Times*, 72; see also Anne Hartell, "Slavery on Long Island," *Nassau County Historical Journal* 6, no. 2 (Fall 1943): 55–71, accessed May 15, 2015, http://longislandgenealogy.com/Slav.htm.

45. See Moss, *Slavery on Long Island*, 100–101. On the New York gradual emancipation statute, see Zilversmit, *First Emancipation*, 180–82.

46. See Olson, "Social Aspects of the Slave in New York," 73; see also, e.g., *Kingston (N.Y.) Plebeian*, March 4, 1805, 3; "Horrid Inhumanity," *New York Spectator*, February 20, 1805, 3; "Slavery!," *Hudson (N.Y.) Bee*, January 8, 1805, 3; *Charleston Courier*, December 29, 1804, 2; *Hudson (N.Y.) Bee*, December 18, 1804, 3.

47. See "Murder!," *Otsego Herald* (Cooperstown, N.Y.), February 25, 1809, 3.

48. McManus, *Black Bondage in the North*, 90–91.

49. Higginbotham, *In the Matter of Color*, 269–70.

50. See Shaw, *Legal History of Slavery*, 17–18; Higginbotham, *In the Matter of Color*, 270–88.

51. Higginbotham, *In the Matter of Color*, 306; see Edward Raymond Turner, *The Negro in Pennsylvania: Slavery, Servitude, and Freedom 1639–1861* (Washington, D.C.: American Historical Association, 1911), 36; Hurd, *Law of Freedom and Bondage*, 1:247–93; Edwin R. Keedy, "History of the Pennsylvania Statute Creating Degrees of Murder," *University of Pennsylvania Law Review* 97, no. 6 (May 1949): 759–64.

52. *Pennsylvania Gazette* (Philadelphia), February 24, 1742, 3.

53. "Excerpt of a Private Letter from Philadelphia, Dated Feb. 23," *Boston Evening-Post*, March 22, 1742, 2.

54. *Pennsylvania Gazette* (Philadelphia), February 24, 1742, 3.

55. *American Weekly Mercury* (Philadelphia), March 4–11, 1741–42, 3.

56. *American Weekly Mercury* (Philadelphia), April 22–29, 1742, 3; *Pennsylvania Gazette* (Philadelphia), April 29, 1742, 3; see Gail Stuart Rowe, *The Embattled Bench: The Pennsylvania Supreme Court and the Forging of a Democratic Society, 1684–1809* (Cranbury, N.J.: Associated University Press, 1994), 87–88; see also *Pennsylvania Journal* (Philadelphia), April 14, 1743, 4 (advertising the sale of a Black Horse Alley house "where William Bullock lately [lived]").

57. "Excerpt of a Private Letter from Philadelphia, Dated Feb. 23," *Boston Evening-Post*, March 22, 1742, 2; *Boston Evening-Post*, November 23, 1741, 2; *Boston Gazette*, May 18–25, 1741, 2; *Pennsylvania Gazette* (Philadelphia), February 11, 1741, 2; *American Weekly Mercury* (Philadelphia), November 5–12, 1741, 2.

58. *A Documentary History of Slavery in North America*, ed. Willie Lee Rose (New York: Oxford University Press, 1976), 45–48, quoting Adolf B. Benson, ed., *Peter Kalm's Travels in North America* (New York: Wilson & Erickson, 1937), 1:204–11.

59. See Zilversmit, *First Emancipation*, 124–37.

60. See Guyora Binder, *Felony Murder* (Stanford, Calif.: Stanford University Press, 2012), 128–29; Keedy, "History of the Pennsylvania Statute Creating Degrees of Murder," 764–73, 773.

61. See *Kline's Carlisle (Pa.) Weekly Gazette*, September 10, 1800, 2–3.

62. See Gigantino, *Ragged Road to Abolition*, 11–12; Cooley, *Study of Slavery in New Jersey*, 11–13; Wolinetz, "New Jersey Slavery and the Law," 2229.

63. See Gigantino, *Ragged Road to Abolition*, 13–14; Graham Russell Hodges, *Slavery and Freedom in the Rural North: African Americans in Monmouth County, New Jersey, 1685–1865* (Madison, Wis.: Madison House, 1997), 4, 23; Shaw, *Legal History of Slavery*, 16–17; Wolinetz, "New Jersey Slavery and the Law," 2229–32.

64. See H. Clay Reed and George J. Miller, eds., *The Burlington Court Book: A Record of Quaker Jurisprudence in West New Jersey 1680–1709* (Washington, D.C.: American Historical Association, 1944; repr., Baltimore: Genealogical Publishing, 1998), 56. The case report states the date of the court proceedings was "the 9th of the 6th Moneth 1686." Ibid. The English year then began on March 25. See Editorial Note, ibid., vii. Kristen Block suggests the trial date was October 8, 1686. See Kristen Block, "Cultivating Inner and Outer Plantations: Property, Industry, and Slavery in Early Quaker Migration in the New World," *Early American Studies* 8, no. 3 (Fall 2010): 530n46.

65. See Reed and Miller, *Burlington Court Book*, 56.

66. See ibid., 57; see also Block, "Cultivating Inner and Outer Plantations," 530.

67. "Instructions for Queen Anne to Lord Cornbury as Governor of New Jersey," in *Documents Relating to the Colonial History of the State of New Jersey, 1687–1703*, ed. William A. Whitehead (Newark, N.J.: Daily Advertiser, 1881), 506, 532; see Gigantino, *Ragged Road to Abolition*, 14–17; Hurd, *Law of Freedom and Bondage*, 1:280n1; Wolinetz, "New Jersey Slavery and the Law," 2232.

68. See New Jersey State Archives, "[The] State v. Barcalow, Monmouth Murder, Inquisition Arthur Barcalow [with] Testimony," file 34201; see also Gigantino, *Ragged Road to Abolition*, 74; Sue Kozel, "'Wench Betty,' Murder of," in *Enslaved Women in America: An Encyclopedia*, ed. Daina Ramey Berry and Deleso A. Alford (Santa Barbara, Calif.: Greenwood, 2012), 329–30.

69. See Kozel, "'Wench Betty,' Murder of," 331, citing New Jersey State Archives, Minutes of the Monmouth County Court of Oyer and Terminer, July 27–August 2, 1784 Nisi Prius, July 27–30, 1784, Minutes July 27, 1784.

70. See, e.g., "Extract of a Letter, Dated Trenton, June 8, 1792," *New-Jersey Journal* (Elizabethtown), June 20, 1792, 3; see also, e.g., *Gazette of the United States* (Philadelphia), June 23, 1792, 28; Shane White, *Somewhat More Independent: The End of Slavery in New York City, 1770–1818* (Athens: University of Georgia Press, 1991), 87; "A Brief History of Lawrence Township, Mercer County, New Jersey," accessed January 25, 2014, http://www.lawrencetwp.com/history.html.

71. See "Extract of a Letter, Dated Trenton, June 8, 1792," *New-Jersey Journal* (Elizabethtown), June 20, 1792, 3.

72. See "Elizabeth-Town, July," *Federal Gazette* (Philadelphia), July 13, 1792, 3; see also, e.g., "New Jersey, Elizabeth-Town, July 11," *Herald of Vermont* (Rutland), August 13, 1792, 2; "Elizabeth-Town, July," *American Mercury* (Hartford, Conn.), July 16, 1792, 3.

73. See Philadelphiensis, "For the Federal Gazette," *Federal Gazette* (Philadelphia), July 19, 1792, 2; see, quoting Workman, David Waldstreicher, *Slavery's Constitution: From Revolution to Ratification* (New York: Hill & Wang, 2009), 120 ("Only greed, and lust for power, could explain how 'the professed enemies of *negro* and every other species of slavery, should themselves join in the adoption of a constitution whose very basis is *despotism* and *slavery*'"); see also Bernard Bailyn, *Ideological Origins of the American Revolution* (Cambridge, Mass.: Harvard University Press, 1992), 334.

74. See Philadelphiensis, "For the Federal Gazette," *Federal Gazette* (Philadelphia), July 19, 1792, 2.

75. See Elmer T. Hutchinson, *Documents Relating to the Colonial History of the State of New Jersey, Calendar of New Jersey Wills, Volume VIII, 1791–1795* (Jersey City, N.J.: Scott, 1942), 192–93.

76. See Elmer T. Hutchinson, *Documents Relating to the Colonial History of the State of New Jersey, Calendar of New Jersey Wills, Volume XI, 1806–1809* (1947; repr., Berwyn Heights, Md.: Heritage Books, 2009), 189.

77. See Barbara Jeanne Fields, *Slavery and Freedom on the Middle Ground: Maryland during the Nineteenth Century* (New Haven, Conn.: Yale University Press, 1985), xii.

78. See Andrew Fede, *Roadblocks to Freedom: Slavery and Manumission in the United States South* (New Orleans: Quid Pro Books, 2011), 88, 120n10; Andrew Fede, *People without Rights: An Interpretation of the Fundamentals of the Law of Slavery in the U.S. South* (New York: Garland, 1992; repr., New York: Routledge, 2011), 46–48, 57nn2–11; Allan Kulikoff, *Tobacco and Slaves: The Development of Southern Cultures in the Chesapeake, 1680–1800* (Chapel Hill: University of North Carolina Press, 1986), 4–6.

79. See Peter Kolchin, *American Slavery 1619–1877*, rev. ed. (New York: Hill & Wang, 2003), 252; Kulikoff, *Tobacco and Slaves*, 23–44, 319–34; Gloria L. Main, *Tobacco Colony: Life in Early Maryland, 1650–1720* (Princeton, N.J.: Princeton University Press, 1982), 9–47, 97–139; Menard, "Making a 'Popular Slave Society,'" 384–95.

80. See Elbert B. Smith, "Maryland, Slavery in," in *Dictionary of Afro-American Slavery*, ed. Randall M. Miller and John David Smith (Westport, Conn.: Greenwood Press, 1997), 443; Kolchin, *American Slavery*, 254; Fields, *Slavery and Freedom on the Middle Ground*, 1–22.

81. See Nelson, *Common Law in Colonial America*, 101–24; Jeffrey K. Sawyer, "English Law and the 'Right of Persons' in Early Maryland," in *Order and Civility in Early Modern Chesapeake* (Lanham, Md.: Lexington Books, 2014), 81–86; Jeffrey K. Sawyer, "The Rhetoric and Realty of English Law in Colonial Maryland, Part I—1632–1689," *Maryland Historical Magazine* 108 (Winter 2013): 395–99; Jonathan L. Alpert, "The Origin of Slavery in the United States—The Maryland Precedent," *American Journal of Legal History* 14, no. 3 (July 1970): 189–221.

82. See Morris, *Southern Slavery and the Law*, 164; Demetri D. Debe and Russell R. Menard, "The Transition to African Slavery in Maryland: A Note on the Barbados Connection," *Slavery & Abolition* 32, no. 1 (March 2011): 134–38; Michael Carlton Tolley, "Maryland and the Anglo-Legal Inheritance," *Journal of Legal History* 11, no. 3 (December 1990): 355–56.

83. See "Instructions to the Governor of Maryland," August 26, 1691, in *America's Founding Charters: Primary Documents of the Colonial and Revolutionary Era Governance*, ed. Jon L. Wakelyn (Westport, Conn.: Greenwood, 2006), 2:352; C. Ashley Ellefson, *The Private Punishment of Servants and Slaves in Eighteenth-Century Maryland* (2010), 4, 59, accessed October 10, 2016, http://www.aomol.msa.maryland.gov/megafile/msa/speccol/sc2900/sc2908/000001/000822/pdf/am822.pdf.

84. See Virgil Maxcy, ed., *The Laws of Maryland* (Baltimore: Philip H. Nicklin, 1811), 1:238; Ellefson, *Private Punishment of Servants and Slaves*, 63–64.

85. Morris, *Southern Slavery and the Law*, 169.

86. See Jacqueline Jones, *A Dreadful Deceit: The Myth of Race from the Colonial Era to Obama's America* (New York: Basic Books, 2013), 6; Warren M. Billings, ed., *The Old Dominion in the Seventeenth Center: A Documentary History of Virginia, 1606–1700* (Chapel Hill: University of North Carolina Press, 1975), 114.

87. See Bernard Christian Steiner, ed., *Archives of Maryland: Proceedings of the Provincial Court of Maryland 1658–1662* (Baltimore: Maryland Historical Society, 1922), 41:190–91, 205–06; see also Jones, *Dreadful Deceit*, 1–46; Fede, *People without Rights*, 82; Helen Brock and Catherine Crawford, "Forensic Medicine in Early Colonial Maryland, 1633–1683," in *Legal Medicine in History*, Cambridge History of Medicine, ed. Michael Clark and Catherine Crawford (New York: Cambridge University Press, 1994), 33; Alpert, "Origin of Slavery in the United States," 193.

88. Steiner, *Archives of Maryland: Proceedings of the Provincial Court*, 190.

89. Ibid., 190–91.

90. Ibid., 191; see Jones, *Dreadful Deceit*, 3–4.

91. Steiner, *Archives of Maryland: Proceedings of the Provincial Court*, 205; see Jones, *Dreadful Deceit*, 4–5.

92. Steiner, *Archives of Maryland: Proceedings of the Provincial Court*, 206.

93. See, Jones, *Dreadful Deceit*, 36.

94. See Ellefson, *Private Punishment of Servants and Slaves*, 63–67.

95. See *Archives of Maryland: Somerset County Court 1687–1689*, Atwood S. Barwisk, transcriber (Lakeville, Ct: Somerset Archaeography, 1999), 91, 84–87; Ellefson, *Private Punishment of Servants and Slaves*, 59–61.

96. See Ellefson, *Private Punishment of Servants and Slaves*, 62.

97. See ibid., 67, 90n70.

98. See Jean B. Lee, *The Price of Nationhood: The American Revolution in Charles County* (New York: Norton, 1994), 68, 310n59; Philip D. Morgan, *Slave Counterpoint: Black Culture in the Eighteenth-Century Chesapeake and Lowcountry* (Chapel Hill: University of North Carolina Press, 1998), 266–67.

99. See "Baltimore County Court," *Baltimore Sun*, February 21, 1845, 1; *Baltimore Sun*, September 9, 1843, 2; *Baltimore Sun*, September 8, 1843, 2; see also Charles B. Tiernan, *The Tiernan and Other Families, Original Letters and Memoranda in the Possession of Charles B. Tiernan* (Baltimore: William J. Gallery, 1908), 72; "Baltimore County Appointments," *American Commercial Daily Advertiser* (Baltimore), March 17, 1846, 2.

100. See Clayton E. Jewett and John O. Allen, *Slavery in the South: A State-by-State History* (Westport, Conn.: Greenwood, 2004), 36–42; Patience Essah, *A House Divided: Slavery and Emancipation in Delaware, 1638–1865* (Charlottesville: University of Virginia Press, 1996), 9–40.

101. See John A. Munroe, *History of Delaware*, 5th ed. (Cranbury, N.J.: Associated University Presses, 2006), 99; William H. Williams, *Slavery and Freedom in Delaware, 1639–1865* (Wilmington, Del.: Scholarly Resources, 1996), 249–50; Essah, *House Divided*, 6–8, 22–26.

102. See William J. Cooper, Jr. and Thomas E. Terrill, *The American South: A History* (Lanham, Md.: Rowman & Littlefield, 2009), 1:215.

103. See Hurd, *Law of Freedom and Bondage*, 2:80; see also, on Delaware's early slave laws, Essah, *House Divided*, 32–35.

104. See Williams, *Slavery and Freedom in Delaware*, 91–92, 98n83; Morris, *Southern Slavery and the Law*, 180; *Vermont Gazette* (Bennington), May 20, 1805, 3.

105. See Williams, *Slavery and Freedom in Delaware*, 91–92; "John Cowgill Corbit," in *Biographical and Genealogical History of the State of Delaware* (Chambersberg, Pa.: J.M. Rank, 1888), 1:577; J. Thomas Scharf, *History of Delaware, 1609–1888* (Philadelphia: L.J. Richards, 1888), 2:107. For the statute prohibiting the sale of slaves for export out of Delaware, see Fede, *Roadblocks to Freedom*, 40, 251.

106. See Jewett and Allen, *Slavery in the South*, 99–107.

107. See Robert M. Ireland, *The Kentucky State Constitution: A Reference Guide* (Westport, Conn.: Greenwood, 1999), 1–11; Bennett H. Young, ed., *History and Texts of the Three Constitutions of Kentucky* (Louisville: Courier-Journal Job Printing, 1890), 84; Hurd, *Law of Freedom and Bondage*, 2:13, 15, 18; see also Matthew Salafia, *Slavery's Borderland: Freedom and Bondage along the Ohio River* (Philadelphia: University of Pennsylvania Press, 2013), 45–55; Stephen Aron, *How the West Was Lost: The Transformation of Kentucky from Daniel Boone to Henry Clay* (Baltimore: Johns Hopkins University Press, 1996), 89–101.

108. See Salafia, *Slavery's Borderland*, 72–78, 209–11; Marion B. Lucas, "Kentucky, Slavery," in Miller and Smith, *Dictionary of Afro-American Slavery*, 383.

109. See "An Act to Amend an Act Entitled 'An Act to Amend the Penal Laws of This Commonwealth,'" approved December 19, 1801, in *The Statute Law of Kentucky*, ed. William Littell (Frankfort, Ky.: William Hunter, 1810), 2:467; see also Boynton Merrill, Jr., *Jefferson's Nephews: A Frontier Tragedy* (Princeton, N.J.: Princeton University Press, 1976), 268; Hurd, *Law of Freedom and Bondage*, 2:13–19; C. A. Wickliffe et al., eds., *The Revised Statutes of Kentucky* (Frankfort, Ky.: A. G. Hodges State Printer, 1852), 247–48; William Littell and Jacob Swigert, eds., *A Digest of the Statute Laws of Kentucky* (Frankfort, Ky.: Kendall and Russell, 1822), 2:986.

110. See "An Act to Enable Owners of Slaves to Protect Them from the Violence of the Wanton and Unfeeling," in *A Digest of the Statute Laws of Kentucky*, ed. C. S. Morehead and Mason Brown (Frankfort, Ky.: Albert G. Hodges, 1834), 2:1481; Morris, *Southern Slavery and the Law*, 204; Merrill, *Jefferson's Nephews*, 270–71.

111. "An Act to Reduce into One, the Several Acts Respecting Slaves, Free Negroes, Mulattoes and Indians," in Morehead and Brown, *Digest of the Statute Laws of Kentucky*, 2:1474; see *Ely v. Thompson*, 10 Ky. (3 A.K. Marsh.) 70 (1820).

112. See "An Act to Amend the Law Concerning Slaves, and for Other Purposes," in *Acts Passed at the First Session of the Thirty-Eighth General Assembly of the Commonwealth of Kentucky* (Frankfort, Ky.: J.G. Dana and A.G. Hodges, Public Printers, 1830), 174–75; see also Hurd, *Law of Freedom and Bondage*, 2:17; "Chapter 617, An Act to Revise the Statutes," adopted May 24, 1851, in *Acts of the General Assembly of the Commonwealth of Kentucky* (Frankfort, Ky.: A.G. Hodges & Co.—State Printers, 1851), 1:207; Morris, *Southern Slavery and the Law*, 183; James Oakes, *Slavery and Freedom: An Interpretation of the Old South* (New York: Norton, 1990), 157–58.

113. See Jay Feldman, *When the Mississippi Ran Backwards: Empire, Intrigue, Murder, and the New Madrid Earthquakes* (New York: Free Press, 2005), 186; Merrill, *Jefferson's Nephews*, 238; Christopher Waldrep, "Egalitarianism in the Oligarchy: The Grand Jury and Criminal Justice in Livingston County, 1799–1808," *Filson Club History Quarterly* 55, no. 3 (July 1981): 256–58.

114. See Feldman, *When the Mississippi Ran Backwards*, 186; Merrill, *Jefferson's Nephews*, 238–39; Waldrep, "Egalitarianism in the Oligarchy," 257.

115. See Merrill, *Jefferson's Nephews*, 269, 411nn14–15.

116. See Feldman, *When the Mississippi Ran Backwards*, 9–11, 103, 147–48, 182–87; Merrill, *Jefferson's Nephews*, 256–302.

117. See Elizabeth B. Clark, "'The Sacred Rights of the Weak': Pain, Sympathy, and the Culture of Individual Rights in Antebellum America," *Journal of American History* 82, no. 2 (September 1995): 465.

118. See "Trials for Murder," *Rhode-Island Republican* (Newport), August 12, 1830, 2; "Trials for Murder," *New York Commercial Advertiser*, August 7, 1830, 5.

119. See, e.g., "Slavery as It Is," *Pennsylvania Freeman* (Philadelphia), August 22, 1839, 3.

120. Morris, *Southern Slavery and the Law*, 181; *Commonwealth v. Theodore H. Davis*, Mercer County, Circuit Court Case Files, Bundle C-138, 1850–51, Kentucky State Department for Archives and History.

121. See *Commonwealth v. Lee*, 60 Ky. (3 Met.) 229, 231–32 (1860).

122. See Edward Long, *The History of Jamaica* (London: T. Lowndes, 1774), 2:493.

123. Frederick Douglass, *Autobiographies: Narrative of the Life of Frederick Douglass: An American Slave, My Bondage and My Freedom, Life and Times of Frederick Douglass* (New York: Library of America, 1994), 205.

124. See Hodges, *Root and Branch*, 38.

125. Mayo-Bobee, "Servile Discontents," 341.

126. See Greene, *Negro in Colonial New England*, 236; see also Melish, *Disowning Slavery*, 25.

CHAPTER 6. Slave Killing in Britain's Southern Mainland Colonies

1. See Christopher Tomlins, *Freedom Bound: Law, Labor, and Civic Identity in Colonizing English America, 1580–1865* (New York: Cambridge University Press, 2010), 428–504; Susan Dwyer Amussen, *Caribbean Exchanges: Slavery and the Transformation of English Society, 1640–1700* (Chapel Hill: University of North Carolina Press, 2007), 129–44; April Lee Hatfield, *Atlantic Virginia: Intercolonial Relations in the Seventeenth Century* (Philadelphia: University of Pennsylvania Press, 2004), 154–61; Richard S. Dunn, *Sugar and Slaves: The Rise of the Planter Class in the English West Indies, 1624–1713* (Chapel Hill: University of South Carolina University Press, 1972), 239–46; Demetri D. Debe and Russell R. Menard, "The Transition to African Slavery in Maryland: A Note on the Barbados Connection," *Slavery & Abolition* 32, no. 1 (March 2011): 134–37; Bradley J. Nicholson, "Legal Borrowing and the Origins of Slave Law in the British Colonies," *American Journal of Legal History* 38, no. 1 (January 1994): 41–53.

2. See, e.g., Tomlins, *Freedom Bound*, 463–75; L. H. Roper, *The English Empire in America, 1602–1658: Beyond Jamestown*, Empires in Perspective, vol. 7 (London: Pickering and Chatto, 2009), 51–83; Thomas D. Morris, *Southern Slavery and the Law, 1619–1860* (Chapel Hill: University of North Carolina Press, 1996), 38–46; Andrew Fede, *People without Rights: An Interpretation of the Fundamentals of the Law of Slavery in the U.S. South* (New York: Garland, 1992; repr., New York: Routledge, 2011), 29–44; A. Leon Higginbotham, Jr., *In the Matter of Color: Race and the American Legal Process: The Colonial Period* (New York: Oxford University Press, 1978), 19–60; Alden T. Vaughan, "The Origins Debate: Slavery and Racism in Seventeenth-Century Virginia," in *Roots of American Racism: Essays on the Colonial Experience* (New York: Oxford University Press, 1995), 128–74; Russell R. Menard, "Making a 'Popular Slave Society' in Colonial British America," *Journal of Interdisciplinary History* 43, no. 3 (Winter 2013): 377–82; Barbara Jeanne Fields, "Slavery, Race, and Ideology in the United States," *New Left Review*, May/June 1990, 95–118.

3. See, e.g., Lorena S. Walsh, *Motives of Honor, Pleasure, and Profit: Plantation Management in the Colonial Chesapeake, 1607–1763* (Chapel Hill: University of North Carolina Press, 2010), 382–93; Philip D. Morgan, *Slave Counterpoint: Black Culture in the Eighteenth-Century Chesapeake and Lowcountry* (Chapel Hill: University of North Carolina Press, 1998), 35–101; Allan Kulikoff, *Tobacco and Slaves: The Development of Southern Cultures in the Chesapeake, 1680–1800* (Chapel Hill: University of North Carolina Press, 1986), 23–44; John C. Cooms, "The Phases of Conversion: A New Chronology for the Rise of Slavery in Early Virginia," *William and Mary Quarterly*, 3rd ser., 68, no. 3 (July 2011): 332–60.

4. See Walsh, *Motives of Honor, Pleasure, and Profit*, 203; Peter Kolchin, *American Slavery 1619–1877*, rev. ed. (New York: Hill & Wang, 2003), 252; Fede, *People without Rights*, 31, 35, 46; see also Clayton E. Jewett and John O. Allen, *Slavery in the South: A State-by-State History* (Westport, Conn.: Greenwood, 2004), 258.

5. See Morgan, *Slave Counterpoint*, 95–101; Robert E. Brown and B. Katherine Brown, *Virginia 1705–1786: Democracy or Aristocracy?* (East Lansing: Michigan State University Press, 1964), 72–76.

6. See Richard S. Dunn, *A Tale of Two Plantations: Slave Life and Labor in Jamaica and Virginia* (Cambridge, Mass.: Harvard University Press, 2014), 1–22; Virginia Bernhard, *A Tale of Two Colonies: What Really Happened in Virginia and Bermuda* (Columbia: University of Missouri Press, 2011); Hatfield, *Atlantic Virginia*, 161.

7. See generally, on the early common law in Virginia, W. Hamilton Bryson, "English Common Law in Virginia," *Journal of Legal History* 6, no. 3 (December 1985): 249–50.

8. William W. Hening, ed., *Statutes at Large of Virginia* (Richmond, Va.: George Cochran, 1819–23), 2:270; see, e.g., Anthony S. Parent, Jr., *Foul Means: The Formation of Slave Society in Virginia, 1660–1740* (Chapel Hill: University of North Carolina Press, 2003), 130; Fede, *People without Rights*, 31–32; A. Leon Higginbotham, Jr., *In the Matter of Color: Race and the American Legal Process: The Colonial Period* (New York: Oxford University Press, 1978), 36.

9. See Paul Finkelman, "Slavery in the United States: Persons or Property?," in *The Legal Understanding of Slavery: From the Historical to the Contemporary*, ed. Jean Allain (Oxford: Oxford University Press, 2012), 114.

10. See ibid., 114n36.

11. See Fede, *People without Rights*, 32.

12. See Kathryn Preyer, "Crime, the Criminal Law and Reform in Post-Revolutionary Virginia," *Law and History Review* 1, no. 1 (Spring 1983): 53–54.

13. Hening, *Statutes at Large of Virginia*, 2:481–82; see ibid., 3:86.

14. Ibid., 3:459; see Fede, *People without Rights*, 65.

15. See "Instructions to Lord Culpeper (Continued)," *Virginia Magazine of History and Biography* 28, no. 1 (January 1920): 43.

16. See Letter of Alexander Spotswood to the Board of Trade, February 7, 1715/16, in *The Official Letters of Alexander Spotswood*, ed. R. A. Brock (Richmond: Virginia Historical Society, 1885), 203; see also Marion Dargan, "Crime and the Virginia Gazette 1736–1775," *University of New Mexico Bulletin*, Sociological Series, 2, no. 1 (May 1, 1934): 15n23; see also Parent, *Foul Means*, 133n50, citing 1727 instruction letter to Lieutenant Governor William Gooch.

17. See Peter Charles Hoffer, "Introduction," in *Criminal Proceedings in Colonial Virginia: [Records of] Fines, Examinations of Criminals, Trials of Slaves, etc., from March 1710 [1711] to [1754] [Richmond County, Virginia] American Legal Records, Volume 10*, ed. Peter Charles Hoffer and William B. Scott (Washington, D.C.: American Historical Association and Athens: University of Georgia Press, 1984), xxxvi.

18. See Hening, *Statutes at Large of Virginia*, 3:389–90; see also ibid., 5:540–41; Oliver P. Chitwood, *Justice in Colonial Virginia*, Johns Hopkins University Studies in Historical and Political Science, series 23, nos. 7–8 (Baltimore: Johns Hopkins University Press, 1905; repr., New York: Da Capo Press, 1971), 96–97; Hoffer, "Introduction," xxxv–xliv.

19. See Darrett B. Rutman and Anita H. Rutman, *A Place in Time: Middlesex County Virginia, 1660–1750* (New York: Norton, 1984), 124, 171, 176; see also Morris, *Southern Slavery and the Law*, 165.

20. See Parent, *Foul Means*, 130–32; see also Morris, *Southern Slavery and the Law*, 165–67; Dargan, "Crime and the Virginia Gazette," 15n23.

21. See Letter of Alexander Spotswood to the Board of Trade, February 7, 1715/16, in Brock, *Official Letters of Alexander Spotswood*, 203; see also Morris, *Southern Slavery and the Law*, 166; Dargan, "Crime and the Virginia Gazette," 15n23; A. Leon Higginbotham, Jr. and Anne F. Jacobs, "The 'Law Only as an Enemy': The Legitimization of Racial Powerlessness through the Colonial and Antebellum Criminal Laws of Virginia," *North Carolina Law Review* 70 (April 1992): 1029–30.

22. See Morris, *Southern Slavery and the Law*, 166–67; Dargan, "Crime and the Virginia Gazette," 15n23; see also Parent, *Foul Means*, 132.

23. Hening, *Statutes at Large of Virginia*, 6:111; ibid., 4:132–33; see Parent, *Foul Means*, 132–33; Fede, *People without Rights*, 65.

24. See Hening, *Statutes at Large of Virginia*, 6:369; see also Morris, *Southern Slavery and the Law*, 344.

25. See Parent, *Foul Means*, 132–34, 132.

NOTES TO CHAPTER SIX 283

26. See Morgan, *Slave Counterpoint*, 312–17.

27. See Hoffer, "Introduction," li; see also Lieutenant Governor Gooch to Duke of Newcastle, June 29, 1729, in *Calendar of State Papers Colonial, American and West Indies, Volume 36:1728–1729* (1837), *British History Online*, accessed September 22, 2014, http://www.british-history.ac.uk/report.aspx?compid=72473; see also Parent, *Foul Means*, 132–33; Morris, *Southern Slavery and the Law*, 167, 475n30.

28. See Dargan, "Crime and the Virginia Gazette," 15; see also Parent, *Foul Means*, 133n50; Higginbotham and Jacobs, "'Law Only as an Enemy,'" 1032; "Hung for Negro Murder," *William and Mary Quarterly* 8, no. 1 (July 1899): 35–36.

29. See Hoffer and Scott, *Criminal Proceedings in Colonial Virginia*, 218–19; see also Morris, *Southern Slavery and the Law*, 167.

30. See Morgan, *Slave Counterpoint*, 296–300.

31. See Morris, *Southern Slavery and the Law*, 168.

32. See *Virginia Gazette* (Williamsburg), April 21, 1775, suppl., 4.

33. Ibid., May 13, 1775, 2.

34. See Morris, *Southern Slavery and the Law*, 168, 475n37.

35. See Dargan, "Crime and the Virginia Gazette," 15.

36. See Alan Taylor, *The Internal Enemy: Slavery and War in Virginia, 1772–1832* (New York: Norton, 2013), 23–27; Gary B. Nash, *The Unknown American Revolt: The Unruly Birth of Democracy and the Struggle to Create America* (New York: Penguin, 2006), 137, 150–66; Philip J. Schwarz, *Twice Condemned: Slaves and the Criminal Laws of Virginia, 1705–1865* (Baton Rouge: University of Louisiana Press, 1988), 180–87.

37. See Gregory H. Nobles, "Historians Extend the Reach of the American Revolution," in *Whose Revolution Was It?" Historians Interpret the Founding*, ed. Alfred F. Young and Gary H. Nobles (New York: New York University Press, 2007), 210–11.

38. See Michael A. McDonnell, *The Politics of War: Race, Class, and Conflict in Revolutionary Virginia* (Chapel Hill: University of North Carolina Press, 2007), 9–10; Michael A. McDonnell, "Class War? Class Struggles during the American Revolution in Virginia," *William and Mary Quarterly*, 3rd ser., 63, no. 2 (April 2006): 314, 320; see also Peter Thompson, "The Thief, the Householder, and the Commons: Languages of Class in Seventeenth-Century Virginia," *William and Mary Quarterly*, 3rd ser., 63, no. 2 (April 2006): 253–80 (discussing the earlier development of white class structure and tensions).

39. See Edward B. Rugemer, "The Development of Mastery and Race in the Comprehensive Slave Codes of the Greater Caribbean during the Seventeenth Century," *William and Mary Quarterly*, 3rd ser., 70, no. 3 (July 2013): 451; see also Matthew Mulcahy, *Hubs of Empire: The Southeastern Lowcountry and British Caribbean*, Regional Perspectives in Early America (Baltimore: Johns Hopkins University Press, 2014), 85–87; Jewett and Allen, *Slavery in the South*, 206–7; Peter H. Wood, *Black Majority: Negroes in Colonial South Carolina from 1670 through the Stono Rebellion* (New York: Knopf, 1974), 3–17.

40. "The Fundamental Constitutions of Carolina," in *Locke: Political Essays*, Cambridge Texts in the History of Political Thought, ed. Mark Goldie (New York: Cambridge University Press, 1997), 180; see Brad Hinshelwood, "The Carolinian Context of John Locke's Theory of Slavery," *Political Theory* 4, no. 4 (August 2013): 562–90.

NOTES TO CHAPTER SIX

41. See Daragh Grant, "'Civilizing' the Colonial Subject: The Co-evolution of State and Slavery in South Carolina, 1670–1739," *Comparative Studies in Society and History* 57, no. 3 (July 2015): 611, 614; see also Mulcahy, *Hubs of Empire*, 87–88; L. H. Roper, *Conceiving Carolina: Proprietors, Planters, and Plots, 1662–1729* (New York: Palgrave Macmillan, 2004), 4–6, 29–40; Higginbotham, *In the Matter of Color*, 163, 429n86.

42. See Wood, *Black Majority*, 13; see also, e.g., Tomlins, *Freedom Bound*, 427–52; S. Max Edelson, *Plantation Enterprise on Colonial South Carolina* (Cambridge, Mass.: Harvard University Press, 2006), 43–44; Walter Edgar, *South Carolina: A History* (Columbia: University of South Carolina Press, 1998), 35–46; Higginbotham, *In the Matter of Color*, 151–54; Jack Kenny Williams, *Vogues in Villainy: Crime and Retribution in Ante-Bellum South Carolina* (Columbia: University of South Carolina Press, 1959), 36; Justin Roberts and Ian Beamish, "Venturing Out: The Barbadian Diaspora and the Carolina Colony, 1650–1685," in *Creating and Contesting Carolina: Proprietary Era Histories*, ed. Michelle LeMaster and Bradford J. Wood (Columbia: University of South Carolina Press, 2013), 49–72; Nicholson, "Legal Borrowing and the Origins of Slave Law," 49–53; Thomas J. Little, "The South Carolina Slave Laws, 1670–1700," *South Carolina Historical Magazine* 94, no. 2 (April 1993): 88–89; M. Eugene Sirmans, "The Legal Status of the Slave in South Carolina, 1670–1740," *Journal of Southern History* 28, no. 4 (November 1962): 463.

43. See Jack P. Greene, "Colonial South Carolina and the Caribbean Connection," *South Carolina Historical Magazine* 88, no. 4 (October 1987): 197; see also Mulcahy, *Hubs of Empire*, 84–85, 88–90.

44. See Rugemer, "Development of Mastery and Race," 452, 456–57; see also Mulcahy, *Hubs of Empire*, 90–96; ; Roper, *Conceiving Carolina*, 6–19; Wood, *Black Majority*, 18–34.

45. See Greene, "Colonial South Carolina and the Caribbean Connection," 205; see also Mulcahy, *Hubs of Empire*, 84–85, 96–101; Wood, *Black Majority*, 36–62; Converse D. Clowse, *Economic Beginnings in Colonial South Carolina, 1670–1730* (Columbia: University of South Carolina Press, 1971), 122–32.

46. See Kolchin, *American Slavery*, 252; Fede, *People without Rights*, 46; Rugemer, "Development of Mastery and Race," 452; Little, "South Carolina Slave Laws," 89.

47. See Robert M. Weir, *Colonial South Carolina: A History* (Columbia: University of South Carolina Press, 1983), 173–75; Grant, "'Civilizing' the Colonial Subject," 614.

48. See, e.g., Mulcahy, *Hubs of Empire*, 104–6; Stephanie McCurry, *Masters of Small Worlds: Yeoman Households, Gender Relations, and the Political Culture of the Antebellum South Carolina Low Country* (New York: Oxford University Press, 1995), 30–33.

49. See Greene, "Colonial South Carolina and the Caribbean Connection," 206; see also Morgan, *Slave Counterpoint*, 96–97.

50. See Fede, *People without Rights*, 47, quoting Winthrop D. Jordan, *White over Black: American Attitudes toward the Negro 1550–1812* (Chapel Hill: University of North Carolina Press, 1968), 103.

51. See Tomlins, *Freedom Bound*, 437–52; Higginbotham, *In the Matter of Color*, 151–215; Grant, "'Civilizing' the Colonial Subject," 614; Rugemer, "Development of Mastery

and Race," 452; Little, "South Carolina Slave Laws," 90–101; Sirmans, "Legal Status of the Slave in South Carolina," 464–66.

52. David J. McCord, ed., *Statutes at Large of South Carolina* (Columbia: A. S. Johnston, 1840), 7:345–47; Little, "South Carolina Slave Laws," 97–98.

53. See "An Act for the Better Ordering of Slaves," March 16, 1695/96, in *Acts of the General Assembly*, Governor Archdale's Laws, vol. 6, March 2–16, 1696, Act No. 141 papers 60–66, South Carolina Department of Archives and History, Columbia, S.C.; see also Roper, *Conceiving Carolina*, 93–116; Weir, *Colonial South Carolina*, 66–67; Thomas Cooper, ed., *The Statutes at Large of South Carolina* (Columbia, S.C., 1837), 2:78, 96, 121; Grant, "'Civilizing' the Colonial Subject," 614; Rugemer, "Development of Mastery and Race," 453–54; Little, "South Carolina Slave Laws," 90–101; Sirmans, "Legal Status of the Slave in South Carolina, 1670–1740," 466. England and its colonies followed the Julian (Old Style) calendar until 1752, when they adopted the Gregorian calendar. March 25 is the first day of each year on the Julian calendar. Accordingly, I use the Old Style form for pre-1752 dates between January 1 and March 24 as follows: January 9, 1692/93. See, e.g., Alvin Rabushka, *Taxation in Colonial America* (Princeton, N.J.: Princeton University Press, 2008), 3–4; Linda L. Sturtz, *Within Her Power: Propertied Women in Colonial Virginia* (New York: Routledge, 2002), 183.

54. McCord, *Statutes at Large*, 7:363–64.

55. See "Instructions to Governor Francis Nicholson," August 30, 1720, in *America's Founding Charters: Primary Documents of the Colonial and Revolutionary Era Governance*, ed. Jon L. Wakelyn (Westport, Conn.: Greenwood, 2006), 2:434–35; see also ibid., 418.

56. McCord, *Statutes at Large*, 7:381.

57. Ibid., 7:393–94.

58. Tomlins, *Freedom Bound*, 446–47.

59. Ibid., 449; see Robert Olwell, *Masters, Slaves, and Subjects: The Culture of Power in the South Carolina Low Country, 1740–1790* (Ithaca, N.Y.: Cornell University Press, 1998), 62–71; Higginbotham, *In the Matter of Color*, 192–98; Wood, *Black Majority*, 308–26.

60. See Olwell, *Masters, Slaves, and Subjects*, 62.

61. McCord, *Statutes at Large*, 7:410–11; see Morris, *Southern Slavery and the Law*, 183–84.

62. McCord, *Statutes at Large*, 7:411; see Morris, *Southern Slavery and the Law*, 184.

63. See *State v. Welch*, 1 S.C.L. (1 Bay) 172 (S.C. Com. Pl. Gen. Sess. 1791) (defendant indicted and tried for slave murder was not entitled to offer exculpatory oath, manslaughter conviction, and fifty-pound fine affirmed); Fede, *People without Rights*, 62, 86. On white class conflict, see Grant, "'Civilizing' the Colonial Subject," 631.

64. See McCord, *Statutes at Large*, 7:402.

65. See ibid., 7:426; see also Aaron J. Palmer, *A Rule of Law: Elite Political Authority and the Coming of the Revolution in the South Carolina Lowcountry, 1763–1776* (Leiden: Brill, 2014), 126.

66. See Olwell, *Masters, Slaves, and Subjects*, 70, 71n57.

NOTES TO CHAPTER SIX

67. See Robert Young, *Domesticating Slavery: The Master Class in Georgia and South Carolina, 1670–1837* (Chapel Hill: University of North Carolina Press, 1999), 49.

68. See Gov. William Bull, "A Representation of the Present State of Religion, Policy, Agriculture and Commerce, Charleston South Carolina, 1770," in *Stono: Documenting and Interpreting a Southern Slave Revolt*, ed. Mark M. Smith (Columbia: University of South Carolina Press, 2005), 30–31; Young, *Domesticating Slavery*, 49–50; see also Edgar, *South Carolina*, 115–16.

69. See Higginbotham, *In the Matter of Color*, 153.

70. See Milton Ready, *The Tar Heel State: A History of North Carolina* (Columbia: University of South Carolina Press, 2005), 68.

71. See Marvin L. Michael Kay and Lorin Lee Cary, *Slavery in North Carolina, 1748–1775* (Chapel Hill: University of North Carolina Press, 1995), 11.

72. See Jewett and Allen, *Slavery in the South*, 186–87; William S. Powell, *North Carolina through the Centuries* (Chapel Hill: University of North Carolina Press, 1989), 39–43.

73. See Ready, *Tar Heel State*, 68–69; Jewett and Allen, *Slavery in the South*, 187.

74. See Ready, *Tar Heel State*, 68–69; Jewett and Allen, *Slavery in the South*, 188–90; Powell, *North Carolina through the Centuries*, 131–46.

75. See Kay and Cary, *Slavery in North Carolina*, 22–24; see also Ready, *Tar Heel State*, 69–70; Kolchin, *American Slavery*, 252, 254; Jewett and Allen, *Slavery in the South*, 186; Fede, *People without Rights*, 46; John Spencer Bassett, *Slavery in the Colony of North Carolina*, Johns Hopkins University Studies in Historical and Political Science, series 14, nos. 4–5 (Baltimore: Johns Hopkins University Press, 1896), 19–26.

76. See "An Act Concerning Servants and Slaves," in *The State Records of North Carolina, Laws 1715–1776*, ed. Walter Clark (Goldsboro, N.C.: Nash Brothers, 1904), 23:62–66; see also Daniel Deacon, "'Willful and Malicious': Slave Personhood and the North Carolina Law of Slave-Killing, 1715 to 1791," *Illumination: The Undergraduate Journal of Humanities*, Spring 2006, 35.

77. "Instructions for Our Trusty and Welbeloved George Burrington, . . . ," December 14, 1730, in *The Colonial Records of North Carolina*, ed. William L. Saunders (Raleigh, N.C.: P.M. Hale, 1886), 3:106; Bassett, *Slavery in the Colony of North Carolina*, 42; Deacon, "'Willful and Malicious,'" 36.

78. "An Act Concerning Servants and Slaves," in Clark, *State Records of North Carolina*, 23:197.

79. Ibid., 23:201–2.

80. See Crown v. Matthew Hardy, Colonial Court Records, Criminal Papers (General and Assize), 1743, CCR 177, State Archives of North Carolina; Ready, *Tar Heel State*, 80; Kristen Fischer, *Suspect Relations: Sex, Race, and Resistance in Colonial North Carolina* (Ithaca, N.Y.: Cornell University Press, 2002), 167, 243n14; Donna J. Spindel, *Crime and Society in North Carolina, 1663–1776* (Baton Rouge: Louisiana State University Press, 1989), 48.

81. "Instructions to Arthur Dobbs . . . ," June 17, 1754, 5:1122, "Minutes of the Upper House of the North Carolina General Assembly, September 30, 1756," 5:660, both in Saunders, *Colonial Records of North Carolina*; see Bassett, *Slavery in the Colony of North*

Carolina, 42–43; Deacon, "'Willful and Malicious,'" 37; R. H. Taylor, "Humanizing the Slave Code of North Carolina," *North Carolina Historical Review* 2, no. 3 (July 1925): 323.

82. See Don Higginbotham and William S. Price, Jr., "Was It Murder for a White Man to Kill a Slave? Chief Justice Martin Howard Condemns the Peculiar Institution in North Carolina," *William and Mary Quarterly*, 3rd ser., 36, no. 4 (October 1979): 595, 597.

83. See ibid., 595, 597–601 (quoting the charge that was published in the Newport, Rhode Island, *Newport News* of May 11, 1772).

84. Ibid., 597–601.

85. See Kay and Cary, *Slavery in North Carolina*, 57–58, 75; Fede, *People without Rights*, 63; William S. Price, Jr., *Not a Conquered People: Two Carolinians View Parliamentary Taxation* (Raleigh: North Carolina Department of Cultural Reserves, Division of Archives and History, 1975), 2–5, 14–33; Higginbotham and Price, "Was It Murder?," 593–97.

86. See Kay and Cary, *Slavery in North Carolina*, 92.

87. "Letter from Josiah Martin to William Legg, Earl of Dartmouth, May 30, 1773," in Saunders, *Colonial Records of North Carolina*, 9:663; see Bassett, *Slavery in the Colony of North Carolina*, 43.

88. See Deacon, "'Willful and Malicious,'" 39; see also Higginbotham and Price, "Was It Murder?," 596.

89. "An Act to Prevent the willful Killing of Slaves," in Clark, *State Records of North Carolina*, 23:975–76; see Kay and Cary, *Slavery in North Carolina*, 75–76; Fede, *People without Rights*, 63–64.

90. See Bassett, *Slavery in the Colony of North Carolina*, 44; William M. Wiecek, "The Statutory Law of Slavery and Race in the Thirteen Mainland Colonies of British America," *William and Mary Quarterly*, 3rd ser., 34, no. 2 (April 1977): 266.

91. "An Act Concerning Servants and Slaves," in Clark, *State Records of North Carolina*, 23:201–2; Fede, *People without Rights*, 64.

92. "Letter from Josiah Martin to William Legg, Earl of Dartmouth, July 13, 1774," in Saunders, *Colonial Records of North Carolina*, 9:1013; see Deacon, "'Willful and Malicious,'" 39.

93. See Watson W. Jennison, *Cultivating Race: The Expansion of Slavery in Georgia, 1750–1860* (Lexington: University Press of Kentucky, 2012), 7; Christopher Leslie Brown, *Moral Capital: Foundations of British Abolitionism* (Chapel Hill: University of North Carolina Press, 2006), 78–85; Betty Wood, *Slavery in Colonial Georgia, 1730–1775* (Athens: University of Georgia Press, 1984), 1–23.

94. See Glenn McNair, *Criminal Injustice: Slaves and Free Blacks in Georgia's Criminal Justice System* (Charlottesville: University of Virginia Press, 2009), 37; Higginbotham, *In the Matter of Color*, 216–53; see generally Paul M. Pressly, *On the Rim of the Caribbean: Colonial Georgia and the British Atlantic World* (Athens: University of Georgia Press, 2013), 11–31; Jennison, *Cultivating Race*, 11–18; Wood, *Slavery in Colonial Georgia*, 24–87; Ralph Betts Flanders, *Plantation Slavery in Georgia* (Chapel Hill: University of North Carolina Press, 1933), 3–22.

95. Allen D. Candler, *The Colonial Records of the State of Georgia*, 26 vols. (Atlanta: Franklin, 1904–16), 1:58; see Wood, *Slavery in Colonial Georgia*, 84.

96. Jennison, *Cultivating Race*, 7; see ibid., 18–22; see also Mulcahy, *Hubs of Empire*, 106–11; Pressly, *On the Rim of the Caribbean*, 1–10, 134–52.

97. See Jewett and Allen, *Slavery in the South*, 82; Fede, *People without Rights*, 46.

98. See Pressly, *On the Rim of the Caribbean*, 28, 135–36; Wood, *Slavery in Colonial Georgia*, 104–9; Flanders, *Plantation Slavery in Georgia*, 52.

99. See Candler, *Colonial Records of the State of Georgia*, 18:102–44; see also Pressly, *On the Rim of the Caribbean*, 150–51; Jennison, *Cultivating Race*, 23–40; McNair, *Criminal Injustice*, 37–38; Wood, *Slavery in Colonial Georgia*, 112–23; Higginbotham, *In the Matter of Color*, 252–62; Flanders, *Plantation Slavery in Georgia*, 23–31.

100. See Candler, *Colonial Records of the State of Georgia*, 18:105–6.

101. See ibid., 18:132.

102. See ibid., 18:134–35.

103. See ibid., 18:132–33.

104. See ibid., 18:106–7.

105. Ibid., 19, pt. 1:209–49; ibid., 18:649–88; see Wood, *Slavery in Colonial Georgia*, 125–30; Flanders, *Plantation Slavery in Georgia*, 23, 31–32.

106. See Jennison, *Cultivating Race*, 24–25; Young, *Domesticating Slavery*, 50; Wood, *Slavery in Colonial Georgia*, 128–30; Elmer Beecher Russell, *The Review of American Colonial Legislation by the King in Council* (New York, 1915), 135–36. On slaves as real, personal, or hybrid property, see Morris, *Southern Slavery and the Law*, 62–80; Roy W. Copeland, "The Nomenclature of Enslaved Africans as Real Property or Chattels Personal: Legal Fiction, Judicial Interpretation, Legislative Designation, or Was a Slave a Slave by Any Other Name," *Journal of Black Studies* 40, no. 5 (May 2010): 946–59.

107. See Candler, *Colonial Records of the State of Georgia*, 19, pt. 1:244–45; ibid., 18:682–83; Oliver H. Prince, ed., *Digest of the Laws of the State of Georgia* (Milledgeville, Ga.: Grantland & Orme, 1822), 348.

108. See Candler, *Colonial Records of the State of Georgia*, 18:683–84.

109. See ibid., 19, pt. 1:245. The 1765 act also imposed a six-shilling fine if a slave was "beaten Bruised Maimed or Disabled" by a person "not having sufficient Cause or Lawfull authority for doing so." See ibid., 18:106–7.

110. See ibid., 19, pt. 1:214.

111. See Jennison, *Cultivating Race*, 34, quoting Governor James Wright to the Board of Trade, June 8, 1768.

112. See Jennison, *Cultivating Race*, 34; see also James Habersham, N. Jones, Lewis Johnson, N. W. Jones, John Milledge, Archibald Bullock, and William Ewen to Benjamin Franklin, May 19, 1768, in *Collections of the Georgia Historical Society Vol. VI: The Letters of Hon. John Habersham, 1756–1775* (Savannah: Georgia Historical Society, 1904), 71–75.

113. See Wood, *Slavery in Colonial Georgia*, 124–28, 124; see also Pressly, *On the Rim of the Caribbean*, 9, 150–51.

114. See Jennison, *Cultivating Race*, 38.

115. See Frank Lambert, *James Habersham, Loyalty, Politics, and Commerce in Colonial Georgia* (Athens: University of Georgia Press, 2008), 1–4, 113–16, 4.

116. See Jennison, *Cultivating Race*, 40.

117. See Flanders, *Plantation Slavery in Georgia*, 26.

CHAPTER 7. Slave Homicide Reform in Virginia

1. See Clayton E. Jewett and John O. Allen, *Slavery in the South: A State-by-State History* (Westport, Conn.: Greenwood, 2004), 258–70; Peter Kolchin, *American Slavery 1619–1877*, rev. ed. (New York: Hill & Wang, 2003), 254; Richard Tadman, *Speculators and Slaves: Masters, Traders, and Slaves in the Old South* (Madison: University of Wisconsin Press, 1989), 12.

2. See W. S. Rossiter, *A Century of Population Growth: From the First to the Twelfth Census of the United States: 1790–1900* (Washington, D.C.: Government Printing Office, 1909; repr., Baltimore: Genealogical Publishing Co., 1969), 135–36.

3. See Kathryn Preyer, "Crime, the Criminal Law and Reform in Post-revolutionary Virginia," *Law and History Review* 1, no. 1 (Spring 1983): 56–70; Gail McKnight Beckman, "Three Penal Codes Compared," *American Journal of Legal History* 10, no. 2 (April 1966): 149–56; "64. Founders Online, National Archives, A Bill for Proportioning Crimes and Punishments in Cases Heretofore Capital, 18 June 1779," in *The Papers of Thomas Jefferson*, vol. 2, *1777–18 June 1779*, ed. Julian P. Boyd (Princeton, N.J.: Princeton University Press, 1950), 492–507, accessed June 8, 2014, http://founders.archives.gov/documents/Jefferson/01-02-02-0132-0004-0064, ver. 2014-05-09.

4. See William W. Hening, ed., *Statutes at Large of Virginia* (Richmond, Va.: George Cochran, 1819–23), 12:681.

5. See A. Leon Higginbotham, Jr. and Anne F. Jacobs, "The 'Law Only as an Enemy': The Legitimization of Racial Powerlessness through the Colonial and Antebellum Criminal Laws of Virginia," *North Carolina Law Review* 70 (April 1992): 1031n345, quoting Philip J. Schwarz, *Twice Condemned: Slaves and the Criminal Laws of Virginia, 1705–1865* (Baton Rouge: University of Louisiana Press, 1988), 25.

6. See William Blackstone, *Blackstone's Commentaries with Notes of Reference, to the Constitution and Laws, of the Federal Government of the United States; and of the Commonwealth of Virginia*, ed. St. George Tucker (Philadelphia: William Young Birch, and Abraham Small, 1803), Appendix, Note H—On the State of Slavery in Virginia, 1, pt. 2: 56; St. George Tucker, *A Dissertation on Slavery: With a Proposal for the Gradual Abolition of It, in the State of Virginia* (Philadelphia: Matthew Carey, 1796), 53.

7. See Blackstone, *Blackstone's Commentaries*, 1, pt. 2: 56, note *; Tucker, *Dissertation on Slavery*, 52, note q.

8. *Thomas Sorrell's Case*, 3 Va. (1 Va. Cas.) 253, 255–58 (Sup. Ct. App. 1786), 258; see Thomas D. Morris, *Southern Slavery and the Law, 1619–1860* (Chapel Hill: University of North Carolina Press, 1996), 478n96; Andrew Fede, *People without Rights: An Interpretation of the Fundamentals of the Law of Slavery in the U.S. South* (New York: Garland, 1992; repr., New York: Routledge, 2011), 66; Higginbotham and Jacobs, "'Law Only as an Enemy,'" 1033–34.

9. See Fede, *People without Rights*, 66–72; see also Alan Taylor, *The Internal Enemy: Slavery and War in Virginia, 1772–1832* (New York: Norton, 2013), 62–69; Jonathan D. Martin, *Divided Mastery: Slave Hiring in the American South* (Cambridge, Mass.: Harvard University Press, 2004), 104–37; Philip D. Morgan, *Slave Counterpoint: Black Culture in the Eighteenth-Century Chesapeake and Lowcountry* (Chapel Hill: University of North Carolina Press, 1998), 288–91, 312–17.

10. See Andrew Fede, "Legitimized Violent Slave Abuse in the American South, 1619–1865: A Case Study of Law and Social Change in Six Southern States," *American Journal of Legal History* 29, no. 2 (April 1985): 113; see also Fede, *People without Rights*, 70–72, 75–76, 100–105; William Goodell, *The American Slave Code* (1853; repr., New York: Negro Universities Press, 1968), 124, 216–17; Higginbotham and Jacobs, "'Law Only as an Enemy,'" 1036, citing *Harris v. Nicholas*, 19 Va. (5 Munf.) 483 (Sup. Ct. App. 1817) (owner cannot recover damages on slave hiring contract when slave was beaten to death by someone not the defendant hirer's agent); *Brown v. May*, 15 Va. (1 Munf.) 288 (Sup. Ct. App. 1810) (affirming $150 judgment against strangers who beat and injured plaintiff's slave); *Kennedy v. Waller*, 12 Va. (2 Hen. & M.) 415 (Sup. Ct. App. 1808) (reversing $450 verdict against defendants who killed hired slave because plaintiffs lacked standing to sue).

11. *Hoomes v. Kuhn*, 8 Va. (4 Call) 274, 1792 Va. LEXIS 40 (1792).

12. See *Hoomes v. Kuhn*, 1792 Va. LEXIS 40, *1–*10; see also *Hoomes v. Kuhn*, Wythe 136, 1791 Va. LEXIS 8 (October 1791) (October 1792).

13. See *Virginia Gazette and Alexandria Advertiser*, January 27, 1791, 3.

14. See *Virginia Gazette and Alexandria Advertiser*, February 17, 1791, 3; ibid. (February 10 1791): 2; see also Michael Lee Pope, *Hidden History of Alexandria* (Charleston, S.C.: History Press, 2011), 75–76; Alex Bontemps, *The Punishing Self: Surviving Slavery in the Colonial South* (Ithaca, N.Y.: Cornell University Press, 2008), 131.

15. See "An Act to Reduce into One, the Several Acts Concerning Slaves, Free Negroes and Mulattoes," in *A Collection of All Such Acts of the General Assembly of Virginia* (Richmond, Va.: Samuel Pleasants, Jr. and Henry Pace, 1803), 188; see also Fede, *People without Rights*, 174–75; B. W. Leigh, ed., *The Revised Code of the Laws of Virginia* (Richmond, Va.: Thomas Ritchie, 1819), 1:426–27; Higginbotham and Jacobs, "'Law Only as an Enemy,'" 1029.

16. See Andrew Fede, *Roadblocks to Freedom: Slavery and Manumission in the United States South* (New Orleans: Quid Pro Books, 2011), 91; see also Taylor, *Internal Enemy*, 35–39.

17. See Taylor, *Internal Enemy*, 39–102; Fede, *Roadblocks to Freedom*, 89–94; Melvin Patrick Ely, *Israel on the Appomattox: A Southern Experiment in Black Freedom, from the 1790s through the Civil War* (New York: Knopf, 2004), 379–80; Morgan, *Slave Counterpoint*, 15–16.

18. See Randolph Roth, *American Homicide* (Cambridge, Mass.: Belknap, 2009), 37–39, 95, 98.

19. See ibid., 95.

20. See ibid., 98–99, 98; see also Steven Pinker, *The Better Angels of Our Nature: Why Violence Has Declined* (New York: Viking, 2011), 94–100.

21. See Roth, *American Homicide*, 99; chapter 6, notes 32–38.

22. William J. Novak, *The People's Welfare: Law and Regulation in Nineteenth Century America*, Studies in Legal History (Chapel Hill: University of North Carolina Press, 1996), 53.

23. See "An Act to Amend the Penal Laws of This Commonwealth," in *The Statutes at Large of Virginia, from October Session 1792, to December Session 1806*, ed. Samuel

Shepherd (Richmond, Va.: Samuel Shepherd, 1835), 2:5–14; see also, e.g., John D. Bessler, *Cruel and Unusual: The American Death Penalty and the Founders' Eighth Amendment* (Lebanon, N.H.: Northeastern University Press, 2012), 150; Guyora Binder, *Felony Murder* (Stanford, Calif.: Stanford University Press, 2012), 128–30; Leonard Birdsong, "Felony Murder: A Historical Perspective by Which to Understand Today's Modern Felony Murder Rule Statutes," *Thurgood Marshall Law Review* 32, no. 1 (2006): 17–18; Guyora Binder, "The Origins of American Felony Murder Rules," *Stanford Law Review* 57, no. 1 (October 2004): 119–20, 149; Preyer, "Crime, the Criminal Law and Reform," 70–85; Beckman, "Three Penal Codes Compared," 156–59; Edward A. Wyatt, IV, "George Keith Taylor, 1769–1815, Virginia Federalist and Humanitarian," *William and Mary Quarterly*, 2nd ser., 16, no. 1 (January 1936): 8–11.

24. See "An Act to Amend the Penal Laws of This Commonwealth," in Shepherd, *Statutes at Large of Virginia*, 2:5–7; "An Act to Amend the Penal Laws of This Commonwealth," in *A Collection of All Such Acts of the General Assembly of Virginia*, 2nd ed. (Richmond, Va.: Samuel Pleasants, 1814), 499.

25. See *Wicks v. Commonwealth*, 4 Va. (2 Va. Cas.) 387, 1824 WL 1065, *4 (Gen. Ct. 1824) (affirming murder conviction).

26. See Binder, *Felony Murder*, 129–30; Birdsong, "Felony Murder," 18.

27. See "An Act to Amend an Act Intituled 'An Act to Reduce into One the Several Acts Concerning Slaves, Free Negroes and Mulattoes,'" in Shepherd, *Statutes at Large of Virginia*, 2:147–48.

28. See "An Act to Amend the Laws Heretofore Made Amending the Penal Laws of This Commonwealth," in Shepherd, *Statutes at Large of Virginia*, 2:405–6; "An Act to Amend the Laws Heretofore Made Amending the Penal Laws of This Commonwealth," in *A Collection of All Such Acts of the General Assembly of Virginia of a Public and Permanent Nature as Have Passed since the Session of 1801* (Richmond, Va.: Samuel Pleasants, Jr., 1808), 2:15–16; *Commonwealth v. Chapple*, 3 Va. (1 Va. Cas.) 184, 1811 WL 350 (Va. Gen. Ct. 1811) (affirming conviction for shooting a slave and noting that 1803 act addressed issues raised under 1796 act).

29. See "William Nelson to the Governor," in *Calendar of Virginia State Papers and Other Manuscripts from January 1, 1808, to December 31, 1835*, ed. H. W. Flournoy (Richmond, Va., 1892), 93.

30. See Inquisition of Bob, 1803 May 16th, Prince Edward County (Va.) Free Negro and Slave Records, 1783–1865 (bulk 1801–64), Local Government Records Collection, Prince Edward County Court Records, Library of Virginia, Richmond, Va.; see also Ely, *Israel on the Appomattox*, 225–26, 549n1.

31. See "Murder!," *Lexington (Ky.) Reporter*, March 2, 1811, 4; "A Devil Incarnate!," *New York Commercial Advertiser*, January 21, 1811, 3.

32. See "Casualties," *Massachusetts Spy or Worcester Gazette*, June 27, 1810, 3.

33. "Crimes, Lynchburgh (Vir.) Nov. 16," *Republican Messenger* (Sherburne, N.Y.), December 25, 1810, 3.

34. See *Baltimore Patriot and Mercantile Advertiser*, February 24, 1819, 3; *Commonwealth v. Cohen*, 4 Va. (2 Va. Cas.) 158, 1819 Va. LEXIS 62 (1819).

35. See Ely, *Israel on the Appomattox*, 225–26.

36. See generally on the Code's adoption, Christopher Michael Curtis, *Jefferson's Freeholders and the Politics of Ownership in the Old Dominion* (New York: Cambridge University Press, 2012), 196n6; see also W. Hamilton Bryson, ed., *Virginia Law Books: Essays and Bibliographies* (Philadelphia: American Philosophical Society, 2000), 18. For Leigh's proslavery views, see Lacy K. Ford, *Deliver Us from Evil: The Slavery Question in the Old South* (New York: Oxford University Press, 2009), 378–80.

37. Leigh, *Revised Code of the Laws of Virginia*, 1:616.

38. See ibid., 1:617–18.

39. See "By the Mails," *Portland (Maine) Gazette*, December 30, 1823, 2.

40. See "Homicides of Adults in Rockbridge County, Virginia, 1778–1900," accessed October 10, 2016, http://cjrc.osu.edu/files/Rockbridge%20County%20homicides.doc.

41. See *Souther v. Commonwealth*, 48 Va. (7 Gratt.) 673, 680–81 (1851), quoting Session Acts of 1847–48, 95; George M. Stroud, *A Sketch of the Laws Relating to Slavery in the Several States of the United States of America* (2nd ed. 1856; repr., New York: Negro Universities Press, 1968), 21, note *; see also *Report of the Revisors of the Code of Virginia Made to the General Assembly in July 1849 Being Their Final Report and Relating to the Criminal Code* (Richmond, Va.: William F. Ritchie, 1849), 939, note *.

42. See *Report of the Revisors of the Code of Virginia*, 940, note *.

43. See *Commonwealth v. Turner*, 26 Va. (5 Rand.) 678 (1827); Fede, *People without Rights*, 105–21.

44. *Souther v. Commonwealth*, 48 Va. (7 Gratt.) 673 (1851).

45. See ibid., 673–83.

46. See 1840 United States Federal Census, Hanover, Virginia, roll 560, p. 104, image 213, accessed November 4, 2013, http://search.ancestry.com.

47. See *Souther v. Commonwealth*, 678–79.

48. See ibid., 673–78.

49. *Commonwealth v. Turner*, 26 Va. (5 Rand.) 678 (1827).

50. See *Souther v. Commonwealth*, 679–80.

51. See ibid., 679.

52. Ibid., 680.

53. Ibid., 681.

54. See, e.g., discussing the case, Curtis, *Jefferson's Freeholders*, 230–32; Jenny Bourne Wahl, *The Bondsman's Burden: An Economic Analysis of the Common Law of Southern Slavery* (New York: Cambridge University Press, 1998), 150; Morris, *Southern Slavery and the Law*, 178–79; Fede, *People without Rights*, 80; Harriet Beecher Stowe, *The Key to Uncle Tom's Cabin* (Boston: John P. Jewett, 1853; repr., New York: Arno Press, 1968), 149–54; Higginbotham and Jacobs, "'Law Only as an Enemy,'" 1034–36; Fede, "Legitimized Violent Slave Abuse," 121–22.

55. See *The Code of Virginia* (Richmond, Va.: William F. Ritchie, 1849), vii–x, 800; *Report of the Revisors of the Code of Virginia*, 938–40; see generally, on the 1849 Code's preparation and approval, Curtis, *Jefferson's Freeholders*, 196–229; Bryson, *Virginia Law Books*, 18. Patton was General George Patton's great-grandfather. See Carlo D'Este, *Patton: A Genius for War* (New York: HarperCollins, 1995), 11. Robinson was Benjamin W. Leigh's son-in-law. See Bryson, *Virginia Law Books*, 121.

56. See *Code of Virginia*, 723.

57. See *Report of the Revisors of the Code of Virginia*, 939, note *.

58. See *Code of Virginia*, 723; *Report of the Revisors of the Code of Virginia*, 940, note *.

59. See *Code of Virginia*, 754.

60. See "Whipped to Death," *New Hampshire Patriot and State Gazette* (Concord), September 10, 1851, 2; *New Orleans Times-Picayune*, September 9, 1851, 1; *Brattleboro (Vt.) Weekly Eagle*, September 8, 1851, 3; "News of the Day," *Alexandria (Va.) Gazette*, August 30, 1851, 2.

61. See "Col. James Castleman," *Alexandria (Va.) Gazette*, October 23, 1851, 2; see also Stowe, *Key to Uncle Tom's Cabin*, 194–95, quoting "Homicide Case in Clarke County, Virginia," *National Era* 5, no. 45 (November 6, 1851): 178.

62. See 1850 United States Federal Census, Clarke, Virginia, roll M432_940, p. 297A, image 416, accessed November 4, 2013, http://search.ancestry.com; 1850 United States Federal Census, Slave Schedules, accessed November 4, 2013, http://search.ancestry.com.

63. See "To His Excellency, John B. Ford," *Alexandria (Va.) Gazette*, February 20, 1849, 2.

64. See "A New Breed of Cattle," *Milwaukee Sentinel*, June 23, 1849, 2.

65. See ibid.; see also, e.g., "Arabian Cattle," *The Plough, the Loom, and the Anvil* 2, no. 4 (October 1849): 231; "Arabian Cattle," *Scientific American*, June 29, 1849, 325; "The Agricultural Fair, Fairfax County, Va.," *Alexandria (Va.) Gazette*, October 26, 1849, 2; "Syrian Cattle," *Brattleboro (Vt.) Semi-Weekly Eagle*, August 6, 1849, 1; "Fine Calves—The Khaisis," *Vermont Journal* (Windsor), July 13, 1849, 1; "Arabian Cattle Introduced," *Republican Farmer* (Bridgeport, Conn.), June 19, 1849, 2; "News of the Day," *Alexandria (Va.) Gazette*, June 2, 1849, 2; "The Twin Calves," *Richmond Enquirer*, February 27, 1849, 2.

66. See "Shenandoah," *Alexandria (Va.) Gazette*, December 7, 1850, 2.

67. See "Jefferson Congressional District," *Richmond Enquirer*, April 11, 1851, 2; *Alexandria (Va.) Gazette*, February 20, 1849, 2; *Richmond Enquirer*, February 5, 1846, 2.

68. See 1850 United States Federal Census, Clarke, Virginia, roll M432_940, p. 175B, image 353, accessed November 4, 2013, http://search.ancestry.com; 1850 United States Federal Census, Slave Schedules, accessed November 4, 2013, http://search.ancestry.com.

69. See "Col. James Castleman," *Alexandria (Va.) Gazette*, October 23, 1851, 2; see also Stowe, *Key to Uncle Tom's Cabin*, 194–95, quoting "Homicide Case in Clarke County, Virginia," 178.

70. See Stowe, *Key to Uncle Tom's Cabin*, 197–98, quoting "Homicide Case in Clarke County, Virginia," 178.

71. See "Railroad Meeting in Loudon," *Alexandria (Va.) Gazette*, March 15, 1852, 2.

72. See "Died," *Alexandria (Va.) Gazette*, March 24, 1854, 2.

73. See 1850 United States Federal Census, Sussex, Virginia, roll M432_978, p. 118B, image 232, accessed April 21, 2015, http://search.ancestry.com; 1850 United States Federal Census, Slave Schedules, accessed April 21, 2015, http://search.ancestry.com; 1840 United States Federal Census, Sussex, Virginia, roll 576, p. 232, image 1142, accessed April 21, 2015, http://search.ancestry.com.

74. See "Sentenced to be Hung," *Richmond Whig*, August 9, 1853, 3; *Richmond Whig*, July 15, 1853, 3.

75. See "A Murder," *Alexandria (Va.) Gazette*, November 8, 1853, 3; see also "Catalogue of Southern Atrocities," *Boston Liberator*, December 2, 1853, 192; *Boston Daily Atlas*, November 14, 1853, 1; "Murder in Sussex," *Trenton (N.J.) State Gazette*, November 10, 1853, 2.

76. See "News of the Day," *Alexandria (Va.) Gazette*, May 3, 1854, 2.

77. See 1860 United States Federal Census, District 1, Sussex, Virginia, roll M653 1380, p. 446, image 451, accessed April 21, 2015, http://search.ancestry.com; 1860 United States Federal Census, Slave Schedules, accessed April 21, 2015, http://search.ancestry.com.

78. See 1850 United States Federal Census, Mecklenburg, Virginia, roll M432_960, p. 97A, image 196, accessed November 4, 2013, http://search.ancestry.com; 1850 United States Federal Census, Slave Schedules, accessed November 4, 2013, http://search.ancestry.com.

79. See "Slave Murder in the United States," *Anti-Slavery Reporter*, new series, 8, no. 12 (December 1, 1860): 308; "The Late Slave Murder Case in Mecklenberg County—Conviction of the Murderer," *New York Herald*, October 3, 1860, 2; see also William A. Link, *Roots of Secession: Slavery and Politics in Antebellum Virginia* (Chapel Hill: University of North Carolina Press, 2003), 42–43, 267n27.

80. A. Wilson Greene, *Civil War Petersburg: Confederate City in the Crucible of War* (Charlottesville: University of Virginia Press, 2006), 130; see Ezra J. Warner and W. Buck Yeats, "Thomas Saunders Gholson (Virginia)," in *Biographical Register of the Confederate Congress* (Baton Rouge: Louisiana State University Press, 1975), 100–101.

81. See *Speech of Hon. Thos. S. Gholson of Virginia on the Policy of Employing Negro Troops, and the Duty of All Classes to Aid in the Prosecution of the War* (Richmond, Va.: Geo. P. Evans, 1865), 4; see also Robert F. Durden, ed., *The Gray and the Black: The Confederate Debate on Emancipation* (Baton Rouge: Louisiana State University Press, 1972), 166–72. On the Davis and Lee proposals and the Confederate Congress's legislation, see Bruce Levine, *Confederate Emancipation: Southern Plans to Free and Arm Slaves during the Civil War* (New York: Oxford University Press, 2006).

82. See "A White Man Convicted of the Murder of a Negro," *New York Commercial Advertiser*, May 24, 1858, 1.

83. Wyatt Espy and John Ortiz Smykla, "Executions in the U.S. 1608–2002: The Espy File Executions by State," 359–82, 398–99, Death Penalty Information Center, accessed March 10, 2016, http://www.deathpenaltyinfo.org/documents/ESPYstate.pdf.

84. See Ely, *Israel on the Appomattox*, 226.

CHAPTER 8. Slave Homicide Reform in North Carolina and the Common Law of Slavery

1. See Clayton E. Jewett and John O. Allen, *Slavery in the South: A State-by-State History* (Westport, Conn.: Greenwood, 2004), 186, 192–93; Peter Kolchin, *American Slavery 1619–1877*, rev. ed. (New York: Hill & Wang, 2003), 254; Richard Tadman, *Speculators and Slaves: Masters, Traders, and Slaves in the Old South* (Madison: University of Wisconsin Press, 1989), 12; John Spencer Bassett, *Slavery in the State of North Carolina*, Johns Hopkins University Studies in Historical and Political Science, series 17, nos. 7–8 (Baltimore: Johns Hopkins University Press, 1899), 77–79.

2. See Bill Cecil-Fronsman, *Common Whites: Class and Culture in Antebellum North Carolina* (Lexington: University Press of Kentucky, 1992), 12–14, 71–72; W. S. Rossiter, *A Century of Population Growth: From the First to the Twelfth Census of the United States: 1790–1900* (Washington, D.C.: Government Printing Office, 1909; repr., Baltimore: Genealogical Publishing, 1969), 135–36.

3. "An Act to Amend an Act, Entitled, 'An Act to Prevent Thefts and Robberies by Slaves, Free Negroes and Mulattoes,' Passed at Tarborough, in the Year One Thousand Seven Hundred and Eighty-Seven; and to Amend an Act, Passed in the Year One Thousand Seven Hundred and Seventy-Four, Entitled, 'An Act to Prevent the Wilful and Malicious Killing of Slaves," in *Laws of the State of North Carolina*, ed. Henry Potter, J. L. Taylor, and Bart Yancey (Raleigh: J. Gales, 1821), chap. 335, §3, 1:654.

4. See "An Act to Prevent the Stealing of Slaves or by Violation, Seduction or Any Other Means, Taking or Conveying Away Any Slaves, the Property of Another; and for Other Purposes Therein Mentioned," in *The State Records of North Carolina, Laws 1777–1788*, ed. Walter Clark (Goldsboro, N.C.: Nash Brothers, 1905), 24:220.

5. See *Philadelphia General Advertiser*, March 13, 1792, 2 (quoting both statutes); see also, on nineteenth-century gambling regulation, William J. Novak, *The People's Welfare: Law and Regulation in Nineteenth Century America*, Studies in Legal History (Chapel Hill: University of North Carolina Press, 1996), 159–61, 313–14.

6. See Bartholomew F. Moore and Asa Biggs, *Revised Code of North Carolina* (Boston: Little, Brown, 1855); see also Guion Griffis Johnson, *Ante-Bellum North Carolina: A Social History* (Chapel Hill: University of North Carolina Press, 1937), 644–82; David Walbert, "Criminal Law Reform," *Learn NC: North Carolina Digital History, North Carolina and the New Nation*, accessed July 10, 2016, http://www.learnnc.org/lp/editions/nchist-newnation/4782; Donna J. Spindel, *Crime and Society in North Carolina, 1663–1776* (Baton Rouge: Louisiana State University Press, 1989), 124–25.

7. *State v. Weaver*, 3 N.C. (2 Hayw.) 77 (Sup. Ct. 1798).

8. Ibid., 78; see *Smith v. Weaver*, 1 N.C. 141, Tay. 58 (Sup. Ct. 1799) (denying Weaver's motion to dismiss Smith's trespass suit filed after Weaver was acquitted at criminal trial).

9. *State v. Piver*, 3 N.C. (2 Hayw.) 247 (Sup. Ct. 1799).

10. See ibid., 248; see also Cecil-Fronsman, *Common Whites*, 77.

11. See Charles R. Holloman, "Bright, Simon," in *Dictionary of North Carolina Biography*, ed. William S. Powell (Chapel Hill: University of North Carolina Press, 1996), 1:227.

12. *State v. Boon*, 1 N.C. 103, Tay. 246 (1801).

13. Ibid., 103–4; Verdict, *State of North Carolina v. John Boon*, Superior Court, Hillsborough District, October Term 1801, in State Archives of North Carolina (SANC), case 1040. On Haywood, see Robert E. Corlew, "Haywood, John," in Powell, *Dictionary of North Carolina Biography*, 3:87–88.

14. See Laura F. Edwards, *The People and Their Peace: Legal Culture and the Transformation of Inequality in the Post-revolutionary South* (Chapel Hill: University of North Carolina Press, 2009), 50; Kemp P. Battle, "An Address on the History of the Supreme Court," 36, delivered February 4, 1889, accessed March 28, 2015, http://www.ncschs.net/siteres.aspx?resid=edf32a30-80ce-4262-bc73-08625be1a2c9.

15. See *State v. Boon*, 114.

16. Ibid., 111–13, 111–12.

17. Ibid., 110–11.

18. Ibid., 104–10, 107.

19. "An Act to Amend an Act, Entitled, 'An Act to Amend an Act, Entitled, An Act to Prevent Thefts and Robberies by Slaves, Free Negroes or Mulattoes, and to Amend an Act, Entitled, An Act to Prevent the Wilful and Malicious Killing of Slaves,'" in Potter, Taylor, and Yancey, *Laws of the State of North Carolina*, chap. 585, 2:948–49; see R. H. Taylor, "Humanizing the Slave Code of North Carolina," *North Carolina Historical Review* 2, no. 3 (July 1925): 323–24.

20. See *State vs. Augustus Benton*, Orange County Criminal Actions, 1806, C.R.073.326.8, inquest report, September 8, 1806, SANC.

21. See ibid., statement of Elias Hawes, September 8, 1806.

22. See ibid., statement of Benjamin Yeargin, September 1, 1806.

23. See ibid., statement of Hugh Nunn, September 8, 1806.

24. See ibid., indictment, undated.

25. See ibid., letter of Ed Jones to A. B. Bruce, March 29, 1820; see also *The Public Acts of the General Assembly of North Carolina* (Newbern, N.C.: Martin & Ogden, 1804), 1:84. For another discussion of this case, see Edwards, *People and Their Peace*, 193–94.

26. See "A Caution to Slave Drivers," *Raleigh Star*, April 19, 1810, 64; see also Johnson, *Ante-Bellum North Carolina*, 501.

27. See "For the Star," *Raleigh Star*, August 9, 1810, 126–27; see also Johnson, *Ante-Bellum North Carolina*, 501.

28. See *Raleigh Star*, October 6, 1815, 3; see also, on Nash, Jacquelin Drane Nash, "Nash, Frederick," in Powell, *Dictionary of North Carolina Biography*, 4:359–60, and on Ruffin, John V. Orth, "Ruffin, Thomas," in *The Yale Biographical Dictionary of American Law*, ed. Roger K. Newman (New Haven, Conn.: Yale University Press, 2009), 471–72 and the articles in the symposium "Thomas Ruffin and the Perils of Public Homage," *North Carolina Law Review* 87, no. 3 (March 2009).

29. See *Raleigh Star*, October 13, 1815, 3.

30. See *Raleigh Star*, October 27, 1815, 3; see also "Horrid Cruelty, in the Murder of a Slave in America," in *Kirby's Wonderful and Eccentric Museum: or Magazine* (London: R. S. Kirby, 1820), 4:400–402.

31. See *Raleigh Star*, November 10, 1815, 4; see also *American Magazine* 1, no. 6 (November 1815): 223–26.

32. See *Raleigh Star*, November 17, 1815, 4.

33. "An Act to Punish the Offense of Killing a Slave," in Potter, Taylor, and Yancey, *Laws of the State of North Carolina*, chap. 949, 2:1407; "An Act to Punish the Offense of Killing a Slave," in *Laws of the State of North Carolina Enacted in the Year 1817*, chap. 18 (Raleigh: Thomas Henderson, State Printer, 1818), 18–19.

34. *State v. Walker*, 4 N.C. 662, Tay 230 (1817); see "Fall Circuit," *Raleigh Star*, November 14, 1817, 3. The Court of Conference after 1804 was called the Supreme Court. See Battle, "Address on the History of the Supreme Court," 36–38.

35. See *State v. Walker*, 4 N.C., 662–69; *Carolina Federal Republican* (New Bern), December 6, 1817, 2; *New York Daily Advertiser*, December 4, 1817, 2; *American Star*

(Petersburg, Va.), December 2, 1817, 3. For Walker's November 19, 1817, pardon petition to the general assembly, see Petition of John Walker, *Digital Library on American Slavery Race and Slavery Petitions Project*, accessed March 28, 2015, http://library.uncg.edu/slavery/petitions/details.aspx?pid=829.

36. See Battle, "Address on the History of the Supreme Court," 39–43. On the changes leading to the creation of the North Carolina Supreme Court, see Edwards, *People and Their Peace*, 50–53, 208–9, 239.

37. See *Litchfield (Conn.) Republican*, December 11, 1820, 2; "Murder," *Alexandria (Va.) Gazette*, August 2, 1819, 2; Indictment, *State of North Carolina v. Mason Scott*, Superior Court, Wake County, March Term 1820, in SANC, case 787.

38. See *State v. Scott*, 8 N.C. (2 Hawks) 24, 1820 N.C. LEXIS 7, *1–*2 (1820); "Mason Scott," *Connecticut Journal* (New Haven, Conn.) (April 25, 1820): 3.

39. See Marshall De Lancey Haywood, "Henry Seawell," in *Biographical History of North Carolina from Colonial Times to the Present*, ed. Samuel A. Ashe et al. (Greensboro, N.C.: Charles L. VanNoppen, 1905), 2:396.

40. See ibid., 2:394–97; see also *State v. Walker*, 4 N.C., 668.

41. See *State v. Scott*, 1820 N.C. LEXIS 7, *8–*10, *8.

42. See ibid., *12–*19.

43. See *Litchfield (Conn.) Republican*, December 11, 1820, 2; *New York Columbian*, November 22, 1820, 2; *Carolina Gazette* (Charleston), October 28, 1820, 1; *Raleigh Star*, October 27, 1820, 3; *New York Spectator*, October 27, 1820, 4; Wyatt Espy and John Ortiz Smykla, "Executions in the U.S. 1608–2002: The Espy File Executions by State," 193, Death Penalty Information Center, accessed March 10, 2015, http://www.deathpenaltyinfo.org/documents/ESPYstate.pdf; see also Cecil-Fronsman, *Common Whites*, 77–78; Seth Koch and Robert P. Mosteller, "The Racial Justice Act and the Long Struggle with Race and the Death Penalty in North Carolina," *North Carolina Law Review* 88, no. 6 (September 2010): 2049.

44. See Marshall DeLancey Haywood, *John Branch: 1782–1863* (Raleigh: Commercial Printing, 1915), 11–12.

45. *State v. Tackett*, 8 N.C. (1 Hawks) 210 (1820).

46. See ibid., 210–13; Indictment, *State of North Carolina v. William Tacket*, Superior Court, Wake County, Spring Term 1820, in SANC, case 1115; see also "Murder!," *Hillsboro Telegraph* (Amherst, N.H.), January 15, 1820, 2; "Murder," *New York Columbian*, December 30, 1819, 2. On slave marriages, see, e.g., Michael Grossberg, *Governing the Hearth: Law and the Family in Nineteenth-Century America* (Chapel Hill: University of North Carolina Press, 1985), 129–33; Tyler D. Parry, "Married in Slavery Time: Jumping the Broom in Atlantic Perspective," *Journal of Southern History* 81, no. 2 (May 2015): 294–95; Darlene C. Goring, "The History of Slave Marriage in the United States," *John Marshall Law Review* 39 (2006): 306–10, 316.

47. *State v. Tackett*, 8 N.C. (1 Hawks), 213.

48. Ibid., 213–14; see *City of Washington Gazette*, October 19, 1820, 2.

49. *State v. Tackett*, 8 N.C. (1 Hawks), 214.

50. Ibid., 214–15.

51. See ibid., 216–17.

52. See ibid., 217.

53. Ibid., 217–18.

54. Ibid., 218.

55. See Moore and Biggs, *Revised Code of North Carolina*, 203–5; Andrew Fede, *People without Rights: An Interpretation of the Fundamentals of the Law of Slavery in the U.S. South* (New York: Garland, 1992; repr., New York: Routledge, 2011), 72–73; see also Saidiya V. Hartman, *Scenes of Subjection: Terror, Slavery, and Self-Making in Nineteenth-Century America* (New York: Oxford University Press, 1997), 83; William E. Wiethoff, *A Peculiar Humanism: The Judicial Advocacy of Slavery in High Courts of the Old South, 1820–1850* (Athens: University of Georgia Press, 1996), 83–84; Russell K. Osgood, review of *The American Law of Slavery 1810–1860: Considerations of Humanity and Interest*, by Mark Tushnet, *Cornell Law Review* 67, no. 2 (January 1982): 434–38.

56. *State v. Hale*, 9 N.C. (2 Hawks) 582 (1823).

57. Ibid., 586–87; see Fede, *People without Rights*, 103–5. On poor white and slave fraternization and violence, see, e.g., Jeff Forret, *Race Relations at the Margins: Slaves and Poor Whites in the Antebellum Southern Countryside* (Baton Rouge: Louisiana State University Press, 2006), 157–83; Fede, *People without Rights*, 72–77, 100–105, 116–21.

58. *State v. Jarrott*, 23 N.C. (1 Ired.) 76 (1840).

59. See ibid., 81–87.

60. *State v. Will*, 18 N.C. (1 Dev. & Bat.) 121 (1834).

61. See, e.g., Cynthia Lee, *Murder and the Reasonable Man: Passion and Fear in the Criminal Courtroom* (New York: New York University Press, 2003), 58–60; Hartman, *Scenes of Subjection*, 83, 148; Thomas D. Morris, *Southern Slavery and the Law, 1619–1860* (Chapel Hill: University of North Carolina Press, 1996), 289–92; Fede, *People without Rights*, 167–76.

62. *State v. Reed*, 9 N.C. (2 Hawks) 454 (1823).

63. See Indictment, *State of North Carolina v. Thomas Reed*, Superior Court, Hertford County, March Term 1823, in SANC, case 1760.

64. See Statement of the Case, *State of North Carolina v. Thomas Reed*, Superior Court, Hertford County, March Term 1823, in SANC, case 1760.

65. See John Hope Franklin, *The Free Negro in North Carolina 1790–1860* (Chapel Hill: North Carolina University Press, 1943), 99–100.

66. See Edwards, *People and Their Peace*, 195–96; Morris, *Southern Slavery and the Law*, 180, 477n95; Archibald D. Murphey to Thomas Ruffin, September 10, 1825, in *The Papers of Archibald D. Murphey*, ed. William Henry Hoyt (Raleigh: E.M. Uzzell & Co., State Printer, 1914), 1:317.

67. See "Effects of Slavery," *Boston Recorder*, July 27, 1822, 120; *Western Carolinian* (Salisbury, N.C.), May 28, 1822, 2; see also Johnson, *Ante-Bellum North Carolina*, 503.

68. See *State of North Carolina v. David Yeates*, North Carolina Supreme Court 1808–1909, in SANC, file 1311; *State v. Yeates*, 11 N.C. (4 Hawks) 187 (1825).

69. See S[amuel] F[inley] Patterson to Hutchins Burton, June 10, 1827, Governor's Papers, SANC; Bertram Wyatt-Brown, *Southern Honor: Ethics and Behavior in the Old South* (New York: Oxford University Press, 1982), 376–77; Bertram Wyatt-Brown, "Barn

Burning and Other Snopesian Crimes: Class and Justice in the Old South," in *Class, Conflict and Consensus: Antebellum Southern Community Studies*, ed. Orville Vernon Burton and Robert C. McMath (Westport, Conn.: Greenwood, 1982), 198.

70. See *Free Press* (Tarborough, N.C.), June 23, 1827, 4; *New Bern (N.C.) Sentinel*, June 23, 1827, 3; *Raleigh Register*, June 22, 1827, 1. The story also was printed in newspapers in the North and in the South. See, e.g., "Horrors of Slavery," *Portland (Maine) Gazette*, July 10, 1827, 2; "Horrors of Slavery," *New York Spectator*, July 6, 1827, 1; *Berkshire Star* (Stockbridge, Mass.), (July 5, 1827), 3; *New York Daily Advertiser*, July 3, 1827, 2; *American* (New York), June 28, 1827, 2; *Charleston Currier*, June 19, 1827, 2.

71. See Wyatt-Brown, "Barn Burning and Other Snopesian Crimes," 198.

72. *State v. Hoover*, 20 N.C. (4 Dev. & Bat.) 393 (1839).

73. See Fede, *People without Rights*, 95–96n83.

74. See *State v. Hoover*, 393–94, 396; Trial Record, *State of North Carolina v. John Hoover*, Superior Court, Iredell County, Fall Term 1839, in SANC, case 2637. The Supreme Court's file includes two handwritten versions of the trial court record, one is dated January 20, 1840, another November 2, 1839. I refer to the 1840 version. See, citing this trial record, Carolyn J. Powell, "In Remembrance of Mira: Reflections on the Death of a Slave Woman," in *Discovering the Women in Slavery: Emancipating Perspectives on the American Past*, ed. Patricia Morton (Athens: University of Georgia Press, 1996), 47–60; Anthony V. Baker, "Slavery and Tushnet and *Mann*, Oh Why? Finding 'Big Law' in Small Places," *Quinnipiac Law Review* 26, no. 3 (2008): 698–707; Anthony V. Baker, "'For the Murder of His Own Female Slave, a Woman Named Mira ...'": Law, Slavery and Incoherence in Antebellum North Carolina" (2006), *Student Scholarship Papers* 18, accessed August 12, 2014, http://digitalcommons.law.yale.edu/student_papers/18. The State Archives file also includes a handwritten version of Chief Justice Ruffin's decision.

75. See Powell, "In Remembrance of Mira," 50.

76. See Baker, "'For the Murder of His Own Female Slave,'" 2n5.

77. See Powell, "In Remembrance of Mira," 50.

78. See Testimony of William B. Jones and John H. McLaughlin, Trial Record, *State of North Carolina v. John Hoover*, 17–19, 18–19; Baker, "'For the Murder of His Own Female Slave,'" 1–4, 3–4.

79. See Testimony of John H. McLaughlin, Trial Record, *State of North Carolina v. John Hoover*, 19; Baker, "'For the Murder of His Own Female Slave,'" 4, 4n18.

80. See Indictment, Trial Record, *State of North Carolina v. John Hoover*, 1–5.

81. See *State v. Hoover*, 393–94; Testimony of witnesses, Trial Record, *State of North Carolina v. John Hoover*, 9–17; Powell, "In Remembrance of Mira," 51–52, 51; Baker, "Slavery and Tushnet," 703–4n51; Baker, "'For the Murder of His Own Female Slave,'" 5–6.

82. See *State v. Hoover*, 394.

83. See Testimony of William B. Jones and John H. McLaughlin, Trial Record, *State of North Carolina v. John Hoover*, 17–19.

84. See Testimony of Dr. Moore, Trial Record, *State of North Carolina v. John Hoover*, 19–20; see also *State v. Hoover*, 393–94; Baker, "'For the Murder of His Own Female Slave,'" 4. Dr. Moore's first name is not stated in the transcript.

85. See Testimony of Mr. Allison, Trial Record, *State of North Carolina v. John Hoover*, 17; Powell, "In Remembrance of Mira," 56. Allison's first name is not stated in the transcript.

86. See *State v. Hoover*, 394.

87. See ibid., 395; Baker, "'For the Murder of His Own Female Slave,'" 6.

88. See Baker, "'For the Murder of His Own Female Slave,'" 6, quoting Superior Court Minutes, *State of North Carolina v. John Hoover*, September 12, 1839, in SANC, 518; see also *New York Liberator*, October 24, 1839, 1.

89. See *State v. Hoover*, 395–97; see also Baker, "'For the Murder of His Own Female Slave,'" 7–8.

90. See *State v. Hoover*, 395–96, 396 (citations omitted).

91. *State v. Mann*, 13 N.C. (2 Dev.) 263 (1829).

92. See *State v. Hoover*, 395. In the handwritten version of the opinion, the sentence "He must not kill" is an interlineation. See *State v. Hoover*, 1.

93. See note 33.

94. See *State v. Hoover*, 395.

95. *State v. Hoover*, 395–96.

96. See Governor Jonathan Worth to C. K. Lenow, 29 May, 1868, in *The Correspondence of Jonathan Worth*, ed. J. G. de Roulhac Hamilton (Raleigh: Edwards and Broughton, 1909), 2:1215; "Executions in Iredell," *Landmark* (Statesville, N.C.), February 13, 1880, 3; see also Powell, "In Remembrance of Mira," 49; Baker, "Slavery and Tushnet," 700n39; Baker, "'For the Murder of His Own Female Slave,'" 8–9; *Tarboro (N.C.) Press*, April 11, 1840, 2.

97. See James A. Wynn, Jr., "*State v. Mann*: Judicial Choice or Judicial Duty," *North Carolina Law Review* 87, no. 3 (March 2009): 1000; Andrew Fede, "Legitimized Violent Slave Abuse in the American South, 1619–1865: A Case Study of Law and Social Change in Six Southern States," *American Journal of Legal History* 29, no. 2 (April 1985): 139.

98. See David Grimsted, *American Mobbing, 1828–1861: Toward Civil War* (New York: Oxford University Press, 1998), 168.

99. See "$400 Reward," *North-Carolina Standard* (Raleigh), March 12, 1845, 3; see also John L. Cheney, Jr., ed., *North Carolina Government 1585–1979: A Narrative and Statistical History* (Raleigh: North Carolina Department of the Secretary of State, 1981), 312.

100. See "Horrid Murder—Escape of the Murderer," *New York Herald*, April 26, 1845, 2, citing *Richmond Star*, April 24, 1845.

101. See James C. Kearney, *Nassau Plantation: The Evolution of a Texas-German Slave Plantation* (Denton: University of North Texas Press, 2010), 280n24; *A Twentieth Century History of Southwest Texas* (New York: Lewis, 1907), 2:403–4.

102. See "Shaver, Mary Ann (Bass) Holloway: Death of Grandma Shaver," *Colorado County Obituaries-Shaver*, accessed May 5, 2015, http://www.coloradocountyhistory.org/obits/s/shaver.htm; "Mary Ann Whathal 'Granny Shaver' Bass Holloway-Shaver," *Find a Grave*, accessed May 5, 2015, http://www.findagrave.com/cgibin/fg.cgi?page=gr&GRid=63653055.

103. Cecil-Fronsman, *Common Whites*, 76.

104. See "Killing a Slave," *Pennsylvania Freeman* (Philadelphia), March 25, 1847, 3; see also "Killing a Slave," *Boston Liberator*, August 20, 1847, 134; Cecil-Fronsman, *Common Whites*, 76.

105. *State v. Robbins*, 48 N.C. (3 Jones) 249 (1855).

106. See ibid., 249–55; Wilma A. Dunaway, *The African-American Family in Slavery and Emancipation*, Studies in Modern Capitalism (New York: Cambridge University Press, 2003), 30; Larry Griffin, "Prominent Wilkes Citizens Were Slave Owners," *The Record*, Internet Edition, no. 783 (October 15, 2014), accessed April 3, 2015, http://therecordofwilkes.com/newsa.asp?edition_number=783&pg=F. On the ambivalent attitudes of many southerners toward domestic slave traders, see Steven Deyle, *Carry Me Back: The Domestic Slave Trade in American Life* (New York: Oxford University Press, 2005), 44–60, 206–44; Robert H. Gudmestad, *A Troublesome Commerce: The Transformation of the Interstate Slave Trade* (Baton Rouge: Louisiana State University Press, 2003), 62–86; see also Don H. Marr, Jr., "Slave Trading and Slave Traders in North Carolina" (M.A. thesis, East Carolina University, May 1995). Nevertheless, between 1820 and 1860, more than two million slaves were sold in the United States and more than two-thirds were sold to local buyers, including commercial sales through agents or brokers. See Deyle, *Carry Me Back*, 157.

107. See *State v. Robbins*, 250–52.

108. See ibid., 252–55; Fede, *People without Rights*, 94–95n82; *Pittsfield (Mass.) Sun*, November 1, 1855, 1; "Look out for Murderer," *Carolina Watchman* (Salisbury, N.C.), July 26, 1855, 2.

109. See *State v. Robbins*, 255.

110. Ibid., 259; see *Boston Liberator*, January 18, 1856, 12.

111. See Governor Jonathan Worth to C. K. Lenow, May 29, 1868, in de Roulhac Hamilton, *Correspondence of Jonathan Worth*, 2:1215; Larry Griffin, "Of Human Bondage: Part Three at a Look at Slavery in Wilkes," *The Record*, Internet Edition, no. 780 (September 24, 2014), accessed March 28, 2015, http://www.therecordofwilkes.com/newsa.asp?edition_number=780&pg=F.

112. See "Atrocious Murder of a Negro, and Acquittal of the Murderers, etc.," *New York Tribune*, October 26, 1858, 3 (emphasis omitted).

113. For other interpretations, see, e.g., Edwards, *People and Their Peace*, 233–44; Mark V. Tushnet, *Slave Law in the American South: State v. Mann in History and Literature*, Landmark Law Cases and American Society (Lawrence: University Press of Kansas, 2003), 30–37; Mark V. Tushnet, *The American Law of Slavery 1810–1860: Considerations of Humanity and Interest* (Princeton, N.J.: Princeton University Press, 1981), 90–123; Bassett, *Slavery in the State of North Carolina*, 20–28; Bryce R. Holt, "The Supreme Court of North Carolina and Slavery," in *Historical Papers Published by the Trinity College Historical Society*, series 17 (Durham, N.C.: Duke University Press, 1927), 12–24; Timothy C. Meyer, "Slavery Jurisprudence on the Supreme Court of North Carolina, 1828–1858: William Gaston and Thomas Ruffin," *Campbell Law Review* 33, no. 2 (2011): 313–39; Omar Swartz, "Codifying the Law of Slavery in North Carolina: Positive Law and the Slave Persona," *Thurgood Marshall Law Review* 29 (Spring 2004): 291–309;

Reuel E. Schiller, "Conflicting Obligations: Slave Law and the Late Antebellum North Carolina Supreme Court," *Virginia Law Review* 78, no. 5 (August 1992): 1219–28; A. E. Keir Nash, "A More Equitable Past? Southern Supreme Courts and the Protection of the Antebellum Negro," *North Carolina Law Review* 48 (1969–70): 200–219.

114. See *State v. Mann*, 13 N.C. (2 Dev.) 263 (1829); *Commonwealth v. Turner*, 26 Va. (5 Rand.) 678 (1827); Fede, *People without Rights*, 105–11.

115. See Edwards, *People and Their Peace*, 193–96, 355–56n42.

CHAPTER 9. Slave Homicide Reform in Georgia and Tennessee

1. Compare A. E. Keir Nash, "A More Equitable Past? Southern Supreme Courts and the Protection of the Antebellum Negro," *North Carolina Law Review* 48 (1969–70): 212.

2. See Clayton E. Jewett and John O. Allen, *Slavery in the South: A State-by-State History* (Westport, Conn.: Greenwood, 2004), 82–84, 224–25; Peter Kolchin, *American Slavery 1619–1877*, rev. ed. (New York: Hill & Wang, 2003), 254; Willard Range, *A Century of Georgia Agriculture 1850–1950* (Athens: University of Georgia Press, 1954), 3–17.

3. See Watson W. Jennison, *Cultivating Race: The Expansion of Slavery in Georgia, 1750–1860* (Lexington: University Press of Kentucky, 2012), 63–64.

4. See *Augusta Chronicle and Gazette of the State*, September 16, 1797, 3.

5. See *Augusta Chronicle and Gazette of the State*, October 7, 1797, 3; see also Jennison, *Cultivating Race*, 64.

6. See Walter McElreath, *A Treatise on the Constitution of Georgia* (Atlanta: Harrison Company, 1912), 266; John Codman Hurd, *The Law of Freedom and Bondage in the United States* (1858 and 1862; repr., Boston: Little, Brown, 1968), 2:101n2; see also Jennison, *Cultivating Race*, 64–65; Melvin B. Hill, Jr., *The Georgia State Constitution: A Reference Guide* (Westport, Conn.: Greenwood, 1994), 5–6, 23; Albert B. Saye, *Constitutional History of Georgia, 1732–1945* (Athens: University of Georgia Press, 1948), 155–95; McElreath, *Treatise on the Constitution of Georgia*, 95–115.

7. See "An Act to Carry into Effect the 12th Section of the 4th Article of the Constitution," in *A Digest of the Laws of the State of Georgia*, ed. Oliver H. Prince (Milledgeville, Ga.: Grantland & Orme, 1822), 456; ibid., 348.

8. See Howell Cobb, ed., *A Compilation of the Penal Code of the State of Georgia* (Macon: Joseph M. Boardman, 1850), 83; see also Thomas R. R. Cobb, *A Digest of the Statute Laws of the State of Georgia* (Athens, Ga.: Christy, Kelsa & Burke, 1851), 2:785; Lucius Q. C. Lamar, ed., *A Compilation of the Laws of the State of Georgia* (Augusta: T. S. Hannon, 1821), 569, 616.

9. See *Jordan v. State*, 22 Ga. 545, 1857 WL 1944 (1857); Howell Cobb, ed., *A Compilation of the General and Public Statutes of the State of Georgia* (New York: Edward O. Jenkins, 1859), 604; see also "Humanity of the Slave Laws of Georgia," *Macon Telegraph*, January 4, 1861, 1.

10. See Lamar, *Compilation of the Laws*, 654; see also Cobb, *Compilation of the General and Public Statutes*, 635; Cobb, *Compilation of the Penal Code*, 181–82. See, for the 1860 law, "An Act to Amend the Twelfth Section of the Thirteenth Division of the Penal Code," in *Acts of the General Assembly of the State of Georgia Passed at Milledge-*

ville at an Annual Session in November and December 1860 (Milledgeville, Ga.: Nisbet and Barnes, 1861), 56; and for the 1851 act, *Moran v. Davis*, 18 Ga. 722, 723 (1855); see generally Thomas D. Morris, *Southern Slavery and the Law, 1619–1860* (Chapel Hill: University of North Carolina Press, 1996), 184.

11. See Morris, *Southern Slavery and the Law*, 185.

12. See Timothy S. Huebner, *The Southern Judicial Tradition: State Judges and Sectional Distinctiveness, 1790–1890* (Athens: University of Georgia Press, 1999), 72.

13. *State v. Abbot*, 1 Ga. Rep. Ann. 203, R.M. Charlton 244 (1822).

14. Ibid., 204–5, 205.

15. See ibid., 204–5.

16. See Anna Stowell Bassett, "Some Georgia Records of John Abbot, Naturalist," *Auk* 55, no. 2 (April 1938): 249–50; see also Pamela Gilbert, *John Abbot: Birds, Butterflies and Other Wonders* (London: Merrell Holberton, 1998), 74–76; H. Wayne Leibee, "John Abbot of Georgia (1751–1840) A Pioneering Naturalist in America," *Southern Lepidopterists' News* 25, no. 4 (December 31, 2003): 110.

17. See Ralph Betts Flanders, *Plantation Slavery in Georgia* (Chapel Hill: University of North Carolina Press, 1933), 241–42.

18. See "Brutal Murder of a Slave by His Owner," *Charleston Currier*, February 9, 1857, 1.

19. See "Whipping a Slave to Death in Savannah," *Boston Liberator*, April 3, 1857, 56; "A Runaway Slave Whipped to Death," *New Bedford (Mass.) Mercury*, February 27, 1857, 2; "Whipping a Slave to Death in Savannah," *Cleveland Leader*, February 24, 1857, 2.

20. See "Brutal Murder of a Slave by His Owner," *Charleston Currier*, February 9, 1857, 1; see also James Campbell, *Crime and Punishment in African American History* (New York: Palgrave Macmillan, 2013), 21.

21. *Bailey v. State*, 26 Ga. 579, 1858 Ga. LEXIS 366 (1858); *Bailey v. State*, 20 Ga. 742, 1856 Ga. LEXIS 143 (1856).

22. See 1850 United States Federal Census, Division 90, Warren, Georgia, Roll M432_86, p. 153B, image 314, accessed July 27, 2014, http://search.ancestry.com; 1850 U.S. Federal Conesus—Slave Schedules, accessed July 27, 2014, http://search.ancestry.com; Jack F. Cox, *The 1850 Census of Georgia Slave Owners* (Baltimore: Clearfield Co., 1999), 14.

23. See *Bailey v. State*, 1858 Ga. LEXIS 366, *1.

24. See "A Proclamation-Georgia," *Macon Weekly Telegraph*, August 31, 1852, 3.

25. See *Bailey v. State*, 1856 Ga. LEXIS 143, *1.

26. See ibid., *1–*7.

27. See *Bailey v. State*, 1858 Ga. LEXIS 366, *1.

28. See ibid., *1–*6.

29. See 1860 United States Federal Census, Georgia Militia District 158, Warren, Georgia, Roll M653_140, p. 8, image 8, Family History Library Film: 803140, accessed July 27, 2014, http://search.ancestry.com.

30. *Cobb v. Battle*, 34 Ga. 458 (1866).

31. See ibid., 461, 468–69.

32. See ibid., 459–70.

33. See ibid., 473–84; see also Aviam Soifer, "Reviewing Legal Fictions," *Georgia Law Review* 20 (Summer 1986): 888–90. For Georgia's evolving manumission restrictions, see Andrew Fede, *Roadblocks to Freedom: Slavery and Manumission in the United States South* (New Orleans: Quid Pro Books, 2011), 98–104.

34. *Martin v. State*, 26 Ga. 494, 1858 Ga. LEXIS 99 (1858); see *Columbus (Ga.) Enquirer*, March 23, 1858, 2; Flanders, *Plantation Slavery in Georgia*, 239–40.

35. See *Martin v. State*, 1858 Ga. LEXIS 99, *1–*14; 1850 United States Federal Census, Division 91, Washington, Georgia, Roll M432_87, p. 224A, image 49, accessed September 27, 2013, http://us-census.org/pub/usgenweb/census/ga/washington/1850/pg0215a.txt; 1850 U.S. Federal Conesus—Slave Schedules, accessed September 27, 2013, http://search.ancestry.com/cgi-bin/sse.dll?indiv=1&db=1850slaveschedules&rank=1&new=1&MSAV=0&msT=1&gss=angs-d&gsfn=green&gsln=martin&msrpn__ftp=Georgia%2c+USA&msrpn=13&msrpn_PInfo=5-%7c0%7c1652393%7c0%7c2%7c3245%7c13%7c0%7c0%7c0%7c0%7c&uidh=649&_83004003-n_xcl=f&pcat=35&fh=0&h=2605403&recoff=17+18&ml_rpos=1.

36. *Martin v. State*, 1858 Ga. LEXIS 99, *1–*14.

37. Ibid., *1–*3.

38. Ibid., *13–*14.

39. Ibid., *3–*13.

40. Ibid., *14–*26; see "Murder of a Slave," *Daily True Delta* (New Orleans), March 30, 1858, 1.

41. See, e.g., Paul DeForest Hicks, *Joseph Henry Lumpkin: Georgia's First Chief Justice* (Athens: University of Georgia Press, 2002), 86–97; Watson Jennison, "Rewriting the Free Negro Past: Joseph Lumpkin, Proslavery Ideology, and Citizenship in Antebellum Georgia," in *Creating Citizenship in the Nineteenth Century South*, ed. William A. Link, David Brown, Brian Ward, and Martyn Bone (Gainesville: University of Florida Press, 2013), 41–43.

42. See *Martin v. State*, *18–*20, *31–*34.

43. Ibid., *27–*30.

44. See U.S. Federal Census Mortality Schedules, 1850–85, and Related Indexes 1850–80 (T655), archive roll 8, census year 1860, Ware Georgia, p. 705, accessed September 27, 2013, http://search.ancestry.com/cgi-bin/sse.dll?db=USMortality&h=396473&indiv=try&o_vc=Record:OtherRecord&rhSource=3530.

45. See Hicks, *Joseph Henry Lumpkin*, 1–62; William E. Wiethoff, *The Insolent Slave* (Columbia: University of South Carolina Press, 2002), 149–59; Huebner, *Southern Judicial Tradition*, 70–86; see also John Phillip Reid, "Lessons of Lumpkin: A Review of Recent Literature on Law, Comity, and the Impending Crisis," *William and Mary Law Review* 23 (Summer 1982): 590–91.

46. *American Colonization Society v. Gartrell*, 23 Ga. 448, 464–65 (1857); see Hicks, *Joseph Henry Lumpkin*, 124–35.

47. See Fede, *Roadblocks to Freedom*, 112–14, 225–31; Huebner, *Southern Judicial Tradition*, 86–95; Reid, "Lessons of Lumpkin," 591–602; Mason W. Stephenson and D. Grier Stephenson, Jr., "'To Protect and Defend': Joseph Henry Lumpkin, the Supreme

Court of Georgia, and Slavery," *Emory Law Journal* 25 (Summer 1976): 582–86; see also, e.g., *Cleland v. Waters*, 19 Ga. 35, 1855 WL 1788, *7 (1855).

48. See Huebner, *Southern Judicial Tradition*, 95; see also Hicks, *Joseph Henry Lumpkin*, 133.

49. See, e.g., Fede, *Roadblocks to Freedom*, 109–14, 373–74, for an evaluation of Lumpkin's proslavery views.

50. *Jordan v. State*, 22 Ga. 545, 1857 WL 1944 (1857).

51. *Camp v. State*, 25 Ga. 689 (1858).

52. See *Jordan v. State*, 1857 WL 1944, *1.

53. Ibid., *2.

54. See ibid., *3–*4.

55. See ibid., *6–*9, *8.

56. See *Camp v. State*, 690.

57. See ibid., 690–92.

58. See ibid., 692.

59. See ibid., 693; see Cobb, *Digest of the Statute Laws*, 2:784.

60. *Jim v. State*, 15 Ga. 535, 1854 WL 1652 (1854).

61. *Jim v. State*, 1854 WL 1652, *6–*7.

62. *Cox v. State*, 32 Ga. 515, 1861 WL 1403 (1861).

63. See *Cox v. State*, 1861 WL 1403, *1–*3, *1.

64. Ibid., *2.

65. Ibid., *3–*4.

66. See ibid., *4–*5.

67. *Neal v. Farmer*, 9 Ga. 555 (1851).

68. See ibid., 599–84; Andrew Fede, *People without Rights: An Interpretation of the Fundamentals of the Law of Slavery in the U.S. South* (New York: Garland, 1992; repr., New York: Routledge, 2011), 70–72, 75–76; Daniel Flanigan, *The Criminal Law of Slavery and Freedom 1800–1868* (New York: Garland, 1987), 158–60, 169–73. For damage suits, see, e.g., *Johnson v. Lovett*, 31 Ga. 187 (1860) (affirming judgment for defendant who beat hired slave, slave's owner suffered no economic loss); *Moran v. Davis*, 18 Ga. 722 (1855) (affirming judgment for hirer sued by deceased hired slave's owner); *Macon & Western Railroad v. Davis*, 13 Ga. 68 (1853) (reversing judgment for owner of deceased slave, but finding that statute making railroads liable for damages done to livestock or other property applied to slaves).

69. See Chase C. Mooney, *Slavery in Tennessee* (Bloomington: Indiana University Press, 1957), 7.

70. See Jewett and Allen, *Slavery in the South*, 224–25; Mooney, *Slavery in Tennessee*, 8; Hurd, *Law of Freedom and Bondage*, 2:89–90.

71. See Jewett and Allen, *Slavery in the South*, 224–25; Richard Tadman, *Speculators and Slaves: Masters, Traders, and Slaves in the Old South* (Madison: University of Wisconsin Press, 1989), 12; Arthur F. Howington, *What Sayeth the Law: The Treatment of Slaves and Free Blacks in the State and Local Courts of Tennessee* (New York: Garland, 1986), viii.

72. See Donald L. Winters, *Tennessee Farming, Tennessee Farmers: Antebellum Agriculture in the Upper South* (Knoxville: University of Kentucky Press, 1994), 135–54; Mooney, *Slavery in Tennessee*, 127–46; see also Jewett and Allen, *Slavery in the South*, 225–26.

73. Howington, *What Sayeth the Law*, ix; see Mooney, *Slavery in Tennessee*, 4–6.

74. See Howington, *What Sayeth the Law*, ix–xi, x–xi.

75. See Chase C. Mooney, "The Question of Slavery and the Free Negro in the Tennessee Constitutional Convention of 1834," *Journal of Southern History* 12, no. 4 (November 1946): 489–98, 498; see also, e.g., Lacy K. Ford, *Deliver Us from Evil: The Slavery Question in the Old South* (New York: Oxford University Press, 2009), 390–417; Durwood Dunn, *An Abolitionist in the Appalachian South: Ezekiel Birdseye on Slavery, Capitalism, and Separate Statehood in East Tennessee, 1841–1846* (Knoxville: University of Tennessee Press, 1997), 3–12; Mooney, *Slavery in Tennessee*, 76–79; Oliver P. Temple, *East Tennessee in the Civil War* (Cincinnati: Robert Clarke, 1899), 111–18; J. H. Henderson, "Slavery in Tennessee," *Proceedings of the Twenty-Third Annual Meeting of the Bar Association of Tennessee* (1904): 173–77.

76. See Mooney, *Slavery in Tennessee*, 79–80; Chase C. Mooney, "Question of Slavery and the Free Negro," 498–502.

77. See Dunn, *Abolitionist in the Appalachian South*, 13–66.

78. R. L. Caruthers and A. O. P. Nicholson, *A Compilation of the Statutes of Tennessee* (Nashville: James Smith, 1836), 676–77; John H. Haywood and Robert L. Cobbs, eds., *The Statute Laws of the State of Tennessee* (Knoxville: F.S. Heiskell, 1831), 1:320; Hurd, *Law of Freedom and Bondage*, 2:89–90; see Howington, *What Sayeth the Law*, 84–85; Mooney, *Slavery in Tennessee*, 8–9.

79. See Fede, *People without Rights*, 212; Cornelia Anne Clark, "Justice on the Tennessee Frontier: The Williamson County Circuit Court 1810–1820," *Vanderbilt Law Review* 32, no. 1 (January 1979): 440; Caleb Perry Patterson, "The Negro in Tennessee, 1790–1865: A Study in Southern Politics," *University of Texas Bulletin*, no. 2205 (February 1, 1922): 44–45.

80. See Return J. Meigs and William F. Cooper, *The Code of Tennessee Enacted by the General Assembly of 1857–'8* (Nashville: E.G. Eastman & William Company, State Printer, 1858), 510, 512–13.

81. See Haywood and Cobbs, *Statute Laws of the State of Tennessee*, 1:320; see also Meigs and Cooper, *Code of Tennessee*, 513; Mooney, *Slavery in Tennessee*, 9.

82. See *Werley v. State*, 30 Tenn. (11 Hum.) 172 (1850); Haywood and Cobbs, *Statute Laws of the State of Tennessee*, 1:251.

83. See Dunn, *Abolitionist in the Appalachian South*, 84. On Birdseye's biography, see ibid., 26–66.

84. See ibid., 40–43, 245n1.

85. See ibid., 245.

86. See ibid., 90–91, 258–59, 91.

87. See Howington, *What Sayeth the Law*, 93; Louise Gillespie Lynch, *Miscellaneous Records: Williamson County Tennessee* (1978–84), 2:5, 5:66.

88. See Howington, *What Sayeth the Law*, 91.

89. See ibid., 93–94, 94; see also *Rowe v. State*, 30 Tenn. (11 Hum.) 491 (1851).

90. See Howington, *What Sayeth the Law*, 94n44; *Jones v. Allen*, 38 Tenn. (1 Head) 626 (1858); see also Jacob I. Corre, "Thinking Property at Memphis: An Application of Watson," *Chicago-Kent Law Review* 68, no. 3 (1993): 1382–86.

91. *Fields v. State*, 9 Tenn. (1 Yer.) 156 (1829).

92. See ibid., 156–57.

93. See ibid., 157–65.

94. See ibid., 162; chapter 8, notes 9–10, 12–18.

95. See *Fields v. State*, 156–61.

96. See ibid., 162–65, 164, 165; see, on Hall's opinion, chapter 8, note 18.

97. See *Nelson v. State*, 29 Tenn. (10 Hum.) 518, 1850 WL 2022, *6 (1850); *Jacob v. State*, 22 Tenn. (3 Hum.) 493, 1842 WL 1984. *16–*18 (1842). On Turley and Green as leading Tennessee jurists, see M. Keith Siskin, "Green, Nathan, Sr.," in *Great American Judges: An Encyclopedia*, ed. John R. Vile (Santa Barbara, Calif.: ABC-CLIO, 2003), 1:304–10; Joshua W. Caldwell, *Sketches of the Bench and Bar of Tennessee* (Knoxville: Ogden Brothers, 1898), 136–44, 150–52.

98. See Kevin T. Barksdale, *The Lost State of Franklin: America's First Secession* (Lexington: University Press of Kentucky, 2009), 176–83; Dunn, *Abolitionist in the Appalachian South*, 22, 48–56; Theodore Brown, Jr., "The Formative Period in the History of the Supreme Court of Tennessee, 1796–1835," in *A History of the Tennessee Supreme Court*, ed. James W. Ely, Jr. (Knoxville: University of Tennessee Press, 2002), 19, 30, 35. For another view of the *Fields* decision as a case in which judges were willing "to allow abstract principles of justice to override clearly applicable, though inhumane, statutory provisions," see A. E. Keir Nash, "Reason of Slavery: Understanding the Judicial Role in the Peculiar Institution," *Vanderbilt Law Review* 32, no. 1 (January 1979): 168–69, 168n568.

99. See Harry H. Johnston, *The Negro in the New World* (New York: MacMillan, 1910), 372; see also Charles Ball, *Slavery in the United States: A Narrative of the Life and Adventures of Charles Ball, A Black Man* (New York: John S. Taylor, 1837), viii–x.

100. *James v. Carper*, 36 Tenn. (4 Sneed) 397, 1857 WL 2493 (1857).

101. See *James v. Carper*, 1857 WL 2493, *1.

102. Ibid. *3.

103. Ibid., *4.

104. See Flanigan, *Criminal Law of Slavery and Freedom*, 171; see also *Wentworth v. McDuffie*, 48 N.H. 402, 1869 WL 2774 (1869) (horse owner's suit against hirer of a horse that died because of immoderate and violent driving). For views of *James*, see, e.g., Fede, *Roadblocks to Freedom*, ix–x; Jonathan D. Martin, *Divided Mastery: Slave Hiring in the American South* (Cambridge, Mass.: Harvard University Press, 2004), 121–23; Robert Westley, "Restitution Claims for Wrongful Enslavement and the Doctrine of the Master's Good Faith," *British Journal of American Legal Studies* 3, no. 2 (Fall 2014): 289–90; Note, "What We Talk about When We Talk about Persons: The Language of a Legal Fiction," *Harvard Law Review* 114, no. 6 (April 2001): 1749n21.

105. *Kirkwood v. Miller*, 37 Tenn. (5 Sneed) 455 (1858).

106. See ibid., 456–59.

107. See ibid., 459–60.

108. See *Polk, Wilson & Co. v. Fancher*, 38 Tenn. (1 Head) 336 (1858), referring to *Wort v. Jenkins*, 14 Johns. 352, 1817 N.Y. LEXIS 89 (N.Y. Sup. Ct. 1817).

109. See Fede, *People without Rights*, 70–72, 100–101, 242.

CHAPTER 10. South Carolina Joins the Homicide Law Reform Trend

1. See Clayton E. Jewett and John O. Allen, *Slavery in the South: A State-by-State History* (Westport, Conn.: Greenwood, 2004), 206, 258; Peter Kolchin, *American Slavery 1619–1877*, rev. ed. (New York: Hill & Wang, 2003), 254; Stephanie McCurry, *Masters of Small Worlds: Yeoman Households, Gender Relations, and the Political Culture of the Antebellum South Carolina Low Country* (New York: Oxford University Press, 1995), 33. On legal inertia, see Richard L. Abel, "Law as Lag: Inertia as a Social Theory of Law," *Michigan Law Review* 80, no. 4 (March 1982): 802–3.

2. See McCurry, *Masters of Small Worlds*, 33, 44.

3. See W. S. Rossiter, *A Century of Population Growth: From the First to the Twelfth Census of the United States: 1790–1900* (Washington, D.C.: Government Printing Office, 1909; repr., Baltimore: Genealogical Publishing, 1969), 135–36.

4. See Jewett and Allen, *Slavery in the South*, 206–7; Steven Deyle, *Carry Me Back: The Domestic Slave Trade in American Life* (New York: Oxford University Press, 2005), 44, 296; Richard Tadman, *Speculators and Slaves: Masters, Traders, and Slaves in the Old South* (Madison: University of Wisconsin Press, 1989), 12.

5. See McCurry, *Masters of Small Worlds*, 33–36, 44–45, 35; see also Matthew Mulcahy, *Hubs of Empire: The Southeastern Lowcountry and British Caribbean*, Regional Perspectives in Early America (Baltimore: Johns Hopkins University Press, 2014), 210–11; Rachel N. Klein, *Unification of a Slave State: The Rise of the Planter Class in the South Carolina Backcountry, 1760–1808* (Chapel Hill: University of North Carolina Press, 1990), 14–15, 150–52, 238–68; Orville Vernon Burton, *In My Father's House Are Many Mansions: Family and Community in Edgefield, South Carolina* (Chapel Hill: University of North Carolina Press, 1985), 15–46.

6. See *State v. Bowen*, 34 S.C.L. (3 Strob.) 573, 1849 WL 2687 *2 (Court of Appeals, Law 1849); John Belton O'Neall, *Negro Law of South Carolina Collected and Digested by John Belton O'Neall* (Columbia: John G. Bowman, 1848), 30.

7. *State v. Gee*, 1 S.C.L. (1 Bay) 163, 1791 WL 207 (S.C. Com. Pl. Gen. Sess. 1791).

8. Ibid., 163.

9. Ibid., 164–65, 164.

10. See *State v. Welch*, 1 S.C.L. (1 Bay) 172 (S.C. Com. Pl. Gen Sess. 1791).

11. See "Charge Delivered by the Honourable Judge Wilds of South-Carolina," *American Law Journal* 1 (1808): 67; see also Warren Moise, *Rebellion in the Temple of Justice: The Federal and State Courts in South Carolina during the War between the States* (Lincoln, Neb.: iUniverse, 2004), 85; Elizabeth Dale, "Getting Away with Murder," *American Historical Review* 111, no. 1 (February 2006): 96.

12. "Charge Delivered by the Honourable Judge Wilds," 68; see, e.g., *New York Spectator*, February 26, 1806, 2; Edwin Anderson Alderman et al., eds., *Library of Southern*

Literature (Atlanta: Martin & Hoyt, 1907–13), 16:121–22; George Armstrong Wauchope, ed., *The Writers of South Carolina with a Critical Introduction, Biographical Sketches, and Selections in Prose and Verse* (Columbia, S.C.: State Co., 1919), 403–6; John Belton O'Neall, *Biographical Sketches of the Bench and Bar of South Carolina* (Charleston: S.G. Courtenay, 1859), 1:102–5; Harriet Beecher Stowe, *The Key to Uncle Tom's Cabin* (Boston: John P. Jewett, 1853; repr., New York: Arno Press, 1968), 189–91.

13. See O'Neall, *Biographical Sketches*, 1:104; Dale, "Getting Away with Murder," 97. O'Neall calculated the maximum fine of 700 pounds currency, 100 pounds sterling, to be $128.57. O'Neall, *Biographical Sketches*, 1:104, note *.

14. See *Charleston Courier*, August 19, 1807, 3. On maritime slavery, see David S. Ceclski, *The Waterman's Song: Slavery and Freedom in Maritime North Carolina* (Chapel Hill: University of North Carolina Press, 2001); Bernard E. Powers, Jr., *Black Charlestonians: A Social History 1822–1885* (Fayetteville: University of Arkansas Press, 1994), 10–11; Philip D. Morgan, *Slave Counterpoint: Black Culture in the Eighteenth-Century Chesapeake and Lowcountry* (Chapel Hill: University of North Carolina Press, 1998), 236–44.

15. See *Charleston Courier*, January 28, 1806, 2.

16. See Howell Meadoes Henry, *The Police Control of the Slave in South Carolina* (Emory, 1914; repr., New York: Negro Universities Press, 1968), 67.

17. See *The State v. Samuel Nettles* (For Burning a Negro), November 1806, Kershaw County Court of General Sessions, Indictments, L28176, box 11, South Carolina Department of Archives and History, Columbia, South Carolina (SCDAH).

18. See *Fitch v. State*, 11 S.C.L. (2 Nott & McC.) 558 (Const. Ct, of App. 1820). The South Carolina courts later held that the criminal common law offense of simple assault and battery could not be committed against slaves. See *State v. Maner*, 20 S.C.L. (2 Hill) 453 (Ct. App. Law & Equity 1834) (affirming conviction of assault with intent to murder); Fede, *People without Rights*, 102–3.

19. See *Charleston Times*, December 8, 1807, 2; *Charleston Courier*, December 3, 1806, 3; Henry, *Police Control of the Slave*, 67.

20. See Laura F. Edwards, *The People and Their Peace: Legal Culture and the Transformation of Inequality in the Post-Revolutionary South* (Chapel Hill: University of North Carolina Press, 2009), 355n42.

21. See *The State v. Davis Cooper* (Murder of a Negro), April 1808, Kershaw County Court of General Sessions, Indictments, L28176, SCDAH; Klein, *Unification of a Slave State*, 292–93. On John Kershaw, see "Kershaw, John (1756–1829)," in *Biographical Directory of the United States Congress*, accessed June 17, 2016, http://bioguide.congress.gov/scripts/biodisplay.pl?index=K000149. On his father Joseph Kershaw, for whom the district was named, see Klein, *Unification of a Slave State*, 31–37.

22. See Merton L. Dillon, *Slavery Attacked: Southern Slaves and Their Allies, 1619–1865* (Baton Rouge: Louisiana State University Press, 1990), 196; Klein, *Unification of a Slave State*, 292–93; Henry, *Police Control of the Slave*, 67.

23. See *Carolina Gazette* (Charleston), June 15, 1810, 4.

24. See *Charleston City Gazette and Commercial Daily Advertiser*, November 10, 1810, 2.

25. See Jack K. Williams, *Dueling in the Old South: Vignettes of Social History* (College Station: Texas A&M University Press, 1980), 66; Yates Snowden, ed., *History of South Carolina* (New York: Lewis, 1921), 1:553, 555; "Legislature of South-Carolina," *Charleston City Gazette and Commercial Daily Advertiser*, December 12, 1812, 3; "To the Editor," *Charleston City Gazette and Commercial Daily Advertiser*, November 30, 1812, 2; "A Devil Incarnate!," *New York Journal*, January 23, 1811, 3; "House of Representatives," *Charleston City Gazette and Commercial Daily Advertiser*, December 13, 1810, 2; see also Matthew A. Byron, "Thou Shall Not Duel: Some Observations regarding the Impotency of Dueling Laws in South Carolina," *Proceedings of the South Carolina Historical Association* (2013): 33.

26. See Henry, *Police Control of the Slave*, 67–68.

27. See ibid., 68.

28. See Dillon, *Slavery Attacked*, 196; Bertram Wyatt-Brown, "Barn Burning and Other Snopesian Crimes: Class and Justice in the Old South," in *Class, Conflict and Consensus: Antebellum Southern Community Studies*, ed. Orville Vernon Burton and Robert C. McMath (Westport, Conn.: Greenwood, 1982), 187; see also Michael Stephen Hindus, *Prison and Plantation: Crime, Justice, and Authority in Massachusetts and South Carolina, 1767–1878* (Chapel Hill: University of North Carolina Press, 1980), 132n8; Jack Kenny Williams, *Vogues in Villainy: Crime and Retribution in Ante-Bellum South Carolina* (Columbia: University of South Carolina Press, 1959), 43.

29. See *The State v. John Havis* (Murder of a Slave), November 1819, Kershaw County Court of General Sessions, Indictments, L28176, box 7, SCDAH; *The State v. John Havis* (Assault and Battery), April 1817, Kershaw County Court of General Sessions, Indictments, L28176, box 7, SCDAH; *Acts and Resolutions of the General Assembly of the State of South-Carolina Passed in December, 1815* (Columbia: D. & J. Faust, State Printers, 1816), 133; "United States Census, 1820," database with images, *Family Search*, accessed June 17, 2016, https://familysearch.prg/pal:/MM9.3.1/TH-1951-25137=21641-88?cc=1803955, July 14, 2015, image 17 of 30, citing NARA microfilm publication M33 (Washington, D.C.: National Archives and Records Administration); accessed June 25, 2016, https://familysearch.org/ark:/61903/3:1:33S7-9YYY-53Y?i=16&wc=3L7F-46M%3A1586984803%2C1586986333%2C1586985320%3Fcc%3D1803955&cc=1803955; "United States Census, 1810," database with images, *Family Search*, image 25 of 35, accessed June 25, 2016, https://familysearch.org/ark:/61903/3:1:33SQ-GYBQ-9282?i=24&wc=QZZZ-MP3%3A1588180002%2C1588181626%2C1588179902%3Fcc%3D1803765&cc=1803765; Edwards, *People and Their Peace*, 196, 355n42.

30. See Edwards, *People and Their Peace*, 356n44.

31. See Henry, *Police Control of the Slave*, 68.

32. See "Message no. 1, from His Excellency the Governor of the State of South Carolina, Delivered to the Legislature, the 27th November, 1820," *Charleston City Gazette and Commercial Daily Advertiser*, December 2, 1820, 2; Henry, *Police Control of the Slave*, 68; Ryan A. Quintana, "Planners, Planters, and Slaves: Producing the State in Early National South Carolina," *Journal of Southern History* 81, no. 1 (February 2015): 100; see also "Geddes, John," in *The Encyclopedia of South Carolina* (St. Clair Shores, Mich.: Somerset, 2000), 1:93–94.

33. See "An Act to Restrain the Emancipation of Slaves, and to Prevent Free Persons of Color from Entering into This State; and for Other Purposes," in *Statutes at Large of South Carolina*, ed. David J. McCord (Columbia: A. S. Johnston, 1840), 7:459–60; see also Andrew Fede, *Roadblocks to Freedom: Slavery and Manumission in the United States South* (New Orleans: Quid Pro Books, 2011), 98; "From Columbia," *Charleston Courier*, December 23, 1820, 2.

34. See "Horrid Murder!" *Washington (Pa.) Reporter*, March 26, 1821, 2.

35. See Michael P. Johnson, "Denmark Vesey and His Co-conspirators," *William and Mary Quarterly*, 3rd ser., 58, no. 4 (October 2001): 966. On Beccaria, see Cesare Beccaria, *On Crimes and Punishments*, trans. Henry Paolucci (1764; New York: Bobbs-Merrill, 1963), 45–52, 74–75; see also John D. Bessler, *The Birth of American Law: An Italian Philosopher and the American Revolution* (Durham, N.C.: Carolina Academic Press, 2014); Marcello Maestro, *Cesare Beccaria and the Origins of Penal Reform* (Philadelphia: Temple University Press, 1973).

36. See Williams, *Dueling in the Old South*, 555; see also "Legislature of South-Carolina," *Charleston City Gazette and Commercial Advertiser*, December 11, 1821, 2.

37. "An Act to Increase the Punishment Inflicted on Persons Convicted of Murdering Any Slave; and for Other Purposes Stated Therein Mentioned," in *Statutes at Large of South Carolina*, ed. David J. McCord (Columbia: A. S. Johnston, 1839), 6:158; *Carolina Gazette* (Charleston), January 5, 1822, 1.

38. See Henry, *Police Control of the Slave*, 68; Edward McCrady, "Slavery in the Province of South Carolina, 1670–1770," in *The Annual Report of the American Historical Association* (Washington, D.C.: Government Printing Office, 1896), 658.

39. *State v. Taylor*, 13 S.C.L. (2 McCord) 483, 1823 WL 811 (Const. Ct. App. 1823).

40. *State v. Taylor*, 1823 WL 811, *1.

41. See Quintana, "Planters, Planters, and Slaves," 96–101, 96–97, quoting William J. Novak, *The People's Welfare: Law and Regulation in Nineteenth Century America*, Studies in Legal History (Chapel Hill: University of North Carolina Press, 1996), 2.

42. See Henry, *Police Control of the Slave*, 108.

43. See Andrew Fede, *People without Rights: An Interpretation of the Fundamentals of the Law of Slavery in the U.S. South* (New York: Garland, 1992; repr., New York: Routledge, 2011), 68, quoting Douglas Hay, "Property, Authority and the Criminal Law," in *Albion's Fatal Tree: Crime and Society in Eighteenth-Century England*, ed. Douglas Hay et al. (London: Allen Lane, 1975), 25; see also E. P. Thompson, *Whigs and Hunters: The Origins of the Black Act* (London: Allen Lane, 1975), 258–69.

44. See *White v. Chambers*, 2 S.C.L. (2 Bay) 70, 1796 WL 552, *1 (Const. Ct. App. 1796).

45. *White v. Chambers*, 1796 WL 552, *3.

46. *Arthur v. Wells*, 9 S.C.L. (2 Mill Const.) 313, 1818 WL 796 (Const. Ct. App. 1818).

47. See *Arthur v. Wells*, 1818 WL 796, *1.

48. Ibid., *2.

49. *Witsell v. Earnest*, 10 S.C.L. (1 Nott & McC.) 182, 1818 WL 851 (Const. Ct. App. 1818).

50. See *Witsell v. Earnest*, 1818 WL 851, *1.

51. See O'Neall, *Biographical Sketches*, 1:125–28.

52. See *State v. Motley*, 41 S.C.L. (7 Rich.) 327 (Ct. App. Law 1854) (affirming murder convictions of Thomas Motley and William Blackledge); Wyatt Espy and John Ortiz Smykla, "Executions in the U.S. 1608–2002: The Espy File Executions by State," 309, Death Penalty Information Center, accessed March 10, 2015, http://www.deathpenaltyinfo.org/documents/ESPYstate.pdf (listing Motley and Blackledge among those executed in 1854); "Sentence of the Slave Murderers," *Boston Recorder*, February 2, 1854, 18 (discussing Judge O'Neall's comments while sentencing Motley and Blackledge to death); see also, e.g., *State v. Smith*, 33 S.C.L. (2 Strob.) 77 (Ct. App. Law 1847) (affirming murder conviction for shooting a young enslaved boy); *Richardson v. Dukes*, 15 S.C.L. (4 McCord) 156 (Ct. App. L. & Eq. 1827) (reversing one dollar judgment as inadequate compensation for owner whose slave, while stealing potatoes from the defendant's property, was shot and killed by defendant); *State v. Cole*, 13 S.C.L. (2 McCord) 117 (Const. Ct. App. 1822) (affirming riot convictions of defendants who allegedly as patrollers whipped William Cattell's female slave, were abusive to Cattell, and killed Cattell's dogs); *Hogg v. Keller*, 11 S.C.L. (2 Nott & McC.) 113 (Const. Ct. App. 1819) (reversing judgment for defendant Keller in civil suit by Hogg, whose slave was whipped by defendants who allegedly were in a slave patrol).

53. *State v. Cheatwood*, 20 S.C.L. (2 Hill) 459, 1834 WL 1530 (Ct. App. L. & Eq. 1834).

54. See G. W. Featherstonhaugh, *Excursion through the Slave States* (London: John Murray, 1844), 2: 346–47; see also Fede, *People without Rights*, 76–77; Hindus, *Prison and Plantation*, 134–35; Henry, *Police Control of the Slave*, 70; Wyatt-Brown, "Barn Burning and Other Snopesian Crimes," 199; *State v. Pemberton*, 13 N.C. (2 Dev.) 281 (1829) (affirming decision granting arrest of judgment after defendants' conviction on common law indictment for playing cards with slaves).

55. See *State v. Cheatwood*, 1834 WL 1530, *2; see also *State v State v. Harden*, 29 S.C.L. (2 Speers) 152 (Ct. App. Law 1832).

56. See Fede, *Roadblocks to Freedom*, 13–19; Fede, *People without Rights*, 68–69, 210–14.

57. See John Jonah Murrell et al., Christ Church Parish, to South Carolina House, 1829, in *The Southern Debate over Slavery, Volume I, Petitions to Southern Legislatures, 1778–1864*, ed. Loren Schweninger (Urbana: University of Illinois Press, 2001), 105–9; see also John Hope Franklin and Loren Schweninger, *Runaway Slaves: Rebels on the Plantation* (New York: Oxford University Press, 1999), 152, 305–9.

58. See *State v. Taylor*, 13 S.C.L. (2 McCord), 491–93.

59. *State v. Raines*, 14 S.C.L. (3 McCord) 533, 1826 WL 710 (S.C. App. 1826).

60. See ibid., at *1–*6.

61. Ibid., *8; see *State v. Cheatwood*, 20 S.C.L. (2 Hill) 459, 1834 WL 1530, *4 (S.C. App. 1826); see also "The State v. Eliza C. Rowand," *Charleston Currier*, May 14, 1847, 2 (quoting Judge O'Neall's jury charge referring to a trial court ruling in "O'Hearn's" case before the *Raines* decision).

62. See *State v. Raines*, 1826 WL 710, *6–*8; Fede, *People without Rights*, 70, 91n34.

63. *State v. Fleming*, 33 S.C.L. (2 Strob.) 464, 1848 WL 2457 (S.C. App. of Law 1848).

64. See *State v. Fleming*, 1848 WL 2457, *1–*4. Judge Evans was both the trial judge and an appellate judge in this case according to the practice often evidenced in ante-

bellum South Carolina appeals. The legislature in 1824 created the state's first Court of Appeals, which was made up of three appellate judges. But the legislature abolished this court in 1835 and in 1836 created Courts of Appeal for law and equity made up of the trial court judges who often wrote appellate decisions affirming their own trial court rulings. In 1859 the legislature again created a Court of Appeals with three appellate judges. See Jasper M. Cureton, "Coming of Age: The South Carolina Court of Appeals" (South Carolina Judicial Department, South Carolina Court of Appeals), accessed October 17, 2016, http://www.judicial.state.sc.us/appeals/history.cfm.

65. See *State v. Montgomery*, 25 S.C.L. (Chev.) 120, 1840 WL 1998 (S.C. Ct. of App. of Law 1840); 1850 Census, St. Michael and St. Phillip, Charleston, South Carolina, roll: M432_850, p. 286B, image 413, accessed June 24, 2015, http://search.ancestry.com; 1840 Census, Place, Charleston, South Carolina, roll 509, p. 82, image 768, Family History Library Film 0022508, accessed June 24, 2015, http://search.ancestry.com; James W. Gibbs, *Dixie Clockmakers* (Gretna, La.: Pelican, 1979), 149.

66. See *Edgefield (S.C.) Advertiser*, November 5, 1845, 4.

67. See Burton, *In My Father's House*, 6, 13–17, 145, 336n10, 379n120.

68. See *State v. Harden*, 31 S.C.L. (2 Rich.) 533, 1846 WL 2237 (Ct. App. of Law 1846); *New Orleans Times-Picayune*, March 28, 1846, 1; *Southern Patriot* (Charleston), March 13, 1846, 2.

69. See "Trial of Russell Harden for Murdering One of His Slaves," *National Police Gazette* (New York), November 7, 1846, 3; "Trial of Russel Harden," *Edgefield (S.C.) Advertiser*, October 21, 1846, 2; see also *Edgefield (S.C.) Advertiser*, February 17, 1847, 3; *Edgefield (S.C.) Advertiser*, February 10, 1847, 3. On Butler, see "Butler, Andrew Pickens (1796–1857)," in *Biographical Directory of the United States Congress*, accessed April 30, 2015, http://bioguide.congress.gov/scripts/biodisplay.pl?index=b001173.

70. See the introduction, notes 1–25.

71. See *State v. Posey*, 35 S.C.L. (4 Strob.) 142 (Ct. of App. of Law 1849) (affirming conviction for Appling's murder); *State v. Posey*, 35 S.C.L. (4 Strob.) 103 (Ct. App. of Law 1849) (affirming conviction as accessory to Matilda's murder by Appling); Dale, "Getting Away with Murder," 97; Elizabeth Dale, "A Different Sort of Justice: The Informal Courts of Public Opinion in Antebellum South Carolina," *South Carolina Law Review* 54 (Spring 2003): 634–37; John Wertheimer, et al., "*State v. Posey*: Criminal Bargains between the Enslaved and Their Enslavers in Antebellum South Carolina" (unpublished manuscript, 2016). On divorce, see Loren Schweninger, *Families in Crisis in the Old South: Divorce, Slavery, and the Law* (Chapel Hill: University of North Carolina Press, 2012), 11; McCurry, *Masters of Small Worlds*, 86–91; Janet Hudson, "From Constitution to Constitution, 1868–1895: South Carolina's Unique Stance on Divorce," *South Carolina Historical Magazine* 98, no. 1 (January 1997): 75.

72. See *State v. Posey*, 35 S.C.L. (4 Strob.), 103–5.

73. See *State v. Sims*, 18 S.C.L. (2 Bail.) 29, 31 (S.C. Ct. of App. of Law and Equity 1831).

74. See *State v. Posey*, 35 S.C.L. (4 Strob.), 103–21.

75. *State v. Posey*, 35 S.C.L. (4 Strob.), 142–66.

76. See *State v. Posey*, 35 S.C.L. (4 Strob.), 166–67; *State v. Posey*, 35 S.C.L. (4 Strob.), 121–41.

77. See *State v. Posey*, 35 S.C.L. (4 Strob.), 128–48, note *.

78. See *State v. Crank*, 18 S.C.L. 92 Bail.), 69–77; *State v. Simmons*, 3 S.C.L. (1 Brev.) 6 (Const. Ct. of App. 1794); Fede, *People without Rights*, 192.

79. See Coroner's Verdict, SCDAH, State vs. L.A. Stubbs, Marlboro County, Court of General Sessions, Indictment 1852 #485, L 35182, box 1.

80. Henry, *Police Control of the Slave*, 70.

81. Thomas D. Russell, "Slave Auctions on the Courthouse Steps: Court Sales of Slaves in Antebellum South Carolina," in *Slavery and the Law*, ed. Paul Finkelman (Lanham, Md.: Rowman & Littlefield, 1997), 336.

82. See Manisha Sinha, *The Counterrevolution of Slavery: Politics and Ideology in Antebellum South Carolina* (Chapel Hill: University of North Carolina Press, 2000), 44; Russell, "Slave Auctions," 336–37; Stephen B. Weeks, *Southern Quakers and Slavery: A Study in Institutional History* (Baltimore: Johns Hopkins University Press, 1896), 266–87; W. Scott Poole, "'Your Liberty in That Province': South Carolina Quakers and the Rejection of Religious Toleration," in *The Dawn of Religious Freedom in South Carolina*, ed. James Lowell Underwood and W. Lewis Burke (Columbia: University of South Carolina Press, 2006), 165; William A. Schaper, "Sectionalism and Representation in South Carolina," in *Annual Report of the American Historical Association for the Year 1900* (Washington, D.C.: Government Printing Office, 1901), 393; J. D. Lewis, South Carolina Home, South Carolina—The Counties, Marlboro County, South Carolina, accessed December 29, 2012, http://www.carolana.com/SC/Counties/marlboro_county_sc.html.

83. See Leonardo Andrea and Joseph Edward Hill, *Abstracts of Divisions of Estates of Stubbs and Allied Families of Marlboro County South Carolina* (1964), 1–4; J. A. W. Thomas, *A History of Marlboro County, with Sketches of Numerous Families* (Atlanta: Foote & Davis, 1897), 184; *Lamb v. Lamb*, 17 S.C. Eq. (Speers Eq.) 289, 1843 WL 2561 (S.C. App. Eq. 1843).

84. See Andrea and Hill, *Abstracts of Divisions of Estates of Stubbs*, 143–44, 146–47, 163; Lynn Steen, "1820 Census Marlborough District," accessed January 5, 2013, http://sciway3.net/proctor/marlboro/census/1820/12.html; Will of Thomas Stubbs, April 6, 1847, recorded June 21, 1847, in will book A, p. 258, case 1, box 27, accessed January 2, 2013, http://sciway3.net/proctor/marlboro/wills/StubbsThomas.html. On the Battle of New Orleans, of which the press became aware after February 4, 1815, see Alan Taylor, *The Civil War of 1812: American Citizens, British Subjects, and Indian Allies* (New York: Vintage, 2010), 420–21; Robert V. Remini, *The Battle of New Orleans: Andrew Jackson and America's First Military Victory* (New York: Penguin, 1999), 191–93. On marriage between first cousins, see, e.g., William Kaufman Scarborough, *Masters of the Big House: Elite Slaveholders of the Mid-Nineteenth Century South* (Baton Rouge: Louisiana State University Press, 2003), 25–26.

85. See Lynn Steen, "1840 Census Marlborough District," accessed December 9, 2012, http://sciway3.net/proctor/marlboro/census/1840/21.html.

86. See Andrea and Hill, *Abstracts of Divisions of Estates of Stubbs*, 146–47; "United States Census, 1850," index and images, L.A.J. Stubbs in household of L A J Stubbs, Marlboro County, Marlboro, South Carolina, United States, citing dwelling 499, family 499, NARA microfilm publication M432, roll 856, accessed December 8, 2012, https://familysearch.org/pal:/MM9.1.1/M8QV-5MP.

87. See Stubbs, Lewis, Sr. of Marlboro District Will Typescript (MSS Will: Will Book A, p. 238, Estate Packet: Apt 26, Pkg. 12), accessed December 31, 2012, http://www.archivesindex.sc.gov/onlinearchives/ViewImage.aspx?imageNumber=S1080930018003260000a.jpg&recordId=303111. L. A. J. Stubbs's brother Thomas J. Stubbs died a single man in 1843. See Andrea and Hill, *Abstracts of Divisions of Estates of Stubbs*, 163.

88. See "United States Census (Slave Schedule), 1850," index and images, *Family Search*, L.A.J. Stubbs, Marlboro County, Marlboro, South Carolina, citing NARA microfilm publication M432, accessed December 8, 2012, https://familysearch.org/pal:/MM9.1.1/MV8M-SBJ; Will of Mary A. Crosland, recorded in Will Book A, p. 219, recorded June 14, 1841, case 1, box 24, accessed December 18, 2012, http://sciway3.net/proctor/Marlboro/wills/CroslandMary.html; "Mary Ann (Sparks) Crosland (1785–1841) and Her Descendants," August 4, 2003, accessed December 28, 2012, http://www.sparksfamilyassn.org/pages/136-F.html; Andrea and Hill, *Abstracts of Divisions of Estates of Stubbs*, 148.

89. See Thomas, *History of Marlboro County*, 23, 29, 44, 176, 276, 44; Indictment, SCDAH, State vs. L.A. Stubbs, Marlboro County, Court of General Sessions, Indictment 1852 #485, L 35182, box 1; see also *State v. McIver*, 2 S.C. (2 Rich.) 25, 25–26 (1870); Lynn Steen, "1850 Census Marlborough County," accessed January 5, 2013, http://sciway3.net/proctor/marlboro/census/1850/011.html; "Charles Pinckney Townsend," accessed December 30, 2012, http://members.valley.net/~townsend?CPTAautobiography.html. Meekin was a chairman of the District's Board of Commissioners and was involved in the construction of a new court house that opened in 1852. Thomas, *History of Marlboro County*, 168.

90. See Coroner's Verdict, SCDAH, State vs. L.A.J. Stubbs, Marlboro County, Court of General Sessions, Indictment 1852 #485, L 35182, box 1; Thomas, *History of Marlboro County*, 168.

91. See Thomas, *History of Marlboro County*, 157–58; Indictment, SCDAH, State vs. L. A. Stubbs, Marlboro County, Court of General Sessions, Indictment 1852 #485, L 35182, box 1; see also Lynn Steen, "1850 Census Marlborough County," accessed January 5, 2013, http://sciway3.net/proctor/marlboro/census/1850/005.html; Lynn Steen, "1840 Census Marlborough County," accessed January 5, 2013, http://sciway3.net/proctor/marlboro/census/1840/14.html.

92. See *St. Louis Daily Missouri Republican*, January 31, 1853, 1; *Boston Courier*, January 24, 1853, 2; *New Orleans Times-Picayune*, January 22, 1853, 1; *Alexandria (Va.) Gazette*, January 22, 1853, 2; *Newark Daily Advertiser*, January 18, 1853, 2; *Charleston Currier*, January 15, 1853, 1; *Daily Placer Times and Transcript* (San Francisco), December 16, 1852, 3; *Charleston Currier*, October 29, 1852, 1; *New Orleans Times-Picayune*, October 29, 1852, 2; *Baltimore Sun*, October 26, 1852, 1; see also Thomas D. Morris, *Southern Slavery and the Law, 1619–1860* (Chapel Hill: University of North Carolina Press, 1996), 180; Hindus, *Prison and Plantation*, 134; Michael L. Radelet, "Executions of Whites for Crimes Against Backs: Exceptions to the Rule?," *Sociological Quarterly* 30, no. 4 (Winter 1989): 534, 538; "Executions in the U.S. 1608–2002: The Espy File Executions by State," 309, Death Penalty Information Center, accessed March 10, 2015, http://www.deathpenaltyinfo.org/documents/ESPYstate.pdf. In 1913, H. M. Henry wrote, "Though

the records are silent, it is the recollection of elderly persons of the community still living that [Lewis] was duly executed for the crime." Henry, *Police Control of the Slave*, 70. I referred to Henry's statement and concluded that this execution was not established. See Fede, *People without Rights*, 81. I am now convinced that Stubbs was executed. Judge O'Neall's 1853 letter stated that "in the past winter a master was hanged in Bennetsville, Marlborough District, S.C." See "Slave Laws—Letter from Justice O'Neal," *New York Daily Tribune*, August 15, 1853, 6.

93. See Jonathan Kennon Thompson Smith, "Death Notices from the *Christian Advocate*, Nashville, Tennessee 1880–1882 (of Those Persons Born up to and Including the Year 1830)," September 9, 1882 (2000), accessed December 28, 2012, http://www.tngenweb.org/records/tn_wide/obits/nca/nca7-07.htm; see also Lulu Crosland Ricaud, *The Family of Edward and Ann Snead Crosland, 1740–1957* (Columbia: State Commercial Printing, 1958), 126; Carroll County Tennessee and History, Slave Transactions, Deed Book K, p. 670, accessed December 31, 2012, http://genealogytrails.com/tenn/carroll/deedslavejk.html.

94. See *St. Louis Daily Missouri Republican*, January 31, 1853, 1; *New Orleans Times-Picayune*, January 22, 1853, 1.

95. See William A. McInnis, Marlboro SC 1860 Slave Schedule Census (2001), accessed January 6, 2013, http://files.usgwarchives.net/sc/marlboro/census/1860/slvo371a.txt, http://files.usgwarchives.net/sc/marlboro/census/1860/slvo344b.txt, http://files.usgwarchives.net/sc/marlboro/census/1860/slvo366b.txt.

96. On brother and brother-in-law rivalry and violence in the antebellum South, see Bertram Wyatt-Brown, *Southern Honor: Ethics and Behavior in the Old South* (New York: Oxford University Press, 1982), 382.

97. See *State v. Bradley*, 43 S.C.L. (9 Rich.) 168, 168–69 (S.C. App. Law 1855).

98. See "Law Court of Appeals," *Charleston Courier*, December 13, 1855, 1; O'Neall, "Wilkes Thurlow Caston," in *Biographical Sketches*, 2:587–88.

99. *State v. Bradley*, 43 S.C.L. (9 Rich.) 168 (S.C. App. Law 1855).

100. See ibid., 169.

101. See Thomas Starkie, *A Practical Treatise on the Law of Evidence and Digest of Proofs in Civil and Criminal Proceedings*, 5th American ed., ed. Theron Metcalf et al. (Philadelphia: P.H. Nicklin and T. Johnson, 1834), 1:446.

102. See *State v. Bradley*, 168–69.

103. See ibid., 170–72; see also Hindus, *Prison and Plantation*, 134.

104. See *Charleston Mercury*, March 5, 1856, 3; *Charleston Courier*, March 4, 1856, 2; "News Summary," *Springfield (Mass.) Republican*, February 27, 1856, 1.

105. See *Charleston Courier*, May 31, 1858, 2; see also *Charleston Mercury*, June 2, 1858, 2. On Simons, see Bruce S. Allardice, *More Generals in Grey* (Baton Rouge: Louisiana State University Press, 1995), 209–10.

106. See *Charleston Courier*, June 2, 1858, 2.

107. See *Charleston Courier*, June 3, 1858, 2.

108. See *Charleston Mercury*, June 14, 1858, 2.

109. See *Charleston Mercury*, February 6, 1861, 2.

110. See *Charleston Courier*, February 16, 1861, 1.

111. See Theodore Rosengarten, *Tombee: Portrait of a Cotton Planter with Journal of Thomas B. Chaplin (1822–1890)* (New York: William Morrow, 1986), 456–58, 458; "Thomas B. Chaplin Sits on a Jury of Inquest," in *A Documentary History of Slavery in North America*, ed. Willie Lee Rose (New York: Oxford University Press, 1976), 210–12; see also Dea H. Boster, *African American Slavery and Disability: Bodies, Property, and Power in the Antebellum South, 1800–1860* (New York: Routledge, 2013), 67; David Grimsted, *American Mobbing, 1828–1861: Toward Civil War* (New York: Oxford University Press, 1998), 168–69; Wyatt-Brown, *Southern Honor*, 376.

112. See W. J. Megginson, *African American Life in South Carolina's Upper Piedmont, 1780–1900* (Columbia: University of South Carolina Press, 2006), 119, 453–54n24; see also *Hester v. Hagood*, 21 S.C.L. (3 Hill) 195, 1836 WL 1509 (S.C. App. L. 1836) (affirming nonsuit judgment against Hester).

113. See *State v. M'Kee*, 17 S.C.L. (1 Bail.) 651, 1830 WL 1354, *1 (Ct. App. Law & Eq. 1830).

114. See *Rowe v. State*, 2 S.C.L. (2 Bay) 565, 1804 WL 409 (S.C. Const. App. 1804).

115. See "A Notable Decision," *New Yorker* 6, no. 11 (December 1, 1838): 171; see also Hindus, *Prison and Plantation*, 134.

116. See Henry, *Police Control of the Slave*, 75.

117. See O'Neall, *Negro Law of South Carolina*, 20.

118. See "Slave Laws—Letter from Justice O'Neal [sic]," *New York Daily Tribune*, August 15, 1853, 6.

119. See Grand Jury Presentment, Fall Term 1853, C 372, Fairfield District, Court of General Sessions, L 20141, Journal 1840–63, pp. 56–58, November 1, 1853, SCDAH; Morris, *Southern Slavery and the Law*, 184.

120. See John Codman Hurd, *The Law of Freedom and Bondage in the United States* (1858 and 1862; repr., Boston: Little, Brown), 2:100; see also Fede, *People without Rights*, 127n82.

CHAPTER 11. The Antebellum States' Law on Slave Homicide

1. See, e.g., Sven Beckert, *Empire of Cotton: A Global History* (New York: Knopf, 2014), 100–122; Walter Johnson, *River of Dark Dreams: Slavery and Empire in the Cotton Kingdom* (Cambridge, Mass.: Belknap, 2013), 3–17; John Craig Hammond, *Slavery, Freedom, and Expansion in the Early American West* (Charlottesville: University of Virginia Press, 2007), 1–75; Adam Rothman, *Slave Country: American Expansion and the Origins of the Deep South* (Cambridge, Mass.: Harvard University Press, 2005), ix–xi, 34–35; John Craig Hammond, "Slavery, Settlement, and Empire: The Expansion and Growth of Slavery in the Interior of the North American Continent, 1770–1820," *Journal of the Early Republic* 32, no. 2 (Summer 2012): 175–206.

2. Edward E. Baptist, *The Half Has Never Been Told: Slavery and the Making of American Capitalism* (New York: Basic Books, 2014), xxi, 2–3, xxi; see W. S. Rossiter, *A Century of Population Growth: From the First to the Twelfth Census of the United States: 1790–1900* (Washington, D.C.: Government Printing Office, 1909; repr., Baltimore: Genealogical Publishing, 1969), 133.

3. See Wyatt Espy and John Ortiz Smykla, "Executions in the U.S. 1608–2002: The Espy File Executions by State," Death Penalty Information Center, accessed March 10, 2015, http://www.deathpenaltyinfo.org/documents/ESPYstate.pdf.

4. See Vernon Valentine Palmer, *Through the Codes Darkly: Slave Law and the Civil Law in Louisiana* (Clark, N.J.: Lawbook Exchange, 2012), 141–62; Thomas Ingersoll, *Mammon and Manon in Early New Orleans: The First Slave Society in the Deep South* (Knoxville: University of Tennessee Press, 1999), 134–39, 234–39, 321–26; Judith Kelleher Schafer, *Slavery, the Civil Law, and the Supreme Court of Louisiana* (Baton Rouge: Louisiana State University Press, 1994), 1–10; Hans W. Baade, "The Law of Slavery in Spanish Louisiana, 1769–1803," in *Louisiana Legal Heritage*, ed. Edward F. Haas (Pensacola: Perdido Bay Press for the Louisiana State Museum, 1983), 43–86; Vernon Valentine Palmer, "The Strange Science of Codifying Slavery—Moreau Lislet and the Louisiana Digest of 1808," *Tulane European & Civil Law Forum* 24 (2009): 83–113; Hans W. Baade, "The Bifurcated Romanist Tradition of Slavery in Louisiana," *Tulane Law Review* 70 (1996): 1481–99; Thomas Ingersoll, "Slave Codes and Judicial Practice in New Orleans, 1718–1897," *Law and History Review* 13, no. 1 (Spring 1995): 23–62; see also Shael Herman, "The Contributions of Roman Law to the Jurisprudence of Antebellum Louisiana," *Louisiana Law Review* 56 (1996): 257–315.

5. See Joe Gray Taylor, *Negro Slavery in Louisiana* (Baton Rouge: Louisiana Historical Association, 1963), 3–20, 21; see also Joe Gray Taylor, *Louisiana: A Bicentennial History* (New York: Norton, 1976), 57–86.

6. See Jenifer M. Spear, *Race, Sex, and Social Order in Early New Orleans* (Baltimore: Johns Hopkins University Press, 2009), 9, 53.

7. See Ingersoll, *Mammon and Manon in Early New Orleans*, xiii; see also Spear, *Race, Sex, and Social Order in Early New Orleans*, 225–26n18.

8. See Spear, *Race, Sex, and Social Order in Early New Orleans*, 19–20, 54–59; Clayton E. Jewett and John O. Allen, *Slavery in the South: A State-by-State History* (Westport, Conn.: Greenwood, 2004), 122–23; Peter Kolchin, *American Slavery 1619–1877*, rev. ed. (New York: Hill & Wang, 2003), 254, 256.

9. Spear, *Race, Sex, and Social Order in Early New Orleans*, 53.

10. See "Code Noir (1685) [sic] in Louisiana," in *Slavery: Oxford Readers*, ed. Stanley L. Engerman, Seymour Drescher, and Robert Paquette (New York: Oxford University Press, 2001), 116–17; see also Palmer, *Through the Codes Darkly*, 43–140; Spear, *Race, Sex, and Social Order in Early New Orleans*, 60–61; Ingersoll, *Mammon and Manon in Early New Orleans*, 234–39; Guillaume Aubert, "'To Establish One Law and Definite Rules': Race, Religion, and the Transatlantic Origins of the Louisiana Code Noir," in *Louisiana: Crossroads of the Atlantic World*, ed. Cecile Vidal (Philadelphia: University of Pennsylvania Press, 2014), 21–43; Ingersoll, "Slave Codes and Judicial Practice in New Orleans," 30–31; chapter 2.

11. See Thomas D. Morris, *Southern Slavery and the Law, 1619–1860* (Chapel Hill: University of North Carolina Press, 1996), 184.

12. "An Act Prescribing the Rules and Conduct to Be Observed with Respect to Negroes and Other Slaves in This Territory, Approved, June 7, 1806," in *A General Digest of the Acts of the Legislature of Louisiana*, ed. L. Moreau Lislet (New Orleans: Benjamin

Levy, 1828), 1:118, "Crimes and Offenses," §16; see Schafer, *Slavery, the Civil Law*, 28; Judith K. Schafer, "'Details Are of a Most Revolting Character': Cruelty to Slaves as Seen in Appeals to the Supreme Court of Louisiana," *Chicago-Kent Law Review* 68, no. 3 (1993): 1284–86.

13. See U. B. Phillips, ed., *The Statutes of the State of Louisiana* (New Orleans: Emile LaSere, 1855), 163; see also Schafer, *Slavery, the Civil Law*, 29.

14. "An Act Prescribing the Rules and Conduct to Be Observed with Respect to Negroes and Other Slaves in This Territory, Approved, June 7, 1806," in Moreau Lislet, *General Digest of the Acts*, 1:118, "Crimes and Offenses," §17; see Schafer, *Slavery, the Civil Law*, 30.

15. See *Civil Code of the State of Louisiana* (1825), 90–91; Schafer, *Slavery, the Civil Law*, 28. An 1856 law permitted courts and juries to order public auction sales of mistreated slaves when their masters were indicted for cruelty, "whether they convict or not." See Morris, *Southern Slavery and the Law*, 186. An 1830 Kentucky act also provided for the sale of slaves cruelly abused by masters. An 1860 Maryland act authorized the freeing of slaves after their masters' third slave abuse convictions. See ibid., 183.

16. See Spear, *Race, Sex, and Social Order in Early New Orleans*, 73; Frank R. Baumgartner and Tim Lyman, "Louisiana Death-Sentenced Cases and Their Reversals, 1976–2015," *Journal of Race, Gender, and Poverty* 7 (Spring 2016): 72–73; Frank R. Baumgartner and Tim Lyman, "Race-of-Victim Discrepancies in Homicides and Executions, Louisiana 1976–2015," *Journal of Public Interest Law* 17 (August 2015): 130n2, 138.

17. See Schafer, *Slavery, the Civil Law*, 31.

18. *State v. Morris*, 4 La. Ann. 177 (1849).

19. Schafer, *Slavery, the Civil Law*, 31–32; *State v. Morris*, 4 La. Ann., 177.

20. See *State v. Morris*, 4 La. Ann., 177; see also Schafer, *Slavery, the Civil Law*, 32.

21. See *State v. White*, 13 La. Ann. 573, 1858 WL 5211, *1 (1858); Schafer, *Slavery, the Civil Law*, 34. Augustus W. Walker also was unsuccessfully prosecuted for the harsh, cruel, inhuman, but not fatal mistreatment of slaves whom he purchased along with a plantation from Joseph S. Cucullu. This prosecution apparently was related to Walker's breach of warranty suit against Cucullu. See Ariela Gross, *Double Character: Slavery and Mastery in the Antebellum Southern Courtroom* (Princeton, N.J.: Princeton University Press, 2000), 106–9; Walter Johnson, *Soul by Soul: Life Inside the Antebellum Slave Market* (Cambridge, Mass.: Harvard University Press, 1999), 209. Schafer also noted that W. H. Davis was convicted for felonious assault on a slave, but his relationship to his victim was not stated. See *State v. Davis*, 14 La. Ann. 678 (1859); Schafer, *Slavery, the Civil Law*, 34–35.

22. See Edwin Adams Davis, ed., *Plantation Life in the Florida Parishes of Louisiana, 1836–1846, as Reflected in the Diary of Bennett H. Barrow* (New York: AMS Press, 1967), 148; see also Morris, *Southern Slavery and the Law*, 180. Barrow's comment is telling because his diary for the years 1840 to 1841 recorded 160 whippings of his 200 slaves—120 of whom were workers during this period. According to Fogel and Engerman, Barrow's slaves endured 0.07 whippings per hand per year. See Robert William Fogel and Stanley L. Engerman, *Time on the Cross: The Economics of American Negro Slavery* (New York: Little, Brown, 1974), 1:145. Gutman replied: "A slave—'on average'—was whipped

every 4.56 days. Three slaves were whipped every two weeks. Among these sixty (37.5 percent) were female." See Herbert G. Gutman, *Slavery and the Numbers Game: A Critique of "Time on the Cross"* (Urbana: University of Illinois Press, 1975), 19. And according to Gutman and Sutch, among the 120 slaves then working, there were 1.19 whippings per hand per year. See Herbert G. Gutman and Richard Sutch, "Sambo Makes Good, or Were Slaves Imbued with the Protestant Work Ethic?," in *Reckoning with Slavery: A Critical Study in the Quantitative History of American Negro Slavery*, ed. Paul A. David, Herbert G. Gutman, Richard Sutch, Peter Temin, and Gavin Wright (New York: Oxford University Press, 1976), 63; see also, e.g., James W. Clarke, *Race, Violent Crime, and American Culture: The Lineaments of Wrath* (New Brunswick, N.J.: Transaction, 1998), 26–29.

23. See "Most Atrocious Case," *New York Commercial Advertiser*, December 15, 1845, 1; see also "Murder of a Slave," *Baltimore Sun*, December 15, 1845, 4.

24. See "Cruelty," *Philadelphia Inquirer*, December 19, 1845, 2. On Preaux, see Caryn Cosse Bell, *Revolution, Romanticism, and the Afro-Creole Protest Tradition in Louisiana, 1718–1868* (Baton Rouge: Louisiana State University Press, 1997), 162–63.

25. See "Horrible Treatment and Murder of a Slave in New Orleans," *Philadelphia Inquirer*, November 30, 1854, 1.

26. See "Two Women Indicted for the Murder of a Slave in New Orleans," *Albany Evening Journal*, January 4, 1855, 2. On Robertson and Larue, see Judith Kelleher Schafer, "The Murder of a 'Lewd and Abandoned Woman': *State of Louisiana v. Abraham Parker*," *American Journal of Legal History* 44, no. 1 (January 2000): 24–25.

27. See "Trial of Two Women for Whipping a Slave to Death," *New York Times*, February 1, 1855, 6; see also Isaac E. Morse, *Annual Report of the Attorney General to the Legislature of the State of Louisiana, January 1855* (New Orleans: Emile La Sere, 1855), 17. On Bermudez, see *Biographical and Historical Memoirs of Louisiana* (Chicago: Goodspeed, 1892), 2:470–72; "Edward Bermudez," *KnowLA: Encyclopedia of Louisiana*, accessed May 3, 2015, http://www.knowla.org/entry/1446/; Ned Hemard, "The Lady and the Sword," *Nostalgia: Remembering New Orleans History, Culture, and Traditions*, accessed May 3, 2015, http://www.neworleansbar.org/uploads/files/The%20Lady%20with%20the%20Sword_6-11.pdf.

28. See *Sacramento Union-Supplement*, April 15, 1858, 2; "Horrible Cruelty and Murder," *Brooklyn Daily Eagle*, March 24, 1858, 2; "Shocking and Murderous Cruelty to a Slave Boy," *Daily True Delta* (New Orleans), March 16, 1858, suppl. 1; "Horrible Brutality and Murder," *New Orleans Times-Picayune*, March 15, 1858, 4.

29. See "Recorder Fabre's Court," *Daily True Delta* (New Orleans), March 20, 1858, 3.

30. See *Sacramento Union-Supplement*, August 17, 1858, 2; *St. Louis Daily Missouri Republican*, July 30, 1858, 2; *Lowell (Mass.) Daily Citizen and News*, July 22, 1858, 2; see also Taylor, *Negro Slavery in Louisiana*, 226.

31. See Schafer, *Slavery, the Civil Law*, 35–57; see also *Barrow v. McDonald*, 12 La. Ann. 110 (1857) (reversing civil judgment for plaintiff who claimed his partner intentionally killed a slave they jointly owned); *State v. Seaborne*, 8 Rob. 518, 1843 WL 3883 (La. 1843) (affirming manslaughter conviction).

32. See John Ray Skates, *Mississippi: A Bicentennial History* (New York: Norton, 1979), 22–78, 43; see generally John Hebron Moore, *The Emergence of the Cotton King-*

dom in the Old Southwest: Mississippi, 1770–1860 (Baton Rouge: Louisiana State University Press, 1988), 1–5; Sylvester John Hemleben and Richard T. Bennett, "Beginnings of the Legal Profession in Mississippi," *Mississippi Law Journal* 36 (1965): 159, 165.

33. See Jewett and Allen, *Slavery in the South*, 158–60; see also Skates, *Mississippi*, 54–55; John Codman Hurd, *The Law of Freedom and Bondage in the United States* (1858 and 1862; repr., Boston: Little, Brown, 1968), 2:142–45; Michael H. Hoffheimer et al., "Pre-1900 Mississippi Legal Authority," *Mississippi Law Journal* 73 (Fall 2003): 198; Michael H. Hoffheimer, "Mississippi Courts: 1790–1868," *Mississippi Law Journal* 65 (Fall 1995): 102–6.

34. See William Kernan Dart, "The Legal Partition of Louisiana and Mississippi," in *Minutes of the Ninth Annual Meeting of the Mississippi State Bar Association* (Jackson: Hederman, Bros., 1914), 70–91; William N. Ethridge, Jr., "An Introduction to Sargent's Code of the Mississippi Territory (1799–1800)," *American Journal of Legal History* 11, no. 2 (April 1967): 148–51.

35. "A Law Respecting Crimes and Punishments," *American Journal of Legal History* 11, no. 2 (April 1967): 166.

36. "A Law for the Regulation of Slaves," *American Journal of Legal History* 11, no. 2 (April 1967): 194, 196.

37. See "An Act for the Punishment of Crimes and Misdemeanors, Originally Passed in June 1802, but Reenacted with Some Amendment in 1807," in *A Digest of the Laws of the State of Alabama: Containing the Statues and Resolutions in Force at the End of the General Assembly in January, 1823*, ed. Harry Toulmin (Catawba: Ginn & Curtis, 1823), §§1–5, 206–7; see also Michael J. Hoffheimer, "Murder and Manslaughter in Mississippi: Unintentional Killings," *Mississippi Law Journal* 71 (2001): 53–57; Hoffheimer, "Mississippi Courts," 103–4n14; Ethridge, "Introduction to Sargent's Code," 148.

38. See Hoffheimer, "Murder and Manslaughter," 57–58 discussing the February 12, 1820, act.

39. See "An Act Respecting Slaves," in Toulmin, *Digest of the Laws*, §16, 631, adopted March 6, 1805; Hurd, *Law of Freedom and Bondage*, 2:143.

40. *State v. Jones*, 1 Miss. (Walker) 83 (1821).

41. Mississippi's first Supreme Court's judges also were the state's Superior Court trial judges who rode a trial court circuit and reviewed their colleagues' decisions on appeal. See George Poindexter, ed., *The Revised Code of the Laws of Mississippi* (Natchez, Miss.: Francis Baker, 1824), 540, 543–47, 550–51; Hoffheimer, "Mississippi Courts," 116–24.

42. *State v. Jones*, 1 Miss. (Walker), 83–84; see Mark V. Tushnet, *The American Law of Slavery 1810–1860: Considerations of Humanity and Interest* (Princeton, N.J.: Princeton University Press, 1981), 73; Kenneth M. Stampp, *The Peculiar Institution: Slavery in the Ante-Bellum South* (New York: Vintage, 1956), 221.

43. *State v. Jones*, 1 Miss. (Walker), 83.

44. See "An Act to Regulate the Several Courts in This Territory, and to Create a Superior Court of Errors and Appeals," in Toulmin, *Digest of the Laws*, §4, 162; Hoffheimer, "Mississippi Courts," 115n69. For the similar procedure authorized in a June 29, 1822, statute enacted after *Jones*, see "An Act to Establish and Organize the Supreme Court, and to Define the Powers and Jurisdiction Thereof," in Poindexter, *Revised Code*, §21, 154.

45. See Gross, *Double Character*, 25; see generally D. Clayton James, *Antebellum Natchez* (Baton Rouge: Louisiana State University Press, 1968).

46. See William Ransom and Edwin Adams Davis, eds., "Introduction," in *William Johnson's Natchez: The Ante-Bellum Diary of a Free Negro* (Baton Rouge: Louisiana State University Press, 1993), 3–12; see also John Ray Skates, Jr., *A History of the Mississippi Supreme Court, 1817–1948* (Jackson: Mississippi Bar Foundation, 1973), 1–5, 10, 81–82, 84, 99, 104–5; Dunbar Rowland, "Supreme Court—1817–32," in *Mississippi: Comprising Sketches of Counties, Towns, Events, Institutions, and Persons in Cyclopedic Form* (Atlanta: Southern Historical Publishing, 1907), 2:755–56.

47. *State v. Jones*, 1 Miss. (Walker), 83–84.

48. Ibid., 84, citing *Commonwealth v. Chapple*, 3 Va. (1 Va. Cas.) 184 (1811) (affirming conviction after indictment of defendant for maliciously stabbing a slave contrary to statute).

49. *State v. Jones*, 1 Miss. (Walker), 84 (emphasis added). On the antebellum definitions of positive law, see John V. Orth, "When Analogy Fails: The Common Law & *State v. Mann*," *North Carolina Law Review* 87, no. 3 (March 2009): 980n9.

50. Lofft 1, 98 Eng. Rep. 499, 20 How. St. T. 1 (K.B. 1772).

51. See *Somerset v. Stewart*, Lofft, 19.

52. *State v. Jones*, 1 Miss. (Walker), 85; see Poindexter, *Revised Code*, 554.

53. *State v. Jones*, 1 Miss. (Walker), 86; see Michael L. Radelet, "Executions of Whites for Crimes Against Backs: Exceptions to the Rule?," *Sociological Quarterly* 30, no. 4 (Winter 1989): 541n6 (Adams County research did not confirm whether Jones was executed).

54. William E. Wiethoff, *A Peculiar Humanism: The Judicial Advocacy of Slavery in High Courts of the Old South, 1820–1850* (Athens: University of Georgia Press, 1996), 146. For other discussions of *Jones*, see, e.g., Colin (Joan) Dayan, *The Law Is a White Dog: How Legal Rituals Make and Unmake Persons* (Princeton, N.J.: Princeton University Press, 2011), 54–55; Thadious M. Davis, *Games of Property: Law, Race, Gender, and Faulkner's Go Down Moses* (Durham, N.C.: Duke University Press, 2003), 30–31; Thomas Szasz, *Liberation by Oppression: A Comparative Study of Slavery and Psychiatry* (New Brunswick, N.J.: Transaction, 2002), 162; Wiethoff, *Peculiar Humanism*, 146, 157–58; Morris, *Southern Slavery and the Law*, 51, 175; Andrew Fede, *People without Rights: An Interpretation of the Fundamentals of the Law of Slavery in the U.S. South* (New York: Garland, 1992; repr., New York: Routledge, 2011), 3, 73–75; Paul Finkelman, *An Imperfect Union: Slavery, Federalism, and Comity* (Chapel Hill: University of North Carolina Press, 1981), 229; Tushnet, *American Law of Slavery*, 72–76, see also Paul Finkelman, *The Law of Freedom and Bondage: A Casebook* (New York: Oceana, 1986), 247–50; Meredith Lang, *Defender of the Faith: The High Court of Mississippi 1817–1875* (Jackson: University Press of Mississippi, 1977), 108–10; Michael P. Mills, "Slave Law in Mississippi from 1817–1861: Constitutions, Codes, and Cases," *Mississippi Law Journal* 71 (Fall 2001): 176–78. On Clarke, see J. Calvitt Clarke, III, "The Life of Joshua G. Clarke: Mississippi's First Chancellor," *FHC Annals: Journal of the Florida Conference of Historians* 20 (May 2013): 1–10; Andrew T. Fede, "Judging Against the Grain? Reading Mississippi Supreme Court Judge Joshua G. Clarke's Views on Slavery Law in Context," *FHC Annals: Journal of the Florida Conference of Historians* 20 (May 2013): 11–29.

55. *Respublica v. Teischer*, 1 U.S. (1 Dall.) 335, 338 (Pa. 1788). See generally, on animal cruelty regulations, Luis Chiesa, "Why It Is a Crime to Stomp on a Goldfish? Harm, Victimhood and the Structure of Anti-cruelty Offenses," *Mississippi Law Journal* 78 (Fall 2008).

56. See "An Act for the Punishment of Crimes and Misdemeanors," in Poindexter, *Revised Code*, chap. 54, §§7, 8, 297; "An Act for the Punishment of Crimes and Misdemeanors, Originally Passed in June 1802, but Reenacted with Some Amendment in 1807," in Toulmin, *Digest of the Laws*, §7, 207, §18, 208; see also *Friar v. State*, 4 Miss. (2 Howard) 422 (Err. & App. 1839) (affirming slave stealing conviction). The penalty for stealing slaves later was reduced to a fine. See generally Charles Sackett Sydnor, *Slavery in Mississippi* (1933; repr., Gloucester: Peter Smith, 1965), 105–6, 160.

57. See Fede, "Judging Against the Grain?," 13, 28.

58. See "An act, for the Punishment of Crimes and Misdemeanors," in Poindexter, *Revised Code*, chap. 54, §§2, 3, 29, and 30, 297, 301; see also Hoffheimer, "Murder and Manslaughter," 58–60 discussing the 1822 act.

59. See "An Act, to Reduce into One, the Several Acts, Concerning Slaves, Free Negroes, and Mulattoes," in Poindexter, *Revised Code*, chap. 73, §44, 379, adopted June 18, 1822.

60. See A. Hutchinson, ed., *Code of Mississippi from 1798 to 1848* (Jackson: Price and Fall, State Printers, 1848), Title II, §§3–26, Title III, §§1–21, 954–59, 957; see also Hoffheimer, "Murder and Manslaughter," 60–72.

61. See Christopher Waldrep, *Roots of Disorder: Race and Criminal Justice in the American South, 1817–80* (Urbana: University of Illinois Press, 1998), 18–21. For other examples of killings of sick or disabled slaves, see, e.g., Dea H. Boster, *African American Slavery and Disability: Bodies, Property, and Power in the Antebellum South, 1800–1860*, Studies in African American History and Culture (New York: Routledge, 2013), 66–67.

62. See William R. Smith, Sr., *Reminiscences of a Long Life: Historical, Political, and Literary* (Washington, D.C.: William R. Smith, Sr., 1889), 1:183–96.

63. Morris, *Southern Slavery and the Law*, 181, quoting *State v. James Paul*, 1843, case 324, file 130–324 (1841–46), Lowndes County Department of Archives and History: Criminal File, Lowndes County Courthouse, Columbia, Miss.; see also Smith, *Reminiscences of a Long Life*, 196.

64. See Smith, *Reminiscences of a Long Life*, 196.

65. See "Life in Texas," *Newport Mercury*, July 17, 1847, 2; "From Texas," *Augusta Chronicle*, July 16, 1847, 2; "Life in Texas," *Albany Evening Journal*, July 10, 1847, 2; "Life in Texas," *New York Commercial Advertiser*, July 9, 1847, 2.

66. "From the New Orleans Picayune, July 10, Later from Texas," *New York Spectator*, July 21, 1847, 2.

67. "Arrest," *Boston Liberator*, June 16, 1848, 4; "Arrest for Murdering a Slave," *Frederick Douglas' Paper* (Rochester), May 5, 1848, 4; "Arrest for Murdering a Slave," *American Traveller* (Boston), April 29, 1848, 3; *Mississippi Free Trader* (Natchez), April 19, 1848, 4; *Charleston Currier*, April 13, 1848, 2.

68. Smith, *Reminiscences of a Long Life*, 201. Paul also was a defendant in a successful freedom suit filed in Tuscaloosa, Alabama, by Cornelius Sinclair, a free black man from Philadelphia who was captured and sold as a slave to Paul in Alabama. See

Judson Crump and Alfred L. Brophy, "Twenty-One Months a Slave: Cornelius Sinclair's Odyssey: Freedom, Slavery, and Freedom Again in the Old South," U.N.C. Legal Studies Research, paper 2469529 (July 28, 2014), accessed November 22, 2014, http://papers.ssrn.com/sol3/papers.cfm?abstract_id=2469529&download=yes.

69. See William Johnson, "The Diary of William Johnson," in *William Johnson's Natchez*, 500.

70. See Skates, *History of the Mississippi Supreme Court*, 14–15.

71. See *State v. Kelly*, 11 Miss (3 S. & M.) 518, 1844 WL 2029 (Err. & App. 1844), *1.

72. See ibid., *2.

73. See ibid., *5.

74. See ibid., *6–*7.

75. See "Convicted of the Murder of a Slave," *Brooklyn Daily Eagle*, January 17, 1855, 2.

76. See William Lewis Sharkey et al., eds., *Revised Code of the Statute Laws of the State of Mississippi* (Jackson: E. Barksdale, State Printer, 1857), chap. 64, art. 165–83, 600–602, 601; see also Hoffheimer, "Murder and Manslaughter," 72–80.

77. *Oliver v. State*, 39 Miss. 526 (Err. & App. 1860).

78. See Don C. Doyle, *Faulkner's County: The Historical Roots of Yoknapatawpha* (Chapel Hill: University of North Carolina Press, 2001), 133.

79. *Oliver v. State*, 527.

80. Ibid., 527–28.

81. Ibid., 529–30.

82. Ibid., 527.

83. Ibid., 535–36. On Barr, see Doyle, *Faulkner's County*, 122–23, 402n3.

84. *Oliver v. State*, 539–40.

85. See Andrew Fede, *Roadblocks to Freedom: Slavery and Manumission in the United States South* (New Orleans: Quid Pro Books, 2011), 316–18; Mills, "Slave Law in Mississippi," 223; see also Skates, *History of the Mississippi Supreme Court*, 26–28, 79.

86. See *Jolly v. State*, 21 Miss. (13 S. & M.) 223, 225 (1849) (affirming Henry R. Jolly's fourth degree manslaughter conviction and two-year prison term for killing Jim, an enslaved man owned by John L. Downs); *Dowling v. State*, 13 Miss. (5 S. & M.) 664 (1846) (reversing Thomas Dowling's second degree manslaughter conviction and five year prison term for killing Dick Smith, an enslaved man owned by Rice C. Ballard, Dowling was Ballard's overseer).

87. *Thompson v. Young*, 30 Miss. 17 (1855).

88. Ibid., 18.

89. Ibid., 18–19.

90. Ibid., 19.

91. See Herbert James Lewis, *Clearing the Thickets: A History of Antebellum Alabama* (New Orleans: Quid Pro Books, 2013), 1–132; Jewett and Allen, *Slavery in the South*, 2; Thomas Perkins Abernathy, *The Formative Period in Alabama, 1815–1828*, rev. ed. (University: University of Alabama Press, 1965), 72–90; Charles S. Davis, *The Cotton Kingdom in Alabama* (Montgomery: Alabama State Department of Archives and History, 1939), 192–96; Hurd, *Law of Freedom and Bondage*, 2:150; see also Paul M. Pruitt, Jr. and David I. Durham, "The Future Alabama in the Mississippi Territory, 1798–1817,"

in *Prestatehood Legal Materials: A Fifty-State Research Guide, Including New York City and the District of Columbia*, ed. Michael Chiorazzi and Marguerite Most (Binghamton, N.Y.: Haworth Information Press, 2005), 1:1–29.

92. See "Constitution of the State of Alabama," Art. VI, "Slaves," §3, in Toulmin, *Digest of the Laws*, 931.

93. See "Constitution of the State of Alabama," Art. VI, §19, in Toulmin, *Digest of the Laws*, 929.

94. See Lewis, *Clearing the Thickets*, 291; Paul M. Pruitt, Jr., *Taming Alabama: Lawyers and Reformers, 1804–1929* (Tuscaloosa: University of Alabama Press, 2010), 18–24.

95. "An Act Regulating Punishments under the Penitentiary System," in *Supplement Aikin's Digest Laws of the State of Alabama*, ed. Alexander B. Meek (Tuscaloosa: White & Snow, 1841), chap. 3, §§5–7, 931.

96. John J. Ormand, Arthur P. Bagby, and George Goldthwaite, eds., *The Alabama Slave Code of 1852* (Montgomery: Brittan and De Wolf, 1852), 561, §§3080–81, 591, §§3295–96; see James Benson Sellers, *Slavery in Alabama*, 2nd ed. (University: University of Alabama Press, 1964), 226–30.

97. See Helen T. Catterall, ed., *Judicial Cases Concerning American Slavery and the Negro* (1926–37; repr., New York: Negro Universities Press, 1968), 3:130–31; Daniel J. Meador, "The Supreme Court of Alabama—Its Cahaba Beginning, 1820–1825," *Alabama Law Review* 61, no. 5 (2010): 896–900. The legislature in 1851 increased the number of judges to five, but reduced it back to three in 1854. See Catterall, *Judicial Cases*, 3:131.

98. See *State v. Jones*, 5 Ala. 666, 1843 WL 269, *1 (1843).

99. See ibid., *1–*2.

100. See ibid., *3–*6.

101. *Ex parte Howard*, 30 Ala. 43, 1857 Ala. LEXIS 35 (1857).

102. See Sellers, *Slavery in Alabama*, 239–40, quoting H. V. Wooten, "Private Journal of Life & Doings," 1:31; see also Davis, *Cotton Kingdom in Alabama*, 108. Wooten later became a prominent physician and author and is credited with starting Alabama's peach growing industry. See "Wooten, Hardy Vickers," in *History of Alabama and Dictionary of Alabama Biography*, ed. Thomas McAdory Owen (Chicago: S.J. Clarke, 1921), 4: 1807–8; "Alabama Peach Industry," *Encyclopedia of Alabama* accessed February 8, 2014, http://www.encyclopediaofalabama.org/face/Article.jsp?id=h-1108.

103. See Morris, *Southern Slavery and the Law*, 180–81, 478n98.

104. *Dave v. State*, 22 Ala. 23, 33(1853).

105. See *Hudson v. State*, 34 Ala. 253 (1859) (affirming Elisha Hudson's second degree murder conviction after Hudson and Thomas C. Carlisle were indicted for murdering Gus, a slave belonging to William Fuller and after a jury acquitted Carlisle and convicted Hudson, who was sentenced to a six month prison term and a $500 fine); *Cobia v. State*, 16 Ala. 781 (1849) (reversing Francis J. Cobia's conviction and ten-year prison term for murdering John, a slave of Alexander P. Crawford, because the verdict did not state the degree of the murder).

106. See *McGrew v. Cato's Executors*, Minor 8, 1820 Ala. LEXIS 8 (1820); see also *Dearing v. Moore*, 26 Ala. 586, 1855 Ala. LEXIS 203 (1855); *Parker v. Mise*, 27 Ala. 480, 1855 Ala. LEXIS 76 (1855); *Townsend v. Jeffries' Adm'r*, 24 Ala. 329, 1854 Ala. LEXIS 36 (1854);

Middleton v. Holmes, 3 Port., 1824 Ala. LEXIS 54 (1836); *Morgan v. Rhodes*, 1 Stew. 70, 1827 Ala. LEXIS 42 (1827); Fede, *People without Rights*, 71.

107. See Diane Mutti Burke, *On Slavery's Border: Missouri's Small-Slaveholding Households, 1815–1865* (Athens: University of Georgia Press, 2010), 19–22; Stephen Aron, *American Confluence: The Missouri Frontier from Borderland to Border State* (Bloomington: Indiana University Press, 2006), 37–105; Harriet C. Frazier, *Slavery and Crime in Missouri, 1773–1865* (Jefferson, N.C.: McFarland, 2001), 7–11.

108. See Frazier, *Slavery and Crime in Missouri*, 19–20.

109. See Burke, *On Slavery's Border*, 27; see also ibid., 22–27; Hammond, *Slavery, Freedom, and Expansion*, 51–75.

110. See ibid.; Jewett and Allen, *Slavery in the South*, 174–75; Frazier, *Slavery and Crime in Missouri*, 96.

111. T. J. Stiles, *Jessie James: Last Rebel of the Civil War* (New York: Knopf, 2002), 38; see also Jonas Viles, "Sections and Sectionalism in a Border State," *Mississippi Valley Historical Review* 21, no. 1 (June 1934): 3–22.

112. See Jeffrey C. Stone, *Slavery, Southern Culture, and Education in Little Dixie, Missouri, 1820–1860*, Studies in African American History and Culture, ed. Graham Hodges (New York: Routledge, 2006), 11–29; Stiles, *Jessie James*, 10–11, 37–55; R. Douglass Hurt, *Agriculture and Slavery in Missouri's Little Dixie* (Columbia: University of Missouri Press, 1992), x–xiv; see also, e.g., Burke, *On Slavery's Border*, 12, 27, 48–51, 95; Walter Schroeder, "Little Dixie," in *The American Midwest: An Interpretative Encyclopedia*, ed. Richard Sisson, Christian Zacher, and Andrew Clayton (Bloomington: Indiana University Press, 2007), 170; Robert M. Crisler, "The Regional Status of Little Dixie in Missouri and Little Egypt in Illinois," *Journal of Geography* 49, no. 8 (November 1950): 337–43; Robert M. Crisler, "Missouri's 'Little Dixie,'" *Missouri Historical Review* 42, no. 2 (January 1948): 130–39.

113. See Stone, *Slavery, Southern Culture, and Education*, 22–23; Hurt, *Agriculture and Slavery in Missouri's Little Dixie*, 80–151; see also Burke, *On Slavery's Border*, 333n14.

114. "A LAW Entitled a Law Respecting Slaves," in *Laws of a Public and General Nature of the District of Louisiana, of the Territory of Louisiana, of the Territory of Missouri, and of the State of Missouri, up to the Year 1824* (Jefferson City, Mo.: W. Lusk & Son, 1842), 27–33, 30; see Aron, *American Confluence*, 119–20; Frazier, *Slavery and Crime in Missouri*, 25–46; William G. Foley, *The Genesis of Missouri: From Wilderness Outpost to Statehood* (Columbia: University of Missouri Press, 1989), 154; Harrison Anthony Trexler, *Slavery in Missouri, 1804–1865*, Johns Hopkins University Studies in Historical and Political Science 32 (Baltimore: Johns Hopkins University Press, 1914), 57–60; Hurd, *Law of Freedom and Bondage*, 2:166–68; Frank O. Bowman, III, "Getting Away with Murder (Most of the Time): Civil War Era Homicide Cases in Boone County, Missouri," *Missouri Law Review* 77 (Spring 2012): 329–30; Hammond, "Slavery, Settlement, and Empire," 196–97; E. M. Violette, "The Black Code in Missouri," *Proceedings of the Mississippi Valley Historical Association* 6 (1912–13): 287–302.

115. See Hurd, *Law of Freedom and Bondage*, 2:168; Frazier, *Slavery and Crime in Missouri*, 127; A. A. King, ed., *The Revised Statutes of the State of Missouri* (St. Louis: Argus Office, 1835), 19; Violette, "Black Code in Missouri," 303–4.

NOTES TO CHAPTER ELEVEN 327

116. See King, *Revised Statutes of the State of Missouri*, 167.
117. See ibid., 168.
118. See ibid., 169–70.
119. See ibid., 171.
120. See ibid., 210; see *State v. Peters*, 28 Mo. 241 (1859); Fede, *People without Rights*, 113.
121. See Stone, *Slavery, Southern Culture, and Education*, 42; Frazier, *Slavery and Crime in Missouri*, 125–44, 135.
122. See Frazier, *Slavery and Crime in Missouri*, 128; Trexler, *Slavery in Missouri*, 68n50.
123. See *Mann v. Trabue*, "Statement of Case and Points Relied on by Appellant," filed May 26, 1827 and "Appellee's Brief," filed May 26, 1827, Missouri Supreme Court file, box 90, folder 16, *Missouri Digital Heritage, Missouri Supreme Court Historical Database*, accessed February 22, 2015, http://www.sos.mo.gov/Images/Archives/SupremeCourt/B090 F16.pdf; *Mann v. Trabue*, 1 Mo. 709 (1827); Frazier, *Slavery and Crime in Missouri*, 142.
124. See Frazier, *Slavery and Crime in Missouri*, 133–34.
125. See George Rollie Adams, *General William S. Harney: Prince of Dragoons* (Lincoln: University of Nebraska Press, 2001), 47; Frazier, *Slavery and Crime in Missouri*, 135. On John Mullanphy, see Michael C. O'Laughlin, *Missouri Irish: The Original History of the Irish in Missouri* (Kansas City, Mo.: Irish Genealogical Foundation, 1984), 91–93.
126. See Adams, *General William S. Harney*, 47; Frazier, *Slavery and Crime in Missouri*, 136.
127. See Letter from George Ihrie to Col. S. Cooper (July 29, 1860), in *Official Correspondence of Brig. Gen W. S. Harney, U.S. Army and First Lt. Geo. Ihrie, late U.S. Army with the U.S. War Department, and Subsequent Personal Correspondence* (——), 5–7 (quoting indictment dated July 28, 1834); see also Adams, *General William S. Harney*, 47; Frazier, *Slavery and Crime in Missouri*, 136–37.
128. See Letter from George Ihrie to Col. S. Cooper (July 29, 1860), in *Official Correspondence of Brig. Gen. W. S. Harney, U.S. Army and First Lt. Geo. Ihrie*, 8 (quoting motion dated November 4, 1834, and order dated November 5, 1834); see also Adams, *General William S. Harney*, 51; Frazier, *Slavery and Crime in Missouri*, 137–39.
129. See Adams, *General William S. Harney*, 48.
130. See Extract of a letter dated July 2, 1834, from Mr. Nathan Cole of St. Louis, Missouri, to Arthur Tappan, Esq., in Theodore Dwight Weld, *American Slavery as It Is: Testimony of a Thousand Witnesses* (New York: American Anti-Slavery Society, 1839; repr., New York: Arno Press, 1968), 89.
131. See ibid., 61. On Nathan Cole and his son Nathan, who in 1869 was elected the St. Louis mayor, see J. C. Maple and R. P. Rider, *Missouri Baptist Biography* (Kansas City, Mo.: Western Baptist, 1914), 1:287–99. On Arthur Tappan and his brother Lewis, see, e.g., David Paul Nord, "Tappan, Arthur" and "Tappan, Lewis," in *Encyclopedia of American Journalism*, ed. Stephen L. Vaughn (New York: Routledge, 2008), 517–18.
132. See Frazier, *Slavery and Crime in Missouri*, 139–41.
133. See *Carpenter v. State*, 8 Mo. 291 (1843); Frazier, *Slavery and Crime in Missouri*, 141.
134. See Frazier, *Slavery and Crime in Missouri*, 141.
135. See ibid., 142.

136. See *Peters v. Clause*, 37 Mo. 337 (1866) (affirming judgment for owner whose slave was injured by inhuman and cruel beating of bailee, applying principle that would apply "[i]f a horse be returned in a damaged condition"); *Nash v. Primm*, 1 Mo. 178 (1822) (reversing judgment for defendant who allegedly shot and killed plaintiff's slave and ordering that judgment be entered for plaintiff); Frazier, *Slavery and Crime in Missouri*, 126.

137. See Jewett and Allen, *Slavery in the South*, 23–25; S. Charles Bolton, *Arkansas, 1800–1860: Remote and Restless* (Fayetteville: University of Arkansas Press, 1998), 61–62, 125–28; Hurd, *Law of Freedom and Bondage*, 2:171; L. Scott Stafford, "Slavery and the Arkansas Supreme Court," *University of Arkansas Little Rock Law Journal* 19 (Spring 1997): 413–15.

138. See Bolton, *Arkansas, 1800–1860*, 61–62, 127–28; Fon Louise Gordon, "From Slavery to Uncertain Freedom: Blacks in the Delta," 99–101, and Donald Holley, "The Plantation Heritage: Agriculture in the Arkansas Delta," 239–41, both in *The Arkansas Delta: Land of Paradox*, ed. Jeannie Whayne and Willard B. Gatewood (Fayetteville: University of Arkansas Press, 1993).

139. See William McK. Ball and Sam C. Roane, eds., *Revised Statutes of the State of Arkansas* (Boston: Weeks, Jordan, 1838), 24, 37; see also Orville W. Taylor, *Negro Slavery in Arkansas* (Durham, N.C.: Duke University Press, 1958), 29–42.

140. See Stafford, "Slavery and the Arkansas Supreme Court," 439n162 (citing newspaper stories referring to two white men who, in 1829 and 1847, were accused of killing their own slaves, but not reporting the results of these alleged crimes); see also Josiah Gould, ed., *A Digest of the Statutes of Arkansas* (Little Rock: Johnson & Yerkes, State Printer, 1858), 327–33; Ball and Roane, *Revised Statutes of the State of Arkansas*, 238–43; J. Steele and J. M'Campbell, eds., *Laws of Arkansas Territory* (Little Rock: J. Steele, 1835), 170–72.

141. *Austin v. State*, 14 Ark. 555 (1854).

142. Ibid., 558.

143. Ibid., 567.

144. Ibid., 567–68 (citation omitted).

145. See *Brunson v. Martin*, 17 Ark. 270, 1856 WL 574, *2–*5 (1856).

146. See ibid., *4–*5.

147. See ibid., *2–*3.

148. Ibid., *3.

149. Ibid., *4.

150. See J. W. Looney, *Distinguishing the Righteous from the Roguish: The Arkansas Supreme Court, 1836–1874* (Fayetteville: University of Arkansas Press, 2016), 97; John Hallum, *Biographical and Pictorial History of Arkansas* (Albany: Weed, Parsons, 1887), 1:296–300; John Livingston, *Biographical Sketches of Distinguished Americans, Now Living* (New York, 1853), 422–25; Weld, *American Slavery as It Is*, 192 (quoting the *Free Press*, August 16, 1838); G. B. Rose, "The Supreme Court of Arkansas," *Green Bag* 4, no. 9 (September 1892): 425–26.

151. See Jewett and Allen, *Slavery in the South*, 68; Hurd, *Law of Freedom and Bondage*, 2:190–94.

152. See Jewett and Allen, *Slavery in the South*, 67–69; see also Edward E. Baptist, *Creating an Old South: Middle Florida's Plantation Frontier Before the Civil War* (Chapel Hill: University of North Carolina Press, 2002).

153. See "An Act Relating to Crimes and Misdemeanors," in *Compilation of the Public Acts of the Legislative Council of the Territory of Florida Passed Prior to 1840*, ed. John P. Duval (Tallahassee: Samuel S. Sibley, 1839), 113–15; see also James M. Denham, *A Rogue's Paradise: Crime and Punishment in Antebellum Florida, 1821–1861* (Tuscaloosa: University of Alabama Press, 1997), 121; Leslie A. Thompson, ed., *A Manual or Digest of the Statute Law of the State of Florida Passed at Its Fourth Session* (Boston: Charles C. Little and James Brown, 1847), 491.

154. See James M. Denham and Randolph Roth, "Why Was Antebellum Florida Murderous? A Quantitative Analysis of Homicide in Florida, 1821–1861," *Florida Historical Quarterly* 86, no. 2 (Fall 2007): 216–39.

155. See Denham, *Rogue's Paradise*, 138. Ferdinand McCaskill was executed in 1857 for stabbing and killing a "negro" at Wolsey, near Pensacola. McCaskill's relationship to his victim and the facts of the crime are not known; nor is it clear if the victim was enslaved. See ibid., 139.

156. See *McRaeny v. Johnson*, 2 Fla. 520, 527 (1849) (citations and quotations omitted); see also *Tallahassee Rail-Road Co. v. Macon*, 8 Fla. 299 (1859); *Kelly, Timanus & Co. v. Wallace*, 6 Fla. 690 (1856); *Forsyth and Simpson v. Perry*, 5 Fla. 337 (1853).

157. See "Justice Thomas Baltzell," *Florida Supreme Court*, accessed May 13, 2016, http://www.floridasupremecourt.org/about/gallery/baltzell.shtml.

158. See Randolph B. Campbell, "Introduction. Human Chattels: The Laws of Slavery in Texas," in *The Laws of Slavery in Texas*, ed. Randolph B. Campbell (Austin: University of Texas Press, 2010), 3; see generally Randolph B. Campbell, *The Peculiar Institution in Texas, 1821–1865* (Baton Rouge: Louisiana State University Press, 1989), 10–49.

159. See "An Act Concerning Slaves," in *A Digest of the Laws of Texas*, ed. Oliver C. Hartley (Philadelphia: Thomas, Cowperthwait, 1850), 195–96, 780–81; "An Act Concerning Slaves," in *Laws of the Republic of Texas Passed at the Session of the Fourth Congress* (Houston: Telegraph Power Press, 1840), 172; see also *Callihan's Ex'rs v. Johnson*, 22 Tex. 596, 601 (1858); *Chandler v. State*, 2 Tex. 305, 310 (1847); Campbell, *Peculiar Institution in Texas*, 144.

160. See Jewett and Allen, *Slavery in the South*, 237–41; Hurd, *Law of Freedom and Bondage*, 2:193.

161. See Campbell, *Peculiar Institution in Texas*, 56–59.

162. See "Constitution of the State of Texas," in Hartley, *Digest of the Laws of Texas*, 76; *Callihan's Ex'rs v. Johnson*, 601; see also Campbell, *Peculiar Institution in Texas*, 144.

163. *Chandler v. State*, 2 Tex. 305 (1847).

164. See ibid., 307.

165. See ibid., 309–10.

166. See "An Act to Amend the Third Section of an Act Entitled 'An Act Concerning Slaves,' Approved February 5, 1848," in Hartley, *Digest of the Laws of Texas*, 786; *Nix v. State*, 13 Tex. 575 (1855); see also *State v. Stephenson*, 20 Tex. 151 (1857) (sustaining indict-

ment against John Stephenson and Edwin S. Cabler for assault and battery on a slave, Malissa, who was owned by Linsay P. Rucker).

167. See "An Act Supplemental to 'An Act Concerning Crimes and Punishments,' Approved March Twentieth, A.D. Eighteen Hundred and Forty-Eight," in *The Laws of Texas, 1822–1897*, ed. H. P. N. Gammel (Austin: Gammel Book Co., 1898), 3:1503; *Callihan's Ex'rs v. Johnson*, 600.

168. See James Willie, "[Preface]," in *The Penal Code of the State of Texas* (Galveston: News Office, 1857), n.p., Texas State Law Library, accessed June 25, 2016, http://www.lrl.state.tx.us/scanned/statutes_and_codes/Penal_Code.pdf; "The Codes of 1856," Texas State Law Library, accessed June 25, 2016, http://www.lrl.state.tx.us/collections/oldcodes.cfm.

169. See *Penal Code of Texas*, 105.

170. See ibid., 110.

171. Ibid., 110–11.

172. See ibid., 113.

173. See ibid., 133.

174. See ibid., 134.

175. See *Echols, Adm'r v. Dodd*, 20 Tex. 190 (1857) (hirer liable for damages when hirer's overseer beat the plaintiff's slave to death); Campbell, *Peculiar Institution in Texas*, 148–52.

176. See Mark Davidson, "The Civil War and Reconstruction in Harris County's Only District Court," *Houston Lawyer* 33 (November/December 1995): 43.

177. See *Wilson v. State*, 29 Tex. 240, 1867 WL 4517 *5 (1867); Campbell, *Peculiar Institution in Texas*, 148; Hans W. Baade, "Chapters in the History of the Supreme Court of Texas: Reconstruction and 'Redemption' (1866–1882)," *Saint Mary's Law Journal* 40, no. 1 (2008): 49; see *Presley v. State*, 30 Tex. 160, 1867 WL 4576 (1867) (reversing conviction for killing a slave belonging to another person).

CONCLUSION. Breaking Out of the Box of Slavery Law

1. Compare Ely Aaronson, *From Slave Abuse to Hate Crime: The Criminalization of Racial Violence in American History* (New York: Cambridge University Press, 2014), 39–49.

2. See Robert Young, *Domesticating Slavery: The Master Class in Georgia and South Carolina, 1670–1837* (Chapel Hill: University of North Carolina Press, 1999), 132–33; see also Lacy K. Ford, *Deliver Us from Evil: The Slavery Question in the Old South* (New York: Oxford University Press, 2009), 141–203; Joyce E. Chaplin, *An Anxious Pursuit: Agricultural Innovation and Modernity in the Lower South, 1730–1815* (Chapel Hill: North Carolina University Press, 1993), 53–68, 123–24, 362–65; Joyce E. Chaplin, "Slavery and the Principle of Humanity: A Modern Idea in the Early Lower South," *Journal of Social History* 24, no. 2 (Winter 1990): 299–315.

3. See Eugene D. Genovese, *Roll, Jordan, Roll: The World the Slaves Made* (New York: Vintage, 1976), 41.

4. See *State v. Davis*, 52 N.C. (7 Jones Law) 52 (1859); *State v. Jowers*, 33 S.C. (11 Ired. Law) 555 (1850); *State v. Harden*, 29 S.C.L. (2 Speers) 152 (Ct. App. Law 1832); see also Andrew Fede, *People without Rights: An Interpretation of the Fundamentals of the Law of Slavery in the U.S. South* (New York: Garland, 1992; repr., New York: Routledge, 2011), 167–76. On the law box, see Robert Gordon, "Introduction: J. Willard Hurst and the Common Law Tradition in American Historiography," *Law & Society Review* 9, no. 1 (Autumn 1975): 10.

5. See *The Penal Code of the State of Texas* (Galveston: News Office, 1857), 7, 158–61.

6. See ibid., 161; see also, discussing the elite's attitudes toward the white poor in American history, Nancy Isenberg, *White Trash: The 400-Year Untold History of Class in America* (New York: Viking, 2016).

7. See Wilbert E. Moore and Robin M. Williams, "Stratification in the Ante-Bellum South," *American Sociological Review* 7, no. 3 (June 1942): 346; see also Robert J. Cottrol, *The Long, Lingering Shadow: Slavery, Race, and Law in the American Hemisphere* (Athens: University of Georgia Press, 2013), 102–9; Ira Berlin, *Slaves without Masters: The Free Negro in the Antebellum South* (New York: New Press, 1974); Leon F. Litwack, *North of Slavery: The Negro in the Free States, 1790–1860* (Chicago: University of Chicago Press, 1961), 64–112.

8. See Randall Kennedy, "The State, Criminal Law, and Racial Discrimination: A Comment," *Harvard Law Review* 107, no. 6 (April 1994): 1267; see also Randall Kennedy, *Race, Crime, and the Law* (New York: Pantheon Books, 1997), 29–36, 76–80.

9. See S. F. Davis, *Mississippi Negro Lore* (Indianola, Miss., 1914), 21–28; see also Melvin Patrick Ely, *Israel on the Appomattox: A Southern Experiment in Black Freedom, from the 1790s through the Civil War* (New York: Knopf, 2004), 435–43, 455–68; Leon F. Litwack, *Trouble in Mind: Black Southerners in the Age of Jim Crow* (New York: Knopf, 1998), 217–79; Neil R. McMillen, *Dark Journey: Black Mississippians in the Age of Jim Crow* (Urbana: University of Illinois Press, 1989), 201–17; I. Bennett Capers, "The Crime of *Loving, Lawrence,* and Beyond," in *Loving v. Virginia in a Post-racial World: Rethinking Race, Sex, and Marriage*, ed. Kevin Noble Maillard and Rose Cuison Villazor (New York: Cambridge University Press, 2012), 120; I. Bennett Capers, "Reading Back, Reading Black, and *Buck v. Bell,*" in *African American Culture and Legal Discourse*, ed. Lovalerie King and Richard Schur (New York: Palgrave, 2009), 13; I. Bennett Capers, "The Trial of Bigger Thomas: Race Gender and Trespass," *New York University Review of Law and Social Change* 31, no. 1 (2006): 7–8; but see, stating, "The logic of common law resisted formation of a distinct 'Negro law,'" Christopher Waldrep, *Roots of Disorder: Race and Criminal Justice in the American South, 1817–80* (Urbana: University of Illinois Press, 1998), 51; see also Christopher Waldrep, *Jury Discrimination: The Supreme Court, Public Opinion, and a Grassroots Fight for Racial Equality in Mississippi* (Athens: University of Georgia Press, 2010), 214.

INDEX

Abbot, John, Jr., 154
Abbot, John, Sr., 154
abolition movement, 27, 28, 57–58, 67; Nathan Cole on, 213–14; Frederick Douglass and, 90; Harriet Beecher Stowe and, 1, 5, 125, 191
Abruzzo, Margaret, xi, 8
Act for Regulating Slaves (Jamaica), 48
Act for the Better Order and Government of Slaves (Jamaica), 49
Act for the Better Ordering and Governing of Negroes (Barbados), 44
Act for the Better Ordering and Governing of Negroes and Other Slaves in This Province (Ga.), 106
Act for the Better Ordering and Governing of Negroes and Other Slaves in This Province (S.C.), 100
Act for the Better Ordering and Governing of Negroes and Slaves (S.C.), 99
Act for the Better Ordering of Slaves (Jamaica), 48
Act for the Better Ordering of Slaves (S.C.), 99
Act for the Better Protection of Slaves of This Island (Barbados), 62
Act for the Better Regulating and Governing Negroes and Other Slaves (Bahamas), 55
Act for the Good Governing of the Rights between Masters and Servants (Barbados), 44–46
Act for the Governing of Negroes (Barbados), 50
Act for the Security of the Subject . . . (Bermuda), 52–53
Act to Prevent the Willful Killing of Slaves (N.C.), 105
Adams, James H., 189
Adkins, Williams, 188
Aiken, William, 184
Alabama, 28, 206–9

Albemarle, Duke of (Christopher Monck), 49
Alfonso X (Spanish king), 25, 27–28, 30
Alfred the Great (Anglo-Saxon king), 35
Allen, A. A., 159–60
Allen, Charles H., 213
Allen, Daniel, 166
Allen, John, 74
Allen, Nazareth, 190
Allen, Samuel, 72
Alsop, Thomas, 119
Andrews John, 117, 118
Andros, Edmund, 71
Anglo-Saxons, 12, 34–35
Anne (English queen), 72, 78
Antigua, 41; demographics of, 50; slave laws of, 51, 61. *See also* Leeward Islands
Antonius Pius (Roman emperor), 9, 17–18, 19
Archdale, John, 99
Argolo, Joao, 31
Arkansas, 215–18
Arrents, Johannes, 177
Arthur, Hargrove, 181
Arthur v. Wells, 181
Ashe, John, 176
Ashton, Thomas, 74
Atkins, John, 50
Atkins, Jonathan, 46
Austin v. State of Arkansas, 215–16, 217

Baas, Jean-Charles de, 29
Badger, George E., 142
Bahamas, 47, 48, 54–55, 59–60
Bailey, Henry, 4
Bailey, Pierce, 156
Bailey, Samuel, 136
Baker, James A., 222
Baldwin, Samuel, 46–47
Ball, Peter, 68, 84
Ball, William, 151
Baltzell, Thomas, 219

INDEX

Barbados, 40–41, 66, 141; demographics of, 52; slave laws of, 6, 43–50, 52–54, 61–63, 69; South Carolina and, 6, 41, 91, 97–98, 182; sugar plantations on, 44, 50; Virginia and, 92
Barber, John, 96
Barcalow, Arthur, 78–79
Barr, Hugh A., 204
Barrow, Bennett H., 195, 312
Bartlett, John E., 155
Bascom, Peter, 260–61n40
Bassett, John Spencer, 105
Battle, Lawrence, 157
Battle, William H., 150
Bay, Elihu Hall, 174
Beaufeau, Alfred, 195
Beccaria, Cesare, 178
Beckles, Hilary, 62–63
Bee, Frances C., 2, 3
Bell, Derrick, 8, 233n44
benefit of clergy, 36, in British island colonies, 49, 59, 60, 62, 63, in North Carolina, 105–7, 131, 133–34, 138, 143, in South Carolina, 101, in Tennessee, 165, 179, in Virginia, 95
Benton, Augustus, 134–35
Berkeley, George, 39
Berkenhead, John, 44
Bermuda, 47, 52–53, 59
Bermudez, Joaquim, 196
Beson, John W., 190
Binkly, Robert, 150
Birdseye, Ezekiel, 165–66, 169
Birdsong, Henry, 126–27, 129
Blackledge, William, 181
Block, Kristen, 276n64
blood feuds, ix, 12, 14; among Anglo-Saxons, 34–35; after Norman Conquest, 35–36; among Visigoths, 23; wergild and, ix, 12, 34–36
Board of Trade and Plantations, 46, 48, 49–50, 108
Body of Liberties (Mass.), 70–71, 73
Bolton, Ellen, 167
Boon, John, 132–33
Bouldin, Wood, 127–28
Bourne, Andrew, 95
Boylan, Michael, 155

Braddock, Guillermo, 30
Bradley, Jackson, 188–89
Bradley, Keith, 15
Bradshaw, Jonas, 143
Branch, John, 139
Brazilian slavery, 15, 27–28
Bright, Simon, 132
British slave laws, 9–10, 33–42; of Atlantic Islands, 43–67; of North America, 68–90
British Virgin Islands, 41, 57, 64–65; demographics of, 56; slave laws of, 56; sugar plantations on, 56
Brocard, Charles, 29
Brooks, William M., 208
Brown, Christopher, 38
Brunson, Robert A., 216–18
Bryan, James W., 149
Bull, William, 100
Bull, William, II, 101–2
Bullock, John, 76
Bullock, William, 68, 76
Burrington, George, 103
Burton, Hutchins G., 136, 143
Bush, Jonathan, 35, 40
Butler, Andrew, 184
Butler, Pierce M., 190
Byrd, William, II, 94

Cahsen, James Santiago, 30
calendars, Julian and Gregorian, 276n64, 295n53
Calvert, Philip, 82
Camp, Newton, 159, 160
Camp v. State of Georgia, 159, 160
Campbell, Leona, 214
Campbell, William, 101
Campfield, Zaba, 88
Canada, 28, 29–30, 68
Cane, Nathaniel, 71
Capers, I. Bennett, 224
Carpenter, Conrad, 214
Carpenter, Dennis, 176
Carper, Sampson, 169–71
Caruthers, Robert, 171–72
Castleman, James, 124–26, 129
Castleman, Stephen D., 124–26, 129
Caston, Wilkes Thurlow, 188
Catron, John, 168

Chambers, Edward R., 127
Chambers, James, 180–81
Chandler, David, 220
Chandler, Job, 83
Chandler v. State of Texas, 220
Chaplin, Joyce, 8
Charles II (English king), 46, 48–49; North Carolina and, 102; Pennsylvania and, 75; South Carolina and, 97
Charleston, S.C., 1–5, 100–101, 175–79, 181, 183–84, 189
Cheatwood, Bob, 182
Cherokees, 11
Chestnut, John, 177
Chindasvind (Visigothic king), 23, 24
clans, ix, 11–15; primitive societies, 12, 235n5; tribal societies, 12, 23. *See also* traditional societies
Clarke, Joshua G., x, 198–200
Claudius (Roman emperor), 17
Clayton, John, 94
Clovis I (Frankish king), 14
Cobb, Howell, 153, 156
Cobb, Jesse, 132
Cobb, Thomas R. R., ix
Cobb v. Battle, 157
Code Noir, 29–30, 58, 194
Código Negro Carolino, 27
Cohen, Abraham, 174
Cohen, Joseph, 118
Colbert, Jean-Baptiste, 29
Colcock, Charles J., 181, 183
Cole, Nathan, 213–14
Commonwealth of Virginia v. Turner, 122
Concalves Carneiro, Antonio, 31
Conner, David, 220
Consolidated Acts (Jamaica), 58–59
Consolidated Slave Act (Bahamas), 59
Consolidated Slave Law (Barbados), 63
Constantine (Roman emperor), 9, 18–19, 241n65
contract societies, 11–13
Cooke, John R., 136–37
Cooley, John, 74
Cooper, Davis, 176
Cooper, Samuel, 74–75
Corbit, William, 86
Cornbury, Lord, 78

coroner, role defined, 2
corpus delicti, 188
Cotton, Elijah, 155
Cox, James, 78
Cox, Thomas W., 161–63
Cox, William, 96
Cox v. State of Georgia, 161–63
cruelty to slaves (nonfatal): Bahamas laws on, 60; Georgia laws on, 107, 108, 153–54, 288n109; Kentucky laws on, 87, 319n15; Louisiana laws on, 193, 194, 319n15; Maryland laws on, 319n15; Mississippi laws on, 198, 200; Missouri laws on, 211; South Carolina laws on, 100, 191; Texas laws on, 220–22; Tobago laws on, 55; Visigoths laws on, 23–25. *See also* mutilation of slaves; punishment of slaves
Crump, Hannah, 96
Cuban slave codes, 27
Cucullu, Joseph S., 319n21
Culpeper, Lord, 93
"culture hearths," 41

Dalton, Michael, 37
Dane, Nathan, 68
Daniel, Joseph J., 139
Datchurut, Jean, 209–10
Davenport, Addington, 71
Davies, Henry L., 117
Davis, Jefferson, 128
Davis, John, 136
Davis, Sidney Fant, 224
Davis, Theodore H., 89
Davis, W. H., 319n21
de jure discrimination, ix, 224
defensor (*sindico procurador*), 27
Delaware, 41, 68, 80; slave homicide cases in, 85–86; slave laws of, 89, 111
Denham, James, 219
DeSaussure, William, 181
Deveaux, J. Porteous, 2–5
DeWolf, James, 72–73
Dick, John M., 141, 145–46
Dietz, Aimes, 195–96
Dimitry, Eliza, 195–96
Dobbs, Arthur, 103
Dodson, Daniel, 132–33
Dominica, 41, 54, 57

336 INDEX

Dongan, Thomas, 71
Donley, Stockton P., 222
Douchenet, Antoine, 194
Douglass, Frederick, 90
Drayton, John, 176
Dudley, Paul, 71
Duke of York, 73
Duke of York's Laws, 73, 75, 77
Dunmore, Lord, 97
Dunn, Richard S., 92
Dunning School, 225n3
Dutton, Richard, 49–50

Earle, Baylis J., 182, 184
Earnest, John, 181
Edwards, Bryan, 60
Edwards, Laura, 151, 177
Elkins, Stanley M., x, 6
Elliot, Hugh, 64
Ellis, Charles Rose, 60
Ely, Melvin Patrick, 117, 118
emancipation, 69, 164–65; Jamaican laws on, 48, 67; New York laws on, 74; Pennsylvania laws on, 76. *See also* manumission
Enlightenment, 7, 58, 67, 111
Ervig (Visigothic king), 23, 24
Ethelbert I of Kent, 35
Euric (Visigothic king), 23
Evans, Josiah J., 183, 312n64
Ewing, William, 167
exculpatory oath, 7, 24, in Georgia, 107–8; in Louisiana, 193–94; in Eliza Rowand's case, 4, 5, 184; in South Carolina, 101, 174, 183, 190–91
exile, 17, 24, 25, 31, 244n24
exploitation colonies, 234n46

factor (factorage), 2
families, ix, 11, 35, 46, 97, 224; discipline within, 153; slave owning, 110, 130, 173, 186; of slaves, 39
Farmer, Nancy, 163
Fendall, Josias, 82
Fergus, Claudius, 58
Fernandez, Domingo, 30
feuds. *See* blood feuds
Field, Richard H., 122
Fields, William, 167–68

Fields v. State of Tennessee, 167–68
Finkelman, Paul, 92–93
Finley, Moses I., 15, 20, 38
Flanders, Ralph Betts, 109, 155
Flanigan, Daniel, 171
Fleming, Josiah, 183
Fletcher, Andrew, 39
Florida, 26, 218–19
Floyd, John B., 124
France, 14; slave laws of, 9, 22, 28–30, 58, 209
Franklin, Benjamin, 108
Franklin, Jason, 150–51
Frazier, Harriet, 209–10, 212, 214–15

Gaillard, Theodore, 175–76
Gaius's *Institutes*, 20
Games, Alison, 47
Gaspar, David Barry, 51
Gaston, William, 141
Gaughan, Judy, 16
Geddes, John, 178
Gee, State of South Carolina v., 174
George III (English king), 55
Georgia, 105–9; constitution of, 153; demographics of, 106, 152, 173; slave homicide cases in, 154–63, 172; slave laws of, 6, 7, 105–9, 130, 152–63
Ghachem, Malick, 29
Gholson, Thomas Saunders, 127–28
Gibbons, Lyman, 209
Glynn, Anthony G., 138
Gooch, William, 95
Goode, Trueman, 142
Goodell, William, ix
Gorton, Samuel, 255n44
gossip networks, 7
Goveia, Elsa, 25, 26, 51–52, 56, 61, 63
Graham, William A., 148
Gray, Samuel, 94
Gray, William, 183
Green, Elizabeth, 185
Grenada, 57, 58
Grenville, Henry, 54
Grey, John, 37
Griffin, Dempsey, 101
Griffin, Miriam, 19
Guadeloupe, 28

Habersham, James, 108
Haddock, Solomon, 155
Hadrian (Roman emperor), 17
Hagar, William, 167
Hagood, Benjamin, 190
Haiti, 28, 31
Hale, Matthew, 37
Hall, Henry M., 208–9
Hall, John, 134, 138, 168
Hammond, Dennis F., 161, 162
Handler, Jerome, 44, 63
Harden, Russel, 184
Hardin, Samuel, 118
Hardy, Matthew, 103
Harney, William S., 213–14
Harper, Kyle, 18, 19
Harper, William, 182
Harris, Iverson L., 157
Harris, John W., 221
Harris, Susanna and Richard, 83–84
Harris, William (scholar), 19
Harris, William L. (judge), 204–5
Hart, John, 51
Hartley, Oliver Cromwell, 221
Hatfield, April, 92
Havis, John, 177
Hawes, Elias, 134
Hawkins, Thomas, 87–88
Hawkins, William, 37
Hawley, Henry, 44
Hayne, A. P, 3, 5
Haywood, John, 132, 168
Heflin, Wes, 136
Henderson, Leonard, 138–39
Henry, Howell M., 179, 315–16n92
Henry, John Joseph, 77
Hertzer, Caroline, 189
Hester, Alfred, 190
Hinkel, Mary, 148
Hodge, Arthur, 57, 64–65
Hodges, Graham Russell, 90
Hoffman, Carl A., 75
Holloway, John, 148
Holloway, Mary Ann, 148–49
Holt, William W., 157, 158
homicide, 16, 35–38, 68; definitions of, 11, 20, 198, 207, 221; excusable, 36–37, 71, 133, 200, 203, 211, 221; justifiable, 36–37, 133;

Kentucky laws on, 87; *Las Siete Partidas* on, 25, 27–28, 30; Pennsylvania laws on, 76; by slaves, 215–16; types of, 36; Virginia laws on, 115–17, 119, 120. *See also* manslaughter; slave homicide
Hoomes v. Kuhn, 112–13, 114
Hooper, William, 104–5
Hoover, John, ix, 10, 149, 150; trial of, 144–48
Hopkins, Keith, 15
Howard, Benjamin, 208
Howard, Martin, 56–57, 103–4
Howard, Phillip, 48–49
Howington, Arthur, 166–68
Hudson, Charles, 127–28, 129
Huff, J., 166
Huff, Thomas, 142
Huggins, Edward, 64
Hunt, B. F., 4–5
Hunt, Samuel, 79–80
Hunt, T. G., 197
Hurd, Justus, 203
Hurst, Hugh C., 167
Huston, John, 111
Hutcheson, Francis, 39
Hutcheson, George, 77
Hutchinson, Thomas, 71

indentured servants, 39, 44, 46; in Maryland, 81; in Pennsylvania, 76; in Virginia, 91, 97
Indians. *See* Native Americans
intendant, 28

Jamaica: demographics of, 47, 50; emancipation on, 67; slave law reforms of, 53–54, 57–59; slave laws of, 44, 47–49, 89, 105; South Carolina and, 98; sugar plantations on, 44, 48
James, Jane G., 169–71
James II (English king), 71
James v. Carper, 169–71
Jarrott, State of North Carolina v., 141, 168
Jefferies, David, 168
Jefferson, Thomas, 1, 88, 111
Jennison, Watson, 108
Johnson, Tom, 118
Johnson, William (free black), 201–2
Johnson, William (overseer), 219
Johnston, Samuel, 133–34

Jones, Isaac, 198–200, 202
Jones, William H., 207–8
Jordan, Randal S., 159–60
Jordan v. State of Georgia, 159–60
Julius, John, 65
jus utendi et abutendi, 21
Justinian (Roman emperor), 17, 19, 20

Kalm, Peter, 76
Kelly, Archibald, 202
Kelly, James, 190
Kentucky: slave homicide cases in, 87–89; slavery in, 68, 80, 86–87
Kershaw, John, 176
King, George, 194
King Philip's War, 70
Kirkwood v. Miller, 171–72
Kuhn, Jacob, 112–13

Lacroix, Jean-Baptiste, 209–10
Landers, Jane, 30
Larnage, Marquis de, 31
Larue, John, 196
Las Siete Partidas (Alfonso X), 25, 27–28, 30
latifundia, 15, 23
Lawless, Luke E., 213
Lee, James, Jr., 83
Lee, Robert E., 128
Lee, William, 96
Leeward Islands, 28, 41, 64–65; demographics of, 50, 52; slave laws of, 48, 51–52, 60–61
Leigh, Benjamin Watkins, 118, 292n55
Leigh, William, 122
Lejeune, Nicholas, 31
Leovigild's code, 23
Lewis, Lilburne, 88
Lewis, Stephen, 200–201
lex Aquilia, 16
lex petronia, 16–17
Lex Salica, 14
lex talionis, 12
Little, Archibald, 202
Locke, John, 97
Long, Edward, 53, 58, 89
Lord, Peter, 104, 105
Louapre, Joseph, 195
Louis XIV (French king), 29–30

Louis XV (French king), 193
Louisiana, 28; demographics of, 193; French influences on, 28, 30, 192–93; slave laws of, 7, 192–97; as Spanish colony, 26, 192
Ludford, Thomas, 65
Lumpkin, Joseph P., 158, 159, 162, 205
Lynch, Thomas, 48
lynchings, 13, 167
Lyon, Richard F., 162–63

Maillart, Pierre, 31
Maine, Henry Sumner, 11, 114
Maitland, Frederic William, 35–36
M'Alister, John & William, 77
Malone, Obadiah, 212–13
Manly, Charles, 138
Mann, Marshall, 212
Mansfield, Lord, 199
manslaughter, 75, 83; Alabama laws on, 207–8; definitions of, 36, 198, 207; Georgia laws on, 160, 162; involuntary, 115, 119, 121, 123, 160, 211; Louisiana laws on, 195; Mississippi laws on, 198, 203; North Carolina laws on, 140; South Carolina laws on, 101, 174, 189; Virginia laws on, 94–95, 111, 115–17, 119, 121. *See also* homicide
manumission, 21, 38, 56; on Barbados, 61–62; in Georgia, 157, 159; in South Carolina, 178; in Virginia, 114, 115. *See also* emancipation
marriage, first cousin, 186
Martin, Green, 156–59
Martin, James, 216–18
Martin, Josiah, 104–5
Martin, Philip, 155
Martin v. State of Georgia, 157
Martinique, 28–29
Maryland, 80; demographics of, 81; slave homicide cases in, 81–85; slave laws of, 48, 111; slavery in, 68, 80
Massachusetts, 41; slave laws of, 48, 68, 70–71
Massachusetts Body of Liberties, 70–71, 73
Mathews, David, 176
Mayo-Bobee, Dinah, 90
McAtee, John, 84–85
Mccay (McCay), Spruce, 133

McCrady, Edward, 179
McDonald, Charles J., 160
McGuire, Abyer, 88–89
McKeown, Niall, 19–20
McKewn, Mary, 189
McKinney, John A., 164
McKinney, Robert J., 170–71, 172
McManus, Edgar, 68, 74
McRaeny, Daniel, 219
Megginson, W. J., 190
Merrick, Edwin, 194–95
Middleton, Joiner, 177
Miller, George, 171–72
Miller, William, 136–37, 138
Milner, John, 101
Minton, Douglas, 177
Mississippi, 28, 192, 197–206
Missouri, 28, 209–15
M'Kee, Francis R., 190
Molyford, Thomas, 47
Monroe, George, 128
Montgomery, Priscilla, 183–84
Montserrat, 41, 50. *See also* Leeward Islands
Moore, Albert A., 190
Moore, Alfred, 132
Moore, Wormley, 219
Moorhead, John, 148
Morgan, Philip, 95
Morocco, 31
Morris, Richard, 8
Morris, State of Louisiana v., 194
Morris, Thomas, 7, 81, 96
Moser, Philip, 176–77, 179
Motley, Thomas, 181
Munro, Robert, 188
Murcheson, Simon, 201–2
murder (as crime), common law, 36–38; reform laws and degrees, 76, 115–16; in Rome, 16
Murphey, Archibald D., 142
mutilation of slaves, 193–94; British law on, 68; French law on, 28–29, 31, 58, 193; Visigothic law on, 24. *See also* punishment of slaves
Myers, William, 117–18

Nash, Frederick, 136
"natal alienation," 13
Native Americans, 3, 11, 15; British enslavement of, 49, 51, 70; French enslavement of, 30; Portuguese enslavement of, 27; Spanish enslavement of, 26
Neal, William, 163
Neal v. Farmer, 163
"negro law," 224
Nelson, William, 117, 122
Nettles, Samuel, 175
Nevis, 41, 50, 52, 64. *See also* Leeward Islands
New England, 48, 70–75, 114; slavery in, 41–42, 68, 69. *See also individual states*
New France, 28, 29–30, 194
New Grenada Slave Act, 58
New Hampshire, 41, 71; slave homicide cases in, 73; slave laws of, 48, 68, 72
New Jersey: demographics of, 69; slave laws of, 48, 77–80
New Netherlands, 73
New York: demographics of, 69, 73; slave homicide cases in, 73–75; slave laws of, 48, 68, 71
Newton, Cornelius S., 186–87
Nicholson, Francis, 99
Nisbet, Eugenius A., 163
Nix, J. D., 220
North, E. W., 2, 5
North Carolina, 102–5, 130–51; demographics of, 102–3, 130; slave homicide cases in, 132–51; slave law reforms in, 103–5, 130–51; slave laws of, 6, 48, 57–58, 103, 168; slavery in, 102; Tennessee and, 152, 164, 165; Virginia slave laws versus, 151
Northey, Edward, 72
Novak, William, 115, 180
Nunn, Hugh, 135

Oliver v. State of Mississippi, 203–5
Olwell, Robert, 101
O'Neall, John B., 4–5, 182, 190–91, 224
O'Neill, Eben, 30
Ordenações Filipinas, 27
O'Reilly, Alejandro, 209
"other slavery," defined, 254n39
Overzee, Symon, 81–82

papel de venta, 27
Parent, Anthony, 95

Parke, Daniel, 51
Parker, Joshua, 181
Patterson, Orlando, 13–15, 223; on Jamaican abolition, 67; on Jamaican slave laws, 58
Patterson, Samuel Finley, 143
Patton, Gen. George, 292n55
Patton, John Mercer, 123
Paul, James, 201, 323n68
Paxton, John, 138
Payne, Hiram, 216
Pearson, Richmond, 149, 224
Peck, Jacob, 168, 169
Pelteret, David, 35
Pendleton, Edmund, 111
Penn, William, 75
Pennsylvania, 41, 58, 75–76, 200; demographics of, 69; slave homicide cases in, 76, 77
Pequot War, 70, 114
Peters, Belvard J., 89
Petigru, James Lewis, 4
Pettit, William, 74
Phenney, George, 54–55
Philip II (Spanish king), 27–28
Philippines, 27
Phillips, Ulrich B., ix, 6, 225n3
Pitman, William, 10, 96–97, 115
plantation society: in Brazil, 27; in Maryland, 80–81; patterns of development, 6, 232n30; in South Carolina, 98; Visigothic, 23. *See also* sugar plantations
Pollock, Frederick, 35–36
Pope, Jacob, 142–43
Porcher, Peter, 3, 5
Portuguese slave laws, ix, 9, 27–28, 31; Roman tradition of, 22; Visigothic tradition of, 25
Posey, Eliza, 184–85
Posey, Martin, 184–85
Posey, Matilda, 184–85
Pottenger, Samuel, 83
Powell, Carolyn, 144, 145
Preaux, Robert, 195
Preston, Bacchus, 57
primitive societies, 12, 235n5; clans, ix, 11–15; tribal societies, 12, 23. *See also* traditional societies
prodigals, 20, 241n72

Puerto Rico, 27
punishment of slaves, 21; in Barbados, 45–46; Brazilian laws on, 28; *Code Noir* on, 29; in Martinique, 28–29; in New England, 68; Portuguese laws on, 28; Roman laws on, 14, 17–18; in South Carolina, 2–3, 5–6; Spanish laws on, 26; Visigothic laws on, 24. *See also* cruelty to slaves; mutilation of slaves
Purdy, Jedediah, 38

Quakers, 75, 77, 86
Quimby, James, 75
Quincey, Edmund, 71
Quinn, Charles, 95
Quintana, Ryan A., 180

Raines, Guy, 183
rape, 21, 36
Rawlins, Henry, 65
Real Cédula de su Majestad sobre la educación, trato y ocupaciones de los esclavos, 27
Reccesvind (Visigothic king), 23
Recopilación de los reyes de los reynos de las Indias, 26–27
Reed, Thomas, 142
Reeve, Tapping, 68
Reglamento para la educación, trato y ocupaciones de los esclavos (Puerto Rico), 27
Rhett, James S., 4
Rhode Island, 104; slavery in, 40, 41, 69, 72–73
Richardson, Millington, 139
Robbins, Christopher, 10, 149–50
Roberts, Justin, 39
Robertson, John Blount, 196
Robinson, Conway, 123
Rogers, Woodes, 55
Roman slave laws, 9, 15–23, 223; adapted by Dutch, 73; adapted by French, 28; adapted by Visigoths, 22; adapted in Louisiana, 192
Romney, Lord, 65
Roth, Randolph, 114–15, 219
Roueche, François, 196–97
Rowand, Eliza, 1–6, 184, 191
Rowand, Robert, 2–4

INDEX 341

Rowe, Benjamin, 167
Ruffin, Thomas, 136, 142, 144, 146–48

sacrifice, human, 11, 14
Saint Kitts (Saint Christopher), 28, 41, 43, 50, 65; demographics of, 50; slave laws of, 61–62. *See also* Leeward Islands
Saint Vincent, 57
Saint-Domingue, 28, 31
Salian Franks, 14
Samuels, Green B., 124
San Domingo, 27
Sandiford, James H., 189–90
Sargent, William, 198
Schwarz, Philip, 111
Scott, Charles, 88
Scott, Christopher C., 216–18
Scott, Mason, 138–39
Scott, Samuel P., 243n11
Scott, Sarah, 96
Seaforth, Lord (Francis Humberston Mackenzie), 61–63
Seawell, Henry, 138–40
Seldon, Samuel, 94
self-defense, 80; in British law, 36, 45–46; in U.S. law, 80, 113–14, 167, 198, 207
serfdom, 13, 35
Settle, Thomas, 148
settler, problematic term, 234n46
settler colonies, 234n46
Shackford, John, 214
Sharpe, Horatio, 83
Shepherd, Jesse G., 150–51
Sides, Henry, 143
Simons, James, 189
Sinclair, Cornelius, 323n68
sindico procurador (defensor), 27
Skene, John, 77
Slater, John, 175
slave homicide, 6, 7, 10, 222, 223; categories of, 14, 223; Frederick Douglass on, 90; by freed blacks, 142, 182; justifiable, 6, 11, 24, 45, 162. *See also* homicide; punishment of slaves
slave rebellions, 2, 58, 97; prevention of, 101–2, 104, 171; Tennessee law on, 165; Texas law on, 221; on Westward Islands, 57
slave trade, internal (U.S.), 301n106

slavery, 22; Joshua G. Clarke on, 198; definition of, 13; Moses Finley on, 38; as punishment for crimes, 70, 178; Justin Roberts on, 39; serfdom versus, 13. *See also individual states*
slaves: abolition of trade in, 57–58; legal complaints by, 18, 27, 29, 30; legal testimony by, 5–7, 29, 63, 75, 161, 166, 267n125; liability for crimes ordered by owner, 3–4, 230n14; marriages, 139, 297n46; murder by, 113–14, 215–16; mutilation of, 24, 28–29; as problematic term, xi; stealing of, 175, 180; trials of, in South Carolina, 3
Smith, Cotesworth P., 205–6
Smith, Gerrit, 166, 169
Somerset v. Stewart, 57, 199
Sorrell, Thomas, 111–12
South Carolina, 1–10; appellate and trial judges, 312–13n64; Barbados and, 6, 41, 91, 97–98, 182; demographics of, 98, 173, 186; Fundamental Constitutions of, 97–98; slave homicide cases in, 1–10, 174–77, 179, 181–90; slave laws of, 48, 97–102, 106–7, 173–91, 193–94, 200; Virginia and, 91–92, 95, 96
Souther, Simeon, 121–22, 129
Souther v. Commonwealth of Virginia, 121–22, 123
southern law, as problematic term, 231n26
Southey, Thomas, 56
Spanish slave laws, ix, 9, 25–27, 30; Missouri and, 209; Roman tradition of, 22; Visigothic tradition of, 25
spendthrifts, 20, 241n72
Spotswood, Alexander, 94, 103
Stampp, Kenneth, 6, 7
State of Georgia v. Abbot, 154
State of Louisiana v. Morris, 194
State of Mississippi v. Jones, 198–200, 202
State of North Carolina v. Boon, 132–33, 168
State of North Carolina v. Hale, 141
State of North Carolina v. Hoover, 144–48, 149, 150
State of North Carolina v. Jarrott, 141, 168
State of North Carolina v. Mann, 141, 148
State of North Carolina v. Piver, 132, 168

342 INDEX

State of North Carolina v. Reed, 142
State of North Carolina v. Robbins, 149–50
State of North Carolina v. Tackett, 139–40, 146–47, 160–61, 168, 182, 202
State of North Carolina v. Walker, 137–38
State of North Carolina v. Weaver, 132
State of North Carolina v. Will, 141
State of South Carolina v. Bradley, 188–89
State of South Carolina v. Cheatwood, 182
State of South Carolina v. Fleming, 183
State of South Carolina v. Gee, 174
State of South Carolina v. Raines, 183
State of South Carolina v. Taylor, 179
Status societies, 11, 12
Stephenson, Mathew, 164
Stowe, Harriet Beecher, 1, 5, 125, 191
Strafford, Ephraim, 177
Stroud, George, ix
Stubbs, Lewis Andrew Jackson, 10, 185–88, 315–16n92
Suetonius, Gaius, 17
sugar plantations, 27, 57; on Barbados, 44, 50; on British Virgin Islands, 56; on Jamaica, 44, 48. *See also* plantation society
Sweatnam, Richard, 83

Tacitus, Cornelius, 12, 14
Tackett, William, 139–40
Tackett rule, 160–61, 168, 182, 202
Tannenbaum, Frank, ix–x
Tanner, Edwin, 214–15
Tasker, Benjamin, 84
Taylor, George Keith, 115
Taylor, John Louis, 133, 138, 140
Taylor, Warner, 142, 151
Taylor, William H., 179
Tennessee, 130, 223; demographics of, 164; North Carolina and, 152, 164, 165; slave laws of, 164–72
testimony by slaves, 5–7, 29, 63, 75, 161, 166
Texas, 219–22
Thatcher, Joseph S. B., 202
Theodosian Code, 19
Thomas, J. A. W., 187
Thomas, Thomas W., 156
Thompson, George, 219
Thompson, John J., 205–6
Thompson, John W., 204

Thompson, Lucas P., 128
Thompson v. Young, 205–6
Tiernen, Luke, 85
Tobago, 41, 54–57
Tomlins, Christopher, 258n10
Tortola, 56, 57, 64–65
traditional societies, ix, x, 12, 14, 23, 223; clans, ix, 11–15; primitive societies, 12, 235n5; tribal societies, 12, 23
Traube, Charles C., 212
tribal societies, 12, 23; clans, ix, 11–15; primitive societies, 12, 235n5. *See also* traditional societies
Trinidad, 57, 66
Tucker, St. George, 111–12, 129
Turner, Commonwealth of Virginia v., 122

Umbricia, 17
Usher, John, 72

Vagrancy Act (1547), 39
Van Zandt, John, 74
VanderVelde, Lea, 7, 8
Vann, Albert, 150
Vesey, Denmark, 2
villeinage, 35, 45, 70, 134
Virginia, 41, 91–97; demographics of, 91–92, 110, 173; homicide rates in, 114; manumission laws of, 114; North Carolina slave laws versus, 151; slave homicide cases in, 94–97, 111–13, 117–29; slave law reforms in, 48, 110–29; slave laws of, 6, 91–94; South Carolina and, 91–92, 95, 96
Visigoths, 9, 14, 22–25, 30, 223

Walker, Augustus W., 319n21
Walker, John, 137–38
Walmsley, Benjamin, 86
Walrond, Humphrey, 44
Ward, Clarence, 194–95
Wardlaw, David L., 189
Warren, Malachi, 208, 209
Watkins, A. B., 89
Watson, Benjamin, 216
Wayne, James M., 154
Weaver, State of North Carolina v., 132
Weber, Max, 12, 13, 15
Welch, John, 66

Wells, David, 181
wergild (wergeld), ix, 12, 34–36. *See also* blood feuds
West Indies slavery, 15; British laws in, 41; Spanish laws in, 26–27, 30
Westbrook, Ira, 149
Westcott, James D., 219
Wheeler, Royall T., 220
White, David, 95
White, George, 194–95
White, Robert, 115–16
White, Sims, 180–81
White, William, 119–20
white letter law, 224
Whyte, Robert, 168
Wiecek, William M., 105
Wilds, Samuel, 175
Williams, Hezekiah, 113
Williams, Mary Wilhelmine, ix–x
Williams, William, 86
Williamson, David, 85
Williamson, Luke Tiernan, 85
Williamson, Thomas, 94
Willie, James, 221
Wills, James, 77–78
Wilson, Frances, 94, 103
Wilson, William (Hill), 119–20
Wilson, William R., 222
Windward Islands, 57
Withers, Thomas Jefferson, 185
Witsell v. Earnest, 181
Wood, Betty, 108
Wood, Peter, 98
Woodley, Andrew, 94
Wooten, Hardy Vickers, 208–9, 325n102
Workman, Benjamin, 79–80
Wright, James, 107, 108
Wythe, George, 111

Yamasee War, 98
Yeargin, Benjamin, 135
York, Duke of, 73; laws of, 73, 75, 77
Young, William, 205–6
Younge, Enrique, 30

Zacek, Natalie, 52